C000247221

PUBLIC LAW IN A MULTI-LAYER

At the beginning of the twenty-first century it appears that the traditional Diceyan model of a unitary constitution has been superseded as power has come to be distributed—particularly in the post-1997 period—between institutions at European, national, devolved and local level. Furthermore, the courts have come to play a powerful role at all levels through judicial review, while forms of regulation and contracting, together with other informal techniques of governance, have emerged. The contemporary constitution can be characterised as involving a multi-layered distribution of power—a situation which raises many key questions about the role of public law. How is the distribution of power between the different levels of the contemporary constitution to be policed? What is the emerging contribution of the courts in regard to EC law, the Human Rights Act 1998 and devolution? What roles should be played by the legislative and judicial bodies at each level? Who should have access to the courts in public law disputes, and on what grounds should the courts regulate the exercise of public power? Can a coherent distinction be maintained between public and private law? The essays in this important collection tackle such questions from a variety of perspectives, aiming between them to provide a dynamic picture of the role of public law in the contemporary, multi-layered constitution.

PUBLIC LAW IN A MULTI-LAYERED CONSTITUTION

Edited by

Nicholas Bamforth

Fellow in Law,
The Queen's College, Oxford

and

Peter Leyland

Senior Lecturer in Law
London Metropolitan University

HART PUBLISHING
OXFORD AND PORTLAND, OREGON
2003

Published in North America (US and Canada) by
Hart Publishing
c/o International Specialized Book Services
5804 NE Hassalo Street
Portland, Oregon
97213-3644
USA

Hart Publishing is a specialist legal publisher based in Oxford, England.
To order further copies of this book or to request a list of other publications
please write to:

Hart Publishing, Salters Boatyard, Folly Bridge, Abingdon Rd, Oxford, OX1 4LB
Telephone: +44 (0)1865 245533 Fax: +44 (0) 1865 794882
email: mail@hartpub.co.uk
WEBSITE: http//:www.hartpub.co.uk

British Library Cataloguing in Publication Data
Data Available

ISBN 1-84113-282-9 (hardback)
1-84113-283-7 (paperback)

Typeset by John Saunders Design and Production
Printed and bound in Great Britain by
Biddles Ltd, *www.biddles.co.uk*

Preface

This collection of essays aims to engage with what we describe as the 'multi-layered' nature of contemporary constitution. The UK constitution has been—and still is—characterised by evolutionary change, but in the last thirty years of the twentieth century it was quite fundamentally and often deliberately refashioned in a number of areas, something which has had important consequences for the role of public law. No single collection of essays could hope to chart every aspect of this process, nor to provide a definitive account of the boundaries and content of the contemporary system of public law. Instead, having sketched out the nature of the refashioning in the first chapter, subsequent chapters analyse some of its key aspects in an attempt to offer some suggestions or tentative conclusions about the architecture of the contemporary constitution. We hope, in consequence, that the essays will be of use to scholars, students, practitioners, and anyone else with an interest in public law.

Early versions of many of the essays were presented at a weekend seminar in April 2002, generously sponsored by Linklaters and Hart Publishing, and held at The Queen's College, Oxford. Thanks are due to the sponsors, to Queen's, and to Sir Stephen Sedley, who chaired several sessions of the seminar. The editorial work would not have been nearly as smooth were it not for the willingness of our contributors to meet deadlines and to make helpful suggestions, and we should like to thank them for this. We should perhaps also say that even in an academic world driven by e-mail, we would not have found our work as editors nearly as straightforward had it not been for the fact that we are relatively close neighbours in north London.

We should also like to express our thanks to Terry Woods and Bridget Shersby at London Metropolitan University, to Richard Hart and April Boffin at Hart Publishing, and to Putachad Leyland for providing Thai refreshments at crucial moments. Finally, we would each like to express our thanks to or, where appropriate, to remember our respective parents: Colin and the late Joyce, and the late Basil and Enid.

London NW1   Nicholas Bamforth
July 2003   Peter Leyland

Contents

List of Contributors

NICHOLAS BAMFORTH is Fellow in Law, The Queen's College, Oxford.

PETER CANE is Professor of Law in the Research School of Social Sciences at the Australian National University in Canberra.

RICHARD CORNES, Barrister and Solicitor of the High Court of New Zealand, is Lecturer in Public Law, School of Law, University of Essex.

CONOR GEARTY is Professor of Human Rights at the London School of Economics and Political Science.

BRIGID HADFIELD is Professor of Law at the University of Essex.

CAROL HARLOW is Professor of Law at the London School of Economics and Political Science.

MURRAY HUNT is a Barrister in Matrix Chambers, London.

PETER LEYLAND is a Senior Lecturer in the School of Law, Governance and International Relations at London Metropolitan University.

MARTIN LOUGHLIN is Professor of Public Law at the London School of Economics and Political Science.

JOANNA MILES is a Fellow of Trinity College, Cambridge.

JOHN MORISON is Professor of Law and Head of School in the School of Law, Queen's University Belfast.

STEPHANIE PALMER, Barrister, is a Fellow of Girton College, Cambridge and a Lecturer in Law at Cambridge University.

MICHAEL TAGGART teaches at the Law School in the University of Auckland, New Zealand.

ADAM TOMKINS is Fellow and Tutor in Law, St Catherine's College, Oxford, and John Millar Professor of Public Law-elect at the University of Glasgow.

1

Public Law in a Multi-Layered Constitution

NICHOLAS BAMFORTH AND PETER LEYLAND

A NY ACCOUNT OF the role, dimensions and mechanisms of public law in a particular jurisdiction must involve—whether as a presupposition or as an explicit proposition—some view of the workings of the constitution of that jurisdiction. Public law, however defined, is concerned with the exercise of power by public bodies and with the mechanisms for controlling such power,[1] so it must follow that the underpinning constitutional provisions—concerning, for example, the role and nature of the state, the allocation of power between constituent institutions of the state, the proper role of the legislature, executive and judiciary, and notions of democratic accountability and representation—will play an important role in delimiting both the territory within which and the way in which public law is to operate. To suggest otherwise would be tantamount to claiming that it is possible to understand and to navigate the geography of a settled area without first comprehending basic notions such as distance, height and terrain, quite apart from more sophisticated concepts such as public and private property. Professors Carol Harlow and Richard Rawlings have made the normative claim that 'behind every theory of the law, there lies a theory of the state'.[2] Our claim—that any understanding of the dimensions of public law presupposes a coherent account of the constitutional terrain—operates in an analogous fashion to this normative claim, but does so at a purely *analytical* level.

In itself, our claim should hardly be contentious. We make it openly only because it provides the analytical foundation for much of what follows in this collection of essays. The central theme running through the collection is that the restructuring of the constitutional architecture of the United Kingdom in the past

---

[1] For rival definitons, see C Harlow and R Rawlings, *Law and Administration* (London, Butterworths,1997), pp 25–28, chs 2–4.

[2] N 1 above, p1. To similar (albeit broader) effect, see also Professor Harold Laski's assertions that 'No theory of the state is ever intelligible save in the context of its time. What men think about the state is the outcome always of the experience in which they are immersed' (H. Laski, *A Grammar of Politics* (London, Allen and Unwin, 1925), p i) and that 'Law cannot transcend the relations it is intended to enforce. Its ultimate postulates are never self-determined, but given to it by the economic system of which it is the expression' (p xxii; see also ch 10, p 544).

thirty or so years—in particular, since 1997—has been fundamental, and poses important questions for the role of public law. In practical terms, power (both legislative and political) has been spread away from the Westminster Parliament, both 'upwards' to the European Union and 'downwards' to the devolved assemblies. There has also been what might be seen as a rebalancing of the roles of the courts and Parliament in holding the executive to account, given the development by the courts—particularly since 1977—of a comprehensive regime of judicial review, a regime which has arguably been strengthened by the passage of the Human Rights Act 1998. The domain of government has also been altered by the processes of privatisation and contracting out, and the administrative processes of government altered by the techniques of 'new public management'. These latter developments require us to think about how we understand the shape of the state and the appropriate methods of regulating state power.

The various changes highlighted here have been prompted by a diverse collection of rationales, justifications and ideologies. The Human Rights Act and the devolution legislation were enacted in the post-1997 period by the New Labour government, for example, while privatisation, contracting out and 'new public management' have their origins in the period of Conservative government from 1979 to 1997 (which is not to say that they were not embraced by the incoming government in 1997). More specifically, it might be fair to say that the package of constitutional reform measures enacted since 1997 does not appear to have been based upon an overall plan.[3] In addition, the development of domestic judicial review has been the responsibility of the courts (whatever one's view as to the constitutional basis of the review jurisdiction) and has not always been welcomed by the government of the day.[4] Looked at in the round, the various developments we have outlined might therefore be felt to have produced something of a patchwork quilt effect, constitutionally-speaking. Nonetheless, the *overall consequence* has been to bring about a profound constitutional change, in that the United Kingdom could now be said to possess what might be described as a *multi-layered* constitution. As mentioned above, there has been a two-way redistribution of power from Westminster level to the European Union and the devolved levels of government, and the European Convention on Human Rights now plays a direct role in national law. Elected public bodies and courts must—to varying degrees—take account of and reflect such changes, and the allocation of power between such bodies might be said to vary according to factors which operate *both* at the same constitutional level as the body itself *and* at higher (or lower) levels within the constitution. Two examples will illustrate this. First, national courts were traditionally said to be concerned to give effect to the Sovereign will of the Westminster Parliament.[5] In

---

[3] Responsibility for drafting the various pieces of legislation was widely spread.

[4] For contrasting perspectives, see C Forsyth (ed), *Judicial Review and the Constitution* (Oxford, Hart, 2000).

[5] Significant examples in relation to statutory interpretation include *R. v Hull University Visitor, ex p. Page* [1993] AC 682; *R. v Secretary of State for the Home Department, ex p. Fire Brigades Union* [1995] 2 AC 513. In relation to Parliamentary Sovereignty, see, eg, *Ellen Street Estates v Minister of Health* [1934] KB 590; *British Railways Board v Pickin* [1974] AC 765.

today's constitution, however, they must read that will (as far as possible) subject to the jurisprudence of the European Court of Human Rights and subject to the over-riding force of European Community law.[6] Secondly, the permissible scope of executive action—whether at UK or at devolved level—is regulated by general United Kingdom-level laws, by the requirements of EC law and the European Convention (via the European Communities Act 1972 and Human Rights Act 1998 respectively) *and*, to varying extents, by the rules delimiting the power of the devolved institutions. In this sense, the constitution might be said to have taken on the appearance of a structure with multiple, but inter-connected and sometimes overlapping layers.

A further complicating factor has been that power— and the mechanisms for regulating its exercise—seem to have diffused sideways as well as vertically upwards and downwards. At both national and EU levels, it is clear that the mechanisms of constitutional accountability must be measured in judicial as well as in political terms. However, the proper boundary between the realms of legal and political accountability remains the subject of fierce debate,[7] the resolution of which has not been helped by the fact that the methods of exercising power have—via processes such as privatisation and contracting out—spread laterally away from a centralised executive. Such developments do not inevitably occur alongside the emergence of a multi-layered constitution—it would be quite possible to conceive of a multi-layered constitution in which they were not present—but they do form an important feature of the contemporary constitutional landscape, and one which has particular resonance given the existence of a multi-layered constitution in that the boundary between state and non-state actors appears currently to have been drawn in different places in different constitutional layers.

The primary purpose of the essays gathered together in this collection is to reflect upon the role of public law in the present, multi-layered constitutional ordering. The contributors focus on a variety of different features of the contemporary constitution and argue from a variety of standpoints. However, each essay has something important to say about the multi-layered theme. In general, the essays are concerned to evaluate specific, practical questions: how do the different layers interact, for example? What is the appropriate role of legal as opposed to political accountability within each layer? Deeper-level questions are, of course, posed by the emergence of a multi-layered constitution. How, for example, do we now understand the idea that the Westminster Parliament is a legally sovereign body? Do we now have competing—or overlapping—notions of sovereignty at different levels of the constitutional structures which apply in Western Europe? Should we see the driving force behind our constitution in a 'top down' way—that is, that it is ultimately determined by the rules and principles of the European Union—or in a 'bottom up' fashion, by stressing the continuing importance of the voluntary adherence of member states to the European Union? These questions

---

[6] On the Convention, see Human Rights Act 1998, s 3; *R. v A.* [2002] 1 AC 45, paras. [44], [108] and [162]. On EC law, see *R. v Secretary of State for Transport, ex p. Factortame (2)* [1991] 1 AC 603.

[7] See, eg the chapters by Tomkins, Harlow, Taggart, Hunt and Gearty in this volume.

have, at various times, been considered elsewhere.[8] By contrast, the aim of this collection is to analyse the ways in which different aspects of the contemporary multi-layered constitution interrelate. While this exercise has a practical, map-drafting focus, certain broader conclusions about the *nature* of that constitution can be drawn from the analysis. In the remainder of this introduction, we will attempt to explain some of the features of the multi-layered model in further detail. We will then explain how the chapters in the collection illustrate the themes we have canvassed. It goes without saying that it would be impracticable, in a single introduction or set of essays, to capture every aspect of the present multi-layered model, or to evaluate all its consequences. We hope, in the present volume, simply to sketch out some of the broader themes.

THE MULTI-LAYERED CONSTITUTION: AN OVERVIEW

Many claims have been made about the post-1997 reforms to the United Kingdom constitution. It has been suggested, for example, that considered in the round, these reforms require us to see the contemporary constitution as less monolithic, less centralised and less political than it previously was.[9] More radically, others have claimed variously that the raft of constitutional legislation amounts to a new constitutional settlement,[10] that it deals 'hammer blows against our Benthamite and Diceyan traditions', or that it entails a shift from a 'political' to a 'law based' constitution.[11] Contestable though these latter claims might be, for the reasons indicated above, it is nonetheless clear that the emergence—over the past thirty years—of a multi-layered constitution is a matter of considerable significance, and it is the purpose of this section of the introduction to sketch out some of its features. In order to do so, a useful starting point is to outline—in order to provide a basis for comparison—the features of Professor AV Dicey's conception of the constitutional order. We are not saying that it follows inevitably from the emergence of a multi-layered constitution that all reference to Dicey's model should necessarily be abandoned. Rather, we present Dicey's analysis as a counter-example to the multi-layered model, something which will enable us to illustrate the differences between the two more clearly.

The primary components of Dicey's model were Parliamentary Sovereignty and

---

[8]   There is a large literature on these topics. See, eg, N MacCormick, *Questioning Sovereignty: Law, State and Practical Reason* (Oxford, Clarendon Press, 1999); 'Symposium: Can Europe Have a Constitution?' (2001) 12 *KCLJ* 1–133; PP Craig, 'Constitutions, Constitutionalism and the European Union' (2001) 26 *EL Rev* 125; I. Pernice 'Multilevel constitutionalism in the European Union' (2002) 27 *EL Rev* 511; N Walker, 'Human Rights in a Postnational Order: Reconciling Political and Constitutional Pluralism', ch 7 in T Campbell, KD Ewing and A Tomkins (eds), *Sceptical Essays on Human Rights* (Oxford, Clarendon Press, 2001).

[9]   C Munro, *Studies in Constitutional Law* 2nd edn (London, Butterworths., 1999), p 12.

[10]   R Hazell and R Cornes (eds), *Constitutional Futures: A History of the Next Ten Years* (Oxford, OUP, 1999), p 1.

[11]   J Jowell and D Oliver, *The Changing Constitution* 4th edn (Oxford, OUP, 2000), p v. D Oliver, *Constitutional Reform in the UK* (Oxford, OUP, 2003), p v.

the rule of law. Parliamentary Sovereignty, in Dicey's classic formulation, was the notion that 'Parliament has the right to make or unmake any law whatsoever, and further that no person or body has the right to override or set aside the legislation of Parliament'.[12] Dicey was not claiming here that there were no limits on Parliament. Rather, he was suggesting that such limits as existed were political, or—at most—took effect via judicial interpretation of legislation. For Dicey, the most obvious political limits on Parliamentary power were what he termed the 'internal' and 'external' constraints: a Parliament would not legislate to bring about certain outrageous consequences—even though it might have the power to do so—due to fear of an adverse political reaction by the electorate, and due to internal constraints of political morality. Dicey's notion of the rule of law might be said to play an analogous limiting function. Parliament would feel politically or morally compelled (even though it was not legally compelled) not to legislate in violation of the rule of law. Professor Paul Craig has thus suggested that a vision of unitary, self-correcting democracy lay behind Dicey's picture of the constitution: all were to be subject to the same law, with political rather than legal redress (hence 'self-correcting') being available for legislative excess.[13] Dicey's account was also noteworthy for his suggestion that the rule of law required 'equality before the law, or the equal subjection of all classes to the ordinary law of the land administered by the ordinary law courts', so that there could be no

> idea of any exemption of officials or others from the duty of obedience to the law which governs other citizens or from the jurisdiction of the ordinary tribunals; there can with us be nothing really corresponding to the 'administrative law' (*droit administratif*) or the 'administrative tribunals' (*tribunaux administratifs*) of France. The notion that lies at the bottom of the 'administrative law' known to continental systems is, that affairs or disputes in which the government or its servants are concerned are beyond the sphere of the civil courts and must be dealt with by special and more or less official bodies. This idea is utterly unknown to the law of England … .[14]

Dicey was also keen to stress, as part of his definition of the rule of law, that the protection of individual rights in the United Kingdom was the task of the ordinary common law, and that no specific rights code was necessary.[15]

Many aspects of Dicey's account have now, it might be claimed, been superseded. The 'unitary' character of the British constitution has been called into question by the introduction of devolution and the transfer of powers to the European level. An intermediate level of national government now exists in Scotland, Wales and, in principle, in Northern Ireland, which is subordinate to Westminster.[16]

---

[12] AV Dicey, *An Introduction to the Study of the Law of the Constitution* 10th edn (London, MacMillan, 1959), pp 39–40.

[13] PP Craig, *Public Law and Democracy in the United Kingdom and the United States of America* (Oxford, Clarendon Press, 2000), p 15 *ff*.

[14] AV Dicey, n 12 above, pp 202–3; see also pp 193–5.

[15] AV Dicey, n 12 above, p 197.

[16] In each case a new institutional framework has been established, with a range of competences. Also, the Greater London Authority Act 1999 restored a strategic level of London wide government with the introduction of a Greater London Authority consisting of a Mayor and Assembly for London. However, comprehensive devolution for England and its regions has thus far been a notable omission,

Although the devolution arrangements which exist are asymmetrical in nature—most obviously, in the present context, in relation to the presence or absence of legislative powers at the devolved level—it might nonetheless be said that they pose a challenge to the 'unitary' nature of the constitutional structure. For example, it was predicted that following devolution the supremacy of the Westminster Parliament would have a 'different and attenuated' meaning so that 'instead of enjoying a regular and continuous exercise of supremacy, [Westminster] will possess merely a nebulous right of supervision ...,'[17] the assumption behind this assertion being that post-devolution, Westminster would find it politically difficult to legislate against the wishes of the devolved bodies.[18] There was, indeed, an expectation that a convention would be established whereby the Westminster Parliament would not normally legislate over devolved matters in Scotland and that this would be an unusual occurrence which would take place with the agreement of the devolved legislature.[19] Furthermore, the law-making powers of the devolved bodies (whether consisting in the making of primary or subordinate legislation) are such that substantively different bodies of law might now be expected to emerge at different levels within the United Kingdom.

Looking to the European level, there has clearly also been a large-scale transfer of power to the EU law-making institutions. National laws must now be 'disapplied' by the courts for incompatibility with directly effective EU law, and national governments may be liable in damages for acting incompatibly with EU law.[20] Depending upon one's interpretation of the effect of EU membership on the concept of legal sovereignty, this development might be felt to affect both the unitary nature of the constitution and its self-correcting aspect.[21] For example, domestic courts must disregard the legislation of the Westminster Parliament—however much popular support there may be for such legislation—if it violates the rules of EU law.[22] The principle of 'subsidiarity' is intended to recognise the importance of ensuring that, where practicable, decision-making takes place at a local level. How successful this principle has been is, however, open to question.[23]

---

although proposals for regional government have recently been made (see the Cornes chapter in this volume).

[17]   V Bogdanor, *Devolution in the United Kingdom* (Oxford, OUP, 1999), p 291.

[18]   See now A Page and A Batey 'Scotland's Other Parliament: Westminster Legislation about Devolved Matters in Scotland since Devolution' [2002] *PL* 501.

[19]   This is referred to as the Sewell Convention. It acknowledges that three types of legislation require the consent of the Scottish Parliament to be proceeded with: Westminster legislation for devolved purposes; Westminster legislation altering legislative competence; and Westminster legislation altering executive competence.

[20]   See, resepctively, *R. v Secretary of State for Transport, ex p. Factortame (No.2)*, n 6 above; *Brasserie du Pecheur v Germany* [1996] ECR I-1029.

[21]   For rival accounts of the significance of *Factortame (2)*, see PP Craig, 'Sovereignty of the United Kingdom Parliament after *Factortame*' (1991) 11 *YBEL* 221; Sir William Wade, 'Sovereignty: Revolution or Evolution?' (1996) 112 *LQR* 568; TRS Allan, 'Parliamentary Sovereignty: Law, Politics, and Revolution' (1997) 113 *LQR* 443.

[22]   *R. v Secretary of State for Transport, ex p. Factortame (No.2)*, n 6 above.

[23]   See, eg, C Barnard and S Deakin, 'European Community Social Policy: Progression or Regression?' (1999) 30 *IRJ* 55.

Dicey's notion that individual rights were the product of the common law can, to a certain extent at least, be seen as having been challenged by the enactment of the Human Rights Act 1998. The Human Rights Act 1998 establishes a direct relationship between domestic law in the United Kingdom and the rights set out in the European Convention on Human Rights. In theory, the Act preserves the sovereignty of Parliament since the courts cannot invalidate primary legislation,[24] and Parliament remains free to legislate in defiance of the Convention. However, the degree to which the Act enables courts to encroach upon Parliamentary intention when construing legislation is a matter for open debate, given that it requires courts to interpret domestic legislation in a way that is compatible with Convention rights.[25] The courts' power to judicially review the actions of public authorities for disproportionality, inspired by section 6 of the Act, also raises questions about the intensity and ambit of judicial review.[26] Another important aspect of the incorporation of the Convention is that the new devolved assemblies are also placed under a statutory duty to act in accordance with Convention rights, arguably requiring the courts to engage—in relation to the assemblies—in an activity akin to constitutional review.[27] Each of these functions is carried out by the courts in order to safeguard a guaranteed list of rights. However, it remains unclear how far the Human Rights Act is affecting the substantive outcomes in judicial review cases.[28] It is, for example, important to remember that the higher courts were concerned to stress their commitment to protecting litigants' common law fundamental rights in the decade before the enactment of the Human Rights Act.[29] Whether or not they did so effectively, they were already content to conceive of the common law in rights-based terms without legislative intervention, a stance which was sometimes associated with the rule of law.[30] At the same

[24] N Bamforth, 'Parliamentary Sovereignty and the Human Rights Act' [1998] *PL* 572; *R. v Secretary of State for the Home Department, ex p. Simms* [2000] 2 AC 115, 131E-132B (Lord Hoffmann); cf, however, *Thoburn v Sunderland City Council* [2002] EWHC Admin 195, [2002] 3 WLR 24, para [62] (Laws L.J.).

[25] C Gearty, 'Reconciling Parliamentary Democracy and Human Rights' (2002) 118 *LQR* 248, 254.

[26] See further P Craig, 'The Courts, the Human Rights Act and Judicial Review' (2001) 117 *LQR* 589; M Elliott, 'The Human Rights Act 1998 and the Standard of Substantive Review' (2001) 60 *CLJ* 301; R Clayton, 'Regaining a Sense of Proportion: The Human Rights Act and the Proportionality Principle' [2001] *EHRLR* 504; N Blake, 'Importing Proportionality: Clarification or Confusion' [2002] *EHRLR* 19.

[27] See, for example, the revised role of the Judicial Committee of the Privy Council in relation to the devolution legislation: see further the Hadfield chapter in this volume; P Craig and M Walters, 'The Courts, Devolution and Judicial Review' [1999] *PL* 274.

[28] Useful bi-monthly surveys of the case law can be found in the 2001 and 2002 volumes of the *EHRLR*. The impact of Convention rights via section 3 of the Act might be felt, to date, to have been more obvious than that under section 6: see *Mendoza v Ghaidan* [2002] EWCA Civ 1533, [2002] 4 All ER 1162; N Bamforth, 'Interpretation and the Human Rights Act 1998: A Constitutional Basis for Anti-Discrimination Protection?' (2003) 119 *LQR* 215.

[29] See, eg, *R. v Secretary of State for the Home Department, ex p. Leech* [1994] QB 198, 209–212; *R. v Secretary of State for Social Security, ex p. Joint Council for the Welfare of Immigrants* [1996] 4 All ER 385; *R. v Lord Chancellor, ex p. Witham* [1998] QB 575; *R. v Secretary of State for the Home Department, ex p. Pierson* [1998] AC 539; *R. v Secretary of State for the Home Department, ex p. Simms*, n 24 above; M Hunt, *Using Human Rights Law in English Courts* (Oxford, Hart, 1997), chs 5 and 6.

[30] For reflection on the rule of law in the context of legislative intention (albeit without specific association with fundamental rights), see *R. v Secretary of State for the Home Department, ex p. Pierson*

time, it was clear, before the Human Rights Act came into force, that courts were developing new principles relating to legitimate expectations and arguably—despite the official prohibition on their doing so, proportionality—and that, in doing so, they were influenced by the supra-national layers of European jurisprudence represented by the ECHR and by EU law.[31]

From a contemporary perspective, it is abundantly clear that a distinctive notion of administrative law has emerged in the United Kingdom, in direct response to the growth of government power in the twentieth century. It seems clear that, at the time of writing, Dicey was in fact mistaken in his view of the nature of French law and of the absence of any type of administrative law in England.[32] As Lord Diplock noted in *R v IRC, ex parte National Federation for the Self Employed,* '[T]he progress towards a comprehensive system of administrative law ... I regard as having been the greatest achievement of the English courts in my judicial lifetime'.[33] We now have an Administrative Court branch of the High Court, which administers judicial review against public authorities, with distinctive grounds of review and distinctive remedies. Many questions surround the appropriate ambit of the judicial review jurisdiction (and it should be noted that private law remedies may still be pursued against public authorities without reference to the Administrative Court), but it should be clear that this major limb of Dicey's definition of the rule of law is not truly representative of the contemporary constitution. This development does not challenge the 'self-correcting' nature of Dicey's vision—the courts do not challenge legislation of the Westminster Parliament head on—but the emergence of judicial review has plainly cast the courts, in the contemporary constitution, as an important counter-weight to executive power.[34]

However, the extent to which there has been a shift in power away from the executive and towards the courts is itself open to question. In part at least, this is because there have been legislative measures which have granted increased powers to ministers and officials[35] and others that have reduced judicial discretion.[36] But

---

[1998] AC 539, 591 (Lord Steyn). References to the rule of law have continued since the Human Rights Act came into force: see *R. v Spear* [2002] UKHL 31, [2002] ACD 97, para [4] (Lord Bingham).

[31]   See G Anthony, *UK Public Law and European Law* (Oxford, Hart, 2002), chs 2 and 3; R Thomas, *Legitimate Expectation and Proportionality in Administrative Law* (Oxford, Hart, 2000). Specifically on proportionality, see G De Búrca, 'Proportionality and *Wednesbury* Unreasonableness: the Influence of European Legal Concepts on UK Law', ch 4 in M Andenas (ed), *English Public Law and the Common Law of Europe* (London, Key Haven, 1998); P Craig, 'Unreasonableness and Proportionality in UK Law', in E Ellis (ed), *The Principle of Proportionality in the Laws of Europe* (Oxford, Hart, 1999).

[32]   I Jennings, *The Law and the Constitution* (London, University of London Press, 5th edn., 1959) and 'In Praise of Dicey 1885–1935' (1935) 13 *Public Administration* 333.

[33]   [1982] AC 617, 641. See also *R. v Secretary of State for the Home Department, ex p. Fire Brigades Union,* n 5 above, 567D-568B (Lord Mustill); Lord Woolf, 'Droit Public-English Style' [1995] *PL* 57, 58–9.

[34]   For a controversial and particularly strong definition of the role of the courts, see the views of Sir John Laws in *Thoburn v Sunderland City Council,* n 24 above, and—speaking extra-judicially—in 'Law and Democracy' [1995] *PL* 72.

[35]   The Immigration and Asylum Act 1999 and the Terrorism Act 2000 confer added powers in the sphere of immigration and state security; the Criminal Justice and Police Act 2001 extends greater powers to the police.

[36]   Eg, Powers of Criminal Courts (Sentencing) Act 2000, ch 3.

also, in the wake of the attacks on the United States on 11 September 2001, statutes have been enacted which might be said directly or indirectly to qualify or undermine Convention rights, demonstrating Parliament's continuing competence to legislate in defiance of the European Convention.[37] For example, the Crime and Security Act 2001 gives the Home Secretary a draconian set of powers directed at immigrants, asylum seekers and alleged terrorists which are perhaps unprecedented in peacetime.[38] Such examples make it difficult to maintain that recent constitutional reforms have simply given rise to a fundamental re-balancing in favour of the courts.

A further crucial aspect of Dicey's account which has been put under severe stress is the notion that there was no distinction between public and private law. Indeed, a more contingent and related question which has arisen in recent years concerns the shape of the state.[38a] Since 1979, the United Kingdom has witnessed privatisation, regulation, deregulation, new public management, the creation of next steps agencies, contracting in the public sector, compulsory competitive tendering in local government, public private partnerships, the citizen's charter, health service reorganisation (to name but a few of the most prevalent initiatives). The tangled interactions between public and private bodies involved in these mechanisms have been further complicated by the operation of divergent patterns of contacting out and regulation at different constitutional layers. There are increasingly dense networks of accountability within which power is exercised, with state institutions being tied into relationships with the business sector and voluntary and consumer groups in many different ways.[38b] These modified approaches clearly have important implications for the shape of our institutions, given that the creation of so much complexity calls into question the predominant role of the state and in particular its capacity to intervene effectively by legislative means. Having said that, the post-1997 period has also witnessed an apparent reiteration of the divisions between public and private institutions at national level due to the obligations imposed specifically upon public authorities by the Human Rights Act 1998[39] and the Freedom of Information Act 2000,[40] and a continuation of the distinction between such institutions in the EC case law concerning the direct effect of directives.[41]

The developments outlined in this section of the introduction suggest that it is no longer realistic (if, indeed, it ever was) to analyse our constitution in terms of a

---

[37] See also the Nationality, Immigration and Asylum Act 2002.

[38] Section 23 allows indefinite detention without trial of a suspected terrorist who is a not a British citizen. See A Tomkins, 'Legislating against terror: the Anti-terrorism, Crime and Security Act 2001' [2002] *PL* 205.

[38a] See M Loughlin, 'The State, The Crown and The Law', in M Sunkin and S Payne (eds), *The Nature of the Crown* (Oxford, OUP, 1999), at p 76.

[38b] See eg, C Scott, 'Accountability in the Regulatory State' (2000) 37 *JLS* 38.

[39] A point made strongly by Morritt V-C in *Aston Cantlow and Wilcote with Billesley Parochial Church Council v Wallbank* [2001] EWCA Civ 713, [2001] 3 All ER 393, para [33].

[40] See the Palmer chapter in this volume.

[41] PP Craig, 'Directives: Direct Effect, Indirect Effect and the Construction of National Legislation' (1997) 22 *EL Rev* 519.

unitary, self-correcting model. The essays in this collection—which are introduced in the next section—seek to build upon this conclusion by highlighting some of the important features of the contemporary, multi-layered constitution, together with the role of public law within it.

THE MULTI-LAYERED CONSTITUTION: THE FEATURES, AS OUTLINED IN THE ESSAYS

It should be stressed that the remit of this collection does not extend to an exploration of the foundations of the contemporary constitution—something which would involve a book in itself. Instead, the various chapters analyse some of the key political and legal features of today's multi-layered constitutional landscape. Broadly speaking, the chapters address—from a variety of standpoints—three key questions. First, what are the similarities, inconsistencies and overlaps between the different layers? Secondly, to what extent should public bodies be regulated—at each layer of the constitution—by legal as opposed to political means? And thirdly, how does the recent reshaping of the structure of the state—using processes such as deregulation, contracting-out and the like—inter-relate with the existence of different constitutional layers? Analytically speaking, the first two questions would be important in *any* multi-layered constitutional arrangement, simply by virtue of the existence of the different layers. The third question is important for the localised and contingent reason that the so-called 'modernisation' of government has been a key feature of recent United Kingdom political history, making some discussion of it crucial if we are to understand the workings of the contemporary constitution.

If we are properly to understand the notion of a multi-layered constitution, however, it is sensible to begin by analysing to some extent the nature of constitutions more generally. This is the purpose of Professor Martin Loughlin's chapter, 'Constitutional law: the third order of the political'. Loughlin suggests that just as 'constitutional' concerns have become important for politicians in recent years, a sceptical strain has emerged among lawyers, whereby constitutional law is seen as 'just politics'. Loughlin, by contrast, seeks to differentiate the legal from the political, thereby explaining the role of law within a constitution.[42] Unusually, he does this by starting with an inquiry into the nature of politics, the results of which are then used to identify what is special about law. Loughlin divides politics into three 'orders'. The first is concerned with the conceptual nature of the political, which relates to disagreement. It is only through the establishment of a state that a group of people within a given territory can become a unity which encompasses the political. By acquiring a monopoly of coercive power, the state is able to keep conflict and disagreement within a framework of order. At the second order level of the political, politics thus emerges within a viable system of government, and is

---

[42] See, at greater length, Loughlin's *Sword and Scales: an Examination of the Relationship Between Law and Politics* (Oxford, Hart, 2000).

concerned with the resolution or containment of disagreement within the parameters set by the system concerned. The cultivation of a belief in the law-governed nature of the state is a powerful aspect of state-building. Constitutional law must be treated as the third order of the political, and Loughlin's analysis of the third order provides the basis for his distinction between law and politics. He suggests that while conflict is an important criterion of politics, a sense of even-handedness is a vital component of state-building, necessitating the cultivation of a belief in the law-governed nature of the state. Constitutional law therefore establishes a framework through which the sovereign authority of the state can be recognised. Loughlin maintains that, while it is possible to see constitutional law as a relatively discrete set of positive rules, the meaning, function and application of those rules is governed by political practice, in which the law is embedded and from which it derives its identity.

This framework provides the basis for Loughlin's critique of much contemporary thinking about constitutions and constitutional law—a critique which is relevant when assessing the arguments developed in later essays. Loughlin suggests that the United Kingdom's traditionally 'political constitution'[43] was an expression of the laws, institutions and practices which made up the processes of governing. Laws regulated many of the key rules of political conduct and ensured a measure of even-handedness, but ultimately only a portion of the rules regulating the political regime were embodied in positive law. By contrast, the more recent tendency has been to treat the legal rules of the constitution as providing the foundation for all political engagement (rather than as the current and perhaps temporary product of such engagement). Loughlin suggests that the emerging modern culture of constitutional legalism misunderstands and downplays the crucial, conflict-centred role of the political, and places too much faith in the rules of positive law as the providers of 'correct' answers to contested questions. Observance of the law is necessary for the maintenance of power, but constitutional legalism obscures the primacy of the political in the operation of any constitution.

Loughlin's analysis is undoubtedly thought-provoking. For present purposes, his essay raises three vitally important questions. First, given that the United Kingdom has traditionally been seen as possessing a 'political constitution', how far have we—in recent years—seen a shift to the type of legalistic model that Loughlin decries, whether in terms of the arrangements that we in fact possess or in our interpretation of them? Is it inevitable that a multi-layered constitution is legalistic in the sense identified by Loughlin? Related to this is the second question, which is whether it is in fact correct to maintain that constitutional legalism misunderstands the role of the political. Murray Hunt's essay, later in the volume, would maintain—for example—that while courts have attempted to accommodate the political when conducting human rights-based judicial review, they have done so in a way which is inelegant and excessively broad, according *too much* deference to

---

[43] This term was used by Professor JAG Griffith as the title to his 1978 Chorley Lecture, 'The Political Constitution' (1979) 42 *MLR* 1. It should be noted that Loughlin's definition of politics is analogous to that used by Griffith (below at pp 12, 19–20; see also Loughlin's *Sword and Scales*, n 42 above, pp 6–9).

political bodies. The scope for disagreement about such matters in a multi-layered constitution is immense, and it is clear that different viewpoints will depend upon competing normative perspectives. The third—and perhaps broadest—question is whether it is meaningful to analyse a constitution using any particular analytical framework, if constitutions are of the provisional character identified by Lough-lin. The argument underpinning this collection of essays is that the traditional, unitary model of the United Kingdom constitution has now been replaced by a multi-layered model. Loughlin's analysis—if correct—forces us to ask ourselves how temporary such an arrangement may be, and whether it is in fact useful to deploy a multi-layered analysis as a basis for understanding the constitution.

The subsequent two essays—by Adam Tomkins and Carol Harlow—comple-ment one another, given that they concentrate on political aspects of our present-day constitutional arrangements. In his essay 'What is Parliament For?', Tomkins analyses the contemporary role of the Westminster Parliament—in particular the House of Commons—in an era characterised by the constitutional layering inher-ent in devolution within the United Kingdom and the transfer of powers to Euro-pean institutions. As a supporter of the 'political constitution' model, Tomkins asks how we can repair the 'political constitution' by improving the performance of Par-liament.[44] He argues that it is a mistake to conceive of Parliament, as Dicey did, principally as a legislative body. Rather, the key task of Parliament is and always has been to hold government to account (of which scrutiny of draft legislation is but one aspect). Parliament at the start of the twenty-first century plays a largely instru-mental role as a legislator: it retains the theoretical right not to enact into law the measures placed before it by the government of the day, but this right is very rarely exercised. Tomkins thus suggests that the primary purpose of Parliament is not to make law, but is instead to scrutinise the government's legislative proposals—something which is a part of its broader scrutiny function. Tomkins argues that it would be sensible officially to recognise the primary role of Parliament as being that of scrutineer, and calls for a radical strengthening of Parliament's powers of scrutiny. Parliament should be placed at the top of a pyramid of accountability, allowing it systematically to draw upon the investigations of outside regulators and commissions. Tomkins's prescription thus involves a re-casting of the methods available at Westminster level for promoting political accountability, one aim being to adjust the notion of a political constitution so as to fit in with a multi-layered constitutional structure. The normative debate concerning the desirability of the political constitution model is of course long-standing,[45] and it would be natural for supporters of the competing positions in this debate to differ in their conclu-sions concerning the merits of Tomkins's aim. A further question—whatever one's normative perspective—will be how far Tomkins's proposals can succeed as a basis for guaranteeing a meaningful constitutional role for the Westminster Parliament.

---

[44]   For Tomkins's normative views, see his 'In Defence of the Political Constitution' (2002) 22 *OJLS* 157, 169–175.

[45]   See eg, C Harlow and R Rawlings *Law and Administration*, n 1 above; M Loughlin *Public Law and Political Theory* (Oxford, Clarendon Press, 1992).

Arguments about scrutiny—this time at European Union level—are pushed further in Professor Carol Harlow's chapter, 'European Governance and Accountability', which critically evaluates what she categorises as the accountability problems which have arisen in the development of a multi-layered constitutional structure. Harlow argues that there has been a transfer of power vertically upwards from national institutions to EU institutions, arguably weakening national political mechanisms for maintaining the accountability of executive bodies (in particular, accountability through national legislatures), as well as a transfer of power within the EU layer from political decision-makers to the European Court of Justice. This argument provides a powerful illustration of some of the developments associated earlier in this introduction with the notion of a multi-layered constitution: legislative and executive power now resides, in practice, at national *and* EU levels, and a significant regime of legal accountability has developed through the courts. At a deeper level, Harlow's chapter also illustrates the definitional difficulties inherent in notions of accountability. Politically, the term can be interpreted in many different ways, each of which has diverse constitutional implications: compare, for example, the idea that elected bodies are held accountable by submitting themselves periodically to the electorate's verdict; the notion that executive decision-makers are held accountable by having to explain their decisions to a legislature; the requirement that officials resign in prescribed circumstances as a mechanism for ensuring accountability; and the view that accountability is fostered by subjecting institutions to periodic auditing by regulators. Legally, the term is associated with controls imposed by the courts, begging the question which controls are appropriate. Harlow suggests that the weight and meaning ascribed to various notions of accountability in the United Kingdom is somewhat unique when considered against a broader European backdrop, something which may help to explain why these notions have generally failed to take hold at a European level. Harlow reiterates her faith in political (in preference to legal) accountability, and uses this as a basis for criticising current proposals—such as the European Commission's White Paper on Governance—for reform of the policy-making processes at EU level. As with Tomkins's arguments, one's view of Harlow's criticisms and conclusions must ultimately depend, at normative level, on one's position concerning the comparative pros and cons of political as opposed to legal accountability.

The subsequent two chapters—by Richard Cornes and Professor Brigid Hadfield—explore some of the important constitutional questions raised by devolution from the Westminster Parliament to Scotland, Wales and (sporadically) Northern Ireland: that is, by the explicit creation of new constitutional layers. Whilst each author is formally concerned with a particular aspect of the post-1997 devolution programme—Cornes with the position of the English regions post-devolution, Hadfield with the role of the judiciary in post-devolution Northern Ireland—both make significant general points about the role of devolution within a multi-layered constitution, and about what is required in order for the process of asymmetrical devolution to work. For example, Professor Hadfield points out that the degree to which each layer in a multi-layered constitution is both discrete and settled will be crucial to the working of the overall structure, and both essays provide useful analyses of the efficacy of the devolved aspects of the United Kingdom's constitution.

In his essay 'Devolution and England—what is on offer?', Richard Cornes engages in a critical analysis of recent proposals for English regional government.[46] Cornes suggests that although such proposals would constitute a further advance for multi-layered governance in the United Kingdom, they do not in fact amount to devolution in any real sense. Based on an analysis of the devolution regimes in Scotland, Wales and Northern Ireland, Cornes argues that the essence of devolution is the transfer of power from Westminster to governing institutions responsible for distinct geographical areas within the United Kingdom, with devolved decision-makers being primarily answerable to their local electorates. Thus defined, genuine devolution of power must be to an area with which the local population identifies, and to locally elected bodies with a legislative/executive division. Furthermore, it is desirable for devolved institutions to be open to judicial review only on the grounds set out in the statute in which power is devolved, rather than on every available common law ground of review. Priority should be given to devolved institutions being held to account by the local electorate, something which would also leave only a residual guardian role for the United Kingdom government and Westminster Parliament. Measured against these criteria, the nature and functions of the proposed English regional bodies, together with the ambit of continuing central government control, would make it inappropriate to describe them as genuinely devolved institutions.

Cornes's analysis serves to remind us that there is no uniquely correct way to allocate power within a multi-layered constitution. For example, as part of his argument, Cornes distinguishes between devolution and other methods for allocating power on a layered basis. According to Cornes, the requirement of local election differentiates devolution from decentralisation, in which central government power is merely delegated to appointed officials or bodies. The United Kingdom's programme of devolution can, he argues, also be distinguished from federalism— under which *each* governing authority enjoys a constitutionally entrenched scope of authority—given that the Westminster Parliament technically retains legal sovereignty, even if it cannot in practice freely exercise its legislative power over devolved areas. In practice, political considerations are likely to determine which devolution arrangement is adopted. Important general lessons can also be learned from Cornes's conclusion, which is that the nature of the union between England, Scotland, Wales and Northern Ireland must be reformulated so that each constituent nation becomes an individual, but co-operating, member state within the European Union. This is a contentious suggestion, but it is important analytically for two reasons. The first relates to Cornes's argument that his proposal provides the only practical basis for managing the relations between the constituent nations. He contends that the asymmetrical devolution regime which has emerged since

---

[46] Made in the White Paper *Your Region, Your Choice: Revitalising the English Regions*, Cm.5511.

1997 does not resolve the anomalous status of England, and that the proposals for regional government will not strike the right balance either. Whether or not this is correct, Cornes draws our attention to the key point that there is ample room for debate about the suitability of a given legal regime to the political and social circumstances in which it must operate: something which may lead us to conclude that a particular method of distributing power on a layered basis either is or is not workable in practice. Secondly, Cornes's conclusion highlights the possibility that an inappropriate legal regime may generate tension or inconsistency between different constitutional layers. Quite apart from the possibility that devolution creates a division between the Westminster Parliament's political and legal capacity to act, the fact that the United Kingdom forms part of the European Union clearly has implications—as Cornes recognises—for how best to allocate power between Westminster and the devolved layers of the UK's constitutional structure. Unless, for example, all four constituent nations of the United Kingdom remain members of the EU—with an overarching EU layer in their constitution(s)—Cornes's substantive conclusion could not in practice work.

In her chapter 'Does the devolved Northern Ireland need an independent judicial arbiter?', Professor Hadfield also suggests that there is a key distinction to be drawn between devolution and federalism. By contrast with Cornes, however, the distinction—for Hadfield—rests upon the presence or absence of a written constitution as much as the presence or absence of a hierarchy of legislative bodies. Hadfield suggests that in a federal system, power is allocated by an overarching written constitution, which can be amended only by using a specific formula involving both central and provincial authorities. Furthermore, central and provincial bodies within a federal structure must each possess areas of exclusive legislative competence—something which is not the case under devolution, in which the 'national' level remains constitutionally paramount. In an evocation of our earlier discussion of the debate between advocates of legal and political controls, Hadfield also implies that one key to understanding a multi-layered constitution—whether constructed on a federal or a devolved basis—is by identifying the custodians, whether legal or political, of the integrity of each layer. Hadfield suggests—in a fashion which, in its emphasis, differs from Cornes's analysis—that responsibility for the evolution of devolution should lie primarily with the elected devolved institutions, *subject to* the presence of other mechanisms for accountability within the multi-layered constitutional system.

However, the appropriate balance between political and legal controls appears—for Hadfield—to be a somewhat contingent matter. In assessing the role of legal controls within the devolved structure that (at present, intermittently) applies in Northern Ireland, Hadfield points out that—in the various devolution experiments which were attempted in Northern Ireland prior to the Northern Ireland Act 1998—the judiciary was given roles, in policing the relevant settlements, of varying widths. Hadfield therefore makes the important suggestion that, while political accountability may often prove to be more effective than legal accountability, this depends upon the *general* efficacy of the judiciary as a mechanism for ensuring constitutional accountability. The implication seems to be that the more effective the judiciary is in general terms, the wider the role it might plausibly be given in policing a devolution settlement. Hadfield thus suggests that any assessment of the 1998 Act must take account of the fact that, at 'national' level, the judiciary has become much more assertive and self-confident in exercising its judicial review jurisdiction than was the case during previous periods of devolution in Northern Ireland. Hadfield concludes that rigorous judicial scrutiny of the respective powers of the devolved institutions *and* central government is vital if the constitutional settlement contained in the 1998 Act is to be properly policed; and that, by contrast with earlier devolution experiments, it is not appropriate to rely overwhelmingly on political mechanisms.

The next four chapters focus, in very different ways, on the sideways diffusion of what might once have been viewed—broadly-speaking—as purely state power. Processes such as deregulation, contracting-out and privatisation have become widespread at all constitutional levels in the last twenty years, as has the (at least partial) reconceptualisation along consumerist lines of the relationship between providers and recipients of public services. These changes raise difficult questions about how (and whether) we should now distinguish between public and private bodies and functions, and how we can best ensure that such functions are exercised accountably.

Professor John Morison's chapter, 'Modernising Government and the e-government revolution', uses Michel Foucault's governmentality approach to the deployment of power in society to analyse the constitutional implications of the contemporary 'modernisation of government' process, in particular the development of e-government. The governmentality approach seeks to shift our focus away from traditional subjects of constitutional scholarship such as the executive and the legislature. Governmental action cannot attain its ends all by itself: instead, it requires the active co-operation of non-state actors (whether individuals or collective bodies) and engagement with existing networks of power in society. By focusing solely on the notion of a sovereign body imposing its will, we lose sight of the fact that the practical *operation* of government is shaped, informed and assisted by civil society. Furthermore, law is only one instrument of governance: one must also think of codes, agreements, understandings, and so on. Foucault argued, using the governmentality approach, that the state diffused its power and developed links with a whole range of power centres in civil society during the nineteenth and twentieth centuries, allowing it to survive social change by moving away from earlier forms of government based on command and territorial control. Morison analyses recent constitutional changes from a similar standpoint, by arguing that globalisation and European integration—together with processes such as privatisation and contracting-out—have generated a multiplicity of sites of power, arranged in a network of mutual influence instead of hierarchical layers. The creation of quasi-governmental agencies and the frequent performance of characteristically 'public' functions by private bodies require us to think of power in terms of a complicated series of networks.

If Morison's advocacy of governmentality is accepted, then public lawyers will need to widen their focus radically. Whatever one's view of this possibility, Morison offers some important observations concerning the re-conceptualisation of government resulting from the 'modernisation' programme. The essential focus of this programme is on developing a consumer orientation for service-delivery, improving public sector performance and taking advantage of new information technology. This involves the notion of government as an enabler, facilitator and regulator rather than as a direct provider of services: something which turns on negotiation, monitoring and the development of networks and partnerships. E-government—which harnesses computer technology as a mechanism for delivering government services and consulting citizens—is a key part of the programme, although it is still at an early stage of development in the United Kingdom.[47] Morison suggests that—if developed radically so as to make *all* government services, at whatever level, available on-line through the same electronic 'gateway'— the project could relegate the distinctiveness of different government departments, as well as the many different layers which characterise the present constitution. The project would require us to redefine the space occupied by government, since a new forum would have opened up in which government, citizens, and other bodies could interact. Therefore, while it appears to dilute our need to think of the state in distinctive terms, e-government may—if fully developed— serve also to blur the distinctions between constitutional layers.

In his chapter 'UK Utility Regulation in an Age of Governance', Peter Leyland evaluates the consequences of the re-conceptualisation and 'modernisation' of government for a specific area of activity which now appears to embrace aspects of both the public and the private, namely the regulation of utility supply. In the wake of privatisation, contracting-out and the introduction of 'New Public Management', the gas, electricity and water industries have become increasingly fragmented, as have the forms of regulation that apply to them. Responsibility for regulating related aspects of the same industry are sometimes distributed to different bodies. This process of fragmentation has been accentuated still further since 1997 by the creation of differing regulatory regimes in different parts of the United Kingdom following devolution. The post-1997 period has also seen the development of informal 'soft law' regulatory techniques for service delivery by the utility sector, further underlining the switch from centralised bureaucratic mechanisms of service delivery to much more fragmented devices. Leyland argues that another consequence of the reconfiguration of the utility sector has been the attenuation of political accountability to the Westminster Parliament through ministers (an argument previously explored by Tomkins). In consequence, utility regulation provides a powerful illustration of the variable mechanisms by which power is exercised and regulated at the national and devolved constitutional layers, and of the difficult question of how best to ensure the accountability of bodies charged with the delivery of services formerly provided directly by state bodies. In developing these arguments, Leyland is sympathetic to the notion (articulated by

[47] See also 'E-government: no thanks, we prefer shopping', *The Economist*, 4 January 2003, p 23.

Colin Scott) that regulation should be seen not so much as a function of government but as a form of governance, characterised by the interdependence of state and non-state organisations, interactions within networks, negotiations between actors, and sometimes by a degree of autonomy from the state.[48] In contrast to Morison's conclusions concerning the development of e-government, Leyland therefore emphasises the on-going importance of the differences between the regulatory regimes operating in different constitutional layers. As we shall see when considering Professor Peter Cane's chapter, different views to Leyland's may also be taken concerning the distinction between state and non-state actors.

Questions concerning the division between public and private power are also raised by the concept of a right to freedom of information. As Stephanie Palmer argues in her chapter, 'Freedom of Information: a New Constitutional Landscape?', freedom of information is an important measure available for the control of power in the contemporary constitution, and is viewed in many jurisdictions as a constitutional right. Traditionally, the democratic objectives underpinning freedom of information have, however, not been seen as relevant to private sector bodies: for information can, from a private sector standpoint, be viewed as private property rather than as a public good. Given the arguable blurring of public and private in the last twenty years, the democratic objectives of freedom of information legislation can therefore be undermined—where public services are contracted out to private bodies—if access to information is denied in such circumstances because the arrangement in play is uncritically accepted as private. It is with this concern in mind, together with an appreciation of the way in which they illustrate the multi-layered theme, that Palmer analyses the similarities and differences between the Freedom of Information Act 2000 and the Freedom of Information (Scotland) Act 2002. While the Acts apply to a broader range of bodies than is typical in many other jurisdictions—thereby alleviating some of the concerns relating to contracting-out—Palmer argues that the exclusion from disclosure of commercially sensitive information contained within the legislation may well be problematical in the light of such concerns. Furthermore, the bodies which are defined as public authorities for freedom of information purposes are not identical to those which count as public authorities under the Human Rights Act 1998—something which may cause confusion both administratively and in terms of future litigation. It therefore remains unclear how far the Acts will enhance either the political or legal accountability of the bodies to which they apply.

The questions raised by Leyland and Palmer concerning the public law-private law divide are analysed in greater depth in Professor Peter Cane's chapter 'Accountability and the Public/Private Distinction'. Cane characterises the current debate as paradoxical. On the one hand, the public law-private law distinction seems to be alive and well in every layer of the constitution: it is embedded in domestic judicial review, in the Human Rights Act 1998 and Freedom of Information Act 2000, and

---

[48]   C Scott, 'The Governance of the European Union: The Potential for Multi-level Control' (2002) 8 *ELJ* 59; 'Private Regulation of the Public Sector: a Neglected Facet of Contemporary Governance' (2002) 29 *JLS* 56.

in the rules concerning direct effect in EC law. On the other hand, there is a common academic view—characterised in much of the scholarship concerning regulation and 'New Public Management'—that the distinction is in some sense outmoded or inappropriate. We seem, Cane suggests, to be caught between wanting to reaffirm (through legislation and case law) that government is different from civil society, and needing to make sense of the array of phenomena—such as regulation—which appear to challenge the distinctions between public and private. Cane's answer rests on making a careful division between the approaches to the distinction. He suggests that functional approaches distinguish between public and private law on the basis of the nature of the function under scrutiny, while institutional approaches employ a blunter distinction based on the nature of the body. While the performance of governmental tasks by non-governmental bodies has reinforced the functional approaches, differing combinations of both can be found in cases concerning the scope of judicial review, the definition of a 'public authority' within section 6 of the Human Rights Act 1998, and the ambit of direct effect under EC law: a point which neatly illustrates the multi-layered nature of the contemporary constitution.

Cane argues that recent criticisms of the public law-private law distinction are analytically flawed. He also engages in detailed scrutiny of the regulation scholarship. Scott's argument concerning governance, Cane suggests, can only be used to undermine a public law–private law distinction understood in institutional terms: it supports no conclusion about the viability or desirability of a functional divide.[49] Cane also suggests that since arguments about a functionally-drawn distinction rest on competing normative considerations of distributive justice, empirical observations concerning the ease or difficulty with which such a distinction works in practice are unlikely to have strong persuasive effect. The paradox identified at the start of his chapter can, Cane argues, be solved only by recognising that supporters and opponents of the public law–private law distinction are talking past each other at normative level. Opponents are making the empirical claim that the distinction misrepresents the way in which power *is* distributed and regulated, while supporters make the normative claim that the distinction embodies an attractive theory of the way power *should be* distributed and regulated. Cane's own formulation of the distinction is therefore normative: he suggests—in stark contrast to Oliver[49a]—that certain values are distinctively public and others (for example, those associated with making profit) distinctively private.

Cane's conclusion is important. We tend to assume in political theory that the role of the state, seen in terms of its duties and responsibilities, is in some sense unique. Cane's values-based distinction helpfully makes this point explicit, and gives us a basis for understanding the apparently contradictory tendencies adopted (empirically speaking) in the areas of regulation and human rights. One could

---

[49] It should also be noted that, from the standpoint of service *delivery*, differences between public and private remain strongly evident: see further S. Prentice, 'People, not structures, hold the key to public services reform' (2002) 10 *Renewal* 48.

[49a] D Oliver, *Common Values and the Public–Private Divide* (London, Butterworths, 1999).

properly say that we would no longer need to overlook one area in order to make sense of the other. What Cane's normative distinction does not do, however, is to free us entirely from empirical argument. For, having recognised the existence of a normative justification for the public law–private law distinction, we are still faced with practical questions about where the distinction should be drawn in individual cases. The role of Cane's normative approach is to supply us with a more honest mechanism for answering such questions. Whatever substantive conclusion one arrives at, it must be noted that the four chapters discussed here all draw attention, from different perspectives, to an important feature of the existence of multiple constitutional layers: namely that definitions of the public—and indeed the significance of the concept of the public—can vary from layer to layer. It is perfectly possible, in a unitary constitution, to argue about the positioning and significance of the public law–private law divide: in a multi-layered constitution, such questions acquire greater importance given the possible variations between the different layers.

The final five chapters focus on the role of the courts in a multi-layered constitution. As such, they focus specifically on the appropriate remit of legal—as opposed to political—controls over public power in different layers of the constitution. As with the earlier chapters by Tomkins and Harlow focusing on political accountability, the arguments relating to legal accountability deployed in the present chapters utilise a variety of approaches. In the first of the five chapters, Nicholas Bamforth engages in a largely analytical exercise by evaluating the response of United Kingdom courts to the emergence of a multi-layered constitution. By contrast, the next three chapters—by Professor Michael Taggart, Murray Hunt and Professor Conor Gearty—focus, from differing normative perspectives, on the proper role of the courts now that the Human Rights Act 1998 is in force. They do so, in particular, by considering the degree to which judges should defer to decisions made by elected bodies. At one level, the chapters are therefore concerned with the distribution of power between the courts, the executive and the legislature, and the comparative merits of legal and political accountability, within the national layer of the constitution. However, the three chapters also contain broader reflections on the interaction between different constitutional layers, specifically by focusing—again, from divergent perspectives—on the implications of the jurisprudence of the European Court of Human Rights for the emerging Human Rights Act jurisprudence at national level. The final chapter—by Joanna Miles—is also concerned both with the divergent role of the courts in different constitutional layers and with the appropriate judicial role, but considers such questions through the specific question of which litigants should have access to the courts.

In 'Courts in a Multi-Layered Constitution', Nicholas Bamforth analyses the implications of the emergence of a multi-layered constitution for judicial decision-making at national level. Bamforth suggests that there have been contradictory tendencies in the case law, leading to a fragmentation between judicial approaches depending upon the area concerned. For example, before the Human Rights Act came into force, proportionality could officially be used as a ground of judicial review only in cases involving EC law points; its use was officially prohibited in purely domestic cases. Nonetheless, considerable evidence exists to show that proportionality-style review was unofficially employed in practice. In similar vein, the official refusal to recognise proportionality could be contrasted with the courts' enthusiasm for developing domestic remedies by analogy with EC law—notably in the areas of injunctive relief against ministers and restitutionary relief against public authorities. The recognition of proportionality as a basis for review in cases falling within the Human Rights Act also raises the possibility of fragmented judicial approaches. It is unclear, for example, whether its availability in Human Rights Act cases will encourage courts to allow proportionality officially to play a role in cases involving no Convention or EC law points, or how Convention jurisprudence will interact with case law of the European Court of Justice in cases where both are relevant. Bamforth argues that such issues will depend, for their resolution, on the degree to which courts accord priority to their perceived role at national constitutional level by contrast to their role in the enforcement of rules emanating from the two European layers of the constitution (a balance which in itself begs many questions concerning the way in which courts understand the constitutional basis of the present multi-layered structure). The case law concerning the Human Rights Act and EC law reflects these competing priorities. At a more theoretical level, Bamforth points out that any account of the appropriate role of the courts in the present-day constitution—whether that account is more sympathetic to the notion of a 'political constitution' or to legal constitutionalism—must now take account of the significance of the two European layers. A simple distinction between a political constitution and legal constitutionalism may no longer be appropriate given that neither standpoint can offer—in and of itself—clear-cut guidance to courts as to the priority (if any) to be accorded to the European layers.

In relation to the national layer, Professor Taggart argues in his chapter 'Reinventing Administrative Law' that the 'classic model' of United Kingdom administrative law—characterised by restrictive grounds of judicial review (most obviously, where the exercise of discretionary power was concerned) and an emphasis on judicial restraint—is being swept away by the advent of 'constitutional', judicial reasoning focused on rights. Taggart illustrates the workings of the 'classic model' by analysing the famous *Wednesbury* decision[50]: which, he suggests, was characteristic of the tendency of the courts at the time to steer clear of apparently 'political' questions. At face value, the 'classic model'—which sought to keep courts away from 'political' questions—contrasts sharply with the inquiry which a court must now carry out when reviewing the exercise of discretionary power in Human Rights Act cases involving 'qualified' rights (that is, rights which may permissibly be overridden in specified circumstances). Courts must now begin by considering the nature of the right allegedly infringed, and then decide whether that right has been justifiably limited in terms of the express qualifications

---

[50] See Lord Greene MR's judgment in *Associated Provincial Picture Houses v Wednesbury Corporation* [1948] 1 KB 223.

imposed upon it. The burden of justifying the restriction falls on the public authority, which must provide clear and sufficient evidence. This 'right-centred' approach, Taggart suggests, requires more focused, consistent and transparent judicial methodology than was the case under the 'classic model'. Taggart argues, however, that judges will still remain wary, under the rights-focused model, of intervening in certain types of case. The central idea behind the 'classic' *Wednesbury* approach—that it is inappropriate for the courts to adjudicate in *every* dispute between citizen and state—lives on. The real distinction between the rights-focused model and the *Wednesbury* approach is that under the former, such an idea must be more clearly articulated in the case law: something which requires the development of a coherent theory of judicial deference which pays close attention to considerations of democratic legitimacy and judicial expertise.

This idea also forms a primary focus of Murray Hunt's chapter, 'Sovereignty's Blight: Why Contemporary Public Law Needs the Concept of 'Due Deference''. Hunt suggests that a proper approach has yet to be articulated, in Human Rights Act cases, concerning when and on what basis judicial deference to elected institutions is appropriate. The notion of a 'discretionary area of judgment'[51] is inappropriate as it presupposes the existence of a definitive constitutional boundary between legal and political redress: a specific *area* within which the judiciary will defer, with matters falling within this area being seen as inappropriate for judicial resolution. Hunt's preferred approach is known as 'due deference'. Since rights can cut across all substantive areas of public decision-making, courts should approach the deference issue in a focused, issue-specific way, with decision-makers being required in each case to show why they deserve judicial deference. Having identified the specific issue in respect of which deference is being claimed, courts should ask—in relation to *that* particular issue—how *much* deference should be shown to the decision-maker. Hunt ties his analysis to what he categorises as a much deeper problem in public law thought. He suggests that modern accounts of public law struggle unsuccessfully to reconcile the traditional Diceyan notion of Parliament's legal sovereignty with the modern constitutional notion of the sovereignty of the individual, with its concomitant respect for constitutional rights. This leads to a public law of competing supremacies, and forces courts to employ uneasy spatial analyses such as the 'discretionary area'. By contrast, Hunt suggests, the 'due deference' approach can steer the courts between the two extremes of judicial submission to elected bodies and judicial supremacy. By focusing on the value of rights and the cogency of the reasons advanced for restricting them, it prevents courts from grounding their analyses in formalistic notions such as the will of Parliament.

Hunt stresses that his 'due deference' approach presupposes that the courts and Parliament *share* a commitment to representative democracy and to certain rights, freedoms and basic values. His project, however, is to develop a suitable methodology for the courts to use, a methodology might also accompany Michael Taggart's notion that judicial deference to elected bodies will continue to be relevant. In his

[51] Stemming from Lord Hope's judgment in *R. v Director of Public Prosecutions, ex parte Kebilene* [2000] 2 AC 326, 380.

chapter 'Civil Liberties and Human Rights', Conor Gearty similarly concludes that the Human Rights Act requires a commitment from Parliament, the executive and the courts, but the scope of this commitment—to those principles of civil liberties which make our society a self-governing community of equals—would appear to be rather different from Hunt's. In particular, Gearty carves out a distinctive—and arguably pre-eminent—role for political accountability. In doing so, Gearty draws a sharp distinction between civil liberties and human rights. Civil liberties are, he suggests, concerned with the freedoms which are essential to the maintenance and fostering of representative government: the right to vote and to stand for election, together with a list of associated rights such as freedom of expression and freedom of assembly. Since civil liberties are rooted in a commitment to the idea of a representative democracy, they may sometimes be qualified in the interest of democratic necessity. Gearty argues that human rights, by contrast, are of a more absolute and general nature, and that arguments about when rights should be qualified are often hard to resolve given that answers cannot be provided by reference to a unifying underlying commitment to representative democracy. Gearty characterises the Convention as a charter of civil liberties rather than human rights, and suggests that this is entirely consistent with the Human Rights Act's protection of Parliamentary Sovereignty via the declaration of incompatibility procedure. Ultimate decisions concerning the restrictions of civil liberties should, he suggests, lie with elected bodies, and courts should adopt a restrained approach to statutory interpretation under section 3 of the Act.[52] Although he stresses the predominant role of political institutions, Gearty is keen to argue that this does not leave civil liberties undefended against a potentially authoritarian legislature. For one thing, any analysis must be politically realistic: it is inevitable, in practice, that undesirable restrictions on civil liberties are sometimes enacted. The appropriate remedy in this situation is political rather than legal. Furthermore, the record of United Kingdom courts in civil liberties cases is, Gearty argues, unimpressive, both in absolute terms and in contrast to the Westminster Parliament. While Gearty does not extend his analysis into the area of deference explicitly, it is clear that he would take a very different view—as a committed supporter of traditional Parliamentary sovereignty—from that advocated by Hunt.

The Taggart, Hunt and Gearty chapters highlight the fact that one's normative view concerning the appropriate division between legal and political accountability is central to any assessment of the proper role of the courts in the contemporary constitution. Hunt believes that constitutional accountability is best protected by giving the courts a principled and clearly articulated role, in which deference to elected institutions (and the scope for mechanisms of political accountability) is carefully calibrated and controlled. A coherent balance must therefore be struck between competing notions of sovereignty. For Gearty, by contrast, legal accountability is better seen as an adjunct to political accountability, with the sovereignty of Parliament remaining pre-eminent. Both approaches beg

---

[52] See further C Gearty, 'Reconciling Parliamentary Democracy and Human Rights', n 25 above.

many questions. A crucial question for Hunt's analysis will be whether the 'due deference' approach in fact keeps the courts away, to a sufficient extent, from questions which are unsuitable for judicial resolution. At a more theoretical level, questions might also be raised about whether the tension he identifies between competing notions of sovereignty is in fact such a crucial underlying issue. Crucial questions for Gearty will be whether the distinction between civil liberties and human rights is in fact as stark as he maintains, given the existence of many competing theories of the nature of human rights; and whether Parliament is in fact as successful a guarantor of civil liberties, and the courts as unsuccessful in this role, as he maintains.

The three essays also highlight the interaction between different layers of the constitution, again in rather different ways. Michael Taggart suggests that the rise of rights-focused, 'constitutional' litigation is related, at least in part, to the growing number of domestic, regional and international human rights instruments around the world. The 'reinvention' of administrative law is underpinned both by the growth of 'constitutionalism' within the United Kingdom and by the internationalisation of human rights standards on a global basis. Taggart does not develop this analysis at length, but it is clear that he sees normative questions concerning the proper role of the courts—and, in consequence, the proper division between legal and political accountability—to be integrally-related to the emergence of a multi-layered constitution. Hunt and Gearty adopt divergent views about the European Convention on Human Rights, in parallel with their contributions to the debate concerning the role of courts at the national layer. Both agree that the Convention is now an important point of reference for national courts, but they differ as to the lessons which the reasoning of the Strasbourg Court might offer at national level. Hunt argues that the Strasbourg Court's 'margin of appreciation' principle suffers from similar deficiencies as the domestic 'discretionary area of judgment', and therefore looks on the principle with disfavour. However, he appears to view the Convention as offering—at least *prima facie*— statements of the value to be attached to particular rights, something which would be important for national courts in deploying a 'due deference' analysis. Gearty's view is (as indicated above) that the Convention is clearly a charter for civil liberties rather than human rights. One aim of the Convention is to promote an effective political democracy, and many of the central Convention rights relate to that aim. The Convention allows for such rights to be qualified in the face of overriding and deeper democratic necessities, and Gearty argues that the Strasbourg Court has generally approached this matter in a principled and coherent fashion. The implication of this, clearly, is that national courts must similarly seek to treat Convention rights as civil liberties.

The final chapter, by Joanna Miles—entitled 'Standing in a Multi-Layered Constitution'—also focuses, albeit in the specific context of the range of litigants who are entitled to litigate in essentially public law disputes—on the appropriate division between legal and political accountability, and on the complexities associated with the existence of multiple constitutional layers. Miles traces—in particular, by using a case study based upon the standing and intervention rights of the pressure group Greenpeace—the differences between standing and intervention rules in Human Rights Act judicial review cases, devolution disputes, EC law cases, and ordinary judicial review under section 31 of the Supreme Court Act 1981. The existence of so many different tests reflects the multi-layered nature of the contemporary constitution, in which courts are required to interpret and apply laws deriving from many different sources. While it may be appropriate to have different tests in different contexts, Miles points out that one difficulty with the present position is that some of the formally separate areas of case law are not in practice discrete. Miles suggests that we can only determine which tests for standing and intervention are appropriate by reference to our views concerning the appropriateness and legitimacy of different types of claimant or intervener raising their arguments in the legal—rather the political—sphere, and concerning the proper role of courts within the constitution. Are courts, for example, supposed merely to safeguard the rights of individuals against the state, or are they concerned to correct illegalities, whoever the litigant happens to be? Miles canvasses a variety of possible answers, but her main concern is to stress the need for any solution to be of a principled nature.

CONCLUSION

We have argued that the United Kingdom can now be said to possess a multi-layered rather than a unitary, self-correcting constitution. The processes whereby such a constitution has emerged have sometimes been controversial, as is demonstrated by the ongoing debate about the basis—as a matter of national constitutional law—for the courts' recognition of the supremacy of EC law. However such deep-level debates are resolved, it is at least clear that the existence of a (and of this particular) multi-layered constitution gives rise to many lower-level practical questions, and it is with such questions that this collection of essays seeks to engage. We cannot claim that the essays in the collection engage with—still less answer—all such questions. Nonetheless, by highlighting the sheer range of questions—particularly concerning the similarities and differences between the different layers, the scope for cross-over between them, the appropriate role of political and legal accountability mechanisms, and the boundaries between state and non-state actors—we hope that they go some way towards sketching a map of the terrain on which debate about the contemporary constitution must nowadays be conducted, and indeed that they stimulate further contributions to that debate.

2

Constitutional Law: the Third
Order of the Political

MARTIN LOUGHLIN*

F OR MOST OF the twentieth century, constitutions were generally regarded—
like most formal legal documents—as being rather dry and dreary matters,
likely to be of interest only to three relatively discrete groups of people: officials with responsibilities relating to the system of government, lawyers who were
occasionally called on to advise and litigate in the circumstances of a particular
dispute, and to a small group of academics who continued to believe in their
importance as objects of scholarly inquiry. Within this last group in particular, the
importance of constitutional investigation seemed during the course of the
century to have diminished. In the latter half of the twentieth century, for example, most political scientists (in the English-speaking world at least) appeared to
have given up on constitutions, as the intellectual orientation of their discipline
shifted away from the study of the institutional framework of public decision-
making and towards the more 'scientific' study of political behaviour. Formal
constitutional arrangements, it was suggested, presented a façade that acted as a
barrier to the acquisition of a scientific understanding of politics as an extended
power play. The field of constitutional investigation was therefore left mainly to a
relatively small group of lawyers who remained interested in studying those basic
rules concerning the allocation of governmental authority.

During the last decade or so, however, this twentieth century trend underwent a
marked reversal. The general interest that recently has been shown in constitutions as frameworks for the control and regulation of government and, perhaps
even more importantly, in constitutionalism as a political theory which expresses
the fundamental values of contemporary society, has been quite remarkable. Both
politically and intellectually, questions concerning the form and nature of

* Earlier versions of this chapter were presented as a Lansdowne Lecture at the University of Victoria,
BC, at staff seminars at Queen's University, Kingston, Ontario and the University of Nottingham, and
at a seminar on 'Governance in Transition' in Belfast, held as part of the ESRC-sponsored programme
on 'Justice in Transition: Northern Ireland and Beyond'. I am most grateful to the organisers of, and
participants in, these seminars for support and constructive comments, and to the Leverhulme Trust
for the award of a Major Research Fellowship in relation to a project of which this chapter forms part.

constitutions have captured an unusual amount of public attention. During the twenty-first century, constitutions might well reacquire the status that they once enjoyed in the nineteenth.

Many factors have contributed to this regeneration of interest in constitutional matters. On the global stage, probably the most important has been the train of events that has followed the collapse of the Soviet Union. This episode, which marks a change of world-historical significance, has led to a major exercise of constitution-making in the newly independent states of the former Soviet empire; and invariably these documents have taken the form of liberal constitutionalist texts, establishing a law-governed democratic republic which pledges to respect the rights and freedoms of the individual.[1] As a result of the growing number of states which have formally pledged to respect constitutionalist principles, international organisations have taken up the challenge of promoting constitutionalism—a theory resting on such basic concepts as the separation of powers, the rule of law, respect for human rights, and the institutionalisation of effective judicial remedies—as a tool of social and economic development. Today, respect for the norms embedded within constitutionalism is often treated as a vital condition for the receipt of aid by western governments or as a precondition imposed on states seeking to join various international clubs.[2]

But it is not only change on the international stage that has shunted constitutional questions higher up the political agenda. Over the last 20 or so years, advanced western democracies, labouring under the pressure of a growing public expenditure burden, have been obliged to undertake a reassessment of the role of the state. This has led to a set of reforms, illustrated by such initiatives as privatisation and 'new public management', which has brought about a restructuring of the welfare state.[3] One consequence of the reconfiguration of government's role is that the state is no longer treated as a general agency for wealth redistribution. Discussion has thus moved away from the language of social justice with respect to governmental programmes that reallocate material resources and towards a more individualised language of rights, whether of minority ethnic groups or of various categories of vulnerable people. The resulting growth in the discourse of human rights within domestic politics has had the effect, implicitly at least, of heightening interest in constitutional concerns. Politics, it would appear, seems increasingly to be concerned with the obligations of government and the rights of citizens.

There are, of course, other more local factors that have led to a revival of interest in constitutions. In Britain, where because of its peculiar political history there

[1] See AE Dick Howard (ed), *Constitution-making in Eastern Europe* (Washington, DC, Woodrow Wilson Center Press, 1993); Ulrich K Preuss, 'The Politics of Constitution Making: Transforming Politics into Constitutions' (1991) 13 *Law & Policy* 107–123.

[2] The Council of Europe, for example, today requires all states seeking membership first to sign and ratify the European Convention on Human Rights and the European Charter of Local Self-Government.

[3] See, eg, David Osborne and Ted Gaebler, *Reinventing Government: How the Entrepreneurial Spirit is Transforming the Public Sector* (New York, Plume, 1993); Christopher D Foster and Francis J Plowden, *The State under Stress: Can the Hollow State be Good Government?* (Buckingham, Open University Press, 1996).

exists no formal constitution of the modern variety, this phenomenon is now often perceived not as a cause of celebration but rather as a deficiency that must be remedied.[4] In Canada, by contrast, the motivating impetus has been the perpetuation of concern about the identity of Canadian society, especially with respect to the status of minority language groups and of the first nations.[5] Whatever the mix, the political message being spread around the Western world is that we are all constitutionalists now.

Political scientists now express much more interest in the institutional aspects of governmental decision-making[6] and even in courts, both as decision-making institutions and as vehicles for the articulation of public values.[7] It is scarcely an exaggeration to suggest that today the concerns of political theorists seem to be dominated by various aspects of constitutionalism, such as rights,[8] constraint theory[9] and constitutional design in general.[10]

However, at more or less the same time that matters constitutional have shot up the agendas of politicians, political scientists and political theorists, a sceptical strain amongst lawyers about the discipline of constitutional law has emerged. This scepticism—cynicism might be a better term—assumed its most ideological and strident form in the work of the American critical legal studies movement of the 1980s, where the objective appeared to be that of questioning many of these liberal constitutionalist values and reducing constitutional discourse to that of partisan politics.[11] But even beyond the confines of that highly politicised movement, many students now tend to come away from constitutional law courses mouthing the slogan (albeit with a more world-weary inflection): 'Well, it's all just politics'.[12]

---

[4] See Institute for Public Policy Research, *A Written Constitution for the United Kingdom* (London, Mansell, 1993).

[5] See, eg, Will Kymlicka, *Multicultural Citizenship* (Oxford, Clarendon Press, 1995); James Tully, *Strange Multiplicity: Constitutionalism in an Age of Diversity* (Cambridge, Cambridge University Press, 1995).

[6] See, eg, JG March and JP Olsen, *Rediscovering Institutions: The Organisational Basis of Politics* (New York, Free Press, 1989).

[7] See, eg, David Robertson, *Judicial Discretion in the House of Lords* (Oxford, Clarendon Press, 1998); Alec Stone Sweet, *Governing with Judges: Constitutional Politics in Europe* (New York, Oxford University Press, 2000).

[8] See, eg, Hillel Steiner, *An Essay on Rights* (Oxford, Blackwell, 1994); Attracta Ingram, *A Political Theory of Rights* (Oxford, Clarendon Press, 1994); Michael Ignatieff, *Human Rights as Politics and Idolatry* (Princeton, NJ, Princeton University Press, 2001).

[9] See Jon Elster, *Ulysses Unbound: Studies in Rationality, Precommitment, and Constraints* (Cambridge, Cambridge University Press, 2000).

[10] See, eg, Russell Hardin, *Liberalism, Constitutionalism, and Democracy* (Oxford, Oxford University Press, 1999).

[11] See, eg, Roberto Unger, 'The Critical Legal Studies Movement' (1982) 96 *Harvard Law Review* 563; David Fraser, 'Truth and Hierarchy: Will the Circle be Broken?' (1984) 33 *Buffalo Law Review* 729; Mark Tushnet, *Red, White and Blue: A Critical Analysis of Constitutional* Law (Cambridge, Mass., Harvard University Press, 1988); Allan C Hutchinson, *Waiting for Coraf: A Critique of Law and Rights* (Toronto, University of Toronto Press, 1995).

[12] The apotheosis of this tendency can be seen in the response to the US Supreme Court's role in *Bush v Gore*, in which, however sophisticated the justificatory or critical explanation, it proved almost impossible to discern a discrepancy between any scholar's legal analysis and their voting behaviour. For a useful overview see EJ Dionne Jr and William Kristol (eds), *Bush v Gore: The Court Cases and the Commentary* (Washington, DC, Brookings Institution Press, 2001).

Although some jurists have directly responded to this trend, much of this work has been geared towards the attempt to explicate law's ideal qualities.[13] From this perspective, it is not difficult to demonstrate how law is capable of being differentiated from politics. But this type of legalistic approach tends to be constructed around an image of the individual pitted against the state and ultimately it seems to be underpinned by a desire to identify law and politics as the positive and negative polarities of modes of public decision-making.[14] Whatever value this approach—which is itself an act of political choice—may have, it is unlikely to be of any help in the search for finding effective means of negotiating differences. Formalism might be a useful device for taking forward the philosophical quest of isolating the phenomenon of the legal. But it acts as a positive hindrance to the exercise of advancing the more sociologically inspired objective of understanding law and politics as competing, but also related, modes of public discourse.

How then are we to proceed? If the reductive position of saying of constitutional law that 'it's all just politics' is uninteresting and the formalist stance of pre-supposing an ideal quality to law—that is, of starting with a transcendental view which elevates law into a realm above politics—is unhelpful, how can matters be advanced? We might begin by noting that what unites these two otherwise directly opposing positions is a common starting position. Both begin by trying to identify what, if anything, is special about law; and it may be the law-centred nature of their inquiry that leads ultimately to a distortion and polarisation of views. Perhaps a better way forward, then, would begin with an inquiry into the nature of politics and from this perspective to identify what seems to be special about law. Rather than starting with law and analysing whether or not it is reducible to politics, we might start with politics and consider how politics is capable of being elevated to law. By taking this line of inquiry, I hope to show that constitutional law can best be understood as what might be termed the third order of the political.

THE CONCEPT OF THE POLITICAL

In his influential essay on the vocation of politics, Max Weber defined politics as an activity through which 'the leadership, or the influencing of the leadership of a *political* association, hence today, of a *state*' is acquired.[15] Weber's definition highlights important aspects of the conduct of politics. Most significantly, perhaps, it suggests that politics is to be conceived as a practice that operates within an

---

[13] See, eg, Ernest Weinrib, 'Legal Formalism: On the Immanent Rationality of Law' (1988) 97 *Yale Law Journal* 949.

[14] See Judith N Shklar, *Legalism* (Cambridge, Mass: Harvard University Press, 1964), esp 1–28.

[15] Max Weber, 'Politics as a Vocation' [1919] in HH Gerth and C Wright Mills (eds), *From Max Weber: Essays in Sociology* (London, Routledge & Kegal Paul, 1948), 77–128, at 77. See also Max Weber, *Economy and Society: An Outline of Interpretive Sociology* (Guenther Roth and Claus Wittich (eds), Berkeley, University of California Press, 1978), 55: politics is public activity aimed at 'exerting influence on the government of a political organisation; especially at the appropriation, redistribution or allocation of the powers of government'.

institutional setting and is primarily concerned with the guidance of public decision-making—that is, with governing the state.

This type of definition is one that is commonly offered today. But although it is
able to provide some explanation of the nature of political practice within an institutional framework, it does not reach to the core of the engagement of politics. It
suggests that politics is action aimed at influencing the leadership of a political
association, thereby laying itself open to the criticism of being self-referential. If
the phenomenon is to be grasped, we cannot start by assuming any particular
form through which the activity of politics is conducted within the state. Rather
than deriving an understanding of the political from a theory of the state, the concept of the state presupposes the concept of the political.

This is the approach adopted by Carl Schmitt, who suggests that if the concept of
the political is properly to be identified, it must rest on its own distinctions. Just as
'in the realm of morality the final distinction is between good and evil, in aesthetics
beautiful and ugly, in economics profitable and unprofitable,' the question, Schmitt
asks, is 'whether there is a special distinction which can serve as a simple criterion
of the political'.[16] The answer he provides—somewhat controversially—is that
political action is action founded on the distinction between friend and enemy.

Schmitt's provocative answer is rooted in the conviction that conflict is a pri-
mordial condition, and it is this basic fact which gives rise to politics. Schmitt's
position is liable to be misunderstood. He is not suggesting that, say, the contest
between opposing political factions within the state is to be understood in terms of
this distinction between friend and enemy. Nor does he maintain that the distinction yields the substance of politics.[17] Schmitt here is not concerned with the practices of politics—what I will be calling the second order of the political—but with
a first order phenomenon: the concept of the political itself.

Schmitt's contention is that at the core of the concept of the political lies 'the
most intense and extreme antagonism', in other words, 'the ever present possibility
of conflict' and even of 'armed combat'.[18] It is the persistence of this threat 'which
determines in a characteristic way human action and thinking and thereby creates
a specifically political behaviour.'[19] Only through this most basic understanding of
the concept of the political, Schmitt contends, are we able to render meaningful
that which otherwise must remain obscure and incoherent. His claim is that the
political is a fundamental and inescapable aspect of the human condition.[20]

[16] Carl Schmitt, *The Concept of the Political* [1932] George Schwab trans (Chicago, University of
Chicago Press, 1996), 26.

[17] This is the error that Agnes Heller appears to make in her assessment of Schmitt: see Agnes Heller,
'The Concept of the Political Revisited' in David Held (ed), *Political Theory Today* (Cambridge, Polity
Press, 1991), 330–43, 332–33.

[18] Schmitt, above n 16, at 29, 32. Cf Heraclitus (535–475BC): 'War is the father of all and king of all,
and some he shows as gods, others as men; some he makes slaves, others free.' See GS Kirk, JE Raven and
M Schofield, *The Presocratic Philosophers: A Critical History with a Selection of Texts* (2nd edn, Cambridge, Cambridge University Press, 1995), Frag 53, Hippolytus, ref IX.9.4.

[19] *Ibid* at 34.

[20] Cf Leo Strauss, 'Notes on Carl Schmitt, *The Concept of the Political*' in Schmitt, above n 16,
81–107, 94: 'The political [for Schmitt] is a basic characteristic of human life; politics in this sense *is*
destiny; therefore man cannot escape politics' (emphasis in original).

By pursuing an understanding of the political to its very foundations, Schmitt seeks to reveal its essential character. That this continues to be a pressing question is illustrated by John Dunn's recent declaration to the effect that:

> Here we all are, loose in history and dubiously at ease within ourselves and with each other. What are we going to do about it? This is certainly the political question: and an eminently practical and exceedingly insistent one too.[21]

The Concept of the Political can therefore be read as an attempt systematically to address a basic issue about politics. But it also goes further and tries to answer to one of the most critical questions posed in classical political thought: how should I live? In *Euthyphro*, Plato asks about the nature of those disagreements that we could not settle and which would cause us to be enemies. The answer offered in the dialogue is not so dissimilar to Schmitt's:

> I suggest you consider whether it would not be the just and the unjust, beautiful and ugly, good and evil. Are not these the things, when we disagree about them and cannot reach a satisfactory decision, concerning which we on occasion become enemies—you and I, and all other men?[22]

Moral values are certainly not irrelevant in politics. The point that Schmitt impresses upon us is that they are not authoritative. Although humans are norm-loving animals, they live in a world comprising a multiplicity of moral maps. And it is the inevitability of clashes between these that determines the political. There is, after all, scarcely a war that has been fought in which all of the combatants did not believe that they had right on their side. The political can thus 'derive its energy from the most varied human endeavours, from the religious, economic, moral and other antitheses.'[23] But, whatever its cause, the 'political entity is by its very nature the decisive entity, regardless of the sources from which it derives its last psychic motives.'[24] The enemy in Schmitt's reading is not an evil person to be reviled: that would be too moralistic. Nor is he a criminal to be punished: that is too legalistic. The enemy is simply a foe to be defeated.

Schmitt reinforces the distinctively political nature of this 'enemy' by highlighting its public aspect. The enemy, he claims, is 'not the private adversary whom one hates' but 'is solely the public enemy': the enemy is *hostis*, not *inimicus*.[25] 'The enemy exists,' he elaborates, 'only when, at least potentially, one fighting

---

[21] John Dunn, 'What is Living and What is Dead in the Political Theory of John Locke?' in his *Interpreting Political Responsibility* (Cambridge, Polity Press, 1990), 9, 21–22.

[22] Plato, *Euthypro*, 7c-d in *The Dialogues of Plato* [c.399–387 BC] RE Allen trans. (New Haven, Yale University Press, 1984), i.47. See also Plato, *The Laws* [c.335–323 BC] RG Bury trans. (London, Heinemann, 1926), Bk1, where Clinias explains why the original Cretan legislator had devised such a warlike polity: 'And herein ... he condemned the stupidity of the mass of men in failing to perceive that all are involved ceaselessly in a lifelong war against all States ... every State is, by a law of nature, engaged perpetually in an informal war with every other State.'

[23] Schmitt, above n 16, 38.

[24] *Ibid* at 43–44.

[25] *Ibid* at 28.

collectivity of people confronts a similar collectivity.'[26] Echoing Hobbes, whose work he much admired,[27] Schmitt argues that it is this potential which underpins the political:

> The political does not reside in the battle itself, which possesses its own technical, psychological, and military laws, but in the mode of behaviour which is determined by this possibility, by clearly evaluating the concrete situation and thereby being able to distinguish correctly the real friend and the real enemy.[28]

Schmitt's work is not without its ambiguities and difficulties.[29] But by focusing on the existential character of the political, his thought yields acute insights into the role of the state, the conduct of politics within a system of governance, and also—especially as Schmitt himself claimed that his studies were of a juristic nature[30]—into the nature and functions of constitutional law.

POLITICS AND THE STATE

Schmitt's work is less clear than it might be on the question of the relationship between the state and the political. Since politics orders everything, he argues that it does not simply function within a particular domain: properly understood, it is an aspect of intensity of conflict. But because Schmitt also indicates the role of politics in managing conflict, on occasions he conveys the converse impression and implies that it is the limitation rather than the intensification of conflict that provides the essence of the political. Consequently, although he starts by asserting

[26] *Ibid*. This distinction also has parallels in classical political thought. See, eg, Cicero, *De Officiis*, III.29: 'There are also rights of war, and the faith of an oath is often to be kept with an enemy … [But] if you should not pay a price for your life, agreed on with robbers, it is no fraud if you should not perform it, though bound by an oath. For a pirate is not comprehended in the number of lawful enemies, but is the common foe of all men.'

[27] Schmitt refers to Hobbes as 'truly a powerful and systematic thinker': *ibid*. at 65. Cf Strauss, above n 20, at 89–93.

[28] *Ibid* at 37. Cf Hobbes, *Leviathan*, ch XIII: 'the nature of War, consisteth not in actuall fighting; but in the known disposition thereto, during all the time there is no assurance to the contrary. All other time is Peace.'

[29] Schmitt's work has recently attracted a great deal of attention from Anglo-American scholars. For valuable critical appraisals see especially: Gopal Balakrishnan, *The Enemy: An Intellectual Portrait of Carl Schmitt* (London, Verso, 2000); David Dyzenhaus, *Legality and Legitimacy: Carl Schmitt, Hans Kelsen and Herman Heller in Weimar* (Oxford, Oxford University Press, 1997), ch 2; David Dyzenhaus (ed), *Law as Politics: Carl Schmitt's Critique of Liberalism* (Durham: Duke University Press, 1998); John P McCormick, *Carl Schmitt's Critique of Liberalism: Against Politics as Technology* (Cambridge, Cambridge University Press, 1997); Chantal Mouffe (ed), *The Challenge of Carl Schmitt* (London, Verso, 1999); William E Scheuerman, *Carl Schmitt: The End of Law* (Lanham,: Rowan & Littlefield, 1999).

[30] Of *The Concept of the Political*, Schmitt later wrote that: 'The challenge that issues from the text itself is aimed primarily at experts on the constitution and jurists of international law'. See Carl Schmitt, *Der Begriff des Politischen. Text von 1932 mit einem Vorwort und drei Corollarien* (Berlin: Duncker & Humblot, 1963), Preface; cited in Heinrich Meier, *Carl Schmitt and Leo Strauss: The Hidden Dialogue* J Harvey Lomax trans. (Chicago: University of Chicago Press, 1995), 3. See also Carl Schmitt, *Political Theology: Four Chapters on the Concept of Sovereignty* [1922] George Schwab trans. (Cambridge, Mass: MIT Press, 1988), 29–31.

that the political must be defined apart from a definition of the state, there is, as Gopal Balakrishnan has noted, a tendency surreptitiously to reintroduce the state, as a vehicle for conflict management, 'as the natural subject of political life.'[31] This ambiguity notwithstanding, Schmitt's objective in building from the concept of the political is useful, especially because it yields a powerful insight into the question of what the intricate exercise of state-formation might involve.

From Schmitt's perspective, it is only through the establishment of the state that a group of people within a certain territory becomes 'a pacified unity encompassing the political.'[32] Once it becomes possible to define a people as a group that is to be differentiated from other political units, what emerges is a sense of 'national consciousness,' by which is meant a minimal degree of cohesion and distinctiveness that is forged amongst a people.[33] With the recognition of a 'we' that can be set against the 'they' of the rest of mankind, the friend-enemy distinction is capable of being externalised. Michael Howard has observed how, from the very beginning, 'the principle of nationalism was almost indissolubly linked, both in theory and practice, with the idea of war.'[34] But it is also a consequence of this process that domestic antagonisms become capable of being managed effectively, thereby remaining below the level of intensity of friend versus enemy.

By acquiring a monopoly of coercive power, the state imposes peaceable order and gradually forges some notion of the unity of a people. This perspective on state formation enables us both to recognise the significance of the distinction, which is often drawn in international relations, between external and internal conceptions of sovereignty[35] and also to appreciate the importance of the ideology of nationalism as a source of state-building energy.[36] Since the state is thus able to institutionalise domestic political antagonism at a lower level of intensity than that of friend versus enemy, one of its most basic achievements is that of being able to keep conflict and disagreement within a framework of order. For these conditions to be realised, however, the tensions that exist within the state must be actively managed. Once this positive role of the state is acknowledged, we can

---

[31] Balakrishnan, above n 29, at 110. This ambivalence is also reflected in Schmitt's treatment of Hobbes who, in the first edition of *The Concept of the Political* he described as 'by far the greatest and perhaps the sole truly systematic political thinker', a position from which he resiled in the light of Leo Strauss's observation (above n 20, at 89–93) that Hobbes's individualistic principles are constructed precisely for the purpose of negating, in Schmitt's sense, the political. See Meier, above n 30, esp at 32–38.

[32] Ernst-Wolfgang Böckenförde, 'The Concept of the Political: A Key to Understanding Carl Schmitt's Constitutional Theory' in Dyzenhaus (ed), above n 29, at 37, 39.

[33] Karl W Deutsch, *Nationalism and Social Communication: An Inquiry into the Foundations of Nationality* (2nd edn, Cambridge, Mass, MIT Press, 1966), 173.

[34] Michael Howard, 'Empires, Nations and Wars' in his *The Lessons of History* (Oxford, Clarendon Press, 1991), 21, 39.

[35] See, eg, RBJ Walker, *Inside/Outside: International Relations as Political Theory* (Cambridge, Cambridge University Press, 1993).

[36] See Benedict Anderson, *Imagined Communities: Reflections on the Origin and Spread of Nationalism* (rev. edn, London, Verso, 1991). Gellner captures something of this spirit when he observes that states are 'groups which *will* themselves to persist as communities': Ernest Gellner, *Nations and Nationalism* (Oxford, Blackwell, 1983), 53.

begin to understand the state to be an artefact or, in Jacob Burckhardt's expression, as 'a work of art.'[37]

Within a relatively stable political regime, such as that of the United Kingdom today, this achievement is in danger of being overlooked.[38] But the fact of the matter is that 'today virtually everywhere in the world, groups of human beings need with the utmost urgency to decide whom to fear and whom to trust, whom to identify with and whom to identify against, with whom and against whom to seek to cooperate or to struggle, even, *in extremis*, whom to seek to kill.'[39] Viewed in this light, state formation must be treated as a complex process through which many of these fears and tensions can be controlled, regulated, and also manipulated. It is at this second-order level of the political, politics within a viable system of government, that what might be called the practices of politics emerge. Here, the political system operates mainly through a range of second-order distinctions, such as those between governors and governed or government and opposition.[40]

POLITICS AS STATECRAFT

Schmitt believed that conflict was not only endemic but also existential: group life without conflict—society without politics—constitutes a denial of the human condition which, if ever realised, would amount to a moral loss.[41] This is a view that Schmitt shared with Machiavelli. But whereas Schmitt concentrated on the existential character of this phenomenon, Machiavelli's overriding aim had been to offer advice to rulers on the most effective way to govern. Furthermore, although both Schmitt and Machiavelli accepted the intrinsically political nature of society and embraced the political reality of conflict, important differences exist between them. The nature of these differences is instructive.

Although Schmitt worked through the concept of the political in a highly systematic manner, he had the rather unsound tendency to raise the inevitability of conflict into a foundational principle. Machiavelli, by contrast, was concerned primarily to demonstrate how, through the cultivation of sound political practice, enmities could not only be handled but positively harnessed. For Machiavelli, a sound politics requires *virtù*, by which he means courage, vigour, vitality and

[37] Jacob Burckhardt, *The Civilisation of the Renaissance in Italy* (Oxford, Phaidon Press, 1945), Pt I.

[38] Nevertheless, the situation in Northern Ireland is instructive. Here, ever since its founding in 1920, and especially over the last 30 years, the integrative function of the state in forging a unity of the people has been placed in question. In this situation, the danger exists that the friend-enemy distinction does indeed become determinative of all significant issues within domestic politics.

[39] John Dunn, 'Specifying and Understanding Racism' in his *The History of Political Theory and Other Essays* (Cambridge, Cambridge University Press, 1996), 148, 151.

[40] See Niklas Luhmann, *Political Theory in the Welfare State* (John Bednarz (trans), (Berlin, de Gruyter, 1990), esp chs 3 and 5.

[41] This explains why Schmitt opposed the forces of technology which he believed to be threatening the political: see McCormick, above n 29. We might also note Joseph Cropsey's comment that, in his attack on modern liberalism, Schmitt believed that liberalism was 'complicitous with communism in standing for the withering away of the political and replacing it with the technological—the reduction of humanity to the last man.' See Cropsey, 'Foreword' to Meier, above n 30, at x.

strength of purpose. By acting with *virtù* and in accordance with the requirements of necessity, *fortuna*—the unpredictable or fortuitous—could be tamed and glory secured.[42] Machiavelli's purpose was to provide guidance on how to handle this contest between freedom and necessity whereas Schmitt, having constructed a political reality based on conflict, appeared simply to celebrate this condition and to 'transform enmity and brokenness into metaphysical principles'.[43] As FR Ankersmit comments, this is 'as if marital quarrels were seen not as an unavoidable aspect of living together, but as its very basis.'[44] As an account of politics within a system of governance, Machiavelli's is to be preferred.

Machiavelli was the first writer to argue that politics, especially once it is understood to be a set of practices relating to the art of the state, rests on its own rules and principles. Emphasising the point that politics is concerned with the pursuit of power, Machiavelli rejects the classical view that it should be understood simply as the art of maintaining 'the good community.' But in order to understand his position, it is necessary first to consider how he develops this notion of the autonomy of the political from his views about human nature. For Machiavelli, the inner life of man (*animo*) is not a sphere of repose, harmony or self-control, but one of continual motion. Man, he suggests, is ruled not by reason but by appetite and ambition, and these characteristics, which provide the source of action, lead to competition and conflict. This analysis of the human condition causes Machiavelli to adopt a novel approach to the issue of scarcity. For the ancients, the phenomenon of scarcity in the world was resolved by self-discipline and education. Machiavelli, by contrast, argues that 'since the scarcity of objects is the result of the nature of appetite and passion, and not the other way around, competition and conflict between men is natural and inevitable.'[45] Machiavelli's innovation was to suggest that man is a political animal precisely because people are required to engage with one another as a means to their own satisfaction. Because people strive not only to achieve material success but also to attain fame and glory—qualities which require some degree of public acknowledgement—politics must be conceived to be a natural condition.

Although Machiavelli here breaks with classical assumptions, his writing should still be interpreted in the context of the early modern revival of the republican idea of politics as a set of practices that evolve within a form of order that seeks to promote the common good.[46] Machiavelli thus employs the term 'politics' to denote those practices operating within a regime of authority that is constrained by laws, and he contrasts such a regime with the unrestrained exercise of power, which

---

[42] Niccolò Machiavelli, *The Prince*, [1513] Stephen J Milner trans. (London, Dent, 1995) chs 25, 26.

[43] FR Ankersmit, *Aesthetic Politics: Political Philosophy Beyond Fact and Value* (Stanford, Stanford University Press, 1996), 127.

[44] *Ibid.*

[45] Martin Fleisher, 'A Passion for Politics: The Vital Core of the World of Machiavelli' in Fleisher (ed), *Machiavelli and the Nature of Political Thought* (New York, Atheneum, 1972), 114, 130.

[46] See Maurizio Viroli, 'Machiavelli and the Republican Idea of Politics' in Gisela Bock, Quentin Skinner and Maurizio Viroli (eds), *Machiavelli and Republicanism* (Cambridge, Cambridge University Press, 1990), 143–71.

generally is called tyranny.[47] Consequently, although Machiavelli displaces the
rule of reason both within the individual and the collectivity, he does not suggest
that politics can be reduced to the pursuit of appetite and desire. While there is no
room in Machiavelli's world for an objective natural law that yields authoritative
precepts of right conduct, this does not mean that politics is reducible simply to
the pursuit of material self-interest.

This last point is one that is central to the understanding of politics as an
autonomous sphere of activity. Machiavelli's work emphasises the gulf that exists
between the private and public spheres, between what Hannah Arendt, echoing
the classical division, called 'the sheltered life in the household' and 'the merciless
exposure of the *polis*.'[48] The activity of attending to the arrangements of the public
sphere, Machiavelli is arguing, requires special skills that go beyond those of
household management. It is for this reason that Arendt suggested that Machiavelli is the 'only postclassical political theorist who, in an extraordinary effort to
restore its old dignity to politics, perceived the gulf and understood something of
the courage needed to cross it.'[49]

Those that seek to rule in the common good, Machiavelli argues, are certainly
obliged to act with vigour and courage. But they must also cultivate the virtue of
prudence. Prudence in politics requires rulers to possess certain skills of practical
reason, including those of being able to speak fluently, to act persuasively and to
deliberate wisely. In chapter 15 of *The Prince*, Machiavelli lists 11 pairs of qualities
that bring a ruler praise or blame: generosity or miserliness; beneficence or greed;
mercy or cruelty; trustworthiness or faithlessness; strength or weakness; humanity
or pride; chastity or lasciviousness; uprightness or guile; flexibility or severity;
seriousness or light-heartedness; religiosity or scepticism. Although recognising
that it would be laudable to find all the good qualities combined in a ruler, he
states that:

> since it is not possible either to possess or wholly to observe them, because human nature
> does not allow it, it is necessary for him to be sufficiently prudent that he knows how to
> avoid the infamy of those vices that will deprive him of his state.[50]

But he also goes on to comment that the ruler:

> should not worry about the infamy incurred by those vices which are indispensable in
> maintaining his state, because if he examines everything carefully, he will find that some-
> thing which seems virtue [*virtù*] can, if put into practice, cause his ruin, while another
> thing which seems a vice can, when put into practice, result in his security and well-
> being.[51]

---

[47] See Niccolò Machiavelli, *The Discourses*, I.25 [1531] Leslie J Walker trans. Bernard Crick (ed)
(Harmondsworth, Penguin, 1983) (contrasting a 'political regime' with 'despotism' or 'tyranny').
[48] Hannah Arendt, *The Human Condition* (Chicago, University of Chicago Press, 1958), 35. Cf Aristotle, *The Politics* [c 335–323 BC] TA Sinclair trans. Trevor J Saunders (ed) (Harmondsworth, Penguin,
1981) Bk I, ii.
[49] *Ibid.*
[50] Machiavelli, *The Prince*, ch 15.
[51] *Ibid.*

Machiavelli here asserts the autonomy of the political by suggesting that, within the sphere of politics, there is no power of reason superior to that of prudence. We must therefore be quite clear about the meaning of this term. In an insightful essay, Martin Fleisher provides a most useful explanation of Machiavelli's conception of prudence.

> Prudence is not to be measured principally by the existing standards of right and wrong but by the assessment of the best means to achieve one's ends. Prudence is not synonymous with caution, nor is it the dominance of reason over the appetites and passions. It is, instead, the cool calculation of what must be done in a given situation to accomplish one's purposes without judgment of the situation being unduly affected by passions or the contemporary conventions and ideals of right and wrong.[52]

Prudence is the ability to assess the situation and adopt the most appropriate course of action. It is to be distinguished from rule-governed action or from following the precepts of conventional morality primarily because new situations require innovative responses. It must also be distinguished from following the dictates of appetite, since the function of prudence is properly to serve the appetites (such as ambition) through an ability dispassionately to assess the requirements of the situation.

It might be noted that missing from the qualities listed above is that of justice. Machiavelli believes that to govern well rulers must be able to cultivate a reputation for being good.[53] But what he is suggesting at base is that the measure of justice is that of prudent rule. Cities and empires that are ruled well increase in glory, reputation and power. Such regimes will be law-governed. But the limits of laws should also be acknowledged and rulers might find it necessary, for the promotion of the common good, to break promises, to proceed deceptively or act belligerently.[54]

In common with Schmitt, then, Machiavelli's conception of politics is built on the belief that there is no single over-arching normative criterion for resolving existential conflicts.[55] His genius was to have recognised so early that there is no one true answer to the classical question: how should I live? Moral and political values are irreducibly plural and conflicts are inevitable: politics arises from the necessity of having to make choices between rival, sometimes incommensurable, goods in circumstances where there can be no authoritative principle or standard for resolving the dispute.

---

[52] Fleisher, above n 45, 139–40.

[53] Machiavelli, *The Prince*, ch 18. In this chapter Machiavelli indicates that political power depends primarily on what the people believe. The distinction between appearance and reality is irrelevant to the pursuit of politics: appearances—what the people believe—is the reality of politics.

[54] See, eg, Machiavelli, *The Discourses*, Bk III, ch 9: 'Piero Soderini [Florence's *Gonfaloniere a vita*, 1502–12] conducted all his affairs in his good-natured and patient way. So long as circumstances suited the way in which he carried on, both he and his country prospered. But when afterwards there came a time which required him to drop his patience and his humility, he could not bring himself to do it; so that both he and his country were ruined'. On Soderini see: Felix Gilbert, *Machiavelli and Gucciardini: Politics and History in Sixteenth Century Florence* (Princeton, Princeton University Press, 1965), ch 2.

[55] See Isaiah Berlin, 'The Originality of Machiavelli' in his *Against the Current: Essays in the History of Ideas* (Oxford, Clarendon Press, 1989), 25–79.

This *agonal* conception of politics, it should be emphasised, is not one that Schmitt shared. Heinrich Meier has convincingly argued that although he located politics in the necessity of action in the face of conflict, Schmitt ultimately answers the critical question—how should I live?—by appealing to a political theology which builds on the necessity of faith and of the truth of divine revelation. Drawing on the authority of biblical teaching,[56] Schmitt affirms the centrality of original sin, believes that these existential questions cannot be solved by reason alone and places his faith in 'the certainty of the God who demands obedience, rules absolutely, and judges in accordance with his own law.'[57] Schmitt's political theology is not content to leave matters of politics to deliberation and contest; he recognises that the battle between faith and errant faith admits of no neutral and must be waged in favour of the truth of divine revelation. This is a path that few can—and none should—follow.

The overriding significance of Schmitt's analysis of the concept of the political is that it helps us to appreciate the true originality of Machiavelli's thought. Although Schmitt explains how the political may have its source in enmity, the conduct of politics—what has been called the second-order of the political—is not built on the celebration of conflict: it is generated by the need to ensure its effective management. Politics is, as Michael Oakeshott expresses it, often an 'unpleasing spectacle':

> The obscurity, the muddle, the excess, the compromise, the indelible appearance of dishonesty, the counterfeit piety, the moralism and the immorality, the corruption, the intrigue, the negligence, the meddlesomeness, the vanity, the self-deception and finally the futility … offend most of our rational and all of our artistic susceptibilities.[58]

But in so far as it succeeds in 'modifying the reign of arbitrary violence in human affairs, there is clearly something to be said for it, and it may even be thought to be worth the cost.'[59]

Politics is cultivated through those practices that enable the activity of governing to be effectively conducted. Through the development of these practices, especially when they are harnessed to the forces of nationalism, bonds of allegiance are strengthened and a sense of the unity of a people is forged. And it is this forging of a sense of common identity, which may be based on ethnicity, culture, language or common history, that provides the key to explaining why the political antecedes the state. As Ulrich Preuss expresses it, 'the common feeling of a group's oneness is the determining state-building social energy.'[60] Understood as a set of practices

---

[56] Genesis 3:15: 'I will put enmity between thy seed and her seed.' In tracing matters back to the doctrine of original sin, Schmitt's thought here displays similarities with the work of de Maistre: see Joseph de Maistre, 'The Saint Petersburg Dialogues' [c.1802–17] in Jack Lively (ed), *The Works of Joseph de Maistre* (London, Allen & Unwin, 1965), 183.

[57] Heinrich Meier, *The Lesson of Carl Schmitt: Four Chapters on the Distinction between Political Theology and Political Philosophy* (Chicago, University of Chicago Press, 1998), 11.

[58] Michael Oakeshott, *The Politics of Faith and the Politics of Scepticism* [c.1952] Timothy Fuller (ed) (New Haven, Yale University Press, 1996), 19.

[59] *Ibid* at 19–20.

[60] Ulrich K Preuss, 'Political Order and Democracy: Carl Schmitt and His Influence' in Chantal Mouffe (ed), above n 29, 155, 157.

operating within a system of government, politics is a significant accomplishment. The nature of this achievement was eloquently voiced by Lord Balfour when he remarked of the British system that 'the whole political machinery presupposes a people so fundamentally at one that they can safely afford to bicker; and so sure of their moderation that they are not dangerously disturbed by the never-ending din of political conflict'.[61]

This conception of politics has its roots in Machiavelli's resoundingly realistic portrayal of the human condition. We begin, Machiavelli argues, without any inheritance. His starting point has been concisely summarised in these terms: 'God did not give us a perfect beginning, as the Bible says, and nature did not provide us with a potentiality for politics, as Aristotle says. We began bare, unprotected, insecure, and justly fearful.'[62] Politics, in Machiavelli's thought, springs from what is necessary to ensure human survival and flourishing and, given the existential nature of enmity and conflict, politics has evolved to ensure that these conflicts are constructively handled.[63]

But this does not mean that politics seeks the elimination of conflict. Machiavelli argues that, far from being a destructive condition, conflict and dissension are vital ingredients of cohesion. Reflecting on the Roman republic, he notes that 'those who condemn the quarrels between the nobles and the plebs, seem to be cavilling at the very things that were the primary cause of Rome's retaining her freedom'.[64] In every republic, he concludes, 'there are two different dispositions, that of the populace and that of the upper class and that all legislation favourable to liberty is brought about by the clash between them'.[65] Machiavelli here impresses on us two important messages: that politics is concerned with the handling, not elimination, of conflict, and that liberty has its source not in ideas or in texts but in the cut and thrust of political struggle.

THE THIRD ORDER: CONSTITUTIONAL LAW

Although conflict remains an important element of politics, the cultivation of a sense of even-handedness constitutes a vital aspect of the project of state-building. For conflict to be positively harnessed, some less partisan framework of rule needs to be devised. This concern brings us directly to the question of constitutional law.

---

[61] Earl of Balfour, 'Introduction' to Walter Bagehot, *The English Constitution* (Oxford, Oxford University Press, 1936), xxiv; cited in Schmitt, *Political Theology*, above n 30, xxiii. See also Ernest Barker, 'The Discredited State: Thoughts on Politics before the War' (1915) 2(o.s.) *Political Quarterly* 101, which emphasises the vital condition of unstable equilibrium in state-society relations as being necessary for the continuation of progress.

[62] Harvey C Mansfield, *Machiavelli's Virtue* (Chicago, University of Chicago Press, 1996), 55.

[63] Cf Michael Oakeshott, *Rationalism in Politics* (London, Methuen, 1962), 127: 'In political activity, then, men sail a boundless and bottomless sea; there is neither harbour for shelter nor floor for anchorage, neither starting place nor appointed destination. The enterprise is to keep afloat on an even keel; the sea is both friend and enemy; and the seamanship consists in using the resources of a traditional manner of behaviour in order to make a friend of every hostile occasion.'

[64] Machiavelli, *The Discourses*, I.4.

[65] *Ibid.*

Many of the ideals associated with law, especially those of the rule of law and the assimilation of law to justice, help to create intimacy, shape identity, generate trust, and strengthen allegiance. The evolution of institutions of government that aspire to operate at one remove from direct manipulation by power-wielders removes certain decisions and disputes from partisan political processes and this too serves to bolster faith in the system. The cultivation of a belief in the law-governed nature of the state is, in short, a means of generating political power and an especially powerful aspect of state-building. But does this mean that law can be said to transcend the political?

The appropriate starting point must be to begin by treating constitutional law as a third order of the political. The establishment of a legal system that operates in accordance with its own conceptual logic and remains free from gross manipulation by power-wielders is, without doubt, an achievement of considerable importance. But whenever this modern idea of the rule of law is invoked, the predominant image is that of the formation of a legal system that serves the purpose of adjudicating between citizens[66] or ensures that rigorous procedures governing the imposition of criminal penalties are maintained.[67] This image is derived primarily from Montesquieu who, in Judith Shklar's words, advocated the establishment of 'a properly equilibrated political system in which power was checked by power in such a way that neither the violent urges of kings, nor the arbitrariness of legislatures could impinge directly upon the individual in such a way as to frighten her and make her feel insecure in her daily life.'[68]

Within a legal system that exists for the purpose of handling civil claims between citizens or for enforcing the norms of criminal conduct, it can be assumed, at least for the purpose of this analysis, that judges perform the important but relatively mundane task of resolving disputes in accordance with the rule system that has been laid down.[69] When we reflect on the idea of constitutional law, however, matters become much more complicated. Here we are concerned not with law as the expression of the sovereign authority of the state, but with law as a means of establishing a framework through which the sovereign authority of the state can be recognised.[70] To put the matter crudely, the image of law as command must, in this context, be jettisoned: law now presents itself as a species of 'political right'.[71]

---

[66] See Ernest J Weinrib, 'The Intelligibility of the Rule of Law' in Allan C Hutchinson and Patrick Monahan (eds), *The Rule of Law: Ideal or Ideology?* (Toronto, Carswell, 1987), 59, 62: 'I wish to argue that in private law the non-instrumental aspect of law shines forth with particular brilliance, so that through reflection on private law we can grasp the Rule of Law as a coherent conceptual possibility.'

[67] See Douglas Hay, 'Property, Authority and the Criminal Law' in Hay *et al* (eds), *Albion's Fatal Tree* (Harmondsworth: Penguin, 1975), 17–63; EP Thompson, *Whigs and Hunters: The Origin of the Black Act* (Harmondsworth: Penguin, 1975), 258–69.

[68] Judith Shklar, 'Political Theory and the Rule of Law' in Hutchinson and Monahan (eds), above n 66, at 1, 4.

[69] See, however, Martin Loughlin, *Sword and Scales: An Examination of the Relationship between Law and Politics* (Oxford, Hart, 2000), ch 6.

[70] Cf Justinian, *Digest* I.1.1: '*Publicum ius est quod ad statum rei Romanae spectat*' [Public law is that which pertains to the constitution of the Roman state.] (Ulpian). [534] Alan Watson trans. (Philadelphia, University of Pennsylvania Press, 1998)

[71] In the exercise of analysing this conception of law, it might be noted that we remain handicapped

I do not propose to elaborate here on the idea of political right.[72] All that need
be said is that, in this context, law is best understood as a set of practices that is
embedded within, and which acquires its identity from, a wider body of political
practices. Whilst it is possible to formulate constitutional law as a relatively discrete set of rules (that is, as positive law),[73] it must be understood that the meaning, function and mode of application of such rules is governed by the practices of
politics.[74] This claim is not meant in the trite sense that constitutional law is rooted in the political because it serves the function of regulating political institutions,
processes and decisions. Following the general approach of Machiavelli and (to a
lesser extent) Schmitt,[75] the claim is founded on three basic convictions. The first
is that of the autonomy of the political. The second is the promotion of a conception of constitutional law as a body of law that is not handed down from above but
which exists as part of the self-regulatory processes of this autonomous political
realm, and which may therefore be conceptualised as principles of political prudence. The third is the belief not only that the political cannot entirely be eliminat-
ed and subsumed into the rule-based logic of legal decision-making but that it
should not be, since, properly understood, the primacy of the political provides a
condition of human flourishing.

Since many of the contemporary misunderstandings of constitutional lawyers
stem from a mischaracterisation of constitutions, it may be helpful to proceed by
analysing the nature of conventional approaches to modern constitutional
arrangements.

CONSTITUTIONS

We might begin by noting that the term 'constitution' is itself a source of
ambiguity. Its most consistent usage in ancient times was as an expression of
formally declared legislation.[76] However, *constitutio* was also used as a translation

by the fact that, while other European languages are able to draw a distinction between *jus, droit, diritto*
and *Recht*, on the one hand, and *lex, loi, legge* and *Gesetz* on the other, there exists no corresponding differentiation in English of the word 'law'.

[72] I discuss this subject further in 'Representation and Constitutional Theory' in Paul Craig and
Richard Rawlings (eds), *Law and Administration in Europe* (Oxford, Oxford University Press, 2003),
ch 3, and 'Ten Tenets of Sovereignty' in Neil Walker (ed), *Sovereignty in Transition* (Oxford, Hart, 2003),
ch 3.

[73] In the British context, this was Dicey's outstanding achievement: AV Dicey, *Introduction to the
Study of the Law of the Constitution* (8th edn, London, Macmillan, 1915), esp ch 1.

[74] This has been the major failure of Dicey (*ibid.* at 199: 'the principles of private law have … been
by the action of the Courts and Parliament so extended as to determine the position of the Crown and
its servants') and his followers.

[75] Cf Robert Howse, 'From Legitimacy to Dictatorship—and Back Again: Leo Strauss's Critique of
the Anti-Liberalism of Carl Schmitt' in David Dyzenhaus (ed), above n 29, at 56, 69: 'Schmitt puts
Machiavelli's teaching in the form of legal scholarship, which at times appears to be a learned internal
critique of an "autonomous discipline", ie, juridical science.'

[76] Justinian, *Institutes* I.2.6: 'whatever the emperor has determined (*constituit*) by rescript or decided
as a judge or directed by edict is established to be law: it is these that are called constitutions'. [534]
Peter Birks and Grant McLeod trans. (London, Duckworth, 1987). That this formulation influenced

of the Greek *politeia*, and therefore stood as a descriptive term for the entire body politic.[77] This latter formulation of the idea of constitution as an expression of the laws, institutions and practices which make up a tradition of governing has been of particular influence in English thought. It is in this sense that we might refer to Britain's distinctively political constitution. This type of formulation enables us to identify the constitution as 'an entailed inheritance.'[78] It also helps us to recognise the intrinsically political character of the governing relationship.

Notwithstanding the breadth of this characterisation, it must be emphasised that the laws are vital ingredients of a political constitution: they regulate many of the basic rules of political conduct, provide a source of stability in governing arrangements and, as a consequence of their handling and interpretation by a judiciary insulated from direct political influence, ensure a degree of even-handedness in rule application. This last aspect is of particular importance because, especially through law's claims to generality and universality, the appeal to the law-bounded character of the system contributes greatly to the maintenance of the system's legitimacy, and hence also capacity. But it is invariably the case that a constitution will leave space for what might be called extra-legal governmental action. The constitution here is following a basic law of political necessity: the necessity of rulers being able to take decisive action for the purpose of ensuring that conflict and dissension is handled effectively.

The form, breadth, and conditional nature of this extra-legal governmental power have varied throughout history. An early version of this power can be identified in the ancient Roman practices of constitutional dictatorship.[79] It appears in the medieval literature in the form of the doctrine of necessity.[80] A more

the work of English jurists is evident in the work of Sir John Fortescue, *De Laudibus Legum Anglie* [1468–71] SB Chrimes (ed) (Cambridge, Cambridge University Press, 1942), 36–37: 'But customs and the rules of the law of nature, after they have been reduced to writing, and promulgated by the sufficient authority of the prince, and commanded to be kept, are changed into a constitution or something of the nature of statutes.'

[77] See Graham Maddox, 'Constitution' in Terence Ball, James Farr and Russell L Hanson (eds), *Political Innovation and Conceptual Change* (Cambridge, Cambridge University Press, 1989), 50–55; Howell A Lloyd, 'Constitutionalism' in JH Burns (ed), *The Cambridge History of Political Thought* (Cambridge, Cambridge University Press, 1991), 254–55.

[78] Edmund Burke, *Reflections on the Revolution in France* [1790] Conor Cruise O'Brien (ed) (London, Penguin, 1986), 119.

[79] See Clinton L Rossiter, *Constitutional Dictatorship: Crisis Government in the Modern Democracies* (Princeton, NJ: Princeton University Press, 1948), ch 2. We might note Machiavelli's assessment (*The Discourses*, I.34) of the Roman practice: 'It is clear that the dictatorship, so long as it was bestowed in accordance with public institutions, and not assumed by the dictator on his own authority, was always of benefit to the state.'

[80] See, eg, FM Powicke, 'Reflections on the Medieval State' in his *Ways of Medieval Life and Thought: Essays and Addresses* (London, Odhams Press, 1949), 135–36: '[T]he lords and knights about Philip the Fair were familiar with a conception of *utilitas* which carries us very far in the theory of statecraft. They could express or at least appreciate the expression of public utility in terms of *necessitas*, and by necessity they meant more than the public need. They meant the right and duty of the king and his agents ... to override positive law in the common interests for which they were responsible. The word 'necessity' had had a long history in ecclesiastical literature. Pope Gregory VII [in the eleventh century] had asserted that the pope in case of necessity could make new laws. A century later we find, applied to policy, the phrase 'necessity knows no law'. ... St. Thomas Aquinas developed a theory of necessity. He argued that, in certain circumstances, necessity knows no law; also that a tyrant can be removed on the

regularised variation exists in the distinction between *gubernaculum*, the inherent power of the king to govern his realm, and *jurisdictio*, a sphere of right in which the king is bound by the law.[81] And many of the English constitutional disputes of the seventeenth century were articulated with respect to the boundaries between the 'absolute' and 'ordinary' prerogatives of the crown.[82] Since the seventeenth century, however, constitutional thought has been underpinned by the necessity of ensuring the accountability of governors to the people. One product of this development has been an understandable concern to express sovereign authority in terms of that institution which has the final word over the course of action that best promotes the *salus populi*.

The British solution—that sovereignty rests in the crown-in-parliament—is sufficiently abstract and general to be capable of providing a plausible response in terms of the mode of political association, whilst at the same time fudging a variety of practical political questions, including that of the nature of any governmental power beyond law. In his opening words to *Political Theology*—'Sovereign is he who decides on the exception'[83]—Carl Schmitt offered a characteristically provocative formulation. The essence of his argument was that: 'The rule proves nothing; the exception proves everything: It confirms not only the rule but also its existence, which derives only from the exception.'[84] Once again, Schmitt is guilty of pushing an astute insight to its extreme, thereby overstating its force. So although he seems correct both in his contention that the exception cannot be banished from the world and also in the observation that the exceptional situation

ground of necessity ... The legists of Philip the Fair gave a more positive direction to the argument. Necessity, in their mind, was more than a sanction of self-protection; it was a call to assert the power of the king, over and above the limits set by custom and tradition, in the interests of his kingdom and of the Christian community of which his kingdom was a responsible part.'

[81]   See Charles Howard McIlwain, *Constitutionalism: Ancient and Modern* (rev edn, Ithaca, NY, Cornell University Press, 1977), ch 4; SB Chrimes, *English Constitutional Ideas in the Fifteenth Century* (Cambridge, Cambridge University Press, 1936), 40–62; Francis D Wormuth, *The Royal Prerogative 1603–1649: A Study in English Political and Constitutional Ideas* (Ithaca, NY, Cornell University Press, 1939), 55–60.

[82]   See *Bate's Case* (1606) *State Trials*, II, 389 per Fleming CB: 'The Kings power is double, ordinary and absolute, and they have several laws and ends. That of the ordinary is for the profit of particular subjects, for the execution of civil justice, the determining of meum; and this is exercised by equitie and justice in ordinary courts, and by the civilians is nominated *jus privatum* and with us common law: and these laws cannot be changed, without parliament ... The absolute power of the King is not that which is converted or executed to private use, to the benefit of any particular person, but is only that which is applied to the general benefit of the people and is *salus populi*; as the people is the body, and the King the head; and this power is guided by the rules, which direct only at the common law, and is most properly named Pollicy and Government; and as the constitution of this body varieth with the time, so varieth this absolute law, according to the wisdome of the King, for the common good.' See Francis Oakley, 'Jacobean Political Theology: The Absolute and Ordinary Powers of the King' (1968) *J of the History of Ideas* 323–46. The Bill of Rights 1689, art 1 abolished this absolute prerogative: 'The pretended power of suspending of laws, or the execution of laws by regal authority, without the consent of parliament, is illegal.'

[83]   Schmitt, *Political Theology*, above n 30, at 5.

[84]   *Ibid* at 15. Schmitt's continuing interest in this question is indicated by the fact that he also published a work specifically on the history of commissarial dictatorship: Schmitt, *Die Diktatur* (Leipzig: Duncker & Humblot, 1921). For analysis, see Balakrisnan, above n 29, at ch 2.

has juristic significance,[85] he goes too far in asserting that the exceptional reveals the essence of the concept of sovereignty.

In modern constitutional thought, this question of the exception has been obscured by the precepts of constitutionalism.[86] The edifice of modern thought has been erected on the principle that the constituent power rests in the body of the people, who delegate a limited authority to government to promote the public good. Governors are thus presented as servants of the people, and they are required to account for the powers entrusted to them. Governments, in Locke's words, are vested with 'only a fiduciary power to act for certain ends'.[87] From here it requires but a short leap of constitutional faith to embrace the idea of an original compact, the belief that the workings of the state are driven by the principle of self-government, and the acceptance of the claim that governmental action is based on enumerated powers. Such beliefs acquired great impetus from the American and French revolutions, which not only brought about a radical shift in notions of the source of governmental authority, but also led to the emergence of a relatively novel understanding of the term 'constitution'. This new understanding was concisely expressed by Thomas Paine, when he argued that a constitution 'is a thing *antecedent* to a government' and that 'a government is only the creature of a constitution.'[88]

In this conception, the constitution assumes the form of a document that receives its authorisation from the people. This constitution ostensibly establishes and delimits the powers of government, lays down the principles of political engagement and determines the relationship between the citizen and the state. By apparently defining the rules of political conduct, the document presents itself as a powerful instrument for controlling the practices of politics and of providing a measure of stability to what otherwise might be a rather volatile contest. Provided this type of constitutional document is recognised to be the product of a political bargain—an attempt to devise a formal framework outlining some of the principal forms and working arrangements of the political constitution—it can provide a useful aid to the activity of statecraft. But once 'the constitution' is assumed to establish the foundation of all political engagement and, further, once it is treated like any other legal text to be interpreted and enforced by lawyers, then we enter a new phase of understanding. Once the modern constitutional text is treated as positive law, an important shift in the idea of the constitution is effected.

---

[85] *Ibid* at 7, 13.

[86] On this matter, Schmitt seems essentially correct: 'All tendencies of modern constitutional development point toward eliminating the sovereign in this sense' (*Political Theology*, above n 30, at 7). But see Rossiter, above n 79

[87] John Locke, *Two Treatises of Government*. [1680] Peter Laslett (ed) (Cambridge, Cambridge University Press, 1988) II § 149.

[88] Thomas Paine, *Rights of Man* [1791–2] in his *Rights of Man, Common Sense and Other Writings* (Mark Philp (ed), Oxford, Oxford University Press, 1995), 122.

CONSTITUTIONAL LEGALISM

The constitution has traditionally been viewed as a set of institutions and practices that serve to identify the character of a political regime, and in accordance with this political constitution only a portion of these arrangements are embodied in positive law. The modern constitution, by contrast, presents itself as a body of 'fundamental law'. Once it is accepted that the precepts of this fundamental law are to be enforced through the institutional mechanism of courts,[89] positive law comes to be viewed—by lawyers at least—as laying the foundations of political order.

This constitutional legalism obfuscates the issue of governmental authority. Operating on the fictions of original grant, self-government and enumerated powers, constitutional legalism radically suppresses the issue of rulership. As a representative institution deriving its power from the people and encompassing the law-making power, the authority of the legislature can readily be acknowledged. As faithful servants of the legislature (and the people), charged with the responsibility of ensuring that the will of the people is given precise effect, the status of the judiciary is given due recognition. But the office of government occupies an ambivalent position. In effect, 'government' is replaced with the notion of 'the executive'. The question is: executive of what? Within modern constitutions, the executive is invariably presented as an agent. But the fact that everywhere and without exception this 'executive' actually exercises a much greater power than any reading of constitutional texts would suggest presents us with a conundrum. Constitutional legalists see this phenomenon as an abuse, one that must be curtailed by a more assertive use of law to curb the executive's power of action. But is it possible that their analyses are rooted in error? Rather than starting with the document for the purpose of drawing conclusions about the activity, perhaps we should start with the character of the activity for the purpose of deriving conclusions about the nature of the document.

If constitutionalist reasoning is indeed rooted in error, what is the root source of this mistake? Here, it may be helpful to return to those early-modern political theorists whose works have helped shape such constitutionalist thinking. Thomas Hobbes has little to contribute on this subject. By focusing on the power-conferring moment, that moment when sovereign power is brought into existence through the voluntary action of rights-bearing individuals, he radically modernised the understanding of government. But Hobbes had little to say about the forms through which governmental power is exercised. In effect, he simplified political power by reducing it almost entirely to the legislative form—the power of command. For the purpose of addressing the question of the constitutional forms

---

[89] The breakthrough with respect to the US Constitution is achieved in *Marbury v Madison* 1 Cranch 137 (1803). See Rogers Smith, *Liberalism and American Constitutional Law* (Cambridge, Mass, Harvard University Press, 1985); Robert Lowry Clinton, *Marbury v Madison and Judicial Review* (Lawrence, Kansas, University Press of Kansas, 1989).

of rule, then, it is necessary to turn to Locke and Montesquieu. On this issue it is worth emphasising that although Locke and Montesquieu are rightly regarded as founders of the modern liberal doctrines of the separation of powers and the rule of law, both recognised the pivotal role of governmental power.

Locke was perhaps the first modern theorist to take seriously the issue of executive power. Recognising three functions of civil government, the legislative, the executive and the federative,[90] he argued that, since there are many things that the law cannot provide for, 'the good of Society requires, that several things should be left to the discretion of him, that has the Executive Power'.[91] The executive power, then, is not simply the power of putting law into effect but includes the 'Power to act according to discretion, for the publick good, without the prescription of the Law, and sometimes even against it.'[92] Locke here explicitly concedes that government cannot be reduced to law; constitutions must, of political necessity, allow for extra-legal governmental action. This is essentially a sphere of prudential action. In Pasquale Pasquino's interpretation of Locke's reflections on this subject, 'the branch that exercises the executive function is not reducible to a machine that applies the law; it is endowed with its own will and responsibility that permit it to face the unpredictable.'[93] What Locke in effect does, then, is to bring within the general framework of the constitution that dictatorial power to act *extra et contra legem* which Machiavelli had argued was an essential safeguard for the state.

Although generally credited with having devised the doctrine of the separation of powers, Montesquieu also gave due recognition to the importance of executive power. The great value of the executive, Montesquieu believed, was that it always is focused on 'immediate things', that is, on those matters of political necessity. But he went further in stressing the function of the executive. 'If the executive power does not have the rights to check the enterprises of the legislative body', he

---

[90] The federative power (derived from *foedus*, the Latin term for treaty) is that power to deal with foreign affairs, and is accepted by Locke as being 'much less capable to be directed by antecedent, standing, positive Laws, than the Executive': Locke, *Two Treatises of Government*, II §147. Notwithstanding the differences in function, Locke recognised that the federative power was invariably vested in the executive (*ibid* § 148). Vile's commentary on the federative power is significant: 'The importance of what Locke has to say here has generally been overlooked, and the failure, particularly on the part of Montesquieu, to take up this point, has contributed greatly to the inadequacy of the classification of government functions. Locke was writing at a time when the supremacy of legislature over the policy of the government *in internal affairs* was being established. The king must rule according to law. But Locke realised … that the control of internal affairs, particularly taxation, presented very different problems from those of external affairs. In matters of war, and of treaties with foreign powers, it was not possible, and still is not possible today, to subject the government to the sort of prior control that is possible in domestic matters': MJC Vile, *Constitutionalism and the Separation of Powers* (2nd edn, Indianapolis, Liberty Fund, 1998), 66. The distinction between ordinary and absolute prerogative has thus, in part, been converted into a distinction between internal and external functions. This issue remains a major source of tension with respect to the continued existence of a sphere of unfettered discretionary power that governments possess to deal with emergencies: see, eg, Jules Lobel, 'Emergency Power and the Decline of Liberalism' (1989) 98 *Yale Law Journal* 1385.

[91] Locke, *Two Treatises of Government*, II § 159.

[92] *Ibid* § 160.

[93] Pasquale Pasquino, 'Locke on King's Prerogative' (1998) 26 *Political Theory* 198, 202.

contended, 'the latter will be despotic'.[94] Placing a modern gloss on Montesquieu's views, Harvey Mansfield has noted that executive power, 'expanding when needed, kept the rule of law from being, in effect, the rule of ambitious legislators and contrary judges'.[95] Its beauty, Mansfield continued, is that it 'can reach where law cannot, and thus supply the defect of law, yet remain subordinate to law'.[96] By recognising the need to maintain a balance between the legal and the non-legal, between rules and prudence, Montesquieu 'shows how liberty *emerges* in a whole which mixes the law with what we would call its conditioning factors in a series of "relations"'.[97]

The error, it would appear, lies not in the work of these political philosophers of liberalism. Instead, it is to be found in the emerging modern culture of legalism. What is particularly noteworthy is that within the framework of constitutional legalism it has proved increasingly difficult openly to acknowledge the real political function of the executive power. In Locke's thought, the legislative and executive powers were left in tension, with any conflict having to be addressed politically, and ultimately being resolved as a result of the people's residual right of rebellion.[98] Although advocating a more formal separation of powers, Montesquieu also recognised the political character of the exercise, believing that, provided each of these roles is properly acknowledged, the three branches of government 'are constrained to move by the necessary motion of things'.[99] With the emergence of constitutional legalism, however, came the belief that solutions to these intrinsically political matters are to be found in, or through, the text. Consequently, whenever —as has been the case in all modern states—the executive has acted to fill those spaces which exist within all constitutional documents,[100] this has been the occasion for disapprobation.

The error of constitutional legalism is of a most basic kind, that of mistaking the part for the whole. Such legalism fails properly to acknowledge the provisional character of constitutional arrangements and that 'the development and acceptance of a constitutional framework can occur only as the contingent result of irresolvable conflict.'[101] Indeed, this must be so, because its object—the activity of governing—is interminable. The arrangements of governing are in a permanent state of disequilibrium, since 'the system has never been designed as a whole, and such coherence as it possesses is the product of constant readjustment of its parts

---

[94]   Montesquieu, *The Spirit of the Laws*, Bk11 [1748] Anne M Cohler, Basia Carolyn Miller and, Harold Samual Stone trans and (ed) (Cambridge, Cambridge University Press, 1989) ch 6.
[95]   Harvey C Mansfield, Jr, *Taming the Prince: The Ambivalence of Modern Executive Power* (Baltimore, Johns Hopkins University Press, 1993), xx.
[96]   *Ibid.*
[97]   *Ibid.* at 221.
[98]   Locke, *Two Treatises of Government*, II [1680] Peter Laslett (ed) (Cambridge, Cambridge University Press, 1988) ch XIX.
[99]   Montesquieu, *The Spirit of the Laws*, Bk.11, ch 6.
[100]   See, eg, Richard M Pious, *The American Presidency* (New York, Basic Books, 1979), 333: 'The President claims the silences of the Constitution.'
[101]   Stephen Holmes, *Passions and Constraint: On the Theory of Liberal Democracy* (Chicago, University of Chicago Press, 1995), 217.

to one another'.[102] What Michael Oakeshott calls 'the system of superficial order' is, of course, always 'capable of being made more coherent'.[103] And while this can often be a useful and positive exercise, 'the barbarism of order appears when order is pursued for its own sake and when the preservation of order involves the destruction of that without which order is only the orderliness of the ant-heap or the graveyard.'[104]

Modern constitutions, especially when colonised by lawyers, are particularly prone to this type of orderliness, presumably because one of the basic legal myths is that an answer to any issue can always be found in the body of the law.[105] What lawyers often fail fully to appreciate, especially when they theorise about constitutions, is that, despite their textuality,[106] they are replete with gaps, silences and abeyances. Further, these silences are not oversights; they are not even truces between opposing defined positions. Abeyances, as Michael Foley notes, are 'a set of implicit agreements to collude in keeping fundamental questions of political authority in a state of irresolution'.[107] Far from being susceptible to orderly compromise, these abeyances 'can only be assimilated by an intuitive social acquiescence in the incompleteness of a constitution'.[108] Being important aspects of the exercise of managing political conflict, such obscurities are functional.[109] Constitutions—and constitutional laws—are as much instruments in the on-going business of state-building as they are constraints on the practices of government.

[102] Oakeshott, above n 58, at 34–35.

[103] *Ibid* at 35.

[104] *Ibid.*

[105] The most prominent contemporary advocate is Ronald Dworkin: see his *Taking Rights Seriously* (Cambridge, Mass, Harvard University Press, 1977).

[106] See Wayne Franklin, 'The US Constitution and the Textuality of American Culture' in Vivian Hart and Shannon C Stimson (eds), *Writing a National Identity: Political, Economic, and Cultural Perspectives on the Written Constitution* (Manchester, Manchester University Press, 1993), ch 1; Steven D Smith, *The Constitution and the Pride of Reason* (New York, Oxford University Press, 1998).

[107] Michael Foley, *The Silence of Constitutions: Gaps, 'Abeyances' and Political Temperament in the Maintenance of Government* (London, Routledge, 1989), xi.

[108] *Ibid* at 10.

[109] See, eg, Albert V Dicey and Robert S Rait, *Thoughts on the Union between England and Scotland* (London, Macmillan, 1920), 191–193. Here the authors analyse art 19 of the Treaty of Union of 1707, which seemed to protect the integrity of Scots law by refusing any jurisdictional claim of the English courts. But the position of the House of Lords was left unmentioned. Dicey and Rait comment: 'Did the Commissioners, one asks, intentionally leave a difficult question [the possibility of an appeal from the Court of Session to the House of Lords] open and undecided? The most obvious and possibly the truest reply is that such was their intention, and that prudence suggested the wisdom of leaving to the decision of future events the answer to a dangerous inquiry which after all might not arise for years. There must have seemed much good sense in leaving a curious point of constitutional law practically unsettled until by the lapse of twenty years or more every one should have become accustomed to the workings of the Act of Union.' This type of analysis could equally be applied to the Anglo-Irish Agreement (Cmnd 9657, 1985) and the Belfast Agreement (Cm 4292, 1999) with respect to governmental arrangements affecting Northern Ireland.

CONCLUSION

That constitutions are to be viewed essentially as instruments of state-building rests on a recognition of the complex nature of political power. Political power is not the same as force; rather, it is generated through authority, that is, through the acceptance by the people of the legitimacy of a governing regime. Thus viewed, the imposition of limitations on the exercise of governmental authority will often provide a method of generating more political power—constraints, in other words, can be enabling.[110] Consequently, although formal authority rests in the institutions of government, the extent of that authority is in reality a product of the character of the political relationship that exists between that institutional structure and the people. In this sense, the political order—the sense of a political unity of a people—must be acknowledged to precede the constitutional order understood as text. The political provides the foundation for the constitutional.[111]

It is this primacy of the political that dictates the ambiguous and provisional character of constitutional texts. By virtue of its character, the text is never able to grasp all the precepts underpinning the practices of politics. But even if it were, the tensions between political practices and more basic conflicts—that is, between the first and second order conceptions of the political that gives politics much of its dynamic quality—retains the potential to destabilise that accommodation.[112] Although this was well understood by early-modern theorists,[113] it seems today in danger of being submerged beneath the rhetoric of constitutional legalism. Ronald Dworkin, one of the principal exponents of this position, occasionally does seem to recognise the sensitive political character of constitutional reasoning.

---

[110] This is the theme that Jon Elster has recently been exploring as an aspect of what he calls 'constraint theory': see Elster, above n 9.

[111] Cf Carl Schmitt, *Verfassungslehre* (Munich, Duncker & Humblot, 1928), esp ch 8; for French translation see Carl Schmitt, *Theorie de la Constitution* Lilyane Deroche trans (Paris, Presses Universitaires de France, 1993). In relation to Schmitt's argument that the political is the pre-constitutional foundation of the constitution, Preuss (above n 60, at 157–8) notes: 'This has a far-reaching consequence—probably one which, next to the notorious friend-enemy theory of the political, has instigated the most fervent resistance, at least among constitutional lawyers: the consequence that the integrity of the political order can—and sometimes even must—be sustained against the constitution, through the breach of the constitution, because the essence of the political order is not the constitution but the undamaged oneness of the people.' On occasions, Schmitt's argument seems to rely on an unresolved ambiguity between the ancient and modern usages of the term 'constitution'. But, again, where he errs is in drawing an overly essentialist (that is, an ethnic rather than a civic) interpretation of the idea of the unity of a people.

[112] It is for this reason that the attempt by John Rawls to resile from his earlier foundationalism (see Rawls, *A Theory of Justice* (Oxford, Oxford University Press, 1972)) and rely on an 'overlapping consensus'—'a consensus that includes all the opposing philosophical and religious doctrines likely to persist and gain adherents in a more or less just constitutional democratic society'—fails adequately to reorientate the idea of 'justice as fairness' as one that emerges within a political tradition: see Rawls, 'Justice as Fairness: Political not Metaphysical' (1985) 14 *Philosophy and Public Affairs* 223, 225–226.

[113] As we have seen, Locke and Montesquieu recognised the necessity of executive action beyond law. That Hobbes rejects the idea of law as foundational of political order is evident in his argument that, when individuals covenant with one another to establish the office of the sovereign, they do so by an act of alienation rather than of delegation.

But more commonly, the political aspects are repressed. 'Some issues from the battleground of power politics' he argues, are called 'to the forum of principle' and in this special constitutional arena such 'conflicts' are converted into 'questions of justice'.[114] But the process of conversion from political to legal remains mysterious, and his call for 'a fusion of constitutional law and moral theory',[115] suggests ultimately that he seeks to circumvent politics by appealing to the transcendental character of law.

Adherence to law, it must be emphasised, is vital. Rulers lose their state, Machiavelli maintained, 'the moment they begin to break the laws and to disregard the ancient traditions and customs under which men have long lived'.[116] But this is not because law is divinely prescribed, it is not because it reflects some natural equilibrium, it is not because it incorporates fundamental moral principles and it is not because it is an expression of transcendent Reason. Governments adhere to law —to the extent that they do—essentially because it is a prudential necessity. Law observance is necessary for power maintenance. Only by openly acknowledging this basic point—one that is rooted in the primacy of the political—are we likely to be able to address the range of political questions that constitutional discourse throws up for consideration in a sensible manner.

---

[114] Ronald Dworkin, 'The Forum of Principle' in his *A Matter of Principle* (Cambridge, Mass, Harvard University Press, 1985), 71.

[115] Ronald Dworkin, 'Constitutional Cases' in his *Taking Rights Seriously* (Cambridge, Mass, Harvard University Press, 1977), 149.

[116] Machiavelli, *The Discourses*, III.5.

3

What is Parliament for?

ADAM TOMKINS

We have been in recess since July, and during that time there has been a fuel crisis, a Danish no vote, the collapse of the Euro and a war in the middle east, but what is our business tomorrow? The Insolvency Bill [*Lords*]. It ought to be called the Bankruptcy Bill [*Commons*], because we play no role.[1]

INTRODUCTION

THESE WORDS WERE spoken in the autumn of 2000 by one the twentieth century's most committed parliamentarians, Tony Benn MP. Even if he was exaggerating a touch with his claim that the euro had collapsed, the question he poses is a pressing one: in the era of sound-bite politics, of government by spin, of decentralisation within the United Kingdom and globalisation without, what is Parliament for? With new (or at least renewed) sites of power emerging at the European level and within the United Kingdom at the regional level, where should national institutions turn? As a partial answer to this question, this chapter offers a vision of how one of our most special and, once, cherished institutions—Parliament—might develop in the opening years of the twenty-first century.

The argument in this chapter has three threads. The first and perhaps the most obvious is that we cannot understand what should become of Parliament until we have first understood something of how we arrived at the situation in which we now find ourselves. As we shall see, when we consider the question of what Parliament was for in the past, we will find that many of our assumptions of what Parliament is now for are rather more contingent and less certain than we might have assumed. This has the consequence, or so it will be suggested, that we should not feel constrained by contemporary views of parliamentary purpose and function, and should feel reasonably relaxed about offering revised interpretations: revisions that might at first glance appear rather far-fetched, but which on further analysis turn out to be more modest.

---

[1] Tony Benn MP, HC Deb, 23 October 2000, col 12.

The second thread is more descriptive. Constitutionally, we live in interesting times, and there is much contemporary debate about the future of Parliament—debate which Parliament itself is deeply engaged in. A substantial portion of this chapter is devoted to surveying these debates, many of which are very recent, indeed still ongoing. Over the past five years especially a series of reform proposals has been put forward by a variety of parliamentary committees, think-tanks, and others. This chapter has as one of its principal goals the task of drawing these proposals and debates to the attention of constitutional lawyers, and of evaluating their various strengths and limitations.

Finally, the chapter contains a proposal of its own: a first, tentative answer to the question posed in the chapter's title. It will be suggested here that we should reconceive of what it is we think Parliament is for, constitutionally. In particular, *we should abandon the notion that Parliament is principally a legislator. We should instead see Parliament as a scrutineer, or as a regulator, of government.* Such is the key claim made in this chapter. We used to see Parliament as being both essential and central to the constitutional order. Now we are not so sure. As we shall set out in a little more detail in the section below, contemporary commentators generally see Parliament as possessing two constitutional functions. The first is to make the law: Parliament is the national legislature. The second is to hold the government of the day to constitutional account: all government ministers are collectively and individually accountable and responsible to Parliament. Lawyers have tended to devote more energy to the first of these than to the second. This may not be surprising: after all, parliamentary sovereignty (that is, the legislative supremacy of Acts of Parliament) is a rule of law, enforceable in the courts, whereas ministerial responsibility is a mere convention of the constitution: a binding political rule, but not a rule to which there is any judicially enforceable sanction attached. The suggestion here is that we should reverse this hierarchy, and place the emphasis not on Parliament's legislative functions, but on its task of holding the executive to constitutional account.

A century ago there was nothing more sacred to constitutional lawyers than the doctrine of parliamentary sovereignty. For Dicey—the foremost expositor of the rule—it was the very keystone of constitutional law. It meant that Parliament could make or unmake any law whatsoever, and that no one had the authority to override or to set aside the laws Parliament made. So much is axiomatic to any law student. In the past 30 years, however, there has been considerable revision of this doctrine, and we now see the European Communities Act 1972, the Human Rights Act 1998, and the Scotland Act 1998 as constituting limitations of varying sorts on the operation of Dicey's doctrine. The literature on this point is considerable, and this chapter does not seek to add to it. The focus of this chapter will be on Parliament's constitutional role as a scrutineer of government, rather than on its legislative functions.

On this aspect of Parliament's role, constitutional lawyers are more and more coming to the view expressed in our opening quotation by Tony Benn that the House of Commons is bankrupt, and that it has ceased to play a meaningful, or at least a leading, role. Rather than regarding Parliament as the institution in which the government should be held to account, for example, constitutional lawyers are increasingly advocating that we should instead be turning to the courts. There is a move in contemporary constitutional affairs away from what has been termed the 'political constitution' model, towards a legal constitutionalism. I have written elsewhere of what I consider to be the dangers of this move.[2] This chapter contributes to the debate not by repeating those arguments, but rather by seeking to move on from them. The issue here is not whether we should abandon the parliamentary, or political, constitution and replace it with a legal, or judicial, constitution. Instead, the focus here will be to consider how we should go about the task of repairing the political constitution: if the parliamentary model of constitutional accountability is broken, how do we best fix it?

SOME HISTORY: WHAT WAS PARLIAMENT FOR?

The first thing that we have to remember about Parliament is that the way in which we conceive of it now is not the way in which we have always conceived of it. We now think of Parliament as if its principal constitutional role is to make the law, to pass statutes and statutory instruments, to be the nation's law-maker, its legislator. Any further parliamentary function is secondary to that. Other functions are identified in the literature. We have all read that Parliament scrutinises the work of the executive; or that Parliament provides us with our executive, that it is through Parliament that the executive must govern; or that Parliament has a representative function—the Commons represents the people who elect it, and the Lords represents the aristocracy. But none of this is taken as seriously as the legislative function. Indeed, many constitutional commentators, when writing about Parliament, write *only* of its legislative power.[3]

It was not always thus. Conceiving of Parliament as being in principal part the nation's sovereign law-maker was a late Victorian invention. As with so many Victorian inventions, the twentieth century has ossified a mere fad into a fixed tradition.[4] By these remarks I am not suggesting that there were no traces of parliamentary sovereignty before the days, or the writings, of Dicey.[5] But I am suggesting that the post-Diceyan fixation with questions of legislative sovereignty has led us into making a mistake about Parliament, and that is to place too much emphasis on Parliament's legislative function at the expense of the other constitutional roles it plays.

---

[2] See, eg, A Tomkins, *The Constitution after Scott: Government Unwrapped* (Oxford, Clarendon Press, 1998), at 266–75; A Tomkins, 'Introduction: On Being Sceptical about Human Rights', in T Campbell, K Ewing and A Tomkins (eds) *Sceptical Essays on Human Rights* (Oxford, Oxford University Press, 2001), 1–11; and A Tomkins, 'In Defence of the Political Constitution' (2002) 22 *Oxford Journal of Legal Studies* 157.

[3] See, eg, E Barendt, *An Introduction to Constitutional Law* (Oxford, Clarendon Press, 1998) and C Munro, *Studies in Constitutional Law* (2nd edn, London, Butterworths, 1999).

[4] See E Hobsbawm and T Ranger, *The Invention of Tradition* (Cambridge, Cambridge University Press, 1983).

[5] For the pre-nineteenth century history and development of parliamentary sovereignty, see J Goldsworthy, *The Sovereignty of Parliament: History and Philosophy* (Oxford, Clarendon Press, 1999).

A rather better Victorian view of Parliament than Dicey's was Bagehot's. To the House of Lords Bagehot ascribed two functions: the power to delay and the power of revision.[6] Its value, he thought, was two-fold: first it imposed on the common mass the value of nobility, but equally, in doing so, it prevented the common mass from having to experience the evils that would replace nobility if it were not there. These alternatives he identified as the rule of wealth, the rule of rank, and the rule of office, all of which would for Bagehot be profoundly inferior to the reverence, respect and obedience which were the qualities associated with noble rule.[7] To the House of Commons Bagehot ascribed five functions. Its 'main function' was to act as the electoral college 'which chooses our president'.[8] Unlike the electoral college of the United States, the House of Commons was permanent. Thus for Bagehot the most fundamental constitutional role of the Commons was to supply the government. We shall return to this point below. The additional functions of the Commons were its expressive function ('to express the mind of the English people on all matters which come before it'); its teaching function ('to teach the nation what it does not know'); its informing function, and finally its legislative function. Bagehot added that for some commentators, the House of Commons possessed as well as these five a sixth function—a financial function—by which the Commons would scrutinise the government's finances. He dismissed this, however, arguing that this sixth was not a discrete function, but rather a particular manifestation of the others.[9]

On the informing function, Bagehot wrote:

> In old times one office of the House of Commons was to inform the sovereign of what was wrong. It laid before the Crown the grievances and complaints of particular interests. Since the publication of the Parliamentary debates a corresponding office of Parliament is to lay these same grievances, these same complaints, before the nation, which is the present sovereign. The nation needs it quite as much as the king ever needed it.[10]

This is an incisive point, more incisive indeed than Bagehot himself realised. In the sixteenth century the existence of Parliament had revolved around the monarch's need for counsel and consent: 'for monarchs, parliaments were occasions on which they could consult a wider range of their subjects than was normally available.'[11] The central importance of parliamentary consultation (as opposed to other forums in which the monarch could consult with his or her subjects) lay in the essential constitutional fact, established even before the reign of the Tudors, that the Crown could raise money from its subjects only with their

---

[6] W Bagehot, *The English Constitution* (London, Fontana, 1993), 133. Bagehot's book was first published in 1867, and is the leading work describing British government in what might be regarded as the golden period of parliamentary government: 1832–1867—the curious period falling after the end of the rule of the Crown but before the beginning of the rule of party.

[7] *Ibid* at 124–26.

[8] *Ibid* at 152.

[9] *Ibid* at 154–46.

[10] *Ibid* at 154.

[11] See J Loach, *Parliament under the Tudors* (Oxford, Clarendon Press, 1991), 1.

consent. From the fourteenth century it had been recognised that it was through the meeting of Parliament that such consent could be obtained. This, historically, is the principal function of Parliament: not to legislate, but to give consent to the Crown's raising of money. Constitutionally the most pressing grievances and complaints which the Commons could lay before the Crown were those which related to money.

In the seventeenth century, Parliaments conceived of themselves as having two functions: the power of the purse, and the powers attendant on being a High Court. As to the latter, Parliament had two powers as a court of law: judicature (the administration of justice) and legislation (the creation of statute). Of these, 'contemporaries perceived no clear distinction between judicature and legislation, and regarded the making and implementation of law as inseparably linked.'[12] Parliament's jurisdiction as a court stemmed directly from its medieval origins, but during the sixteenth century Parliament's judicature began to be eclipsed by the common law courts, by the courts of chancery, and by the prerogative courts. However, the revival of parliamentary judicature is a notable feature of the early seventeenth century, and represents Parliament's growing dissatisfaction with the constitutional positions adopted by the common law courts. Parliamentary judicature took many forms: the Lords heard appeals, petitions, and cases enforcing privilege, and the Commons acting jointly with the Lords employed two centrally important procedures: attainder and impeachment.[13] An attainder was an Act of Parliament 'declaring an individual guilty of treason or some other felony.'[14] Attainder was little used between 1603 and 1641, as it proved difficult for the Commons to secure the Lords' assent.[15] Impeachment played a much more significant role.[16] Maitland described the early seventeenth century as 'the era of impeachments' but he warned that we should 'not think of impeachments as common events. During the whole of English history there have not, I think, been seventy, and a full quarter of all of them belong to the years 1640-1642.'[17] The procedure for impeachment was generally that the Commons would prepare

---

[12] See D Smith, *The Stuart Parliaments 1603–1689* (London, Arnold, 1999), 32. Smith argues that 'the modern demarcation between the judiciary and the legislature was entirely alien to seventeenth-century England. Contemporaries regarded the judicial and legislative functions as part of a single process whereby the Houses collaborated with the Crown to redress grievances and resolve problems both general and specific.' (*Ibid* at 38).

[13] The Commons had little judicature when acting alone, other than in enforcing its own privileges, as it lacked the power to hear evidence under oath: see Smith, *ibid* at 35.

[14] Smith, *ibid* at 35.

[15] That said, however, attainder was used in 1641 to remove Strafford, and was employed again against Lilburne and others during the Commonwealth. Attainder was last used in England in 1696: see Smith, *ibid* at 35.

[16] Impeachment appears to have originated in 1376, but was not used after 1459 until it was revived in 1621 to be used in the cases against the monopolists Sir Francis Mitchell and Sir Giles Mompesson, as well as against Francis Bacon. The impeachments of Mompesson and Mitchell were not of great constitutional significance, as they were both commoners, impeached for 'fraud, violence and oppression'. Bacon's impeachment, however, was far more telling, as when he was impeached (for bribery) he was one of the King's principal ministers—indeed he was the Lord Chancellor. See F Maitland, *The Constitutional History of England* (Cambridge, Cambridge University Press, 1908), 246.

[17] Maitland, *ibid* at 317.

articles of impeachment which would form the basis of a trial before the Lords, with managers from the Commons acting as prosecutors. As Smith has explained: 'impeachment was particularly useful because it allowed the Houses to try to dislodge "evil counsellors" and "enemies of the commonwealth" without attacking the monarch personally.'[18] It was from this ancient power that the modern doctrine of ministerial responsibility emerged.

For all Parliament's growing powers in the early seventeenth century, and its growing willingness to use them, one core fact must not be forgotten, and that is that Parliament was called, prorogued and dissolved entirely at the behest of the Crown. Parliaments, as van Caenegem has reminded us:

> were created by the Crown as sounding boards and providers of funds. Their primary function was to listen to royal policy declarations, to agree to them and provide the required financial means.[19]

The great breakdown of English government in the early seventeenth century was caused in part by the King's failure to appreciate the importance to England's constitution of his working with, and not against, Parliament. The result was that Parliament stood its ground and simply refused to vote the sums which the Crown needed.[20] The consequences were fatal: Charles I called no Parliament between 1629 and 1640, and tried to govern without it. He tried too to raise taxation without parliamentary consent, most notoriously in the form of ship-money.[21] Despite the judges supporting him, eventually he was forced to reconvene Parliament. Less than two years later England was at civil war.

The point here is that, taking a longer historical view than merely gazing back lazily to Dicey, suggests that there is nothing revolutionary in reconceiving of Parliament as if it is not an institution which is primarily concerned with legislation. The argument here is radical in the sense that it is taking us back to our roots—it is seeking to remember why we have Parliament in the first place. But perhaps this is sufficient history for now. Let us turn our attention back to the present.

PARLIAMENT SINCE 1990

To read the standard literature, you would think that modern Parliament is in a bad way. Not only is it being reported less and less in the media: now it is also being written out of the constitutional law textbooks. The classic example is *The Changing Constitution*. This influential and widely-read collection of essays contained in its earlier editions an excellent essay by Colin Turpin on the conventions of individual and collective ministerial responsibility to Parliament. The essay was axed

---

[18] Smith, above n 12, at 36.

[19] R van Caenegem, *An Historical Introduction to Western Constitutional Law* (Cambridge, Cambridge University Press, 1995), 85.

[20] Smith writes that 'during the mid and late 1620s, the costs of war were such that the Crown probably needed in the region of £1 million a year. Parliamentary supply amounted to £353,000 in 1624, £140,000 in 1625, and £275,000 in 1628.' See Smith, above n 12, at 54.

[21] On ship-money, see *R v Hampden* (1637) 3 St Tr 825.

from the most recent edition (published in 2000) because, its editors tell us, 'the doctrine of individual ministerial responsibility has been significantly weakened over the last ten years or so, so that it can no longer be said, in our view, that it is a fundamental doctrine of the constitution'.[22] This is strong and uncompromising stuff, but it is misjudged. No fair-minded constitutional commentator would deny that ministerial responsibility has taken a severe knocking over the last decade or so. The scandalous and clearly unconstitutional rewriting of the rules on ministerial responsibility by cabinet ministers and senior civil servants during the Major years has been well documented elsewhere. Sir Robin Butler's spurious distinction between full ministerial responsibility and mere accountability; Michael Howard's refusal to resign and his dismissal of Derek Lewis over management in prisons in 1995; and William Waldegrave's refusal to resign over the deceitful way he had reported to Parliament as disclosed in the labyrinthine Scott Report on 'arms to Iraq' in 1996 were all deeply troubling episodes for those who continue to respect the ideal of the parliamentary constitution.[23] As Diana Woodhouse has damningly but rightly expressed it:

> the effective operation of the convention [of individual ministerial responsibility] depends upon the integrity of the minister concerned and the extent to which the acceptance of responsibility is a matter of principle rather than political pragmatism. Neither integrity nor principle was a characteristic associated with the Conservative governments of the 1990s.[24]

Nonetheless, it is an exaggeration to suggest as Barendt has done that 'it is rare for the House of Commons to hold an individual minister to account.'[25] Similarly, Jowell and Oliver have acted prematurely in writing the obituary of ministerial responsibility. It might have been thought that with its unsightly and (frankly rather embarrassingly) large majority, the Labour government that has been in power since 1997 would have behaved, if anything, even more obnoxiously than did its Conservative predecessor. After all, is the conventional wisdom not that parliamentary accountability of the government is likely to be stronger when the government's majority is smaller? Major and Blair have combined effectively to

---

[22] See J Jowell and D Oliver (eds), *The Changing Constitution* (4th edn, Oxford, Oxford University Press, 2000), viii. Ours is not the only time in which commentators have lamented the apparent decline of Parliament—indeed, it may be that every generation considers Parliament, rather like the (now defunct) satirical magazine *Punch*, to be 'not as good as it was'. In the early 1960s there was a glut of books published on this theme: see, eg, B Crick, *The Reform of Parliament* (London, Weidenfeld and Nicolson, 1964); A Hill and A Whichelow, *What's Wrong with Parliament?* (Harmondsworth, Penguin, 1964). A number of the proposals and recommendations in books such as these found their way (eventually) into parliamentary practice from the late 1970s. Perhaps the lesson here is that Parliament *always* gets a bad press, but that it does learn, adapt, and improve, such that it would always be folly to write it off.

[23] For a full discussion of these episodes, see A Tomkins, *The Constitution after Scott*, above n 2, at 25–67.

[24] D Woodhouse, 'Individual Ministerial Responsibility and a Dash of Principle', in D Butler, V Bogdanor and R Summers (eds), *The Law, Politics and the Constitution* (Oxford, Oxford University Press, 1999), 102.

[25] Barendt, above n 3, at 116.

turn this wisdom on its head. Following the 1992 general election the Conservative majority in the House of Commons was 21. This number shrank during the life of the Parliament, as Tory MPs died and their party lost by-election after by-election. By the end, the Conservatives were reliant on the Ulster Unionists for survival. Yet this was exactly the period of Howard and Waldegrave. In contrast, the Labour Party enjoyed a majority of 179 after the 1997 election, and this was dented by only the smallest margin in the 2001 election. How has Parliament fared since 1997? Has the enormity of the Labour majority been as unhealthy for Parliament as was widely feared? Or has the principle of ministerial responsibility begun to recover? Has the Labour government conducted itself with any more integrity and principle than the Conservative government did?

The record since 1997 is actually quite positive. Three instances can be cited each of which constitutes a significant and considerable improvement on the Conservative legacy. The first concerns pensions. The parliamentary ombudsman had found that the department of social security had failed to inform those who might be affected that widows and widowers would inherit only half of their spouses' State Earnings Related Pension (SERPS). He further found that this failure amounted to what he termed a 'systemic failure' on the part of the department.[26] Who should be held responsible for this? The system? The department? The Secretary of State? The internal auditors? In evidence given to the House of Commons the Permanent Secretary blamed the accounting officers, but the Secretary of State (Alistair Darling) stepped forward and contradicted her, saying that it is ministers who are responsible for what happens in their departments and 'if you let the ministers off then you are never going to hold anyone to account really'.[27]

The second instance concerns the Sandline affair in 1998, relating to foreign policy and Sierra Leone. It was alleged that foreign office officials had authorised the supply of military equipment to Sierra Leone.[28] The Foreign Secretary, Robin Cook, responded by establishing an inquiry, whose report was published, and by working alongside the House of Commons Foreign Affairs Select Committee in implementing a programme of some 60 reforms. Mr Cook told the House of Commons that Parliament, through the Foreign Affairs Committee, should make sure that 'the Foreign Office and I are harried, pursued and kept up to scratch in putting in place the programme of reform.'[29] The government's handling of this matter stands in stark contrast to the way in which initial allegations of 'arms to Iraq' had been handled by Conservative ministers in the late 1980s and early 1990s.[30] The third instance concerns the way in which the Home Secretary, Jack

---

[26] See D Woodhouse, 'The Reconstruction of Constitutional Accountability' [2002] *Public Law* 73, 81.

[27] Public Administration Committee, *Report of the Parliamentary Ombudsman* (HC 305, 1999–2000), minutes of evidence, Q 117: cited by Woodhouse, *ibid* at 81.

[28] See Woodhouse, *ibid* at 84.

[29] HC Deb, 18 May 1998, col 609. See Woodhouse, above n 26, at 84. See also I Leigh, 'Secrets of the Political Constitution' (1999) 62 *Modern Law Review* 298, 303–4.

[30] On which, see Tomkins, *The Constitution after Scott*, above n 2, at 95–112.

Straw, responded to the difficulties in the passport office in 1999. Woodhouse tells the story thus:

> The home secretary not only explained what had happened but apologised personally to those queuing at the Petty France Passport Office. He also took amendatory action, intervening in some cases to ensure that passports were issued in time, compensation was paid to those whose travel plans had been disrupted and extra staff were employed to clear the backlog. Moreover, while his explanations and actions implied that the crisis was the result of agency mismanagements, he did not publicly blame and punish the chief executive, as Michael Howard had done in the case of the Prison Service Agency. His emphasis was rather on putting things right … Before the Home Affairs Select Committee, the permanent secretary, David Ormand, gave a full explanation.[31]

Each of these episodes represents a serious attempt to make parliamentary accountability work. These stories would be unlikely to command many column-inches on the front pages of national newspapers, as ministerial heads did not roll, and the drama of resignation was avoided. But to equate responsibility with resignation was always a mistake—and indeed to expect resignation may well operate so as to dilute, rather than to strengthen, accountability, as it ups the stakes to such a point that political game-playing replaces genuine responsibility. What these stories are about is Parliament trying to do better, and government trying to do better.

PARLIAMENT AND IMPROVING SCRUTINY

Liaison

For all Woodhouse's splendid invective against the hollow Major government, the operation of ministerial responsibility and the success of the parliamentary or political constitution actually depends on more than governmental integrity and principle. It also depends on parliamentary will. The early 1990s witnessed not only a constitutionally bankrupt executive in Britain, but also a pathetically supine Parliament. Such change as we have seen since 1997 might well be more a change in the latter characteristic than the former. While some ministers in the Blair government have clearly sought to subject themselves and their departmental work to greater parliamentary scrutiny than did their Conservative predecessors, it is not as if the Blair government generally treats Parliament with great respect. The Prime Minister himself, of course, rarely attends the House of Commons save for the weekly half-hour Prime Minister's question time. The Speaker has had to remind the government on numerous occasions of the constitutional importance of ministers making policy statements in the House first, rather than in media studios or press interviews. And, as our opening quotation from Tony Benn makes clear, Parliament under Blair has enjoyed spectacularly long holidays.

---

[31] Woodhouse, above n 26, at 85.

In any consideration of politics under New Labour, allegations of government by spin and control-freakery abound. Power is devolved to Scotland, but the London party leadership exerts its influence to keep dissidents such as Dennis Canavan away.[32] Power is devolved to Wales, but the Prime Minister wants Alun Michael not Rhodri Morgan to be First Minister.[33] London has a mayor but on no account will Ken Livingstone be Labour's candidate.[34] Immediately following the 2001 election the government tried to act in a similar way over Parliament. But just as it was unsuccessful in Rhodri Morgan's and Ken Livingstone's cases, so too was it unsuccessful with regard to Parliament. The government sought to manipulate the membership, and in particular the chairmanship,[35] of the Commons select committees. Most notoriously, the government whips sought to oust Gwyneth Dunwoody from the chair of the Transport Committee, and to oust Donald Anderson from the chair of the Foreign Affairs Committee. Even worse, Mr Anderson's replacement was to be the luckless Chris Smith, who throughout the 1997–2001 Parliament had been a member of the cabinet, as Secretary of State for Culture, Media and Sport. The departmental select committees are the unique preserve of backbench MPs. While Mr Smith was a backbencher (as the Prime Minister had reshuffled him out of the Government following the 2001 election) he had been one for less than a month. Parliament—and in particular the parliamentary Labour Party—revolted, and in an unusual show of defiance voted down the government's proposed membership.[36] The whips had to think again, Mrs Dunwoody and Mr Anderson were reinstated as the chairs of their committees, and the House approved the revised list of nominations.[37]

There is nothing unusual in the government, through its whips, seeking to control membership and chairmanship of select committees. After the 1992 election the Conservative whips sought to prevent Nicholas Winterton from being reappointed to the chair of the Health Select Committee. Mr Winterton, a Conservative MP, had been the chair of the committee since 1983, and under his chairmanship the committee had published a number of reports critical of the government's programme of reforms to the NHS. Mr Winterton objected, but the whips had a defence: they argued that it was a party rule that no member would serve as chair of the same committee for more than two Parliaments. Unfortunately for the whips Sir John Wheeler had served as chair of the Home Affairs Committee for two Parliaments. Unlike Mr Winterton's committee, the Home Affairs Committee had not been especially critical of the Home Office during the 1980s, and it was not in the

---

[32] Mr Canavan claimed the support of 95% of his local party, but the national party successfully kept him off the list of Labour candidates for the Scottish Parliament. Mr Canavan stood for election as an independent, and was successfully elected.

[33] Alun Michael lost a vote of confidence in the Welsh Assembly, and was replaced by Rhodri Morgan, in February 2000.

[34] Ken Livingstone left the Labour Party and stood as an independent candidate. He won the election to become London's first elected mayor in May 2000.

[35] The House of Commons continues to refer to each committee having a 'chairman'. I will use the term 'chair'.

[36] See HC Deb, 16 July 2001.

[37] See HC Deb, 19 July 2001.

government's interest for him to be replaced, but the price to paid for removing Mr Winterton was that Sir John Wheeler also had to be removed, although he (unlike Mr Winterton) was compensated through subsequent elevation to ministerial office. Both positive and negative conclusions can be drawn from these stories. On the plus side, they suggest that select committees are sufficiently powerful, prestigious and effective to be taken seriously by the government and its whips. If select committees were worthless, or ineffective, why go to the bother of seeking to manipulate their membership and direction? But on the minus side, of course, these committees are supposed to be rigorous and independent committees of inquiry. If the whips can so easily remove thorns from the government's flesh, will that not discourage rigour? If the whips have control over membership, does that not dilute the extent to which the committees can truly be said to be independent of government? What was unusual about the events of July 2001 was not that the whips tried it on, but that Parliament stood up to them, and won.

Select committees are set up at the beginning of each new Parliament. Their membership is formally a matter for the Committee of Selection. When the system of departmental select committees was established in 1979 it was the intention that through the Committee of Selection the political parties in the House of Commons would be obliged to submit their nominations for committee membership to the prior scrutiny of backbench MPs before they were put to the House. However, the Committee of Selection has come to interpret its role as being limited to the confirmation of the proposals put to it by the party managers (ie the whips). What the events of July 2001 clearly showed was that this mechanism of appointment to select committees no longer enjoyed the confidence of the House. Why did Parliament bite back in this way in 2001, whereas it had not done so in 1992?

One reason is that throughout the lifetime of the 1997–2001 Parliament concern gradually developed on all sides of the Commons as to the continuing effectiveness of the departmental select committee system. The House of Commons was well aware of the way it was perceived by public and press. Its reputation had plunged before 1997 and was showing few signs of recovery under New Labour. While the government had delivered notable constitutional reform with regard to devolution and the passing of the Human Rights Act 1998, Parliament had been left relatively untouched, unimproved, and unmodernised. The House of Lords Act 1999 had not even managed to remove all the hereditary peers. The Jenkins Report on reform to the electoral system for elections to the House of Commons had apparently sunk without trace.[38] In 1997 a Modernisation Committee had been established to plot the ways in which the arcane procedures and practices of the Commons could be, well, modernised, but it was a lacklustre committee, without overall strategy, which published rather mundane reports on second-order issues.[39] The Modernisation Committee is a unique committee in that it is chaired

---

[38] See *Report of the Jenkins Commission on the Voting System*, (Cm 4090, October 1998).

[39] That said, however, the Modernisation Committee did publish reports on two important issues during the 1997–2001 Parliament: on sittings in Westminster Hall, and on the carry-over of public

not by a backbench MP but by a cabinet minister: the Leader of the House. But to make modernisation work the House needed a leader in the Richard Crossman mould,[40] and neither Anne Taylor nor Margaret Beckett fitted it.

Instead of coming via the Leader of the House and the Modernisation Committee, parliamentary leadership in the Commons came in the 1997–2001 Parliament from the rather unlikely source of the Liaison Committee. This normally quiet and sleepy committee is composed of all the chairs of the departmental and other[41] select committees. In the 1987 and 1992 Parliaments it barely met and reported only cursorily at the end of each Parliament—in general terms and without great effect—on the difficulties encountered by select committees during the Parliament.[42] However, during the 1997–2001 Parliament the Liaison Committee stirred. Its first and most important step was to publish in March 2000 a report entitled *Shifting the Balance: Select Committees and the Executive.*[43] This powerful, and for a select committee well-publicised, report sought to provide the impetus for a revision and strengthening of select committees. When the report was published it had been more than 20 years since the last reorganisation, and the Liaison Committee in 2000 aimed to achieve for parliamentary scrutiny in the first decade of the twenty-first century what the 1978 report of the Procedure Committee had achieved for the 1980s and 1990s.[44] For the Liaison Committee, the starting point was that:

> the 1979 select committee system has been a success. We have no doubt of that. At a bargain price, it has provided independent scrutiny of government ... it has exposed mistaken and short-sighted policies and, from time to time, wrong-doing both in high places and low. It has been a source of unbiased information, rational debate, and constructive ideas. It has made the political process less remote, and more accessible to the citizen who is affected by that process—and who pays the bill. Its very existence has been a constant reminder to Ministers and officials, and many others in positions of power and influence, of the spotlight that may swing their way when least welcome.[45]

However, despite the fact that the committee system had 'shown the House of Commons at its best' the committee acknowledged that the performance of select committees had 'not been consistent' and that their success had not been 'unalloyed'.[46] The purpose of the committee's report was to find ways of making parlia-

Bills. On these, see 2000–01 HC 906 and 1997–98 HC 543. Other matters on which the committee reported included: sittings on Thursdays; timing of votes; facilities for the media; voting methods; scrutiny of European business; and explanatory material for Bills. The rather more impressive work of the Modernisation Committee since the 2001 election is considered below.

[40] Crossman was Leader of the House in Harold Wilson's reforming government of the 1960s. He was the minister responsible for steering the Parliamentary Commissioner Bill through the House in 1966. This was the measure which introduced the ombudsman into British constitutional practice. A gifted and committed constitutionalist, it was the same Richard Crossman who wrote the introduction (first published in 1963) to Bagehot's *The English Constitution.*

[41] Eg, Public Administration Committee and Public Accounts Committee.

[42] See, eg, 1996–97 HC 323.

[43] 1999–2000 HC 300, 3 March 2000.

[44] See Select Committee on Procedure, *First Report*, 1977–78 HC 588.

[45] Liaison Committee, *Shifting the Balance*, above n 43, at para 4.

[46] *Ibid* at paras 5–6.

mentary scrutiny of the government more effective, by reinforcing the select committees.[47] The various recommendations contained in the report of the Liaison Committee can be analysed as falling into eight main categories, as follows.

Appointment and Nomination

The committee recommended that nomination should be taken out of the hands of the whips; that at the very beginning of each new Parliament, at the same time as the Chairman and Deputy Chairmen of Ways and Means are appointed, a Chairman and two Deputy Chairmen of Committees should be appointed, all of whom would be senior and respected backbench members of the House, who would invite names for appointment to select committees, the nominated membership of each committee being put before the House within two weeks; the committee further recommended changes to the way in which appointments are made to committees during Parliaments, when members of committees leave—the very high level of turnover, and delays in replacing members, caused considerable concern in the 1997–2001 Parliament.

Payment and Remuneration

The committee recommended that in order to make chairmanship of committees more attractive, and in order to provide for a career structure in the Commons to complement the ministerial career ladder, that such matters as paying chairmen of committees should be urgently considered by the Senior Salaries Review Body.

Debates and Questions on Reports

The committee suggested that the tendency to use the frequency of debate of select committee reports as a criterion of success was somewhat crude, and stated that while more parliamentary time could usefully be deployed in this way, such a reform would not be sufficient of itself:

> what is needed is a new way of giving timely and effective exposure to reports. We propose that, once a week after Questions, there should be a period of half an hour devoted to a report—normally one published within the previous fortnight.[48]

Timing and Quality of Government Replies

The committee noted that the rule was clear: namely that government departments should reply to select committee reports within two months; the committee

---

[47] A number of the ideas underpinning the committee's recommendations were drawn from the early experience of the Scottish Parliament, which has experimented valuably with committee mandate and structure in a number of ways.

[48] *Ibid* at para 40.

further noted that this deadline was very frequently missed; the committee further noted that the quality of government replies was 'patchy: some are exemplary but too many are superficial.'[49]

Follow-up on Recommendations

The committee reported that some select committees were already in the habit of regularly following-up on their recommendations—the Agriculture and Defence Committees were cited as examples; the committee recommended that all select committees adopt this procedure; the committee further recommended that all select committees should draw up annual reports which should be submitted to the Liaison Committee so that the Liaison Committee too could follow-up on committees' recommendations.

Improving the Scrutiny of Draft Legislation

The publication of draft bills was an innovation of the 1997–2001 Parliament, with 12 being published in all; draft bills were scrutinised by select committees (not standing committees) and this was felt by the Liaison Committee to be a valuable use of select committee resources, although a number of improvements to the procedure were recommended by the committee, particularly as regards timetabling and notice.

Ensuring Greater Co-operation between Committees

Like the introduction of draft bills, the publication of joint committee reports (following joint inquiries) was a further innovation of the 1997–2001 Parliament. The leading example to date is the quadripartite inquiry into arms exports conducted by the Defence, Foreign Affairs, International Development, and Trade and Industry Committees. The Liaison Committee welcomed this innovation, although it stated that here again certain procedural improvements and clarifications were needed.

Staffing and Resources Issues

The committee noted that 'no-one could accuse select committees of being profligate in their staffing' and noted that the House employs 107 permanent staff who serve some 25 committees and sub-committees. As a way of helping select committees improve the quality of their financial scrutiny of government departments the Liaison Committee recommended that the Committee Office should establish a unit specialising in public expenditure. The committee further recommended that if select committees are to engage in more pre-legislative scrutiny the Committee Office should also establish a unit of staff with specialisation in that.

[49] *Ibid* at para 47.

This adds up to a comprehensive and intelligent package of reforms. Yet it was comprehensively and quite unintelligently rejected by the government.[50] The Liaison Committee stated that the government's reply was:

> both disappointing and surprising. We found it disappointing because our proposals were modest. We did not suggest line-by-line scrutiny of the Estimates as a condition for their approval; we did not suggest any change in the powers of select committees: for example, to allow them to require papers from government departments or to summon Ministers—for all of which there are strong cases.[51]

The government rejected out of hand the committee's recommendations on reforming the way in which members of committees are nominated at the beginning of Parliament. It further rejected the committee's suggestion that prime Commons time (immediately after questions once every week) should be devoted to questions and/or short debates on a recently published committee report, the so-called 'select committee half hour'. On improving conditions for scrutiny of draft legislation the government was non-committal at best. On facilitating co-operation between committees the government was unhelpful, as it was on the committee's suggestions for improving the timing and quality of government replies to select committee reports. None of the government's positions persuaded the Liaison Committee, which subjected the government's reply to a forensic and devastating critique.[52]

The report of the Liaison Committee was debated twice in the Commons, once on an adjournment debate in November 2000, and once on a substantive motion on an opposition day in February 2001.[53] But despite persistent parliamentary pressure the government stood firm. One year on from the publication of its first report the Liaison Committee published a further report, *Shifting the Balance: Unfinished Business*,[54] in which the committee revisited its core recommendations, and repeated them. Not all of the committee's recommendations required government action or approval, of course. Of the eight sets of recommendations outlined above, those relating to nomination and appointment, to payment and remuneration, to government replies, and to scrutiny of draft legislation would require government action. However, those relating to improving follow-up procedures, to co-operation between committees, and to staffing matters were recommendations for the attention of the House as a whole, and not principally for the government. In its *Unfinished Business* report, while the Liaison Committee remained disappointed by the response of the government, it was able to report substantive progress on many of its non-governmental recommendations. Committees had started to produce annual reports which the Liaison Committee could (and did) use as the basis of further scrutiny. One major advantage of this was that the Liaison Committee could identify 'best practice' and encourage all

---

[50] The government's reply to the committee was published on 18 May 2000 as Cm 4737.
[51] Liaison Committee, *Independence or Control?* 1999–2000 HC 748, 25 July 2000, para 3
[52] *Ibid.*
[53] See HC Deb, 9 November 2000, cols 473–540; and 12 February 2001, cols 80–128.
[54] 2000–01 HC 321, 15 March 2001.

the committees to adopt it. Another was that the committee could obtain a fuller picture of the contribution which select committees were making. From the annual reports which the Liaison Committee reviewed in March 2001 it could conclude, for example, that in two respects in which Parliament (and in particular the House of Commons) is usually regarded as being particularly weak in terms of scrutiny, considerable improvements had been made: first as regards scrutiny of treaties,[55] and secondly as regards scrutiny of EU matters.[56] Further, staffing in the Committee Office had improved, and in particular the Comptroller and Auditor General had authorised the secondment of staff from the National Audit Office (NAO) to the Committee Office to help select committees in matters of financial scrutiny. Finally, the Committee could report that in another development which was contributing to the growing reach and range of select committees' activity, a number of committees had conducted hearings into public appointments: this was true of the Treasury Committee (which took evidence from all the members of the Monetary Policy Committee); the Health Committee (who interviewed the chairman-designate of the National Institute for Clinical Excellence); the Transport Committee (who took evidence from the newly appointed chairman of the Strategic Rail Authority); and of the Health and Agriculture Committees (who jointly interviewed the chairman of the new Food Standards Agency); as well as others.[57]

Hansard Society

In its endeavour to raise the profile of the Commons scrutiny function, and to persuade both Parliament and the government to take scrutiny seriously, the Liaison Committee played a leadership role, but it was not alone. The Hansard Society, the think-tank and pressure group which seeks to 'promote effective parliamentary democracy' appointed in the autumn of 1999 a working party to conduct an

---

[55] The Procedure Committee conducted a review of parliamentary scrutiny of treaties (see 1999–2000 HC 210) and had found that while select committees have frequently performed expertly in scrutinising treaties, there was one improvement which could be made. The Liaison Committee reported that the Government had accepted the recommendation of the Procedure Committee to the effect that if a select committee requests a debate before ratification of a treaty raising major political, military or diplomatic issues, the request would be acceded to.

[56] The Liaison Committee reported that 'there is increasing emphasis on European Union subjects: not only broad policy, but also specific proposals and documents. The Home Affairs Committee has stepped up its work on Justice and Home Affairs business in the EU; the International Development Committee has produced three reports on EU development policy; the Welsh Affairs Committee has examined European Structural Funds as they affect Wales; the Environmental Audit Committee reported on a greening agenda for the Helsinki summit; and the Health Committee looked at the proposed EC Directive on Tobacco Advertising. These are only a few examples; and for some committees, such as Foreign Affairs and Trade and Industry, the EU dimension is present in much of their work. We particularly welcome the co-operation between the European Scrutiny Committee and other committees in the examination of issues on the EU agenda. This relationship has been underlined by the new provision in Standing Order 143(11) under which the European Scrutiny Committee may seek an opinion on a European document from another committee before deciding whether to clear a document or to recommend a debate.' See 2000–01 HC 321, at paras 87–88.

[57] See *ibid* at para 93.

inquiry into and to report on ways in which Parliament's scrutiny functions could be improved. In the early 1990s the Hansard Society had commissioned a report on improving Parliament's legislative procedures. That report was widely read, respected and influential.[58] Now the Hansard Society sought a similarly weighty and authoritative report on scrutiny. In July 2001 it got one: the report was called *The Challenge for Parliament: Making Government Accountable.*[59] Building on the foundations laid by the Liaison Committee in 2000, this was a formidable report, well researched, thoughtful and well argued.

Unlike the Liaison Committee, the Hansard Society report did not focus exclusively on select committees. Rather, it sought to evaluate Parliament's strengths and limitations as regards scrutiny in the round. It considered both Houses—not only the Commons—and it discussed the chamber of the Commons as much as it considered committees. The report set out its many detailed recommendations as if based on seven overarching principles. Some of these principles are rather banal, but we should briefly set them out. They are: Parliament should be at the apex; Parliament must develop a culture of scrutiny; committees should play a more influential role within Parliament; the chamber should remain central to accountability; financial scrutiny should be central to accountability; the House of Lords should complement the Commons; and Parliament should communicate more effectively with the public.

This may all sound obvious enough. But the core idea of the report is rather more far-reaching than these principles might suggest. This core idea is that while Parliament cannot itself scrutinise everything that central government does, Parliament ought to do a great deal more than it does at present to consolidate and to review the variety of regulation and scrutiny to which the government is subjected. To some limited extent this happens already: both the parliamentary ombudsman and the National Audit Office are already relatively well 'plugged-in' to the parliamentary process. But most other external regulators are much more divorced from Parliament: this is true not only of the utility regulators (Oftel, Ofwat, and so on)[60] but also of such bodies as the Law Commission, the Civil Aviation Authority, the Electoral Commission, the Health and Safety Executive, the Office for Standards in Education (Ofsted), the Office of the Rail Regulator, the Financial Services Authority, the Food Standards Agency, the Press Complaints Commission, the Securities and Investment Board, and a whole host of ombudsmen covering such fields as banking, insurance services, pensions, legal services, and so on. The Hansard Society found that while the House of Commons currently keeps no central list of bodies which lay reports before the House, 'it is estimated that over 500 bodies present reports to Parliament, some on an annual basis, others less frequently. During the 1999–2000 session of Parliament 247 reports were

---

[58] See Hansard Society, *Making the Law: Report of the Hansard Society Commission on the Legislative Process* (London, Hansard Society, 1993).

[59] Hansard Society, *The Challenge for Parliament: Making Government Accountable* (London, Vacher Dod, 2001). For commentary, see D Oliver, 'The Challenge for Parliament' [2001] *Public Law* 666.

[60] See Peter Leyland, ch 7 below.

officially laid before MPs'.[61] Yet less than 14 per cent of select committee reports deal with any of this wealth of material.[62]

The core recommendation of the report was that Parliament should place itself at the apex of this pyramid of accountability: it should systematically and rigorously draw on the investigations of outside regulators and commissions, thereby on the one hand providing a framework for their activities, so they feel less ad hoc than at present, and on the other hand also drawing on their expertise and resources to enable Parliament more effectively to perform its function of holding ministers to constitutional account.[63] This recommendation is pushing in exactly the right direction. Stronger parliamentary links with external regulators would be welcomed not only by select committees[64] but also by the regulators.[65] It would transform the culture of regulation in the United Kingdom: the external commissions and regulators would no longer be seen as alternatives to Parliament, but as complementary to it, or even as part of it. One of the strengths of this idea is that it builds on preexisting good practice. At its best the House of Commons already behaves in this way. This can be seen by examining the way in which the parliamentary ombudsman and the National Audit Office work with the Commons committees—not only their own committees (the Public Administration Committee and the Public Accounts Committee) but also with the departmental committees. A good recent example of this matrix working well together is the case of the Child Support Agency. Consider the following pattern:[66]

1993   Child Support Agency established

1994   Social Security Select Committee publishes two reports (March and October) highlighting deficiencies of the CSA

1995   January: ombudsman lays first report on the CSA before Parliament

1995   January: Government publishes White Paper *Improving Child Support* and amending legislation which becomes Child Support Act 1995

1995   March: Select Committee on the PCA publishes report responding to ombudsman's concerns

1995   November: Public Accounts Committee publishes report on financing the CSA

1996   January: Social Security Select Committee publishes its third report on the CSA

---

[61]   Hansard Society report, above n 59, at para 3.14.

[62]   *Ibid.*

[63]   To this end the Hansard Society report recommended that both Houses should maintain a central list of all those organisations obliged to report to Parliament. This list should be distributed to every committee, so that every departmental select committee is aware of the organisations which come under their jurisdiction. See *ibid* at para 3.24.

[64]   See, eg, the efforts of the Education Committee to include the work of Ofsted in its oversight: see 1998–99 HC 52; and see *ibid* at para 1.27.

[65]   See evidence of Sir Ian Byatt, Director General of Ofwat, and of Elizabeth France, Information Commissioner, cited *ibid* at paras 1.28–1.29.

[66]   This table is drawn from the Hansard Society report, above n 59, at para 8.25.

1996   March: ombudsman lays second report before Parliament
1996   June: Social Security Select Committee publishes its fourth report on the CSA
1997   March: Public Accounts Committee publishes its second report on the finances of the CSA
1997   March: Social Security Select Committee publishes its fifth report on the CSA
1997   April: the CSA Independent Case Examiner is introduced to assess cases of maladministration
1997   July: Labour Government publishes Green Paper on CSA reform
1999   July: Government publishes White Paper on CSA reform which leads to new legislation introducing major changes

Here we see the departmental select committee producing five reports in three years, buttressed by two special reports from the ombudsman, one report from the ombudsman's committee, and two reports from the Public Accounts Committee (both of which were based on reports compiled by the NAO). The Social Security Select Committee took evidence from ministers, senior civil servants, CSA chief executives, pressure groups, and members of the public personally affected by the CSA. Both the Conservative and Labour governments responded—the amendatory legislation of 1995 was introduced in principal part because of parliamentary pressure and was shaped both by the evidence amassed by the committees and the ombudsman and by their recommendations.[67] The aim behind the Hansard Society report is to make this sort of experience the ordinary routine of Parliament, rather than the unusual exception. The other point which should be made here is that no one else could have done this. From no other source could such persistence of pressure have been forthcoming. No other institution (the courts included) could have achieved the extent of the changes which the Conservative and Labour governments were, in effect, forced to make.

In addition to this core idea, the Hansard Society report made a series of detailed recommendations covering a wide variety of parliamentary practices. We do not have space to consider them all here, but the key recommendations as regards committees, and as regards the Commons chamber, can briefly be listed. First, on committees, the report proposed that: every backbench MP should be expected to serve on a select committee; all but the largest government departments should have only one PPS (thereby increasing the number of non-governmental MPs); key posts on select committees should be paid; MPs who chair committees should receive a salary equivalent to that of a minister; select committees should be given a set of core duties, and 'to improve the coverage of issues, to utilise the work of the regulators and to give the committees a continuity to their work they should meet pre-agreed objectives over the course of a Parliament'[68] to be agreed with and

---

[67] See *ibid* at paras 8.22–8.33. See also C Harlow, 'Accountability, New Public Management, and the Problems of the Child Support Agency' (1999) 26 *Journal of Law and Society* 150.
[68] Hansard Society report, above n 59, at para 3.25.

monitored by the Liaison Committee; committees should use rapporteurs to gather evidence and produce background papers; committees should publish follow-up reports two or three years after reporting on an issue to assess the extent to which their recommendations have been implemented. On the Commons chamber, the report recommended that Parliament should have a non-ministerial steering committee responsible for the management of the parliamentary timetable, the effect of which would be to take this issue out of the government's hands. On the chamber the report stated that:

> the chamber's role in contributing to the scrutiny and calling to account of government has three main components, namely authorising government action, debating issues of political significance and calling ministers to account for their actions through questions and debates. The chamber's role is distinct in that it provides a broader oversight role than that of the committees which can engage in more detailed investigation.[69]

Modernisation

The story we have been telling is one of growing parliamentary dissatisfaction with the way in which the government is held to political account. We have seen how in the 1997–2001 Parliament the Liaison Committee took the lead in seeking to rejuvenate Parliament's committee structure. We have seen also how the government comprehensively and depressingly rejected the committee's suggestions for reform. We have seen how Parliament bit back in July 2001 when it defeated the government—the first defeat the Blair government had suffered on the floor of the House since coming to power in 1997—on the question of select committee membership. And finally, we have seen how in this endeavour Parliament has received a considerable boost from the authoritative and thoughtful report of the Hansard Society. So where are we now?

If all this left the ball in the government's court, the government have responded surprisingly positively since the summer of 2001. In the post-election reshuffle the Prime Minister handed the critical position of Leader of the House to Robin Cook, the former foreign secretary. Unlike his immediate predecessors, Mr Cook was, potentially, a Leader with both the political gravitas and the vision to become a reformer as influential as Richard Crossman.[70] After having been appointed, the new Leader of the House surrounded himself with advisers who seemed to share his commitment to parliamentary reform (including Meg Russell, formerly of the Constitution Unit, and Greg Power, who acted as secretary to the Hansard Society Commission which drew up the report discussed above, and who indeed drafted that report). Under Mr Cook, the first work undertaken by the Modernisation

---

[69] *Ibid* at para 4.4.

[70] In opposition Robin Cook was one of the Labour Party's most effective and proficient parliamentary performers. He established his credentials as a committed parliamentarian in leading the opposition on the parliamentary reception of the Scott Report on 'arms to Iraq' in early 1996. Mr Cook resigned from the government in March 2003 and was replaced as Leader of the House first by John Reid and subsequently by Peter Hain. Whether Mr Hain will continue in the Cook vein remains to be seen.

Committee concerned the future of select committees. The Committee reported on this issue in February 2002.[71] The nature and tenor of its report and of the recommendations contained within it were much more closely in tune with the work of the Liaison Committee and the Hansard Society than might have been expected given the government's response to the Liaison Committee in 2000. The Modernisation Committee is a committee of the House of Commons, of course, and not of the government. But it is chaired by a cabinet minister and while its recommendations are not officially representative of government policy, it does seem implausible that the Leader of the House would allow the committee to veer too far away from that which would be acceptable to the government. The committee's key recommendations were as follows:

- on nomination and appointment, the committee recommended that at the start of each Parliament a Committee of Nomination should be set up under the Chairman of Ways and Means; the membership of this committee should be a matter for the Speaker and not subject to any party interest of lobbying and should be prescribed in the Standing Orders;[72]
- on payment and remuneration, the Committee recommended that the chairs of the principal investigative select committee should be paid an additional salary;
- on select committees following-up on their recommendations, the Committee agreed with the Liaison Committee that committees should produce annual reports which should form the basis of further inquiry by the Liaison Committee;
- on staffing, the Committee made recommendations very similar to those from the Liaison Committee and from the Hansard Society.

In all these respects, it is clear that the Modernisation Committee moved substantially towards the position of the Liaison Committee. In some respects, indeed, the Modernisation Committee went further than the Liaison Committee. The Modernisation Committee recommended, for example, that a statement of core tasks should be adopted for each committee; that committees should experiment with rapporteurs; that there should be a two-term limit imposed on those who may chair committees; that the standard size of committees should be increased from 11 to 15; that those with poor attendance records should be swiftly replaced; and that the departmental select committees should be renamed 'scrutiny committees'.

---

[71] Modernisation Committee, *Select Committees*, 2001–02 HC 224.

[72] It will be recalled that the Liaison Committee had recommended a committee of three to perform this task. This was criticised as being too small and the recommendation did not find support when the House debated the report. The Modernisation Committee recommended that the Committee of Nomination should consist of the Chairman of Ways and Means (who should not have a vote) and nine others: these nine should be the most senior backbencher on the government side; the most senior backbencher on the opposition benches; and seven members of the Chairman's Panel, chosen with broad regard to party balance, reflecting gender balance and based on length of service. Four of the seven would be from the government side (including at least one woman) and three from the opposition parties (also including at least one woman).

In March 2002 the Liaison Committee published a report responding to, and broadly welcoming, the recommendations of the Modernisation Committee.[73] It supported the Modernisation Committee's proposals with regard to nomination and membership of committees. It supported the thrust of the committee's proposals with regard to remuneration, although the Liaison Committee could not see the justification for limiting the additional salary only to those who chaired the 'principal' committees, as the Modernisation Committee had suggested. The recommendations of the Modernisation Committee as regards the drawing up of a statement of core tasks for committees; on the use of rapporteurs; and on swiftly replacing members of committees with poor attendance records were also approved. The Liaison Committee did not, however, approve of the recommended two-term limit for chairs of committees; nor of the increase of the standard size to 15; and nor of the renaming of select committees as scrutiny committees.

The Modernisation Committee's proposals were debated and voted on in the House of Commons on 14 May 2002. Unhappily, not all of the proposals met with support. Most notably, plans for the new Committee of Nomination were rejected (albeit narrowly: the vote was 209 to 195), with the result that membership of select committees will continue to be a matter for the whips. The House supported the bulk of the remainder of the Committee's proposals, however, and voted (by 197 to 175) in support of the proposal to pay the chairs of select committees a higher salary—this matter has now been referred to the Senior Salaries Review Body. The House also agreed that no member would be able to serve as chair of the same committee for more than two Parliaments (or eight years).

There has been one further reform. On 26 April 2002 the Prime Minister announced that he would appear every six months before the Liaison Committee to answer questions concerning the government's policies and performance. This will be the first time any Prime Minister has appeared before and given evidence to a select committee, and represents another modest step in the direction of buttressing Parliament's ability to hold the executive to account.

FUTURE DEVELOPMENTS: A PROPOSAL

What are we to make of this range of reform measures, both proposed and adopted? On the positive side, it is clear that there is considerable political and parliamentary realisation that Parliament could do better. While in the past quarter-century there has been significant improvement in the way Parliament holds the executive to account (most notably, but not only, due to the establishment in 1979 of the system of departmental select committees), there appears to be both room for, and more importantly the political will to find, ways of making further improvements. There has in recent years been a healthy and widespread political conversation about taking parliamentary scrutiny forward, and

[73] Liaison Committee, *Select Committees: Modernisation Proposals*, 2001–2002 HC 692.

this is hugely to be welcomed. On the more cautious side, however, it is equally clear that there remain powerful forces for conservatism (to use one of the Prime Minister's favourite phrases). Nowhere is this more apparent than in the government itself. For all its reformist and modernising zeal, this is a government that has very little appetite to subject itself to greater parliamentary accountability, the Prime Minister's appearances before the Liaison Committee notwithstanding. It can hardly be blamed for this: only the spectacularly naïve would expect it to be different.

The combined efforts of the Liaison Committee, the Hansard Society and (belatedly) of the Modernisation Committee have produced a promising range of reform measures, a good number of which will translate relatively easily and swiftly into rejuvenated parliamentary practice. Even if the question of membership of committees is to remain in the hands of the whips—which is a shame— the profile, importance and political influence of the select committees of the House of Commons has been heightened by the events and reports described in this chapter. The reforms we have outlined are to be taken seriously, and should be welcomed.

That said, however, there is something dispiritingly cautious about even the most progressive of these measures. Welcome as they are, these are modest reforms. Even in the report of the Hansard Society there is little in the way of deep thinking. Revamping committees is all well and good, but it has something about it of the famous image of rearranging the deck-chairs on the *Titanic*. Perhaps the analogy is inapt: Parliament may be unfashionable, but it is not about to sink. Nonetheless, we do have to ask the question of whether reducing the power of the whips, increasing the authority of committee chairs, integrating the plethora of extra-parliamentary scrutiny into a parliamentary framework, and beefing up the resources that committees may employ, is really all that we ought to be doing. Certainly, we can see that these are moves in the right direction, but perhaps they represent nothing more than a holding position. This is not the great leap forward: what we have here is a programme of consolidating measures, designed to keep the parliamentary show afloat while we look elsewhere for a more profound inspiration.

For all their many qualities, the various reports and sets of recommendations considered in this chapter share two major omissions: nowhere is there an analysis of how Parliament's scrutiny functions should be accommodated alongside its legislative functions, and nowhere is there an analysis of how the two Houses of Parliament should operate together. This latter omission is particularly surprising given the recent reforms to the composition of the House of Lords provided for under the terms of the House of Lords Act 1999 and the ongoing debate about the next stage of House of Lords reform. Indeed, all of the reform proposals we have discussed rest on two assumptions: that Parliament will continue to be composed of two Houses, and that Parliament will continue to serve as the national legislature, as well as being a vehicle for executive scrutiny. Both of these assumptions might usefully be challenged. Let us start with the latter issue.

It is largely a myth that Parliament is a legislator. It does not make law. Almost all legislation is made within and by the executive of the day.[74] This is true of primary legislation just as much as it is for secondary legislation. Of course, Parliament is and remains the organ through which the executive must give its legislative proposals the force of law. But the reality is that Parliament plays an instrumental role only—not a sovereign role at all. Parliament retains the theoretical right not to enact into law the measures which the government of the day place before it, but this is a right which is exceptionally rarely exercised. It was exercised only once during the eleven years of Mrs Thatcher's premiership, and has yet to be exercised at all under Mr Blair. Parliament's legislative role is in practice one of scrutiny. Through a variety of means, ranging from the second reading debate on the principles underpinning the measure to the line by line scrutiny of each clause in standing committee, Parliament scrutinises the government's legislative proposals and policies. Sometimes the government will be forced to accept an amendment, and many times the government will itself suggest amendments (sometimes at Parliament's suggestion, often times not), but on the whole all governments— even John Major's governments[75]—manage relatively easily to get the vast bulk of their proposals safely through Parliament.

This being the case, why do we persist with the nineteenth century perception that the purpose of Parliament is to make the law? The legislative purpose of Parliament is not to make the law, but is rather to scrutinise the government's legislative proposals. The critical word here is scrutinise. The whole of this chapter has been concerned with issues of parliamentary scrutiny of government. For over a century constitutional commentators have seen Parliament's legislative function as being distinct from (and more important than) its scrutiny function. The argument here, however, suggests that this may be a false dichotomy. A better view might be that Parliament's legislative function is not different from its scrutiny function, but should rather be conceived as being an aspect of it.

This is a reconceptualisation that sits surprisingly comfortably with recent developments in legislative parliamentary practice. As is well known, the government has started to publish some of its Bills in draft, to enable greater pre-legislative scrutiny than was previously possible. Such scrutiny is carried out by select committees—not by standing committees. If pre-legislative scrutiny can be so carried

---

[74] Occasionally Parliament will pass a Private Member's Bill, that is, a Bill sponsored not by the executive but by a non-ministerial Member of Parliament. However, executive control of the parliamentary timetable is such that it is practically impossible for such a measure to be passed without the government's active support. A number of Private Member's Bills are in fact measures that the government would itself have sponsored but for lack of parliamentary time: in other words, some Private Member's Bill are Private Member's Bills in name only and are really government Bills passed in Private Members' time.

[75] After the 1992 election the Conservatives had a relatively small majority in the House of Commons. The smaller the government's majority, the more difficult it will be for the government to push its legislation through the Commons. But even John Major's government had few problems on this front except in the context of the European Union. The number of eurosceptic Conservative MPs was greater than the government's Commons majority, thereby giving the eurosceptics a considerable degree of leverage: see R Rawlings, 'Legal Politics: The United Kingdom and Ratification of the Treaty on European Union' [1994] *Public Law* 254 (Part 1) and 367 (Part 2).

out, why not also legislative scrutiny? This is not a theoretical question. Select committees, including departmental select committees, are beginning to play a much more visible role in legislative scrutiny. The Anti-terrorism, Crime and Security Act 2001 provides an excellent example. This measure was the subject of no fewer than five reports from select committees during the course of its accelerated passage through Parliament in November-December 2001.[76]

This is what is meant by the suggestion (which now looks a little less radical than it might at first sight have seemed, perhaps) that we should abandon the notion that Parliament is a legislator, and conceive of it instead as a scrutineer. There are three aspects to its scrutiny, two of which have been considered here. The first is administrative scrutiny, the traditional function of the departmental select committee. The second is legislative scrutiny. The third, which we have not had time to consider in any detail in this chapter, is financial scrutiny, an exceptionally important yet still under-researched area the lead role in which is played by the Public Accounts Committee, with considerable and expert support being offered by the National Audit Office.[77]

To what extent is this tripartite scrutiny function capable of being carried out by the House of Commons alone? If the functions of Parliament are to be reconceived along the lines suggested above, does the Westminster Parliament need to continue to operate on a bicameral model? It may be that it does: it may be that Commons scrutiny could be organised (much as it now is) along departmental lines, with House of Lords committees organised along more cross-cutting lines. Thus, there is in the House of Lords a committee on science and technology, a committee on the European Union, and a new committee on the constitution, for example. It may be, however, that the House of Lords has now passed its use-by date and that its abolition would force the Commons to take itself more seriously: without the Lords for back-up, the Commons would have to take more responsibility for itself. No particular position on these issues is advocated here, save that these are ripe questions, and they should be under more serious consideration both within Parliament and beyond than is currently the case. Despite the recent, modest, reforms to the composition of the House of Lords, and despite the Royal Commission on further reform that reported in 2000,[78] there has been very little critical analysis within Parliament of the future of the functions and powers of the House of Lords.[79]

---

[76] The Joint Committee on Human Rights published two reports on the Bill, and the Select Committee on Home Affairs, the Select Committee on Defence, and the House of Lords Select Committee on Delegated Powers each published one report on the Bill: for details and commentary, see A Tomkins, 'Legislating against Terror: The Anti-terrorism, Crime and Security Act 2001' [2002] *Public Law* 205.

[77] A number of changes have recently been proposed and adopted affecting the area of parliamentary financial scrutiny: see Procedure Committee, *Resource Accounting and Budgeting*, 1997–98 HC 438 and Procedure Committee, *Procedure for Debate on the Government's Expenditure Plans*, 1998–99 HC 295. For commentary, see K Hollingsworth and F White, 'Public Finance Reform: the Government Resources and Accounts Act 2000' [2001] *Public Law* 50.

[78] *Royal Commission on the Reform of the House of Lords* (Cm 4534, January 2000).

[79] It has been the House of Commons that has traditionally taken the lead in matters of scrutiny. This is particularly the case in the context of financial scrutiny. There are signs, however, that the House of Lords has very recently started more seriously to consider questions of its role as a scrutiner of government: see for example the *Report by the Group Appointed to Consider how the Working Practices of the*

Of course, the continuation of Westminster as a bicameral Parliament is not the only institutional issue brought into question. The relationship in each House between committee work and the floor, or chamber, is a critical issue. It may be that Parliament needs to become much more a Parliament of committees, along the lines perhaps of the European Parliament, than it has hitherto been prepared to accept. It may be that it should be rather smaller. In a unicameral Commons of 500 members, 125 could be government ministers, leaving 375 non-governmental members to be divided into (say) 25 scrutiny committees of 15 members each. Commons time could be very differently organised. Currently about half its time is spent on legislation. Perhaps a better balance would be to spend 50 per cent of time on departmental and administrative scrutiny, 25 per cent of time on financial scrutiny, and 25 per cent of time on legislative or policy scrutiny? These are just some of the issues that would be under consideration if we were serious about revitalising Parliament.

As things stand, however, there is a sense that Parliament has become confused about what it really is, and what it is really for. At present it legislates only indirectly, yet neither does it focus sufficient energies on scrutinising the government (although as we have seen its record here is not as miserable as many would have us believe). However, it is clear that improvements are needed. Equally clearly they are attainable. There is the political will, and there are the parliamentary means. By sharpening Parliament's 'mission statement', perhaps it will perform its key tasks better. One reason why it sometimes performs badly now is that it is unsure of itself, caught between the two stools of legislator and scrutineer. By reconceiving of it so that the legislative function becomes part of the scrutiny function, perhaps a way can be found for Parliament to perform its scrutiny functions that much more effectively. Otherwise, what is the point in Parliament? If we are not prepared to take Parliament sincerely, why not simply abandon it? We could simply elect our government every four or five years, subject it to the ad hoc, sporadic and peripheral scrutiny of ombudsman, auditor, regulator and law court, and make do.

House of Lords can be Improved, 2001–02 HL 111, published in May 2002. For an excellent extra-parliamentary commentary on the powers (as well as the composition) of the House of Lords, see M Russell, *Reforming the House of Lords: Lessons from Overseas* (Oxford, Oxford University Press, 2000).

4

European Governance and Accountability

CAROL HARLOW*

QUESTIONS ABOUT ACCOUNTABILITY

U NLIKE THE doctrine of ministerial responsibility which, with the notions of legislative supremacy and the rule of law, forms part of our classical constitutional law vocabulary, accountability is not a term of art for lawyers. According to Mulgan, the word was until a few decades ago used 'only rarely and with relatively restricted meaning. [It] now crops up everywhere performing all manner of analytical and rhetorical tasks and carrying most of the burdens of democratic "governance".[1] As the punctuation indicates, 'governance' is another semantic interloper, as prevalent as it is imprecise. Rhodes has identified at least six streams of usage,[2] ranging from the popular and overworked term 'global governance', through technical uses by experts in systems analysis or 'policy network' theory, both gaining credence as methods of studying EU governance,[3] to the 'good governance' advocated by devotees of 'NPM'—a pushy intruder into the vocabulary of public administration.[4]

This new vocabulary all originates in the English-speaking world and translates badly. Wright, for example, describing for a French audience the management revolution within the public service, found difficulty in finding a suitable vocabulary to express himself. He had to make do with the phrase '*état évaluateur*', describing the phenomenon of NPM as 'la mise en place d'un système d'évaluation ex post quantifié et externe'.[5] Mulgan cannot find an exact equivalent in the

---

[1] R Mulgan, '"Accountability": an Ever-Expanding Concept?' (2000) 78 *Public Administration* 555.

[2] R Rhodes, 'The New Governance: Governing Without Government' (1996) 44 *Political Studies* 652.

[3] K-H Ladeur, 'Towards a Legal Theory of Supranationality: The Validity of the Network Concept' (1997) 3 *European Law Journal* 33. See also S Hix, 'The Study of the European Community: The Challenge to Comparative Politics' (1994) 17(1) *W European Politics* 1.

[4] C Hood, 'A Public Management for All Seasons' (1991) 69 *Public Administration* 3; G Drewry, 'The New Public Management', in J Jowell and D Oliver (eds), *The Changing Constitution*, (4th edn, Oxford, Clarendon, 2000).

[5] V Wright, 'Le cas britannique: le démantelement de l'administration traditionnnelle', in L Rouban and J Ziller (eds), Special Issue, *Les Administrations en Europe: D'une Modernisation à l'Autre* (1995) 75 *Actualité Juridique, Droit Administratif* 355, 356.

European literature for the term 'accountability,'[6] while Avril states decisively that Italian, Spanish and French possess no equivalent for the term. All need to borrow the English word if they wish to indicate its portmanteau sense of 'la responsabilité des gouvernants devant le peuple, au double sens de lui rendre compte et de tenir compte de lui.'[7] Avril believes this is no mere chance but indicates a wider lack of correspondence. He suggests, for example, that ministerial responsibility has no exact equivalent in the French political system, explaining the variance by reference to sharply differing attitudes to the functions of Parliament in the two neighbouring societies. Perhaps too, the significant semantic transition from 'responsibility' to 'accountability' reflects a change of practice in the English political system[8] which has not occurred or is incomplete in other European systems. This would help to explain the apparent lack of interest in accountability in institutional studies of the European Union[9] and the dangerous failure to come to grips with the problem of holding the EU institutions accountable at both theoretical and political levels.

In its recent White Paper on Governance the Commission promises to start a process which will respond to 'the disenchantment of many of the Unions' citizens'[10]. It recognises the need to construct a genuine, European civil society, based not only on information but also on active and effective communication with the general public. In the White Paper, information and communication are seen as 'strategic tools of governance', with which to combat the negative image of the European Union in public opinion. The White Paper also lists accountability as one of several values considered essential to good governance,[11] saying:

> Roles in legislative and executive processes need to be clearer. Each of the EU institutions must explain and take responsibility for what it does in Europe. But there is also a need for greater clarity and responsibility from Member States and all those involved in developing and implementing EU policy at whatever level.

This is an unorthodox idea of accountability, focused on the policy-making process. It pays minimal attention to the more traditional obligation of government to render an account of its doings, and there is almost no reference in the White Paper to classical definitions of responsibility and accountability as recognised within the democratic systems of government of the Member States. The White Paper also seriously downplays the role of Parliaments, reducing them to the level of pressure groups and other organisations of civil society, to which the Commission wishes to entrust the task of collecting and collating public opinion—hardly consonant with the view of Lord and Beetham that accountability

---

[6]   Mulgan, above n 1.

[7]   P Avril, 'Les Fabriques des politiques', in N Wahl and J-L Quermonne (eds), *La France presidentielle* (Paris, Presses de la FNSP, 1995), 65.

[8]   G Drewry and D Oliver, *Public Service Reforms: Issues of Accountability and Public Law* (1996).

[9]   But see C Lord, *Democracy in the European Union,* (Sheffield Academic Press, 1998).

[10]   European Commission, *White Paper on European Governance* (COM(2001) 428 final, Brussels, July 2001), 32.

[11]   White Paper, above n 10, at 10.

'seems both to be expected of the EU by the public, and to follow from the logic of its own mission statements.'[12]

This chapter sets out to explore the concept of accountability as it operates in the European Union and to evaluate the existing machinery for accountability. It seeks to consider the respective importance of traditional, political and managerial accountability in the EU system of governance. A political 'accountability gap' is identified, caused in part by the weak European political system, in part by structural factors. The vertical transfer of functions to the institutions of a transnational system of governance which, it is argued, are not designed for purposes of accountability, has weakened national accountability systems. It has led to a horizontal transfer of functions at national level from the sphere of domestic policy in which government is subjected to the controls of a representative parliamentary assembly, to the historically less accountable pillar of foreign affairs. This is one form of 'perversion of democracy'[13] introduced by the phenomenon of transnational governance. The second takes the form of a transfer of powers from the institutions of representative democracy to an autonomous and unrepresentative judiciary, a marked feature of global governance systems dominated, as the European Union is, by the values of the market and institutions of capitalism. Economic actors, as Shapiro observes, feel comfortable with the apparent certainty of law and legal liability.[14] Whether a 'judicial liability system' is truly a form of accountability and whether, if so, it is an adequate substitute for, or is superior to, the democratic accountability which rates highly in national, democratic systems, is a question which needs to be addressed. Arguably, the controls of the European Court of Justice on which the European Union has relied so heavily for accountability, have helped to erode the control systems of national Parliaments and processes of democracy—the second perversion of democracy.

DEMOCRATIC AND POLITICAL ACCOUNTABILITY

In the case of the European Union, the elemental notion of democratic accountability in the sense of a process by which a government has to present itself at regular intervals for election, and can be ousted by the electorate,[15] can be quickly passed over. At EU level, governments are not elected. There is not, nor is it likely that in the immediate future there will be, an elected government at EU level and although it has been suggested[16] that the Commission could be indirectly elected,

---

[12] C Lord and D Beetham, 'Legitimizing the EU' (2001) 39 *Journal of Common Market Studies* 443, 446.

[13] See D Wincott, 'Does the European Union Pervert Democracy? Questions of Democracy in New Constitutionalist Thought on the Future of Europe' (1998) 4 *European Law Journal* 411.

[14] M Shapiro, 'The European Court of Justice', in P Craig and G de Burca (eds), *The Evolution of EU Law*, (Oxford, Oxford University Press, 1999).

[15] S Gustavvson, 'Reconciling Suprastatism and Accountability: a View from Sweden', in C Hoskyns and M Newman (eds), *Democratizing the European Union, Issues for the Twenty-first Century* (Manchester, Manchester University Press, 2000).

[16] S Hix, 'Linking National Politics to Europe', available at www.Network-Europe.net

whether by the European Parliament or by national Parliaments, both outcomes seem unlikely. The best that can be hoped for is the status quo of choice of President and Commissioners by the Member States, subject nowadays to the 'approval' of the directly elected European Parliament (EC Treaty Article 14), a chink opened up by the Amsterdam Treaty and used by the European Parliament rather skilfully to heighten its political powers.[17] This is, however, hardly the same as direct election of a government.

The absence of democratic accountability in this primary sense helps to explain the general apathy and indifference which marks European political space.[18] Without an elected, democratic government, the European Union lacks the polarity of a party system. Party systems appeal to citizens, as they simplify electoral choices. A strong, transnational, party system, capable of rising above national politics, would, Hix believes.[19] help to align European democracy with traditional domestic politics. But an elected European government does not seem to rate high on political agendas, though a *Eurobarometer* question asking whether there should be a European government responsible to a European Parliament, has once received a positive answer. Nor does statistical evidence show the European electorate queuing up to exercise their democratic rights. The current clamour for European constitutions and constitutional rights does not emanate from the people but from an European elite, motivated by a search for self-legitimation.

This is not, however, the end of political accountability. At the heart of the concept in the European tradition, we find some obligation for government to answer or account to a democratically elected parliament or assembly. The idea is perhaps at its strongest in the classical British doctrine of ministerial responsibility to Parliament, which requires individual ministers to give an explanation to the House of Commons both of policies and of the way in which they have been implemented in their department, taking responsibility in this capacity for their public servants.[20] Other systems of government may treat this obligation as less fundamental. As already stated, Avril downplays the force of the doctrine in the French political system, virtually denying to the National Assembly the scrutiny function without which accountability can never be a reality. His thesis is to some extent borne out by, and helps to explain, the limited control exercised by the French Assembly over its government's conduct of European affairs. The problem is undoubtedly heightened by the near immunity of French governments from scrutiny of their foreign affairs policies, constitutionally a presidential function. It has too been said that Italy's long period of fragmented political parties, weak

---

[17] R Corbett, F Jacobs and M Shackleton, *The European Parliament* (4th edn, Harlow, Longman, 2000) 234–38.

[18] P Magnette 'European Governance and Civic Participation: Can the European Union be Politicised?' (Harvard, Jean Monnet Working Paper No 6/01).

[19] See for exposition S Hix, *The Political System of the European Union* (Basingstoke, Macmillan, 1999).

[20] C Turpin, 'Ministerial Responsibility' in J Jowell and D Oliver (eds), *The Changing Constitution* (3rd edn, Oxford, Clarendon, 1994). For a sceptical account, see F Ridley, 'There is no British Constitution: A Dangerous Case of the Emperor's Clothes' (1988) 41 *Parliamentary Affairs* 340. See also Adam Tomkins, Chapter 2 above.

coalition government and consequential reliance on votes of confidence, has led to governments accountable rather to political parties than to Parliament as a whole.[21] The scrutiny function is, in Italy, a late arrival on the scene; parliamentary questions are a new introduction, and there is no equivalent to the European Parliament's subject-based committees or the departmental select committees of the UK Parliament.[22] Such a restricted view of parliamentary accountability would rebound on the Italian Parliament's grasp over the field of European affairs.

Immunity from accountability may on occasion result in opening a gap between government and popular opinion. In the referendum to ratify the treaty of Maastricht, for example, there was near disaster. The fact that Maastricht necessitated an amendment to the French Constitution was exploited by the National Assembly, which seized the opportunity to add on to the amendments an article greatly expanding its own powers in European affairs,[23] described as 'a complete break with the French tradition of the executive being the sole player in international negotiations'.[24] On this occasion, popular accountability through the instrument of a referendum came together with representative democracy to provide a starting point for a new accountability to the democratically elected and representative assembly. Similar developments have taken place in other Member States, including the United Kingdom. Here too ratification of the Maastricht Treaty of European Union was a turning point when the Government of John Major was saved by a whisker from falling.[25] Concern over the delegation of powers to Europe has led more recently to reform of the parliamentary select committee system so as to enhance parliamentary control.[26] Fear that the Treaty of European Union would heighten the accountability gap between people, government and parliaments led also to the celebrated judgment by the German Federal Constitutional Court warning the German government that cession of powers to the European Union would not be tolerated indefinitely and might, if it went too far, be seen as unconstitutional.[27]

[21] A. Manzella, 'La transition institutionelle', in S Cassese (ed), *Portrait de l'Italie actuelle*, (Paris, *La documentation française*, 2001), 60–61.

[22] P Furlong, 'The Italian Parliament and European Integration: Responsibilities, Failures and Successes' (1995) 1 *J Legislative Studies* 35, 44. See, similarly, P Leyland and D Donati, 'Executive Accountability and the Changing Face of Government: UK and Italy Compared' (2001) 7 *European Public Law* 217, 234.

[23] See F Rizutto, 'The French Parliament and the EU: Loosening the Constitutional Straitjacket', Special Issue, *National Parliaments and the European Union* (1995) 1 *J Legislative Studies* 46.

[24] R Ladrech, 'Europeanization of Domestic Politics and Institutions: The Case of France' (1994) 32 *Journal of Common Market Studies* 69.

[25] R Rawlings, 'Legal Politics: The United Kingdom and Ratification of the Treaty on European Union (Part One)' [1994] *PL* 254.

[26] A process starting with Select Committee on Procedure, 4th Report, *European Community Legislation* (HC 622-I 1989/90); Government Response (Cm 1081, 1990); Select Committee on European Legislation, 27th Report, *The Scrutiny of European Business* (HC 51–xxvii, 1995/6). See also Reports of the Select Committee on European Legislation at www.parliament.uk/commons/selcom/enrolhome.htm.

[27] *Bundesverfassungsgericht*, 2nd Chamber (Senat) Cases BvR 2134/92 and 2 BvR 2159/92 (12 October 1993) BVerfGE 89, 155; in English, *Brunner v European Union Treaty* [1994] 1 CMLR 57. For comment see P Kirchhof, 'The Balance of Powers Between National and European Constitutions' (1999) 5 *European Law Journal* 225.

'Accountability' in the sense of political responsibility may entail no more than the giving of an 'account' in the sense of explanation; governments, indeed, would by and large prefer to believe that this was the extent of their duty. The classical doctrine of responsibility, as adopted in Oliver's definition of accountability, however, entails more than this: the actor is required not only to give an account or explanation of the disputed actions, but also, where appropriate, to 'suffer the consequences, take the blame or undertake to put matters right if it should appear that errors have been made'.[28] Accountability is, in other words, amendatory. In blatant defiance of tradition, the argument has been seriously advanced to a Select Committee of the British House of Commons that full ministerial responsibility, carrying the sanction of censure and resignation, should arise only where the *personal involvement* of a minister could be shown. Accountability, for these purposes carefully distinguished from responsibility, would then indicate no more than a ministerial obligation to 'give an account' of the department's performance to Parliament and the public. This altogether weaker meaning was not surprisingly rejected out-of-hand by the Committee.[29] New opportunities for weakening the classical concept of responsibility have also been created through the hiving-off of central government functions to autonomous or semi-autonomous agencies. Again, this is a process which has gone much further in some Member States than others, though all have been affected. In the United Kingdom, the development is closely related to the phenomenon of 'New Public Management', discussed further below. In Sweden, and to a lesser extent in other Scandinavian countries, administration has always been to a large extent conducted by autonomous administrative agencies, though apparently without a lessening of parliamentary accountability.[30] Agencies of this type, with extensive regulatory or administrative powers, have not yet taken root in the European Union, and the existing agencies, which exist largely to collect and collate information, have not as yet, with one exception discussed below, created serious accountability problems.

The European Parliament takes accountability seriously. It likes to present itself as the only democratic European institution, and sees success in holding 'the government' to account as a vital component of the power struggle in which it is engaged against Council and Commission. It has used the various powers which it has wrested rather painfully from institutions and Member States during the process of Treaty amendment skilfully and to good effect.[31] In addition to the powers it has acquired from the Council with regard to Commission appointments, progress has been made on legislative and budgetary fronts. To take the lat-

---

[28]   D Oliver, *Government in the United Kingdom: The Search for Accountability, Effectiveness and Citizenship* (Buckingham, Open University Press, 1991) 22.

[29]   A Tomkins, *The Constitution After Scott* (Oxford, Oxford University Press, 1998), 59–63. See also Public Service Committee, *Ministerial Accountability and Responsibility* (HC 813, 1995/6), para 170.

[30]   J Ziller, 'European Models of Government: Towards a Patchwork with Missing Pieces" (2001) 54 *Parliamentary Affairs* 102. See also Special Issue, 'Delegation and Accountability in European Integration, The Nordic Parliamentary Democracies and the EU' (2000) 6 *J Legislative Studies* 33.

[31]   Many of the most important are in inter-institutional agreements, such as the celebrated *modus vivendi* ([1996] OJ C/102) by which the European Parliament started to gain control of the Comitology (below).

ter first, an important stage in the struggle for power over Community finance was reached in the early 1970s, resulting from Budgetary Treaties with the Council in 1970 and 1975. In 1975, the European Parliament gained the significant power to grant formal discharge of the budget, supported by the power of the Court of Auditors (ECA) to make a declaration of assurance on which discharge is based. Three European Parliament committees deal with financial matters: an active and powerful policy-making Committee on Economic and Monetary Affairs; a Committee on Budgets to deal with the allocation of the Community budget, to which the Commission makes regular interim reports; and the Committee on Budgetary Control, which prepares the way for the annual discharge of the Community accounts, to which the ECA makes its annual reports.[32] After further years of struggle, the European Parliament has finally gained an added concession of some importance. EC Treaty Article 270 now prohibits the Commission from acting outside the parameters of the budget, giving an assurance that the *overall budget* will not be exceeded without recourse to the European Parliament. The European Parliament has also secured a measure of budgetary control and a power of audit over the affairs of agencies. Budgetary powers allow the European Parliament to extend its authority into areas from which it has been deliberately excluded by the Council, notably the Common Foreign and Security Policy (the 'Second Pillar'), which must ultimately involve substantial expenditure. It has even been predicted that the combination of audit power with limited power over the appointment process will in time be used to exact political responsibility from the powerful and largely autonomous European Central Bank and perhaps ultimately the wider European banking system, designed though it is to be autonomous and largely free from political accountability.[33]

Whether the legislative process truly forms part of an accountability system is a moot point; the amendatory element central to the notion of accountability at least points to retrospectivity.[34] However this may be, from the standpoint of Parliaments in Europe, legislative accountability is problematic. True, there has been steady progress from the so-called 'old-style procedures', under which the Council can either legislate alone, or after a non-binding consultation of the European Parliament. The most modern variant of the 'co-decision procedure' (EC Treaty Article 251, as amended at Amsterdam) effectively gives the European Parliament a power of final veto, if agreement cannot be reached during the conciliation procedure between Council and European Parliament. The problem is, however, that this procedure is easily by-passed. There is (as yet) no written constitution and the Treaties contain no formal division of powers. Since Maastricht, the elusive subsidiarity principle is supposed to 'guide the action of the Union's institutions', exhorting them 'to leave as much scope for national decision as possible'[35] Effectively, however, the

---

[32] For further details, see Corbett *et al*, above n17, Table 17, at 116.
[33] W Buiter, 'Alice in Euroland' (1999) 37 *Journal of Common Market Studies* 181.
[34] The point is discussed more fully in C Harlow, 'Accountability, New Public Management, and the Problem of the Child Support Agency' (1999) 26 *JLS* 150.
[35] EC Treaty Protocol 30 on the application of the principles of subsidiarity and proportionality.

Council possesses an override; competence can be transferred to EU level as and when the Council, representing national governments, sees a need. National parliaments do not necessarily have to be consulted. New Treaty articles can at present revert to 'old-style procedures', undercutting the legislative accountability of Council to European Parliament. When, for example, the 'Third Pillar' justice and home affairs powers, were transferred to the Community at Amsterdam, the consultation procedure was retained for a transitional, five-year period (EC Treaty Article 67).

Again, the Council may resort to outline legislation, relying on the Commission's implementation powers (EC Treaty Article 211) together with their own supervisory powers under the Comitology Decision, which allows regulations to be made by the Commission subject only to the advisory opinions of a network of committees appointed by, and responsible to, the Commission.[36] Comitology has been the subject of sustained criticism from academics, on the ground of its impenetrability [37] and is greatly disliked also by the European Parliament on the ground that it usurps its place in the legislative process. In contrast to the present EU agencies, which in general possess no legislative powers, Comitology virtually escapes parliamentary control.[38] Currently the Commission is leaning away from Comitology and, largely for reasons of expertise, towards agencies with clearly delimited powers.[39] This is not, however, a recipe for accountability, as the history of agencies in national systems, where the choice of an agency rests often on the need—or desire—for autonomy and reduced accountability, clearly shows. Moreover, the creation of agencies at EU level as the centre of a 'policy network' of national agencies and other policy actors is likely seriously to diminish the input of national Parliaments at both policy-making and scrutiny stages.

A wide variety of informal methods of collaboration are at the disposal of Member States when they wish to avoid the legal and institutional controls of the EU Treaties. Use of the Third Pillar is indicative. Over the years, the co-operation of Member States in the fields of migration policy led to unaccountable, executive policy-making. The format was one of informal, intergovernmental co-operation, conducted through ad hoc groups, working groups and committees designed to exclude the Community institutions under the pretext of lack of formal EC competence in the field. Not only did this avoid a transfer of scrutiny powers to the

---

[36] Council Decision 99/468 of 28 June 1999 laying down procedures for the exercise of implementing powers conferred on the Commission, JO L184/23.

[37] See essays in M Andenas and A Turk (eds), *Delegated Legislation and the Role of Committees in the EC*, (Dordrecht, Kluwer Law International, 2000); C Joerges and E Vos (eds), *EU Committees: Social Regulation, Law and Politics* (Oxford, Hart Publishing, 1999); RH Pedler and GF Scheafer (eds), *Shaping European Law and Policy. The Role of Committees and Comitology in the Political Process* (Maastricht, European Institute of Public Administration, 1996).

[38] On the history of the relationship, see K St C Bradley, 'The European Parliament and Comitology: On the Road to Nowhere?' (1997) 3 *European Law Journal* 230.

[39] European Commission, *White Paper on European Governance* (COM(2001) 428 final, Brussels, July 2001), 234. See generally J Vervaele, 'Shared Governance and Enforcement of European Law: From Comitology to a Multi-level Agency Structure' in C Joerges and E Vos (eds), above n 3. For an example of current thinking on agencies, see Regulation 187/02 of the European Parliament and Council laying down the general principles and requirements of food law, establishing the European Food Safety Authority and laying down procedures in matters of food safety.

European Parliament but it had a seriously detrimental effect on control by national Parliaments.[40] Thus the important Dublin Convention on asylum applications,[41] a document with dramatic effect on the rights of third country nationals, was a product merely of the 'Schengen group' of national representatives, while the Schengen agreement on open borders was drafted by working groups and input into the text of the rules from representative assemblies or civil society organisations was almost entirely lacking. Yet these texts were later to form the basis of EU migration policy.[42] Notably, Third Pillar matters have never been properly brought within the formal EU structure. The justice and home affairs agenda has a tendency to grow invisibly, spawning agencies such as Europol, over which there is little control from any Parliament in the European Union, and programmes such as the Corpus Juris programme for collaboration and harmonisation of the criminal justice process throughout the European Union, conducted in great secrecy by Council working groups with the help of academics.[43] This typifies the way in which informal co-operation can result in erosion of parliamentary democracy: the powers of national parliaments are undercut by transfer of competence to European but not EC level yet no commensurate political accountability to the European Parliament is substituted.[44] National Parliaments have not been adequately incorporated into the EU structure, hence necessary documentation is often not available to them as occurred when the United Kingdom House of Commons debated the European arrest warrant.

For the European Parliament, the high-point of accountability so far was reached with the resignation of the Santer Commission in 1999, following an unsuccessful vote of censure tabled against the College of Commissioners in the European Parliament.[45] The resignation followed an investigation carried out on behalf of the European Parliament into allegations of fraud and mismanagement by the Commission. The Commission's slow and inadequate response to the allegations led the European Parliament to freeze 10 per cent of the Commissioners' salaries. Following further allegations, the European Parliament adopted a resolution calling for a Committee of Independent Experts to be established, to report jointly to Commission and Parliament. Publication of their Interim Report on

[40] E Guild, 'The Constitutional Consequences of Lawmaking in the Third Pillar of the European Union' in P Craig and C Harlow (eds), *Lawmaking in the European Union*, (London, Kluwer Law International, 1998).

[41] The Dublin Convention determining the state responsible for examining applications for asylum lodged in one of the Member States of the European Communities (15 June 1990).

[42] E Guild and C Harlow (eds), *Implementing Amsterdam* (Oxford, Hart Publishing, 2000).

[43] M Delmas Marty (ed), *Corpus Juris Introducing Penal Provisions for the Purpose of the Financial Interests of the European Union* (Paris, Economica, 1997); European Commission, Green Paper on criminal-law protection of the financial interests of the Community and the establishment of a European Prosecutor (Brussels, 11.12.2001, COM (2001) 715 final). For comment see J Spencer, 'The Corpus Juris Project and the Fight Against Budgetary Fraud' (1999) 1 *Cambridge Yearbook of European Legal Studies* 77; W van Gerven, 'Constitutional Conditions for a Public Prosecutor's Office at the European Level', in G de Kerchove and A Weyenbergh, V*ers un éspace judiciare pénal européen (*Paris, Editions ULB, 2000).

[44] J Lodge, 'The European Parliament', in S Andersen and K Eliassen, *The European Union: How Democratic Is It?*, (London, Sage Publications, 1996).

[45] A Tomkins, 'Responsibility and Resignation in the European Commission' (1999) 62 *MLR* 744.

15 March 1999 occasioned the unprecedented resignation not merely of individual Commissioners at the behest of President Santer but of the Commission as a whole, nominally accepting a principle of collective responsibility.

The Experts' analysis is couched primarily in terms of the classical terminology and doctrine of political responsibility. In their terse and celebrated conclusion, they speak of the 'growing reluctance among the members of the hierarchy to acknowledge their responsibility' and suggest that it is 'becoming difficult to find anyone who has even the slightest sense of responsibility'.[46] Towards the end of the conclusions, however, the Experts make an important statement of principle:[47]

> The principles of openness, transparency and accountability… are at the heart of democracy and are the very instruments allowing it to function properly. Openness and transparency imply that the decision-making process, at all levels, is as accessible and accountable as possible to the general public. It means that the reasons for decisions taken are known and that those taking decisions assume responsibility for them and are ready to accept the personal consequences when such decisions are subsequently shown to be wrong.

The incoming President, Romano Prodi, picked this up in a speech, where he said:[48]

> I am firmly convinced that increasing the *efficiency and accountability* of the Commission in future largely depends on greatly reducing the grey areas which currently tend to blur demarcation lines of autonomy and responsibility between those performing more political tasks and those more involved with administration.

Prodi acknowledged the concern of the public with good government and promised reform. 'Once we have increased the Commission team's capacity to provide political direction, we will be able to set about increasing the *transparency, efficiency and accountability* of their departments, as required by the Treaty of Amsterdam and demanded by European public opinion'. In this way, the two reports of the independent experts[49] had brought accountability into the vocabulary and on to the political agenda of the European Union. Essentially, this was taken to mean the responsibility, collective and individual, of the College of Commissioners to the European Parliament. There is little reference to national Parliaments in the Experts' Reports yet to close the yawning accountability gap, a much greater input is required from national Parliaments.

At present, the degree of control exercised over EU matters by national parliaments depends essentially on two variables: the balance of power inside the national system between Parliament and government; and the degree of parlia-

---

[46] Committee of Independent Experts, *First Report on Allegations Regarding Fraud, Mismanagement and Nepotism in the European Commission* (Brussels, 15 March 1999), para 9.4.25 (Interim Report).

[47] Interim Report, above n 46, para 9.3.3.

[48] Commisssioner Prodi's speech to the European Parliament available at http:// europa.eu.int/ comm/commissioners/prodi/speeches/130499 en.htm (emphasis added).

[49] Committee of Independent Experts, *Second Report on the Reform of the Commission, Analysis of Current Practice and Proposals for Tackling Mismanagement, Irregularities and Fraud* (10 September 1999).

mentary control over the conduct of foreign affairs, an aspect of the first, larger
question. Different Parliaments conceive their roles very differently and prioritise
different aspects of their functions, with the result that their contribution to
accountability, and the seriousness with which they undertake their scrutiny function, may vary greatly. Some Parliaments have reacted more forcefully than others
to the challenge of law-making by the Community. The most stringent control is
through mandate, but this is exceptional; the Danish Folketing is the only successful example of this model. The Folketing has assumed the power to mandate ministers in policy-making and, on accession to the Community, this rule was simply
extended.[50] No other national Parliament has taken political accountability to
such limits, and it is, indeed, doubtful if the European Union could function if
mandate were to be tried more widely.

Attempts to tie national Parliaments into the EU system are presently at a stale-
mate. Protocol 8 on the Role of National Parliaments in the European Union
added to the EC Treaty at Amsterdam tries to address the problem. It requires the
Commission to forward all consultation and Green and White Papers 'promptly'
to national parliaments, while Commission proposals for legislation 'shall be
made available in good time'. Access to documentation, essential for the work of
legislative scrutiny, has been a perennial cause for complaint, and is only just
beginning—if it is beginning—to be resolved. Protocol 8 again speaks to the desire
of the institutions to 'encourage greater involvement of national parliaments in
the activities of the European Union and to enhance their ability to express their
views on matters which may be of particular interest to them'. The inter-parlia-
mentary Conference of European Affairs Committees (COSAC) is now able to
scrutinise proposals forwarded to it by Member State governments, and is empowered make *joint* contributions to the legislative process, more specifically in the
area of freedom, security and justice or concerning the rights and freedoms of
individuals. It may in addition address to the institutions 'any contribution which
it deems appropriate on the legislative activities of the Union, notably in relation
to the application of the principle of subsidiarity, the area of freedom, security and
justice as well as questions regarding fundamental rights'. It is, however, questionable whether this is a useful power or, indeed, whether a committee of this type
can claim adequately to represent 15 and more parliaments and their several thou-
sand representatives of diverse political parties and groupings. The institutions,
more especially the European Parliament, which has a direct interest in the outcome, are undoubtedly keen to find a place for national Parliaments in the EU policy-making process but the dilemma which goes to the heart of the relationship is
spelled out in Protocol 8, which was, after all, drafted for and signed by Member
State governments. The Preamble to the Protocol demonstrates fear on the part of
the European Council, representing national *governments*, of being seen to trespass on sensitive *parliamentary* terrain. In a significant caveat, the High Contracting Parties recall 'that scrutiny by individual national parliaments of their own

---

[50] D Arter, 'The Folketing and Denmark's "European Policy": The Case of an "Authorising Assembly"' in Special Issue, *Parliaments in Western Europe* (1990) 13 *W European Politics* 110.

government in relation to the activities is a matter for the particular constitutional organisation and practice of each Member State', while the Protocol concludes with the timorous assertion that 'contributions made by COSAC shall in no way bind national parliaments or prejudge their position'.

Martin Westlake, who describes national Parliaments as 'partners and rivals', notes their tendency to 'talk past one another'.[51] Yet for the accountability gap to be closed, it is essential for *national Parliaments* to take matters into their own hands; they need to ensure that relationships *between* national Parliaments are strong and in good repair. By collaborating with *each other*, they could achieve greater success in securing accountability for EU affairs. Only if national Parliaments can use influence enhanced by collaboration at the EU level to secure the stricter observance of the subsidiarity principle can they play their full part in EU governance. Robin Cook, when Foreign Secretary, called for a forum in which national Parliaments could meet to discuss problems of subsidiarity.[52] But the risk national Parliaments face is that such a forum would operate to provoke turf wars between the three tiers of European Parliaments, the outcome being a huge and unwieldy 'forum', enlarged to accommodate regional Parliaments. This could minimise Parliamentary input into policy and decision-making, while seeming to enhance it. It would also undermine the scrutiny role of Parliaments. Yet if national Parliaments are to retain their central place in European democracy, it is essential that they should find innovative ways to collaborate with each other. Even without the help and resources of the European Parliament, a programme of close co-operation between European Parliaments is both possible and urgently needed.

AUDIT AND ACCOUNTABILITY

Christopher Hood describes financial control as 'deeply embedded in the European tradition of constitutional (limited) government and formal public accountability in financial affairs'.[53] Financial accountability is certainly seen as an essential ingredient of 'good governance' throughout the Member States; it may, indeed, be the common element in definitions of the elusive concept. Financial probity figures high too on the list of issues important to the European public.[54] The fall of the Santer Commission was precipitated by charges of fraud and fiscal irregularity. The collegial resignation after the Interim Report of the Committee of

---

[51] M Westlake, 'The European Parliament, The National Parliaments and the 1996 Intergovernmental Conference' (1995) *Political Quarterly* 59, 70.

[52] *The New Statesman*, 14 August 1998.

[53] C Hood, 'The Hidden Public Sector: the "Quangocratization" of the world', in F-X Kaufmann, G Majone and V Ostrom (eds) *Guidance, Control and Evaluation in the Public Sector*, (Berlin, de Gruyter, 1986).

[54] The Annual Reports of the ECA and of the British NAO are regularly reported in the quality press. See S Grey, *Tackling Fraud and Mismanagement in the European Union* (London, Centre for European Reform, 2000).

Independent Experts not only attracted an unusually high level of media attention but also focused public attention on the work of the European Parliament, raising its profile in a Eurostat survey by a figure of 8 per cent. This suggests that focus on its budgetary functions would provide the European Parliament with an easy path to greater legitimacy.

In a sense, the Committee of Independent Experts usurped the place of the European Court of Auditors, in whose annual reports the Santer affair first surfaced. For a number of reasons, the ECA has found difficulty in establishing a firm role for itself in the EU political space.[55] The ECA itself attributes its difficulties to the absence of a powerful Ministry equivalent to the French Ministry of Finance or British Treasury, which has meant that management and audit were never basically 'pushing in the same direction'.[56] Lack of interest and firm support on the part of the Council, and occasional outright hostility from the Commission, are other important factors. Before the independent experts reported, internal audit of the Community finances was overseen by DG XX of the Commission—equivalent in national terms to siting the Treasury in a major spending ministry. The Commission ethos is not geared towards audit or accountability; it views itself as policy-maker and engine of the European Union, whose function it is to push the Member States down the path of European integration.[57] Financial responsibility is made harder by old-fashioned systems of personnel management, a problem only just beginning to be addressed by reforms set in place by Vice-President Neil Kinnock as a response to the strictures of the Independent Experts.[58] The most important reforms to result from the Reports of the Committee of Independent Experts were undoubtedly of the Commission's internal audit system, moved to a unit directly responsible to the President, and of the *Office européen de lutte anti-fraude* (OLAF), responsible for the investigation of frauds against the Community budget, which was given greater autonomy and put under the supervisory jurisdiction of a new and active committee which reports to the European Parliament.[59]

These were rather basic, though necessary, reforms. A much more radical programme of improvements is necessary to generate public confidence in the European Union fiscal system and how to achieve this is more problematic. The financial structures of the EU are notably complex, partly due to the vast number of cross-border financial transactions, partly to the EU administrative system. The European Commission is not the equivalent of a national or federal public service. It does not

[55] B Laffan, 'Becoming a "Living Institution": The Evolution of the European Court of Auditors' (1999) 37 *Journal of Common Market Studies* 251.

[56] Report in response to the conclusions of the European Council of 18 June 1983, [1983] OJ C287/1. See F White and K Hollingsworth, *Audit, Accountability and Government*, (Oxford, Clarendon, 1999), 194–96.

[57] B Laffan, 'From Policy Entrepreneur to Policy Manager: the Challenge Facing the EC' (1997) 4 *Journal of European Public Policy* 422.

[58] European Commission, *Reforming the Commission*, (COM 200 (2000)); European Commission, *New Staff Policy* (IP/01/283, Brussels, 28 February, 2000); followed by a further series of internal Commission working papers (SEM).

[59] See *First Report of the Supervisory Committee of the Anti-fraud Office* (OLAF), [2001]OJ C365 (20.12.2001).

itself engage in service delivery. The programmes which it operates, notably the two largest, the common agricultural and structural funding programmes, are administered on its behalf by national and sub-national administrations, or national agencies in the Member States. In addition, the Commission enters into contracts with private companies, and operates through the voluntary sector, whose books may not be subject to public audit. These complex programmes involve in the region of 18 billion individual financial transactions annually, of which it seems that *more than one in seven* may be procedurally irregular.[60] As the investigations of the Committee of Independent Experts proved beyond a shadow of doubt, the Commission has been a lax and inefficient manager. It has not devised techniques for the effective co-ordination of networks nor does its reform programme so far prove that it is capable of so doing.[61] The ethos of the Commission is not managerial. It has not been wholly receptive to public management techniques as increasingly adopted in national administration,[62] though they are beginning to find a place in the Kinnock programme of reform. Not only have its own audit systems proved inadequate but the Commission has also failed signally to set in place in respect of its major progammes of structural funding, grants and subsidies, the 'audit trails' which are the *sine qua non* of modern audit systems.[63] Long before they came up against the magisterial reproofs of the Committee of Independent Experts, the Commission's arrangements for scrutiny of EU finances were severely criticised by the European Court of Auditors in its Annual Reports. Disparities in national audit systems add to the problems of auditing a set of already exceptionally complex transactions. In its Annual Report for 1998, the ECA noted that 'the separate accounts kept by the Member States contained significant errors,'[64] while a House of Lords inquiry has questioned 'how far national audit institutions are actually able to police the expenditure of Community funds once the money has been paid over to national governments'.[65] There are at present few incentives for national authorities to deal with fraud within their boundaries, even if they have the capacity to do so, and the Commission has been slow in trying to provide them. Techniques of audit also differ widely within the Member States, and there are at least four variants of audit body.[66] The ECA can only operate through a system of 'spot sampling' according to which about 600 of 360,000 transactions are on average examined—in the view of accountancy experts, too small a base from which to extrapolate.[67] The external

---

[60] *Annual Report of the ECA 1998*, paras 2.41–2.52.

[61] L Metcalfe, 'The European Commission as a Network Organization' (1996) *Publius: The Journal of Federalism* 43; 'Reforming the Commission: Will Organizational Efficiency Produce Effective Governance?' (2000) 38 *Journal of Common Market Studies* 817; and 'Reforming the European Governance: Old Problems or New Principles?' (2001) 67 *International Review of Administrative Sciences* 415.

[62] C Pollitt *et al*, *Performance or Compliance? Performance Audit and Public Management in Five Countries* (Oxford, Oxford University Press, 1999); D Farnham *et al*, *New Public Managers in Europe* (Basingstoke, Macmillan, 1996).

[63] M Power, *The Audit Society: Rituals of Verification*, (Oxford University Press, 1999).

[64] Annual Report, above n 60, para 1.11.

[65] House of Lords Select Committee on the European Communities, *Court of Auditors* (HL 102 (1986–7)), 11, para 22 (Mr Jo Cary).

[66] National Audit Office, *State Audit in the European Union* (London, NAO, 1996), as updated.

[67] Power, above n 63, at 89. The comment is based on interviews with auditors.

audit system operated by the ECA is thus far from foolproof, even with help from national audit offices, on whose assistance it is entitled to draw. To iron out the differences and weld the disparate systems into a new, and more professional, audit structure for the European Union will involve hard choices, made harder, as indicated, by the absence of an independent Treasury, and a Commission ethos neither geared to audit nor to managerialism.

Antipathy to public management is reflected too in suspicion of 'value-for-money' auditing, a technique which allows auditors, by recourse to comparators of performance, to identify practical ways in which managers may better target their efforts, but also allows them gradually to extend their remit deep into policy-making, an aspect of audit which has made it most attractive to public managers.[68] The ECA has for some time been anxious to extend its activities into VFM auditing, building on the word 'sound' in EC Treaty Article 188(c). The ECA hopes that the introduction of VFM audit could stiffen Commission accountability in financial matters; it would also favour the extension of accountability for the execution of policy through the introduction of NPM techniques. The Commission, on the other hand, is jealous of its position as the policy motor of the Community, and keen to preserve the discretionary monopoly to which it has became accustomed. Since VFM audit is now in place in a majority of Member State public audit systems, it can only be a matter of time before it permeates Commission practice. In practice, the Commission would certainly find VFM helpful in the construction of management networks designed to render the various operators accountable for implementation of EU policy; to put this differently, VFM would seem to be an essential ingredient of a system of managerial control of EU administration networks.

Accountability through audit will, however, never be easy in the European Union. Driven on by the European Parliament and ECA, and latterly by the OLAF supervisory committee, the Commission has at last recognised the necessity of introducing a minimum degree of uniformity into the management of EU finances. It is, for example, currently negotiating protocols on management and audit with Member States participating in the administration of structural funds. Enlargement is, however, likely to make everything more difficult. Boundaries will be widened, audit chains lengthened, new, perhaps less effective, systems and techniques of audit introduced. In case of fraud, there will be the necessity of intervention from a greater number of police forces and new systems of criminal justice. To date, it should be remembered, there has never been a successful prosecution of an EU official for fraud, with the Commission normally claiming diplomatic immunity if charges are threatened.[69] Whether the difficulties can be overcome through the new arrangements for co-ordinated criminal justice policies pushed forward at Laeken[70] is very questionable.

---

[68]   M Power, *The Audit Explosion* (London, Demos, 1994).

[69]   Grey, above n 4, at, 4.

[70]   Presidency's conclusions on justice and home affairs, Laeken, 17 December, 2001. See also proceedings of Council, Justice, Home Affairs and Civil Protection, Brussels, 16 November 2001, OR 13758/01.

Some commentators see the way forward through alignment of audit methodologies to produce 'the beginnings of a "Community" model of financial control and audit.'[71] But an audit system must be chosen for effectiveness and efficiency, and not because it combines elements of all or most of the audit models in use through the Community. Such a hybrid would probably fail as an administrative transplant, and might actually undercut the efficiency of the most effective national systems, in which case it would be heavily resisted by those Member States with most to lose. The House of Lords has asked in contrast only for *minimum standards*, accepting that 'differences between systems of control are justified so long as each system is effective.'[72] This is a more sensible approach, though it begs the crucial question: are they or can they be made so?

ACCOUNTABILITY THROUGH LAW

The relationship between courts and government is not usually formulated in terms of accountability. Lawyers, including EU lawyers, prefer the classical vocabulary of rule of law, guaranteed, with liberty, democracy and respect for fundamental rights and freedoms, as fundamental values by the Treaties. In states with strong systems of public law, however, law is not only the framework within which government is held accountable but stands also at the centre of the constitutional system of accountability. Equal, or even greater, trust is placed in courts than Parliaments. Oliver links the two ideas of rule of law and accountability when she describes accountability as creating:[73]

> a framework for the exercise of state power in a liberal-democratic system, within which public bodies are forced to seek to promote the public interest and compelled to justify their actions in those terms or in other constitutionally acceptable terms (justice, humanity, equity); to modify policies if they should turn out to have been ill conceived; and to make amends if mistakes and errors of judgement have been made.

This is the role which lawyers traditionally allocate to the rule of law.

Sometime in the nineteenth century, the term 'control' lost its close link to financial audit and entered the standard vocabulary of administrative law: jurisdictional control or judicial review of administrative action began to be recognised as a way to hold government answerable to courts. During the twentieth century, judicial review has tended to expand its empire, becoming the standard means of challenge to administrative action. The chief medium by which judicial review protects private interests and exercises control over administrative decision-making is through a cluster of procedural rights, recognised in slightly variant forms in all major European legal systems.[74] Reasoned decisions are also a

---

[71]   White and Hollingsworth, above n 56 at 194–96.

[72]   House of Lords, Select Committee on the European Communities, *The ECA: the case for reform* (HL 63, 2000/1) Conclusions, para 13.

[73]   D Oliver, *Government in the United Kingdom: The Search for Accountability, Effectiveness and Citizenship*, n 28 above.

[74]   See for the EU, H-P Nehl, *Principles of Administrative Law*, (Oxford, Hart Publishing, 1998).

basis for administrative accountability; indeed, for Shapiro, they provide the basis for all judicial review of administrative discretion and arguably, of all judicial review.[75] EC Treaty Article 253 (ex 190) contains an obligation for the institutions to 'state the reasons on which [their decisions] are based' and the European Court of Justice has not been slow to recognise its potential; its standard formula justifying the reasoning of decisions stresses the control function of judicial review. It also contains a reference to an embryonic principle of transparency, a second area in which courts can act strongly to enhance accountability; recently, the Court of First Instance has begun to take transparency very seriously.[76]

From a procedural point of departure, many supreme courts have been able to add to their portfolio the function of 'higher law judicial review'.[77] When they rule in this way on the validity of legislation, constitutional courts undoubtedly hold government to account. Boundary demarcation based on the Treaties and on a body of constitutional principle developed by the Court has emerged as a primary function of the European Court of Justice,[78] allegedly built into its competence by the Treaty obligation 'to ensure that, in the interpretation and application of this Treaty, the law is observed' (EC Treaty Article 220). The Court possesses (or has assumed, according to one's viewpoint) the last word in interpreting the Treaties. It polices the competences of the European Union, decides on the validity of European Union legislation and in so doing preserves the 'institutional balance' of the Treaties, maintaining the balance of power between the EU institutions.

A further body of constitutional jurisprudence concerning the relations between the EU legal order and that of the Member States has been developed from the seminal case of *van Gend en Loos*.[79] Many EU lawyers see this jurisprudence as the culmination of the integration process; European democracy may be in deficit, but the European legal order emphatically is not (the antithesis is deliberate and habitual). The jurisprudence has by and large been both activist and integrationist in character, the objective being to create an effective legal system by which EU law can be enforced. It is primarily the Member States, rather than the EU institutions, which are being held accountable, a process requiring the acquiescence and, occasionally, active co-operation of national courts. Essentially, co-operation is based on a legal fiction that national courts function in a dual

[75] M Shapiro, 'The Giving Reasons Requirement' (1992) *University of Chicago Legal Forum* 179, 180.
[76] D Curtin, 'Citizens' Fundamental Right of Access to EU Information: An Evolving Digital Passepartout?' (2000) 37 *CML Rev* 7. See also Case T-174/95 *Svenska Journalistforbundet v Council* [1998] ECR II-2289; Case T-14/98 *Hautala v Council* [1999] ECR II-2489 and, on appeal, 6 December 2001 (Opinion of A-G Leger, 10 July 2001); Case T-111/00 *British American Tobacco International (Investments) Ltd v Commission*, 10 October 2001; Case T-188/98 and T-211/00 *Aldo Kuijer v Council* (6 April 2000 and 7 February 2002).
[77] Defined by M Shapiro, 'The European Court of Justice', above n 14 at 321 as 'the invalidation of laws enacted by the normal or regular legislative process, because they are in conflict with some higher law, typically a constitution or treaty'.
[78] For the start of this practice, see A Lorenz, 'General Principles of Law: Their Elaboration in the Court of Justice of the European Communities' (1964) *American Journal of Comparative Law* 12; A Akehurst, 'The Application of General Principles of Law by the Court of Justice of the European Communities' (1981) 52 *British Yearbook of International Law* 29.
[79] Case 26/62 *Van Gend en Loos v Nederlandse Administratie der Belastingen* [1963] ECR 1.

capacity as courts of the national legal systems but also as EU courts.[80] The machinery which links the two tiers of the EU legal order is the preliminary reference procedure put in place by the Treaties (EC Treaty Article 234), whereby national courts refer points of EU law which arise in cases before them to the ECJ for a ruling. This procedure has, until recently, been used very freely and generally speaking in an integrationist fashion,[81] again with the objective of creating an effective legal system by which EU law can be enforced.

For Mulgan, the law is not in itself an accountability mechanism, nor is compliance with the law an act of accountability; the legal accountability mechanism is confined to that part of the law which lays down enforcement procedures.[82] Here Mulgan seems to be separating law's standard-setting or declaratory function, prioritised by constitutional courts and EU lawyers, from the machinery by which administration is brought to account and law is enforced. This tallies with the views of Lord, who sees legal accountability as one of the four elements which go to make up democracy's 'irreducible core'. For Lord, democratic accountability requires that citizens must be able to access a court 'with a complaint that power-holders are seeking to evade or distort the rules by which they are themselves brought to account'.[83]

The ECJ is conscious of the importance of enforcement and, again with effectiveness in mind, has gone some way to harmonise the system of legal remedies available from courts in the European Union.[84] Two celebrated cases are particularly significant in this respect. In *Factortame*,[85] where interim relief pending a ruling from the ECJ on legality was claimed from English courts, the ECJ answered questions posed in an Article 234 reference by saying that:

> [T]he full effectiveness of Community law would be ... impaired if a rule of national law could prevent a court seised of a dispute governed by Community law from granting interim relief in order to ensure the full effectiveness of the judgment to be given on the existence of the rights claimed under Community law. It follows that a court which in those circumstances would grant interim relief, if it were not for a rule of national law, is obliged to set aside that rule.

In *Francovich*,[86] the ECJ, walking boldly on to uncharted terrain, authorised the *creation* of a remedy in damages against Member States for failure, deliberate or otherwise, to implement EU directives. While this development could be seen as

---

[80] I Maher, 'National Courts as EC Courts' (1994) 14 *Legal Studies* 226.

[81] See T de la Mare, 'Article 177 and Legal Integration' in P Craig and G de Burca (eds), *The Evolution of EU Law*, (Oxford University Press, 1998).

[82] R Mulgan, '"Accountability": an Ever-Expanding Concept?' (2000) 78 *Public Administration* 555 .

[83] C Lord, *Democracy in the European Union* (Sheffield, Academic Press, 1998), 96 (emphasis added).

[84] J Steiner, 'From Direct Effects to *Francovich*: Sifting Means of Enforcement of Community Law' (1993) 18 *European Law Review* 3.

[85] Case C-213/89 *R v Secretary of State for Transport, ex parte Factortame (No 3)* [1990] ECR I-2433.

[86] Joined Cases 6, 9/90 *Francovich and Bonafaci v Italy* [1991] ECR I-5357. And see Joined Cases C-46/93 and C-48/93 *Brasserie du Pecheur SA v Germany; R v Transport Secretary ex parte. Factortame (No 4)* [1996] ECR I-1029 and Case C-392/93 *R v HM Treasury, ex parte British Telecommunications* [1996] 3 WLR 203, [1996] ECR I-1631.

paralleling the liability of the institutions under the Treaties to pay compensation for loss caused through their actions (EC Treaty Articles 235 and 288), in practice it took some time for the ECJ to recognise the need for equality in this respect[87]— not the only case in which the legal accountability of the Member States under European Union law has allegedly been greater than that of the European Union and its institutions. On these two cases, the ECJ could have predicated an integrated system of legal remedies, greatly strengthening the elements of enforceability and reparation in legal accountability. Instead, an apparent loss of confidence has brought a period of unpredictable and unstable case law.[88]

Courts which take seriously their function of constitutional adjudication and use the process of judicial review to bring government to account are likely to face questions about their own accountability. The ECJ is no exception to the rule. It has been attacked as integrationist, activist, and for usurping the policy-making function.[89] On the other hand, it can be argued that the curious structure of the EU judicial system contains a guarantee of 'judicial balance'. So long as the ECJ and CFI satisfy their main 'interlocutors',[90] keeping on the right side of national courts, the precarious balance between holding government to account and self-accountability inherent in the public law function of the judiciary is probably being maintained. This may be one explanation for a decline in the integrationist enthusiasm of the early years, another being the introduction of the subsidiary concept by the Treaty on European Union (above), with the weight of public opinion beginning to tip decidedly in the direction of subsidiarity.

CONCLUSIONS

Two opportunities for reform lie before the European Union as it faces the enormous challenge of enlargement. The first is the Convention set up by the European Council at Laeken with a mandate to 'identify the key issues for the Union's future developments and the various possible responses'.[91] The Laeken Declaration invites the Convention to concentrate on four broad themes: reorganisation of the Treaties, competences, legislative procedures and the efficiency and democracy of the institutions. This broad brief would allow the rambling European structure of

---

[87] See now Case C-352/98P, *Laboratoires Pharmaceutiques Bergaderm and Goupil v Commission*, 4 July 2000.

[88] R Crauford Smith, 'Remedies for Breaches of EU Law in National Courts: Legal Variation and Selection' in P Craig and G de Burca (eds), above n 81; T Tridimas, 'Liability for Breach of Community Law: Growing Up and Mellowing Down' (2001) 38 *CML Rev* 301.

[89] Famously by H Rasmussen, *On Law and Policy in the Court of Justice* (Hague, Martinus Nijhoff, 1986). See, for a different slant, T Hartley, 'The European Court, Judicial Objectivity and the Constitution of the European Union' (1996) 112 *LQR* 95.

[90] A term introduced by J Weiler, 'A Quiet Revolution: The European Court of Justice and its Interlocutors' (1994) *Comparative Political Studies* 510. And see R Dehousse, *The European Court of Justice* (Basingstoke, Macmillan, 1998).

[91] See Conclusions of the Laeken Council, above n 70.

'bits and pieces'[92] to be made more coherent, helping on the one hand to heighten the doubtful legitimacy of the EU and on the other to close the accountability gap which so frightens citizens and undercuts and threatens legitimacy. A significant first step in the right direction would be to complete the unfinished business of Amsterdam by removing all policy-making in the fields of justice and home affairs from unaccountable committees and working groups. This could be done either by bringing it formally within the perimeters of the Treaties or by decisively returning policy-making to the Member States, restoring the responsibility of national Parliaments. A further improvement in the field of law-making would be to shift the balance decisively in favour of representative and democratically elected Parliaments. The present hiatus, which allows the Council to revert at will to the 'old procedures' and act as sole legislator, with or without consultation of the European Parliament, should be reconsidered in the context of qualified majority voting. Co-decision procedure should become the norm.

Moves of this type in the direction of definition and clarity would unfortunately go against the grain of the Commission's White Paper on European Governance,[93] the European Union's main attempt to tackle problems of efficiency and legitimacy of the governance process and its second opportunity for reform. As already indicated, the White Paper includes accountability in the list of values recognised as essential for good governance but it uses a highly unorthodox definition. Rather than taking its rightful place as a 'core attribute of democratic rule',[94] accountability has here been reduced to an element in the policy-making process. It has become prospective rather than retrospective, internal rather than external, in this way departing from traditional understandings. Moreover, key questions of accountability, notably who is to be accountable for what to whom,[95] are entirely glossed over in this White Paper.

Again, there is little or no reference to the programmes of reform underway in the Commission in the wake of the Reports of the Independent Experts, designed to strengthen financial accountability and to introduce the Commission to the basic precepts of NPM. Perhaps the Commission sees these as a private affair, for which it is not publicly accountable. This could explain (though not justify) the omission from the White Paper of any reference to the right of every person, established by Article 41 of the recent European Charter of Fundamental Rights, 'to have his or her affairs handled impartially, fairly and within a reasonable time by the institutions of the Union'. This is the more surprising in that, according to the European Ombudsman, 'The Charter is the first in the world to include a right to good administration as a fundamental right in a human rights declaration.'[96] The right is, of course, expanded in the European Ombudsman's recently published

---

[92] D Curtin, 'The Constitutional Structure of the Union: A Europe of Bits and Pieces' (1993) 30 *CML Rev* 17.

[93] European Commission, *White Paper on European Governance* (COM(2001) 428 final).

[94] C Lord and D Beetham, 'Legitimizing the EU' above n 12, 446.

[95] See C Scott, 'Accountability in the Regulatory State' (2000) 27 *JLS* 38.

[96] J Soderman, 'The Struggle for Openness in the European Union', speech of 21 March 2001, available at www.euro-ombudsman.eu.int.

Code of Good Administrative Behaviour. The omission to mention either Code or Charter in the White Paper was heavily criticised by the European Parliament, which expressed regret that:

> although the White Paper mainly deals with matters falling under good administration, the Commission has not been able to take a position on the European Parliament's and the European Ombudsman's initiative on good administration.[97]

This underlines the fact that the Commission's interpretation of the term 'governance' is as one-sided as its definition of accountability. Ignoring those aspects of the myriad meanings of the imprecise term which emphasise the efficiency targets of NPM, the Commission has produced its own novel definition in a footnote[98] to mean the 'rules processes and behaviour that affect the way in which powers are exercised at European level, particularly as regards openness, participation, accountability, effectiveness and coherence'. The Commission has *incorporated its own agenda* of participatory democracy into its definition. It has then proceeded at the level of macro-governance, presenting a bundle of vague and inchoate suggestions for consultation of civil society and its organisations, without any proper analysis of the way in which these may impact on the existing structure of the European Union.

Member State governments, European Councils and the Commission, have on numerous occasions expressed their concern at the lack of popular support for the European Union, and the lack of interest in its institutions and policy-making. The Council is inclined to focus on transparency, a value which it sees as very important—so long, at least, as its own privileges are not too greatly affected.[99] It has also emphasised, though without specific proposals, the role of national Parliaments. Both are essential elements in democratic accountability. The Commission, in contrast, puts its faith in stimulating the growth of a truly European civil society, a much tougher proposition. It suggests that the problems are largely systemic, that 'many people are losing confidence in a poorly understood and complex system to deliver the policies that they want.'[100] Their response, to involve society and sections of society in policy-making, would in fact shift political and rule-making power to the Commission without increasing either its efficiency or its accountability towards the public and the Member States. More serious still, the Commission's recommendations seem capable of undercutting the institutions of representative democracy, on which the public tends to rely for exacting accountability from government. In the rush to promote participation by civil society and non-governmental organisations, adequate consideration has not been given to the question whether the Commission's proposals may not undercut more orthodox representative machinery. Strengthening the place of regional assemblies is, for example, likely in the end to prove impractical for logistical reasons, but at the

---

[97] European Parliament, Constitutional Affairs Committee, *Report on the Commission White Paper on European Governance* (Rapporteur: Sylvia-Yvonne Kaufman), 23.

[98] White Paper, p 8.

[99] *Hautala v Council*, above n 76.

[100] White Paper, above n 93, at 3.

same time to weaken national Parliaments. Practical proposals to enhance the representative institutions of Europe and encourage the participation of the people of Europe through traditional representative machinery, on which the Commission is supposed to have been working since Protocol No 8 was added to the Treaties at Amsterdam, are, on the other hand, entirely wanting. It is to be hoped that this critical obligation will surface on the agenda of the Convention. Again, the proposals for 'framework legislation', leaving space for the Commission to fill in 'technical details', and for 'co-regulation', which would instal a general regulatory framework to be implemented by various actors through legal and non-legal instruments [101] is, from the standpoint of legislative accountability, highly suspect. No doubt it would avoid problems of delay and complexity but once again it would succeed in evading legislative accountability at both European and national levels, undercutting the authority of both the European Parliament and national Parliaments.

The White Paper, in short, does not adequately address the numerous questions of accountability which plague the European Union nor are its proposals truly democratic in terms of the democratic systems of government to which the people of Europe are accustomed. Yet fears over accountability are, as Micosi stresses,[102] amongst the deepest fears of people in the face of European union. This is partly why public opinion seems unfavourable to further transfers of national sovereignty and does not seem to want the full democratic accountability of the Commission as an elected government on which President Prodi has set his sights. As Micosi describes the process of integration, the expansion of EU tasks has been driven by Member States in response to the demands of large and powerful constituencies within European society, notably the transnational business community, without the explicit approval either of the peoples of Europe or of their elected representatives. Integration is thus the de facto consequence of a series of incremental and piecemeal decisions taken at various intergovernmental conferences and by the institutions, for which governments have largely escaped political accountability to national Parliaments. 'Public opinion may have supported each increment, but Europe's citizens are unhappy with the overall result because of their inability to exercise control.'[103]

A written constitution, federal in character and with a clear list of those powers which are devolved to the European Union and those retained by Member States, although it has powerful advocates, notably in Germany,[104] is not the most likely outcome of the Convention on the Constitution. Nor is essential structural change, controversial at the Nice IGC, likely to prove less so in the context of the Convention. The White Paper, with its pretentious though vague agenda, is another missed opportunity. The struggle for accountability is always formulated at the

---

[101] White Paper, above n 93, at 20–23.
[102] S Micosi, 'The mandate of the Convention' in *Institutional Reforms in the European Union, Memorandum for the Convention* (Rome, Europeos, 2002).
[103] *Ibid* at 10.
[104] C Dorau and P Jacobi, 'The Debate over a "European Constitution": Is it Solely a German Concern?' (2000) 6 *European Public Law* 413.

macro level of structures, institutions and constitutions. In truth it needs to start at a lower and more pragmatic level: in the practice of politicians and officials within the EU institutions and, above all, in national Parliaments.

This chapter was completed before the Convention had started to publish working papers and drafts. No attempt has been made to incorporate these or its newly published draft Constitution into the text or footnotes.

5

Devolution and England:
What is on Offer?

RICHARD CORNES*

INTRODUCTION

IN MAY 2002, John Prescott, Deputy Prime Minister and Stephen Byers, then Secretary of State for Transport, Local Government and the Regions, set out the Government's proposals for a new level of regional government within England in a white paper entitled *Your Region Your Choice: Revitalising the English Regions* ('the White Paper').[1] The next indication of the Government's plans for England came in the speech from the throne on 13 November 2002, in which a Bill allowing for referendums in the English regions on establishing regional assemblies, was promised. That Bill, the Regional Assemblies (Preparations) Bill 2002, was passed in 2003. It empowers the Secretary of State, having assessed the level of regional interest in a regional assembly, to call one or more regional referendums.[2] The Act contains no further detail as to the precise structure and organisation of the proposed assemblies; that detail will only be forthcoming once at least one region has voted for a regional assembly. At that point the:

> Government [will] … introduce a second Bill, when Parliamentary time allows, to enable regional assemblies to be set up where people have voted for them. Elections for those assemblies would be held within months of the second Bill becoming law. This should allow the first regional assembly to be up and running early in the next Parliament.[3]

Until that Bill is introduced the only detail available about the proposed regional assemblies is contained in the White Paper; and an analysis of that document from the perspective of constitutional law is at the heart of this chapter.

---

* My thanks to the editors and other contributors to this volume for their comments on an early outline of the chapter discussed at a weekend seminar in Oxford at Easter 2002. I am also particularly grateful to Leigh Oakes and my colleagues Meris Amos and Deidre Fottrell for reviewing a draft of this chapter.

[1] *Your Region Your Choice: Revitalising the English Regions* (Cm 5511, 2002).
[2] Regional Assemblies (Preparations) Act 2003, s 1.
[3] 'Bill Paves the Way for England's First Directly Elected Regional Assemblies' (News Release 122, Office of the Deputy Prime Minister, 14 Nov 2002). On 16 June 2003 referenda were announced for three northern regions during 2004. 'Prescott go-ahead to devolve regions', *The Guardian*, 16 June 2003.

In the preface to the White Paper, the Prime Minister promises that it will, 'build on the success of devolution elsewhere in the UK,' while the Deputy Prime Minister and Secretary of State, state that, 'by devolving power and revitalising the regions we bring decision-making closer to the people and make government more efficient, more effective and more accountable.'[4] However, what the White Paper offers England is a series of weak regionally-based assemblies, certainly not comparable to the new Parliament in Scotland or the new Assembly in Northern Ireland, of even more limited scope than the National Assembly for Wales; and not, it will be argued, worthy of the title 'devolution.'

By purporting to extend the devolution process to the English regions, a further development of multi-layered governance within the United Kingdom, the government also implicitly seeks to answer what has become known as the 'English Question.'[5] The question refers to the fact that now power has been devolved to other parts of the United Kingdom, with the consequence that Members of Parliament at Westminster may no longer discuss devolved issues, Members of Parliament elected from Scotland, Wales and Northern Ireland are still entitled to take part in decision-making on matters concerning only England.[6] This chapter will argue, based on a definition of devolution arising from an examination of its history to date, that the White Paper's proposals do not amount to devolution. It will end with the suggestion that the answer to the English Question may not be one which can be answered by proposing new levels of government for England. Rather, it will be suggested, the question the United Kingdom needs to address is that of the Union itself between England, Scotland, Wales and Northern Ireland; and that only by dealing with the future, and nature, of that Union, in the context of continuing European integration, can the anomaly highlighted by the devolution process to date be adequately addressed.[7]

[4] *Ibid.*

[5] Relevant to this book's concern with multi-layered government is Noreen Burrows' comment that in the absence of regional government within England, 'the United Kingdom, taken as a whole, is not characterised as having multi-layered government—that description only applies at the moment to Scotland, Northern Ireland and Wales. However, even where devolution has occurred …[it] is a differentiated process. Thus the United Kingdom as a whole may be said to have *multi-textured* government in the sense that the layers of government are uneven throughout': Noreen Burrows, *Devolution* (London, Sweet & Maxwell, 2000), 189–90, (emphasis added and footnote omitted).

[6] See discussion of the English Question in O Hood Phillips and P Jackson, *Constitutional and Administrative Law* (London, Sweet & Maxwell, 2001) paras 5–042 and 5–046; Selina Chen and Tony Wright (eds) *The English Question* (London, Fabian Society, 2000); and *An Unstable Union: Devolution and the English Question* (London, Constitution Unit, 2000), in which Robert Hazell characterises England as, 'the gaping hole in the devolution settlement' (at 7).

[7] I acknowledge that reform of the Union itself is not on the agendas of the three major pan-United Kingdom political parties (Labour, Liberal Democrat and Conservative). However, one of the purposes of academic discourse is to raise issues for debate which might otherwise not be discussed. Furthermore, the issue of the Union could quite conceivably *have* to be addressed if, for instance, the Scottish National Party (the second largest party in the Scottish Parliament, and committed to an independent Scotland within the European Union) won power north of the border. The Northern Ireland Act 1998 also contains provisions contemplating the end of the Union's inclusion of Northern Ireland if the required majorities there voted to leave the Union and form a united Ireland. In some respects the only inhabitants of the United Kingdom who do not think about the issue of the Union are the English. Compare Krishnan Kumar, *The Making of English National Identity* (Cambridge, Cambridge University Press, 2003).

The argument will proceed as follows: first a brief introduction to the Blair Government's devolution programme will be set out; then, drawing on this brief history and the accepted sources of constitutional law and principles in the United Kingdom, a set of defining characteristics for devolution will be proposed; following this, the defining characteristics will then be used to assess the White Paper's proposals and the relevant provisions of the Regional Assemblies (Preparations) Act 2003, leading to the conclusion that they do not amount to devolution, but merely decentralisation (unless the definition of devolution is so altered as to rob it of all significance);[8] finally, the chapter's conclusion will argue that the proposals for English regional assemblies fails to answer the English Question, and that the solution to that question should be sought in the possibility of reformulating the Union between England, Scotland, Wales and Northern Ireland so that they become co-operating (here we may look to the members of the Nordic Council for inspiration)[9] but distinct and individual members of what the Scottish constitutional lawyer, Neil McCormick, has referred to as 'the European Commonwealth.'[10]

DEVOLUTION AND NEW LABOUR[11]

The Labour Government elected in May 1997 moved rapidly on its manifesto promises on devolution. Within three months of the election, White Papers were published outlining elected assemblies for Scotland and Wales.[12] By July 1997, the Referendums (Scotland and Wales) Act 1997 had received Royal Assent and by September, the referendums had been held. Both Scotland and Wales voted for devolution (and, in Scotland, a minor tax varying power), though in Wales the majority was slight, a meagre 1 per cent. The following year the Scotland, Government of Wales, and Northern Ireland Acts were all passed. Northern Ireland was then the first to elect its new legislature with polls held on 25 June 1998.[13] On 6 May 1999, Scotland and Wales followed; with elections to the first Scottish Parliament in 300 years,[14] and the first elected national assembly for Wales ever.[15]

---

[8] For a definition of the difference between 'devolution' and 'decentralisation' see below n 50 and accompanying text.

[9] The Nordic countries (Denmark, the Faroe Islands, Greenland, Finland, the Åland Islands, Iceland, Norway and Sweden) co-operate at both parliamentary and ministerial levels. The co-operation allows inter alia a common Nordic position to be put forward to the European Union; this is especially significant given that not all the Nordic countries are members of the European Union See Mads Qvortup and Robert Hazell *The British-Irish Council: Nordic Lessons for the Council of the Isles* (London, Constitution Unit, 1998).

[10] See Neil MacCormick, *Questioning Sovereignty: Law, State, and Practical Reason in the European Commonwealth* (Oxford University Press, 1999), especially chs 8, 9, 11 and 12.

[11] For a history of devolution in the United Kingdom see Vernon Bogdanor, *Devolution in the United Kingdom* (Oxford University Press, 1999).

[12] *Scotland's Parliament* (Cm 3658, 1997); *A Voice for Wales* Cm 3719 (1997).

[13] As a result of the Belfast Agreement (also referred to as the 'Good Friday Agreement') of Easter 1998; see *The Agreement Reached in Multi-Party Negotiations* (Cm 4292, 1998).

[14] The Parliament has 129 members elected on a proportional electoral system. The executive is led by a First Minister who is elected by the Parliament, appointed by the Queen, and who in turn nominates other ministers for endorsement by the Parliament prior to being appointed by the Queen.

[15] The Assembly has 60 members elected on a proportional electoral system. Those 60 elect one of

Of the three devolved institutions so far established, the new Scottish Parliament has the greatest degree of power. The Scotland Act 1998 grants the new Parliament the power to pass what it calls 'Acts of the Scottish Parliament', terminology which suggests that, in some way at least, the instruments are to be viewed as 'primary'.[16] A similar general grant of power is also made to the Scottish Executive.[17] Both general grants are then subject to specific restrictions.[18] The restrictions are the classic set of functions retained in federal systems: eg foreign affairs and defence. These 'big ticket' exclusions are supplemented by a very detailed set of more specific exceptions—it is in relation to these that Craig and Walters raised an early alarm about the potential for conflict over the boundaries of the Parliament's powers.[19]

The Northern Ireland Act 1998 creates a legislative body along the lines of the Scottish Parliament with general legislative authority subject to certain reservations.[20] The 108-member Assembly is elected on a proportional basis. The most intriguing feature of the Northern Ireland scheme is the form of the executive. It is in effect a forced coalition, with the executive departments being distributed between the Assembly parties based on the number of seats held in the Assembly. Furthermore, the First and Deputy First Ministers are in effect equal in authority. Currently, the First Minster is drawn from the moderate unionist party and the Deputy from the moderate nationalist party.[21] The entire scheme requires equal power-sharing at all levels. It is well known that the devolution process in Northern Ireland has regularly been thrown into turmoil by difficulties in the peace process, an issue which will not be addressed here.[22]

The devolution settlement in Wales can justly be described as extraordinarily complex.[23] Not only is it that, it is also significantly less generous than the Scottish

their number as First Secretary; the First Secretary then appoints up to eight other Assembly Secretaries and to them is delegated power by the Assembly. The Government of Wales Act 1998 used the term 'Secretaries'. However, in perhaps an early example of the 'ratchet up' effect of devolution, the term First Minister and Minister is now being used in Wales, mirroring the terminology in Scotland and Northern Ireland. There has been no amendment to the Act to reflect the changed usage.

[16]   Scotland Act 1998, s 28. The nature of 'devolved power' and the meaning of 'primary legislation' in the context of the Scottish Parliament is discussed in greater detail, below n 55 and accompanying text.

[17]   Scotland Act 1998, s 53.

[18]   See Burrows, above n 5, 65–68.

[19]   Paul Craig and Mark Walters 'The Courts, Devolution, and Judicial Review' [1999] *Public Law* 274.

[20]   Northern Ireland Act 1998, s 5. See also Brigid Hadfield, 'The Nature of Devolution in Scotland and Northern Ireland: Key Issues of Responsibility and Control' (1999) 3 *Edinburgh Law Review* 3.

[21]   Although at the time of writing (June 2003) the devolved government in Northern Ireland was once again in suspension, see also below, n 58.

[22]   For further detail, see eg, Rick Wilford and Robin Wilson, 'A Bare Knuckle Ride: Northern Ireland' in Robert Hazell (ed), *The State and the Nations: The First Years of Devolution in the United Kingdom* (London, Academic Imprint, 2000). See also discussion, below n 66 and accompanying text; and see Brigid Hadfield, chapter 6 below.

[23]   The Law Society, making submissions to the National Assembly's operational review in 2001 made the startling comment that it was becoming increasingly difficult for lawyers to provide advice to clients as to exactly what the Assembly's powers are. For the full report of the operational review see www.wales.gov.uk/subiassemblybusiness/procedures/assemblyreview.htm For discussion of the Welsh scheme, see Richard Rawlings, 'The New Model Wales' (1998) 25 *Journal of Law and Society* 461.

and Northern Irish schemes. Unlike Scotland, Wales does not enjoy a general delegation of legislative power subject only to specific exceptions. The Assembly has been delegated executive decision-making authority in specific subject areas—there are no 'Acts of the Welsh Assembly.' Powers previously exercised by the Secretary of State for Wales under a range of statutes are now exercised by the Assembly. Where Scotland has general power, the Assembly has power only in those specific areas delegated to it by statutes, past and future. The initial transfer of powers was accomplished by the National Assembly for Wales (Transfer of Functions) Order 1999, SI 1 1999/672 (UK), a huge and detailed document. A significant weakness of the Welsh scheme, and one likely to lead to tension, is the Assembly's lack of general primary legislative authority. If it wants to act in a novel area, it has to persuade Westminster to pass a statute empowering it.[24] That concludes our review of the Government's devolution programme to date. We now move on to develop a definition of devolution based upon established constitutional principles, and the history of devolution to date.

DEFINING DEVOLUTION

The United Kingdom's Uncodified Constitution

Most states can look to a written constitution for the rules which define the nature of their constitutional arrangements. Even in, for example, asymmetrical, non-federal, regionalised polities such as Spain, there is greater clarity about the nature of the sub-national bodies, and the process by which new devolved governments are established. In Spain the fact of asymmetry does not mean that the constitutional nature of the 17 Autonomous Communities is uncertain. They were established after a nationwide constitution-making process in which Spain, as a state, set out a set of constitutional principles and rules for the development of regional government.[25] In the United Kingdom, to identify the underlying principles and rules of the constitution we have to look to: statutes, common law sources (including for example, judicial precedents), constitutional conventions, the law and customs of Parliament, parliamentary debates themselves, European Community law, European Convention on Human Rights law, and authoritative academic works.[26]

[24] Something which the Assembly has so far not had much luck in achieving. In 2001 the Assembly passed a resolution seeking four Bills in the coming Westminster session: power to improve collaborative working and responsibility in the National Health Service in Wales; providing greater cohesion in the education, training and careers systems in Wales; giving the Assembly authority to approve census forms for use in Wales; and making St David's Day a holiday in Wales (National Assembly for Wales *Record*, 13 March 2001). In the event only one of the Assembly's wishes was included in the Queen's Speech (concerning the NHS in Wales), and even that was subsequently subsumed in an English NHS Bill.

[25] Though the settlement in Spain, like that in the United Kingdom, remains subject to the continuing pressure for further autonomy—see eg 'Independence? Let's have a vote', reporting on plans by the nationalist government of the Basque region to hold a referendum on greater autonomy from Spain, *Economist*, 5 Oct 2002, 38.

[26] Given the uncodified nature of the UK constitution, there is of course no magic to this list of

In contrast then to, for example, the Spanish system of Autonomous Communities, but in keeping with the historic flexibility of British constitution-making, devolution has proceeded in an ad hoc manner, driven by the specific desires and interests of the respective majorities in Scotland, Wales and Northern Ireland. While, thus far, incrementalism has been an accepted characteristic of constitutional development in the United Kingdom, the lack of any serious and detailed attempt (beyond the mantras of 'modernisation' and 'pragmatism') to set out a coherent guiding set of principles, or core characteristics, of devolution is nevertheless unfortunate, and increasingly beginning to attract adverse comment.[27] The fact that 'pragmatism rather than principle [has] long been a dominant theme of British governance ... and [that] the system of government is a mix of structures and institutions inherited from the past, adopted and adapted in seemingly haphazard fashion to meet the needs of contemporary society' is no longer (certainly not in the context of deciding upon the future structure of the state) a sufficient excuse for this traditionally informal, British approach to constitutional change. [28]

Earlier on in the debate about devolution, political scientists Michael Keating and Howard Elcock opened a special edition of the journal *Regional and Federal Studies* devoted to devolution with the comment that the Labour Government's programme of constitutional reform could be described as, 'piecemeal, with little regard to an overall plan, or even consistency.'[29] Indeed, the degree of incrementalism and pragmatism has led one leading constitutional lawyer, Professor Noreen Burrows, to characterise the devolution process as 'haphazard,' rather than merely asymmetrical.[30] Burrows goes further:

> underlying the current devolution process, there is no clear constitutional model... there has been no attempt to provide a legal framework within which the regional governments will operate. ...What appears to be lacking at present is the recognition of the need for constitutional principles within which the various devolution settlements can operate. It is here that New Labour's modernisation process is weakest. There is an absence of constitutional rules and principles to be applied to the United Kingdom's constitutional structure as a whole.[31]

potential sources: see eg S de Smith and R Brazier *Constitutional and Administrative Law* (8th edn, London, Penguin, 1998), 21–27; O Hood Phillips and P Jackson, above n 6, at 18–21; Hilaire Barnett, *Britain Unwrapped: Government and Constitution Explained* (London, Penguin, 2002), 3–24; from a Scottish perspective, Ashton and Finch, *Constitutional Law in Scotland* (Edinburgh, Green, 2000), 26–48; and more discursively, Barendt, *An Introduction to Constitutional Law* (Oxford University Press, 1998), 26–50.

[27]   See Polly Toynbee and David Walker's audit of the first term of the Blair Government, *Did Things Get Better? An Audit of Labour's Successes and Failures* (London, Penguin, 2001). Toynbee and Walker evaluate the Government's progress in devolution under the heading, 'Modernisation', 207–11.

[28]   Barnett, above n 26, Preface. For further discussion on the nature of constitutional change in the United Kingdom, see Michael Foley *The Politics of the British Constitution* (Manchester, Manchester University Press, 1999) and the fourth report of the House of Lords Committee on the Constitution, *Changing the Constitution: the Process of Constitutional Change* (HL 69, 2002).

[29]   Michael Keating and Howard Elcock, 'Introduction: Devolution and the UK State' in *Remaking the Union: Devolution and British Politics in the 1990s* (1998) 8 *Regional and Federal Studies*.

[30]   Burrows, above n 5, at 27.

[31]   *Ibid.*

Alan Ward entitles his discussion of devolution in *The Changing Constitution*, 'Devolution: Labour's Strange Constitutional "Design"',[32] while Bradley and Ewing, writing in 2002, still felt able to note that 'devolution is not a term of art in constitutional law.'[33]

In this section I am going to suggest that a set of defining principles, or characteristics, of devolution can be derived from an examination of what it has entailed in practice in each of Scotland, Wales and Northern Ireland;[34] Thus, the defining characteristics proposed below will have their origins in description. This has the advantage of the precision gained from resting the definition upon what devolution actually is, rather than potentially obscuring its characteristics by way of definition by analogy—consider, for example, use of the tag 'quasi-federalism' to describe devolution.[35]

Once we have elaborated a set of defining characteristics of devolution we can then use them as a base line against which the White Paper's proposals can be considered. I do not entirely, or necessarily, suggest that such progressive incremental change should no longer play *any* role in constitutional reform in the United Kingdom. Rather, what I hope the defining principles can do, used as a prescriptive benchmark, is to force policy makers to adopt a more programmatic and principled approach to constitutional change. Deviation from the established benchmarks must be justified, rather than simply being assumed and allowed. The aim, as it were, is to encourage some 'method to this madness.'

What is devolution?

The very essence of devolution is the transfer of power from Westminster to governing institutions responsible for distinct geographical areas within the United Kingdom, in such a way that the devolved decision-makers are primarily answerable to their local electorate. That statement suggests the following five questions: 1. What geographical areas? 2. What type of institutions? 3. With what kind of power? 4. Controlled in what ways? 5. Established in what way? By answering these questions, which we can do by reference to the history of devolution to date, and the

---

[32] Alan J Ward, 'Devolution: Labour's Strange Constitutional "Design"', in Jowell and Oliver (eds), *The Changing Constitution* (Oxford University Press, 2000).

[33] AW Bradley and KD Ewing, *Constitutional and Administrative Law* (13th edn, Harlow, Longman, 2002), 42; though in fact Bradley and Ewing then go on to provide a succinct definition of devolution.

[34] Following Burrows (above n 5, at 189 at Burrows n 5) I do not treat the Greater London Assembly and the Regional Development Agencies established under the Regional Development Agencies Act 1998 as coming within the term 'devolution', The reason for this, and for their more appropriate characterisation as examples of local government, and decentralisation, respectively, will become clearer during the discussion later in this section.

[35] To which the author pleads guilty to using and recants: see Richard Cornes, 'Intergovernmental Relations in a Devolved United Kingdom: Making Devolution Work' in Robert Hazell (ed), *Constitutional Futures: A History of the Next Ten Years* (Oxford University Press, 1999), 156. The danger that the federal analogy would obscure more than it illuminates about devolution was discussed by Brigid Hadfield in her *Current Legal Problems* lecture 'Towards an English Constitution', 7 March 2002, University College London.

sources for constitutional principles noted above, I suggest we can arrive at a set of more detailed defining characteristics for devolution. In respect of each question the issue will be what, in respect of the issue the question raises, is necessary in order to achieve the basic goal, or the essence, of devolution. For each question there will be a general discussion, referring to accepted sources of constitutional law noted above (the *descriptive element*), which will lead an answer which will be presented as a defining statement of principle (the *prescriptive element*).

What Geographical Areas?

Historically, the geographical units to which the devolution of power has been contemplated have been the constituent nations of the United Kingdom; the nineteenth century idea of 'Home Rule all round' entailed establishing institutions in each of England, Ireland, Wales and Scotland. Home Rule all round of course never eventuated; however, the principle of devolving power to the nations which constitute the United Kingdom survived, and so in 1997 the first devolution statutes concerned Scotland, Wales and Northern Ireland.[36]

The predominant view in the academic literature is that the basis of devolution is the transfer of power to the sub-UK nations. De Smith and Brazier in their 1998 text, presumably written prior to the Belfast Agreement of that year, implicitly speak of devolution with specific reference only to Scotland and Wales.[37] Likewise, Eric Barendt in his *Introduction to Constitutional Law*, in which he implicitly contrasts devolved power, the power transferred to local government, and federalism.[38] Bogdanor notes that 'the setting-up of the Scottish Parliament and the Welsh Assembly ... imply that the United Kingdom is becoming a *union of nations*, each with its own identity and institutions.'[39] In 2002, Bradley and Ewing write, 'In the United Kingdom, devolution has come to mean the vesting of legislative and executive powers in elected bodies in *Scotland, Wales and Northern Ireland*.'[40] They end their chapter on devolution by noting the anomalies arising as a result of devolution (ie the English Question), and saying that, 'a possible response to the challenge [presented by these anomalies] would be to create devolved forms of government at a regional level in England.'[41] The authors of Hood Phillips and Jackson simply define devolution as the 'delegation of central government powers'

[36] While the status of Northern Ireland as a constituent part of the Union may be a highly contested point, its existence as a thing with which all its people identify with is not. Protestants will couple their Northern Irish identity with a British one; while nationalists, even if they reject the Union with Great Britain and seek reunification with the South, must still have an identity as inhabitants of one of the northern counties which make up Northern Ireland, and their support of the Belfast Agreement in the referendum subsequent to it may be taken as evidence of an endorsement of the North as an entity, even if for the contingent purpose of moving towards an eventual reunion with the rest of Ireland. For analysis of the constitutional implications of the Belfast Agreement for the Union, see Brigid Hadfield, 'The Belfast Agreement, Sovereignty and the State of the Union' [1998] *Public Law* 599.
[37] de Smith and Brazier, above n 26, 63.
[38] See Barendt, above n 26, at ch 3, 'Federalism and Devolution'.
[39] Above n 11, at 287.
[40] Above n 33, at 42. We will return to their comments concerning the type of power vested below.
[41] *Ibid* at 48.

without specifying to what entity those powers are delegated; though in subsequent discussion they deal only with Scotland, Wales, Northern Ireland and note that the Regional Development Agencies Act 1998 could be viewed as a 'first step towards regional devolution in England.'[42] The Scottish constitutional lawyer, Professor Noreen Burrows, in her book *Devolution*, states:

> Devolution is the recognition in law of the national identities and national boundaries that exist inside the nation state that happens to be called the United Kingdom, but which could easily fall into a definition of a union kingdom.[43]

In a footnote shortly after this quote Burrows notes that:

> The creation of a mayor and Assembly in London does not fall into the definition of devolution used in this book. It is however another element in the process of decentralisation and modernisation.[44]

Similarly, Hood Phillips and Jackson deal with the new institutions in London in their chapter on local government. In contrast, Hilaire Barnett opens her discussion of regional and local government with the observation 'historically, the oldest form of devolved power has been to local government'. However she then goes on to discuss devolution to Scotland, Wales and Northern Ireland as distinct from the organisation of local government.[45] Barnett does, however, appear to treat the establishment of the Greater London Authority, and proposals for similar structures in other major cities, as well as possible regional bodies within England, as part of what may be called the 'devolution agenda,' rather than simply as a matter of local government development.

I suggest that the common relevant factor, for the purposes of answering the first question posed 'what geographical area?' concerns *identity*: what matters is that there is a geographical entity with which its inhabitants identify.[46] Such identities in the devolution process have historically been based on being Scottish, Welsh or Northern Irish (whichever side of the sectarian divide). However, in drawing a conclusion for the purposes of the definition of devolution it seems appropriate to allow that the 'identity factor' should be drawn widely enough to take into account the point of view of those living within England. A recent poll for the BBC revealed that more people identified with their local community or region (36 per cent) than England (with which 27 per cent identified), Britain (with which 22 per cent identified), or Europe/the world, which the BBC termed 'cosmopolitan' (which attracted just 13 per cent).[47] The answer therefore should be that, when devolving power in England, it should be transferred to geographical regions with which

---

[42] See O Hood Phillips and P Jackson, above n 6, at 83 and 105.

[43] Above n 5, at 189.

[44] *Ibid* at Burrows n 5.

[45] See Barnett, above n 26, at 216–63.

[46] See MacCormick, who argues 'there is a new diffusion of power [within the United Kingdom] that answers to the growth, all over the world, of what can justly be called the politics of identity'. above n 10, at 193.

[47] 'English want regional assemblies', BBC News, 21 March 2002, http://news.bbc.co.uk.hi.english /uk_politics/newsid_1883000/1883944.stm

people identify. In this context the requirement of a referendum prior to establishing a new devolved entity, fulfilling as it does the requirement for consent, which Burrows identifies as a 'fundamental principle underlying the entire process of devolution' is a useful check that the geographical area identified for devolution is the correct one.[48]

What Type of Institution?

The next relevant issue is the nature of the institution to which power is transferred. This raises three related sub-issues: how the devolved body is constituted; secondly, the existence of a legislative/executive division within the devolved body; and thirdly, the ability of the legislative element to scrutinise the executive element and, preferably, also play a role in initiating policy-making.

Each of the devolved institutions established to date have been formed by local elections using some kind of proportional electoral system.[49] The requirement for local election clearly differentiates the devolved institutions from mere decentralisation—the delegation of central government power to officials, or agencies, appointed by central government, and answerable primarily to central government.[50] The local election of the devolved administrations ensures that they do effect a transfer of power from central government decision-makers to local decision-makers, answerable directly to their electorate.

The Government Offices for the Regions, established in 1994 to co-ordinate central government activities in the English regions, and now strengthened by the establishment, in April 2000, of the Regional Co-ordination Unit, are clearly on this test an example of decentralisation, rather than devolution. It is also argued that while the regional development agencies do work in conjunction with a voluntary regional chamber, where one has been designated as 'suitable' by the Secretary of State (under section 8 of the Regional Development Agencies Act 1998), that the lack of election to the voluntary chamber, and the continuing strong role of the Secretary of State, also mean that the regional development agencies are more appropriately classified as examples of decentralisation. They may be a step on the path to devolution, but they do not yet amount to it.

We now move to the second issue, the existence of a legislative/executive division within the devolved bodies. All three devolved bodies established so far may be said to be composed of distinct legislative and executive components. Beneath that common truth there lies differentiation in the detailed structure of each entity. Scotland has the system most like that of a classic Parliament on the Westminster model, ie an elected Parliament with the executive drawn from it (though its operation is of course modified by the presence of coalition government which

[48] Burrows, above n 5, at 24. See also the discussion below in relation to question 5 concerning how the devolution scheme is given effect to.

[49] See above nn 14 and 15 and accompanying text.

[50] See also O Hood Phillips and P Jackson, above n 6, at 83: '[devolution] should be distinguished from "decentralisation", which is a method whereby some central government powers of decision-making are exercised by officials of the central government located in the regions.'

tends to be the result of the proportional electoral systems chosen); Northern Ireland has its distinct 'forced coalition' of nationalist/republican and unionist/loyalist ministers based on their respective parties' strengths in the Assembly; while in Wales the process of devolution to date has resulted in a greater differentiation between the executive and other members of the Assembly, with the two developing more distinct identities, than was perhaps originally envisaged.[51]

The final issue under this heading concerns the role of the 'legislative' element of the assembly, specifically, the requirement that it be able to scrutinise the work of the executive (again, ensuring that devolution does in fact produce greater local democratic accountability), and, desirably, be able to play a role in policy-making. Turning first to scrutiny, all of the devolution statutes make clear that the 'executive' arms of the new devolved institutions must be accountable, via the legislative element of the institution, to their local electorate. Similarly, all in varying degrees play a role in developing policy, either at their members' own initiatives, or by providing a conduit for their electorates' ideas to be transmitted to the executive. As with much of devolution, how these two functions are carried out varies significantly between each devolved system. For the purposes of this chapter it will not be necessary to go into the operation of the established institutions further.[52]

The answer proposed to the second question is that devolution entails the transfer of power to: (a) a locally elected body in which; (b) there is a legislative/executive distinction, and in which: (c) the legislative element has the ability to scrutinise the activities of the executive element, as well as, desirably, playing a role in policy development.

What Type of Power is Transferred?

In this section I will argue that the transfer of power to a devolved institution is qualitatively different from the transfer of power to local government. There are three issues to deal with under this heading. First, internally, what is the nature of power to be transferred to a devolved entity? Broadly, the answer will be that either legislative competence, executive authority, or both types of power (or some variant on them) are transferred. Secondly, externally to the devolved entity, what is the nature of its power vis-à-vis Westminster? Here the issue will be the degree of autonomy the entity possesses, with a local authority being at the lowest end of the

[51] This is of course a gloss on the complexities of each system, provided for the purpose of illustrating the underlying similarity of a legislative/executive division in each. For detail, see Burrows, above n 5. In Wales, the problematic nature of the relationship between the Assembly and the executive was the subject of a letter from the First Minister to the Presiding Officer (on 5 July 2001); a greater distinction is progressively being drawn between the executive and Assembly in Wales than was perhaps originally envisaged in the Government of Wales Act 1998.

[52] Again, see Burrows, above n 5, particularly at chs. 2, 4 and 5. Analysis of the operation of the Northern Irish Assembly and Scottish Parliament can be found in Rick Wilford and Robin Wilson, *A Democratic Design?:The Political Style of the Northern Ireland Assembly* (London, Constitution Unit, 2001), and Barry K Winetrobe, *Realising the Vision: A Parliament with a Purpose: An Audit of the First Year of the Scottish Parliament* (London, Constitution Unit, 2001). No similar audit of the National Assembly for Wales has yet been published.

scale, and the Scottish Parliament being at the highest. Thirdly, a devolved entity must enjoy fiscal autonomy. Lack of, at the very least, discretion over what money is spent on would interfere with the basic notion of devolution—that power to decide is as a matter of political reality (legal sovereignty aside) *transferred*.

In relation to the first issue, whatever the nature of the power transferred (whether legislative, executive, both, or some variation on them) the key is that the devolved institution must have the capacity to act, to play a meaningful role in relation to the governance of the subject areas it is supposed to have power over.[53] Scotland and Northern Ireland are relatively uncomplicated in this respect, given that both have primary as well as secondary legislative power (the meaning of those terms in the context of devolution will be discussed shortly), as well as executive power, vested in their executives. The Welsh scheme is, however, problematic. As has been noted above, only secondary legislative authority has been delegated to Wales. Judging the Assembly by its activity to date, however, it has certainly shown that it has the capacity to act (it has so far passed some thousands of instruments). However, as was noted in the brief introduction above, the Assembly's continuing dependence on Westminster for primary legislation is proving to be an irritant.[54]

The second issue is the nature of the devolved entities' power vis-à-vis Westminster. On the strict, Diceyan view of the constitution (in which the Westminster Parliament is sovereign) it is clear, as Bogdanor puts it that 'constitutionally, devolution is a mere delegation of power from a superior body to an inferior' and that, 'devolution involves the creation of an elected body, *subordinate* to Parliament.'[55] The position is, in relation to Scotland, for example, made clear by section 28(7) of the Scotland Act 1998 which stipulates that, 'This section [which sets out the Parliament's scope of authority] does not affect the power of the Parliament of the United Kingdom to make laws for Scotland.' In the first cases concerning the devolution settlements, the judges have emphasised this aspect. Lord Rodgers, now a Lord of Appeal in Ordinary, at the time the most senior Scottish judge, said in an early case concerning the new Parliament, '[it] is a body which, *like any other statutory body*, must work within the scope of [its] powers. If it does not do so, then in an appropriate case the court may be

---

[53]   It is assumed, for the purposes of this chapter, that from the point of view of constitutional law the issue of the range of subjects transferred to a devolved institution is neutral to the issue of whether a scheme amounts to devolution as a matter of legal principle (unless of course so little was being transferred as to make the exercise meaningless). The range of subject areas to be transferred is relevant from a public policy/political science point of view. However, such an analysis will not be offered here. In relation to the mix of subject headings proposed for transfer to the English regions in the White Paper, Mark Sandford, from a political science perspective, comments 'there does not appear to be any guiding logic to the range of subject areas assemblies are to play a role in, or the type of power (strategy making, executive functions or influencing role) they have to play their role. … It is quite apparent that the range of functions to be offered to elected regional assemblies owes everything to political bargaining and little to rational analysis': Mark Sandford *A Commentary on the Regional Government White Paper, Your Region, Your Choice: Revitalising the English Regions Cm 5511, May 2002* (Constitution Unit, 2002), para 23, p 11.

[54]   Instruments promulgated to date by the National Assembly for Wales can be viewed at: http://www.hmso.gov.uk/legislation/wales/w-stat.htm. The downgrading of the position of Secretary of State for Wales in the 12 June 2003 cabinet re-shuffle may also exacerbate the weaknesses of the Welsh scheme.

[55]   Above n 11, at 287–88.

asked to intervene and will require to do so.'[56] The mark of a federal system, in which each of the governments enjoys a constitutionally entrenched sovereign scope of authority, is completely lacking in devolution.

However, quite apart from this view not accounting for the cogent arguments concerning the binding nature of the Treaty and Acts of Union put forward by Scottish constitutional lawyers, a bare statement of Westminster's continuing legal sovereignty without qualification would be a misleading description of the constitutional nature of the contemporary devolution settlement.[57] This is so because the technical *legal* retention of sovereignty is only half of the picture. Arguably the more important part of the picture, because it is the operational part, is the *political reality* that power to make decisions in certain areas has in effect been transferred to the new devolved institution. Westminster no longer has more than a residual, perhaps at times partnership, role to play in those areas which have been devolved. As Bogdanor points out, 'politically… devolution places a powerful weapon in the hands of the Scots and the Welsh.' While 'constitutionally, the Scottish Parliament will clearly be subordinate … politically, … it will be anything but … The Scotland Act creates a new locus of political power.' Westminster in effect could not take power back from Scotland without an invitation from Scotland to do so. While legally it retains the power to do so, it is inconceivable that it would exercise it without Scotland's consent except in extraordinary circumstances: 'power devolved, far from being power retained, will be power transferred; and it will not be possible to recover that power except under "pathological circumstances." '[58]

How, though, may we reckon whether the transfer of power to a devolved institution, while not transferring *legal* sovereignty, has transferred *political* sovereignty in such a way to count as an example of devolution? One way to differentiate between the level of autonomy enjoyed by devolved institutions versus that enjoyed by local government is by recourse to judicial decisions—in particular, how the courts approach challenges to the exercise of power transferred by Westminster. All bodies exercising power delegated to them by a Westminster statute are subject to the supervisory jurisdiction of the higher courts, exercising their power of judicial review, to ensure that the delegate remains within the bounds of the authority delegated—a point made with perhaps over-zealous clarity by Lord President Rodger in

[56] *Whaley v Watson* [2000] SC 340; [2000] SCLR 279, emphasis added. For further discussion see Barry Winetrobe, 'Scottish Devolved Legislation and the Courts' [2002] *Public Law* 31, 37. Winetrobe's analysis concerns the first case to reach the Judicial Committee of the Privy Council in which an Act of the Scottish Parliament was challenged for vires (an alleged breach of Article 5(1)(e) of the European Convention on Human Rights by the Mental Health (Public Safety and Appeals) (Scotland) Act 1999). The case was *Anderson, Reid and Doherty v Scottish Ministers* (2002) HRLR 6; (2002) UKHRR 1.

[57] See discussion of the constitutional nature of the union between Scotland and England in O Hood Phillips and P Jackson, above n 6, at paras 4–006 to 4–009; and Neil MacCormick 'Does the United Kingdom have a Constitution? Reflections on *MacCormick v Lord Advocate*' (1978) 29 *Northern Ireland Law Quarterly* 1.

[58] See V Bogdanor, above n 11, at 291. Such 'pathological circumstances' have unfortunately been seen in Northern Ireland where, in order to preserve the peace process, devolved government has been suspended by two Secretaries of State for Northern Ireland, exercising their powers under the Northern Ireland Act 2000, three times now.

the quote from *Whaley v Watson*, set out above. However, the grounds upon which a local authority may be judicially reviewed (the classic set of illegality, procedural unfairness, irrationality and now breach of section 6 of the Human Rights Act 1998) are arguably different from those upon which a true devolved authority may be reviewed.[59] A body which is subject to review both for acting outside of the scope of its empowering statute *as well as* being open to challenge on the traditional common law grounds for review, is more likely to be an example of local government, than of devolution. The distinction will become clearer by considering some of the cases which have arisen to date concerning the new institutions.

The Judicial Committee of the Privy Council has so far had one opportunity to consider a challenge to the vires of an Act of the Scottish Parliament. In *Anderson, Reid and Doherty v Scottish Ministers*, the petitioners sought to argue that the first Act of the Scottish Parliament, the Mental Health (Public Safety and Appeals) (Scotland) Act 1999, was incompatible with Article 5(1)(e) of the European Convention on Human Rights and therefore outside of the Parliament's competence.[60] Opening his analysis of the case, Winetrobe addressed the issue of whether Acts of the Scottish Parliament should be reviewable on the ordinary common law grounds (for example, illegality and procedural unfairness), or whether a more narrow approach is appropriate. Under the narrow approach the only ground upon which an Act could be reviewed would be if it contravened one of the specific limitations set out in section 29 of the Scotland Act.[61] Commenting on the decision upholding the impugned Act, Winetrobe notes that 'the Judicial Committee's approach to the reviewability of Scottish legislation appeared implicitly to be tending towards a narrow rather than broad form of scrutiny.'[62]

On 31 July 2002, Lord Nimmo Smith in the Outer House of the Scottish Court of Session decided the most recent case involving a challenge to the vires of an Act of the Scottish Parliament. In *Trevor Adams and others v Advocate General for Scotland and the Scottish Executive*, the petitioners challenged the legality of the Protection of Wild Mammals (Scotland) Act 2002 and its corresponding commencement order.[63] The challenge to the Act (which makes it a criminal offence to hunt foxes on horseback and with dogs) was based both on the ground that it was outside the competence of the Parliament because it interfered with Convention rights, *as well as* on traditional common law grounds that the Act was ultra vires for procedural impropriety and unreasonableness.[64] The case thus pre-

---

[59]   The issue is also discussed by Craig and Walters, above n 19, and by Brigid Hadfield, 'The Foundations of Review, Devolved Power and Delegated Power' in Christopher Forsyth (ed), *Judicial Review and the Constitution* (Oxford, Hart, 2000), 194.

[60]   Above n 56. A summary of the facts of the case, and analysis, may be found in Barry Winetrobe, 'Scottish Devolved Legislation and the Courts' [2002] *Public Law* 31.

[61]   Section 29(1) provides that 'An Act of the Scottish Parliament is not law so far as any provision of the Act is outside the legislative competence of the Parliament' and then goes on to stipulate the circumstances in which a provision would be outside of competence, which include contravening one of the rights provided in the European Convention on Human Rights.

[62]   Above n 60, at 36. The case is on appeal to the Inner House.

[63]   [2003] SLT 366 (OH).

[64]   *Ibid* at para 4.

sented directly the issue of the range of grounds upon which the Scottish Parliament could be challenged. Tellingly, for our purposes, Lord Nimmo Smith's approach was one which, on Winetrobe's analysis, may be characterised as 'narrow'. He said:

> What appears to me to be of significance is that the Scotland Act is clearly intended to provide a comprehensive scheme, not only for the Parliament itself, but also for the relationship between the courts and the Parliament. ... Sections 28, 29, 100, 101, 102 and Schedule 6 [which set out the scope of the Parliament's competence] are definitive of the extent of the court's jurisdiction and of the procedure to be followed when a devolution issue is raised. It *necessarily follows that traditional common law grounds of judicial review are excluded*, and that there is no room for the implication of common law concepts in considering the competence of the Parliament.[65]

Though not a devolution issue in terms of the Northern Ireland Act, we also have the benefit of comments by the Law Lords sitting in the Appellate Committee as to the nature of the Northern Irish devolution scheme in the Northern Irish case of *Robinson v Secretary of State for Northern Ireland*.[66] What is of interest for the purposes of this chapter is not the specific issues in dispute in the case but comments by the Senior Law Lord, Lord Bingham, about how the courts should characterise the Northern Ireland Act, and accordingly, the interpretive approach they should take to it. Lord Bingham indicated that a generous and purposive approach should be adopted, the Northern Ireland Act being 'in effect a constitution,'[67] while Lord Hoffmann characterised the Act as 'a constitution for Northern Ireland framed to create a continuing form of government against the background of the history of the territory and of the principles [of the Belfast Agreement].'[68] These comments illustrate that while the Northern Ireland Act may technically be an ordinary statute, the courts will take note of the political reality that a devolution statute is of a special significance. It is notable that, at least with regard to Northern Ireland and Scotland, there is a common theme developing of regarding Acts establishing the new devolved bodies as of special, constitutional, significance. This approach sets the new institutions apart from traditional local government institutions which remain open to review on all the traditional common law grounds. [69]

The approach of the Administrative Court to an Order of the National Assembly for Wales provides, however, a contrast. It is unnecessary to recite the facts of *R (on the application of South Wales Sea Fisheries Committee) v National Assembly for Wales;*[70] what is significant is that the judge considered the challenge to the Order

---

[65] *Ibid* at para 63, emphasis added.

[66] [2002] UKHL 32, 25 July 2002. The facts in *Robinson*, and an analysis of it are contained in Brigid Hadfield, chapter 6 below.

[67] [2002] UKHL 32, para 11. See also Hadfield in chapter 6, n 51.

[68] *Ibid* at para 25.

[69] While *Kruse v Johnson* [1898] 2 QB 91 did indicate that local government is entitled to some deference in the making of by-laws, it nevertheless indicated that a by-law could still be held invalid for unreasonableness.

[70] [2001] EWHC 1162, QBD; Admin. Ct, 21 Dec 2001.

not just on the basis that the Assembly had acted outside of the scope of its authority under the relevant statute but also whether the Order was invalid on ordinary common law grounds (including for example, failure to take into account relevant considerations when making the Order). It may be of some consequence that the Order in question was adopted rapidly using the 'executive procedure' which allows for:

> The normal requirements of notification or consultation, submission of a draft Order to the Business Committee, consideration of a report from the Legislation Committee, the laying of a draft Order before the Assembly and its approval by a resolution of the Assembly [all to be] disapplied on the basis that they were not 'reasonably practicable'.[71]

In other words, the Order had followed a more 'executive' route, than a 'legislative' one. This is unlikely to be the end of the debate with respect to the Welsh system, and will possibly further encourage the campaign for the Welsh Assembly to have powers more akin to those enjoyed by its Scottish and Northern Irish counterparts.

Also relevant, by way of contrast, are two recent cases involving the Greater London Authority and its Mayor. Both cases involved the application of the ordinary common law grounds of judicial review. The first, *R (on the application of Transport for London) v London Underground Ltd*, involved the Mayor's challenge, via Transport for London, to the public/private partnership (PPP) scheme proposed by central government for the London Underground on the basis that it was directly in conflict with the Mayor's transport strategy; a strategy which the court, in the course of judgment, held was lawful.[72] The case is significant for our purposes for two reasons. First, the entire matter, including consideration of whether the Mayor's transport strategy was lawful, was dealt with on ordinary judicial review principles; there was no suggestion that special weight should be given to the lawfully adopted policy of the elected Mayor. Secondly, from the point of view of devolution it illustrated that while the rhetoric was that the Mayor would have power to decide transport strategy, the manifesto upon which he was elected could not prevail over (lawful) Whitehall policy concerning the London Underground.[73]

The second case involved a direct challenge to a Greater London Authority policy: the congestion charge on vehicles entering designated areas in the heart of London. In *R v Mayor of London, ex parte Westminster City Council and others*, the claimants sought judicial review of the Greater London (Central Zone) Congestion Charging Order 2001.[74] Again, it is not necessary to recite the facts for the

---

[71]   *Ibid* at para 36.

[72]   The PPP scheme will entail the leasing off of track and other infrastructure of the Underground, for periods of approximately 30 years, to three private companies. Operation of the Underground, and underlying title in the infrastructure, will remain with London Underground Ltd (and in due course Transport for London, which is to be the successor public body). See discussion in Ben Pimlott and Nirmala Rao, *Governing London* (Oxford University Press, 2002), ch 7.

[73]   Contrast the position in Scotland, where there has been no question of Westminster or Whitehall seeking to interfere in Scotland's more generous policies on tuition fees for university students, or provision of free long-term care for the elderly.

[74]   [2002] EWHC 2440, QBD; Admin Ct, 31 July 2002. See also Pimlott and Rao, above n 72.

purposes of this argument; what is of significance is that the grounds for challenge advanced once again included traditional common law grounds such as an allegation that the respondent had failed to take into account relevant considerations. The claimants failed, but the case nevertheless illustrates the difference in judicial approach when dealing with local government, as opposed to devolved, power.

The third issue relating to the type of power devolved concerns the issue of fiscal autonomy. Finance is obviously of direct relevance to the amount of autonomy a devolved body will have. A power to make policy will be meaningless if a devolved entity either does not have the funds to implement its policies, or receives funds from central government on the condition that they be spent on priorities stipulated by central government. With the exception of the Scottish Parliament's power to vary income tax in Scotland by +/- 3 per cent, all three devolved administrations are dependent on block transfers from the central UK government for their funds. The devolved administrations do, though, have discretion as to how they spend the money they receive. However, as the sum of money they receive is linked to changes in central government spending in relation to England, the amount of the block grant can go up as well as down as central government reassess its spending priorities in England.[75] There is the potential therefore, not yet realised, for central government to use its control over finance to interfere with desired policy choices of a devolved administration. This would clearly interfere with the basic purpose of transferring decision-making over certain matters, which is at the heart of devolution.

The answer proposed to the third question is that devolution entails the transfer of the ability to act, whether by way of legislative or executive competence (or some combination or variation thereof). Secondly, ideally the devolved institution will be reviewable only on the grounds set out in the statute in which the power is delegated (and not on the general grounds available in judicial review). Finally, the transfer should be accompanied with sufficient fiscal autonomy so that the devolved entity has the freedom to choose between different policies in the subject areas it has responsibility for.

Controlled in What Ways?

Devolved power must, like all power, be to subject to control. We have seen one method of control in the preceding discussion of judicial review of devolved bodies. In addition to judicial review there are three other avenues by which devolved power may be monitored: local democratic accountability; supervision by the UK executive, via the roles provided for the respective Secretaries of State for each of Scotland, Wales and Northern Ireland, and the respective UK law officers, in each

---

[75] Discussion of the operation of the Barnett formula, under which changes in the block grants are calculated, and its potential to restrict the policy autonomy of the devolved administrations can be found in Richard Cornes and Robert Hazell, 'Financing Devolution: the Centre Retains Control' in Robert Hazell (ed), *Constitutional Futures: A History of the Next Ten Years* (Oxford University Press, 1999).

devolution statute;[76] and finally, Westminster, which retains the potential to legislate for each of the devolved areas.

In order for the basic rationale of devolution to be given effect it follows that the
dominant method for controlling, or holding devolved power to account, should
in the first case be the local democratic process. If a devolved assembly pursues a
policy (within its scope of authority as set out in its establishing statute) which its
electorate disapprove of then it should be for that electorate to vote the disap-
proved-of devolved administration out of power. Next comes the potential for
judicial review. As this has been discussed above the only comment that needs to
be made here is that the possibility of judicial review on traditional common law
grounds in addition to exceeding the competence provisions in the establishing
statute, would be an indication (though not a definitive one) that an institution is
better described as an example of local government than devolution.

If the rationale of devolution is not to be thwarted, the other two methods for control, the continued roles of the Secretaries of State (or lower level Ministers within the
Department of Constitutional Affairs) and UK law officers, and Westminster's continuing ability to legislate, should necessarily be used sparingly, if at all. The role of the
UK executive officers must, of course, be considered discretely, taking into account the
particular circumstances of each devolution settlement. At one end of a scale of
involvement would be the Minister responsible for Scotland who, except, for example,
in the (hopefully) exceptionally rare occasion where she might have to exercise her
power under section 35 of the Scotland Act to prevent a Bill receiving Royal Assent,
functions for the most part as London's emissary to the Scottish administration (and
vice versa).[77] In contrast the Minister responsible for Wales has a continuing role as
the primary link to Westminster for the Assembly; a link of particular importance
because of the Assembly's need to obtain primary enabling legislation from Westminster if it wants to make policy in an area not already covered by a primary enabling
Act.[78] At the other end of the scale, and for reasons which will be obvious, the Secretary of State for Northern Ireland retains a crucial role in the governance of that
province, overseeing as he does the implementation of the Belfast Agreement and during periods of suspension of devolved government, resuming direct responsibility for
governing the province.[79] In respect of all three, however, it is clear that their position
is not one of playing a central role in relation to the matters which have been devolved.

---

[76] On the role of the Secretary of State and the courts in relation to Northern Ireland see Brigid
Hadfield, ch 6 below. The apparent transfer of the positions of Secretary of State for Scotland and Wales
respectively to a new Department of Constitutional Affairs, as a result of a Cabinet reshuffle on 12 June
2003, has created some confusion in this area.

[77] Section 35 of the Scotland Act 1998 empowers the Secretary of State for Scotland to prohibit the
Presiding Officer of the Scottish Parliament from presenting a Bill for Royal Assent if she believes its
provisions are incompatible with any international obligation, would raise issues of national defence or
security, or would adversely affect the law as it applies to reserve matters. To date of course we have only
witnessed the interaction of Scottish administrations and Secretaries of State from the same political
party. It will be interesting to observe how, for example, a Conservative government in London relates
to a Labour, or perhaps even Scottish National Party, administration in Scotland.

[78] As noted above (n 24) this is not something the Assembly has, as yet, been particularly successful in
doing.

[79] See discussion in Hadfield, above n 20.

Finally, there is Westminster's continuing power to make legislation in relation to all matters, including devolved subjects. Clearly, this is a power which should not ordinarily be used, for 'to do so would frustrate the purposes of devolution.'[80] A convention has already been established in relation to Scotland that Westminster will not legislate for Scotland without the prior consent of the Scottish Parliament.[81] While Westminster obviously retains a role in relation to Wales, a requirement for consultation by the UK government (via the Minister responsible for Wales), with the Assembly has been elaborated.[82] Northern Ireland, with the exceptions arising from the interaction between devolution and the ongoing peace process, is in a situation similar to Scotland. In relation to all three, however, there is a common thread; Westminster may legislate, except in extraordinary circumstances, only in consultation with the devolved administration.

The answer proposed for question 4 then is that a devolved institution is one which is primarily held to account by its local electorate, with judicial review available preferably on what Winetrobe would characterise as the 'narrow approach,' while the UK executive and Westminster retain only a residual guardian role.

How Established?

This question is straightforward and can be answered briefly. First, as Burrows notes, 'the fundamental principle underlying the entire process of devolution is one of consent.'[83] Accordingly, prior to the adoption of all the schemes to date the consent of the people within the area to receive devolved power has been sought in a referendum. Secondly, matching the consent of the devolved area is the consent of the Westminster Parliament which gives effect to the devolution scheme by passing the necessary statute. The answer to the final question then is that a system of devolved government is one which is sanctioned by a referendum in the area concerned (thus confirming that the area identified is the correct one for the purposes of question 1 above), and establishing the devolved administration's political sovereignty (for the purposes of question 3 above), and put in place by an Act of the Westminster Parliament (confirming, necessarily, Westminster's retention of legal sovereignty).

Summary: a Working Definition of Devolution

To reiterate, what is set out here is not claimed to be an unalterable set of defining characteristics—the flexible nature of the UK constitution militates against that.

---

[80] Bradley and Ewing, above n 33, at 45.

[81] Known as the 'Sewel convention'. Bradley and Ewing report that 'such consent has readily been given since 1999': *ibid* at 45 at their n 63. Noreen Burrows commented critically on the frequency of use of the Sewel Convention in 'Devolution: Lessons from Scotland?', a paper delivered at the 2001 SPTL Annual Conference, 10 Sept 2001. See also Alan Page and Andrea Batey, 'Scotland's Other Parliament: Westminster Legislation About Devolved Matters in Scotland Since Devolution' [2002] *Public Law* 501.

[82] For detail see Burrows, above n 5, at 79–82.

[83] Burrows, above n 5, at 24.

This is simply an exercise in clarifying the defining principles or characteristics of devolution by reference to what has been put in place in Scotland, Wales and Northern Ireland: if a persuasive case is made for amending the defining characteristics, then so be it. In any event, it is not suggested that every example of devolution should meet all the defining characteristics. What is crucial is that any variations should not obviate the fundamental rationale of devolution: the transfer of central government power to governing institutions responsible for distinct geographical areas within the United Kingdom, answerable primarily to their local electorate for decisions in relation to the subject matters devolved.

In summary then the answers to the five questions posed above are as follows. In a devolution scheme, the area to which power is devolved should be one with which the people within it identify (whether on the basis of national or regional identity). The governing institutions to which power is transferred should be (a) locally elected, (b) contain distinct executive and legislative elements, with the (c) legislative element able to scrutinise the activities of the executive element, and desirably, also play a role in policy development. The power transferred should (a) give the devolved institution the ability to act (whether executively, legislatively or via some combination or variation of both); (b) be reviewable (preferably) only for exceeding the terms of the establishing Act (ie not on the wider range of common law grounds of judicial review); and accompanied with sufficient fiscal autonomy for the devolved body to be able to carry out its functions. The primary avenue for the control of the devolved body should be the local democratic process, complemented by judicial review. While the UK executive may retain, via the relevant Secretaries of State, some role, and the Westminster Parliament continues to be sovereign, these powers should not be exercised except (a) at the request of the devolved body (eg pursuant to the Sewel convention), or (b) in the case of Northern Ireland, the need to ensure public order and the continuance of the peace process. Finally, a devolution scheme should be effected by a Westminster statute only after the consent of the area to receive devolved power has been obtained in a referendum.

WHAT IS ENGLAND BEING OFFERED?

Introduction

Prior to the White Paper's proposals, and the Regional Assemblies (Preparations) Act 2003, there were three components to the Government's programme for the decentralisation of power within England. First, in April 1998, pursuant to the Regional Development Act of the same year, eight regional development agencies (RDAs), with boards appointed by the Secretary of State, were established with responsibility for co-ordinating and implementing economic development in

---

[84] The RDAs cover the following regions: the East, East Midlands, North East, North West, South East, South West, West Midlands and Yorkshire and Humberside.

their regions.[84] Next, in London on 6 May 2000, pursuant to the Greater London Authority Act 1999, a new Assembly and Mayor were elected. Finally, the Local Government Act 2000 was passed, allowing local authorities, subject to a local referendum vote in favour, to introduce directly elected mayors (similar to the model already established in London).

Supplementary to those developments, the Government also endorsed the setting up of voluntary regional chambers within England. Under the Regional Development Agencies Act, a voluntary chamber has been designated to work with each region's RDA, acting as a sounding board and providing some level of local scrutiny of the RDA. However, these voluntary chambers, rather than being elected, are made up of 'regional stakeholders,' primarily business people and representatives from unions and the education sector. In March 2001, a fund of £15 million was established by central government in order to strengthen the ability of the eight regional chambers to scrutinise their respective RDAs and thereby 'strengthen regional accountability.'[85]

The latest proposals for devolution in England, contained in the White Paper *Your Region, Your Choice: Revitalising the English Regions* and the Regional Assemblies (Preparations) Act, continue the theme of the regionalisation of England.[86] England's regions are offered what the White Paper refers to as 'assemblies', though these 'assemblies' are already being referred to as Parliaments, or mini-Parliaments. The leader of the Newcastle City Council was reported as saying that it would be a source of pride for the North East if it became the first English region to have a 'parliament.'[87] The *Independent*'s report read, 'England is to get up to eight new mini-parliaments with tax-raising powers.'[88] In the debate following the announcement of the White Paper in the House of Commons, supporters of further regional devolution stated, 'what Scotland has, Yorkshire and Humberside need.'[89] Relevant, however, to our question in this section, ie, whether England is being offered devolution, is the pointed remark of another MP:

> If the benchmark is Scotland and Wales, how on earth does [the Deputy Prime Minister] think that representative democracy, or real accountability, is served by a handful of neither nowt nor summat representatives, representing several hundred thousand electors in tiny assemblies that have no proper link with their electorate?[90]

Replying, the Deputy Prime Minister put the Government's position:

> [Regional devolution in England] is different from what we did in Scotland, Wales or London. ... We are not establishing parliaments in the regions—that is a fundamentally

---

[85] Department of Trade, Local Government and the Regions, *Regional Chambers* at http://www.regions.dtlr.gov.uk/chambers/index.htm

[86] Above n 1.

[87] *Daily Telegraph*, 10 May 2002.

[88] *Independent*, 10 May 2002.

[89] Austin Mitchell, Hansard, HC Deb, 9 May 2002, col 285.

[90] David Curry, Hansard, HC Deb, 9 May 2002, col 285.

[91] John Prescott, Hansard, HC Deb, 9 May 2002, col 285.

different proposition—we are establishing directly elected assemblies.[91]

What then, addressing the five questions suggested in the previous section, are we to make of the White Paper's proposals? Are the Deputy Prime Minister's directly elected assemblies worthy of the title of devolution he implicitly claims for them in the Foreword to the White Paper?

Evaluating the White Paper's Proposals: Is this Devolution?

To What Geographical Area?

Chapter 6 of the White Paper outlines the proposed boundaries for the proposed regional assemblies.[92] The proposals in chapter 6 are confirmed in section 28 of the Regional Assemblies (Preparations) Act 2003. The regional boundaries chosen are inter alia congruent with those of the already established RDAs, and have, according to the White Paper, a 'reasonably high legal of public recognition.'[93] In support of this statement a 1999 *Economist* survey is quoted which:

> Found that in six out of the eight Government Office regions [which match the boundaries proposed for the regional assemblies] outside London over three-quarters of respondents could name the administrative region in which they lived. Only in Yorkshire and the Humber (66 per cent) and the East of England (52 per cent) was the figure below this level.[94]

Accepting that 'it could be argued that there is an important difference between public recognition of a region and public acceptance or allegiance' the White Paper refers to the requirement for a referendum vote in favour of establishing an assembly prior to one being established.[95] With the possible exception of historically distinct areas within the proposed regions (for example Cornwall, which comes within the South-West),[96] the White Paper's proposals may be said to meet the first requirement of devolution, that power be devolved to geographical entities with which people identify.[97]

What Type of Institutions are Proposed?

[92] See above n 84.
[93] Above n 1, at para 6.2, p 49. 'Regions' are defined in section 28 as being the regions '(except London) specified in Schedule 1 to the Regional Development Agencies Act 1998 (c.45).'
[94] *Ibid.*
[95] *Ibid.*
[96] If the scheme proceeds it is to be hoped that the particular concerns of regions such as Cornwall are answered to the satisfaction of their populations. See also discussion in the Standing Committee on Regional Affairs on Governance in England, 18 Dec 2001; and 'Tories reject South West assembly,' BBC News, 12 Dec 2001(http://news.bbc.co.uk/1/hi/england/1706501.stm). For further detail of the local campaign for a Cornish assembly see http://www.senedhkernow.freeuk.com/
[97] It should be noted that publication of the Regional Assemblies (Preparations) Bill prompted the emergence of voices within other sub-regions expressing similar concerns to those of some inhabitants of Cornwall. See 'County "not part of East Midlands"' (concerning Lincolnshire), BBC News, 21 Nov 2002 (http://news.bbc.co.uk/1/hi/england/2498957.stm); and 'MP rejects regional assembly plan' (concerning West Sussex), BBC News, 20 Nov 2002 (http://news.bbc.co.uk/1/hi/england/2496715.stm).

Will They be Locally Elected?   The White Paper proposes that assembly members be elected using an additional member system (AMS) every four years.[98] The majority of an assembly's members will be elected on a first past the post basis from individual constituencies, with the balance being elected on the basis of regional lists. The regional list members will then be allocated to ensure proportionality. A 5 per cent minimum vote in the region will be required before a party is eligible for a list seat—a provision to avoid the assembly membership being fragmented by representatives of minority parties. Apart from providing a measure of proportionality, the system will have the benefit of ensuring regional representation, a particularly important point in regions with distinct sub-regional units such as Cornwall in the South-West. The White Paper proposals may then be said to meet the requirement of local election.

Is There as Assembly/Executive Distinction Within the Institution?   The assemblies will be small, with a minimum of 25 and a maximum of 35 members.[99] The basic split in these new bodies will be between the 'executive' and the 'scrutiny' members. An executive must be provided from the 25 to 35 members. The White Paper proposes that the executive have a maximum membership of six, ie leaving 19 to 29 members to provide the 'scrutiny' function. The 'scrutiny' members will be assigned to scrutiny committees. The number of these is unknown. However, assuming there was just one committee for each of the 10 areas in respect of which an assembly will prepare a strategy,[100] with each committee having five members, an assembly of 50 members would be required if each scrutiny member were to focus on one subject area. Clearly, the 19 to 29 non-executive members are likely, therefore, to have to sit on more then one committee; yet the White Paper indicates that these members are only going to be required to attend, and be paid, for three days a week. So, while there will be a legislative (or rather scrutiny)/executive split within the regional assemblies, the design requirement of 'smallness' is a concern; it may be that there are insufficient 'legislative/scrutiny' members effectively to carry out the tasks they will be given.

A further novelty in democratic design, and possibly one with the potential to detract from the clarity of the assembly/executive demarcation is the continued role of the RDAs. These bodies almost appear to be alternate regional executives. They retain the task of developing the regional plan, although the assemblies may direct that changes be made to the plan prior to it being published.[101] While the RDAs are to retain day-to-day operational independence, they will now answer to the assembly for their performance. The chair and members of the RDAs will be appointed by the assembly and are expected to have business knowledge.[102] Assemblies will provide funding from their own block grants—the extent to which

[98]   Above n1, at para 6.9, p 50.
[99]   Being 'small' is in fact one of the design guidelines (along with, inter alia, being 'democratic') set out in the White Paper, above n 1, at para 7.1, p 52.
[100]   See below n 108.
[101]   See the White Paper, above n 1, at para 4.22, p 38.
[102]   *Ibid* at para 4.22, p 38.

they seek to dictate to the RDA how the money is spent is at their discretion—though notably the Government expresses a preference that the assemblies continue to permit the RDAs budgetary flexibility.

Will the Legislative Element Play a Role in Scrutinising the Executive and in the Formulation of Policy?   The task of scrutinising the executives will rest with both the assembly as a whole and the scrutiny committees. The scrutiny committees are to be the primary forum in which the executives are held to account. The White Paper indicates that the Government intends to give the assemblies some latitude about how they establish and run the scrutiny committees. They may carry out post-event scrutiny, act as a 'sounding board,' or as a source of ideas as policy is developed.[103] Importantly, no executive members will sit on the committees; this should lessen the potential for them to be co-opted by the regional executive.

As with the committees of the Scottish Parliament the scrutiny committees are also expected to play a role in the development of policy.[104] Experience in Scotland suggests, however, that while the scrutiny and policy development role may be combined, the combination of both can be onerous.[105] Recalling comments made above concerning the size of the assemblies, and in particular the proposal that non-executive members will only be paid for three days a week, it is likely that members will find it difficult to perform satisfactorily all of their roles in the time allowed. Accordingly, our overall conclusion in relation to the second question must be that while *prima facie* the structures proposed may be appropriate, the small size of the assemblies may make it difficult for their members effectively to carry out their functions.

What is the Nature of the Power Transferred?

Legislative, Executive, or Both?   The assemblies' primary instrument of policy-making will be their power to promulgate *strategies*. Three levels are proposed: high level targets; strategies concerning specific subject areas; and an overarching regional strategy. First, the assemblies will set high level 'targets' which they will agree with government.[106] These targets will concern, for instance, the region's economic performance. Assemblies will be rewarded by central government for meeting the target with extra funding. Unlike in Scotland, for example, where the Parliament and executive are left to their own devices, receiving an annual block grant to do with as they will (so long as the policies they pursue are within the competencies granted them under the Scotland Act 1998), the English regions will

---

[103]   *Ibid* at para 7.5, pp 52–53.
[104]   *Ibid* at para 7.6, p 53.
[105]   For analysis of how the Scottish Parliament's committees worked in their first year see Barry Winetrobe, *Realising the Vision: a Parliament with a Purpose—An Audit of the First Year of the Scottish Parliament* (London, Constitution Unit, 2001). For a similar analysis of the Northern Ireland Assembly, see Rick Wilford and Robin Wilson, *A Democratic Design? The Political Style of the Northern Ireland Assembly* (London, Constitution Unit, 2001).
[106]   See the White Paper, above n 1, at ch 4 generally and para 4.7, p 35.

have central government sitting over them like a hybrid upper house of review.

In order to achieve their high level targets, the assemblies will have the power to produce a series of 'regional strategies'. These regional strategies are a novel type of instrument in British constitutional law. They are to contain 'detailed plans' indicating how the assembly will achieve its 'high level targets.'[107] The assemblies will be under an obligation to ensure that their strategies, which will cover 10 areas, are consistent with each other; [108] and will be 'encouraged' to achieve this consistency by producing 'an "overarching" strategy setting out their vision for the region and their key priorities on the range of issues for which they have responsibility.'[109] Presumably their 'vision for the region' will either be, or encompass, the 'key objectives' for the region contained in the 'high level targets' agreed with central government. Finally, the White Paper stresses the government's desire that the 'regional vision' represent a 'shared goal' and, in order for that to be achieved, indicates that assemblies will be expected to consult and work with a wide range of community groups in formulating both the overarching and individual strategies.[110]

Until the Bill setting out the detailed constitution of the proposed assemblies is produced, subsequent to the first regional referendum in favour of an assembly, it is not possible to provide any deeper evaluation of the 'strategies' which assemblies will produce. Care will be needed to ensure that the three different levels of strategies work well together; there is the potential for the proposed scheme to be overly complex.[111]

On What Basis Will the Institution be Reviewable? Given the similarity of the instruments proposed for the regional assemblies to those produced by the Greater London Authority, and possibly also to the instruments produced by the National Assembly for Wales, it is likely that the assemblies' strategies will be open to review not only on the basis of exceeding the powers of their statute, but also the full range of traditional common law grounds. However, it will not be possible to be any more certain about the answer to this question until a Bill to implement a regional assembly is published: the White Paper simply does not contain enough detail on this point.

Will the Institution have Sufficient Fiscal Autonomy? The area of expenditure is another area where there is ambivalence about the degree of power to be devolved. On the positive side, assemblies will receive their money in a block grant, which

---

[107] *Ibid* at para 4.8, p 35.

[108] *Ibid* at box 4.1, p 36: sustainable development; economic development; skills and employment; spatial planning; transport; waste; housing; health improvement; culture (and tourism); biodiversity. Annex D to the White Paper provides details of the regional strategies currently prepared by a range of bodies (including the RDAs, voluntary chambers, and relevant government office for a region) for each region.

[109] *Ibid* at para 4.11, p 35.

[110] *Ibid* at para 4.13, p 36.

[111] As experience in Wales indicates, an overly complex scheme is likely to draw adverse comment. See above n 23.

they will be at liberty to spend as they see best. However, the White Paper indicates that in return the government will 'expect each assembly to help achieve in their region a small number—perhaps six to ten—of targets agreed with the Government.'[112] The means by which an assembly meets its targets will be left to each assembly. However, those assemblies which meet their targets will be rewarded with extra money. No such mechanism for central government to influence the policies of a devolved institution is provided in any of the three established devolution schemes.

The assemblies will be able to supplement their grant income by a precept on council tax; a power also enjoyed by the Greater London Authority. This discretion is to be guided by the government's policy that 'we expect council tax payers (non-domestic rates and business taxes are outside assemblies' powers) in any region with an elected assembly to contribute the equivalent of around five pence a week for a Band D council tax payer.'[113] There is yet another super-scrutiny provision included, for the initial period, there will be a capping system on the precepts similar to that used vis-à-vis local authorities. [114] Finally, in what Sandford describes as an 'innovative' move, the assemblies will have the power to borrow (subject however to Treasury approval) in order to fund capital expenditure, as well as a temporary borrowing power for cash management purposes.[115] The White Paper appears therefore to promise a reasonable degree of fiscal autonomy. The two drawbacks, the incentive scheme for meeting targets agreed with central government, and the capping provisions, are relevant when considering question 4, to which we now turn.

Will the Primary Means of Oversight/Control be the Local Democratic Process?

The degree of central control allowed for in the White Paper is one of the most significant weaknesses of the Government's proposals. The proposed assemblies will be undermined in two respects: first, by provisions detracting from an assembly's ability to function as a devolved institution, and secondly, by provisions allowing for continued direct control (or interference) by Whitehall departments.

Provisions of the first sort include: the possibility for tension between the elected executive and their RDAs; the size of the assemblies, discussed above in terms of the assembly/executive division (there may simply be too few members to run an effective institution); and the proposal that non-executive members only be paid for three days a week (discussed above as regards scrutinising the executive: if these members are to sit on more than one committee, perform scrutiny and policy making functions, three days is likely to be insufficient).

Provisions of the second sort include: the suggestion that central government

---

[112]   *Ibid* at para 5.3, p 44.

[113]   Above n 1, at para 5.8, p 46.

[114]   Compare the development through the nineteenth century of central government's control over local government in Martin Loughlin, *Legality and Locality: The Role of Law in Central-Local Government* (Oxford University Press, 1996).

[115]   See the White Paper, above n 1, at para 5.10, p 46; Sandford, above n 53 para 42, p 17.

will monitor the directions assemblies give their RDA as to how the RDA allocates its budget;[116] the requirement that the assemblies agree their high level targets with central government;[117] the requirement that assemblies consult central government concerning the detail of their regional economic strategy, including the power for central government to require changes in the strategy—either to comply with 'national priorities', or if central government considers it likely that the strategy could have a detrimental effect on areas outside the region;[118] the requirement that assemblies consult central government on individual appointments to their local RDA;[119] the funding arrangements which allow for assemblies to be rewarded for meeting targets agreed with central government;[120] and the presence of a capping system, similar to that used in respect of local government.[121]

The combined effect of these factors will result in assemblies which, unlike those in Scotland, Wales and Northern Ireland, are much more subject to continued, and potentially intrusive, scrutiny by Whitehall civil servants. This, together with the likelihood that the assemblies will be reviewable on the same bases as the National Assembly for Wales and the Greater London Authority, is the most serious flaw in the proposals.

Will the Process Proceed with the Consent of the People in the Area Concerned?

The process suggested for devolution to the English regions may be said, with one caveat, to meet this requirement.[122] A devolution scheme will not be prepared for a region unless there is interest in the region.[123] Once a region has been assessed as interested in regional government, detailed proposals for the reorganisation of local government within the region to achieve a unitary system will be prepared.[124] A referendum on the following question will then be held: 'Should there be an elected assembly for the *(insert name of region)* region?'[125] If there is a majority in favour of a regional assembly then a second Bill will be prepared which will set out the detailed provisions for establishing the assembly.[126]

A caveat has already been raised in discussion under question 1 above concerning the position of areas like Cornwall which have a strong identity distinct from that of the region within which they lie. There is an argument that proceeding to hold a referendum in which such a 'sub-region' was effectively outvoted by a majority from the rest of the region as a whole would breach what Burrows refers

[116] See discussion above regarding 'what is the nature of the power transferred?'
[117] See discussion above n 106 and accompanying text.
[118] See the White Paper, above n 1, at para 4.34, p 38.
[119] *Ibid.*
[120] See above at p 100.
[121] See above n 114 and accompanying text.
[122] For the implementation process see the White Paper, above n 1, at ch 9, p 63.
[123] Above n 1, at paras 9.1 and 9.3, p 63 and the Regional Assemblies (Preparations) Act 2003, s 1.
[124] Regional Assemblies (Preparations) Act 2003, Pt 2.
[125] *Ibid* at s 3(1).
[126] See the press release which accompanied the Bill, above n 3. The Government appears to contemplate one empowering statute under which all the assemblies would be established after a positive referendum vote (above n 1, at para 9.12, p 67).

to as the fundamental principle of consent. It may be that in relation to areas such as Cornwall either a special consultation process is required or that they should even be offered an assembly of their own.

Summary: Does the White Paper Offer England Devolution?

The Government claims its aim is to 'strengthen England by empowering the regions' and that regional government does not mark the break-up of England. [127] The claim made in the Foreword to the White Paper (see the introduction to this chapter) is that the proposals for England can be seen as the next stage in the devolution process. They cannot. The White Paper's proposals, especially in their desire to allow Whitehall a significant continuing role even after the establishment of the regional assemblies, can more appropriately be characterised as the next step in English local government reform, not the next step in the devolution process (at least measured against the standards set so far for that process). [128]

The White Paper proposals may introduce a valuable layer of regional government within England, but the regional assemblies cannot be classed as devolved institutions alongside the new Parliament in Scotland, or the Assemblies in Wales and Northern Ireland. Though meeting certain of the defining principles, the proposals are simply too weak in key respects to justify the label of 'devolution': too little power is effectively devolved, and too much central control is retained. Altering the defining principles set out above to encompass what is proposed for England would, I suggest, result in the watering down of the fundamental principle of devolution (ie the transfer of power) to such an extent as to rob the term and the process of any significance.

CONCLUSION: COULD THE ENGLISH QUESTION BY ANSWERED BY ADDRESSING THE UNION QUESTION?

While not amounting to devolution, does the White Paper nevertheless have the potential to solve the English Question? Traditionally, answers to the English Question fall into one of two classes. The first class involves suggestions for some form of English Parliament and the full federalisation of the United Kingdom. The compelling argument against this solution is simply that a federation in which one part, England, would contain nine-elevenths of the population would be unworkable; as MacCormick points out, 'federal government presumes some equilibrium between the federated units, and a reasonable balance that can be struck between

---

[127]   *Ibid* at para 8.2, p 58.
[128]   The provisions in Pt 2 of the Regional Assemblies (Preparations) Act which provide for the reform of regional local government into a unitary form, prior to a regional assembly being established, could be seen (at least by the cynical) to support such a characterisation. See also 'Testing times for regional assemblies', *Economist*, 21 June 2002, 340.

central government and state governments.'[129] The other class of answers itself falls into two further classes: first, the regionalisation of England; and secondly, alterations to the Westminster Parliament itself, to create within it distinct forums and procedures for dealing with matters which concern only England.[130]

The White Paper seeks to address the English Question via the regionalisation of England. However, accepting that the heart of the English Question is an objection to the continued involvement by Scottish, Welsh and Northern Irish members of Parliament in the making of legislation for England, the regional structures proposed cannot be a sufficient answer—for England will continue to depend on Westminster as its sole de facto legislature, and nothing in the White Paper alters this.[131] The only way this strategy could work is if the English regions were given devolved institutions along the lines of those in Scotland and Northern Ireland, with the ability to pass their own primary devolved legislation.[132] Yet as MacCormick points out, this would necessarily require the 'regional sub-division of the English common law', which no one is seriously likely to suggest given the obvious complexities it would entail.[133] Furthermore, there is an argument that pursuing the regionalisation of England in such a way that Scotland lost its distinctive position as one of the founding nations of the Union, becoming instead comparable to an English region, would be so unpopular in Scotland as to itself destabilise the Union.[134]

The solution to the English Question, it is suggested, lies not in considering the relationship of the English regions to the Union, or tinkering with Westminster's procedures to provide distinct methods for dealing with English matters, but in addressing directly the relationship of England as a national whole, to Scotland, Wales and Northern Ireland—ie, by asking the Union Question. The White Paper's answer to the English Question—along with the other answers commonly proposed—all have one thing in common, a concern to manage the natural dominance of England within the Union. The politics of devolution (from the nineteenth century onwards) is marked by a continuing search for new strategies to balance this dominance with the historical fact that the United Kingdom was formed by the union (though on varying terms) of distinct nations. This is also illustrated in the tension between the strict legal definition (in English constitu-

---

[129] Above n 10, at 195. See also Hazell who argues that such a federal settlement would be 'grotesquely over-balanced': above n 6, at 8.

[130] For discussion of these strategies, which will not be discussed further here, see Hazell, *ibid* at 10–21; and Brigid Hadfield, 'Towards an English Constitution', above n 35.

[131] Westminster's continuing English role is specifically noted in the White Paper, above n 1, at para 8.11, pp 59–60. At least in relation to Welsh primary legislation (also made by Westminster) the Welsh Assembly has an accepted role (see above n 82)—no comparable co-operative relationship appears to be contemplated for the proposed English regional assemblies.

[132] The complexities and problems of the Welsh Assembly (including, significantly, its lack of devolved primary legislative competence) do not make it a recommendable model for the English regions. Further, as noted above, it seems likely that its inadequacies may in any event prompt the evolution of the Welsh system into one more like those in Scotland and Northern Ireland. This is the policy at least of the Welsh Liberal Democrats and the Welsh Nationalist Party, Plaid Cymru.

[133] Above n 10, at 194.

[134] *Ibid.*

tional law)[135] of the United Kingdom as a *unitary* state, as opposed to the political science characterisation of the United Kingdom as a *union* state.[136] We end then with the suggestion of reformulating the Union so that the constituent parts of the United Kingdom become individual (though co-operating) members of the European Union. Such a reformulation would not necessarily need to mark the complete end of the Union within the British Isles: as MacCormick notes, it would be prudent, drawing on the example set by the co-operation between the Nordic countries in the Nordic Council, to build on the structure provided by the Council of the Isles (arising from the Belfast Agreement of 1998) to create new Union institutions which 'would [help to] maintain community in policy and … [harmonise] aspects of law among the various parts of this archipelago once (or if) they became mutually independent member states of the European Union.'[137] In such a scenario the European Union would in effect be used as the counterweight to England's dominant position within the reformulated United Kingdom; while the new co-ordinating institutions, linking the nations currently bound together in the United Kingdom, could preserve the collective strength of the new Union's members within the wider European Commonwealth. Clearly further work will need to be carried out to provide the detail of how such a reformulation would be carried out, and what the governing institutions of the new Union and its members would be. That will however have to await another time.[138] Whatever path for the future is chosen, however, the aim should be making the Union (in whatever form) a collective exercise of the will of all the people who live within it.

---

[135]   The term 'English constitutional law' is used deliberately: Scottish constitutional lawyers may, as noted above, n 57, have a different perspective on this point.

[136]   See Burrows, above n 5, at 189–92; MacCormick, above n 10, at chs 4 and 5; Michael Keating *Plurinational Democracy: Stateless Nations in a Post-Sovereignty Era* (Oxford University Press, 2001); Michael Keating, 'So Many Nations, So Few States: Territory and Nationalism in the Global Era' in Alain-G Gagnon and James Tully (eds), *Multinational Democracies* (Cambridge University Press, 2001); and more generally, Stein Rokkan and Derek Urwin *Economy, Territory: Identity. Politics of Western European Peripheries* (London, Sage, 1983).

[137]   Above n 10, at 197.

[138]   MacCormick has begun to sketch out some of the issues:above n 10, at 199–204; as has Michael Keating in 'Beyond Sovereignty: Nations in the European Commonwealth', ch 5 in his *Plurinational Democracy: Stateless Nations in a Post-Sovereignty Era*, above n 136. See also Arthur Aughey, *Nationalism, Devolution and the Challenge to the United Kingdom State* (London, Pluto Press, 2001).

6

Does the Devolved Northern Ireland Need an Independent Judicial Arbiter?

BRIGID HADFIELD

INTRODUCTION

W ITHIN THE BROAD theme of public law in a multi-layered United Kingdom a clearly crucial issue entails the non-static nature and extent of the constitutional discreteness of each layer. If devolution is a new layer or tier of public power brought into the constitution through the coming into force of the Scotland, Northern Ireland and Government of Wales Acts 1998, it becomes important to identify not only the politico-constitutional consequences of the interposition of that layer but also the custodians of its constitutional integrity. In terms of constitutions which divide power on a territorial basis, devolution is most readily compared with federalism. It is relatively easy to identify the key characteristics of devolution and to contrast them with federalism, although this is not to suggest that either is a rigid and uniform construct.

In a federal system, power is allocated by an overarching written constitution, the sole legal source of central and provincial power; in the devolved United Kingdom, the Westminster Parliament is and remains sovereign and is itself the source of devolved authority. In a federal system, the written constitution is amendable only through a formula which involves both central and provincial authorities; in the devolved United Kingdom, the Westminster Parliament alone possesses the power to amend (indeed even repeal) the devolution Acts. In a federal system, the central and provincial powers are of co-ordinate status (allowing for a mixture of independence and interdependence), each possessing areas of exclusive competence; in the devolved United Kingdom, the Westminster Parliament has, but the devolved legislatures do not have, exclusive legislative competence. In terms of layers of governance, the relationships in devolution are most clearly those of the legally superordinate and its subordinate rather than of co-ordinate levels of power. The key characteristics of devolution, however, permit its modification or reinforcement by a variety of different means in varying political contexts. There may be a (flexible) understanding that the Westminster Parliament will not legislate in the devolved domain without the consent of the relevant legislature; the West-minster Parliament may itself legislate on an ad hoc basis to expand or restrict the devolved legislative competence; a combination of political factors and (lack of) inter- governmental co-operation may impact upon the exercise of a Westminster reserve power which may become either a bludgeon or atrophied. The focus of this chapter, however, will be specifically on a consideration of the varying perceptions of the judicial role within the different patterns of devolution in Northern Ireland. Consideration will be given to those powers which directly, or indirectly (by con-ferring a power itself subject to judicial review), the Westminster Parliament has conferred upon the judges as well as to specific 'devolution issues'. Also, detailed consideration will be given to the decision in *Robinson v Secretary of State for Northern Ireland*, which at its heart involves the power of the Secretary of State for Northern Ireland (not) to bring forward the scheduled date for elections to the devolved Assembly in a significant exercise of power, not least in the context of ownership of the devolved constitution and its evolution.

DEVOLUTION AND THE JUDGES: EARLIER VERSIONS

From one point of view, the expectations and the reality of the judicial role were in general terms so different during the first six or seven decades of the last century that extrapolations from them or comparisons with judicial attitudes to devolu-tion now are at best of limited value. The sea-change wrought by an active judicial review jurisdiction, the jurisprudence of the European Courts of Justice and of Human Rights, the presence of legal aid, the relaxation of the Kilmuir Rules and the higher media profile of the judiciary cannot be underestimated. As against that, to consider the two earlier schemes of devolution which operated in North-ern Ireland, one for 50 years, one for four to five months, should serve to illustrate not only the range of possibilities open to the Westminster Parliament but also the consequences for the operation of devolution which flow from a limited judicial role, whether it be de facto or de jure.

The Government of Ireland Act 1920 incorporated a similar but not totally identical pattern of devolving powers to the Northern Ireland Parliament as was followed in the 1998 Acts for both Scotland and Northern Ireland. Certain matters were withheld from it and reserved to the Westminster Parliament but this was coupled with an otherwise general grant of legislative power to the Northern Ire-land Parliament. Following the then colonial or imperial grant of power, the Northern Ireland Parliament was given the power to legislate for the 'peace, order and good government' of Northern Ireland subject to the matters excepted (and reserved) from it. That Parliament was also precluded from legislating in a way (initially) which had particular effects, for example, interfered with religious equality or entailed the taking of property without compensation. The 1920 Act provided no test to guide the courts with regard to any vires questions which might have arisen concerning the validity of Northern Ireland legislation, although section 50 of the Act sought to ensure that such questions could be heard (after a court of first instance) by the Northern Ireland Court of Appeal. Under the 1920 Act, the main way in which such questions would arise was to be in inter partes legal proceedings after the enactment of the piece of legislation in question. Section 51 of the Act, however, did make special provision for—in the famous words of its side-note—'decision of constitutional questions'. In brief, where it appeared to the Governor or a (Westminster) Secretary of State 'to be expedient in the public interest that steps shall be taken for the speedy determination' of the validity of a (provision in a) Bill or Act of the Northern Ireland Parliament, or whether any service was a transferred service under the Act, the Governor or Secretary of State could request the Sovereign in Council to refer the question to the Judicial Committee of the Privy Council. This power was without prejudice to the power of the Sovereign in Council to refer questions to the Judicial Committee under section 4 of the Judicial Committee Act 1833, which provides that:

> it shall be lawful for His Majesty to refer to the … Judicial Committee for hearing or consideration any such … matters whatsoever as His Majesty shall think fit.[1]

Under section 51(2) of the 1920 Act, the Judicial Committee was empowered on the hearing of the question to permit 'such persons as appear [to it] to be interested' to appear and be heard as parties to the case.

It is essentially otiose to rehearse in this context the details of the two central cases from this era, *Gallagher v Lynn*[2] and (the sole case actually to be decided under section 51) *In re section 3 of the Finance Act (Northern Ireland) 1934*[3] (usually known as the *Education Levy* case). The two issues arising from these cases which are relevant to the theme of this chapter are: (1) the location of the power to make a reference to the Judicial Committee and (2) the principles, if any, articulated by the courts in their resolution of the *vires* questions at issue in these cases.

Section 51 specifically located the power to request a reference to the Judicial Committee in the Governor or a Secretary of State (effectively the Home Secretary) in a subjective grant of power which, at that time and in the context of the personnel empowered, would not have rendered it susceptible to judicial review. Section 51, however, was silent as to who, if anyone, could request the specified parties to make the requisite request to the Sovereign in Council and, more specifically, whether section 51 could be utilised with regard to inter partes proceedings capable of resolution by the Northern Ireland courts. Sir Arthur Quekett in his classic and invaluable commentary on the 1920 Act wrote:

> It may, however, be assumed that neither a Governor nor a Secretary of State would exercise his discretion of making a representation to His Majesty in Council in such a way as

---

[1] This power was exercised in two important NI cases, namely, *In the matter of the reference as to the [Boundary Commission] under Article 12 of the Schedule to the Irish Free State Agreement Act 1922* (provided in full in Sir Arthur Quekett, *The Constitution of Northern Ireland* (1933), vol 1, 170–75), and *In re MacManaway* [1951] AC 161 concerning the application of the House of Commons (Clergy Disqualification) Act 1801 to clergy in the (Anglican) Church of Ireland.

[2] [1937] AC 863.

[3] [1936] AC 352.

to conflict with, or oust, the jurisdiction of the Northern Ireland Courts in a litigation *inter partes.*[4]

Although other petitions were addressed to the Governor and Home Secretary to exercise their powers under section 51, all bar that in the *Education Levy* case were unsuccessful, including a request made in the course of the various proceedings resolved by the House of Lords in *Gallagher v Lynn.*[5] In the *Education Levy* case, Belfast Corporation asked the Governor who asked the Home Secretary who asked the King in Council to refer the validity of section 3 of the Finance Act (Northern Ireland) 1934 to the Judicial Committee. Given the silence of the 1920 Act on procedural matters, the Judicial Committee had first to resolve certain preliminary questions, including who would be regarded as the appellants (Belfast Corporation) and as the respondents (the Northern Ireland Government). The opinion of the Judicial Committee is brief. The issue was resolved in favour of the validity of the Act, for, as explained by Lord Thankerton:

> Such an examination as counsel for the Corporation invited their Lordships to enter upon would tend to narrow the legislative powers of taxation of the Parliament of Northern Ireland almost to vanishing point whereas (by section 21(1) of the 1920 Act) legislative powers are conferred in general terms, subject only to specified exceptions.[6]

Section 53 of the Act provided that decisions of the Judicial Committee (on which no specific provision was made for Northern Ireland judges to sit) on legislative vires and other questions referred to it under the Act 'shall be final and conclusive and binding on all courts.' Given the then jurisprudence, this included the Judicial Committee itself.

The decision in the *Education Levy* case was reinforced by the equally brief decision of the House of Lords in *Gallagher v Lynn*. The unsuccessful challenge to the validity of an Act of the Northern Ireland Parliament arose collaterally in the course of criminal proceedings taken under the Act. Equating the allocation of powers between Westminster and Northern Ireland under the 1920 Act with those in a federal constitution, Lord Atkin (giving the decision of the House) employed the Canadian 'pith and substance test'—(wrongly) upholding the validity of the Act.[7] Hence an Act which had impacted on the excepted domain of cross-border trade in milk was judicially saved because its pith and substance was ascertained solely from the provisions of the Act (and by counsel's concession) as being to regulate the health of the people of Northern Ireland by ensuring quality control over its milk supply. The pith and substance test was in fact more complex than it might at first sight appear (and would be rendered more so in the post *Pepper v Hart*[8] era). Its prime meaning is that incidental effects in a precluded domain do not

---

[4] See Sir Arthur Quekett, *The Constitution of Northern Ireland* (1946), vol 3, 53.

[5] *Ibid* at 52, n 1.

[6] [1936] AC 352 at 358–59.

[7] See H Calvert, 'Gallagher v Lynn Re-examined: A Legislative Fraud' [1972] *Public Law* 11.

[8] [1993] AC 593. See also Further Memorandum to the Joint Select Committee on Parliamentary Privilege by Professor Anthony Bradley (1998–99, HL 43-III, HC 214-III).

invalidate the Act if it otherwise in substance falls in the permitted area. Lord Atkin, however, somewhat unhelpfully went on to state:

> The legislation must not under the guise of dealing with one matter *in fact* encroach upon the forbidden field. Nor are you to look only at the object of the legislator. An Act may have a perfectly lawful object … but may seek to achieve that object by invalid methods.[9]

The pith and substance test consequently is or becomes a test which is capable of expanding or contracting devolved legislative power depending on judicial choice. It is a test which, in the words of one eminent judge, 'lends itself to emphatic asseveration, but it provides but little illumination.'[10] The later case of *R (Hume) v Londonderry Justices*[11] has a bearing on this. The case was decided in February 1972, the start of the worst year of the Northern Ireland 'Troubles,' a month after Bloody Sunday and a month before the Northern Ireland Parliament was prorogued never to be restored. The issue in *Hume* concerned the validity of a piece of Northern Ireland delegated legislation extending certain law and order powers already (lawfully) vested in the police to certain members of the armed forces of the Crown. It was outside devolved power to make a law in respect of the armed forces. As Lowry LCJ held, the conferment of the power on the army was not an incidental effect of legislating for the peace and order of Northern Ireland but rather the achievement of a lawful object by unlawful methods. This he contrasted with the facts in *Gallagher* where the lawful object (health) was sought to be obtained by lawful methods (a licensed control of the milk supply) rather than unlawful (a direct ban on the cross-border trade in milk). That is, in *Hume* but not in *Gallagher* the impugned provision was expressly directed to the precluded power. The ruling of invalidity in *Hume* was immediately rectified by a retrospective Act of the Westminster Parliament—and later, as will be seen, had an impact on the provisions in the Northern Ireland Constitution Act 1973. In both *Gallagher* and *Hume*, however, it could be argued that the test of 'in fact encroaching', articulated in *Gallagher* itself, was satisfied, whatever the 'guise' of the legislation. On the other hand, the test of factual encroachment was itself somewhat unhelpful, not necessarily per se but certainly when placed in the amorphous pith and substance context. Interestingly, in a Canadian case (*Shannon*)[12] after *Gallagher* and involving the validity of a British Columbian Act, Lord Atkin adverted to this part of the test whilst at the same time (wrongly) seeking to lock the judicial approach to the Northern Ireland constitutional structures into the federal context. Lord Atkin said:

> The appellants did not dispute that there was a *bona fide* intention by the Province to confine itself to its own sphere, but they contended that, whatever the intention, the

---

[9] [1937] AC 863 at p. 870.
[10] Latham CJ in *Bank of New South Wales v The Commonwealth* 76 CLR (1947–1948) 1 at 185. Quoted by Lowry LCJ in *R (Hume) v Londonderry Justices* [1972] NI 91 at 110.
[11] [1972] NI 91.
[12] *Shannon and others v Lower Mainland Dairy Products Board (A-G for British Columbia intervening)* [1938] AC 708 (JC). See Quekett, above n 4, at 37.

Province had in fact encroached upon the [Federal] sphere. If they could have established that contention, they would have been in a stronger position. *In this respect* their Lordships desire to quote a passage from the opinion of Lord Atkin in the House of Lords in *Gallagher v Lynn* which … *it will be convenient to bring into the line of authority on constitutional cases arising in the Dominions.*[13]

Lord Atkin then quoted his key passage from *Gallagher* addressed above and immediately concluded on the British Columbian Act:

The pith and substance of this Act is that it is an Act to regulate businesses entirely within the Province and it is therefore *intra vires* of the Province.[14]

In terms of seeking to answer the question asked as the chapter title (and to extrapolate in part from this brief historical excursus), what evaluation may be made of the role of the judges under the Government of Ireland Act 1920? The obvious conclusion relates to the air of judicial detachment manifested not least in their failure to engage with the nature of devolved (cf federal) power. Of course, given that judges can only deal with cases actually brought before them, it is also true to state that this detachment was not their sole responsibility, except in so far as blame may be attached to them for the then quiescent era of what we now call judicial review. What it is important to note in this regard, however, is not solely that the courts failed to engage fully with devolved power but that they failed to engage at all with Westminster's reserve powers. The Westminster Parliament may be sovereign, the Westminster government is not, but the wording and the location of the referral power under section 51 made it (like other reserve powers) an effective dead letter. This, in turn, relates to other factors which impinge directly on the judicial role, for judicial attitudes are but one factor in any evaluation of the judicial contribution. In brief, successive Westminster governments regarded the devolved Northern Ireland as apart from, rather than a part of, the United Kingdom. There was relatively little intergovernmental political engagement and, like a province in a federation, the Northern Ireland Parliament was 'mistress in her own house.' Coupled with this external 'light touch' was the absence internally of patterns of accountability. Given the politico-religious balance of the Northern Ireland population, the voting patterns and the electoral system used, the Northern Ireland Parliament was not, in any politically real sense, answerable to the electorate, and the devolved government effectively had no opposition in the Parliament. Thus instead of patterns of political and judicial accountability—the triangle of power shared between the courts, the Westminster government and the devolved institutions, balanced on the doctrine of parliamentary sovereignty—there were patterns of detachment or disengagement. These patterns left as dominant, within and with regard to devolution in Northern Ireland, the Northern Ireland Parliament, particularly the government itself. There are two points to be made in this regard. One is the inevitable one peculiar to Northern Ireland and

---

[13]   [1938] AC 708 at 719 (emphasis added).
[14]   [1938] AC 708 at 720.

may be termed the arguments on abuse of a dominant position, involving the various political and civil libertarian critiques made of the exercise of its power in the absence of (any) countervailing factors. There is, however, a more general point to be made. The presence of one overdominant player in the field—whatever that player is—stymies the fulfilment of devolution's most basic rationale. That may be stated to be the preservation of the United Kingdom (whose constitution may itself, at least in time past, have been stunted by the unalloyed doctrine of parliamentary sovereignty) and the concomitant provision of elected regional-national control over regional-national affairs. It is also submitted that an inherent element of this must be that the responsibility for the evolution of devolution should lie primarily with the elected devolved institutions but only as operating within the matrix of the triangle of accountability. Northern Ireland well illustrates the reworded dictum of John Donne: 'No constitution is an island, entire of itself'. The need for the impetus for change to lie primarily with the devolved region or nation is reinforced by the extent to which the devolved constitution may be regarded as autochthonous. This may be indicated by the holding of a referendum or the resolutions of a constitutional convention but its absence to any significant extent will clearly enhance central government power.

The point above about the dangers to devolution of any one institution being or becoming dominant is further illustrated by the provisions of the Northern Ireland Constitution Act 1973 which provided for a system of legislative devolution which operated in Northern Ireland for the first five months of 1974. What is interesting about the 1973 Act is its often unremarked but remarkable desire significantly (if not completely) to oust the jurisdiction of the courts in all but anti-discrimination cases.[15] This was coupled with provisions in the Act establishing a crucial role for the (new office of) Secretary of State for Northern Ireland and what may be termed not widespread (and indeed diminishing) support within Northern Ireland for the devolved institutions (either per se or in the context of the projected Council of Ireland), a factor which, when conjoined with a very high incidence of civil unrest, was hardly conducive to the stability of the devolved institutions. Given, however, that the Westminster government at the least hoped that this form of devolution would last, what was the rationale of its attempt to exclude the courts—or, as it were, to regard all devolution issues (bar ones involving anti-discrimination) as ones to be resolved solely in the political and not in the judicial sphere? It should first be remembered that at this stage (1973–1974) the impact on the United Kingdom's legal system of the jurisprudence of the European Courts of Justice and of Human Rights was in its early stages. Certainly the classic cases of the 1960s had reactivated the substance of judicial review—and the 1973 Act's provisions must be read in their light—but the then procedures were restrictive of its availability.

---

[15] For a consideration of those cases which did arise under the anti-discrimination provisions of the Constitution Act (see now the Northern Ireland Act 1998, s 76), see B Hadfield, 'The Northern Ireland Constitution Act 1973: Lessons for Minority Rights' in P Cumper and S Wheatley, *Minority Rights in the 'New' Europe* (1999), 129–46.

In brief: the 1973 Act provided for a Northern Ireland Assembly (elected by proportional representation) and a power-sharing executive to which were to be devolved all legislative and executive power other than matters reserved to Westminster and also those permanently excepted from the Assembly's competence. Reserved matters, which included law and order, were potentially within the Assembly's legislative competence but only with the consent of the Secretary of State for Northern Ireland and of the Westminster Parliament. They otherwise remained the responsibility of the Westminster Parliament. Excepted matters (for example, those of national concern and those which when previously devolved had caused division in Northern Ireland) were absolutely withheld from the Assembly unless and only unless the legislative provision in question was ancillary to a devolved matter. Section 5(7) defined 'ancillary' narrowly (more narrowly arguably than its application in *Gallagher v Lynn*) as meaning

> necessary or expedient in making [the devolved provision] effective or which provides for the enforcement of those other provisions or which is otherwise incidental to, or consequential on, those provisions.

Sections 17 (and 19) of the Act provided that the Assembly could not legislate (nor the executive lawfully take any action) in a way that discriminated 'against any person or class of persons on the ground of religious belief or political opinion.'

Combined with a consent power with regard to reserved and indeed ancillary-excepted matters,[16] the Secretary of State by section 18 (the equivalent in some respects to section 51 of the 1920 Act) was empowered to refer the validity of an Assembly Measure, proposed or enacted, to the Judicial Committee of the Privy Council on the grounds of it being void under section 17 (and only under section 17). The key similarities between section 17 (1973 Act) and section 51 (1920 Act) are to be found in the terms of the grant of power—'appears', 'expedient in the public interest' and 'speedy' decision or determination—and in the location of the power in the political office of a Westminster Secretary of State. The key difference is that section 51 incorporated *any* vires question concerning the Northern Ireland Parliament under the 1920 Act. By contrast, section 4(5) of the 1973 Act expressly stated:

> It is hereby declared for the avoidance of doubt that a Measure is *not invalid* by reason of any failure to comply with the provisions of section 5, 6, 14 or 18(2), (5) or (6) … and *no act or omission under any of those provisions shall be called in question in any legal proceedings* (emphasis added).

Section 5 related to the Secretary of State's consent for Assembly legislation on reserved and excepted-ancillary matters, section 6 to the requisite Parliamentary consent in these regards; section 14 related to the proceedings required in the Assembly on certain financial Measures; and section 18(2), (5) and (6) to aspects of the Judicial Committee referral procedure in the context of a provision in a *proposed* Assembly Measure.

---

[16] Constitution Act 1973, s 5.

The role of the courts under the 1973 Act was, thus, confined to its jurisdiction under section 18 (Judicial Committee only) and with regard to those anti-discrimination cases brought under sections 17 and 19 (any appropriate court). Cases like *Gallagher* and *Hume* were precluded by section 4(5), and an *Education Levy* type scenario was still possible only if involving anti-discrimination arguments. These provisions thus made not the courts but the Secretary of State on unarticulated criteria, other than with regard to excepted-ancillary matters, the custodian of the vires of Assembly Measures, a position assisted by the different ways of legislating on reserved matters. Review of any 'error' by the Secretary of State of substantive categorisation of a matter or of procedure was ousted by the wording of section 4(5). It is highly unlikely that the courts' triumphant approach in *Anisminic*[17] would have carried over to a challenge to the wording of section 4(5), not least given the intention of the 1973 Act and the surrounding political— and violent—context.

Further, judicial review of the Secretary of State's other powers under the 1973 Act was also unlikely: certainly in the 1970s, but also highly probably so even if the system had endured longer than it did. These powers included both the commencement and the discontinuation of the devolved scheme—and both were used. Under section 2(1)(b) no devolution of legislative power could take place until it appeared to the Secretary of State:

> that a Northern Ireland Executive could be formed, which having regard to the support it commands in the Assembly and to the electorate on which that support is based, is likely to be widely accepted throughout the community

and that, having had regard to those matters, there was 'a reasonable basis' for the establishment of a government by consent.[18]

By section 27(5) and (6) of the Act, the Secretary of State (in effect) could make an Order in Council for the dissolution, prorogation or further prorogation of the Assembly, if these power-sharing requirements could not be met 'and that it is in the public interest that the Assembly should be dissolved' or prorogued.[19] In addition the Secretary of State possessed the usual powers in the non-devolved areas and had a key role in the development of an all-Ireland dimension, which, unlike that 1998 model of devolution, was largely not contained (even referentially) in the 1973 Act.

The 1973–1974 Constitution, similar but by no means identical to the 1998 Act, ultimately lacked all but a relatively small amount of 'ownership' within Northern Ireland. Preceded by a border poll (but not a wider referendum on the devolved

---

[17] *Anisminic v Foreign Compensation Commission* [1969] 2 AC 147.

[18] Devolution under the 1973 Act commenced in Northern Ireland on 1 January 1974, with a power-sharing executive drawn from the UUP, SDLP and Alliance Party, which had won 24 seats (29.3 per cent of the poll), 19 seats (22.1 per cent) and 8 seats (9.2 per cent) respectively in the 78 member Assembly. See S Elliott and WD Flackes, *Northern Ireland: A Political Directory 1968–1999* (4th edn, rev'd 1999), 533.

[19] The Assembly was prorogued in May 1974 (initially for a period of four months, eventually for some 25 years) under s 27(6) when, during the Ulster Workers' Council strike, the UUP members resigned from the power-sharing executive.

proposals) the June 1973 elections to the Assembly were boycotted by republicans. The Democratic Unionist and other smaller Unionist parties opposed power-sharing and the later Council of Ireland, the emergence of which also led to further loss of support within the deeply divided Ulster Unionist Party. In the aftermath of the February 1974 UK General Election, in which 11 of the then 12 Northern Ireland Westminster seats were won by Unionists opposed to power-sharing and/or the Council of Ireland, the hostility deepened and the Ulster Workers' Council strike of May 1974 effectively terminated Devolution Mark II.

The courts had a very limited 'power' base in Northern Ireland in the early to mid 1970s: limited powers under the Act; limited availability of judicial review; limited exposure to European jurisprudence; limited by some public distrust as being 'too unionist'[20]—an element which in itself, when also generalised into 'political' shows that consideration of an enhanced judicial role (through devolution or otherwise) is likely to bring concomitant changes in the procedures and principles of their appointment. Against that background and that of one of the worst times during the Troubles (1972–74), it was hardly surprising that the Conservative Government through the 1973 Act placed the Secretary of State for Northern Ireland in such a dominant position. When the main issue is the continuance of devolution rather than its operation, the political mechanisms of decision-making are likely to be more effective than the judicial, even if this brings devolution closer to a 'delegated model'. Arguably, however, the pendulum went from too much Westminster disengagement to too much involvement. Presumably the 1973 Act was not intended to fail; indeed it was designed to take Northern Ireland away from the Troubles and into calmer waters. The Act, therefore, should have drawn a clearer distinction between 'continuity' and 'operational' questions and left vires issues in the hands of the judges and not the Secretary of State. The Act's flexibility or potential for growth was to be determined by the Secretary of State alone (albeit on occasions with some involvement of the Assembly and/or Westminster). As will be seen below, however, where a constitution is more autochthonous, even continuity questions should not be solely the responsibility of Westminster.

When Legislative Devolution Mark III appeared in the form of the Northern Ireland Act 1998, the judicial role, in contexts outside devolution, had developed out of all recognition. What impact is this expanded role likely to have on the operation of the provisions of the Northern Ireland Act itself? Will the minimalisation of the judicial role in the context of devolution continue?

NORTHERN IRELAND ACT 1998: NEW CENTURY DEVOLUTION?

When considering public law in a multi-layered UK constitution and the provision of formal devolved structures, one particularly pertinent factor is the ownership of the devolved constitution. Its point of anchorage needs to be identified. A

---

[20]   See B Dickson, 'Northern Ireland's Troubles and the Judges', in B Hadfield (ed), *Northern Ireland: Politics and the Constitution* (1992), ch 9.

wide variety of devices was resorted to in Northern Ireland over three decades: talks between the Secretary of State and the parties individually, multi-party talks, a Constitutional Convention, a deliberative Assembly, a Forum, a referendum. In Northern Ireland, ownership of devolution has had (both intra and inter) communal dimensions. Ownership, however, has individual dimensions too (although these two aspects are not mutually exclusive): issues will arise which concern the extent of individual input into the legislative process or standing to bring judicial review proceedings in matters concerning the exercise of devolved power. The details of the Northern Ireland Act 1998 must be briefly examined before dealing with the four broad categories of legal proceedings possible under the Act.

The multi-party Belfast Agreement, containing in outline only the key principles of the proposed new devolved Northern Ireland (with a strong all-Ireland dimension), was put before the people of Northern Ireland in a referendum in May 1998. On its acceptance by a clear majority taken over the whole of Northern Ireland (unlike the referendums in Scotland and Wales there was no separate constituency or area voting), the much fuller details were found in the implementing Northern Ireland Act 1998. The relationship between the Agreement and the Act will be considered below.

This Act, like those of 1920 and 1973, established three categories of legislative power: excepted matters (Westminster's), transferred or devolved matters (the Assembly's) and the intermediate reserved category on which three legislative procedures are possible: either by Act of the Westminster Parliament, (Westminster) Order in Council or the Assembly with Secretary of State's consent subject to Westminster's oversight.[21] To elaborate: under section 6(2)(b) excepted matters are in substance totally outside the Assembly's legislative competence. It is precluded from *dealing with* an excepted matter unless the provision concerned is *ancillary* to other provisions dealing with reserved or transferred matters. The definition of 'ancillary' is provided in section 6(3) and is identical (although slightly re-ordered) to section 5(7) of the 1973 Act quoted above. 'Deals with' is defined in section 98(2) as meaning dealing with 'the matter, or each of the matters, *which it affects otherwise than incidentally*' (emphasis added). Good-bye to *Gallagher v Lynn* and all that—presumably. Some consideration should be given to section 98(2)'s similarity or otherwise with the equivalent provision of the Scotland Act 1998, namely section 29(3). The latter places outside the legislative competence of the Scottish Parliament any provision which 'relates to' a non-devolved matter, a question which is to be determined by reference to the purpose of the provision 'having regard (among other things) to its effect in all the circumstances.' The relevant minister in the parliamentary debates on this provision in the Scotland Bill, Lord Sewel, (somewhat blithely) placed this form of wording in the context of *Gallagher v Lynn*: the Scottish courts will have to seek the provision's true nature and character, its pith and substance.[22] It should also be remembered that Lord

---

[21]   Northern Ireland Act 1998, ss 8 and 85.
[22]   HL Deb, vol 952, col 818. See CMG Himsworth and CR Munro, *The Scotland Act 1998* (Current Statutes Annotated), commentary on s 29(2)(b).

Atkin also regarded as ultra vires legislation which under the guise of 'dealing with' (*sic*) one matter 'in fact encroached upon the forbidden field.' He also indicated that it was not sufficient to consider the object alone; the object must not be sought by invalid methods. It would appear, however, that the Scottish courts may have rather more to do in this regard than their Northern Ireland counterparts. A Northern Ireland Office Summary Guide to the Northern Ireland Act, having provided the section 98(2) definition, elaborated:

> it is not necessary to identify any one predominant concern of the provision. So if it affects more than incidentally a reserved or excepted matter, even though it is mainly concerned with transferred matters, it will need the Secretary of State's consent.[23]

The last part of that phrase must not be taken to mean that the Secretary of State can consent to the Assembly legislating in substance on an excepted matter. He cannot do this. His consent, however, is required by section 8 for a provision which 'deals with' an excepted matter and is ancillary to other provisions, and also a provision which 'deals with' a reserved matter.

It is possible that the Northern Ireland courts may not take the narrower line adverted to in the *Northern Ireland Office Guide*, but the differences in the wording between the Scotland and Northern Ireland Acts (and Northern Ireland's recent legislative history) would seem to indicate that a line less expansive of the Assembly's power be taken in the courts, leaving the matter (in part) in the hands of the Secretary of State. That is, the preclusion of Assembly legislation on *excepted* matters is to be regarded strictly: the flexibility of the Assembly's competence over reserved matters (dependent on Secretary of State consent, but *possible*) reinforces this, leaving the expansion or constriction of its powers over reserved matters under political not judicial control. More generally, however, as will be considered further below, all those parties entrusted with pre-enactment scrutiny responsibilities will have to address the meaning of 'deals with'. This language is likely to be used in later statutes too; this is illustrated by the Justice (Northern Ireland) Act 2002 which, when it is brought into force, will by section 84, for example, require Assembly cross-community support for a Bill which contains any provision which 'deals with (otherwise than incidentally)' appointment to judicial office.

There is no general grant of power to the Northern Ireland Assembly; the Act itself leaves within the devolved legislative competence all that is not withheld from it. Sections 6 and 7 of the Act provide that it is outside its legislative competence not only to legislate on excepted matters, but also with extraterritorial effect, incompatibly with any rights under the European Convention on Human Rights and with Community Law, to discriminate against any person or class of person on the ground of religious belief or political opinion or to modify an entrenched enactment, for example, the European Communities Act 1972, the Human Rights Act 1998 and certain provisions of the Northern Ireland Act itself. These 'entrenched' provisions are either excepted or reserved matters.

---

[23]   22 July 1999 (www.nio.gov.uk/guidepub.htm).

The guardians of the Assembly's legislative competence are at least six in number. The powers of the Secretary of State for Northern Ireland in this regard—he has other reserve powers too—have been referred to. Secondly, the Presiding Officer/Speaker of the Northern Ireland Assembly must scrutinise every Bill and if he decides that any of its provisions are outside the Assembly's legislative competence the Bill may not be introduced or continued with.[24] Thirdly, under section 9 of the Northern Ireland Act, the Sponsoring Minister of a Bill must make a written statement that in his or her opinion the Bill is within the Assembly's legislative competence. Fourthly, paragraph 27 of the (inter-governmental) Memorandum of Understanding states that 'the devolved administrations will notify legislative measures to the relevant *UK Departments and Law Officers* both when they are proposed and when they are adopted.'[25] This ties in, fifthly, with section 11 of the Northern Ireland Act to be considered further below which currently empowers the Attorney General for Northern Ireland to refer the question of whether a provision in an Assembly Bill is within its legislative competence to the Judicial Committee. It should be noted that at the present time—and since 1973[26]—the Attorney General for England and Wales is also the Attorney General for Northern Ireland. Section 22 of the Justice (Northern Ireland) Act 2002, which is not yet in force, however, provides for the Attorney General for England and Wales to be no longer Attorney General for Northern Ireland. When that provision comes into force, however, the Westminster government's 'legal oversight' of devolution will continue because under section 27 of the 2002 Act the Attorney General for England and Wales will, by virtue of that office, become Advocate General for Northern Ireland. Section 11 of the Northern Ireland Act 1998 will then be amended to confer the power to refer to the Judicial Committee on both the Advocate General and the Attorney General for Northern Ireland. The sixth body having oversight over the legislative competence of, inter alia, the Northern Ireland Assembly is the Northern Ireland Human Rights Commission which has the duty of advising the Assembly of the compatibility of the proposed legislation with 'human rights.'[27] This duty covers much wider ground than the European Convention on Human Rights[28] but does not encompass the full range of vires questions to be considered by the other 'guardians'.

In addition to the powers vested in the Secretary of State already mentioned, he also possesses various 'reserve' powers, three of which may be mentioned as particularly significant. Under section 14 it is the Secretary of State who submits an Assembly Bill for Royal Assent. Under subsection (5), the Secretary of State may decide not to submit for Royal Assent a Bill which contains a provision which *he considers* '(a) would be incompatible with any international obligations, with the interests of defence or national security or with the protection of public safety or

---

[24] Northern Ireland Act 1998, s 10.

[25] Cm 5240, December 2001, (emphasis added).

[26] Constitution Act 1973, s 10(1), not repealed by the Northern Ireland Act 1998.

[27] Northern Ireland Act 1998, ss 13(4) and 69(4).

[28] *Ibid* s 69(11)(b).

public order' or (b) would have an adverse effect on the operation of the single market in goods and services in the United Kingdom. It may be relevant (for judicial review purposes) to note that section 35(1) of the Scotland Act (which makes no reference to the protection of public safety or public order) uses the more objective 'has reasonable grounds to believe'.

The second power vested in the Secretary of State by section 80 of the Northern Ireland Act (the key wording being the same under section 107 of the Scotland Act) is, by order, 'to make such provision as *he considers necessary or expedient* in consequence of any provision of an Act (not Bill) of the Assembly 'which is not, or may not be', within the Assembly's legislative competence. Such an order (which is an affirmative resolution Westminster statutory instrument under section 96(2) of the Northern Ireland Act) may, inter alia, make provision having retrospective effect. The third power, which will be considered in detail below as it has now been addressed by the House of Lords, is to be found in section 32(3), which requires the Secretary of State to propose (to the Queen in Council) a date for an (extraordinary) Assembly General Election in the absence of an election by the Assembly within the requisite period of a First and Deputy First Minister.

Against that general background, it is possible to identify four broad types of legal proceedings which may arise under the Northern Ireland Act.

First, there is the pre-enactment reference power under section 11 to the Judicial Committee whose decisions, under section 82, are binding in all legal proceedings other than proceedings before the Committee itself. This is not the same as the power found in section 51 of the 1920 Act and section 18 of the 1973 Act. First, it relates only to the pre-Royal Assent stage, that is, only to Bills. Secondly, the power is vested *not* in a Secretary of State but in the Westminster government's (and in due course too the devolved government's) law officer. Paragraph 26 of the Memorandum of Understanding indicates that the Westminster government regards such a power as a 'matter of last resort', hoping to avoid any difficulties through discussion 'so as to avoid any action or omission by the devolved administration having an adverse impact on non-devolved matters'—although this is not a rewording of the vires tests.

The second way in which the courts may be called upon to resolve vires questions concerns (mainly post-enactment) *devolution issues*, which phrase has a technical definition which does not include all questions which may arise in connection with the operation of devolution. Schedule 10 of the Northern Ireland Act (which will in due course be amended by Schedule 7 to the Justice Act 2002 inserting in various places references to the Advocate General for Northern Ireland) lays down the various procedures which may be invoked: by the governments' law officers, by the First Minister and Deputy First Minister of Northern Ireland and by any individual with standing directly through judicial review or, indeed, collaterally as occurred in both *Gallagher* and *Hume*. For our purposes, the definition of devolution issue includes 'a question whether any provision of an Act of the Assembly is within the legislative competence of the Assembly' and also the rather broadly phrased 'any question arising under this Act about excepted or reserved matters'. It is not immediately clear what this means, although section 96(1) (the definition section) refers both 'excepted matters' and 'reserved matters' back to section 4(1). There 'excepted matter' and 'reserved matter' mean 'any matter falling within a description specified' in respectively Schedules 2 and 3, which thus constitute broad headings of subjects not definitive lists. It may be, therefore, that the inclusion of this phrase under the heading of 'devolution issue' is intended to be confined to a consideration of, for example, what 'matters' fall within the description of, for example, 'human genetics,' 'civil defence' or 'the subject-matter of the Human Fertilisation and Embryology Act 1990.' It may be, however, that the phrase in Schedule 10 will not be as narrowly confined.

The third category of case—and as it falls outside Schedule 10, the various procedures there may not be utilised—concerns cases arising out of the operation of devolution but which do not fall under the definition of devolution issue. As Professor Noreen Burrows points out,[29] these cases include procedural matters and the issues involved in cases such as *Whaley v Watson*[30] in Scotland, and also the intragovernmental issue in *In re Campbell and Morrow*[31] in Northern Ireland.

The fourth category of case relates to judicial review of the Secretary of State's 'reserve' powers. As far as members of the public are concerned, with regard to this category of case (and also to a greater or lesser extent categories 2 and 3 also) standing could still be problematic. The Northern Ireland Act 1998 introduces a system of devolution which is to a considerable degree, if not totally, autochthonous and consociational or inter-communal. It also has a far wider or multi-layered context within which to operate as compared with its predecessors: it operates in a more widely devolved United Kingdom; there is a series of Irish dimensions; there is the context of the widening, and deepening, European Community/European Union; there is the evolutive jurisprudence of the European Court of Human Rights; there is the British-Irish Council. Judicial review, as will be considered elsewhere in this book, has changed beyond recognition since 1973. This question for devolution, however, remains: what will the response of the courts be to what may be termed 'political questions' in the devolved domain. This is a specific question in the context of, for example, the level of judicial scrutiny that is appropriate (or the degree of deference due) to the decisions of elected bodies in the Human Rights Act jurisprudence. Here it will be considered in the context of the one devolution case to reach the House of Lords, namely *Robinson v Secretary of State for Northern Ireland*.[32] The issues at stake in it were particularly acute, involving a decision of the Secretary of State not to call an early Assembly General Election in Northern Ireland. In the light of the June 2001 General Election results, the Democratic Unionist Party and Sinn Fein could be expected at the next Assembly Election to make inroads on the Ulster (Official) Unionist Party and the SDLP respectively. It needs little imagination to state that a DUP/Sinn Fein

---

[29] N Burrows, *Devolution* (2000), 144.
[30] *Whaley v Lord Watson* 2000 SC 125.
[31] 16 January 2002.
[32] [2002] UKHL 32, 25 July 2002.

First Minister and deputy First Minister (or even vice versa?) is an unlikely partnership in Northern Ireland. Hence in *Robinson* the future of devolution was potentially at issue—not for the first time in Northern Ireland.

It is not being suggested at least initially that this case is of general application throughout the devolved United Kingdom. Some Scottish cases might not be either—not in the same way at least as human rights and European Community law devolution cases. Such cases will not be considered here, however, as in one crucial regard they cast little light on the operation of devolution *qua* devolution. The principles of the supremacy of EC law apply to all law in the United Kingdom, including that enacted by the Westminster Parliament and although under the Human Rights Act 1998 that Parliament retains its supremacy with regard to Convention rights, they are nonetheless scrutinised for their compatibility with them. Further, as already mentioned, courts considering both Westminster and devolved legislation have to engage with the doctrine of due deference to elected power. *Robinson*, however, specifically raises questions directly pertinent to the nature of devolution in Northern Ireland, not least in terms of the areas of the devolved 'settlement' subject to central control. Consequently, the case is, in that light alone, of importance for an understanding of the multi-layered constitution, and of judicial understanding of the nature of the 'new settlement' and of its 'custodians.'

ROBINSON V SECRETARY OF STATE FOR NORTHERN IRELAND

The issues involved in *Robinson* may be briefly stated. Under section 16(8) of the Northern Ireland Act:

> When the offices of the First Minister and the deputy First Minister become vacant at any time an election shall be held under this section to fill the vacancies within a period of six weeks beginning with that time.

Under section 32(3), if the period mentioned in section 16(8) ends without such an election 'the Secretary of State shall propose a date for the poll for the election of the next Assembly.' Such an election would be an 'extraordinary' general election as opposed to the ones scheduled to be held once every four years. The next scheduled ordinary election would have been 1 May 2003.

The First Minister, David Trimble resigned on 1 July 2001, that automatically meaning that the then Deputy First Minister (Seamus Mallon) also ceased to hold office. When the first period of six weeks had run its course and with the likelihood of a successful section 16(8) election being non-existent, the Secretary of State acting under his powers contained in the Northern Ireland Act 2000 suspended the Assembly for a day (an action which in itself seemed to be an acknowledgement of his need otherwise to exercise his section 32(3) powers). A further six week period commenced, ran and was concluded with another one-day suspension of the Assembly, the Secretary of State indicating that he would not resort to the one-day suspension device again. The next six week period expired on Sunday

4 November 2001 at midnight. An attempt by the Assembly on the preceding Friday to elect David Trimble and Mark Durkan (who had replaced Seamus Mallon) as First Minister and Deputy First Minister failed, the requisite cross-community consensus not being satisfied.[33] After members of a non-designated party changed their designations for cross-community purposes, the vote was taken again on 5 and 6 November and the two candidates for office were elected. The Secretary of State for Northern Ireland accepted that as the election was outside the requisite six weeks he was under an obligation to nominate a date for an extraordinary general election under section 32(3) and actually nominated the date of the next scheduled ordinary election, 1 May 2003, some 18 months on from the date of his decision.

The issues, therefore, before the court in *Robinson* (heard by the Northern Ireland High Court[34] and Court of Appeal[35] and the House of Lords[36]) were twofold:

(1) was the 'out-of-time' election of the First Minister and Deputy First Minister under section 16(8) valid; and
(2) was the Secretary of State entitled to propose as the date for the extraordinary general election the date specified in the Act for the next ordinary election.

Before turning to consider the courts' responses to these questions, some material not referred to by the judges will be provided, in order to facilitate a fuller consideration of the role discharged by the judges in *Robinson* in terms of the material they relied upon and the emphasis it received.

First, we may consider the legislative history of the Northern Ireland Act 1998, whose long title (rather surprisingly referred to by some of the lower court judges as its (non-existent) preamble) states it to be an Act 'to make new provision for the government of Northern Ireland for the *purpose* of implementing' the Belfast Agreement (emphasis is added) . It is, obviously, the case that the Belfast Agreement did not—and could not—contain all the detail necessary for inclusion in the later Act, although as the Bill progressed through Parliament, there was full liaison/discussion between the Secretary of State and the (participating) Northern Ireland parties.

The Northern Ireland Assembly has (once its initial 'shadow' phase ran out) a fixed four-year term.[37] In such a situation it is wise to provide for an earlier dissolution, and to do so in such a way as not to enhance the electoral chances of any one party. In the Bill as originally published, neither what became section 16(8) nor section 32(3) appeared. The Bill did, however, contain a power *vested* in the Queen in Council, effectively of course the *Secretary of State*, to dissolve the Assembly early, thus causing an Assembly election to be held. This was *in addition*

---

[33] See Northern Ireland Act 1998, ss 4(5) and 16(3). Those MLAs who choose not to designate themselves as either 'nationalist' or 'unionist' remain in the 'other' category, a category which does not count for cross-community voting purposes.

[34] Kerr J, 21 December 2001.

[35] Nicholson and McCollum LJJ, Carswell LCJ dissenting, 21 March 2002.

[36] [2002] UKHL 32, 25 July 2002.

[37] Northern Ireland Act 1998, s 31(1). See now the Northern Ireland Assembly Elections Act 2003 and the Northern Ireland (Elections and Periods of Suspension) Act 2003.

to a power vested in the Queen in Council to prorogue or further prorogue the Assembly. What was clause 24(4) stated:

If at any time it appears to Her Majesty—
(a) that the persons who are the [First Minister and Deputy First Minister] and the Northern Ireland Ministers are not able to carry out their functions;
(b) that, if they were to resign, the persons who would be likely to succeed them would not be able to carry out their functions; and
(c) that it is in the public interest that the Assembly should be dissolved, then she (having taken account of any relevant Assembly vote) may direct that an Assembly election take place on a date earlier than 1 May 2003.

During the Committee stage in the House of Lords (a quite crucial stage given the allocation of time order on the Bill in the Commons), several pertinent amendments were made to the Bill. First, when the Bill left the Commons, what became section 16(8) read (as clause 14(7)):

Where the offices of the [First Minister and Deputy First Minister] are vacant, an election shall be held under this section to fill the vacancies.

The clause was amended (both with regard to section 16(8) and section 16(1) on the duty of an assembly to elect a First Minister and Deputy First Minister immediately after an election) through the addition of the six week timescale. The main debate (indeed the sole debate) took place on what became section 16(1), section 16(8) being amended in turn 'on the back' of the earlier debate. Lord Dubs (Junior Minister in the Northern Ireland Office said): 'I do not think that six weeks is too short a period'[38] and in response to questions that six weeks was too long or indeed too short as well as concern about the consequences of breach of the six week period, he said:

(I am) asked what would happen if no election took place for [First Minister and Deputy First Minister] within the six week period. If the Assembly fails to make such an election within six weeks, it will be dissolved and the Secretary of State then sets the date for an extraordinary election. That is not unreasonable. Six weeks is a sufficiently long period to deal with a matter of importance to the government of Northern Ireland.[39]

This specific quotation from Lord Dubs (alone of all the parliamentary material mentioned here) was referred to by some of the judges in *Robinson*, but it has, it is submitted, to be further viewed in light of two other amendments to the Northern Ireland Bill not mentioned by them.

Later in the Committee stage, the government successfully proposed the deletion of clause 24(4) quoted above. Lord Dubs said:

In the Bill as it stands, the Secretary of State may dissolve the Assembly and call fresh elections if she believes the Northern Ireland Ministers are unable to carry out their functions. *This was seen as leaving too much power in the hands of the Secretary of State, and planning for failure. Accordingly … [we propose to leave] the power to call early*

---

[38] HL Deb, 19 October 1998, vol 593, col 1227.
[39] HL Deb, 19 October 1998, vol 593, col 1229.

elections to the Assembly on a majority of two thirds of all members … In addition, a fresh election will be triggered if the Assembly fails within six weeks to elect a [First Minister and Deputy First Minister].[40] (emphasis added)

As will be elaborated on below, Lord Dubs indicated that this would bring the Northern Ireland Bill's provisions on extraordinary elections 'more into line'[41] with the provisions of the Scotland Bill.

The third amendment to the Bill was the deletion of the Secretary of State's power to prorogue the Assembly. Lord Dubs, indicating that such emergency powers were 'planning for failure' and 'as a result might make failure more likely,'[42] referred to the already secured deletion of clause 24(4):

> *In discussions with the Northern Ireland parties* there was considerable opposition to the kind of emergency powers represented by [the prorogation clause]. We have already debated the powers to call emergency dissolutions and fresh elections. *As a result,* the *Secretary of State's powers in this field have instead been given to the Assembly.*[43] (emphasis added)

As Lord Dubs indicated, the Northern Ireland Bill's provisions on extraordinary general elections were brought 'more into line' with what became the relevant provisions in the Scotland Act—'more into line' but with one key difference. Section 32 provides for an extraordinary general election after the passing of a resolution of the Assembly with the support of two-thirds of the Members, (the equivalent in the Scotland Act is section 3(1)(a)). Also, an extraordinary general election shall be called in the situation indicated by section 32(3), a provision at the heart of *Robinson* and quoted and discussed above. This is the equivalent of section 3(1)(b) of the Scotland Act concerning the nomination of Scotland's First Minister within the period of 28 days specified in section 46. In Scotland, the 'triggering agent' of an extraordinary election is the Presiding Officer/Speaker; in Northern Ireland, the Secretary of State. The key difference between the two Acts, however—ignoring, for once, the surrounding political contexts!—is that under the Scotland Act, the calling of an extraordinary election does not displace the next scheduled ordinary election. It will take place as scheduled,[44] the extraordinary election becoming an additional election. In Northern Ireland this is not the case.

Given the emphasis placed in *Robinson* on the role of the Belfast Agreement, as will be mentioned below and given the wording of the Northern Ireland Act's long title, it should be pointed out that the Agreement itself does indicate precisely the post-Agreement/Act role of the Secretary of State. It encompasses responsibility for Northern Ireland Office non-devolved matters; to approve and lay before the Westminster Parliament any Assembly legislation (to which he or she will have

---

[40] HL Deb, 19 October 1998, vol 593, col 1295. The power of the Assembly to resolve to call an early Assembly election is to be found in s 32(1).

[41] *Ibid.*

[42] HL Deb, 21 October 1998, vol 593, col 1442.

[43] *Ibid.*

[44] Subject only to the proviso of the extraordinary election being held within six months of the next scheduled ordinary election.

consented) on reserved matters; to represent Northern Ireland interests in the UK Cabinet; and the right to attend the Assembly upon invitation.[45]

This material has been provided, as mentioned above, in addition to or in comparison with that actually relied on or referred to by the judges. In terms of judicial espousal or disavowal of a soft-edged role with regard to decisions involving the 'deployment of political judgment'[46] the material presented to them and/or relied upon by them is of prime importance. Consideration also needs to be given to the appropriateness of the chosen test when the case involves competing political arguments—as *Robinson* itself did—otherwise the test may simply become one of preserving the validity of the decision challenged whatever the challenge mounted.

Also relevant too is the presence of the sovereign Westminster Parliament, as the enactment of the Northern Ireland Act 2000 illustrates. The suspension of the Assembly by a Westminster Secretary of State acting under the (legal-political) authority of the Westminster Parliament was not envisaged by the Belfast Agreement but it happened. Indeed, given the two suspensions of the Assembly under the Act in the summer of 2001, 18 weeks (rather than six) elapsed between the resignation and re-election of the First Minister and of the Deputy First Minister. To put it more broadly, when considering the political context or consequences, what weight should a judge give to the presence and powers of a sovereign Parliament which, in spite of government protestations to the contrary, has shown itself well able to legislate rapidly and fully should the (perceived) need arise? In the devolved context, is it constitutionally preferable for the courts to uphold a 'reserve' power of a Secretary of State under soft-edged review, or to overturn it, if necessary, under hard-edged review leaving the issue to be resolved, if thought necessary, by the exercise of Westminster's legislative powers? Frankly, given the present balance of powers in the UK constitution, does it really matter in practice at all?

The judgments in *Robinson* delivered in the Northern Ireland High Court and Court of Appeal are essentially pitched low in that they reveal few traces of a new form of constitutional reasoning. Kerr J, in the High Court, whose decision was upheld by Nicholson and McCollum LJJ in a split Court of Appeal, indicated that the arguments on section 16(8) (the 'out-of-time' election of First Minister and Deputy First Minister) and section 32(3) (the date set by the Secretary of State for the extraordinary general election) had to be kept distinct, although resolution of the former question would undoubtedly affect that of the second. The question to which section 16(8) gave rise was whether an election of First Minister and Deputy First Minister outside the prescribed period was valid. Given the wording of the Act's long title, Kerr J noted that its interpretation had to be informed by the Belfast Agreement (and beyond that the 'political realities' of Northern Ireland). The Agreement itself was totally silent on any such time limit. The limited quotations

[45] *The Belfast Agreement* (Cm 3883, April 1998), Strand 1, para 32.
[46] See *In re Michelle Williamson* (a case involving the decision of the Secretary of State for Northern Ireland on whether or not the IRA was maintaining a complete and unequivocal ceasefire); NIHC, 19 November 1999, Kerr J, at 16 of transcript.

from Lord Dubs as recorded in Hansard, he stated, were not sufficiently unequivocal as to settle the question of the proper construction of sections 16 and 32 and therefore could not be relied on. Given that background, Kerr J held that section 16(8) should not be applied in a rigid or inflexible manner: rather in determining whether the six-week period should be classified as a mandatory or directory requirement, the consequences which might flow from non-compliance should be considered. In light of all that (and indeed what is termed 'substantial' compliance with the requirement), he held that the six week requirement could not be classified as mandatory and consequently its terms did not preclude a valid election after the six weeks had run.

Kerr J regarded the discretion given to the Secretary of State under section 32(3) as wide: he was entitled to take the valid election of First Minister and Deputy First Minister into account (and the prospect of continued stable government) and therefore the choice of 1 May 2003 was lawful. Kerr J also referred to the *Williamson* principle:

> a decision such as this is taken in a political context and the political considerations which inform it place it firmly in the category of soft-edged review *where it is inappropriate for the courts to intervene.*[47] (emphasis added)

The 'political considerations' which may have lain behind the Secretary of State's decision were referred to twice by Nicholson LJ in the Court of Appeal, in the context of the meaning to be given to section 16(8):

> It may become apparent to the Secretary of State or the Government that a successful election of [a First Minister and Deputy First Minister] could be held shortly after the expiry of the period under section 16(8) which, if valid, would *obviate the necessity for a fresh election* that *might imperil the Belfast Agreement* ... In view of the date which he did propose ... he obviously thought it was not in the public interest to have an early election for the next Assembly but to allow the existing Assembly to seek to establish public confidence in it ... They must have considered that a fresh election was not in the public interest and at the very least that such an election was *liable to imperil the Belfast Agreement.*[48] (emphasis added)

Indeed, Nicholson LJ indicated that section 32(3) could be used in order to apply pressure on the Assembly to elect a First Minister and Deputy First Minister, 'certainly if compliance with the requirements of section 16 could be met within a short time.'[49]

The Lord Chief Justice, Sir Robert Carswell, dissented. Concentrating primarily on the first issue and placing greater weight on the words of Lord Dubs as well as the policy and objects of the Northern Ireland Act 1998, he held that section 16(8) precluded a valid election outside the prescribed time and that therefore the election of the First Minister and Deputy First Minister was invalid. He further held that the date specified by the Secretary of State under section 32(3) was invalid.

---

[47] Above n 34, at 17.
[48] Above n 35, at 17–19 of transcript.
[49] *Ibid* at 19.

The Lord Chief Justice concluded:

> It is a difficult and invidious task for judges sitting in a court of law to adjudicate upon matters which have a highly charged political context, where the exercise of political judgment is at the centre of decision-making. That task is, however, imposed on us by law and we have to discharge our function in the manner required of a judicial tribunal, looking only at those matters which are properly within our purview. Those matters are concerned solely with the interpretation of the governing statute, and I have sought to construe its terms in such a way as to ascertain and give effect to the intention of Parliament, eschewing all other considerations.[50]

The House of Lords, by a three to two majority, upheld the decision of the majority in the Northern Ireland Court of Appeal. Lord Hutton (a Northern Ireland judge) and Lord Hobhouse dissented on the import of sections 16(8) and 32(3), but all were agreed that no reliance could be placed on the Hansard quotations which had been referred to (not necessarily relied on) in the courts below. The majority held that the interpretation to be given to the Act in general and the two subsections in particular should be the generous and purposive approach appropriate to what is 'in effect a constitution' (per Lord Bingham).[51] He also referred, more surprisingly, to the Secretary of State as the 'non-partisan guardian of the constitutional settlement.'[52] Lord Hoffmann referred to the Act as 'a constitution for Northern Ireland framed to create a continuing form of government against the background of the history of the territory and of the principles'[53] of the Belfast Agreement.

That stated, however, the approach of their Lordships was not notably different from the lower courts in upholding by a majority the validity of an election of First Minister and Deputy First Minister outside the time prescribed under section 16(8), and of the decision under section 32(3), in the unusual circumstances of the case and allowing for the fact that an election under section 16(8) had been secured shortly outside the six week period. Lord Hoffmann stated on the latter point that:

> the question of when the election should be held will be a matter for the Secretary of State and will be informed by his political judgment as to the likelihood of the Assembly being able to elect two Ministers. But that does not mean that your Lordships are making a political decision.[54]

CONCLUSION

There are two specific and conjoined points to consider arising from *Robinson* before addressing the broader themes raised by the title of this chapter.

---

[50] Above n 35, at 23 of transcript.
[51] [2002] UKHL 32, para [11].
[52] *Ibid* at para [14].
[53] *Ibid* at para [25].
[54] *Ibid* at para [34].

The first concerns the use of the Belfast Agreement in the interpretation of the Northern Ireland Act; the second the resort to the Bill's legislative history and to Hansard. First, the Agreement, at least until it is reviewed, will set the parameters for the political debate in Northern Ireland. Secondly, as some of its provisions are directly incorporated by reference into some of the sections in the Act it must in some situations be used as the express and dominant guide to meaning. Thirdly, its inclusion in the long title of the Act gives it a general interpretative role. The Agreement itself, however, is not a detailed blueprint for Northern Ireland any more than the White Papers (albeit of a different genesis) which preceded the referendums in Scotland and Wales deal with all issues later enacted in the Scotland and Government of Wales Acts. Consequently, selective overreliance should not be placed on the silences of the Agreement. As Lord Hutton (dissenting) said in *Robinson*, in effect countering the argument that the Agreement made no reference to any timescale for the election of First Minister and Deputy First Minister:

> the Agreement contains no express provision stating what would happen if cross-community government was not established or did not continue. But Parliament had to provide for this contingency and did so by the provisions of section ... 16(8) and section 32 [55]

and, one might add, by the Northern Ireland Act 2000.

This ties in to the second point. There was extensive discussion during all the Parliamentary stages of the Northern Ireland Bill between the Northern Ireland Office and the 'participating' Northern Ireland political parties. This is one reason for the several hundred amendments made to the Bill in the House of Lords as they addressed the detailed 'outworking' of the Belfast Agreement. In this context, the actual legislative history of the Bill is of significance in its own right and should be fully used, along with, if necessary, a fuller resort to the Hansard debate on the legislative changes. The Belfast Agreement *cannot* stand alone from these later debates and the detailed provisions.

Does the devolved Northern Ireland (remembering that it is not just a part of the devolved United Kingdom but also a part of a wide set of all-Ireland dimensions) need an independent judicial arbiter? Yes, but it is submitted first that there should not be undue reliance on the *Williamson* dictum (which did not really feature at all in the higher courts). Soft-edged judicial review has value but not in the context of litigation in which all the parties have clearly different political perspectives. It would then simply serve the purpose of preserving automatically the impugned decision. More broadly, however, if the post-devolution courts are to fulfil their role as independent arbiters, especially in litigation with parties involving different political mandates, they must be as rigorous in their review of central *government* power as of devolved power. There is no a priori reason to regard the territorial Secretary of State as the sole (or even independent) arbiter of the constitutional settlement. Judicial rigour across the board of such decision-making is

[55] *Ibid* at para [61].

essential, not least when accompanied by changes in judicial appointment processes and the introduction of Judicial Appointment Commissions.

The Northern Ireland experience, through the lack of its case law, shows the difficulties that can arise through unaccountable political power. The remaining checks and balances are now in place. Judicial reserve or caution is justified no longer.

7

Modernising Government and the E-Government Revolution: Technologies of Government and Technologies of Democracy

INTRODUCTION

T HIS CHAPTER LOOKS at the general initiative of the UK government that is associated with the *Modernising Government* programme, and in particular at the development of e-government within this wider process, in order to illustrate a more general argument about how we can now best understand the practice of government and the nature of power through developing the insights of the governmentality approach.

At a theoretical level, the chapter seeks to make some general remarks about the value to constitutional theory of the governmentality approach that is associated with the later writing of Michel Foucault and some important subsequent criticism. The chapter looks critically at the conceptualisation of the practice of government within much public law scholarship, where the emphasis remains on very particular ideas of power that are associated with territory, sovereignty and law. It suggests instead that attention be afforded to insights from the governmentality approach that emphasise the creation and deployment of a whole range of technologies connecting multiple centres of power within an exercise of government

* The author wishes to acknowledge the help and support of a number of bodies and individuals. In particular, thanks must be extended to Roger Cotterrell and his colleagues at Queen Mary, University of London where the author enjoyed a semester as a Visiting Research Fellow with financial assistance from the British Academy. The Institute of Governance at Queen's University also provided a congenial environment to continue research leave with additional support from the Royal Irish Academy. Thanks are also due to a number of individuals in the Cabinet Office and the e-Envoy's Office who provided useful background and to academic colleagues including particularly Ray Geary, Elizabeth Meehan, David Newman, Stephen Coleman, Philip Leith, Dave Wall, Fernando Galindo and Terry Woods, as well as the other authors and editors of this book who met up for a valuable workshop in Oxford in April 2002.

that is wider and more complex than that which is contained within traditional understandings of the role of government and the nature of the state.

It is argued that although some public lawyers are beginning to come to terms with changes in the site of government—and this can be seen in the acceptance of the concept of governance over simpler ideas of government—there is not yet a similar development in understanding how the practice and techniques of government operate now. To a large extent ideas of state, and state power expressed through law, remain the central way of understanding the business of government. This chapter develops a model of changing governance that indicates how the nature of public power, and practices of government have changed so far beyond the framework provided by traditional public law scholarship that it is now necessary and useful to develop insights from the governmentality approach. These changes are presented in general terms before the emphasis moves to looking at the 'modernisation of government' process, and the related drive towards e-government. Focusing on e-government as both a new space in government and as new strategy for government, the chapter considers the value of deploying the governmentality approach to understand how a technology of government must also be supplemented by a technology of democracy.

GOVERNMENTALITY AND CONSTITUTIONAL THEORY

The governmentality approach, which is becoming an important way of understanding how power is arranged in society and how government is to be conceptualised, has its origins mainly in the later writings of Michel Foucault, and some subsequent criticism which develops understandings of how programmes, strategies and techniques of government have been organised in advanced liberal societies.[1]

---

[1] See particularly, M Foucault, 'Governmentality' in JD Faubion (ed) *Michel Foucault, Power: The Essential Works vol 3* (London, Allen Lane Penguin Press, 2000); L Martin, H Gutman and P Hutton (eds) *Technologies of the Self: A Seminar with Michel Foucault* (London, Tavistock, 1998) and P Rabinow (ed), *Michel Foucault: Ethics* (London, Penguin, 1997). Important later work, developing these ideas, includes studies in criminology, notably D Garland, '"Governmentality" and the Problem of Crime: Foucault, Criminology and Sociology' (1997) 1 *Theoretical Criminology* 173; P O'Malley, L Weir and C Shearing, 'Governmentality, Criticism and Politics' (1997) 26 *Economy and Society* 501–17 and N Rose, 'Government and Control' (2000) 40 *British Journal of Criminology* 321. There are also a number of important collections of essays including G Burchell, C Gordon and P Miller (eds) *The Foucault Effect: Studies in Governmentality* (London, Harvester Wheatsheaf, 1991); A Barry, T Osbourne and N Rose, (eds) *Foucault and Political Reason: Liberalism, Neo-Liberalism and Rationalities of Government* (London, UCL Press, 1996) and R Smandych (ed) *Governable Places: Readings on Governmentality and Crime Control* (Aldershot, Gower, 1999). Perhaps most importantly among those who have developed Foucault's work in general terms there is N Rose, *Powers of Freedom: Reframing Political Thought* (Cambridge, Cambridge University Press,1999) and M Dean, *Governmentality: Power and Rules in Modern Society* (London, Sage, 1999). There have been some efforts to apply governmentality to law generally, most notably A Hunt and G Wickham, *Foucault and Law: Towards a Sociology of Law and Governance* (London, Pluto Press, 1994); V Tadros, 'Between Governance and Discipline: The Law and Michel Foucault' (1998) 18 *Oxford Journal of Legal Studies* 75; P Leyland, 'Oppositions and Fragmentations: In Search of a Formula for Comparative Analysis?' in A Harding and E Örücü *Comparative Law in the 21st Century* (London, Institute of Advanced Legal Studies, 2002), 211–34 and D Cowan and D Lomax 'Policing unauthorized Camping' (2003) 30 *Journal of Law and Society* 283.

Foucault's earlier account of discipline, with its emphasis on 'docile bodies' as surfaces for the inscription of power, has been supplemented by later work which stresses the importance of the active subject as the entity through which and by means of which power is actually exercised. Here Foucault is asking questions that are far from the usual ones put in conventional political analysis. There is little by way of explanation or discovery of causes or even connections to other phenomena. Instead, emphasis is on the mentalities of rule: how certain ways of thinking and acting came to be and how particular objects of government came to be selected and thought possible to be governed. The later writers within the governmentality approach too are concerned with 'the fundamental role that knowledges play in rendering aspects of existence thinkable and calculable, and amenable to deliberated and planful initiatives … the invention of new forms of thought …[and] the ethical conditions [under] which it became possible for different authorities to consider it legitimate, feasible and even necessary to conduct such interventions.'[2]

Overall, Foucault is deploying the term 'government' in a very different sense from the conventional idea of state executives and legislatures. The state, sovereignty and law here play a limited role. As he puts it in an often quoted remark, 'Political theory has never ceased to be obsessed with the person of the sovereign. Such theories still continue today to busy themselves with the problem of sovereignty. What we need, however, is a political philosophy that isn't erected around the problem of sovereignty, nor therefore around the problems of law and prohibition. We need to cut off the King's head: in political theory that still has to be done'.[3] In a sense this needs to be done too in constitutional legal theory. We know that the role of the state and of government has changed. Most constitutional theorists now accept in general terms that there has been a movement from government to governance, and that the role of the state has changed from being a guarantor and provider of security, wealth and law towards being more of a partner or facilitator for a variety of other bodies and agencies as they concern themselves with such issues. Nevertheless, constitutionalists remain focused too exclusively on models of power that fail to capture how government now works. Foucault complains that when he first studied power relations there were no tools of study:

> 'we had recourse only to ways of thinking about power based on legal models, that is: what legitimates power? Or we had recourse to ways of thinking about power based on institutional models, that is: What is the state?'[4]

This approach still dominates constitutional thinking. However, the governmentality approach can provide us with a valuable way of understanding how power is exercised indirectly and at a distance. Governmentality puts less emphasis on ideas of high constitutionalism—of Parliament, Cabinet, statute and budget—and

---

[2] P Miller and N Rose, 'Governing Economic Life' (1990) 19 *Economy and Society* 3.
[3] *Power/Knowledge: Selected Interviews and Other Writings 1972–1977* (C Gordon (ed), New York, Pantheon, 1980), 121.
[4] M Foucault, 'The Subject and Power' in Faubion (ed), above n 1, at 327.

stresses instead the importance of the *active subject* as the entity through which and by means of which power is actually exercised beyond traditional state boundaries. The emphasis is much less on the government of a territory, and ideas of judicial sovereignty and law, and more on the management of things—people, resources, ideas—as part of the multiform tactics of government. Instead of state action (or rather in addition to it), there is the important quality of the freedom of the subject. Governmental action by itself cannot attain its own ends; it requires the willing co-operation of the individual subject participating in their own governance. In other words, the site and the agents of government are more than the state and passive subjects; they include also a whole range of persons and agencies co-opted into a wider exercise of power. Rather than simply concentrating on how the state controls and disciplines the body, governance is now involved in two aspects: there are the forms of rule by which authorities govern populations, and there are the 'technologies of the self' through which people shape their own subjectivity and 'make themselves up' as active subjects of power who can make choices.

In this way the governmentality approach sees power diffused through a diverse number of sites, both traditional in the sense of law, police, courts, and legal system, and extended, by way of families, experts, professions, counsellors, churches etc who are all concerned with governmentality, or the 'conduct of conduct' as Foucault terms it. The governmentality approach involves a realisation that government action by itself cannot attain its ends; it needs to 'govern through freedom' where individuals 'make themselves up' (or come to understand themselves and their situation) in ways that coincide with the objectives promoted by the governing authorities. Government involves not simply issuing orders but engaging with existing networks of power in a much more sophisticated approach that takes people as they are, with all their beliefs and understandings of the world, and engaging with these to shape conduct.

As Nicolas Rose puts it (and the quotation is worth presenting at length as it captures much of what is important and interesting about governmentality to the constitutionalist) the governmentality approach has:

> reframed the role to be accorded to the 'the state' in analyses of control and regulation. Centres of political deliberation and calculation have to act through the actions of a whole range of other authorities, and through complex technologies, if they are to be able to intervene upon the conduct of persons, activities, spaces and objects far flung in space and time—in the street, the schoolroom, the home, the operating theatre, the prison cell. Such 'action at a distance' inescapably depends on a whole variety of alliances and lash-ups between diverse and competing bodies of expertise, criteria of judgment and technical devices that are far removed from the 'political apparatus' as traditionally conceived. … 'the state' is neither the only force engaged in the government of conduct nor the hidden hand orchestrating the strategies and techniques of doctors, lawyers, churches, community organizations, pressure groups, campaigning groups, groups of parents, citizens, patients, survivors and all those others seeking to act upon conduct in the light of particular concerns and to shape it to certain ends.[5]

---

[5] 'Government and Control' (2000) 40 *British Journal of Criminology* 321, at 323.

Government thus has multiform tactics: in addition to straightforward state action in the form of law, sanctions, budgets and administrative action there is the important quality of the freedom of the subject and how this freedom is managed. In contrast to simple domination which involves crushing the capacity for action of the dominated, government, properly understood, involves recognising that capacity and mobilising it. To govern is to act upon action. It involves understanding how those who are to be governed think and operate, and using and shaping this in order to guide conduct in the desired direction. As Foucault expresses it, 'the exercise of power is a "conduct of conducts" and a management of possibilities.'[6] Government thus presupposes and depends upon individual freedom and the way in which people see themselves as free, choosing individuals holding all sorts of beliefs and understandings about the world. Foucault refers to the 'technologies of the self' to indicate how people shape their own subjectivity or make themselves up, and are not simply passive objects of power, but rather active subjects of power who can make their own choices. This subjectivity, people's way of thinking about themselves and the world which they inhabit, is shaped by all sorts of pre-existing patterns and habits, complex chains of constraint, obligations and fear as well as new calculations of interest that may be made in relation to new interventions by government and other agencies seeking to effect change. The art of government within the governmentality paradigm involves cultivating this subjectivity in specific forms, aligned to particular government aims. New ways of thinking about the world and understanding particular problem issues are introduced. For instance, the language of managerialism—of risks and rewards, choice, targeting and economic rationalism—may become a dominant way of thinking about issues and problems. Expert discourses are enlisted in the project of seeming to understand the world. 'Scientific fact' is expostulated, and statistical and actuarial information classifies and regroups people and recalibrates risk. New experts and fresh sources of authority arise to replace older traditional or theological sources of knowledge.[7] It is in this way that particular areas of life are reshaped and understandings about specific issues are changed.

Generally then, the governmentality perspective suggests that power and ideas beyond the formal state operates sovereign will. As Foucault reminds us:

> the analysis of power relations within a society cannot be reduced to the study of a series of institutions, not even to the study of all those institutions which would merit the name 'political'.[8]

---

[6] 'The Subject and Power' in Faubion (ed), above n 1, at 341.

[7] As Pavlich puts it, 'governmentality involves a power which operates through "truth". In … "advanced liberal societies" … power relations defer to scientific truths about individuals, selves, democracy, ethics and freedom. Governance operates, that is, by inscribing its subjects in the realms of discourse, and requiring them to recognise themselves in the mirrors of truth that it holds out': G Pavlich, 'The Art of Critique or How Not to be Governed Thus' in G Wickham and G Pavlich, *Rethinking Law, Society and Governance* (Oxford, Hart Publishing, 2001), at 151–52.

[8] M Foucault 'Afterword, The Subject and Power' in H Dreyfuss and P Rabinow *Beyond Structuralism and Hermeneutics* (Chicago, University of Chicago Press, 1982), 224.

Thus, in addition to the formal state there are other bodies that have a role in the operation of government. Power relations are rooted in the system of social networks. Civil society, local government, the private sector, the individual consumer, citizen, voter, expert or whatever are all 'active subjects' who not only collaborate in the exercise of government but also shape and inform it. Government is thus a domain of strategies, techniques and procedures (or 'technologies') through which different forces and groups (including the formal state but reaching far beyond it too) attempt to render their own various programmes operable. The governmentality approach also locates the activity of government generally within the micro level and, in particular, within specific ways of thinking (or 'rationalities') which structure how we see and understand problems, their solutions, as well as the framework within which they exist. This understanding of power takes us away from the state and the formal commands of law as such, and suggests that the space of government is extended far beyond the formal aspects of the constitution. Indeed, the insights of the governmentality approach suggest a chain or network of enclosures where disparate technologies, drawing upon a whole range of resources and techniques, struggle to instantiate particular programmes of action. Different idioms of political power here struggle with one another to be translated from one context to another and to establish themselves in programmes of action which can enlist enough of the various disparate forces to become realisable. Formal government, in the sense of the institutions of the constitution, of course is not absent from this vision: the traditional state retains many resources, including the ability to coerce, and so remains powerful. However, is not the only or even perhaps the main actor in a much more complex process where the problems and solutions of government, and the technologies devised to deal with these, exist in a variety of networks and strategies beyond the formal constitution.

The role of law here is different too. Just as the spaces of government can be seen to extend beyond the traditional boundaries of the constitutional, so too the techniques or technologies of government can be seen to encompass much more than just law in the sense of command. Law is now part of the framework that may establish and go towards defining a space of government. Law does provide much of the context and it underpins and gives effect to many of the ways in which various technologies of government are expressed in ideas of partnership, standards, excellence, best value, audit, performance measure, earned autonomy or whatever. But law in the sense of command, sanction and sovereignty is no longer central.

In this way, the governmentality approach widens our idea of what government involves both in relation to the sites of government and in terms of the technologies of government. It also strips away the perceived 'naturalness' of many of the techniques of governance and allows us to see that even very fundamental ideas such as 'public', 'private', 'citizen' or 'voter', no less than more recent inventions such as 'modernisation', are themselves part of the technology of government.

In sum, the governmentality approach suggests that power exists beyond the state and that the centres and levels of governmental power, like its objectives and its techniques, are multiple and differentiated. Power is less about imposing sovereign will and more about engaging with the many networks and alliances that make up a chain or network which translates power from one locale to another. Individuals relate to power not as simple coerced objects, but as autonomous subjects whose objectivity is shaped by their active engagement with the powers that govern them and by which they 'govern themselves'. Government is a domain of strategies, techniques and procedures through which different forces and groups attempt to render their programme operable. Instead of thinking about one, overarching, single web of the public or the constitutional, with law as its sole or main expression, we should be considering the countless, often competing, value systems and their various methods of promulgation that exist across state and non-state institutions and centres of power and expertise. Law is an important element in this but its role is part of the multiform tactics of government. There are many spaces for government and many technologies of government. This means that the proper subject of an analysis of contemporary forms of government should be those networks and alliances which exercise 'government at a distance' instead of, or as well as, the formal constitution, the state itself and its expression in law.

GOVERNMENT, GOVERNANCE AND GOVERNMENTALITY

This governmentality approach, it is argued, would seem to provide a fuller framework for understanding how government now operates than more traditional constitutional ideas based on sovereignty, law and sanction. It will allows us to consider the problem of government outside the juridical framework of sovereignty and the state. As Rose puts it, governmentality 'rejects the view that one must account for the political assemblages of rule *in terms of* the philosophical and constitutional language of the nineteenth century, or that one must underpin this misleading account with a theoretical infrastructure derived from nineteenth-century social and political theory which accords "the state" a quite illusory necessity, functionality and territorialisation'.[9] Governmentality allows us to look at the complex of governmental strategies, technologies and powers that exist across many different centres of power and that are framed or expressed in law (as well as in other ways) but are not exhausted by reference to the state and law. Governmentality allows us to look at what Foucault termed the 'governmentalisation of the state'[10] which emerged in the nineteenth century and developed in the course of the last century. Foucault is here referring to the way in which the state has diffused within a whole range of other political centres and linked up with a whole range of micro centres of power in order to develop a mode of governing that will allow it to survive within contemporary power relations and escape from the irrelevancy of older, seventeenth and eighteenth century modes of government based on discipline,

[9] Rose, *Powers of Freedom: Reframing Political Thought*, above n 1, at 17–18.
[10] See 'Governmentality' in *Michel Foucault: Power, The Essential Works*, above n 1, at 220–21.

sovereignty and territory. In this way governmentality is directing us to a whole series of heterogeneous fields of government activity where various bodies, authorities and forces have sought to govern 'populations' and their conduct through a whole range of strategies and techniques. Governmentality is thus widening the scope of constitutional study far beyond the traditional institutions and figures such as Parliament, the Prime Minister and the senior judges. It is taking us beyond formal statute and case law and even the more informal practices and understandings of the major figures within the formal constitution. It is directing study to a space of government that encompasses the traditional political institutions but extends far beyond them to include a whole range of other discourses and vocabularies, mechanisms and strategies, rationalities and technologies.

This widening of the remit for constitutional lawyers may seem to reflect, at least in part, the move from 'government' to 'governance'. Almost everywhere, and even among many constitutional law scholars, there has been a realisation that the nature and location of government has changed. Much of this is captured in the idea of a move from government to governance. Figure 7.1 indicates elements of the changing focus for constitutionalists.

Components of government and democracy	The traditional state (and formal democracy)	The 'modernised' state (and organic democracy)
Guardian of Democratic values	Parliament (Demos); Constitution; Bills of Rights; tradition and convention	Parliament (as meta sovereign, guarantor of process); international standards and enforcement mechanisms
Key Agents/ Institutions	Parliaments; political parties and politicians; government including ministries, public servants, welfare bureaucracy, local authorities;—'Big Government'	Quangos, executive + independent agencies; private + voluntary sectors in 'partnerships'; civil society including single issues groups, NGOs; 'democratic citizens'; international/ transnational bodies; 'government as enabler, facilitator'; 'cross-cutting' task forces + 'tsars'
Resources for Governance	Taxation, central national exchequer; local authority rates and grants	Tax revenues funding various resource centres including local, national and european levels of government + distribution across functional lines; private and charitable, matching funds, private finance initiative
Policy Aims/ Core Activities	Macro-economic management; complete welfare provision; managing the 'national interest'	Correcting market failures; regulation and co-ordination of other providers; risk management; management of 'wicked issues' residual direct welfare provision function

Role of public or citizen	Taxpayer, voter, passive recipient of 'entitlements'	Active customer re service delivery; active citizen or stakeholder re policy development
Sphere of public debate and decision	Parliament + assemblies and councils; ('the usual channels'—press, etc.); a single 'national' public sphere	Formal (parliaments and assemblies) and informal—multiple public spheres; self-organising agents; a globalised public sphere
Deliberative form	Parliamentary deliberation, national debate; devolved assemblies; commissions and committees— consensus building	Multiple—open access; multi-level, European Parliament, WTO etc; local assemblies and parliaments; organically constituted local and interest-based forums, e-based; discursive and participatory
Process	Representation (electoral nexus), consultation of politicians with public, liaison with officials— co-operation	Involvement (non-electoral representation?) of civil society, participation of citizens, NGOs and government—in partnership; 'enabling'
Modes of Action/ Instruments	Taxation and public spending; budgets and formal contracts; civil service action; formal legal norms, statute law and case law of domestic courts	Agreements, compacts and concordats; licensing + franchising; networks; 'project-based'; 'contracts'; rule-making, standard + target setting; regulation; incentives—local Public Service Agreements, performance pay; peer review; monitoring + enforcement
Accountability Mechanisms	Direct—visibility of key decision centres, Parliament, PM and ministerial questions, ministerial responsibility; professional norms, ideas of 'public interest'	Indirect—invisibility of key decision centres, legal, consumer/contractual, market disciplines; audit + benchmark; patronage; adjudication of complaints and grievances supranational enforcement mechanisms; domestic courts adjudicating rights, judicial review
Role of Courts	Rule of law; policing boundaries and limits, legality; separation of powers; guaranteeing positive rights; correcting individual injustices; 'red light model'; law as 'imperium'	Emphasising participation, giving access, wide rules of standing; public interest litigation; ensuring information flow; judicial review— balancing rights, interpreting international standards and developing human rights; 'green light model'; law as 'community'

FIGURE 7.1: *'Government to governance': the emergence of 'modernised government'*

This involves a change in the site of government. Government does not now take place only within a single, unified national territory or by means of a unified, single system. The effects of globalisation mean that territory, like economy and culture, are increasingly multiple and plural rather than unified and national. In this context government acts not so much by simply issuing commands or making law but by developing strategies, techniques and procedures which operate across the countless, often competing value systems and concentrations of power that exist across state and non-state institutions and centres of power and expertise. Ideas of multi-level government have evolved from a simple recognition that there are layers beyond the national state to more sophisticated ideas of how power is dispersed into a multiplicity of sites, constituting nodes in a heterarchical network rather than layers in a hierarchical pyramid, which operate in a relationship of mutual influence rather than control.[11] There are also ideas emerging that the activity of government is complex and *multi-format* too. There are now many more agencies and bodies from civil society and the private sector, as well as from government and quasi-government, and these operate at every level from the local, regional, national and European to deliver both the policy and services of government. As well as formal institutions we need to examine also networks, partnerships and project groups. As Skelcher, a commentator from a public administration perspective sees it,[12] we have moved in the last four or five decades from the 'overloaded state' which attempted to manage the economy, deliver the welfare state and underwrite public sector provision through to the 'hollowed out state' of the 1980s where the delivery mechanisms for public services are reallocated to the private sector and the machinery of the state was replaced by structures at one remove from the political centre. Now we are experiencing the 'congested state' where there is a complex of networked relationships between public, private, voluntary and community actors, which has produced a dense, multi-layered and largely impenetrable structure of public action. There is now a flowering of collaborative activity involving a whole range of partnerships across the public policy agenda where government is not necessarily the lead agency. As figure 6.1 seeks to indicate, this has produced a whole new set of agencies, resources, modes of action and policy aims. It has changed the roles of citizens and courts and offered up new spaces both to find accountability and to develop participation. It has certainly changed the nature of the subject of constitutional law.

Some of this change is captured well in ideas of governance. Furthermore notions of 'good governance', promoting values of transparency, democracy and human rights, do provide something of a normative framework to begin to evaluate new forms of governance. But governmentality offers another important

---

[11] See, eg, N Bernard, *Multilevel Governance in the European Union* (2002) or M Keating's account of the 'reterritorialisation of politics' as involving 'a dual process of sub-state mobilisation and supra-state integration' and a 'search for new levels of political action' in 'Europe's Changing Political Landscape' in P Beaumont, C Lyons and N Walker (eds), *Convergence and Divergence in European Public Law* (Oxford, Hart Publishing, 2002), 7.

[12] 'Changing Images of the State: Overloaded, Hollowed out, Congested' (2000) 15 *Public Policy and Administration* 3.

dimension too. It directs us to all the indirect and persuasive controls, soft law and the strategies of government at a distance, where authorities seek to shape and control the actions of others indirectly through moulding the conditions where individuals, communities and societies make themselves up as rational, choosing, consuming and responsibilised citizens, and thereby govern themselves. While traditionally public lawyers tend to think of law mainly in terms of straightforward power—of issuing commands and imposing sovereign will—much of government power is less about the state and law and more related to engaging with the many networks and alliances that make up the chains or networks in society which translate power from one locale to another. The governmentality perspective stresses that the mentalities of post-liberal government cannot be found only in the statute book, the upper court judgment or the text setting out the meta-constitutional framework. In addition we need to look at framework documents, standards and codes, initiatives and programmes, social practices, guidelines, the outworkings of myriad schemes and the language in which all this is expressed.

This poses a challenge to legal scholarship, even in its most interdisciplinary forms. In addition to the traditional techniques such as statutory interpretation, case analysis and the toolbox of sociolegal studies (including particularly ethnography) we must develop the perspectives of governmentality. We must apply the outlook of what Foucault terms a 'history of the present' whereby we strip away the naturalness of programmes and practices and ask why did problems come to be seen in this way and why did particular solutions emerge? This involves developing a standpoint from which to view the creation of governable spaces and the production of governable subjects. Indeed we may say that where governance describes the practice, governmentality is the theory that analyses and critiques. Rose talks in terms of governmentality opening 'a space for critical thought', of how approaches within governmentality seek an open and critical relation to strategies for governing, attentive to their presuppositions and their assumptions.[13] Governmentality provides us with a perspective to see the multiform tactics of governance in ways that introduce a particular critical attitude to things that are otherwise seen as given, as natural or unquestionable. In particular, within a governmentality perspective, as Rose argues, 'programmes and technologies of government ... are assemblages which may have a rationality, but this is not one of a coherence of origin or singular essence ... To analyse, then, is not to seek for a hidden unity behind this complex diversity. Quite the reverse. It is to reveal the historicity and the contingency of the truths that have come to define the limits of our contemporary ways of understanding ourselves, individually and collectively, and the programmes and procedures assembled to govern ourselves. By doing so, it is to disturb and destablise these regimes, to identify weak points and lines of

---

[13]   Rose, above n 1, at 19. As Cotterrell argues, 'the strength of Foucault's work for legal scholarship has been to emphasise the ubiquity of power.... As Foucault revolutionised views of power, sociolegal scholarship should revolutionise views of law.... Law, like power should be seen as a resource operating routinely in innumerable sites and settings'. 'Subverting Orthodoxy, Making Law Central' (2002) 29 *JLS* 632, 639.

fracture in our present where thought might insert itself *in order to make a differ-ence*'.[14] In this way, governmentality directs us to the detail of various technologies of government in terms of their assemblages of modes of thinking and acting and to their wider role within broader ideas of what it is to govern. It also enables us to intervene. It is important within the governmentality viewpoint that power is not seen as a top down exercise where those with most resources (particularly of course the state) marshal them and deploy the art of government to attain some overarching end. Governmentality suggests that people need to be willing partici-pants in their own government. They have choices. Alternatives are possible and resistance is endemic to power relations.[15] Power only works, and is only trans-lated from site to site or among nodes, if it is accepted (or else modified) by those who it passes through. The governmentality approach does not necessarily involve a detached observation of technologies of government but can and should urge resistance, contestation and alternatives.

In what remains of this chapter, the focus will be upon a particular technology of government, namely that relating to the programme of modernisation in general and the development of electronic government in particular. An effort will be made to examine this as an exercise in governmentality which requires us to examine the multiform tactics through which various bodies and agencies strug-gle to instantiate it. Also, this particular programme of government is contested and a critical view is offered of the programme and its assumptions. Indeed, an alternative 'technology of democracy' is outlined.

MODERNISING GOVERNMENT

The New Public Management initiatives of the 1980s and 1990s had enormous impact on the practices of public administration. The challenge of performing additional tasks within a declining budget forced government to develop new ideas in order to increase revenues or reduce costs. Cost transparency and cus-tomer orientation became strategic goals. It became axiomatic that the formal state machinery should be engaged in steering rather than rowing—to use the ter-minology that became well-known.[16] The state was hollowed out and the private sector was brought in to perform functions that formerly were discharged by the state.[17]

The public sector and its technologies of government are still changing. Now, however, the driver is best described under a general rubric of 'modernisation'. This is a worldwide trend which shares several common elements based essentially

---

[14] *Ibid* at 276–77 (emphasis added).

[15] As Foucault says, 'where there is power, there is resistance': *Discipline and Punish: The Birth of the Prison* (London, Penguin, 1977), 187.

[16] This phrase comes of course from the influential book by D Osbourne and T Gaebler, *Reinventing Government: How the Entrepreneurial Spirits is Transforming the Public Sector* (New York, Plume, 1992).

[17] See further, eg, R Rhodes, *Understanding Governance: Policy Networks, Governance, Reflexivity and Accountability* (Buckingham, Open University Press, 1997).

on developing consumer focus, improving public sector performance and taking advantage of new information and communication technology.[18] In the United Kingdom this is a complex, constantly changing and somewhat indistinct phenomenon. It encompasses much of what is more or less straightforward reform, such as the modernisation of Parliament and reforms to political party funding. It also provides a 'brand' to describe general processes of change in the health service, education and, particularly, local government. It also, however, involves a more general orientation in the organisation of government. This involves a new approach or *style* in government operations. This is oriented essentially around reinvigorating public services by bringing in different concepts of efficiency, including elements of private sector efficiency, but without ceding control to the same extent as with earlier versions of privatisation[19]. Figure 7.1 again suggests some of the main general elements of this. Ideas of partnership are key: government is to be the enabler, facilitator or regulator rather than a main provider. Targeting resources, monitoring and enforcement and measuring satisfaction are important. Benchmarking and performance management is a particular feature. Initiatives are typically project-based, cross-cutting and joined up. As the original key document, the White Paper *Modernising Government* (Cm 4310, 1999) expresses it, the aim is to ensure that the public sector will operate in a way that is 'as efficient, dynamic and effective as anything in the private sector' (para 11). Indeed according to the preface of the White Paper, modernising government is not just 'a series of measures that the government will implement now' but also 'a clear statement by the Government of what government is for'. This is undoubtedly an important idea for the Labour Government. The White Paper itself, however, is a complex mixture of the banal and the important: (with characteristic New Labour disregard for syntax) the document claims to offer 'Not Government for those who work in government: but government for people, people as consumers, people as citizens'. The 'Overall Vision' outlined in chapter 1 sees the public sector 'with a culture of improvement, innovation and collaborative purpose' (para 10). It suggests that this can be achieved by the twin goals of seeking to meet users' needs more effectively and improving departments' performance. The White Paper then goes on to develop this in more detail through three 'aims' and five 'key commitments' which are to guide a long-term programme of 'modernisation'.

For the second term, the delivery mechanisms for modernised government have changed but the emphasis on public sector reform has intensified. Now the initiative is supported by the Prime Minister's Delivery Unit and the Office of Public Services Reform. A new document, *Reforming Our Public Services: Principles into Practice* has been published in March 2002. This offers 'four principles of public

---

[18] For the phenomenon of modernisation worldwide see http://www.servicefirst.gov.uk/2000/modernising/worldgovernments.htm

[19] As A Giddens puts it, 'the restructuring of government should follow the ecological principle of "getting more for less", understood not as downsizing but as improving delivered value'. *The Third Way: The Renewal of Social Democracy* (Cambridge, Polity Press, 1998) 74.

sector reform' which turn out to involve national standards; devolution and delegation; flexibility; and expanding choice.[20] Some of the initial modernisation programmes have been retained, some have mutated and some have withered away.[21] Indeed the picture here is one that seems to be constantly changing, with a whole variety of initiatives building on past programmes and emerging from a range of teams and groups within the Cabinet Office. For example, originally there was the Modernising Public Services Group as part of the 'Better Government' initiative and within it there was the Effective Performance Division. Its main initiative called 'Service First' was launched in 1998 as part of an exercise to raise the standards of public services and make them more accountable to users. In 2001 the Government announced a new 'consumer focus' for public services involving regular use of its (now discontinued) Peoples' Panel to carry out consumer surveys across a range of public services.[22] This built upon The Citizen's Charter produced by John Major's Government in 1991 which was relaunched as the New Charter Programme with six key themes and nine principles in place of the original six.[23] Now, in addition to the Delivery Unit and the Office of Public Services Reform, there is a Centre for Management and Policy Studies which offers nine principles of public service delivery and concerns itself with spreading ideas of best practice across the public sector. There is a Good Practice Database, a set of Best Practice Links and a library of best practice guides, although it is for individual service providers to give effect to these principles of public service delivery by issuing their own charters and charter standard statements. Among the numerous best practice guides produced there is even a guide to drawing up charters with a checklist of eight standards to guide the production of standards.[24] There are the Service First Quality Networks[25] (currently 24 in number) which seek to develop and disseminate good practice regionally. There is the Charter Marks scheme which assesses performance against 10 criteria (to be redefined to six in autumn of 2003). This accredits public service organisations as 'Investors in People', or one of the other indicators of excellence, and which may in turn lead to qualification in the Central Government Beacon Scheme.[26] In addition there is the Public Sector Benchmarking Service which sets standards for performance and encourages 'organisational learning'.[27] There is even a system for finding and linking up with European benchmarking partners.[28]

[20] See further www.number-10.gov.uk/output/page5624.asp

[21] See further www.cabinet-office.gov.uk/eeg/secondphase.htm. Activity here is almost constant. For example, the 2002 Comprehensive Spending Review added 130 additional targets to the 300 or so targets that were announced in the 1998 Comprehensive Review. Meanwhile it has been estimated that, for example, Home Office Ministers announced some 46 initiatives within 10 months and the Education Secretary issued 4,500 pages of policy guidance within 17 months in 2001–2002.

[22] See www.servicefirst.gov.uk/consumerfocus/guide_general.htm

[23] See further www.servicefirst.gov.uk/1998/introduc/nine.htm and also G Drewry, 'Whatever happened to the Citizen's Charter?' [2002] *Public Law* 9.

[24] *Service First: The New Charter Programme*, at 4.9.

[25] See www.servicefirst.gov.uk/index/nethome.htm

[26] See further http://www.chartermark.gov.uk/ andwww.cgbs.org.uk

[27] See www.benchmarking.gov.uk

[28] See further http://forum.europa.eu.int/irc/euradmin/eubenchmarking/info/data/en/ebnsite/page1b.htm

Within wider ideas of modernisation there are Public Service Agreements setting targets and establishing performance indicators across the public services for modernisation and reform and introducing criteria for assessment. Within the 'Best Value' programme, which controls the way in which local authorities operate in their various roles as regulators, procurers and providers of services, there is a whole new approach which emphasises fundamental performance reviews of how local services are organised and provided. It brings in the '4Cs' (challenge, consult, compare, compete) which provide an entire new operational philosophy suggesting that local authorities should provide services directly only where it can be established that they are best placed to do so, and here their role must be closely monitored by performance indicators and benchmarking. The creation of a scheme of model 'beacon councils' under the Local Government Act 1999 allows relaxation of various statutory controls on councils which are performing excellently (although significantly it is Whitehall still that distributes 75 per cent of the funding). The introduction of a new power to 'promote community well-being' in the Local Government Act 2000 provides a further mechanism for controlling at a distance how different parts of government operate.[29] This idea of 'earned autonomy' for bodies that are performing within the measures provided has been extended to the health service with 'foundation hospitals' being afforded more resources and less direct control. Even where civil society in the form of the community and voluntary sectors are enlisted in the process of government through discharging certain of the service delivery and policy-making functions in partnership with government, there is a whole framework of semi-formal 'Compacts' setting out the terms on which such partnership should ideally take place.[30]

All this complexity associated with the general modernising government initiative is presented here to suggest that what is occuring can best be seen in terms of governmentality. The whole exercise in Modernising Government is one of capturing an area, describing it in certain terms, devising measures for what is happening, and regulating and controlling it through a massive injection of government effort to implement another way of looking at the world. This involves much more than a legislative programme but encompasses the development of a whole strategy of 'governmentality'. Of course, some aspects of this do not work: some concepts do not translate across the various enclosures or nodes of power. Indeed the constantly changing face of the modernisation programme, where various initiatives have fallen by the wayside, indicates that not everything

---

[29] See further, generally, I Leigh, *Law, Politics, and Local Democracy* (Oxford, Oxford University Press, 2000). Indeed, local government seems particularly open to new measures, with the White Paper, *Strong Leadership, Quality Public Services* (2001) (available at www.local-regions. dtlr.gov.uk/sll/index.htm providing further suggestions for yet another layer of framework of performance indicators, evaluations and rewards.

[30] See further J Morison, 'The Government-Voluntary Sector Compacts: Governance, Governmentality, and Civil Society' (2000) 27 *Journal of Law and Society* 98 for details of how these compacts were drawn up across each of the four regions/nations of the United Kingdom and how these form the basis for further more detailed, local agreements controlling the relationship between central, devolved and local government and the sector. (This essay also attempts to view this process within an account of governmentality.)

that government offers translates or is given effect. However, the overall effect is that the general environment is changed. New 'truths' are revealed and the world recalibrated so that institutions, agencies and people begin to make themselves up in different ways and act accordingly. 'Government', in the sense of acting upon action or managing possibilities, is undoubtedly occuring.

Clearly in this context the activity of government is not accurately to be seen as simply the state issuing commands but rather as a much more complex process involving aspects of government in conjunction with myriad other actors developing strategies, techniques and procedures which operate across all the various value systems and concentrations of power existing within the formal state and outside it in enclosures of political, professional and scientific power. Here the language of standards, benchmarks and performance indicators operates to provide a framework within which people and agencies operate. Concepts such as 'efficiency', 'quality', 'responsiveness', 'best practice', 'best value', 'excellence' or 'mission' are used to introduce basic controlling concepts around which people and agencies can organise themselves and their practices. Techniques of accountability such as centrally set but locally managed budgets and a whole set of practices of evaluation and auditing now provide the means by which agencies, people and communities must orient their actions and make up their lives. A governmentality perspective allows us to see the modernising government programme as being, in the words of Rose and Millar, 'a domain of strategies, techniques and procedures through which different forces seek to render programmes operable'.[31] In this way it can be understood that the power of a government or any individual agency comes from the assemblage of forces by which particular objectives and injunctions can be activated to shape the actions and calculations of others. To understand how power operates, how an actor or agency is able to enlist and mobilise all these diverse forces in pursuit of its roles, we need to look at all the details of how different parts of government set about engaging with the many networks and alliances that make up the chain that translates power from one locale to another. We need make no apology for looking at the detail rather than simply Acts of Parliament or upper court judgments. As Foucault urges as what he terms 'a methodological precaution', we must:

> conduct an *ascending* analysis of power, starting, that is, from its infinitesimal mechanisms ... and then see how these mechanisms of power have been—and continue to be—invested, colonized, utilized, involuted, transformed, displaced, extended, etc. by ever more general mechanisms and by forms of global domination.[32]

This is very far from ideas simply of sovereignty and state. It puts the focus instead on the details of the technologies of government, those strategies, techniques and procedures through which different forces and groups (including the formal state but beyond it too) attempt to render their programmes operable. This

---

[31] N Rose and P Miller, 'Political Power beyond the State: Problematics of Government' 43 *British Journal of Sociology* 173, 183.

[32] 'Two Lectures' in *Power/Knowledge: Selected Interviews and Other Writings 1972–1977*, above n 3, at 142.

understanding of the activity of government and of the technologies of government provides a way of comprehending how power in more informal or unofficial formats operates generally and, in particular, how new technologies of government sit within the constitution. With this approach we can turn to e-government as a more sustained example both of how government seeks to structure government-citizen interaction and how this may be contested and shaped in favour of a more democratic approach.

E-GOVERNMENT: UK ONLINE AS A TECHNOLOGY OF GOVERNANCE

The use of information and communication technology (ICT) is a significant aspect of many of the modernisation processes that are occurring in administrations worldwide.[33] There seems to be a general belief that the processes of government can be improved by drawing upon the ability of ICT to store, process and communicate large amounts of data. This has led to the development of ideas of e-government.[34] Generally this may be defined in terms of using the power of ICT to help transform the accessibility, quality and cost-effectiveness of public services and to help to revitalise the relationship between citizens and government through improved consultation and participation in governance.[35]

In the United Kingdom, e-government is a centrally important element in the general modernisation of government process. UKonline (www/ukonline.gov.uk), launched in December 2000 as the portal through which citizens and others eventually will interact with government online, is central to the modernisation strategy. It is intended that UKonline.gov.uk will be the principal entry point of access for citizens to government information and to services online. The White Paper *Modernising Government* (1999) put a particular emphasis on 'Information Age Government' and how it is important to 'modernise the business of government itself, achieving joined up working between different parts of government and providing new, efficient and convenient ways for citizens and businesses to communicate with government and receive services'.[36] UKonline is to lead the drive to better integration of government services. ICT has been identified by the Head of

[33] There is a webpage at www.gksoft.com/govt/en/ linking governments across the world who are on the World Wide Web.) There are a number of surveys and evaluations of government websites. The Cyperspace Policy Research Group (CyPRG) has tracked the spread and deployment of the Web in 192 governments around the world since 1996 and established a comprehensive database of national public agency websites which can be accessed online. See further www.cyprg.arizona.edu.

[34] See further, eg, R Traunmüller and K Lenk (eds), *Electronic Government: First International Conference , EGOV 2002, Aix-en-Provence, France, September 2002 Proceedings* (Berlin, Springer, 2002) (also available at htttp:link.springer.de/series/lncs/) for a large number of examples from across the world of attempts to modernise government through ICT. See also www.gksoft.com/gov/en/ for webpage linking to governments across the world who are on the World Wide Web and also Silcock 'What is e-government? [2001] *Parliamentary Affairs* 88 and Y. Akdeniz, C Walker, and D Wall, *The Internet, Law and Society* (Harlow, Longman, 2000).

[35] The principal ICT is the Internet, accessible through a variety of means including personal computers and kiosks, mobile phones including text messaging (SMSS), and digital television.

[36] *Modernising Government* (Cm 4310, 1999) ch 5, para 5.

the Civil Service as one of the key enablers to achieve the goals of reform and delivery in the Civil Service.[37] The second phase of modernisation, introduced by *Reforming our Public Services: Principles into Practice* (2002), refers to the 'huge opportunity to harness new technologies to raise standards in public services'[38] and it has endorsed the target of 100 per cent of key services available online by 2005 set in the original *Modernising Government* paper.[39] The role of the e-envoy within the Cabinet Office in promoting e-government and moving government towards its target is also significant.[40] The work of this post is supported both centrally and in the devolved administrations by e-ministers within each department charged with developing departmental strategy and e-champions drawn from senior officials within departments.[41]

In addition to ideas about service delivery, the consultation aspect of e-government also is particularly important in the context of many of the newer policies involved in wider ideas of modernisation. The Cabinet Office and the e-envoy have launched a large-scale consultation on a policy for electronic democracy based on the premise that ICT can 'facilitate, broaden and deepen' participation.[42] This fits in well with general policies which require increasingly that services are targeted and delivery mechanisms monitored; e-government is particularly appropriate for local government too in this context as both improved service delivery and enhanced consultation are central to new approaches to local services. For example, ideas about community leadership duties contained in the Local Government Act 2000 (and proposals outlined in the recent White Paper, *Strong Local Leadership, Quality Services*[43]) put an emphasis on articulating and developing a vision for the community to be obtained after extensive dialogue and consultation. The Best Value regime also involves commitment to consult all sections of the local community on key best value priorities and on the effectiveness of service delivery. More directly, £350 million has been allocated to local government online funding. Targets have been set within public service agreements and, for example, the Best Value Performance Indicator (BVPI 157) provides measures of progress for local authorities in meeting e-government targets where crucially one of transactions identified as suitable for delivery in electronic form is consultation.

Beyond the modernisation programme there is also optimism about e-government in a wider role of reinvigorating traditional democracy. This extends beyond

[37] See paper by Sir Andrew Turnbull to the Civil Serivce Management Board, June 2002, available at www.cabinet-office.gov.uk/2002/news/turnbullpaper.doc and I Holliday, 'Steering the British State in the Information Age' in *Government and Opposition* (2000), 314–29.

[38] *Reforming our Public Services: Principles into Practice* (2002), 14.

[39] It is now expected that only 80% of services will be accessible via the internet by the end of 2005 but of more concern is evidence that despite the internet is being used enthusiastically for shopping, citizens take-up of on-line government services is not growing as expected and in some areas has actually fallen. (See *The Economist*, 4 January 2003.) See also n 52.

[40] See further www.e-envoy.gov.uk

[41] See www.e-envoy.gov.uk/EStrategy/Echampions/fs/en

[42] *In Service of Democracy: A Consultation Paper for Electronic Democracy* (2002).

[43] Above, n 29. See also DTLR and LGA, *e-gov@local: Towards a National Strategy for Local E-Government* (2002) and FITLOG, *Role Models for the Information Age: Using Information Technology to support the New Political Management Arrangements* (2001).

rather limited experiments in e-voting,[44] to notions of establishing a better dialogue between the governed and the governors, perhaps ushering in a whole series of ideas about dialogic or participatory democracy and better forms of decision-making.[45]

Indeed, as some aspects of the formal modernisation programme struggle to find their way into the second phase of the programme, the e-government component is thriving. 2002 *alone* has seen the production of eight major reports from different aspects of government on various aspects of e-government, from local services and participation in local government to e-voting and the state of development.[46] It is also significant that the same period has seen an increasing number of reports and responses from various bodies and interest groups outside government.[47] There is no doubt that e-government is becoming a space for government and it is one that is being contested and shaped as it is increasingly rolled out.

The development of government online should be seen accordingly as an evolutionary process. The rate of evolution depends on complex factors including much more than simply the development of the technology. For example, research from the Cyber Policy Research Group looking at the factors which influence the development of government websites suggests that factors such as the structure and personnel of government and, particularly, the influence of commercial companies and standards drawn from the private sector are influential.[48] Government, of course, remains a major figure in this development. Figure 7.2 provides a model for the general evolution of government online. This development begins with a straightforward posting of information online where communication is one-way and simple. It may then evolve into a more interactive exchange between government and citizens where simple transactions such as renewing passports or paying taxes can be completed. Later services will be combined at a single point of entry and more complex personalisa-

[44] See further the work of the Hansard Society on the use of Internet technology in the United Kingdom's general election in 2001 in S Coleman (ed), *2001: Cyber Space Odyssey: The Internet in the UK Election* (London, Hansard Society, 2001) and the Electoral Commission, *Modernising Elections: a Strategic Evaluation of the 2002 Electoral Pilot Schemes* (2002) at www.electoralcommission.org.uk/publications.htm#anchor1

[45] For example, Tony Blair has declared that, 'I believe that the information society can revitalise our democracy' and he has referred to how 'innovative electronic media [is] pioneering new ways of involving people of all ages and backgrounds in citizenship through new internet and digital technology … that can only strengthen our democracy'. Quoted on Hansard Society, *E-Democracy Programme* webpage at www.hansard-society.org.uk/eDemocracy.htm. Stephen Coleman of the Hansard Society argues for a 'civic commons in cyberspace' which would involve creating an enduring structure to fulfil the democratic potential of the new interactive media. See *Realising Democracy Online: A Civic Commons in Cyberspace* (2001).

[46] National Audit Office, *Government on the Web II*; Audit Commission, *Better Public Services through E-Government*; Audit Commission, *Councils and E-Government*; Improvement and Development Agency, *Local E-Government Now, 2002*; DTLR and LGA, *e-gov @ local*; OGC/Office of e-envoy, *In the Service of Democracy: A Consultation Paper on a Policy for Electronic Democracy*; Electoral Commission, *Modernising Elections: a Strategic Evaluation of the 2002 Electoral Pilot Schemes*.

[47] See, eg, IPPR, *E-Participation in Local Government*; SOCITM, *Better Connected 2002?*; SOCITM and IDEA, *Local E-Government Now: A World Wide View*; Hansard Society, *Technology: Enhancing Representative Democracy in the UK*

[48] See T La Porte, C Demchak and C Friis, 'Webbing Governance: Global Trends Across National Level Public Agencies' in *Communications of the ACM* (2001) which draws upon interviews with 150 webmasters worldwide.

Evolutionary stage	*Level of service available*	*Type of communication*	Form of government organisation
1. Information publishing/ dissemination	Departments set up basic websites, list services and contact points	One–way, 'push', ie analogous to broadcast, 'electronic notice-board' adverts for hardcopy publications	Developed and organised by individual departments. for own use
2. Official two-way transactions	Customers/citizens able to transmit information; limited e-publishing	Two-way communication, 'push' and 'pull'—ie data on request, downloadable documents; electronic signatures for simple transactions	Individual departments or central IT unit initi-ating e-services for use in departments to duplicate existing mechanisms
3. Multi-purpose portals	Single point of entry to multiple government services allowing multiple transactions	Bi-directional communication—send and receive information plus monetary transactions	Interdepartmental co-operation, some cross-cutting organisation
4. Portal personalisation	Individual customer preferences and interests	Customised individual service	Increased cross-cutting of departments
5. Clustering of common services	Perceptions of government as multiple entity replaced by transaction-led interaction across government as a whole	One-touch access; full range of links across to private and voluntary sectors and rest of government	Individual-led interac-tion with 'Government' as single entity; cross-cutting or fully integrated services requiring modified departmental structures;
6. Full integration and transformation	Technology integrated, distance between front and back office shortened or eradicated; services totally integrated across what were formerly department boundaries	Fully interactive; zero touch technologies; proactive alerts; supporting online voting, consultation and discussion	Budgets and culture follow traffic mix; 'isocratic' administra-tion; a revolution in government?

FIGURE 7.2: *The evolution of e-government services*

tion of citizen's entry points can take place. Here communication may be more inter-active and unprompted. A final stage might well involve the joining together of con-sultation processes with service delivery functions within a single portal where all government-citizen interaction takes place in a seamless way.

Such an evolution does, of course, require an associated change in the structure of government as the fourth column of Figure 7.2 indicates. This is a very impor-tant issue. As the technological front office develops, and the old departmental boundaries are blurred in an effort to ensure that the citizen can access the service required directly (rather than simply the department that deals with one or another aspect of his or her problem), so too will the back office change and develop within a general process of integration of services. If citizens are accessing services organised by issues or life events then government departments may find themselves necessarily involved in more and more cross-cutting organisation and, eventually, perhaps in providing more fully integrated services that will challenge the organisation of traditional departments.

At its highest stage of evolution, a fully integrated online government inevitably would bring *huge* changes in the structure of the administration as budgets and culture would follow the direction of traffic making use of individualised, zero touch technologies. From the point of view of the citizen he or she would not be interacting with individual government departments but with 'Government' as a single entity. Indeed at this level (beginning at stage 5 and covering mainly stage 6 of Figure 7.2 above) the whole idea of e-government *involves* and *requires* changes in how government itself is organised.

There is in this way an architecture to e-government requiring links between different parts of government and routes to individual citizens in order to conduct authenticated transactions. The way in which the citizen accesses government, the means by which that that inquiry is routed, and the part of government that deals with the inquiry, are thus intimately linked within the model of e-government. Figure 7.3 shows the framework that is involved.

FRONT END ⟶	MIDDLEWARE ⟶	BACK END
(the principal point of entry departments, entry for the citizen)	(the tier that enables government to join up in a coherent way)	(government local authorities + other sectors delivering services

FIGURE 7.3: *E-government framework*

Within the UK context, ambitions are set at a high level. (Indeed, because of the particular architecture of UKonline there are issues about how technology can expect to change government structures and cultures even at lower evolutionary stages, for example around stages 3 and 4 and moving towards stage 5 in Figure 7.2.) The idea is that www.ukonline.gov.uk will be the 'front end', the principal entry point for citizens to access government information and services online. According to the stated policy of the e-envoy, it will be 'the key driver in

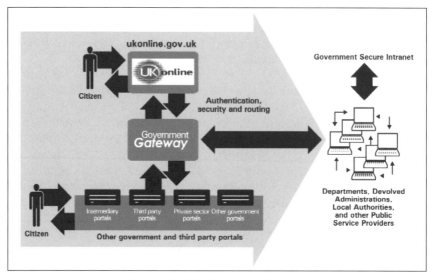

FIGURE 7.4: *The Government Gateway*

transforming the way in which public services are organised and delivered, and in leading the drive to better integration of government services'.[49] While there will be other portals too (for example in the devolved administrations and through local government sites), the idea is 'bring together all public sector portals and web-sites under the UK online brand'.[50]

The 'middleware' is provided by the Government Gateway (see Figure 7.4). This is a sophisticated piece of secure infrastructure with intelligent routing and authentication software opening up different parts of government (and related bodies in the public, private and voluntary sectors) to interact with each other and conduct transactions with the public. The Government Gateway is being developed to ensure that all government information and services are aggregated in one place. It is intended to provide joined up and transparent access to all parts of government and also to ensure that the necessary and appropriate security and authentication is available to enable different parts of government to conduct electronic transactions with citizens.

This is an important piece of governmental architecture and its place within the overall framework designed to transform citizen inquiries into government business has profound consequences for the shape and design of government. It is intended to perform an immense role in routeing and authenticating communications between citizens and all the different parts of government, including devolved and local service providers as well as those other providers drawn from

---

[49] See *UK Online.gov.uk: Connecting You with Government Information and Services* (2001) available online at www.e-envoy.gov.uk
[50] *Ibid* at 12.

other sectors. Within the model, as information flows and budgets are allocated in response to traffic so too will the structure of government need to change to accommodate the supposed reality of citizen experience. (Indeed even services in traditional formats will follow this flow as they are bundled together with the online versions.) Information management and technology is to be the driver for a revolution in the organisation of government where departmental boundaries are eroded by a technological interface that is supposed increasingly to render them obsolete. This may result in what some scholars of public administration term 'isocratic administration' where structures of government are submerged below an interface which intercedes between government and the citizen, and in turn shapes how government organises itself to respond to the citizen. In other words, there may be a process of real structural change in the shape of government that accompanies changes in access to government and the flow of information that results.

Of course we may well doubt if such a revolution is realistic. There must be serious reservations as to whether the macro and micro political cultures of government, accustomed to working within individual departments and with separate budgets, can be transformed merely by technological innovation. Also, there should be significant question marks over the whether such an ambitious project of information engineering were possible—even if it were thought desirable. The record of success in large-scale e-government projects is not good and what is proposed here is even larger.[51]

However, we should consider the Government Gateway as attempting to promote a structural change that would have fundamental *constitutional* implications too. This system is offering a profound re-engineering of government. The Government Gateway offers to link up not only all aspects of central government but also devolved and local government and 'other public service providers' with little regard for the constitutional proprieties and relative competences of different branches and levels of government. Ideas of separation of powers, rule of law and basic principles of legality do not seem to have troubled the information systems engineers. From the standpoint of formal constitutional theory, not only are there issues over the penetration of the voluntary and private sector into government but also there should be concerns over the deployment of information gathered in one (public) context within another (private) one and vice versa. These issues are particularly important in the context of multi-level, multi-agency and multi-format government and give rise to a whole host of other issues about privacy, data

---

[51] The total cost of cancelled and over-budget government IT projects may exceed £1.5bn over the last 6 years according to *Computing* (March 2003). *The Economist*, 4 May 2002, details the record of e-government failures which include the computerisation of the Passport Office which resulted in increased delays and added £40m, projects within the Inland Revenue where costs doubled adding an additional £1.4bn and the Home Office scheme to computerise aspects of immigration applications which was abandoned after costing £77m. The examples could be multiplied. There is even evidence from a report published by the business process solution company eiStream that many governments across Europe are building transactional e-government portals without introducing electronic processing in the back office, with the result that data will either have to be converted to and from digital and paper formats or governments will need to maintain hybrid, dual systems, leading to reduced efficiency. (see *E-Government Bulletin*, January 2003 or http://www.eistream.com

FIGURE 7.5: *UKonline home-page*

protection and confidentiality and human rights. In its fullest form, the e-government revolution would effect a transformation in government and it is unimaginable that the Government Gateway could ever provide what it terms 'authentication, security and routing [sic]' that would be capable of taking into account the legal and constitutional issues involved.

Even in its present form as UKonline, the Government is putting considerable effort and resources into this technology of governance in its attempt to structure the interaction between itself and citizens. As the UKonline home page suggests, the Government's present strategy works on a model of the citizen as *consumer*. It offers a service that essentially facilitates the customer of government services. The home page offers links to five other options. (See Figure 7.5.) 'Quickfind' is a search engine that links to various government departments. The 'Your Life' button is a public information service themed around life-changing events across eight 'Life Stages'. 'Newsroom' is another government information service. 'Do it Online' offers the opportunity to apply directly online for an (as yet limited) number of services such as passport, TV licence, fishing licence and tax self-assessment. Although there has been some research about which services online users would use,[52] this has not amounted to more than market research about demand for products. It has not by any means amounted to a more sustained discussion about how government-citizen relations more generally should be structured.

There is, however, also a CitizenSpace site (currently under review[53]). This is an embryonic consultation forum where government offers online versions of traditional consultations. Here Government seeks views but in a highly systematic and regulated way, even specifying 'tips' to those consulted in order to maximise effectiveness. (It seems that the ideal citizen within CitizenSpace must not only be an active one but also read diligently all the material, be brief, provide evidence, respond to questions as the tips suggest.) It is perhaps significant that although this is 'government-direct', without the intermediary influence of an elected representative, it can not be characterised as 'democracy-direct'. Even the planned relaunch of CitizenSpace outlined in the recent consultation paper[54] will not develop consultation beyond a fairly tightly controlled interaction where, essentially, citizens offer their views on proposals already made in the same way as consumers might make suggestions about products or services. Indeed, there seems to be a view that the Cabinet Office Code of Good Practice and some official best practice guidance[55] represents the highest stage of evolution of government-citizen dialogue. This is far from the case and the essential idea that citizens simply obtain, read and then comment upon lengthy documents from government departments remains officially unchallenged.

Indeed, it is easy to critique UKonline as attempting to restructure the relationship between government and citizen into something closer to that between government and consumer.[56] Listing services online and offering this as an alternative way of doing business does not necessarily amount to doing any more than most medium-sized corporations do in relation to selling their products and establishing ways to complain. In relation to consultation, simply operating a website with contact points may amount to little more than an electronic 'suggestion box' or a survey of those who both have the technology and a desire to engage with government online.

---

[52] See, eg, Cabinet Office, *Electronic Government: the View from the Queue* (1988) which contains the detailed research about potential customer take-up of online services and the Oftel surveys into residential consumer use of Internet services www.oftel.gov.uk/publications/research/indez.htm and the Office of National Statistics' figures on Internet access at www.statistics.gov.uk/pdfdir/intacc0402.pdf There are also studies about the wider use of the Internet for connecting with a range of public officials. See, eg, S Coleman, (ed), *Democracy Online: What Do We Want from MP's Web Sites?* (2002) and more general studies such as H Margetts and P Dunleavy, *Cultural Barriers to e-government* (2000) London: Audit Office.

[53] A review of CitizenSpace is one of the aims of the consultation *In the Service of Democracy: A Consultation Paper on a Policy for Electronic Democracy* (2002) which aims to capture for government some of the enthusiasm that interactive television shows such as Pop Idol and Big Brother have engendered in Britain and elsewhere. For details of this consultation see further www.edemocracy.gov.uk

[54] *Ibid*. This suggests that 100% of government public consultation should be online and that Green and White Papers should include a moderated public discussion forum. Significantly, this is to be hosted by government.

[55] See www.cabinet-office.gov.uk/servicefirst/2000/consult/code/consultationCode.htm and www.servicefirst.gov.uk/1998/guidance/users/index#cont

[56] See further J Morison and D Newman, 'On-line Citizenship: Consultation and Participation in New Labour's Britain' (2001) 15 *International Review of Law, Computers and Technology* 171.

In fact it can be seen from a governmentality perspective that what is occurring is an exercise in governmentality: a new technology of governance is being attempted. An issue has been identified about how to 'modernise' and ideas of information technology have been enlisted as part of a possible solution. Resources are being directed towards identifying and establishing e-government as a space for government. Specialist personnel and expertise are being created and new vocabularies are developed to describe and control this as a governable area. Concepts are being developed to analyse and manage the various issues found there. Links are being made to concentrations of expertise, particularly in private sector IT companies, and 'solutions' are being developed. The overall effect is that the interaction between government and citizens is being mediated, shaped and controlled.

E-GOVERNMENT: A TECHNOLOGY OF DEMOCRACY

Having characterised e-government through the UKonline initiative as being concerned with creating and controlling a space, and establishing it as a governable area, an important clarification must now be added. There is, of course, more involved in e-government than the initiatives of government itself. The idea of governmentality is not simply about accounting for how the state exercises power and control. Indeed to tell the story of e-government from the perspective only of UKonline is as misleading as a history that is about only kings and queens. The governmentality approach stresses how power operates only through networks, through bodies and individuals taking up ideas or rejecting them, modifying initiatives, suggesting alternatives and shaping, influencing and directing how programmes are carried out. There are many players in the e-government arena in addition to those parts of the formal system involved in UKonline. While one story of e-government is about various bodies and agencies (more or less) within government endeavouring to establish and control a governable space, there is another narrative of bodies, agencies and individuals outside formal government, engaging only to degrees with government efforts, and at the same time offering alternatives by way of critique, good practice exemplars, codes of practice etc. The full story of this is far beyond the limits of this chapter. However, it is possible to highlight some of the major democratic issues that have been identified there. It is these that should be of particular concern to constitutionalists.

With regard first to the provision of services online, there is sometimes a belief that the Internet is somehow automatically open and accessible, and therefore more democratic. This is not necessarily the case. Indeed there is a view that e-government development can occur in several styles or formats with varying characters and degrees of democratic potential.[57] More practically, a number of

---

[57] The SOCITM and IDEA, *Local E-Government Now: A World Wide View* report produced in 2002 characterises e-government development as falling into three broad categories: 'e-services', concerned with securing and providing government services by electronic means; 'e-governance', concerned with

organisations have developed measures to evaluate the provision of services. The Society of Information Management (SOCITM)'s *Better Connected 2002* Survey[58] provides an overall review of best practice across local authority websites in Great Britain. It also reports on a test carried out on the ability of local authority websites to respond to the sort of needs that a range of local authority customers, such as a business expanding in a new location or a family moving house, might have. Using various scenarios, the test examines the degree to which government is joined-up, the use of interactive applications, community leadership and usability. Overall, performance across government websites is very patchy. Some do not even provide contact telephone numbers or basic contact addresses. Ratings are also given on how websites performed on specific tasks such as answering e-mails, providing access for those with disabilities[59] and technical performance. The resulting performance tables and 27 pages of advice for website managers is a valuable tool for improving both content and usability of government websites generally.

The Arizona-based research team, CyPRG, has developed the Website Attribute Evaluation (WAE) system.[60] This offers a 43 point scale to measure, at least in part, some of the democratic attributes of systems. The WAE measures openness in terms of the two goals of *transparency* and *interactivity*. Transparency relates to the minimal information that is necessary to navigate the organisation as depicted in the information on the site. Interactivity is a measure of visitor convenience and assesses the extent to which the site is navigable to the user or 'clickable'. This WAE system provides a stern critical voice against those who believe that the technology is by nature open and that e-government automatically equals efficient, open and more democratic government. The global average score for transparency at the last measure was 7.4 out of a possible 21 and for interactivity it is 2.6 out of a possible 18. It may be that constitutional lawyers would wish to add extra dimensions relating to accountability, confidentiality, data protection and privacy. Indeed, one of the major points of this chapter is to argue that establishing such criteria is now necessarily the business of constitutional lawyers. Moreover, there must be issues about access. Although services may be available outside office hours on a '24/7' basis, the issue of a digital divide remains. There may be many individuals and groups, including particularly those who are low income, elderly or otherwise

---

linking up citizens, stakeholders and elected representatives to participate in the governance of communities; and 'e-knowledge' where the emphasis is on developing the skills and ICT infrastructure to exploit knowledge for competitive advantage. The Republic of Ireland (along with Brazil, Hong Kong and Singapore) is characterised particularly as having an 'e-knowledge' quality with the emphasis on community-based economic and social regeneration. The United Kingdom meanwhile is characterised as being within an e-services model.

[58] SOCITM, *Better Connected 2002? A Shapshot of All Local Authority Websites* (2002). See also the e-envoy's guidance to official webmasters (www.e-envoy.gov.uk/webguidelines.htm).

[59] Various organisations dealing with disability provide guidelines for best practice in this field also. For example the RNIB offer a 'See it Right' accreditation to websites that provide accessibility to people with visual impairment (http://www.rnib.org.uk/seeitright).

[60] See C Demchak, C Friis and T La Porte, 'Webbing Governance: National Differences in Constructing the Face of Public Organisations' (2000) (available via www.cyprg.arizona.edu/wea.html).

vulnerable, who do not have access to ICT.[61] It is important that e-government does not introduce any sort of an idea of IT competence as a qualification for meaningful or enhanced citizenship and services.

When we move on to consider the role of e-government in consultation and its contribution to democratic participation there is again a large agenda beyond UKonline and its limited idea of CitizenSpace. Once more it should be stressed that there is nothing about ICT that necessarily improves consultation or enhances democracy. Indeed, Barber believes that it is important to distinguish between different types of democracy—plebiscitary, representative and participatory—and appreciate that some aspects of ICT may enhance certain forms more than others.[62] For example, the speed of new technology will be an attraction to plebiscitary systems while its interactive quality will appeal to proponents of more participatory forms of democracy. Barber also expresses a view, developed further by Sunstein,[63] that the Internet may in fact operate against proper deliberative democracy because it fragments communities by allowing us to screen out the sort of unwanted information that often in normal life forms a common experience and encourages truly joint, endogenous decision-making.

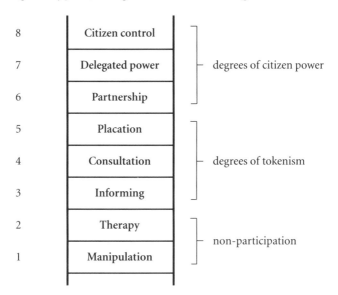

FIGURE 7.6: *Eight rungs on a ladder of citizen participation*

---

[61] Figures on IT use suggest that 56% of the population has now used the Internet and time spent online is increasing. The majority of 15-24 year olds are using the internet at home and 82% of this group have accessed the Internet at some time. See Office of National Statistics, *Internet Access: Households and Individuals* (April 2002) and Oftel Residential Survey, *Consumers' Use of the Internet* (February 2002).

[62] B Barber, 'Which Technology for Which Democracy? Which Democracy for Which Technology?' (2001) *International Journal of Communications Law and Policy* 1. (See www.ijclp.org)

[63] C Sunstein, *Republic.com* (Princeton, Princeton University Press, 2001).

Consultation model	Type of interaction	Examples
Question and answer	Simple public web-page with questions and 'voting'	Youth question Florida Governor http://www.myflorida.com/ eog/kidspage/Questions.htm BBC Talking Point http://newsvote.bbc.co.uk/hi/ english/talking_point/default.stn
Electronic petitions	View a petition online, sign or amend and join discussion forum	Petitioning the Scottish Parliament www.scottish.parliament.uk/ parl_bus/petitions.html Petitions to 10 Downing Street www.number-10.gov.uk/ output/page598.asp
Document + policy comment	Respondents add comments to policy document, can include 'threads' and horizontal communication between groups and individuals	e-democracy toolkit developed by International Teledemocracy Centre http://www.ict.napier.ac.uk/ ITC_Home/ITC/e-toolkit.asp Dutch experience of interactive consultation collected at http://www.inbzl.nl/international/ documents/pab907.htm
On line guests/ panel	Decision-makers or experts on a virtual stage answering questions on pre-chosen topic for agreed time	Young peoples' views on human rights in East Belfast http:www.eastbelfast.com/youth/ US Presidential debate http://www.webwhiteblue.org/rcd/
Online conference	A conference replicated online over a period of days or weeks including workshops, breakout sessions, 'coffee time chats' etc	Scottish Youth Summit http://www.youthsummit.org.uk World Bank Development Forum http://www.worldbank.org. devforum/ongoing.html
Online spatial decision support systems	Virtual modelling of planning options and interactive questioning of planners and community	Pilot studies carried out by geographers from Leeds University at http://www.ccg.leeds.ac.uk
Communities of practice/interest relating to particular topic or consultation process	Online tools for e-mail list group, informal or more structured and focused information exchange. Can include questionnaire, opinion polls, brainstorming etc	Law Commission 290 pp. consultation on housing law in questionnaire form http://www.landlordlaw.co.uk Bologna civic network http://lipoerbole.bologna.it/ Research for public policy-making http://www.yougov.com or http://www.prforum.com
Live chat events	Interact in real-time, Q and A with politicians and (especially) youth groups or hard to reach minorities in structured process hosted by facilitators	Politicians talk to East Belfast Youth http://www.eastbelfast.com/youth/ EU Commission Europa Chats http://europa.ue.int/comm/chat

Consultation model	Type of interaction	Examples
Live multi-media events	'Lunch speaker' or press conference with interactive tv or webcast, poll, questions, text available online etc.	Wisconsin Interactive TV Project http://itv.wpt.org/examples NASA Mars Teaching Training Conference http://quest.arc.nasa.marsconf London's Camden Council engaging with young people www.camden.gov.uk/young/index.cfm
Online deliberative poll	Public consultation with 'quick votes' from both self-selecting and representative samples	By the People – A National Conversation about America in the world http:www.pbs.org/newshour/btp/polls.htm

FIGURE 7.7: *Methods and examples of online consultation*

More simply it can be noted that there is a significant difference between consultation that involves participation and leads genuinely to citizen empowerment and more superficial forms of consultation where views are sought but with little effect. Figure 7.6 indicates a ladder of participation with only the top three rungs amounting to genuine active citizenship where citizens as civil masters can control the policies and activities of civil servants and representatives.[64] Any technology must be judged in terms of how it contributes to meaningful participation. Again there are exemplars, standards and codes available to suggest best practice. The Hansard Society work is particularly valuable in this regard.[65] Much of this is summarised in the view expressed by Coleman that 'democratic deliberation is best conducted within the context of a neutral public space, under the aegis of a fiercely independent, non-partisan organisation.'[66] There are also other sources such as Stephen Clift's *e-government Briefing Book* with its top ten tips[67] and the Institute of Public Policy's *Good Practice Guidelines*.[68] In a paper written with David Newman, the author sketched out a model of consultation that was participatory, based on conversations where preferences are shaped in an interactive

[64] Figure 7.6 is taken from a classic article by S Arnstein, 'A Ladder of Citizen Participation' [1969] *Journal of American Institute of Planners* 216–224, 217.

[65] See particularly S Coleman, *Realising Democracy Online: A Civic Commons in Cyberspace* (London, Hansard Society, 2001); S Coleman, 'UK Citizens Online Democracy: An Experiment in Government-Supported Online Public Space' in *G8 Democracy and Government On-Line Services: Contributions from Around the World* (available at http://www.statskontoret.se/gol-democracy/foreword.htm); N Hall, *Building Digital Bridges: Creating Inclusive Online Parliamentary Consultations* (London, Hansard Society, 2001).

[66] *Realising Democracy Online: A Civic Commons in Cyberspace* (2001).

[67] http:www.netcaucus.org/books/egov2001/

[68] IPPR, Code of Practice in *E-Participation in Local Government* (2002), 19. See also the Consultation Charter provided by the Consultation Institute at http:// www.consultationinstitute.org and the IDeA Knowledge toolkit available at http://www.idea-knowledge.gov.uk

process of discussion rather than simply counted in an exercise to identify the majority position.[69] It is a model drawn from literature on mediation and has the advantage that there are a range of computer support tools to sustain it. Indeed, there are many such models available and many instances of innovative democratic technology being matched with novel information and communication technology to produce improved participation and decision-making. Figure 7.7 shows several examples of good practice from consultations that are have actually taken place using a range of democratic and ITC techniques.

All of these, along with the codes of practice, guidelines and standards urged by various bodies and individuals, can act as a corrective to the idea that UKonline, with all that it entails for the nature and quality of government, is the only way of developing e-democracy.

CONCLUSION

The critique of UKonline with which this examination of e-government has concluded is not intended to suggest that there are not any advantages to offering services online or providing electronic forms of consultation. The potential of e-government to connect citizens with government services and to widen and deepen participation must not be underestimated. However, the main thrust of this chapter has been to argue that e-government should be seen within the context of a wider modernising government initiative. This in turn relates to broader changes in the nature of government as it has mutated towards ideas of governance where the role of the state and its levels and forms of operation have changed.

It has been argued that these wider changes, and their effect on public law understandings of state, law and power, are best understood from a perspective that develops the insights of the governmentality approach associated with the work of Michel Foucault. Such an approach takes us to wider questions. Why did e-government come to be seen as governable space? How does this relate to the modernising government programme and the wider assumptions about the role of the state? How does law combine with other tactics and strategies to mobilise power across various networks? How does this affect our understandings of what the state is and the ways in which it governs? What effect does putting government online have on the structures and relationships of government more generally? How does government seek to structure the interaction between citizens and the administration through controlling the interface by means of which they meet? Are there alternative ways of developing and managing this space? How can we widen our understanding of the nature of government to encompass all this and develop the democratic potential that is entailed?

---

[69]   Above n 56. See also the 'very general' checklist for designing and facilitating web events provided by Full Circle Associates at http://www.fullcir.com/community/designingonlineevents.htm.

   The governmentality perspective begins to provide answers in terms of developing an idea of government as involving the creation and deployment of a whole range of technologies connecting multiple centres of power within an exercise of government that is wider and more complex than that which is contained within traditional understandings within public law scholarship. This is a critical perspective that enables us to strip away the naturalness of the workings of government and see the activity of government encompassing the creation of governable spaces where technologies of government compete with technologies of democracy to realise individual programmes within wider schemes of governance.

8

UK Utility Regulation in an Age of Governance

PETER LEYLAND*

INTRODUCTION

T HIS CHAPTER DISCUSSES UK utility regulation in a constitutional and legal
context and in doing so encounters a number of issues that are central to
this collection of essays. For example, it will be apparent that any discussion
of regulation is closely related not only to how different layers of power are exercised in the contemporary state but to understanding the range of mechanisms
that are available to control the exercise of this power.

The public utilities of gas, electricity and water not only remain of great importance to the national economy but their operation and performance have enormous
economic, political and environmental implications, and although the Labour party
came to power in 1997 having accepted privatisation as a permanent feature of the
economic landscape, the performance of the privatised utilities in particular has
continued to be a matter of pressing public concern.[1] In this chapter, I will first consider the shifting position of public utilities and their regulation in constitutional
and legal terms, but another important theme is an assessment of the different types
of regulation and the impact of devolution on the regulatory process. In recent years
the utilities have been reformulated into 'a complex network of service delivery
arrangements'[2] which have been further compounded by the introduction of a layer
of devolved government for Scotland, Wales and Northern Ireland. In relation to the
utilities, it would appear that a number of diverse statutes has led to a redistribution

---

* I would like to thank Tony Prosser, Mike Taggart and Nicholas Bamforth for their extremely helpful comments on an earlier draft of this chapter.
[1] Nevertheless, it was believed by Labour Party policy-makers that some of the utilities had been dis-
posed of below their market value and this anomaly was tackled by a 'one off' windfall profits tax of
£5.2bn, introduced in the budget of July 1997, following Labour's first general election victory for 18
years. See P Stephens 'The Treasury under Labour' in A Seldon (ed), *The Blair Effect: The Blair Government* 1997–2001 (London, Little Brown, 2001) at pp 195.
[2] A Midwinter and N McGarvey, 'In Search of the Regulatory State: Evidence from Scotland' (2001)
79 *Public Administration*, (No 4) 825.

of powers and functions among the devolved executives and regulators, but that this has taken place without any regional strategy.[3]

At an institutional level we will see that, in the contemporary state post-privatisation and devolution, the channels of accountability to Parliament through ministers have been significantly modified and only operate indirectly as one of a number of mechanisms through which the activities of the utility sector are made accountable.[4] Most obviously this has included the introduction of utility regulators for each industry who 'now play a critical role in national economic management, exercise a power to make decisions worth literally billions of pounds to the stock market value of companies, and are second only to the Chancellor of the Exchequer in the influence they wield over the family budget.'[5]

In seeking to regulate in this sector, regulatory authorities very often intervene in what would otherwise be an economic arena. The problem then becomes deciding upon the degree to which socio-political considerations will be allowed to interfere with the more technical questions that are likely to be involved with economic regulation.[6] In fact throughout this discussion it will be evident that there are distinct and often conflicting objectives for regulators which are usually recognised by and incorporated in the legislation itself, and although the competing weights given to these considerations are of vital importance, no clear formula for resolution is provided by the statutory framework under which they operate. For instance, on the one hand, should the task of regulation be predominantly concerned with promoting competition, controlling prices, safeguarding profitability, promoting one industry in preference to another? Or, on the other hand, should it be concerned with protecting consumer interests and safeguarding the environment? This problem presents itself because social and economic priorities cannot be resolved at an entirely technical level and this may set limits on what any form of statutory regulation can achieve on its own. Indeed, the intention behind exposing these industries to market forces was to place aspects of their operation beyond the domain of public law, while at the same time exercising a substantial degree of control over other aspects of their operation in the public interest. In demonstrating how utility regulation features on a map of public and private power it will be evident that the privatised utilities continue to be contested territory between the public and the private[7] and that this is an area that illustrates a shift in the role of the state from when it exercised a more active 'rowing' function towards it having a rather less intrusive 'steering' function.[8]

Moreover, despite being significant players in the regulatory game, statutory

---

[3] See later discussion of the gas, electricity and water industries.

[4] C Scott, 'Accountability in the Regulatory State' [2000] *Journal of Law and Society* 38, 48.

[5] C Harlow and R Rawlings, *Law and Administration* 2nd ed (London, Butterworth, 1997), 313.

[6] T Prosser, *Law and the Regulators* (Oxford, OUP, 1997), 4 *et seq.*

[7] J Allison, *A Continental Distinction in the Common Law : A Historical and Comparative Perspective on English Public Law* (Oxford, Clarendon, 1996), 101–3.

[8] See D Osborn and T Gaebler, *Reinventing Government* (New York, Addison Wesley, 1992) and M Taggart 'Reinvented Government, Traffic Lights and the Convergence of Public and Private Law. Review of Harlow and Rawlings: *Law and Administration*' [1999] *Public Law* 124, 133.

regulators are by no means the only participants.[9] It will become evident as we proceed with our discussion that there is an intricate web of interrelated issues that surround utility regulation and a 'regulatory space metaphor' has been employed to indicate that the resources relevant to holding regulatory power are dispersed and fragmented.[10] This is further evidenced by the lack of any easily identifiable public/private law distinction.[11] Furthermore, regulation is not restricted to formal state authority derived from legislation or from contracts.[12] Rather, our understanding must be related to the complexity of policy networks which are now characteristic of modern governance and which involve an interplay between government and an expanding range of public, private and hybrid bodies leading to 'complex, dynamic and horizontal [relationships] involving negotiated interdependence.'[13] There are various accountability methods which operate uniquely within each policy domain and these have the character of a system of checks and balances in which particular forms of behaviour are inhibited or encouraged by the overall balance in the system at a particular time.[14] In the case of the privatised utilities, this process includes several regulators and the consumer groups they serve.[15] In fact, the need for a multi-layered engagement with such issues has been recognised by the Government itself as essential.[16] The 'Modernising Government' initiative has encouraged moves towards 'joined up' government.[17] Any such approach clearly has important implications for institutional

[9] For example, it has been suggested that the supervision of service delivery takes place at different degrees of formalism. In this regard executive departments need to be distinguished from the task of regulation where the regulator has real power. See Midwinter and McGarvey, above n 2, at 833.

[10] See L Hancher and M Moran, 'Organising Regulatory Space' in L Hancher and M Moran, *Capitalism, Culture and Regulation* (Oxford, Clarendon, 1989), 271.

[11] Peter Cane explains, in chapter 10 below, n 67, how the concept of 'hybridisation' has been developed by regulation scholars to describe and analyse certain social activities regardless of their institutional form.

[12] The mechanism of the licence is crucial as it sets the levels of competition and is required by the regulated industry to carry on its business. See T Prosser, 'Regulation, Markets and Legitimacy' in J Jowell and D Oliver, *The Changing Constitution* (4th edn, Oxford, Oxford University Press, 2000), 240.

[13] C Scott, 'Analysing Regulatory Space: Fragmented Resources and Institutional Design' [2001] *PL* 330. For an analysis of evolving techniques for the exercise of public and private power in the context of 'e-government' and governance more generally, see John Morison, ch 7 above.

[14] Scott, above n 4, at 55.

[15] This discussion will be concerned with setting out and analysing institutional relationships at an empirical level in terms of structure, constitutional and wider accountability, but it is worth recognising that explanatory models have been proposed as a tentative framework for revealing horizontal and vertical 'directions' of accountability which arise in regard to these overlapping policy networks. A vertical axis registers whether this is to a higher authority, to a parallel institution; or to lower level institutions or groups. The horizontal axis deals with the objective of the accountability identified in terms of economic values (including financial probity and value for money); social/procedural values (such as fairness, equality and legality); continuity security values (such as social cohesion, universal service and safety). See Scott, above n 4, at 42.

[16] See R Rhodes 'The Civil Service' in A Seldon (ed) *The Blair Effect: The Blair Government 1997–2001* (London, Little Brown, 2001), 100. It is pointed out that there has been a significant shift in regulatory philosophy under Labour, with a growing awareness of the cost of regulation and the need for consistency of practice between regulators.

[17] *Better Regulation Task Force: Economic Regulators, 2001* (Cabinet Office, 2001); White Paper *Modernising Government* (Cm 4310, 1999); and the manual from the Performance and Innovation Unit, *Wiring It Up* (2000).

design, since recognising this degree of complexity also has the effect of questioning the predominant role of the state and its capacity to intervene effectively.[18] We shall see that, in practice, there is limited coherence between regulatory bodies, and between the other watchdog and co-ordinating mechanisms which have often been improvised to fulfil a particular policy role.[19]

FROM PUBLIC TO PRIVATE OWNERSHIP/STANDARD FORM OF NATIONALISATION

The nationalised industries, and particularly the utility and transport sector, are of vital strategic importance to the national economy, but this needs to be related more precisely to their legal status and their constitutional position. In this section we will briefly consider the organisation under state ownership in order to demonstrate how the strands of power and the system of accountability evolved from the public corporation model established by nationalisation.

The extension of public ownership was pursued by the Labour government, mainly during the post-war administration between 1945–1951, but as Ewing notes:

> although many of the instruments of production, distribution and exchange were socialised in terms of ownership ... this did not necessarily lead to the effective accountability of these institutions to the people on behalf of whom they were owned.[20]

Indeed, the rationale and the form of nationalisation as it was introduced had more to do with the economic failures of the industries in question[21] and to their strategic importance to the overall performance of the economy, than to any clear commitment to radical social ownership. In particular, the public utilities, which are the main concern of this chapter, were large scale monopolies relying heavily upon state subsidy.[22] Also, the post-war Labour Government and the Labour Governments of the 1960s were committed to economic planning. In consequence, 'in all of these examples, a strong pragmatic case existed, in line with classical principles of free competition, for eliminating private monopoly by taking essential utilities into public ownership.'[23] A broadly Keynesian approach to economics identified a key role for governments in managing a tendency toward imbalance. The formula attributed to Herbert Morrison and applied to London Transport in the 1930s became a model for nationalisation. This typically involved Parliament passing an

---

[18]   Scott, above n 13, at 346.

[19]   One such example is the invention of the 'Strategic Rail Authority' as a response to shortcoming in the rail industry. See the Transport Act 2000.

[20]   See K Ewing, 'The Politics of the British Constitution' [2000] *Public Law* 418.

[21]   A Taylor, *English History* 1914–45 (London, Penguin, 1970), 616 notes that 'British industrialists had got into the habit during the inter-war years of turning to the state when they ran into difficulties.

[22]   It should be noted that in the transport sector the four oligopolistic and loss-making UK rail companies were nationalised in 1948 to form British Rail. This was subsequently privatised under the provisions of the Railways Act 1993.

[23]   P Clarke, *Hope and Glory: Britain 1900–1990* (London, Penguin, 1996), 225.

enabling statute which established a separate corporate identity for the industry and exclusive ownership by the state. The corporation could be financed independently from borrowing, with the statute sometimes containing provision to raise capital by the issue of bonds. These industries often received substantial government subsidies and were exempted from direct parliamentary financial control. The internal conditions of operation varied according to each industry but they were not staffed by civil servants. Personnel were recruited and paid under conditions established by the corporation on standard contracts of employment.

It is also important to consider the mechanisms for ensuring constitutional accountability for the operation of these corporations. In virtually every case, under the enabling statute the relevant minister appointed a Chairman and a Board which was given responsibility for the day-to-day running of the corporation/nationalised industry, while the minister gave final approval for strategic issues involving capital investment. But government involvement did not end here, since the minister could not only insist on being supplied with information, but in some cases could give directions of a general nature as to the exercise or performance by the Board of their functions in relation to matters appearing to the minister to affect the public interest.[24] In fact this power was hardly ever used, but it is widely recognised that ministers increasingly intervened in operational matters such as price-setting, employment and wages.[25] In regard to ministerial accountability to Parliament and before select committees it was a problem, in practice, to distinguish between day-to-day operations which were deemed the responsibility of the Board, and general policy, which was the responsibility of the minister.

The hand of government was felt in other ways too. For instance, the Treasury was in a position to intervene by setting financial targets and by subjecting each industry to cash limits in relation to any subsidy that was provided. The Monopolies and Mergers Commission (MMC) conducted reviews of efficiency and was responsible for the imposition of effective methods of financial control.[26] The obvious problem in the utility sector was a familiar one, namely, how to give the nationalised industries adequate commercial freedom, while simultaneously maintaining sufficient public control to ensure that they followed the government's overall economy strategy and social objectives.[27] The point that must be stressed is that from the formation of the nationalised industries under public ownership, the Government still had to set a balance between the social and public interest aspects of the industry as against its commercial viability and profitability. Indeed, we will see throughout our discussion that such considerations have remained a fundamental underlying issue. For example, the Herbert Report stressed, in relation to the electricity industry, the importance of pursuing self interest as a commercial concern as the best means of serving the national economy and later drew the conclusion that the industry ought

---

[24] A Hanson and M Walles, *Governing Britain* (4th edn, (London, Fontana, 1990), 207 *et seq.*

[25] See M Thatcher, 'Institutions, Regulation and Change: New Regulatory Agencies in the British Privatised Utilities' (1998) 21 *West European Politics* 120, 122–23.

[26] See J McEldowney, *Public Law* (London, Sweet & Maxwell, 1997), 433. Now the Competition Commission. See below n 75.

[27] Hanson and Walles, above n 24, 206.

not to be absolved from economic and commercial justification.[28] An identical tension between commercial and social considerations remains in place under revised arrangements which exist post-privatisation.

   Under nationalisation the economic performance of the utilities could easily be manipulated to favour government policy. As we have seen, the Board was appointed by and indirectly responsible to the minister for matters of overall strategy. However, the fixing of pricing levels was a matter left to the Treasury, and the charging parameters for these essential services could be used as a form of surrogate taxation.[29] Prior to privatisation, these industries were encouraged to follow commercial business practices and they were allowed to charge market rates for some of their services.[29a] Other services were deliberately offered at a loss and several of the utilities were in receipt of public subsidy. In spite of limited accountability and a strong tendency towards monopoly domination, nationalisation succeeded in delivering a remarkably universal standard of utility services throughout the entire United Kingdom. In terms of energy policy this meant that the Government was in a position to make strategic decisions about long-term investment and on what emphasis to place on the use and exploitation of the various sources of energy that were available.

PRIVATISATION AND REGULATION

Privatisation was pursued as one of the main ideological objectives of the Thatcher/Major Governments. A general intention was to apply market driven solutions to the structural problems of governance.[30] Publicly owned industries were characterised as beached whales that were considered both inefficient and a burden on the tax-payer. The plan was to turn them into the glowing beacons of a new enterprise culture.[31] Moreover, the Treasury stood to benefit from the proceeds of privatisation as the government sold off its stake. Also, the flotation of shares on the stock exchange provided the opportunity to further a wider aim, namely, to create a shareholding democracy by extending the scope of private share ownership. The ultimate goal for advocates of this policy was to produce a truly competitive market

---

   [28]   A White Paper published by the Conservative Government, *Financial and Economic Obligations of the Nationalised Industries* (April 1961). See A Sampson, *The Anatomy of Britain* (London, Hodder & Stoughton, 1961), 537.
   [29a]   See eg *Financial and Economic Obligations of the Nationalised Industries* (Cmd 1961), Nationalised Industries: A Review of Economic and Financial Objectives (Cmnd. 3437 (1967)).
   [29]   T Prosser, *Nationalised Industries and Public Control* (Oxford, Blackwell, 1986), 63–69. The Treasury imposed high pricing levels to provide more funds for the Government without having to raise taxes.
   [30]   Governance is employed as a broader concept than government which, for example, takes account of the changing boundaries of the state and the interaction between public, private and voluntary sectors in the implementation of policy. For detailed discussion see Morison ch 7 above p 138, and R Rhodes, *Understanding Governance* (Buckingham, Open University Press, 1997).
   [31]   British Airways might be cited as an example of a privatised industry which has operated successfully as a private company exposed to competition without a regulator. But BA was given enormous economic advantages over competitors by having the pick of the most profitable air routes.

environment for these industries, replacing the need for regulation by imposing market simulating disciplines which in turn would reduce prices for consumers.

The problem was that regulation of privatised utilities confronted many of the same problems as those encountered under public ownership. They were turned into large companies, often exercising monopolistic power, which meant that the performance of the utilities continued to have a vital impact on the nation's economic infrastructure and the broader competitiveness of the national economy. In consequence, any system of regulation had to take account of the obvious public interest in allowing universal access to utility services by controlling price levels and preventing anti-competitive practices. Thus, from the outset utility regulation was required to accommodate often conflicting objectives by navigating a path between social, commercial and environmental considerations. Nevertheless, regulation of some kind was essential since the exercise of monopoly power in the utility sector has many repercussions which relate to the prices consumers have to pay, the level of investment and the standard of the service itself, all of which will have to be controlled to varying degrees.[31a]

Privatisation of state-owned public utilities and transport[32] between 1984 and 1995 changed the industrial structure of the nation[33] and in doing so presented many difficult legal challenges for the Government.[34] In brief, the approach was for Parliament to approve legislation that enabled the Government to transfer ownership of each industry to shareholders, transforming the utilities into autonomous self-financing businesses. On a formal basis this legislation subjected many aspects of the operation of these enterprises to regulation by means of regulatory institutions that were part of the state and accountable to ministers. At the same time, there has been an increasingly significant legal involvement by a process of indirect regulation which relied on drawing up carefully drafted licences and contracts.[35] It has been observed that this meant that the role of the state was recast rather than reduced.[36]

Many of the regulatory provisions were based on a formulation that was established in the Telecommunications Act 1984, although this varied somewhat with each industry. In outline the legislation imposed certain duties in respect of the delivery of the service in question and the statutory regulation of the public utilities[37] but this generally allowed scope for the style of regulation to develop accord-

---

[31a] See pp 202 ff below.

[32] Eg, gas, electricity, power generation, water services and British Rail. British Telecom is something of a hybrid between these categories, as many of its services have been opened up to wider competition.

[33] Clarke, above n 23, 381; C Graham and T Prosser, *Privatizing Public Enterprises: The Constitution, the State and Regulation in Comparative Perspective* (Oxford, Clarendon Press, 1991).

[34] See A Bradley and K Ewing, *Constitutional and Administrative Law* (12 edn, London, Longman, 1997) 326, 336 *et seq*; and see also T Prosser, 'Regulation, Markets, Legitimacy' in J Jowell and D Oliver, *The Changing Constitution* (3rd edn, Oxford, Oxford University Press, 1994).

[35] Harlow and Rawlings, above n 5 at 320.

[36] W Maloney, 'Regulation in an Episodic Policy-Making Environment: the Water Industry in England and Wales' (2001) 79 *Public Administration* (No 3) 625, 626.

[37] J Burton, 'The Competitive Order or Ordered Competition?: The 'UK Model' of Utility Regulation in Theory and Practice' (1997) 75 *Public Administration* (Summer) 157, 164.

ing to the priorities of the regulator for each industry. Indeed, the lack of regulatory philosophy was recognised as a problem from the outset.[38] It has meant that there has been no standardised regulatory system in the United Kingdom.

The office of the regulator was commonly placed under a statutory duty to maintain a universal service, and in doing so, was required to take into account the social consequences of the operation of the industry. There were primary duties to perform,[39] in particular, the control of pricing levels based on a price-cap formula. This was set at the retail price index minus X amount, the idea being to fix this figure at a progressively lower level as this would operate as a strong incentive to greater efficiency. A duty of equal importance, particularly in view of the wider objectives of the Conservative Government (1979–97), was intervention by the regulator to promote competition, often by the regulator acting as a surrogate form of competition.[40] Many of the economic arguments in support of privatisation were to achieve increases of efficiency, primarily through greater competition. But, as we observed in the introduction to this section, the system of regulation is faced with having to achieve some kind of balance by controlling pricing levels, ensuring access to essential services, protecting consumers, maintaining quality of service, while at the same time promoting competition and now also having regard to the profits of shareholders. This task was and still remains highly problematic because of the need to find a way through potentially conflicting interests.[41] In regard to the utilities, the fact that these are often irreconcilable objectives undermines some of the assumptions which inspired the entire privatisation project.[42] (Later, we shall see that the revised approach to structuring Welsh Water tends to confirm many of the deficiencies in the original privatisations and the same point can be made regarding the relaunch of Railtrack in 2002.)

Constitutional Accountability: Ministers and Regulators

Under public ownership, the state had direct responsibility for the operation of public utilities and there was an assumption that the intervention of government would serve a wider public interest. By contrast, the accountability of ministers to Parliament over the operation of these industries was transformed with privatisa-

[38] Initially, the privatised utilities had regimes of regulation that were based on the Conservative Government's reliance on market models, eg, the formula for pricing under these reports (see S Littlechild, '*Regulation of British Telecommunications' Profitability*') (Department of Trade and Industry, 1984); *Economic Regulation of Privatised Water Authorities* (Department of Environment, 1986).

[39] Thatcher, above n 25, at 125 *et seq*.

[40] The issuing and enforcement of licences will be considered later in relation to gas and electricity. Typically other duties were to oversee standards of service; to ensure that a universal service is provided and to safeguard the right of access for consumers.

[41] We can see that typical choices lie between: (1) promoting short term interests by allowing the distribution of profits to shareholders and a longer term view which demanded investment in an infrastructure; (2) pricing the service at market levels as against the social interest of low prices to protect vulnerable consumers; (3) maintaining a standard universal service and promoting competition by opening up the market (see *Better Regulation Task Force Report 2001*, Recommendations 7(1)).

[42] The collapse of Railtrack during the autumn of 2001 provides an illustration of this.

tion. The privatised structure was devised to avoid certain kinds of direct political interference. However, the fact that ministers performed the pivotal task of issuing licences to these businesses has allowed them to decide the timing, progress and extent of what normally is a natural monopoly and also to determine the progress towards a genuinely competitive environment. Further, it has been suggested that this is consistent with accepted notions of ministerial responsibility.[43] But in constitutional terms it appears that privatisation contributed to a further reduction of ministerial responsibility. Post privatisation, the industries were deliberately distanced from direct ministerial responsibility through the adoption of the status of non-ministerial government departments,[44] most obviously because of the parliamentary dimension to accountability since privatisation placed many more aspects of the industry beyond the routine gaze of Parliament.[45] An effect of the change in status when privatisation took place was to transform the channel of accountability. This change of status prevented MPs from asking parliamentary questions to the minister not only about the industry, but about many aspects of the regulation of the industry.[46] At the same time the role for the subject specific Parliamentary Select Committee on the Nationalised Industries (which operated between 1956–79) disappeared with the introduction of the new departmental select committees. These committees now shadow government departments and not the regulatory bodies, nevertheless the utility regulators have been regularly called to give evidence before departmental select committees and have been the subject of significant investigations and reports, some of which have been highly critical and have suggested reforms to the regulatory structure.[47] The National Audit Office and the Public Accounts Committee also perform an important function in overseeing the role of regulation and regulators.[48]

Ministerial responsibility has been eroded for a number of other reasons. First, the regulator in the form of a Director-General (DG) is appointed by and responsible to the minister. This is under a renewable five-year term but to ensure independence the power to dismiss the DG is restricted to incapacity or misbehaviour, and cannot be exercised merely because the regulator's style is deemed unsuitable or the approach adopted seems to be out of step with government policy. Second-

---

[43] See CD Foster, *Privatisation, Public Ownership and the Regulation of Natural Monopoly* (Oxford, Blackwell, 1992), 270–71.

[44] Prosser, above n 12, 239.

[45] In some ways there has been more openness since privatisation as a great deal of information is placed in the public domain. However, it should be noted that the Freedom of Information Act 2000 puts commercially sensitive information in a protected category, see s 43(2).

[46] Bradley and Ewing, above n 34, 344.

[47] See eg, the Employment Committee's report on '*The Remuneration of Directors and Chief Executives of Privatised Utilities*' (HC 159, 1994–95) and the Trade and Industry Committee, '*The Domestic Gas Market*' (HC 681, 1993–94). Adam Tomkins ch 3 above, points out that the Hansard report recommends that Parliament should be at the apex of accountability and in this roles it should systematically draw on the investigations of outside regulators and commissions. He also notes that regulators have also welcomed stronger links.

[48] For a recent examples see *Better Regulation: Making Good Use of Regulatory Impact Assessments* (HC 329, 2001–02) and Office of Gas and Electricity Markets, *Giving Customers a Choice of Electricity Supplier* (HC 85, 2000–01).

ly, the introduction of devolution has had an impact, for example, the regulation of Scottish Water under its regulator is not by way of the minister to the Westminster Parliament but to the Scottish Executive and the Scottish Parliament (see later). Thirdly, the allocation of ministerial competences between departments cuts across regulatory issues relating to the energy industry, eg gas and electricity regulators have reported to the Department of Trade and Industry while environmental concerns and energy efficiency are part of the remit of the Department of Environment, Food and Rural Affairs. Fourthly, the legislation is designed in order to restrict direct ministerial involvement since the office of the regulator functions as a non-ministerial government department with the minister unable to interfere with the day-to-day operation of the department.[49] In practice, the Director-General is granted substantial powers which are broadly defined and divided into primary and secondary duties. A particularly important problem has been establishing clear lines of demarcation between the regulator and the minister.[50] Under nationalisation we observed that there was a lack of clarity when it came to distinguishing between policy matters which were regarded as the responsibility of the minister, and operational issues which were dealt with by the Board. Now there is some overlap in relation to the issuing of licences and referrals to the Competition Commission. As we shall see, this lack of clarity has resulted in calls to refine and proceduralise the process of regulation.[51] Such shortcomings have also led to subsequent legislation to correct regulatory failures.[52]

Lastly, it should also be recognised that, at a different level, legal intervention might constrain the regulator. This is in the sense that judicial review, as a remedy of last resort, acts as a threat that will keep the regulator within the bounds of the discretion set out under the statutory framework.[53]

Gas and Electricity Regulation

We will now consider gas and electricity in order to show how strategies of formal regulation have developed in response to changing circumstances and to perceived failures. In view of the problems attached to the provision of utility services[54] it

[49] See eg Electricity Act 1989 ss.11, 12, 23 and 25 and Proser, above n 12, 239.

[50] In assessing the extent of the autonomy of the Director General it is important not to underestimate the importance of the informal contacts and interventions by ministers, including comments on policies that are pursued by the regulator. Although this process often takes place behind the scenes and is difficult to measure, there have been highly visible ministerial interventions, eg John Prescott in regard to the failure of Railtrack to improve the rail infrastructure. (See Thatcher above, n 39, 130).

[51] C Graham, *Regulating Public Utilities: A Constitutional Approach* (Oxford, Hart Publishing, 2000), 32. Such approaches have been discussed at various levels of theoretical abstraction: see eg, J Black, 'Proceduralising Regulation: Part I' [2000] *OJLS* 597; T Prosser, 'Theorising Utility Regulation' [1999] *MLR* 209.

[52] Eg the Water Act 1999, the Utilities Act 2000 and introduction of the Strategic Rail Authority under the Transport Act 2000.

[53] Prosser, above n 6, 94.

[54] W Hutton, *The State We're In* (London, Verso, 1995), 217 *et seq.*

was obvious at the outset that these industries could not be simply privatised without regulation. Furthermore, the need for regulation has not diminished post privatisation[55] and accountability[56] under current conditions of governance has to be linked to the effectiveness of regulation.

Regulation has remained an important means for the government to achieve its policy objectives[57] and these powers have been strengthened by the post 1997 Labour Government with the introduction of new forms of additional regulation.[58] In some respects this has become more specialised with greater complexity and formality but approaches have become increasingly informal in others ways too. This will be particularly apparent in the later sections of this chapter (See under Regulators 'Joining Up'). Also, there has been a growing emphasis on co-ordination, for example by the use of concordats and a committee co-ordinating the work of regulators. However, as will become clear, the devolution arrangements only partially address the issue of cross-border regulation and between the many different bodies involved.[59]

From the outset there were contrasting approaches to gas and electricity privatisation and regulation. The initial arrangements for gas privatisation were modified in response to criticism over the lack of competition which can be attributed to the way the UK gas industry had been privatised by the Gas Act 1986 as a single entity. The problem was that British Gas was not broken down into 12 regional gas companies, which would have encouraged greater competition. This option was chosen because in the short term it could have had damaging political consequences by increasing the cost of gas to consumers and slowing down the Government's privatisation plans.[60] The original privatisation empowered the Secretary of State after consultation with the Director-General to authorise the public supply of gas by issuing a licence,[61] and the regulator was made responsible for policing the licensing arrangements.[62] Furthermore, the minister was able set targets for competition.[63] The Act

---

[55] The failure to set in place regulation following bus privatisation has meant an unchecked decline in standard and frequency of service delivery and in safety. See W Hutton, *The State to Come*, (London, Verso, 1997), 20.

[56] Accountability in this context can be broadly defined as 'an obligation for a person or organisation to justify actions to another body in terms of some authorisation for the activity given by that body including assignment of duties or purposes, answerability, overseeing performance, incentives for good performance and penalties for inadequate performance.' See O James, 'Regulation Inside Government: Public Interest Justifications and Regulatory Failures' [2000] *Public Administration* 327, 328.

[57] C Harlow and R Rawlings, above n 5, 295.

[58] The reform of the Post Office is the latest example of this. See *Post Office Reform: A World Class Service for the 21st Century* (Cm 4340, 1999) and the Postal Services Act 2000. Postcomm, the industry regulator under the Postal Services Act, published its decision on the introduction of competition for the UK postal market on 29 May 2002.

[59] White Paper, *Modernising Government* (Cm 4310, 1999). Regulation continues as a priority in latest UK government thinking, with an emphasis upon comparing the performance of public bodies against 'quality' systems in the private sector.

[60] P Craig, *Administrative Law* (4th edn, London, Sweet & Maxwell, 1999), 349 *et seq.*

[61] See Gas Act 1986, ss 7 and 8.

[62] This power has now been conferred on the regulator but with the minister retaining a power to determine the conditions: see Gas Act 1995 s 8 and Utility Act 2000, ss 33 and 34.

provided a complex formula for pricing which had to be agreed with the Director-General of Gas Supply. However, the channels of control and accountability were significantly modified by the conferment of private sector status, in that the Gas Act 1986 conferred primary duties on the Director-General (and not the minister). These were first to ensure that the supply of services met all reasonable demand; secondly, to ensure that suppliers were able to finance the provisions of their services; and thirdly s/he was required to promote competition.[64] However, a serious flaw was that the Director-General was not given power to change the legal structure of the industry, in particular to introduce competition[65] and the Director-General could only encourage effective competition in gas supply for consumers above a certain volume which was exclusively to the benefit of large commercial users.

The concerns that had been raised over gas contributed to a different approach when it came to privatising the electricity industry. The state generating company was broken up into National Power, Powergen and Nuclear Electric. Transmission was left in the hands of the National Grid, but the 12 regional supply companies for England and Wales were transferred to the private sector as separate companies.[66] Such an approach was in line with the essential facilities doctrine which tackles the problem of how to introduce competition without duplicating existing infrastructure. This goal is achieved by setting out rules that allow competitors to have access to these facilities and the next stage is to enable competition to take place between existing and new operators.[67]

Regulation of the electricity sector under the Electricity Act 1989 was granted primarily to a Director-General of Electricity Supply who was given broadly similar primary and secondary duties to other regulators. However, one of the most important powers—namely, that of licensing—was shared with the Secretary of State. The minister was granted a power of veto over any modifications to licences.[68] This turned the Secretary of State into the licensing authority by making it possible for him or her to intervene in the work of the regulator, first determining the degree to which competition would be encouraged by deciding upon the number of licences to be issued and second by setting the licensing conditions themselves.[69] However, this remained a power to issue rather than enforce licences (this power remained with the regulator).

[63]   In practice, ministers have continued to play an active part. For example, Peter Hain, as Energy Minister, intervened at a political level on Ofgem's behalf in later March 2001. This was after OFGEM was obliged by the Competition Commission to remove the market abuse licence condition (MALC) which had been intended to be written into contracts to prevent abuse of market power. It was recognised that failure to include this could undermine the regulatory process.

[64]   In addition, there were a number of secondary duties which included promoting and protecting the interests of consumers in relation to pricing; preventing dangers from gas transmission and protecting the environment.

[65]   Prosser, above n 6, 93

[66]   M Grenfell, 'Can Competition Law Supplant Utilities Regulation' in C McCrudden, *Regulation and Deregulation: Policy and Practice in the Utilities and Financial Services Industries* (Oxford, Clarendon Press, 1999), 222–23.

[67]   *Ibid* at 225.

[68]   Electricity Act 1989, s 6 allows the minister to delegate the power to the Director-General of Electricity Supply.

[69]   Prosser, above n 6, 47.

The decision to liberalise the market in the gas and electricity sector by allowing the domestic customer to chose between suppliers was a very significant change of policy. A critical Competition Commission report prompted further legislation in the form of the Gas Act 1995,[70] which imposed a duty on the Director-General to promote competition by opening up the domestic gas market. This was achieved by splitting up the production and distribution and thus making access through pipes owned by British Gas available to any licensed supplier. At this point, the Secretary of State and the Director-General were made responsible for drawing up more detailed rules for the new system. This was by a process that has been termed 'administrative decision-making'.[71] The upshot was that this introduced an element of competition that had been absent from the original privatisation arrangements. Customers were offered the prospect of a reduction in the price of their energy bills but this coincided with a relaxation in regulatory conditions that potentially allowed for variations in pricing on a regional basis.[72]

This incidentally had an unexpected implication, since it also meant that another form of regulation was needed for a different and unforeseen purpose, namely the protection of customers from being tempted into unfavourable deals from new suppliers, who were using unscrupulous methods to mislead the public when inducing them to change from their original gas or electricity provider. As a result of the concerns that were raised, trading standards officers were brought into the process of regulation and consumers were given consumer guidance on the Internet as to the relative merits of the deals on offer.[73]

It should also be remembered that another dimension to regulation is achieving the desired distribution of benefits between different categories of consumers.[74] This can result in the multi-layered involvement of regulators and has been apparent with references from the Office of Fair Trading (OFT) to the Competition Commission (formerly the Monopolies and Mergers Commission) over pricing policy. For instance, the Competition Commission makes an important contribution to the process when the pricing formulae and other licence modifications cannot be agreed by the regulator and the service provider. In this context, the Competition Commission not only has an adjudicatory role but plays a part in setting out future guidelines for pricing. The Competition and Services (Utilities) Act 1992 should also be mentioned since this strengthened the powers of regulators on matters of quality, enabling them to set out standards of supply, reliability and customer service. This legislation introduced

---

[70] Amendments to the Gas Act 1986 followed the report: Monopolies and Mergers Commission, *Gas* (Cm 2314, 1993).

[71] Graham, above n 51, 175 *et seq.*

[72] *Ibid* at 176.

[73] The Office of Fair Trading website provides consumer guidance on the relative merits of the deals on offer. See eg, http://www.energywatch.org.uk

[74] See Prosser, above n 6, 273 for a discussion of the role of the Monopoloies and Mergers Commission (MMC), now the Competition Commission. It was supposed that this role would diminish with increasing competition but there has been little sign of this happening. The Competition Commission is an independent public body established by the Competition Act 1998 and it replaced the MMC on 1 April 1999. Competition Act 1998, s 54 and Sch 10 now determine the Commission's role in regard to utility regulation.

Citizen's Charter values across the utility sector in an attempt to achieve guaranteed standards of service.

REGULATION AND NEW LABOUR: CORRECTION, REPAIR AND CONSULTATION

When Labour was elected in 1997 it was confronted with a number of problems that arose from previous privatisations. For instance, the Labour Government's subsequent attempts to improve regulation have been undertaken against a background of falling standards of service in parts of the sector (eg British Gas lost its Charter Mark and the rail industry has lurched from crisis to crisis). Although Labour was careful to avoid a specific commitment to return any industry to public ownership it modified existing schemes of regulation in response to perceived failures and assumed a much more active role in social and environmental matters.[75] Another prominent feature of this most recent phase of regulation—which is a major concern for this discussion—is that it has a multi-layered character which has become increasingly evident. It has been noted that 'while several agencies were involved in the regulatory process prior to privatisation, this regime was less complex (and less rigorous) than the post privatisation structure'.[76] Accordingly, in the current situation we need to understand the relationship between different layers of government and the relationship between a range of different regulators. An equally important issue for regulators has been the need to undertake their task with a lack of integrated information upon which to base their decisions.

Utilities Act 2000: Statutory Refinement of UK Energy Regulation

The lack of uniformity in the approach to the regulation of gas and electricity, already discussed, is addressed by the Utilities Act 2000 which applies to England, Wales and Scotland. It provides a single regulatory authority for both industries and in setting out to promote effective competition it is intended to reflect increasing convergence between the two industries. This is already very evident from the interpenetration of utility companies with interests in gas, electricity and water in various combinations. However, the role of the new regulatory authority, Ofgem, reaches beyond a purely economic agenda and the Utilities Act differs from previous legislation by placing much greater emphasis on protecting the interests of consumers. For example, under section 13, the Act contains provisions to enable the gas and electricity sectors to make an appropriate contribution to the govern-

---

[75] See White Paper, *A Fair Deal for Consumers: Modernising the Framework for Utility Regulation* (Cm 3898, 1998) and Graham, above n 51, 61 *et seq*. See later section on 'Environmental Regulation of Water'.
[76] Maloney, above n 36, 630.

ment's social and environmental objectives.[77] The Secretary of State has new powers to intervene to adjust charges to help disadvantaged groups.[78] For example, this could be exercised if one group of consumers is treated less favourably than others.[79] In addition, sections 44–50 placed increased restrictions on disconnecting consumers.

In terms of our multi-layered model it is relevant to note that one of the reasons for further regulation is that in the energy sector the government has had to respond to initiatives originating from the European Commission.[80] This is conducted, in part, through powers that are exercised by the Director-General of Fair Trading and now the Competition Commission, concerning in particular intervention to prevent anti-competitive agreements and the abuse of market dominance. The Utilities Act 2000 modifies the structure and regulatory regime for the gas and electricity sector to facilitate further competition in line with EC directives which require that Member States create appropriate mechanisms for regulation to achieve 'competition in generation; a limited form of competition in supply; and unbundling.'[81] It achieves this, as was mentioned earlier, by giving the Competition Commission a significant role in the regulatory process. The Commission has concurrent powers of enforcement with sectoral regulators. In consequence, overlapping layers of formal regulation, both from Europe and through the intervention of other domestic regulatory institutions illustrate the multi-layered nature of the current system.[82]

The Utilities Act 2000 also introduces alignment of the licensing and regulatory systems for gas and electricity (for example by including the concept of standard conditions for electricity licences). Each licence has an accompanying set of standard conditions which set out the obligations and duties that each licensee must adhere to. The Act gives the Gas and Electricity Markets Authority (OFGEM) power to grant licences for gas and for the generation, transmission, distribution and supply of electricity,[83] but the standard conditions of any licence are determined by the Secretary of State.[84] Any such conditions may be modified by

---

[77] See section 70 and 99. The regulator has published a succession of Social Action Plans. For example, newsletter for Social Action Plan No 5 (June 2002) refers to best practice in delivery of energy efficiency advice, debt collection, providing an information campaign for pensioners and promoting awareness of energy issues.

[78] Utilities Act 2000, section 69 and section 98.

[79] C Graham, 'The Utilities Bill' (2000) 11 (3) *Util Law Rev* (May-June) 101.

[80] See EC Directive 96/92 for electricity; and 98/30 for gas.

[81] Graham, above n 51, 122.

[82] It is interesting to compare the French approach to opening up the gas market in response to the EC Directive 96/92 which also involves creating a common regulatory body for electricity and gas 'Commission de Regulation de l'Electricite et du Gaz' (CREG). See Du G Puy-Montbrun and B Martor, 'French Electricity and Gas Regulation' (2000) 11(6) *Util Law Rev* 11 190, 191, who point out that the majority of regulatory powers remain in the hands of the French government, through the Minister for Energy; but the CREG may through its opinions and decisions set the framework for the French regulatory system. These powers are described as minimal in comparison with the United Kingdom, especially as it is the Energy Minister who remains in control of price levels.

[83] See Utilities Act 2000, part IV and part V.

[84] See Utilities Act 2000, s 33 for electricity and s 81.

OFGEM, subject to the giving of notice and reasons. However, the Secretary of State has the power to reject proposed modifications.[85] This is not the end of the regulatory road, since the Competition Commission also has appellate powers, which allow it to override modifications to licensing conditions, if certain conditions are met.[86] Although this crucial licensing procedure has been standardised by the Act, it remains a complex process which only partly clarifies where ultimate authority lies between these competing agencies, and if the focus of decision-making is blurred, this makes it difficult to pinpoint where accountability is actually located.[87]

It is also important to note that the Act establishes a primary duty to protect the interest of consumers[88] and provides a greater element of consumer representation and consultation.[89] This stronger emphasis on consultation takes up an important New Labour theme which encourages participation and citizenship and which characterises many other initiatives that pervade central and local government,[90] but equally this can be seen as a response to dissatisfaction with the previous arrangements. In place of the Gas Consumers' Council and the Electricity Consumers' Council, the Act introduces a Gas and Electricity Consumers' Council which has a general remit for both obtaining and keeping under review information about consumer matters, and for making proposals and providing advice on such consumer matters to public authorities.[91] An important question—in terms of actual accountability—is what, if any, effect such consultation has on the eventual decision-making process itself, since under the Act the consultation only has to be taken into account.

A further issue which will be considered later is the placing in the Utilities Act 2000 of an increased emphasis on environmental considerations. For example, it contains new powers under sections 62–64 for the Secretary of State to make regulations to promote energy efficiency and to encourage the generation of electricity from renewable sources. The Secretary of State is required to issue periodic statutory guidance to the authority on the government's social and environmental objectives and suggest ways in which the authority might contribute to these objectives. The authority must take this guidance into account when it acts.[92] We will observe that the problem here is how this concern is reconciled with the regulator's other duties, and how this policy can be applied consistently throughout the United Kingdom in view of the division of competences which are central to the devolution arrangements.

---

[85]   See C Graham, 'The Utilities Bill' (2000) 11(3) *Util Law Rev* (May–June) 94.
[86]   See above n 75.
[87]   This has important implications regarding the lobbying of interest groups. See conclusion.
[88]   DTI, *A Fair Deal for Consumers: The Response to Consultation* (2000). See Graham, above n 51, 32.
[89]   See Utility Act 2000 s 2 and 5.7 and part III. This now applies to all the utilities: see the Water Act 1999, discussed below.
[90]   See White Paper, *Modernising Government* (Cm 4310, 1999); and John Morison, chapter 7 above.
[91]   Water Act 1999, ss 18–19.
[92]   Utilities Act 2000, ss 10–14.

UTILITY REGULATION AND DEVOLUTION

This section discusses utility regulation in the context of the recent devolution legislation and will reveal that looking at this issue from a territorial perspective further illustrates the complexity of the conditions of modern governance.[92a] In fact the former constitutional position (pre-1999) which was based on a single sovereign state tended to mask a situation which already recognised special territorial arrangements in which the regions enjoyed a certain amount of autonomy. Moreover, the privatisation measures by the Conservative Government were most obviously incomplete in Scotland, Wales and Northern Ireland. This was because of a combination of local hostility to privatisation proposals and because of differences in local conditions of operation of these industries. Since the change of government, devolution has been superimposed on to an already existing structure. This has resulted in an even more diverse and asymmetrical distribution of power between the various parts of the United Kingdom.

A further point to mention is that UK devolution might be regarded as part of a wider European trend[93] which is driven by economic imperatives such as the availability of EU funding on a regional basis.[94] There has been a growing interest in the region as a locus of political, economic and cultural activity which points to the declining capacity of the nation state, with the development of the idea of a Europe of the regions. The current phase of economic restructuring is typically seen as a significant factor in promoting a new role for regional government. Added to this is a view that economic efficiency is facilitated by encouraging regional variations. For example, it has been pointed out that regulatory change and innovation can be 'attributed to the competitive interplay between rival jurisdictions, seeking to develop a regulatory regime which is attractive to mobile factors of production, such as capital.'[95] Such competition can be linked to bringing decision-making closer to those affected by it. Further still, this can be more specifically associated with a growing interest in environmental sustainability. Environmentalists have coined the phrase 'think global act local,' but in reality this is often constrained by larger national and international forces. Nevertheless, there are obvious advantages in dealing with these issues at a local level.[96]

Turning first to the energy sector, regulation of gas and electricity is a matter that the devolution legislation does not deal with directly as an issue in its own right[97]

[92a] See n 30 above.

[93] For references to Spain and Italy, see J Hopkins, *Devolution in Context: Regional, Federal and Devolved Government in the European Union* (London, Cavendish, 2002).

[94] See P Leyland, 'Devolution, the British Constitution and the Distribution of Power' [2002] *NILQ*, Vol 53, n 4, 408–435 at p 428.

[95] Scott, above n 13, 341.

[96] J Tomaney and N Ward, 'England and the "New Regionalism"' [2000] *Regional Studies* 471, 473.

[97] See the Scotland Act 1998, Sch 5 which lists energy and transport under reserved matters but environmental regulation up to the three mile offshore limit as devolved. In addition, powers over land-based operations in support of offshore oil and gas operations under the Offshore Petroleum Development (Scotland) Act 1975, and functions under the Pipe-lines Act 1962 relating to approval of land-based pipe-lines beginning and ending in Scotland, are devolved to the Scottish Executive under SI 1999/1750.

and it is apparent that the changes in administration were not linked to any discernible strategy for the containment of functions and powers, including those by regulators that are exercised across borders and within the United Kingdom.[98] The respective statutes simply specify which areas remain under the control of the Westminster government and which fall within the remit of the devolved executives. So if political power is being divided up by means of devolution, it follows that the accompanying mechanisms for accountability remain a matter of concern. In certain ways, devolution adds to the accountability problem by distributing at least some of this responsibility more widely to the ministers in the new executives and to the devolved Parliaments and assemblies. Indeed, we shall soon see that the organisation of the utilities and the scheme of regulation is significantly different in Scotland, Wales and Northern Ireland.

Perhaps the most obvious divergence arose from the strong resistance to privatisation of the water industry in Scotland, which resulted in the plans eventually being shelved. But in addition to this, there are some significant variations across the energy sector. Although economic regulation of gas and electricity in Wales is on the same footing as in England, the situation is different in Northern Ireland where electricity was privatised in 1992, with the formation of Northern Ireland Electricity. This company deals with power procurement by means of contracts that were formed prior to privatisation. This was undertaken in a manner that keeps power generation distinct from distribution and transmission. This means that trading conditions in Ulster are different from the remainder of the United Kingdom. Northern Ireland Electricity is a monopoly which is regulated by Ofreg, the same regulator as for gas. The company has been able to charge higher prices than elsewhere in the United Kingdom.[99] Also, there have been disputes over price controls between the Director-General for Electricity Supply and the Competition Commission.[100]

Electricity regulation in Scotland is a reserved matter but market conditions differ somewhat from those in the rest of the United Kingdom. First, the industry was not broken up into different companies when it was privatised, although since privatisation the structure and control of the power companies has been radically transformed.[101] Secondly, Scotland was originally left with a fully integrated system of generation and distribution provided by Scottish Power and Scottish Hydro-Electric. Thirdly, the Electricity Act 1989 sets out to guarantee that urban

---

[98] For topical in depth discussion of the issue of accountability and regulation, see eg, G Majone, 'The Regulatory State and its Legitimacy Problems' (1999) 22 *Western European Politics* (No 1, January) 1–24; C Scott, 'Accountability in the Regulatory State' (2000) 27 *Journal of Law and Society* (No 1, March) 38–60 particularly at 48.

[99] C Graham, *Regulating Public Utilities* (Oxford, Hart Publishing, 2000), 113–14.

[100] *Ibid* at 51 and 113 for further details.

[101] For example, Scottish Power has taken over other utility companies, most notably MANWEB and Southern Water. This has turned it into a cross-sector utility player not only across the United Kingdom but also the North West USA. It provides electricity generation, transmission, distribution and supply services. It also supplies gas, provides water, wastewater, telephone and Internet services. Scottish Hydro-Electric has been absorbed by Scottish and Southern Electric, another large utility conglomerate which is active across the energy sector in England and Wales.

and rural consumers in Scotland would be charged on a common basis with the rest of the United Kingdom and that competing suppliers in Scotland should not be put at disadvantage.[102] Graham has pointed out that the appointment by Offer/Ofgem of a Deputy Director-General for Scotland provides evidence of a territorial dimension to regulation and he further suggests that the allocation of competences under the Scotland Act 1998 has the potential to affect the task of regulation itself. For example, the onset of competition in the relationship between customers and utilities will increasingly be a question for Scottish private law, falling under the competence of the Scottish Parliament, while regulation is left with the national regulator. Such incongruities, Graham argues, make the case for a separate regulatory system for electricity in Scotland, reporting to a minister from the Scottish Executive.[103]

The Utilites Act 2000 attempts to ensure that consumer interests in Scotland and Wales are dealt with on a local basis by giving the Gas and Electricity Consumer Council the function of obtaining and keeping under review information about consumer matters, and this involves canvassing the views of consumers in different areas. The Council is obliged to establish one or more committees for both Wales and Scotland to perform this task and the Act also requires the Council to maintain at least one office in each of England, Wales and Scotland at which consumers may apply for information.[104]

Regulating the Water Industry Post-Devolution

Before discussing the position following devolution, it is worth reminding ourselves that privatisation of water in England and Wales proved to be a very difficult undertaking. The water sector under public ownership had operated as a 'professional bureaucratic complex' with minimal state interference and a much less complex regulatory structure than was later imposed.[105] The Government's proposals were highly controversial because they introduced new conflicts between providing returns for shareholders and the need to invest in a crumbling infrastructure, and the equally important need to control charges. Moreover, the industry has been described as a natural monopoly *par excellence*. This is because prohibitive economic costs make it virtually impossible for potential competitors to install rival networks for distribution.[106]

Privatisation in England and Wales involved establishing a new structure for 10 public water authorities and 29 private water companies, and at the same time it called for related environmental and health implications to be adequately controlled.[107] The main task of economic regulation (as opposed to environ-

---

[102] Electricity Act 1989, s 3(2)(a) and (b). Tariff equalisation duty applies to northern Scotland.
[103] Graham, above n 99, 111, 112, n 10.
[104] See Utilities Act 2000, s 18.
[105] Maloney, above n 36, 629.
[106] *Ibid* at 631.
[107] See the Water Act 1989 and the Water Industry Act 1991.

mental: see later) following privatisation was performed by the Office of the Water Regulator (OFWAT) which in common with the other regulators is a non-ministerial government department independent of DEFRA. Under the Water Act 1991 the Director-General for Water Services (DGWS) was given two primary duties.[108] The first was to ensure that the functions of the privatised water and sewerage company met all reasonable demand and were properly carried out. The second was to ensure that water companies were able to finance the provision of these services by securing a reasonable rate of return on their capital.[109] Ofwat followed a similar regulatory pattern on pricing by controlling the annual increase by means of RPI minus X for a given number of years. If a water company contested this formula the Monopolies and Mergers Commission (MMC) had an appellate function in overseeing the regulation of charges by adjudicating on the pricing reviews of the DGWS. This role has led to a tendency for negotiated agreement and accommodation to avoid referral to the MMC. In fact it has been suggested that there has been too much readiness to reach a consensual outcome. In addition to this, the MMC performs an important role in England and Wales in respect to mergers, take-overs and licensing conditions.[110]

Furthermore, additional legislation was necessary in England and Wales to deal with the question of charging because the controversial objective set out earlier of extending metering was not attainable in the time span originally set out. Ofwat called for the Director-General's duty to protect the interests of customers to be made the regulator's single primary duty, putting customers' interests clearly at the heart of water regulation. The regulations and guidance following the Water Act 1991 assists with this by giving the Secretary of State powers partly to determine tariff schemes. This scheme of regulation has been modified by the Water Act 1999. It changes the emphasis by sanctioning an approach that gives the minister powers to make regulations, but also empowers the minister to issue detailed guidance to the regulator. The Secretary of State has the power to make regulations with regard to charging schemes and the Director-General for Water Services has been given power to approve charging schemes.[111] This guidance addresses some of the problems to do with reaching an accommodation between the conflicting considerations, and marks a shift in emphasis from the previous Water Act 1991.

---

[108] Under the Water Act 1989, the Director General for Water Services' secondary duties were to customers: (i) to ensure that no undue preference is shown; (ii) to ensure that there is no undue discrimination in the way companies fix and recover charges; (iii) that rural customers should not be at a disadvantage; (iv) to ensure that the quality of service is protected.

[109] The shortcomings of regulation were brought to prominence during the drought in Yorkshire in 1995. The local population suffered cuts in supply and the regulator responded by imposing penalties on Yorkshire Water. There was also a lack of sensitivity to consumer views, especially over the adoption of metering policies. See Ofwat, *Report on Conclusions from Ofwat's Enquiry into the Performance of Yorkshire Water Services* (Birmingham, 1996); Graham, above n 99, 114, 115.

[110] Maloney, above n 36, 639.

[111] Graham, above n 99, 57.

To a considerable extent the English water industry maintained a regional element which is determined by where the water comes from, in contrast to power which has a national grid that can distribute the supply on a national basis. But although the water industry has retained some characteristics of vertical monopoly with regard to extraction, distribution and supply, since privatisation the separate companies with responsibility for providing water services to the various regions in England have been rearranged through a number of mergers and take-overs (for example, Northumbrian Water, owned by French group Suez, and Thames, owned by Germany's RWE). The point to note here is that this has tended to confound the regulator's task in this field, since the Director-General is faced with informational asymmetries from the various companies which has meant that the information, technical knowledge and expertise required by the regulator is not necessarily available in the form required.[112]

Water in Wales

In Wales, the industry has a distinctive form of ownership. Glas Cymru/Welsh Water—the company that provides water and sewerage services to Wales and some adjoining areas of England—has emerged from exactly the type of corporate rejigging just alluded to. The company was part of the Hyder Group which was taken over by Western Power Distribution in September 2000. Glas Cymru then acquired Welsh Water from Western Power Distribution in May 2001. However, the water industry in Wales is under the same statutory regime of economic regulation as in England. The Government of Wales Act 1998 does not refer to water regulation but it does specify that the Welsh Executive is responsible for the environment.[113] Although the task of regulation remains with Ofwat following changes in ownership Welsh Water/Glas Cymru now has a unique commercial structure within the utility sector. It is a company limited by guarantee and owned and controlled by members instead of by ordinary shareholders. This means that it does not pay dividends in the normal way, allowing the advantages of any reduction in costs to be channeled directly for the benefit of its customers. After having restored ownership and control of the industry to Wales the company has set out its intention to both lower bills for its customers and to secure a £1.2 billion investment programme. This is financed by the efficient device of high quality bonds raised in the City. Because of a combination of efficiency and other organisational advantages, this corporate structure has been

---

[112] Maloney, above, n 36, 626.

[113] See Government of Wales 1998, s 22 and Sch 2(6) which provides that functions are to be transferred for the environment and water and flood defences). However, the Act allows intervention by the Secretary of State if the transferred environmental function has a serious adverse impact on water resources, water supply or the quality of water. (*Ibid* Sch 3 P II(6)). Schedule 3 P III recognises that water issues straddle England and Wales due to the flow of rivers and thus the Welsh Assembly will have some functions over cross-border areas.

proposed as a model that could be used more widely across the utility sector as an alternative to public ownership.[114]

Water in Scotland

Turning next to Scotland, in contrast to the position with gas and electricity, the Scottish Parliament was given legislative competence for the Scottish water industry, and the Scottish water regulator is made accountable to the relevant minister in the devolved executive.[115] The fact that the industry has remained under public ownership means that there is a distinct regulatory culture in Scotland. The main concern is promoting the interests of consumers and customers rather than that of investors or shareholders.[116] Moreover, the failure to introduce competition should not be regarded as a weakness in the sense that is the case for gas and electricity, since the monopolistic character of the industry has prevented competition from being introduced in the remainder of the United Kingdom. It has already been noted that the Scottish water industry, which had been under local authority control, managed to escape the very unpopular privatisation proposals of the Conservative Government. Nevertheless, its structure has been remodelled. The Local Government (Scotland) Act 1994 abolished regional councils and established three public sector water and sewerage authorities as public corporations within the public sector. It put in place a Scottish regional structure with three authorities, designed to achieve significant economies of scale and to ensure the provision of a high quality service and value for money. Their individual areas of responsibility were split to cover the north, east and west of the country. The authorities were placed under a duty to promote conservation and the effective use of water, while at the same time providing adequate water supplies throughout Scotland.[117] As part of these arrangements Scottish Office ministers (prior to devolution) remained responsible for regulation which was performed by means of an annual corporate plan setting financial limits and efficiency targets.[118]

---

[114] In the case of Northern Ireland the Water Service is an executive agency within the Department for Regional Development and it consists of a Chief Executive of Water Services with five other directors. The agency operates under the minister and Permanent Secretary and its stated objective is to provide water and sewerage services in a cost-effective manner to meet the requirements of customers. It also seeks to contribute to the health and well-being of the community and the protection of the environment but the Northern Ireland Water Service is not subject to a comparable regime of statutory regulation.

[115] See Scotland Act 1998, ss 52, 53 and 29.

[116] After the election in 1997 the Labour Government set up a review which identified five aims for the industry. These were to achieve local democratic accountability; to facilitate investment; promote efficiency; ensure continuity of water supplies and protect public health; and minimise disruption to the industry. It has been suggested that in certain ways Scottish regulation is superior. For example, (1) advice by the Commissioner on charging has to be published; (2) the minister has to give reasons for acceptance or rejection; (3) there is assessment of financial parameters; (4) superior forms of consultation are included. See T Prosser, 'Regulating Public Enterprises' [2001] *Public Law* 505, 519.

[117] Water Act 1999, s 65.

[118] See Prosser, above n 116, 515.

Recently, the Scottish Parliament has passed the Water Industry (Scotland) Act 2002 which makes provision to combine the three authorities into a single body to be called Scottish Water[119] which will have a Chief Executive and a board appointed by ministers of the Scottish Executive.[120]

Water regulation in Scotland is also divided in three ways: (1) the Water Industry Commissioner for Scotland is responsible for economic and customer service regulation of the water authorities; (2) the Scottish Executive is responsible for regulating drinking water quality;[121] (3) the Scottish Environment Protection Agency (SEPA) regulates discharges into the environment and is responsible for the control of pollution. The Water Industry Act 1999 introduced a Scottish economic regulator[122] whose role can be contrasted with his English/Welsh counterpart. Clearly, there is not the same pressure to distinguish distribution of efficiencies between shareholders and customers. Rather all benefits ultimately reside with the consumer. The Scottish Executive and Parliament, working in harness with the regulator, decide in what ways the benefits are going to be enjoyed by the consumer. The Water Commissioner for Scotland is required to provide the Scottish Executive with advice about the levels of charges set for the authorities[123] and s/he must also see that the drinking water quality and environment protection standards necessary to protect public health and the water environment are met. This calls for a substantial and ongoing investment programme,[124] although this still involves making a choice between some of the same considerations, namely environmental improvements, lower charges and reductions in expenditure. The Commissioner has a statutory obligation to promote the interests of customers of the water and sewerage authorities.

In addition, the Water Industry Scotland Act 2002 sets up water customer consultation panels for Scotland which perform an important role as a conduit for customer views and has the general function of advising the Commissioner on the promotion of the interests of customers.[125] The Commissioner is required to have regard to any advice given to him by the panel in respect of the water authority.[126]

[119] See Transport and the Environment Committee, *Report of the Inquiry into Water and the Water Industry* (SP362) 9th Report 2001.

[120] Water Industry (Scotland) Act 2002, Sch 3.

[121] The Ministry for Transport and the Environment in Scotland cannot adequately discharge this role without also being integrated with water industry regulation. Also, this has to be understood by reference to the relevant Concordats discussed below. Part II of the Water Industry (Scotland) Act 2002 introduces a regulator for drinking water quality.

[122] Water Industry (Scotland) Act 1999, s 12 introduced a new Water Industry Commissioner for Scotland, appointed by the Secretary of State for Scotland (Sch 9A). The Commissioner has a 'general function of promoting the interests of customers of the new water and sewerage authorities.' See also C Roper, *Economic Regulation of the Scottish Water and Sewerage Industry* (London, HMSO, 2000).

[123] Water Industry (Scotland) Act 2002, s 33.

[124] From *Water Quality and Standards* (1999). See also Graham, above n 99, 113.

[125] See Water Industry (Scotland) Act 2002, s 2.

[126] See the Water Industry (Scotland) Act 2002. Under P I, s 1(2), the Commissioner has the general function of promoting the interests of customers of Scottish Water in relation to the provision of services by it in the exercise of its core functions. Under s 1(3), the Scottish Ministers may, after consulting the Commissioner, give the Commissioner directions of a general or specific character as to the exercise of the Commissioner's functions; and the Commissioner must comply with any such direction.

It should be remembered that the Commissioner advises the minister on charging schemes and that this advice is published. In doing so account has to be taken of considerations such as the economy, efficiency and effectiveness with which Scottish Water is using its resources when exercising its core functions.[127] The Secretary of State after consultation with the Commissioner is empowered to give binding directions of a general or specific character as to the exercise of his functions. It should be noted that the Commissioner has left the politically sensitive question of protecting low income consumers from increases in charges for the Scottish Executive to determine.[128] It has also been observed that on the basis of the information available the regulator advises the Scottish minister on charges, but final approval lies with the minister.[129] Recommendations are not necessarily accepted. A recent proposal for a firm price cap for two years and a highly likely price cap for a third year was not fully accepted by the minister.[130] Such an approach suggests that there is an on-going attempt to establish a link between service improvement and prices that are charged. Nonetheless, in these arrangements we can identify a channel of accountability between the regulator and the Scottish Executive, which in turn is answerable to the Scottish Parliament, and the consultation requirement introduces a process of mediation with the relevant diverse interest groups.

UTILITY REGULATION, CONCORDATS AND ENVIRONMENTAL PROTECTION

In this section it will be suggested that the dissipation of power has to be considered beyond privatisation and economic regulation. This is because the utility sector necessarily involves the overlapping and integrally related question of environmental policy and regulation.[131] As noted already, the statutory framework calls for environmental considerations to be taken into account by regulators and the privatised industries. In the first place, as we have already observed, this requirement has to be reconciled with other priorities (eg lower prices leading to higher consumption and less incentive for energy efficiency). Secondly, this becomes a more complex task when there is a separate regime of environmental regulation which imposes its own constraints on regulatory discretion. The backdrop to this is not merely a Climate Change Strategy[132] which applies to the whole

---

[127] Water Industry (Scotland) Act 2002, s 33(3).

[128] Prosser, above, n 116, at 518. The Commissioner has published a strategic review for 2002–06 which recommends continued charge capping, a single water authority, cost reflective tariffs.

[129] The minister must give reasons for accepting or rejecting any such advice.

[130] See Prosser, above, n 116 at 517. There have been data collecting problems which have impacted on the capacity to take decisions in this area.

[131] For example, the Scottish water industry strategic review for 2002–06 endorses a joint multi-agency project between the Water Industry Commissioner, SEPA and the Water Quality Regulator.

[132] See eg Royal Commission on Environmental Pollution (RCEP) Report (CM 5459, 21 March 2002).

of the United Kingdom, and includes an overall commitment by central government to achieve sustainable development by hitting environmental targets[133] but it also must be remembered that policy-making in this area takes place at a wider European and global level. Environmental initiatives require the implementation of the provisions of international treaties[134] and EU directives[135] which are imposed on national institutions.[136] The Concordat of European Union Policy Issues can be cited as an example of how the devolution arrangements fail adequately to resolve one of 'the symbolic issues of devolution,' namely the representation of the devolved administrations in EU policy formulation.[137]

However, we find that responsibility for many aspects of environmental policy has been given to the devolved executives. This runs counter to a recent trend which has seen administration of environmental policy veer incrementally towards central government (see eg Environment Act 1995 which took away the management of waste disposal from local authorities and gave it to the Environment Agency). Moreover, it has been recognised that given the type of physical and political considerations surrounding environmental issues, it is problematic, to say the least, to attempt a separation of powers as part of a devolved or quasi-federal system of government, since this is an area 'not readily susceptible to a vertical disaggregation of functions still less ... amenable to what might be described as horizontal compartmentalisation of responsibilities.'[138] In the following section we will see how the task of compliance with national and supranational strategies has been affected by spreading the burden more widely and by allowing standards to vary as between England, Scotland, Wales and Northern Ireland.

Environmental Regulation of Water

The water industry is taken to illustrate how environmental regulation overlaps with economic and other levels of regulation. At a supragovernmental level the imposition of EU directives has contributed to the regulation of the environmental aspects and an obvious tension is caused by regulatory responsibilities for environmental issues being divided and granted to the Environment Agency. At a national level the Department (DEFRA) has issued guidance about environmental concerns which make clear that 'the promotion of water efficiency and water conservation are essential steps in mitigating the environmental impact of society's

---

[133] See the 'Greening Government' initiative from the Department of the Environment, Food and Rural Affairs (DEFRA).

[134] Eg the 1992 United Nations Conference on Environment and Development and Kyoto Protocol 1997.

[135] See eg EC Directive 80/778 on quality of water supply, Urban Waste Directive 91/271 and Water Framework Directive 2001/60.

[136] See eg United Kingdom Response to European Commission White Paper on Environmental Liability: http://www.scotland.gov.uk/library3/environment/UKresponse.asp

[137] See R Rawlings, 'Concordats of the Constitution' (2000) 116 *LQR* 256, 272–73.

[138] R Macrory, 'The Environment and Constitutional Change' in R Hazell (ed), *Constitutional Futures: A History of the Next Ten Years* (Oxford, Oxford University Press, 2001), 178–95 at 179.

demand for water and in protecting the aquatic environment for future generations'.[139] It goes on to recommend a wide range of measures to reduce demand for
water. These include: requiring water companies to reduce leakage from their
pipes; providing free leak detection and repair services for household consumers;
reducing demand by installing water-efficient equipment in the home and
encouraging water efficiency audits. Further, there is a recommendation that
water efficiency and reduction in demand should be rewarded by discounted rates
for low income households who undergo audits. Any drive for efficiency to protect
the natural environment has to be reconciled with charging on the basis of the volume of water used. It will already be evident that environmental implications flow
from Ofwat's decisions, particularly to do with obtaining the right trade off
between quality and price. Also, introducing meters for domestic customers has
the potential advantage of lowering demand from consumers and benefiting the
environment. But how can lower consumption be achieved without leading to a
reduction in revenue, and what kind of incentive will there be for business customers who might require high volumes of use to maximise their industrial production? Resolving such questions may boil down to determining whether
charging levels ought to provide sufficient revenue for satisfactory management of
the infrastructure and environmental improvement. Another problem is that
there is evidence to suggest that in England, where the profit motive is stronger,
water companies have used an exaggerated projected cost of environmental obligations as a reason for justifying inflated charges to the Director-General for Water
Services and have then managed to meet their environmental obligations for
much less than estimated.[140]

In England and Wales, environmental regulation is carried out by the Environmental Agency[141] by means of fines and penalties to achieve enforcement compliance (rather than negotiated compliance) and in Scotland (SEPA) regulates
discharges into the environment and is responsible for the control of pollution.
This body was established in 1996 for the protection of the environment in Scotland. Its responsibilities cover air and water pollution, waste and radioactivity discharges and integrated pollution control and its task is performed in partnership
with other players.[142] A ministerial group on Sustainable Scotland meets biannu-
ally to deliver a commitment to integrate the principles of environmentally and
socially sustainable development into all government policies.[143]

---

[139] See Ministerial Guidance re Water Act 1999 http://www.defra.gov.uk/environment/
consult/wia99regs/response/02.htm, at para 2.20.

[140] Maloney, above n 36, at 634.

[141] The Environmental Agency has responsibility for river quality and the quality of inland coastal
waters; land drainage and flood control; management of water resources; fisheries; recreation and conservation; and the improvement and maintenance of non-marine navigation.

[142] For example, s 53 of the Water Industry (Scotland) Act 2002 requires the Scottish Ministers and
Scottish Water, in exercising its functions, to further environmental conservation and enhancement of
natural beauty.

[143] The Northern Ireland Executive has a Department of the Environment with responsibility for
planning control, the environment, pollution control and sustainable development. Once again, the
department's strategic objectives are to conserve, protect and improve the natural and built environ-

In respect to the regulation of the environment we have recognised a primary role for public authorities but there has also been an emerging involvement of public interest groups. Such groups have brought environmental damage issues before the courts.[144] Indeed, there need to be effective ways to ensure that public authorities discharge their obligations to require the restoration of damaged environments. This should be related to supporting the availability of funding for litigation aimed at protecting the environment. It is suggested that where public authorities have functions that involve imposing requirements on polluters for remedying damage to the environment, public interest groups should be entitled to seek review of any failure of such authorities to discharge these functions adequately.[145] Finally, there is a consultation requirement and this is achieved by establishing consultative committees and a domestic consumers' panel of 2,250 members with a larger users' group.

CO-ORDINATING REGULATION

One of the most frequently declared objectives of the Labour Government has been to make sure that policy-making is more 'joined up and strategic.'[146] To achieve this, new initiatives have abounded in almost every area and at many different levels. Concordats and the Regulators' Joint Statement can be taken as two examples of a 'soft law' approach which are of particular relevance to this discussion. In essence this demonstrates evidence of multi-layered regulation of varying degrees of formality.

Concordats

Concordats between central government and the devolved administrations are a significant feature of the devolution arrangements which illustrate how the finer details have been resolved without resort to legislation. They can be regarded as a soft law technique[147] which has involved a mutual commitment to inform and consult closely over devolved and non-devolved matters.[148] Such arrangements also demonstrate the extent to which regulatory responsibilities are interrelated.

---

ment and place the concept of sustainable development at the head of the Department's policies which are to be promoted across the Northern Ireland executive.

[144] For an English case see *R v Inspector of Pollution, ex parte Greenpeace* [1994] 1 WLR 570 but it is worth noting that the rules of standing are narrower in Scotland, with a different concept of 'associational standing.' See Joanna Miles, ch 15 below.

[145] See eg United Kingdom Response to European Commission White Paper on Environmental Liability: http://www.scotland.gov.uk/library3/environment/UKresponse.asp

[146] R Rhodes, 'New Labour's Civil Service: Summing-up Joining Up' [2000] *Political Quarterly* 151.

[147] J Poirier, 'The Functions of Intergovernmental Agreements' [2001] *PL* 134, 144.

[148] See R Rawlings, 'Concordats of the Constitution' (2000) 116 *LQR* 256, 258. This article presents an in-depth critical evaluation of Concordats. See also M Laffin, A Thomas and A Webb, 'Intergovernmental Relations After Devolution' [2000] *Political Quarterly* 233.

There is an overarching Memorandum of Understanding between the UK government and the devolved administrations setting out more general principles which
are supported by bilateral concordats between individual government departments and the devolved administration. The individual concordats are relevant to
particular areas of policy-making. For example, if we turn first to Wales, we find
that the Transport, Planning and Environment Group of the National Assembly of
Wales has responsibility for environmental issues, including climate change policy,
sustainable development and planning issues. The Welsh Executive is committed
to the full integration of environmental and socially sustainable development
throughout all government policy, but it faces similar problems of liaising with
England. Thus a Concordat has been drawn up between the Cabinet of the
National Assembly for Wales and the Department of Environment, Transport and
the Regions to achieve an appropriate degree of co-operation. The Concordat sets
out a mutual commitment to involvement and consultation when there is a possibility that a proposed policy or decision (eg on planning guidance) may have an
impact on, or be connected with, a matter. This must be in good time and in adequate detail. There is a further commitment to share information, analysis and
research and a procedure for dispute resolution.[149]

The closely related Concordat drawn up between the DTI and the Scottish Executive starts from the standpoint of acknowledging the high degree of interrela-
tionship that exists in the energy sector, for example, noting that English and
Welsh companies in the energy field are of key importance to the Scottish economy while the activities of companies located in Scotland are correspondingly
important to the UK economy. The Concordat further acknowledges that wider
issues connected with the energy industries, including international negotiations,
also have an impact on Scotland and that the DTI needs advice on Scottish energy
issues when considering UK energy policy. Such considerations require the DTI
Energy Group and the Energy Division of the Scottish Executive to communicate
and consult closely. It may sometimes be necessary for the Energy Division to consult widely within the Scottish Executive on energy policy matters which have
broader (eg environmental) implications, and the Energy Division is DTI's initial
point of contact with Scottish Executive on all such broader energy matters.

In essence, the Concordat recognises a reciprocal duty to consult when exercising the various overlapping strategic powers that have been divided up. On the one
hand, the Scotland Act 1998 makes the generation, transmission, distribution and
supply of electricity in Scotland, together with powers to license generation and
supply of electricity in Scotland, a reserved matter for Westminster, but with the
proviso that DTI ministers can only exercise these powers after consultation with
the Scottish Ministers. On the other hand, the powers and duties under the electricity legislation listed in Appendix 1 to the Concordat are the subject of executive
devolution (under SI 1999/1750). The Concordat specifies that before carrying

---

[149]   See Concordat, Annex I which deals with sustainable development and environmental change
and covers reservoir safety, management of cross-border river catchments, waste policy, inland water-
ways.

out any of these powers and duties that might have a UK application or may set a precedent, the Scottish Executive will consult the DTI.

The Concordat drawn up between the Department of Transport, Local Government and the Regions (now the Office of the Deputy Prime Minister) with the Scottish Executive which co-ordinates aspects of environmental policy operates on very much the same basis, and is composed in similar language to the Concordat with the DTI. It involves regular meetings between senior officials to discuss matters of mutual interest (Annex I deals with sustainable development and environmental protection). The split in responsibility for energy regulation has led to the devolved Scottish Parliament and Welsh Assembly each drafting a strategy for the environment concerning their respective parts of the United Kingdom. The Scottish Executive Environment Group has responsibility for policies regarding climate change and sustainable development. In March 2000 the Scottish strategy was published at the same time as the broader UK strategy was released. A major difficulty is that because energy remains the responsibility of central Government, many of the measures that might be necessary to combat climate change, either are not within the remit of the Scottish Executive, or if they are, need to be co-ordinated with the rest of the United Kingdom. This means that they will have to work in close partnership with DEFRA to develop those aspects of Scotland's climate change policy. Scotland has set up its own initiatives such as the Scottish Energy Efficiency Office to promote energy efficiency, and it has established its own Renewables (Scotland) Obligation.

In a somewhat different way a Concordat has also been employed to co-ordinate the implementation of the Utilities Act 2000. The Gas and Electricity Markets Authority and the Gas and Electricity Consumer Council have reached an agreement that recognises the need to work together closely to achieve the shared aim of protecting the interests of consumers effectively, which includes a commitment to regular meetings to consider issues ranging from price levels, company performance, compliance with licensing conditions, the selling practices of companies and consumer complaints.[150]

Regulators 'Joining Up'

The 'soft' law approach is not confined to Concordats but arises in regard to another interesting development, the Regulators' Joint Statement, which again is very much in line with the 'modernising government' theme of ensuring that the policy process meets people's needs.[151] This is realised by delivering policy in a consistent way across institutional boundaries. Essentially, it is an attempt to co-

---

[150] Memorandum of Understanding between the Gas and Electricity Markets Authority and the Gas and Electricity Consumer Council (November 2000).

[151] See N Williams, 'Modernising Government: Policy Making within Whitehall' (1999) 70 *Political Quarterly* (No 4) 452; and *Modernising Government* (Cm 4310 J1999) para 23 identifies the need to 'align the boundaries of public bodies.'

ordinate the work of regulators by bringing them together in a number of differ-ent ways.[152] This initiative also implicitly reflects the complexity of the tasks con-fronting regulators in the current environment.[153] For example, we have already seen that the Office of Fair Trading exercises concurrent powers and is able to intervene in the process of utility regulation. In relation to this overlap, the state-ment commences by recognising the importance of the convergence of powers relating to reviewing prices and investigating anti-competitive agreements as a result the Competition Act 1998 and the Utilities Act 2000 (on this point there is also a European dimension). In order to address how such concurrent powers with the OFT are used, a Concurrency Working Party, chaired by the OFT, has been established. It seeks to promote a consistent and co-ordinated approach. It appears that this committee has assumed a prominent informational function by issuing guidance on the way powers under the Competition Act 1998 will be used. This is supported by guidelines which are published by other regulators on how such powers will apply in particular sectors.

In addition, there is a managerial dimension to this initiative, with regulators collectively expressing a desire for effective and efficient organisation and this aspect is to be co-ordinated by a group comprising of principal establishment and finance officers and chief operating officers of the regulatory organisations.[154] Also, there is a more general commitment to sharing best practice in relation to risk management, electronic data, recruitment and staff training, pay and grading structures.

The Regulator's Joint Statement has some practical use, but having recognised such affinities and the advantages to common approaches, it is important to be aware of the limitations of initiatives of this kind. Crucially, there is no procedure to resolve conflicts of interest and disputes that might arise. Also, such informal arrangements cannot adequately address the regulatory shortcomings originat-ing directly from the many disparate pieces of legislation. There are obvious advantages in both providing a common regulatory framework (the Utilities Act 2000 was intended to apply more widely across a number of sectors) and in set-ting out more clearly the respective roles, responsibilities and the directions of accountability of the diverse and overlapping regulatory bodies. Thus it would seem that further legislation is required to deal with many of the remaining struc-tural problems.

---

[152] There has been a general call for greater regulatory consistency which could be achieved by building on the co-ordinating regulation initiative with general practice statements.

[153] See the Regulators' Joint Statement, July 2001.

[154] WS Atkins, *Efficiency Review* (London, HM Treasury, May 2001), considered the working prac-tices of OFTEL, OFGEM, OFWAT and ORR The Chief Secretary then made a statement on the WS Atkins review on 2 July 2001. These financial consultants recognised that regulators were professional-ly run organisations, whose costs were very small in comparison both with the revenue of the indus-tries regulated and with the benefits received by consumers. Their report identified three main areas of concern relating to the information needed to judge efficiency, the cost of support services and staff structure.

CONCLUSION

Regulation has been discussed in a UK context as part of a governance narrative. This is an approach which seeks to investigate how power is exercised in the contemporary state. We have considered the institutional framework in terms of nationalisation, privatisation and regulation before proceeding to outline the impact of devolution and other less formal strategies which have changed the form and practice of government. This can be viewed as part of a shift from a welfare state model towards a regulatory model in the United Kingdom. In sum, we now find a policy sub-system of increasing complexity comprising of a wide range of public and private actors that are involved in policy formulation and implementation processes in the utility sector.[155]

In the first place this has had a profound impact on the crucial issue of accountability. In a formal sense regulators remain accountable to ministers and ultimately to Parliament (either central or devolved) under a statutory regime. However, the division of responsibilities between central and devolved government and between varying types of regulators at different levels has led to overlapping responsibilities which, for example, apply to establishing the terms of licences, setting price levels and determining the exercise of monopoly power and take-overs. In practice, we find that each industry operates as part of a process of circuitous decision-making, but beneath this veneer of statutory functions lies a masked reality of behind the scenes negotiation by the central players. Indeed, attribution of responsibility for the decisions that emerge is so unclear that lobbying on regulatory issues is targeted at ministers, regulators and the industries themselves.[156]

Secondly, at an operational level it is important to stress that certain structural deficiencies in the legislation have hampered the regulatory process. For example, it will be apparent that the original statutes failed to set out in sufficient detail the role and responsibility of regulators which allowed a personalised agenda of negotiated regulation based on bargaining and accommodation[157] to emerge for each industry.[158] Another disturbing tendency has been that regulators, although appearing to be as 'referees standing above the players in the game [and balancing conflicting interests]... in reality they can all too easily become involved in the game' by becoming too closely associated with their client industry.[159] Thirdly, it is evident that decisions by regulators require detailed financial information. The problem is that this is often generated by the client industry and such information may be manipulated so that it might be insufficient or superabundant to suit the

---

[155] Maloney, above, n 36, 627.

[156] See Sue Slipman, *Better Regulation Task Force* (July 2001).

[157] S Wilks, 'Utility Regulation, Corporate Governance, and the Amoral Corporation' in Wilks and Doern (eds), *Changing Regulatory Institutions in Britain and North America* (University of Torronto Press, 1998), 143.

[158] Thatcher, above n 25, at 132.

[159] J Morison and S Livingstone, *Reshaping Public Power* (London Sweet & Maxwell, 1995), 69. See in relation to Ofwat and Yorkshire Water, and the ORR and Railtrack.

purpose of compounding or evading the issue under consideration by the regulator.[160] In response to this difficulty it would appear that more rigorous accounting techniques need to be developed. Fourthly, a common criticism is that regulators have been deprived of the powers to make their own local regulatory rules which are essential to support many of the most sensitive decisions.[161]

This subject is normally discussed with regard to regulators, regulatory agencies and regulatory policies. However, it has been argued that any analysis of utility regulation must be directed at revising the nature of the corporate businesses which are themselves subject to regulation.[162] This has a particular resonance with the recent failure of Railtrack and the collapse of Enron and the resulting implications for the national economy, infrastructure and employment. The point is that improved performance requires more than changes to regulation. It calls for basic reforms to corporate governance that take into account wider issues of social responsibility and allow a substantially reduced role for financial markets. It has been suggested that this may also involve moving towards a corporate compliance model. Although the present Government is still attempting to blend 'the lean efficiency of the private sector with the social goals once exclusively associated with public ownership,'[163] it seems as clear now as it was during the first half of the twentieth century that there are certain natural monopolies that should remain under state control. This is because of the need to establish a structure which, rather than promoting the pursuit of profit, prioritises and rewards the public interest elements of universal access, safety, environmental protection, reliability and punctuality.[164]

---

[160] Foster, above n 43 at 235.

[161] Further, regulators were not given powers to make their own regulatory rules which were necessary to support their decisions. See M Loughlin and C Scott, 'The Regulatory State' in P Dunleavy, A Gamble, I Holliday and G Peele (eds), *Developments in British Politics* (Basingstoke, Macmillan, 1997), 209.

[162] Approaching this from a criminal law perspective, it has been pointed out that identifying corporate responsibility in the contemporary situation is fraught with difficulty and requires new forms of liability to be invented suitable for an organisational elite. 'Corporate regimes will either bargain organisational régimes to suit themselves or relocate elsewhere': see A Norrie, *Crime, Reason and History* (2nd edn, London, Butterworths, 2001), 103.

[163] Wilks, above n 157, at 133 and 154 *et seq.* For example, it is suggested that, 'regulators working together could insist upon internal changes in organisation and process that would make the utilities more orientated towards regulatory compliance'. Also, the principle of mandatory consultation could be extended to all interested groups, including employees, customers and suppliers.

[164] J Freedland, 'These Hybrid Monsters,' *Guardian,* 27 March 2002.

9

Freedom of Information: A New Constitutional Landscape?

STEPHANIE PALMER

F REEDOM OF INFORMATION laws are increasingly accepted as a necessary feature of advanced economic countries. Transparency and access to information has also been recognised as an important value in the European Union.[1] The United Kingdom has lagged behind most other Western countries in this respect but recent years have seen a marked change of policy. The Freedom of Information Act (FOIA) 2000 was introduced as one aspect of the Labour Party's commitment to modernise British government through constitutional change. The Lord Chancellor has promised that the government 'will govern with a new spirit of openness ... [in] partnership with the people.'[2] More recently the Scottish Parliament has passed its own legislation on freedom of information.

Freedom of information laws are closely linked to liberal political thought regarding the role of the state. Access to information about governmental decision-making is couched in terms of a democratic right: a right to know in which all citizens share. In this sense, freedom of information is a constitutional right, perhaps 'the most fundamental of our civic and political rights.'[3] These provisions are justified as enhancing democratic participation in government but they are also linked to accountability through increased oversight. In breathing new life into our traditional accountability mechanisms, freedom of information can be regarded as an important measure available for the control of power in the contemporary constitution. It can also play an instrumental role: a mechanism for improving public authority decision-making. The idea of greater openness, imposed through an Act of Parliament on a constitutional structure traditionally concerned with preserving secrecy, is potentially radical.

---

[1] EC Treaty Article 255. See S Peers, 'From Maastricht to Laeken: The Political Agenda of Openness and Transparency in the EU, in V Deckmyn (ed), *Increasing Transparency in the European Union* (Maastricht, EIPA, 2002).

[2] Lord Irvine of Lairg, 'Constitutional Reform and a Bill of Rights' [1997] *EHRLR* 483.

[3] C Harlow, 'Freedom of Information and Transparency as Administrative and Constitutional Rights' (1999) 2 *Cambridge Yearbook of European Legal Studies* 285.

This legislation gives UK citizens for the first time a statutory right to official information. It extends to all information[4] except that which the FOIA defines as exempt. Other positive aspects of this legislation include independent scrutiny by the Information Commissioner and provision for a system of active disclosure through publication schemes.[5] The FOIA applies to public authorities in England, Wales and Northern Ireland. It received the Royal Assent on 30 November 2000 but it will not come fully into force until January 2005. In Scotland, the Freedom of Information (Scotland) Act (FOISA) 2002 was passed by the Scottish Parliament on 24 April, 2002. Application for access under the FOISA cannot be made until December 2005.

Any discussion concerning the regulation of information reveals certain tensions. On the one hand, information can be perceived as a public good, a resource or commodity necessary to support political rights and the market. On the other, much information is understood as inherently private or as property and not suitable for access or disclosure without potential damage to legitimate commercial concerns or to competitiveness.[6] In order to mediate between these competing claims on information the law regulates information in a different manner in the public and private spheres. The traditional view has been that the democratic objectives underpinning freedom of information are not relevant to private sector bodies. Hence the openness required of the public sector under freedom of information legislation should not be demanded of the private sector. Yet the new reality is that the distinction between the public and private sectors has become blurred. Across the Western world the apparatus of the state is shrinking. The 'hollowing out' of the state is a feature of modern government in the wake of privatisation, contracting out and Next Step Agencies amongst others.[7] In those circumstances then, where public services are contracted out to private sector bodies, there is a threat to the democratic objectives of freedom of information if access is automatically denied because the transaction is uncritically categorised as private. Underlying many of the contentious exemptions contained in the FOIA is this public/private divide.

This chapter will initially focus on the background to the freedom of information legislation in the United Kingdom and the principles underpinning it. It will then critically analyse the freedom of information schemes and assess whether the new legislation could provide greater public scrutiny of the process of government and strengthen accountability. In particular, the exemptions to information which concern the formulation of policy, investigations by public authorities, protection of commercial interests and information provided in confidence will be analysed. The main focus of the chapter will be on the FOIA but some reference to the FOISA will be made. This chapter concludes that the FOIA is significant in establishing the first enforceable freedom of information regime in the United Kingdom. Nevertheless, the legislation may not adequately promote a change to the ethos of secrecy in governance.

[4] See FOIA, s 84.
[5] FOIA, s 19.
[6] A vast amount of material held by public authorities has been obtained from third parties.
[7] R Rhodes, 'The hollowing out of the state: The changing nature of public services in Britain' (1994) 65 *Political Quarterly* 138. See Peter Cane, ch 10 below.

BACKGROUND

In 1997, the Government quickly acted on its election promise to introduce freedom of information by publishing a White Paper outlining its proposals for a Freedom of Information Act and inviting public comment.[8] It was acknowledged in this White Paper that:

> Unnecessary secrecy in government leads to arrogance in governance and defective decision-making. The perception of excessive secrecy has become a corrosive influence in the decline of public confidence in government. Moreover, the climate of public opinion has changed: people expect greater openness and accountability from government than they used to.[9]

This statement is a clear reaction to the ethos of secrecy that has been a hallmark of the Westminster style of government. The traditional position in the United Kingdom is that all official information is secret unless governments choose to disclose it. Openness and transparency have been alien concepts in British government administration as the priority has been to protect official information. Stringent secrecy laws and the absence of any general statutory right of access to government-held information have permitted governments the freedom to regulate the public dissemination of information. The government controls the form in which information is released as well as the timing of any release. This authoritarian position aroused suspicions that governments could, and indeed would, elevate their interests over all others. These suspicions seemed confirmed by the inquiry into the 'arms to Iraq' affair and the collapse of the *Matrix Churchill* trial. Sir Richard Scott's report on the affair commented upon the 'consistent undervaluing by government of the public interest that full information should be available to Parliament'[10] which had contributed to a lack of governmental accountability.

The secrecy ethos of British governments has also been buttressed by the criminal law through the Official Secrets Act. The Official Secrets Act 1911 protected all government information regardless of its public interest or its importance. This 'blanket ban' on the release of all unauthorised official information made it impossible to argue directly for freedom of information legislation: a necessary prerequisite was the repeal of the notorious section 2 of the Official Secrets Act 1911. As David Williams stated in 1965:

> Our knowledge of the workings of the central government nowadays is to a very large degree controlled by the Official Secrets Acts. Outsiders cannot look in. Insiders can look out, but they dare not speak out. Solemn and stern reminders of the terms of the Official Secrets Acts have engendered a general attitude of caution.[11]

---

[8] *Your Right to Know* (Cm 3818, 1997).

[9] White Paper, above n 8, at para 1.1.

[10] *Report of the Inquiry into the Export of Defence Equipment and Dual-Use Goods to Iraq and Related Prosecutions* (HC 115, 1995–6), para D1.165.

[11] David Williams, *Not in the Public Interest* (London, Hutchinson, 1965), 208.

Civil servants remain subject to disciplinary proceedings for any disclosures of information violating internal civil service rules and instructions.

Although the old discredited Official Secrets Act was reformed in 1989, the specified categories of information protected by the criminal law are still broad and there is no provision for a public interest defence.[12] In the recent decision in *R v Shayler*, concerning the effect of the Human Rights Act 1998 on the operation of the Official Secrets Act 1998, Lord Bingham commented on the issue of secrecy in a democratic state:

> Modern democratic government means government of the people by the people for the people. But there can be no government by the people if they are ignorant of the issues to be resolved, the arguments for and against different solutions and the facts underlying those arguments. The business of government is not an activity about which only those professionally engaged are entitled to receive information and express opinions. It is, or should be, a participatory process. But there can be no assurance that government is carried out for the people unless the facts are made known, the issues publicly ventilated.[13]

Shayler was a former member of the security and intelligence services, who released intelligence documents to the public. He claimed that he was acting in the public interest. In spite of acknowledging the tension of secrecy laws in a democratic state, the Law Lords concluded that there was no opportunity for Shayler to claim disclosure was justified in the public interest.[14] This decision has not fractured, as some commentators had hoped, 'the national security-official security nexus' that has proved an enduring feature of the British constitutional structure.[15]

In the United Kingdom there has been a gradual trend towards less secrecy in government.[16] We have come a long way since the 1976 'Croham Directive,' instructing heads of departments to publish 'as much as possible of the factual and analytical material used as the background to major policy studies' but which remained secret until leaked some years later. In 1993 the previous Conservative Government published a White Paper, *Open Government.*[17] It proposed the introduction of a Code of Practice on Access to Government Information.[18] This non-statutory Code came into force in April 1994 and is still in operation at this date. One result of the introduction of the Code was that it raised expectations of greater openness in the public sector. The Code requires government departments to

---

[12] See S Palmer, 'Tightening Secrecy Law: The Official Secrets Act 1989' [1990] *Public Law* 243.

[13] [2002] 2 WLR 754.

[14] Although such a conclusion was a restriction on the right to freedom of expression, it was justifiable under ECHR Article 10(2) on the basis of national security. In the subsequent trial the focus was on the official position held by Shayler rather than on whether the material released damaged national security or showed wrongdoing in the operations of the security service.

[15] N Whitty, T Murphy and S Livingstone, *Civil Liberties Law: The Human Rights Act Era* (London, Butterworths, 2001), 368.

[16] During the 1980s and 1990s some progress had been made in establishing a right of access to certain categories of information. See eg Local Government (Access to Information) Act 1985, Environmental Information Regulations 1992, s 1 1992/3240, the Data Protection Act 1984 and more recently, 1998.

[17] Cm 2290, 1993.

[18] *Ibid* at 32.

respond to requests for information but it does not make the disclosure of official information obligatory. It also contained wide class-based exemptions. The Parliamentary Commissioner for Administration has been given a role in investigating complaints that departments have not complied with the Code,[19] yet there have been few complaints to the Commissioner concerning breaches of the Code. The reason for the paucity of complaints can probably be explained by the fact that there is no direct access to the Commissioner: individuals have to proceed through their Member of Parliament.[20] Overall these modest changes have not reversed the established atmosphere of secrecy in government. It is clear that a far more radical approach would be required in order to achieve a truly open system of government.

In December 1997, the newly elected Labour Government published a White Paper that set out proposals for the introduction of freedom of information legislation. These proposals seemed to signal the intention of the Government to effect a fundamental change to the administrative culture in the United Kingdom. The scope of the proposed Bill was to have an impressively wide application. The White Paper stated that it would cover not only government departments but, amongst others, privatised utilities, quangos, local bodies, universities and public service broadcasters. Services performed for public authorities under contract would also be subject to the new freedom of information. According to these proposals, exemptions should be limited to the following seven areas: national security; defence and international relations; law enforcement; personal privacy; commercial confidentiality; the safety of the individual, the public or the environment; information supplied in confidence; and the integrity of the decision-making and policy advice processes in government. The test for disclosure was based on an assessment of harm that disclosure might cause, and the need to safeguard the public interest.[21] In order to guarantee that decisions on disclosure would be based on a presumption of openness, the appropriate test for most categories of information was a substantial harm test. Of particular significance was the White Paper's total rejection of a ministerial veto or conclusive certificates mechanism. It was proposed that freedom of information legislation should be enforced by an Information Commissioner who would have the power to order disclosure of records and information. In addition the new legislation was to be accompanied by a policy of 'active' disclosure.

In spite of some flaws, the White Paper proposals were largely welcomed[22] but after the first year in office and a number of embarrassing disclosures, the govern-

---

[19]   Code of Practice, cl 11.

[20]   In 2001, Home Office ministers refused to abide by the decision of the Commissioner to release information concerning how often they had declared a possible conflict of interest to their colleagues under the ministerial code. This was the first time that a recommendation of the Commissioner has been refused.

[21]   White Paper, above n 8, at para 3.4.

[22]   See P Birkinshaw, 'An "All Singin' and All Dancin'" Affair: the New Labour Government's Proposals for Freedom of Information' [1998] *Public Law* 176; R Hazell, *Commentary on the Freedom of Information White Paper* (Constitution Unit, 1998) and S Palmer, 'Freedom of Information—Principles and Problems: A Comparative Analysis of the Australian and Proposed UK Systems' in Cambridge Centre for Public Law (ed), *Constitutional Reform in the United Kingdom: Practice and Principles* (Oxford, Hart Publishing, 1998), 147.

ment developed cold feet. Justice Michael Kirby has identified 'seven deadly sins of FOI.' The first was 'strangled at birth.' He reports an Australian politician as saying 'that it was imperative for any government proposing a freedom of information law to get the legislation enacted within the first year of office, lest the skeletons accumulating in the governmental cupboard thereafter render the prospect of enforceable rights of access to information too politically uncongenial to press on with.'[23] Unfortunately, the first sin had been committed. In July 1998, responsibility for freedom of information was moved from the Cabinet Office to the Home Office after the sacking of the minister responsible for its publication and amidst rumours that the White Paper proposals would be severely watered down.

In May 1999, the Government published a draft Freedom of Information Bill[24] for further consultation and for pre-legislative scrutiny by the House of Commons Select Committee on Public Administration[25] and the House of Lords Delegated Powers and Deregulation Committee.[26] This disappointing Bill abandoned many of the principles contained in the 1998 White Paper. Although providing a right to information, the draft Bill contained numerous devices ensuring that secrecy could be maintained by a government determined to do so.

Subsequently, in November 1999 the Government finally presented its long-awaited Freedom of Information Bill to Parliament. Although the Home Secretary responded to some of the criticisms of the draft Bill,[27] the Act has emerged as a 'pale shadow' of the proposals outlined in the White Paper. Any initial optimism that new freedom of information legislation would sweep aside the atmosphere of secrecy and radically alter the administrative culture in the United Kingdom has faded. In Scotland, the development of freedom of information shared some similarities to that South of the border. The new Scottish Executive initially published proposals for an freedom of information Bill in Scotland that rejected many of the key elements of the Bill before Westminster. In particular, its proposals concerning the publication of policy advice and the power of the Scottish Commissioner to order disclosure differed from the draft Bill before Westminster.[28] As we shall see below, the FOISA still retains some important differences from the FOIA but the final result shares similarities with the Act passed by Westminster.

Whether openness in government can be converted from hollow rhetoric to vibrant reality depends in large measure on the extent to which the reforms are

[23] Justice Michael Kirby, 'Freedom of Information: The Seven Deadly Sins' [1998] *EHRLR* 245, 249.
[24] *Freedom of Information: Consultation on Draft Legislation* (Cm 4355, 1999).
[25] House of Commons, Public Administration Select Committee, Third Report session 1998–99, *Freedom of Information Draft Bill* (HC 570, July 1999).
[26] *Report from the Select Committee Appointed to Consider the Draft Freedom of Information Bill*, session 1998–99 (HL 97, July 1999).
[27] The Home Secretary made some important concessions in the second draft Bill. For example, the time for responding to requests was reduced to 20 working days; the remarkable 'jigsaw' exemption which allowed information to be withheld if it could be harmful in combination with other information was abandoned as was the right of the authorities to insist on knowing why an applicant wanted information or to disclose information on condition it was not given to a journalist.
[28] See *An Open Scotland. Freedom of Information: A Consultation.* This document was laid before the Scottish Parliament by the Scottish Ministers in November 1999.

grounded in democratic principle. The next section will outline the arguments justifying openness in government and freedom of information in the context of a constitutional right. These grounds are not self-contained and tend to overlap with each other. The final section will assess whether the government's new legislation can ensure the effective enjoyment of the citizen's right to know.

PRINCIPLES OF FREEDOM OF INFORMATION

Knowledge is a fundamental prerequisite to democracy. Although democracy itself is a contested concept, most would agree that democratic rights include the institutions and procedures of representative government, backed up by human rights operating in a constitutional system dedicated to the rule of law.[29] Although these features of a democratic system are important, even essential, democratic systems hold out the promise of far more than the legitimating of government through participation in periodic elections. A broader understanding of democracy would perceive it as a force for enhancing a culture of participation and equality among citizens.

Legislation on freedom of information could provide an important tool to promote these broader democratic aims. Access to information, as a fundamental democratic right in which all citizens share on an equal footing, is increasingly recognised as a significant aspect of institutional accountability. Such accountability lies at the heart of any conception of political responsibility: governments must answer to a democratically elected Parliament and ultimately to the electorate. Public bodies must be able to justify their actions by demonstrating that they are acting in the public interest.[30] The need for accountability and scrutiny through access to information is increasingly recognised as a necessary feature of a vigorous and vigilant public sphere. Indeed it is an idea which has been given prominence on the political agenda of Western democratic societies for many years.[31]

It is possible to distil a bundle of democratic themes underlying freedom of information legislation, some of which have already been touched upon. As citizens in a democratic society, there is an expectation to be fully informed about the government's actions, policies and decisions. Without information, individuals are unable to exercise their rights and responsibilities effectively. There is also an accompanying expectation by citizens to be able to participate in and perhaps even to influence government policy-making. This feature of democracy distinguishes it from other more authoritarian aspects of political organisation.[32]

---

[29] See S Marks, *The Riddle of All Constitutions* (Oxford, OUP, 2000), ch 3 and D Held, *Democracy and the Global Order: From the Modern State to the Cosmopolitan Governance* (Cambridge, Polity Press, 1995).

[30] See the discussion in Carol Harlow, ch 4 above.

[31] C Harlow, 'Freedom of Information and Transparency as Administrative and Constitutional Rights' (1999) 2 *Cambridge Yearbook of European Legal Studies* 285.

[32] See Marks, above n 29, at 51.

Freedom of information legislation could serve to strengthen the conventional arrangements underpinning our constitutional system. In our political system the executive is not sufficiently responsible to Parliament. The political reality is that the executive has significant control over Parliament. Without openness, the principle of responsible government is undermined. The work of select committees, the efficacy of parliamentary questions, the effectiveness of opposition parties and pressure groups all depend on the availability and accessibility of information. Power is at the heart of secrecy in government, and power and information are inextricably linked.[33] The executive has possession of a vast amount of information and is in a position to authorise selective disclosure in a manner and at a time convenient for the government. Partial disclosure may distort accountability.

The constitutional conventions of individual and collective ministerial responsibility are frequently used to legitimate the maintenance of government secrecy, by 'enforcing an internal governmental discipline in the control of information.'[34] The traditional theory of ministerial responsibility has led to the practice whereby ministers decide for themselves what information should or should not be disclosed to Parliament. Yet the reality is that the doctrine has been eroded to the point where it has been described as deserving 'the status of a legal fiction.'[35] The Matrix Churchill affair and the ensuing report by Scott highlighted the fact that the conventions operated as an obstacle to the availability of information and to holding the government to account. Woodhouse concludes that, even post-Scott, the convention of ministerial responsibility 'remains opaque and incoherent.'[36] Nevertheless, Adam Tomkins contends that to assume the doctrine of ministerial responsibility is no longer 'a fundamental doctrine of the constitution' is misjudged.[37] He argues that in recent years the principle of ministerial responsibility has been having a revival and that it is possible for parliamentary accountability to work, particularly through the reformed select committees of the House of Commons.[38] Undoubtedly, a strong freedom of information culture could contribute to such a revival and enhance the accountability of government and the influence of Parliament.

Ministers frequently use their powers to 'leak' information or give non-attributable briefings to journalists when it is politically expedient. The manipulation of information is inevitable. For example, it would seem that members of the government selectively leaked details of their White Paper proposals on competitiveness to the press before the documents were presented to Parliament. These actions led to questions being raised in Parliament.[39] The problem of leaking is compounded by the widely held belief that government information is the property of the gov-

[33] See EW Thomas, 'Secrecy and Open Government' in PD Finn (ed), *Essays on Law and Government: Principles and Values* (Sydney, Law Book Company, 1995).

[34] C Turpin, *British Government and the Constitution* (4th edn, London, Butterworths, 1999), 523.

[35] D Feldman, 'Public Law Values in the House of Lords' (1990) 106 *LQR* 246, 254.

[36] D Woodhouse, 'Ministerial Responsibility: Something Old, Something New' [1997] *Public Law* 262, 280.

[37] Adam Tomkins, ch 3 above, quoting J Jowell and D Oliver (eds), *The Changing Constitution* (4th edn, Oxford, Oxford University Press, 2000), viii.

[38] *Ibid.*

[39] See Points of Order, HC vol 363, cols 483–4 (15 February 2001).

ernment, even though this valuable resource is created and maintained at the tax-payers' expense. The Official Secrets Act also encapsulated the concept that all official information is vested in the administration. In other words, such information is 'owned' by the government and subject to protection as a property right.

Freedom of information legislation is a potentially important tool to redress the imbalance in power. It also enables more effective supervision of the executive within Parliament. In Australia, the opposition parties have made extensive use of the access to information provisions under the Freedom of Information Act 1982. On the one hand, the theory assumes that the potential exposure to criticism should enhance the government's performance. On the other, the threat of increased criticism makes a strong freedom of information legislation a highly unattractive prospect for governments. Yet one of the fundamental purposes of freedom of information legislation should be to strike a balance between competing public interests of openness and secrecy: neither are absolute values. In order for freedom of information legislation to satisfy the democratic mandate, the unfettered discretion accorded to governments to control the release of information must be subordinated to wider public interest considerations. These ideas have received judicial recognition in freedom of expression decisions such as *Derbyshire County Council v Times Newspapers Ltd*,[40] which stressed the importance of uninhibited criticism of government bodies as an important part of the democratic process: and *in Spycatcher (No 2)*,[41] where Lord Keith cited with approval from the Australian High Court:

> It is unacceptable, in our democratic society, that there should be a restraint on the publication of information relating to government when the only vice of that information is that it enables the public to discuss, review and criticise government action.[42]

A further justification for increased openness in government and freedom of information legislation focuses on the public's needs as consumers.[43] Public authorities hold a very wide range and quantity of information. This includes important economic information about the market, public services, and information supplied by individual companies. The Government has specifically recognised the role of people as citizens and consumers in their White Paper, *Modernising Government*.[44] Yet whether this information should fall within the public or private sphere is not so obvious. Information on consumer and environmental issues preserves political rights by providing citizens with the opportunity to make informed decisions as well as contribute to the public debate, while businesses which submit information to the government are concerned that any subsequent disclosure of that information could destroy proprietary interests in their research or trade secrets.

---

[40] [1993] 2 WLR 449.

[41] *Attorney-General v Guardian Newspapers Ltd (No 2)* [1990] 1 AC 109.

[42] *Ibid* at 258, citing from *Commonwealth of Australia v John Fairfax and Sons Ltd* (1980) 147 CLR 39 at 52.

[43] See D Oliver, *Government in the United Kingdom: The Search for Accountability, Effectiveness and Citizenship* (Milton Keynes, Open University Press, 1991), 169.

[44] Cm 4310, 1999.

Historically, freedom of information legislation has been justified as enhancing the democratic values of accountability and increased participation. The focus has been on the role of the state, its policy-making and government-held information. Yet the hiving-off of many traditional government functions through policies such as privatisation and outsourcing, means that power in the modern democratic state is fragmented. Non-government actors are increasingly carrying out traditional public functions that raise, perhaps even more starkly, the same accountability concerns as with governmental bodies.[45] We have new constitutional structures that are characterised by interdependence among a host of different public/private actors. In many circumstances these arrangements defy easy division into secure public or private compartments. In this new economic paradigm, distinguishing between governmental and private institutions may no longer even be useful.[46] Arguably, our traditional understandings of accountability and responsibility have not been adequately modified to respond to these challenging developments. Jody Freeman states that: 'If we are concerned about accountability…then the question is not how to make agencies accountable, but how to make regulatory regimes ... accountable?'[47] Does the new freedom of information legislation in the United Kingdom adequately provide for this new political reality? Are the traditional values of our public law system that underlie freedom of information, even adequate to meet the challenges posed by the 'hollowing-out' of the state?

Freedom of information also raises questions about the relationship between access and privacy. There is a natural and healthy desire by citizens to know what information the government holds about individuals and, if necessary, to check and correct inaccurate data. Although as outlined below, these rights of access to data are further buttressed by Article 8 of the European Convention on Human Rights, personal information is already protected in the United Kingdom by the Data Protection Act 1998 which provides for access to personal information. These rights have been further extended by the FOIA. Carol Harlow refers to these personal rights, providing for individuals to seek access to personal information about themselves, as administrative law rights rather than constitutional rights.[48] The focus of this chapter is on constitutional rights, those rights to which individuals should have access without showing any special interest.

A further justification for the enactment of freedom of information provisions rests on the general right of freedom of expression. Without access to

[45] See J Freeman, 'The Real Democracy Problem in Administrative Law' in D Dyzenhaus (ed), *Recrafting the Rule of Law* (Oxford, Hart Publishing, 1999), 331.

[46] P Grabosky, 'Using Non-Governmental Resources to Foster Regulatory Compliance' (1995) 8 *Governance* 527, 529.

[47] Freeman, above n 45, at 369. Maloney points out that the water industry is subject to '"heavier" regulation in the private sector ... than sponsoring departments ever did under the public ownership model.' W Maloney, 'Regulation in an Episodic Policy-Making Environment: the Water Industry in England and Wales', (2001) 79 *Public Administration* 625, 640–41. Maloney also points out that regulation raises the a classic principal/agent problem of information asymmetries: regulation depends on detailed technical knowledge that only the regulatee possesses. See also Peter Leyland, ch 8 above.

[48] Harlow, n 31, at 287.

information, freedom of expression is markedly diminished. Article 10 of the European Convention on Human Rights guarantees the right to receive and impart information. There is, however, rather surprisingly, no express guarantee for the right of access to information in the European Convention on Human Rights.[49] ECHR Article 10 provides for a right to 'receive information' which has been held to be limited to receiving information 'that others wish or may be willing to impart.'[50] More recently, the European Court of Human Rights has developed a limited right of access to information by way of a positive obligation under Article 8 (respect for private and family life). In the case of *Gaskin v United Kingdom*,[51] the Court found that in some circumstances an obligation on the government to impart information may arise. The United Kingdom was found to have violated the principle of proportionality in Article 8 because it failed to provide for an independent authority to decide on the issue of disclosure. The United Kingdom procedures were unsuccessfully challenged in *McGinley and E.E. v United Kingdom*.[52] The case concerned two servicemen who were exposed to nuclear bomb tests in the Pacific 40 years ago and had been denied access to their medical records. The European Court found no violation of either Articles 6 or 8. Nevertheless, the Court stated:

> Where a Government engages in hazardous activities, such as those in issue in the present case, which might have hidden adverse consequences on the health of those involved in such activities, respect for private and family life under Article 8 requires that an effective and accessible procedure be established which enables such persons to seek all relevant and appropriate information.'[53]

Lord Justice Sedley notes that there is something odd about 'discovering a right to information in the entrails of Article 8, which says nothing about information,' while refusing to develop adequately this right under Article 10 which specifically refers to information.[54]

The Human Rights Act 1998 will underpin the access provisions for individuals who are seeking information about themselves but will not directly provide equivalent support for the other aspects of freedom of information legislation. It is crucial therefore that the legislation reflects the constitutional arguments and democratic principles outlined above by providing a freedom of information system that can achieve a real cultural shift in public administration. The next section will focus on the central issues in the FOIA.

---

[49] See G Malinverni, 'Freedom of Information in the European Convention on Human Rights and in the International Covenant on Civil and Political Rights' (1983) 4 *Human Rights Law Journal* 443.

[50] *Leander v Sweden* Series A No 116, 29, para 74 (1987).

[51] (1990) 12 *EHRR* 36. See also *Guerra v Italy* (1998) 26 *EHRR* 357.

[52] (1998) 27 *EHRR* 1.

[53] *Ibid* at 45.

[54] S Sedley, 'Information as a Human Right' in J Beatson and Y Cripps (eds), *Freedom of Expression and Freedom of Information* (Oxford, Oxford University Press, 2000), 245.

THE NEW FREEDOM OF INFORMATION LEGISLATION

In the 1997 White Paper that preceded the legislation, the Government acknowledged that it is in the best position to champion the cause of open government and
to challenge the entrenched secrecy culture that has been an established feature of
the administration of the United Kingdom government. This section will assess
the extent to which the new legislation will achieve these objectives.

Section 1 of the FOIA provides for a general right of access to information held
by public authorities. Pursuant to this section, a public authority has two distinct
duties: the duty to confirm or deny whether it holds the requested information
and the duty to communicate it. Each exemption provision specifies whether these
duties apply or are exempted. The right conferred under this section covers 'information'[55] as well as original documents.

It is disappointing that the government decided not to include a 'purpose
clause' in the FOIA.[56] The advantage of including the objective in the legislation
itself is that it is likely to encourage an interpretation of the law that is consistent
with its democratic purpose by establishing a clear presumption in favour of disclosure. These provisions are in evidence in other freedom of information legislation: in Australia, New Zealand and Ireland.[57] In New Zealand, for example, 'the
Ombudsmen have stressed time and time again that the Act must receive such fair
large and liberal interpretation as will best attain the objects of the Act set out in
sections 4 and 5.'[58] Experience from Australia suggests that it is essential that the
object of the legislation should include the underlying principle of the Act.[59] The
section setting out the objectives of the Australian Freedom of Information Act
has led to some interpretative difficulties: it was possible to conclude that the right
of access provided by that Act was an end in itself, whereas an object clause which
explained the broader public interest to be served by enabling access to government documents would encourage an interpretation favourable to disclosure.[60]

---

[55] See FOIA, s 84. Information 'recorded in any form' is covered as well as unrecorded information:
FOIA, s 51(8).

[56] See eg the views of the Data Protection Registrar, Elizabeth French, given in her evidence to the
House of Commons Select Committee on Public Administration (28 June 1999), paras 2.4–2.6. The
Scottish Executive signalled that the Scottish legislation might contain a 'purpose clause' but the FOISA
does not include such a clause.

[57] See the Australian Federal Freedom of Information Act 1982, s 3; New Zealand Official Information Act 1982, ss 4, 5. The purpose of the Irish Act is set out in the long title of the Freedom of Information Act 1997.

[58] I Eagles, M Taggart and G Liddell, *Freedom of Information in New Zealand* (Auckland, OUP,
1992), 4.

[59] Australian Law Reform Commission, Report No 77, Administrative Review Council, Report No
40, *Open Government: a Review of the Federal Freedom of Information Act 1982* (hereafter referred to as
'ALRC'). Section 3 of the Australian Freedom of Information Act states that the object of the legislation
is 'to extend as far as possible the right of the Australian community to access information in the possession of the Government of the Commonwealth'.

[60] ALRC, above n 59, at paras 4.4–4.6. See also the comments of Dr Clark, HC Deb, 7 December
1999, vol 340, col 741.

The new legislation contains some very positive points. First, a statutory right of access to information, as opposed to a Code, has a major psychological as well as legal effect. The FOISA also makes provision for children to exercise rights under the legislation.[61] Secondly, the legislation will be fully retrospective which will avoid any problems with an 'access gap' in respect of documents created less than 30 years ago but before 1999. Thirdly, these public rights of access are determinable and enforceable by an authority independent of government, namely an Information Commissioner. The FOIA provides for free access to the Information Commissioner and an appeal to a tribunal. Finally, there are strict limits on the response times. The Home Secretary took the advice of the Select Committees and reduced the usual response time from 40 to 20 working days following the date of receipt. [62]

The FOIA covers public authorities and this includes a wide range of organisations at all levels of government. Section 3 sets out the different ways in which a body can be a public authority. Any body or organisation listed in Schedule 1 is a public authority for the purposes of FOI; bodies, persons or office holders designated as public authorities by order of the Secretary of State;[63] and publicly owned companies.[64] Obvious public authorities such as government departments, the Houses of Parliament, local authorities, NHS bodies, educational institutions, and police bodies are included in Schedule 1. In addition, the list of public authorities also includes such diverse bodies as the Advisory Committee on Hazardous Substances, the Law Commission, the Parole Board and the Zoos Forum.[65] Private organisations, such as bodies working on contracted–out functions and privatised utilities, may be designated as public authorities in relation to their public functions.[66] The breadth of the FOIA, then, is wider than many overseas freedom of information legislation. The broad coverage in this era of outsourcing is to be welcomed. Nevertheless, as discussed below, freedom of information applications concerning private bodies discharging public functions are subject to structural limitations inherent in the FOIA. [67]

It is striking that, for the purposes of FOI, the Government chose to include a list of authorities in a schedule rather than leave it primarily for the courts to determine what is a 'public authority', as in the Human Rights Act 1998. In the majority of circumstances, a public authority for the purposes of the Human Rights Act will also be considered as such in the FOIA. Yet, some differences may exist. For example, the security and intelligence services are not included in Schedule 1 to the FOIA but Convention rights should still be applicable.

[61] FOISA, s 69.
[62] FOIA, s 10(1).
[63] FOIA, s 5.
[64] FOIA, s 6.
[65] The Secretary of State has power to add further bodies if certain conditions are met: FOIA, s 4(1).
[66] FOIA, s 5. See also HC Standing Committee B, 11 January 2000, col 67.
[67] See M McDcDonagh, 'FOI and Confidentiality of Commercial Information' [2001] *Public Law* 256.

THE EXEMPTIONS

General Points

The efficacy of an enforceable right of access to official information could be undermined if there are extensive exceptions from the general principle of openness. Exemptions are a feature of all overseas freedom of information legislation.[68] Lessons from overseas also indicate that the sharpest debates concern the exemptions. This is hardly a surprise, as it is the exceptions to the principles of freedom of information that endanger the likelihood of achieving greater transparency.

Part II of the FOIA sets out the circumstances where a public authority is under no duty to provide information. In some circumstances, an authority is entitled to refuse even to state whether or not the information is held. Exemptions to the right of access are features of all freedom of information legislation. In fact, such exempt categories largely coincide. The purpose of the exemption provisions is to balance the objective of providing access to government information against legitimate claims for protection.[69] Inevitably, a tension exists between the principle of a right to know and any claim a government is permitted to make to resist disclosure of a document or information. The scope of exemptions in freedom of information legislation and the degree of independent supervision are crucial. If the exemptions are too extensive, they make a mockery of such legislation. In effect, the efficacy of any system of freedom of information is judged by the extent of departures permitted from the general principle of access to official information.

In the White Paper, the Government proposed that 'the test for disclosure [of exempt material] under freedom of information should be based on an assessment of the harm that disclosure might cause, and the need to safeguard the public interest.'[70] In order to guarantee that decisions on disclosure would be based on a presumption of openness, the appropriate test for most categories of information should be a substantial harm test.[71] This set a high hurdle for the public authority to establish. This formulation suggested that it would be necessary to demonstrate that substantial harm would flow from the release rather than merely could do so. Only a limited number of interests were to be protected by the harm test and disclosure was to be assessed on a 'contents basis' rather than a 'class

---

[68] For example the FOIA in the USA has nine exemptions which protect classified national defence and foreign relations information, internal agency rules and practices, information prohibited from disclosure by another law, trade secrets and confidential business information, interagency or intra-agency communications protected by legal privileges, information covering personal privacy, information compiled for law enforcement purposes, information relating to the supervision of financial institutions and geological information. The Access to Information Act in Canada provides for 14 exemptions including information obtained in confidence, advice, protecting the economic interests of Canada, solicitor-client privilege and notice to third parties.

[69] See discussion in ALRC, above n 59, at para 8.1.

[70] White Paper, above n 8, at para 3.4.

[71] *Ibid* at para 3.7. A small category of public bodies, for example Parliament and the security services, were to be excluded from the legislation.

basis.'[72] The seven exemptions in the White Paper, in contrast to the 15 set out in the 1994 Code of Practice, were national security, defence and international relations, law enforcement, personal privacy, commercial confidentiality, the safety of the individual, the public and the environment, information supplied in confidence and decision-making and policy advice.

The FOIA departs from the White Paper suggestions on a number of important issues. In those areas dealing with a harm exemption, the Act has adopted the far weaker test of 'prejudice' or 'is likely to prejudice.'[73] The two Select Committees recommended that the appropriate test should be 'substantially prejudice' for at least some of the exemptions.[74] During parliamentary debates, the Home Secretary stated that the test referred to a probability of harm and not a possibility.[75] The same point was made in the Consultation Document (on the Bill) where it was stated that 'the prejudice must be real, actual or "of substance"'.[76] If this is the test considered appropriate, it seems a missed opportunity for the government to have failed to qualify the word prejudice by either 'serious' or 'substantial.' In contrast, the Scottish legislation has adopted the 'substantial harm' test.[77]

In stark contrast to the proposals in the White Paper, the FOIA (as well as the FOISA) introduces a key distinction between 'class' and 'harm based' exemptions. As set out in the White Paper, the harm-based exemption requires the public authority to show that disclosure of the requested information would, or would be likely to, cause prejudice to the protected interest specified in the exemption. Class-based exemptions permit all information within a particular class to be withheld, regardless of any harm. This includes information relating to security and intelligence, formulation of government policy, court records, parliamentary privilege, legal privilege, communications with Her Majesty, trade secrets, vexatious requests, costly requests, investigation and proceedings carried out by a public authority, prohibitions on disclosure because it would breach, for example, the Official Secrets Acts or lead to contempt of court and material supplied in confidence.[78]

The Act draws a further distinction between those provisions in Part II that confer an absolute exemption and those that provide for a non-absolute or qualified exemption. Where information falls within the scope of an 'absolute' exemption, it excuses the public authority from an obligation to communicate it to an applicant and the duty to confirm or deny. In contrast, where the information falls within

---

[72]   The reference to contents and class-based exemptions is borrowing terminology from public interest immunity claims.

[73]   See FOIA, ss 24, 26, 27, 28, 29, 31(2), 33, 36, 38, 43.

[74]   HC 570, para 71; HL97, para 25.

[75]   HC Deb, 7 December 1999, vol 340, col 717.

[76]   Cm 4355, 1999 para 36.

[77]   See FOISA, ss 28, 30, 32, 33, and 35.

[78]   FOIA, s 23 (security and intelligence), s 35 (formulation of government policy), s 32 (court records), s 34 (parliamentary privilege), s 42 (legal privilege), s 37 (communications with Her Majesty), s 43(1) (trade secrets), s 14 (vexatious requests), s 12 costly requests, s 30 (investigation and proceedings carried out by a public authority), s 44 (breach of other statutory provision or lead to contempt of court), s 41 (material supplied in confidence). Note also class exemptions where information is accessible from another source (FOIA, s 21) and where personal information is covered by the Data Protection Act 1998 (FOIA, s 40(1)).

the scope of a qualified exemption, a public authority is required to release the information unless 'in all the circumstances of the case, the public interest in maintaining the exemption outweighs the public interest in disclosing the information.' The FOIA also provides for 'public interest disclosures' for information falling under some of the class exemptions and almost all of the harm exemptions.[79] The effect of the public interest test is to deter the public authorities from automatically withholding requested information because it falls within an exemption. As a consequence, public authorities must engage in a balancing exercise to weigh up the effects of disclosure in each individual case. Access on public interest grounds is the only means to seek the disclosure of qualified class exemption information.

The public interest is not defined in the FOIA. Arguably the identifying and weighing of public interests would have been easier with a clearly stated purpose clause. Nevertheless, as section 1 of the FOIA sets out a general right of access to information, the presumption should be in favour of disclosure. Information should only be withheld if the public interest in withholding it is greater than the public interest in releasing it. It does seem, however, that the public interest test will vary in its application to harm-based and class exemptions. If an authority was seeking to withhold information under a harm-based exemption, it must identify the harm that would flow from the release of information and then show, in addition, that the specific harm outweighs the public interest in disclosure; whereas in relation to a class-based exemption, the authority could argue that the disclosure would have harmful effects but also 'that the public interest would be harmed by any disclosure from within the relevant class of documents, regardless of the consequences of releasing the actual information in question.'[80]

This chapter will now explore in greater detail the exemption provisions of most relevance to the constitutional themes of this chapter: on the one hand, promoting accountability in government and on the other, the issue of governmental transparency in the economic era of contracting out and privatisation.

Policy Advice

A highly controversial issue in most freedom of information legislation is whether decision-making and policy advice should be disclosed. Such information will be of great interest to the media, opposition MPs and pressure groups as well as individual citizens. Achieving greater transparency in government requires more of this type of information to be released but this is precisely the sort of material that most governments seek to keep confidential. Premature disclosure of policy advice could genuinely interfere with the government's ability to develop policy. Nevertheless some internal discussion could be disclosed without harm and would be

---

[79] FOIA, s 2.
[80] Campaign for Freedom of Information, *Briefing Notes on FOI Bill*, House of Lords ,Third Reading, 21 November 2000, 10.

consistent with the open government principle. Considered assessments of a publicly announced policy are highly unlikely to be harmful to policy development. The decision of the Government to release the minutes of the monthly meetings between the Chancellor of the Exchequer and the Governor of the Bank of England, just six weeks after the meeting had taken place, has not been detrimental to the decision-making process.[81]

Section 35 of the FOIA is a class exemption that includes virtually all information relating to the formation of government policy. More specifically, it exempts information held by government or the National Assembly of Wales if it relates to the formulation or development of policy; ministerial communications; advice or requests for advice by the law officers; or the operation of any ministerial private office. The duty to confirm or deny does not arise in relation to information falling within these categories. During the passage of the Bill through Parliament, one minor concession was made: once a decision has been taken, statistical information 'used to provide an informed background' to the formulation of government policy or which relates to 'ministerial communications' may be disclosed.[82] There is no doubt that it is impossible for governments to operate and develop policies in a goldfish bowl but the sweeping effect of these exemptions go far beyond what is necessary to achieve this aim.

The public interest test is applicable to this exemption. Section 35(4) is the only provision in the FOIA that provides some specific guidance on how the public interest balancing test should be exercised. It provides that in carrying out the balancing exercise, 'regard shall be had to the particular public interest in the disclosure of factual information which has been used, or is intended to be used, to provide an informed background to decision-taking.'[83] This section assumes that it is feasible to distinguish between policy advice and the factual information upon which that advice is based. Indeed the 1997 White Paper had drawn this distinction and suggested that factual and background material should be made available. Even if the public interest test is understood to signal strongly that factual information should be made available in the public interest, there is no guarantee of disclosure.[84]

The policy advice exemption is further buttressed by section 36. This is another wide-ranging, harm-based exemption intended to shield the conduct of public affairs from excessive scrutiny. The breadth of this exemption is truly astonishing, especially when considered in conjunction with the section 35 class exemption that seems to cover the same ground. It exempts government information or information held by any public authority that would, or would be likely to, prejudice the maintenance of the convention of collective responsibility or inhibit (a) the free and frank provision of advice, or (b) the free and frank exchange of views

---

[81] Campaign for Freedom of Information, *Key Issues* (1997), 6. Compare the decision of *Burmah Oil Co v Bank of England* [1980] AC 1090.

[82] FOIA, s 35(2). The wording in FOISA, s 29(2) is the same.

[83] FOISA, s 29(3) is very similar.

[84] See M Supperstone and T Pitt-Payne, *The Freedom of Information Act 2000* (London, Butterworths, 2001), 45.

for the purposes of deliberation, or (c) would otherwise prejudice, or would be likely otherwise to prejudice, the effective conduct of public affairs. Birkinshaw aptly states that this final clause 'could [potentially] cover just about everything and is truly reminiscent of the spirit of the Official Secrets Act.'[85] The Campaign for Freedom of Information have concluded:

> There would be no right to know about purely descriptive reports of existing practice, research reports, evidence on health hazards, assumptions about wage or inflation levels used in calculating costs, studies of overseas practice, consultants' findings or supporting data showing whether official assertions are realistic or not.[86]

There are a number of problems with this clause. Who defines the scope or ambit of the convention of collective responsibility for the purposes of freedom of information? The underlying purpose of the convention is to preserve the appearance of Cabinet solidarity. If the purpose of the convention is not kept in mind it is easy to transform the convention into a general rule of 'cabinet secrecy'.[87] What if there is no disagreement among ministers? How then can collective responsibility be affected by disclosure of Cabinet discussions? Does the widespread practice of ministerial leaks undermine the unanimity principle underlying the convention?

The exemption also seeks to preserve the efficacy and frankness of Civil Service advice. After a policy decision has been made and acted upon, it is hard to justify such a broad limitation on disclosure. Civil servants fear the loss of their anonymity. Yet in order for the FOIA to achieve its aim of promoting democracy, policy advice and alternative policy proposals must be disclosed in order to foster public debate. Without this information, the new legislation is merely paying lip service to freedom of information principles. Increased transparency in decision-making could even be beneficial for governments—for example, background material could show a policy decision was made for objective reasons and not for short-term political gain. Knowledge that analysis may be exposed to outside scrutiny could even improve the quality of advice. All this material could be adequately protected by a harm test. The equivalent exemptions in the FOISA are similar but the 'substantial prejudice' test promises a more powerful right of access than in the FOIA.

The exemptions in sections 35 and 36 potentially undermine the purpose of the FOIA. It is true that information which falls within both these exemptions are subject to the public interest test. If, however, it is information held by a government department and the Commissioner orders release on the grounds of public interest, the ministerial veto could still prevent the disclosure of the information.[88]

---

[85] P Birkinshaw, *Freedom of Information: The Law, the Practice and the Ideal* (3rd edn, London, Butterworths, 2001), 314.

[86] Campaign for Freedom of Information, *Briefing Notes on FOI Bill*, House of Lords Committee Stage, 19 October 2000, 1.

[87] See analysis in I Eagles, M Taggart and G Liddell, above n 58, at 348 and *et seq*.

[88] See discussion below.

Investigations and Proceedings by Public Authorities

A further controversial class exemption covers information held by public authorities such as the police, prosecuting authorities and a wide range of regulatory
bodies such as health and safety executive officers.[89] The purpose of the exemption is to exempt investigations relating to the conduct of legal proceedings as well
as information obtained from confidential sources relating to certain investigations and proceedings. The exemption applies to information which has 'at any
time been held' relating to investigations that may lead to criminal proceedings. In
a response to the recommendations of the Public Administration Select Committee *Report on the Freedom of Information Draft Bill*, the Government argued that
this exemption was necessary 'to preserve the judicial process and to ensure that
the criminal courts remain the sole forum for determining guilt.'[90] The potential
effect of this exemption is to provide protection for any evidence of wrong-doing,
incompetence or default. Miscarriages of justice and reports into accidents could
be shielded from scrutiny. As the Campaign for Freedom of Information commented: 'The results of safety inspection of the railways, nuclear plants and dangerous factories would be permanently exempt. This is the information that most
people assume FOI legislation exists to provide.'[91] It seems that the Government
has already forgotten the questions raised by the Macpherson Report into the
Stephen Lawrence murder inquiry. The report proposed: 'that a freedom of information Act should apply to all areas of policing, both operational and administrative, subject only to the "substantial harm" test for withholding disclosure.'[92] It is
harder to justify the need for such a broad class exemption when section 31 already
permits information to be withheld in circumstances where it might 'prejudice the
administration of justice' or 'the prevention or detection of a crime.' This harm-
based exemption should ensure that no information is released which could damage law enforcement or crime detection.

The public interest test is of considerable importance in this context as it is the
only way that this type of information may be released under the FOIA.[93] Even if
an authority has concluded that the information falls within the protected class,
the public interest test must be considered. The Commissioner can also assess
whether, in the public interest, this information should be released. As a considerable amount of this information will not be held by a government department, his
or her decision will not be subject to the ministerial veto.

---

[89] FOIA, s 30. FOISA, s 34 is also a class exemption.
[90] Government Response to the Public Administration Select Committee on the FOI Draft Bill, 22
October 1999.
[91] *Briefing Notes on FOIA Bill*, House of Lords Committee Stage, 19 October 2000.
[92] *The Stephen Lawrence Inquiry: Report of an Inquiry by Sir W Macpherson* (Cm 4262, 1999), Recommendation 9.
[93] The public interest test is set out in FOIA, s 2.

Commercial Interests

The availability of commercial information under the FOIA is likely to be a hotly contested exemption. It is in this context that the public/private divide raises especially difficult questions. To what extent will the FOIA apply to organisations carrying out public functions or services under contract? The FOIA provides two exemptions to protect the confidentiality of commercially sensitive information. The underlying rationale of protecting commercial information is that it is an important factor in the success of the market economy.[94] According to this argument, release of sensitive information, such as tender prices, will not increase competition, rather it will irreparably damage the process and may lead to the withdrawal of parties from the process. In other words, it will ultimately render the market less competitive.[95]

There are also important public interest considerations that favour disclosure of commercially sensitive information. Information about the terms of government contracts and grants and the standards of performance of public functions contracted out to private bodies is essential to enhance accountability in government and to ensure effective oversight of public expenditure. The very opportunity for secrecy carries with it a risk of abuse. Arguably public information access considerations should not be diluted where the public is the ultimate recipient of the 'public' service, even where supplied through a private organisation.

Section 41 is designed to protect information provided in confidence. It covers information received from another body or person in confidence.[96] Information is exempt where disclosure by the public authority holding it 'would constitute a breach of confidence actionable by that or any other person.'[97] At first glance this section appears to be absolute (the section 2 public interest test does not apply) and there is no requirement to show prejudice. Section 41, however, retains the equitable action for breach of confidence which contains an inherent public interest test and perhaps a need to show detriment.

A duty of confidence may be imposed by an express or implied contractual term but it may also exist independently of any contract. Equity may intervene to restrain disclosure where confidential information comes to the knowledge of a confidant, in circumstances where he or she has knowledge, or is held to have agreed, that the information is confidential.[98] In order for a breach of confidence claim to succeed, three criteria must be satisfied, as described by Megarry J in *Coco v A.N. Clark (Engineers)*:[99]

---

[94] M McDonagh, 'FOI and Confidentiality of Commercial Information' [2001] *Public Law* 256.
[95] *Ibid.*
[96] Note FOIA, s 81(2). This exemption cannot be used to deny access to information exchanged between government departments unless the duty of confidence is owed to another person or body. FOISA, s 36 (confidential information) is very similar to FOIA, s 41.
[97] FOIA, s 41(1).
[98] *Attorney General v Observer Ltd and others* [1990] 1 AC 109 (the 'Spycatcher' case).
[99] [1969] RPC 41 at 47.

First, the information itself … must 'have the necessary quality of confidence about it.' Secondly, that information must have been imparted in circumstances importing an obligation of confidence. Thirdly, there must be an unauthorised use of that information to the detriment of the party communicating it.

Public authorities hold a vast amount of confidential information supplied from private bodies. This information is supplied for various reasons such as under a statutory obligation or as the result of a tender for a contract. Are public authorities exempt from the duty to disclose this information? Has the information been imparted in circumstances importing an obligation of confidence? This aspect of the confidentiality test has evolved significantly in recent years, largely due to the influence of Article 8 of the European Convention on Human Rights. In particular, there is no need to construct an artificial relationship of confidentiality: the obligation will arise whenever the party subject to the duty knows or ought to know that the other person can reasonably expect his privacy to be protected.[100] These developments suggest that the exemption in section 41 is very broad and would apply to any information that is inherently confidential.[101]

Special considerations arise where the party seeking to rely upon breach of confidence is the Crown, since the justification for private citizens—that the protection of their private lives is inherently worthy of protection—cannot apply, and so the burden of proof is placed upon the Crown to show that the protection of a confidential relationship would be in the public interest.[102] Thus any public authority seeking to rely on the confidentiality doctrine would have to satisfy this additional test. As a consequence the scope of the exemption is more limited in circumstances where information has been obtained by a public authority in confidence from another public authority.

Although section 41 is not subject to the section 2 public interest test, the courts will not enforce an obligation of confidence if it would be contrary to the public interest. [103] What is unclear is whether this public interest test is the same as the one under the FOIA. During parliamentary debates, it was considered that the public interest test in an action for breach of confidence was more limited than the public interest test in the FOIA.[104] The section 2 public interest test starts with the presumption that the public have a right to access information. The public interest test in the law of confidentiality appears to be narrower and, the court has held,

---

[100] *Douglas v Hello!* [2001] QB 967 and *Attorney General v Guardian Newspapers Ltd (No 2)* [1990] 1 AC 109.

[101] See the discussion in J Wadham, J Griffiths and B Rigby, *Blackstone's Guide to the Freedom of Information Act 2000* (London, Blackstone Press, 2001), 82–84.

[102] *Guardian (No 2)*, above n 100, at 256 and 283. Lord Griffiths regarded this as equivalent to a requirement that the Crown must show that detriment to the public interest is required. It remains unclear whether detriment to the party to whom the duty is owed is necessary (whilst Rose J in *X v Y* [1988] 2 All ER 648 at 657 and Simon Brown LJ in *R v Department of Health, ex parte Source Informatics* [2001] QB 424 suggested that there is no such requirement, Lightman J in *Campbell v MGN* [2002] EWHC 328 (Ch) unreported at 40 and Lord Keith and Lord Griffiths in *Guardian (No 2)* at 255 and 270 suggested that this was required, but that the criterion was fulfilled very easily).

[103] See eg *Gartside v Outram* (1856) 26 LJ Ch 113 and *Lion Laboratories v Evans* [1985] QB 526

[104] HL Deb, 25 October 2000, vol 618, cols 413–419.

does not include everything that the public is interested in.[105] In those circumstances where the defence of iniquity is relied upon, the court will consider
whether more limited disclosure, for example to the police, would suffice to satisfy
the public interest.[106] Although there are differences between the two tests, it
seems likely and preferable that the underlying principles of FOIA and the Human
Rights Act 1998 will influence the future development of the breach of confidence
public interest test.[107] In Ireland, which has a similar exemption in their freedom
of information legislation, the Information Commissioner has applied the same
public interest considerations to the action for breach of confidence as are relevant
to balancing the public interest test under the statute.[108]

There is a danger, when entering into contracts, that public authorities
implicitly accept obligations of confidence or are pressured into confidentiality
agreements by private companies or organisations. Pursuant to section 45, the
Lord Chancellor is required to issue a Code of Practice providing guidance to public authorities on administrative matters concerned with the discharge of their
functions under the legislation. The Code, still in draft form, requires public
authorities to refuse to accept unjustified obligations of confidentiality, 'so that
information relating to the terms of the contract, its value and performance will be
exempt from disclosure unless this is commercially unavoidable.'[109] It goes on to
state that the acceptance of such confidentiality must be for good reasons and capable of being justified to the Commissioner. The only guidance for public authorities
on public sector contracts is set out in the Code of Practice. The consequences of a
breach of the Code are not set out in the FOIA. The Commissioner will not be able
to enforce compliance if a public authority fails to adhere to the Code. Robert
Hazell observes that relegating key elements to codes of practice is a negative signal
to public servants: 'Even if the legal effect is essentially the same, the political effect
is different. Civil servants are very astute in reading political messages.'[110]

In order to avoid any 'implicit' acceptance of obligations of confidence, it would
be preferable for public authorities to inform all parties in advance of what sort of
information will be disclosed. The National Consumer Council suggests that public authorities should not give undertakings that they will accept information in
confidence unless there are compelling reasons to do so. They suggest that if confidentiality is accepted then it should be explicit, in writing and expressed with a
date for expiry or review.[111] This last clause is important as commercial sensitivity

---

[105] *Lion Laboratories v Evan* 1985] QB 526, 537.

[106] *Francome v MGN* [1984] 1 WLR 892, 898 and *Guardian (No 2)* above, n 100.

[107] Note also, Human Rights Act 1998 s 12. In order to obtain injunctive relief to prevent a public
authority from releasing confidential information, a strong case on the merits at the injunction application stage would have to be shown. See *A v B Plc* [2002] 3 WLR 542 and *Douglas v Hello!* [2001] QB
967.

[108] *Re McAleer and Sunday Times and Department of Justice, Equality and Law Reform*, Information
Commissioner, unreported, Decision No 98158, 16 June 2000 cited in McDonagh, above n 94, at 261.

[109] Draft Code of Practice on the Discharge of the Functions of Public Authorities under Part 1 of
the Freedom of Information Act 2000 ('Code of practice under s 45').

[110] R Hazell, *Commentary on Draft Freedom of Information Bill* (Constitution Unit, 1999), 23.

[111] National Consumer Council, *Guidance on the Release of Commercially Sensitive Information by
Public Authorities* (London, 2001), 5.

may decline over time. There is widespread agreement that marking documents 'confidential' should not be sufficient. The Irish Information Commissioner has recently considered the equivalent confidentiality provision in the Irish Freedom of Information Act. In considering whether prices relating to a tender competition for the supply of army trucks were given in confidence, the Commissioner concluded that there must be a mutual understanding between the parties. He added:

> Indeed, one would have to question, having regard to the coming into force of the Freedom of Information Act, how any public body could have an understanding that the details of its expenditure of public money would be kept confidential.[112]

Commercial information is also protected by the exemption in section 43. It provides that a public authority is exempt from the duty to communicate information where information 'constitutes a trade secret' or where disclosure 'would, or would be likely to, prejudice the commercial interests of any person (including the public authority holding it).' Trade secret is not defined in the FOIA. There is no generally accepted definition in English law. The House of Lords Select Committee defined it as 'information of commercial value which is protected by the law of confidence.'[113] In any event, the sweeping scope of the phrase 'likely to prejudice the commercial interests of any person' will include a trade secret whatever definition is accepted. In fact, the breadth of sections 41 and 43 suggests that there is very little commercial information that will not fall within one of these exemptions. Relying on section 43(2), public authorities could even refuse to disclose information as it is 'likely to prejudice commercial interests' of the public authority itself. The standard of proof may be relatively easy to satisfy. Some commentators have concluded: 'The potential for self-serving reliance upon the exemption in such circumstances is clearly great; particularly where so many public authorities are increasingly involved in commercial ventures.'[114]

Both trade secrets,[115] a class exemption, and commercial interests,[116] a harm-based one, are subject to the overriding public interest test in section 2.[117] The capacity of the FOIA to deliver greater transparency in the commercial dealings of public authorities may depend to a considerable extent on robust decisions of the Information Commissioner. The Campaign for Freedom of Information expressed concern that this provision would prevent disclosure of information such as poor safety records or the sale of dangerous goods.[118] Although information of this kind would fall under the exemption, the public interest override

[112] *Henry Ford & Sons Ltd, Nissan Ireland and Motor Distributors Ltd and the Office of Public Works,* Information Commissioner, unreported, Decision No 98058, 16 June 2000.

[113] *Report from the Select Committee appointed to consider the Draft Freedom of Information Bill,* 27 July 1998, para 45. Note also judicial interpretations of the term in *Faccenda Chicken v Fowler* [1987] 1 Ch 117 (per Neill LJ) and *Lansing Linde v Kerr* [1991] 1 WLR 251.

[114] J Wadham *et al,* above n 101, at 107.

[115] FOIA, s 43(1).

[116] FOIA, s 43(2).

[117] FOISA, s 33 has a similar structure but the relevant harm test must satisfy the higher threshold of 'prejudice substantially'.

[118] Campaign for Freedom of Information *Bill Briefing Notes on FOIA* House of Lords Committee Stage, 19 October 2000, 1.

should ensure that this type of information is disclosed. Nevertheless, it would have been preferable for section 43 to be limited to protecting information that could result in serious commercial disadvantage.[119]

Disclosure through the public interest test provides the only opportunity for access to an enormous amount of information held by public authorities, especially information falling within many of the class exemptions.[120] Where harm-based exemptions are involved, information whose disclosure could lead to prejudice might still be disclosed on the grounds of overriding public interest. As a consequence, public authorities must engage in a balancing exercise to weigh up the effects of disclosure in each individual case. The test requires evidence that the public interest in maintaining the exemption in question is greater than the public interest in releasing it. The public interest test strengthens both the oversight and the instrumental role played by the FOIA. In this sense, it is a mechanism for improving public authority decision-making.

Some of the key factors that should be taken into account when considering the release of commercially sensitive information by public authorities have been suggested by the National Consumer Council. They conclude that 'public interest' in this context should include:

(1) the need to ensure that the expenditure of public funds is subjected to effective oversight, in particular so that the public obtain value for money and to avoid fraud, corruption and the waste or misuse of public funds;
(2) the need to keep the public adequately informed about the existence of any danger to public health or safety or to the environment;
(3) the need to ensure that any statutory authority with regulatory responsibility for a third party is adequately discharging its function.[121]

The Irish Information Commissioner has considered similar issues in determining whether information that fell within the scope of the commercial information exemption should be released in the public interest.[122] An additional factor that he considered was the public interest in requesters exercising their rights under the Irish legislation. In effect, he was confirming the democratic rights underpinning the legislation.

At the very least, it would seem prudent for public authorities contracting with private bodies to carry out a public function to ensure that appropriate arrangements are made to supply public information access rights. The Australian Law Reform Commission has recommended that the Freedom of Information Commissioner should provide guidance to authorities on what arrangements are advisable in particular contacting out situations. In addition, the Commission suggests that the Commissioner should monitor contracting out agreements and

---

[119] McDonagh, above n 94, at 263.
[120] Security and intelligence (FOIA, s 23) is an important exemption not subject to the public interest test.
[121] National Consumer Council, above n 111, at 17.
[122] *Henry Ford & Sons Ltd and the Office of Public Works*, above n 112, at 18–19. See also McDonagh, above n 94, at 264–66.

report on whether satisfactory arrangements are being made in relation to the accessibility of relevant information.[123]

THE INFORMATION COMMISSIONER AND INDEPENDENT SCRUTINY

An effective and independent system of enforcement of the public right to access is essential if a freedom of information system is to operate effectively. The Information Commissioner is given a prominent place under the FOIA. The critical factor is the Commissioner's powers of independent scrutiny and enforcement. Without this feature in a freedom of information system, there will be minimal public confidence in its operation. The Commissioner is given the power to substitute his or her judgment for that of a public authority in relation to whether information falls within an exemption as well as the public interest balance. The most important power of the Commissioner is the enforcement notice which 'requir[es] the authority to take, within such time as may be specified in the notice, such steps as may be so specified for complying with those requirements.'[124] If a public authority fails to comply with the notice, the FOIA provides that the Commissioner may certify this failure to the High Court, which may deal with the authority as if it had committed a contempt of court.[125] There are also provisions for appeal to the Information Tribunal.[126]

Although the Commissioner has the power to order the disclosure of nearly all information on public interest grounds, such a decision could be overridden by a ministerial veto.[127] This veto will be exercised by an 'accountable person', usually a Minister of the Crown who is a member of the Cabinet.[128] This feature of the legislation has the potential to undermine the operation of the public interest override and the independent scrutiny of the freedom of information operation. The existence and scope of the ministerial override strikes at the heart of freedom of information legislation as it maintains ministerial control over disclosure. The fear is that this power could be abused to protect ministers and public authorities from embarrassment. Even if an authority has been negligent or complacent, it may avoid scrutiny. The only remaining option would be to seek judicial review. The ministerial veto power is a critical weakness at the heart of the legislation.

[123] Australian Law Reform Commission, *Open Government: A Review of the Federal Freedom of Information Act 1982* (Canberra, 1995), 202.

[124] FOIA, s 52(1).

[125] FOIA, s 52(2).

[126] FOIA, s 57. There is no equivalent tribunal in Scotland.

[127] FOIA, s 53 applies to decision or enforcement notices served on public authorities by the Information Commissioner relating to a failure on the part of the authority to comply with the duty to communicate information. The minister is given the power to issue a certificate to the Commissioner stating that he has formed the opinion that there was no such failure. Where the minister issues such a certificate, the Commissioner's notice will cease to have effect.

[128] FOIA, s 53(8).

CONCLUSION

It is difficult to predict with any certainty the impact of the new freedom of information legislation in the United Kingdom. Some of the problems outlined above suggest that it may not ensure that the culture and practices of secrecy in government and other public authorities are set aside for good. The right of access is eroded by the wide exemptions, especially in the areas of policy advice, information from investigations and commercial information. The public interest test provides the only opportunity to access a considerable amount of exempt material but the existence of a ministerial veto makes it possible to conceal harmless information. This feature of the FOIA will encourage judicial review applications. A strong commitment to openness would give the independent Information Commissioner a public interest override and the power to order disclosure with few exceptions. The new legislation hardly signifies a new relationship between the state and its citizens.

Yet even with its limitations on rights of access, it is likely that the FOIA will improve the accountability of government to some extent. Decision-makers will be acutely aware that their decisions must be based on relevant factors. The reaction of those at the 'coal face' who are responsible for implementing the new legislation is also crucial. A successful education programme stressing the democratic underpinnings of freedom of information is one way of attempting to change the culture of secrecy that has characterised governance in the United Kingdom. Changing the attitude of those who are responsible for making freedom of information decisions may be one of the most important factors in determining the success or failure of this legislation. Access to information must be perceived not as a threat but as an opportunity for government and public authorities as well as citizens.

In sum, freedom of information holds out the promise of a new constitutional arrangement but this legislation contains devices ensuring that secrecy can be maintained by a government or public authority determined to do so. The doctrine of ministerial responsibility remains at the centre of the FOIA through the operation of the ministerial veto, yet this convention can still operate as an effective cloak for secrecy. This constitutional reform, with its object of democratic renewal, may not have gone far enough. The deeper constitutional structures that maintain the culture of secrecy have not been disrupted, even if, as a result of the more generous freedom of information regime which exists in Scotland, the overall provision for freedom of information now reflects the differential structure of the British constitution. In consequence, there will be some increased oversight and accountability as a result of this new legislation but it could prove to be more cosmetic than a fundamental constitutional reform.

10

Accountability and the Public/Private Distinction

PETER CANE

INTRODUCTION

T HERE IS A paradox in legal thinking about the organisation of social life
and, in particular, about the relationship between 'the governors and the
governed.'[1] On the one hand, the public/private distinction seems alive and
well. The 1977 reforms of judicial review procedure (originally found in RSC
Order 53 and now in CPR Part 54) are still firmly in place, and there is now a specialist Administrative Court in England. These changes are widely considered to
have precipitated the introduction of the public/private distinction into English
administrative law and to have marked the end of its long love affair with Dicey,
who famously rejected the distinction. The distinctions between public and private bodies and public and private functions have an important place in EC law
(where, for instance, directives have direct effect only against organs of the state)
and in the provisions of enactments such as the Public Supply Contracts Regulations 1995, S1 1995/201, the Human Rights Act (HRA) 1998 and the Freedom of
Information Act 2000. English courts are disinclined to apply the (private) law of
tort in unmodified form to organs of government. In the USA, the public/private
distinction is deeply entrenched in the jurisprudence of the US Supreme Court,
where the 'state action' doctrine marks the boundary of application of the Bill of
Rights.[2] The picture is similar in Australia where, for instance, the Administrative
Appeals Tribunal exercises statutory jurisdiction to review decision-making by
government officers and bodies; and where judicial review, under the Commonwealth Administrative Decisions (Judicial Review) (ADJR) Act 1977, is available only
in respect of 'decisions of an administrative character made under an enactment.'

---

[1] To adopt a somewhat question-begging but not unhelpful phrase.
[2] J Freeman, 'The Private Role in Public Governance' (2000) 75 *New York ULR* 543, 575–80;
D Barak-Erez, 'A State Action Doctrine for an Age of Privatization' (1995) 45 *Syracuse LR* 1169. For a
recent contribution to the parallel Canadian debate on the reach of the Charter, see A Reichman, 'A
Charter-Free Domain: In Defence of *Dolphin Delivery*' (2002) 35 *UBCLR* 329.

On the other hand, by contrast, there is a common view amongst scholars that as a means of understanding and analysing social life, the public/private distinction is outmoded as a result of the 'revolutions' popularly and compendiously referred to by terms such as 'Thatcherism,' 'Reaganism,' 'the new public management' (NPM) and 'the regulatory state.' According to stronger versions of this view, what has happened is not just that relations between the public and private spheres have become more complex and multi-faceted in the wake of 'privatisation' of 'public' utilities, contracting-out of the provision of 'public' services, joint 'public/private' infrastructural projects (under the Private Finance Initiative (PFI), for instance),[3] corporatisation of government business enterprises,[4] creation of administrative ('Next Steps') agencies and 'internal markets' (most notably within the NHS), and a wide variety of 'responsive' alternatives to traditional command-and-control regulation.[5] Rather, the two spheres have become inextricably interwoven in a process better analogised to the scrambling of an egg than to the weaving of a two-stranded rope.

There are at least three different lines of criticism of the public/private distinction to be found in the legal literature. One is that the distinction is descriptively inaccurate, or at least unhelpful, as a way of explaining legal and social structures and institutions. A second criticism is that scholars who think about control of and accountability for the exercise of power in terms of the public/private distinction tend to focus on formal and hierarchical avenues of accountability and control, such as judicial and parliamentary supervision, at the expense of other less formal and non-hierarchical mechanisms. A third strand of criticism of the public/private distinction is more explicitly normative. It says that legal procedures and rules of legal liability and accountability should not distinguish between governor and governed, public bodies and private bodies, public functions and private functions, because all subjects of the law, whether they be individual citizens, commercial corporations, government agencies, or whatever, should be equal before the law.

That, then, is the paradox: public/private is dead. Long live public/private! How can this legal schizophrenia be explained? One possibility might be to say that to the extent that the law is built on a public/private distinction, it is simply out of step with (or lagging behind) political developments. It might be argued, for instance, that measures such as the Australian ADJR Act are products of a past era that should be scrapped and replaced with something more consonant with the way the world works.[6] However satisfying such a response might be in the case of a piece of legislation that predated the neo-liberal revolution of the 1980s and 1990s and is now about 25 years old, it hardly seems adequate to explain, for instance, the struc-

---

[3]   M Freedland, 'Public Law and Private Finance: Placing the Private Finance Initiative in a Public Law Frame' [1998] *PL* 288.

[4]   M Allars, 'Private Law but Public Power: Removing Administrative Law Review from Government Business Enterprises' (1995) 6 *Public Law Review* 44. For a discussion of many of these various phenomena from an American perspective see J Freeman, above n 2.

[5]   N Gunningham and P Grabosky, *Smart Regulation* (Oxford University Press, 1998), ch 2.

[6]   This is Dawn Oliver's view about judicial review procedure: D Oliver, 'Public Law Remedies and Procedures: Do We Need Them?' [2002] *PL* 91.

ture of the legal regime established by the English Human Rights Act 1998. In fact, we seem to be caught between wanting to reaffirm that government is different, and ought to be treated by the law differently, from civil society, while at the same time needing to make sense of the array of phenomena that seem to challenge distinctions between governor and governed, the public and the private. Another initially tempting explanation of the paradox might be to say that unease about the public/private distinction is a preoccupation of academics not shared by judges and legislators. But this suggestion will not stand up to closer scrutiny. For instance, the wisdom of the regime of judicial review procedure has been the cause of debate amongst policy-makers as much as academics; and use of the public/private distinction in the HRA was the subject of considerable public and parliamentary as well as academic debate.

The aim of this chapter is to analyse and better understand the nature of the paradox that I have identified and its implications for broad themes of this volume—the distribution and regulation of power. The first step will be to discuss in some detail certain of the legal regimes in which the public/private distinction plays a significant role. Next comes an analysis of some prominent recent attacks on the public/private distinction. Finally, I will suggest that the paradox can be resolved by distinguishing between two quite different versions of the public/private distinction—one institutional/functional, and the other values-based.

THE PUBLIC/PRIVATE DISTINCTION IN OPERATION

The first part of this section deals with the concept of a functional public/private distinction by focusing on the HRA, and the second with the concept of an institutional public/private distinction, referring to judicial review of executive action and several other legal regimes.

Human Rights and the Concept of Public Functions

'Fundamental human rights' as traditionally conceived are rights against the government or the state, not against other citizens. This is as true of the rights guaranteed under the amendments to the US Constitution as it is of rights enshrined in more recent international and national human rights documents. According to this conception, human rights law rests on a fundamental distinction between the governors and the governed, the state and 'civil society' (ie the non-state), the 'public' and the 'private.' In the amendments to the US Constitution, some of the rights are expressly drafted as rights against the government. The first amendment (freedom of speech) and the fourteenth amendment (equal protection) are the best-known examples. Certain amendments, by reason of their subject matter, only apply to state action. The seventh amendment (trial by jury) is an example.[7]

---

[7] Although, of course, there is nothing intrinsic to the practice of 'judgment by one's peers' that marks it as public. Limitation of trial by jury to public legal proceedings is a political choice.

But even those amendments that are not limited to state action by their terms or content have been interpreted as applying basically only to 'state action.'[8]

Some of the rights contained in the European Convention on Human Rights (ECHR) (by which the United Kingdom was bound under international law for many years before the enactment of the HRA in 1998, and by which it remains bound) are, by virtue of their content, rights against the state. But there is nothing in the express terms of the provisions of the Convention that would prevent them applying to citizens as well as to government. Being an international treaty, the ECHR imposes obligations only on nation states and not on individuals; but those obligations (for instance, to bring domestic law into conformity with the Convention) may relate not only to dealings between citizens and government but also to relations between citizen and citizen.

It was against this background that the question of the scope of application of the HRA arose. The Act deals separately with 'primary and subordinate legislation' on the one hand and 'acts' (of 'public authorities') on the other. Under section 3, primary and subordinate legislation must, as far as possible, be 'read and given effect in a way that is compatible with Convention rights.' Section 4 confers jurisdiction to make a declaration that primary or subordinate legislation is incompatible with a Convention right. Acts of public authorities are dealt with in section 6, which renders unlawful acts that are incompatible with Convention rights. Whereas incompatibility of primary legislation with a Convention right is expressly stated not to affect its legal validity, the making of incompatible subordinate legislation would constitute an (unlawful) act under section 6.[9] There is no statutory definition of the concept of 'an act' beyond the provision that it includes 'failure to act' (except failure to introduce in or lay before Parliament a proposal for legislation, and failure to make any primary legislation or remedial order).

A provision of primary or subordinate legislation that requires or authorises breach of a Convention right will be incompatible with the Convention regardless of whether the breach constitutes 'state action.'[10] So, for instance, legislation regulating defamatory speech would be incompatible with Article 10 of the ECHR (on freedom of expression) if it permitted one citizen to infringe another citizen's Convention right of free expression. In other words, the regime under sections 3 and 4 provides protection against breaches of Convention rights that are 'legally regulated'—in the sense of required or authorised by primary or subordinate legislation—by whomever they are committed.[11] Nevertheless, the subject matter of the regime established by sections 3 and 4 of the HRA is legislation, not the conduct that it requires or authorises. Unlike primary legislation, subordinate legisla-

---

[8] For a useful brief discussion see R Clayton and H Tomlinson, *The Law of Human Rights* (Oxford University Press, 2000), 208–17.

[9] Primary legislation and remedial orders made under the Act do not constitute 'acts' for the purposes of s 6: HRA s 6(6)(b).

[10] N Bamforth, 'The True 'Horizontal Effect' of the Human Rights Act 1998' (2001) 117 *LQR* 34.

[11] It has also been argued that although only a 'victim' may challenge an act under s 6, anyone may invoke ss 3 and 4: M Elliott, 'The Human Rights Act 1998 and the Standard of Substantive Review' [2001] *CLJ* 301.

tion also falls within the regime established by section 6 of the HRA, provided it can be attributed to an 'act of a public authority.' Furthermore, because courts and tribunals are public authorities for the purposes of section 6, they are under a duty not to act incompatibly with Convention rights in making and developing the common law.[12] The result of all this is that while the HRA only imposes obligations to respect Convention rights on Parliament and public authorities, it will also have profound indirect effects on the legal position of 'private' individuals and bodies by reason of its direct impact on law-making activities. In the result, the public/private distinction is most important to the operation of human rights law in relation to activities other than law-making.

The statutory concept of a 'public authority' is complex. It has both institutional and functional elements. On the institutional side, 'the House of Lords in its judicial capacity' is a public authority (s 6(4)). But the House of Lords in any other capacity is not; nor is the House of Commons (proviso to s (3)). On the functional side, 'any person certain of whose functions are functions of a public nature' is a public authority (6 (3)(b)), except in relation to 'acts of a private nature' (s 6 (5)). The juxtaposition of 'function' and 'act' is slightly puzzling. An act may or may not involve the performance of a function. For instance, engaging in a recreational pursuit seems to be the very antithesis of performing a function. On this basis, the phrase 'act of a private nature' could embrace both acts done in performance of private functions and 'private acts'. So the word 'act' in the phrase 'act of a public authority' should be understood to refer to an act or a failure to act regardless of whether it was referable to the performance of a function. The obligation not to act incompatibly with Convention rights attaches to acts, not functions.

The term 'public authority' is also defined to include 'a court or tribunal' (s 6 (3)(a)). This seems to be a mixed institutional/functional criterion of public authority status. For instance, the High Court—a paradigmatic court—would qualify as a court 'institutionally' as it were; and a Social Security Appeal Tribunal—a paradigmatic tribunal—would qualify as a tribunal institutionally. But it is well established that a body may, by reason of its functional characteristics, be a 'court' (for certain purposes at least) even though it is not called a court.[13] By parity of reasoning, the same should be true of tribunals.[14] So in principle at least, a body could be a court or tribunal, and hence a public authority, solely by virtue of (certain of) its functions. Beyond this, the HRA gives no guidance as to what the

---

[12] There is a large literature on the nature and content of this obligation examined in terms of the nature of the HRA's 'horizontal effect.' See, eg, M Hunt 'The "Horizontal Effect" of the Human Rights Act' [1998] *PL* 423; G Phillipson, 'The Human Rights Act, "Horizontal Effect" and the Common Law: A Bang or a Whimper?' (1999) 62 *MLR* 824; N Bamforth, 'The Application of the Human Rights Act 1998 to Public Authorities and Private Bodies' [1999] *CLJ* 159; R Buxton, 'The Human Rights Act and Private Law' (2000) 116 *LQR* 48; HWR Wade, 'Horizons of Horizontality' (2000) 116 *LQR* 217; J Morgan, 'Questioning the "True Effect" of the Human Rights Act' (2002) 22 *LS* 259.

[13] *Pickering v Liverpool Daily Post and Echo Newspapers plc* [1990] 1 All ER 355 (CA); [1991] 2 AC 370 (HL).

[14] HRA, s 21(1) defines 'tribunal' in terms of 'legal proceedings.' Clayton and Tomlinson (above n 8 at 207–8) suggest that 'legal proceedings' should be understood in terms of the exercise of judicial power, ie functionally.

term 'public authority' means. This is troubling because section 6 is understood to set up a contrast between what are called 'core' and 'hybrid' public authorities. According to this reading, hybrid public authorities are persons 'certain of whose functions are of a public nature'. But except in relation to the House of Lords in its judicial capacity and 'paradigmatic' courts and tribunals, the HRA says nothing about what a core public authority is.[15]

In *Aston Cantlow and Wilmcote with Billesly PCC v Wallbank*[16] the entity in question was a parochial church council, that is, a statutory corporation and part of the (established) Church of England. The council served a statutory notice on the defendants requiring them to repair a church building. The defendants disputed their liability, arguing that the (common) law that established the liability was incompatible with Article 1 of the First Protocol to the ECHR. The House of Lords held, unanimously, that the council was not a core public authority; and, by a 4–1 majority (Lord Scott dissenting), that it was not a hybrid public authority. There is an unfortunate lack of uniformity in the reasons variously given for these conclusions. Lord Nicholls (at [8] and [14]) and Lord Hope (at [47]) took an institutional approach to the concept 'core public authority'. Noting that under Article 34 of the ECHR, only 'persons', 'groups of individuals' and 'non-governmental bodies' can qualify as 'victims' entitled to complain of breaches of s 6 of the HRA, they concluded that core public authorities are 'governmental bodies', and that the council was not a core public authority because it was a 'religious', not a governmental body.[17] By contrast, Lord Rodger understood the concept 'core public authority' functionally, concluding that the council's 'general function' was religious, not governmental (at [144], [159], [166]). Lord Hobhouse hedged his bets, saying that a core public authority 'has a governmental character and discharges governmental functions' (at [87]); although the tone of his discussion is more functional than institutional.[18]

On the other hand, all of the Law Lords adopted a functional approach to the concept 'hybrid public authority'. Lord Nicholls (at [16]) and Lord Hope (at [41],

---

[15]   One might think that since a hybrid public authority is an entity certain of whose functions are public, a pure public authority would be an entity all of whose functions are public: *Aston Cantlow and Wilmcote with Billesley PCC v Wallbank* [2003] UKHL 37 at [85] (Lord Hobhouse); [143] (Lord Rodger). Such an exhaustive definition would be extremely difficult to apply in practice, even assuming it to be desirable in principle. Clayton and Tomlinson, above n 8, at 191–92 suggest as the criterion of a pure public body that its functions are 'largely or predominantly of a public nature.'

[16]   [2003] UKHL 37.

[17]   Both judges refer to an article by Dawn Oliver, 'The Frontiers of the State: Public Authorities and Public Functions under the Human Rights Act' [2000] *PL* 476. Oliver argues that 'public authority' should be understood narrowly rather than broadly because public authorities 'may' not be entitled to complain of breaches of the ECHR: it would be undesirable, she argues, that 'fringe bodies' should not be entitled to rely on the Convention. She does not discuss ECHR Article 34, and seems to assume that neither hybrid nor core public authorities can assert Convention rights. By contrast, Lord Nicholls and Lord Hope seem to equate 'core public authority' with 'governmental body' and 'hybrid public authority' with 'non-governmental body'. On that basis they apparently believe that while core public authorities cannot rely on the Convention, hybrid public authorities can—at least in relation to their private acts/functions: Lord Nicholls at [11].

[18]   Unfortunately, the judgments do not always distinguish clearly between 'governmental' and 'public', or between 'non-governmental' and 'private', either in their application to bodies or to functions, even though s 6 of the HRA does not use the term 'governmental'. Similarly, only Lord Hobhouse (at [88]) distinguishes between (private) functions and (private) acts.

[63]) could be interpreted as going further and arguing that unless the defendant is a core public authority, the application of s 6 of the HRA depends entirely on whether it was performing a public function (or a public act). According to this approach, a hybrid public authority is not a person or body 'certain of whose functions are functions of a public nature' (s 6(3)(b)), but rather a person or body performing a public function (or act). This would mean that an entity, other than a core public authority, could be a public authority only in relation to a particular (public) act. The effect of this approach is to collapse the distinction between public authorities and public functions (/acts) in relation to persons or bodies other than core public authorities. For these judges, then, s 6 applies to all acts of governmental entities, and to all public acts/functions by whomever performed.

Underlying this discussion is a point of fundamental importance. In the modern period, the public/private distinction seems to have developed, in political and legal thinking anyway, in the eighteenth and nineteenth centuries as a result, on the one hand, of the centralisation and expansion of government and, on the other, of the growth of ideas about the importance of the individual (as distinct from the community) associated with the Enlightenment. In this context, the distinction was conceived institutionally in terms of a contrast between government and non-government. Using French law as his model, John Allison has argued that there is an important link between a political conception of the state as a separate entity and the distinction between public law and private law.[19] In the French system, the public/private distinction has institutional roots, and it has also borne institutional fruit in the shape of the Conseil d'Etat. AV Dicey who, in his *Introduction to the Study of the Law of the Constitution*, first published in 1885, argued for the principle of equality before the law, understood that principle in institutional terms, with government on one side of the equation and citizens on the other. On that basis, he rejected both a substantive distinction between public and private law and an institutional arrangement under which the two bodies of law would be administered by different agencies.

Ironically, the first edition of Dicey's work was published only about 12 years after the French Tribunal des Conflits, in the case of *Blanco* (1873), adopted the essentially functional criterion of *service publique*[20] to define the boundary between the respective jurisdictions of the Conseil d'Etat and the ordinary courts.[21] More importantly for present purposes, political and legal developments of the last 25 years have seriously undermined the institutional understanding of

---

[19] J Allison, *A Continental Distinction in the Common Law: A Historical and Comparative Perspective on English Public Law* (Oxford, Clarendon Press, 1996); also T Daintith, 'State Power' in *The New Palgrave Dictionary of Economics and the Law* (London, Macmillan, 1998), 524. On the history of the public/private distinction more generally see MJ Horwitz, 'The History of the Public/Private Distinction' (1982) 130 *U of Penn LR* 1423.

[20] This was originally conceived as a mixed functional/institutional criterion; but as it developed it became more and more functional: LN Brown and JS Bell, *French Administrative Law* (5th edn, Oxford University Press, 1998), 129–32.

[21] Brown and Bell, above n 19, at 5, 129. On the infiltration of this concept into English law see T Prosser, 'Public Service Law: Privatization's Unexpected Offspring' (2000) 63 *Law and Contemporary Problems* 63.

the public/private distinction. We now see clearly that non-government institutions are implicated in various ways in governmental tasks ('governance') and, conversely, that government participates in various ways alongside its citizens in social and economic life.[22] One result has been a shift from conceiving the public/private distinction in institutional terms to thinking about it in functional terms. Partly, no doubt, because the ECHR was conceived and drafted at a time when the public/private distinction was understood primarily in institutional terms (and because it is a treaty), the conceptual structure of section 6 of the HRA is ambivalent as between institutional and functional understandings of the province of public law in general, and of human rights law in particular. Understood in institutional terms, human rights are rights against government. Understood in functional terms, human rights are designed to impose constraints upon the performance of governmental tasks, activities or functions.

An important contrast between the institutional and functional understandings of the concept of publicness is that whereas institutional approaches are commonly based on reasonably hard-edged factual criteria, the idea of a public function is widely acknowledged to rest on value judgements about the interest that society can legitimately claim in regulating the lives of individual citizens. Under the functional approach the public/private divide is not between government and non-government but between society, or community, and the individual. Because of its evaluative nature, the functional approach is context-specific. Judgements about which activities are public and which are private will depend on the purposes for which the distinction is being drawn. For instance, the fact that an activity is classified as public for the purposes of human rights law does not mean that it will be classified as public in other legal contexts.

Andrew Clapham takes a rather different functional approach to the scope of human rights law.[23] His starting point is that the distinction between the state (public) and non-state (private) actors should not mark the line between application and non-application of human rights law. At the same time, the focus of his approach is not on identifying those activities in the conduct of which human rights must be respected. Rather he starts with the functions of human rights. In broad terms (but with particular reference to the ECHR), he says that these are to protect and promote democracy on the one hand, and individual dignity on the other.[24] In his view, it is only conduct that has 'a public element' that attracts the protection of 'democracy-enhancing' human rights. By contrast, 'dignity-enhancing'[25] human rights protect conduct regardless of whether it has a public element. This can be put in terms of duties: people have a duty to respect dignity-enhancing rights in all situations, whereas democracy-enhancing rights need only be respected in public situations. And, whilst the functional public/private distinction embodied in section 6 of the HRA relates to the scope of the obligation to protect

---

[22] For a recent general statutory encouragement of such participation see Local Government Act 2000, especially ss 2 and 4.

[23] *Human Rights in the Private Sphere* (Oxford University Press, 1993).

[24] *Ibid*, especially at ch 5.

[25] These descriptions of rights are mine, not Clapham's.

human rights, Clapham's use of the distinction relates to the conduct protected by human rights.

At first sight this is an attractive approach because it relates the scope of application of human rights to their underlying purpose. Democracy and dignity may be interfered with by non-state actors as well as by the state, and by those engaged in private activities as well as by public functionaries. On reflection, however, Clapham's account seems less satisfactory. One problem arises out of the fact, expressly acknowledged by Clapham, that at least some human rights protect both democracy and dignity. More importantly, it seems at least arguable that although only some human rights protect democracy, they all protect dignity by virtue of the fact that they belong to individuals as human beings. If all rights protect dignity, they should, according to Clapham's reasoning, all apply to private as well as public activities because people's dignity ought to be respected at all times. If this is so, the distinction between public and private activities does no work. Rather the scope of applicability of any particular right would depend solely on its content. Rights will be applicable to some situations but not to others merely by virtue of their terms and substance. But because people's dignity ought to be respected in all situations, the distinction between democracy (public) and dignity (private) is irrelevant to deciding the scope of application of any particular right because all rights protect dignity.

It is clear that there is something amiss with Clapham's analysis when one considers the examples he gives of how the democracy/dignity distinction affects the application of rights. Suppose (he says) that the members of a small Christian community refuse to allow a coven of witches to address them; and, by contrast, that witches are banned from holding meetings.[26] In the latter situation (says Clapham) democracy is threatened, but not in the former. However, it is hard to see how anything follows from this about the scope of freedom of speech. In the latter situation (it seems) both democracy and dignity are threatened; and so the right to speak is (doubly) engaged. In the former situation—so Clapham's discussion implies—the witches' freedom of speech is not infringed. This seems to be because their dignity is not threatened. But it is by no means clear that the concept of 'dignity' could be elaborated to produce this conclusion independently of some reference to the lack of a public element in the activity of the Christian group.

Clapham's position is further complicated by his insistence that he is not recommending abolition of the public/private distinction.[27] So, he says, whereas 'private individuals' have a right to privacy that can be set against another's 'right to information,' 'the State' has no such right to privacy but only a 'claim to *secrecy*.'[28] This example takes us right back to an institutional public/private distinction. In the end, I would argue, the logic of Clapham's position precisely requires abandonment of the public/private distinction and determination of the scope of human rights solely by reference to their substantive terms and without reference,

[26] Clapham, above n 23 above, at 146.
[27] *Ibid* at 134.
[28] *Ibid* (original emphasis).

in terms of a public/private distinction, *either* to the characteristics of those bound to respect them or of the functions and activities they engage in, *or* to the characteristics of activities protected by human rights.

Judicial Review and the Institutional Public/Private Divide

If the HRA reflects a shift to a functional understanding of the public/private distinction, there are other areas in which institutional understandings are still dominant or at least very important. The Freedom of Information Act 2000, for instance, applies to information held by a 'public authority'; and Schedule 1 contains a very long list of bodies that qualify as such for the purposes of the Act.

At the opposite extreme—in terms of conceptual complexity, anyway—are the common law rules governing the scope of 'judicial review' in the sense of proceedings brought in accordance with Civil Procedure Rules (CPR) Part 54. CPR Part 54 is the successor to the version of Order 53 of the Rules of the Supreme Court (RSC) that came into operation in 1977. The previous version of Order 53 dealt only with applications for the 'prerogative writs' of certiorari, prohibition and mandamus.[29] The procedural restrictions that surrounded applications for these remedies were so adverse to applicants that declarations and injunctions (the procedures for which were laid down in other Orders of the RSC and were less restrictive) came to be used as alternatives to the prerogative writs. The 1977 amendments to Order 53 regularised this situation by providing that prerogative orders (formerly 'prerogative writs') could be claimed only in accordance with the Order 53 procedure, but that declarations and injunctions could be applied for either under Order 53 or in accordance with the procedures for seeking these remedies laid down in other Orders of the RSC. A perhaps unanticipated result of making injunctions and declarations available 'either way' was the enunciation by the House of Lords in *O'Reilly v Mackman*[30] of the so-called 'exclusivity principle' to the effect that declarations and injunctions could be sought under Order 53 only in 'public law matters.' The exclusivity principle proved to be extremely controversial, and various exceptions to it were quickly developed.[31] However, the basic idea that judicial review under RSC Order 53, and now under CPR Part 54, is the appropriate procedure for 'public law claims' has become entrenched in the law, thus creating a procedural public/private divide.

The case law concerning the meaning of 'public law claim' and, hence, the scope of CPR Part 54, is extremely complex and has several strands. One strand rests on a distinction between public law rights and private law rights. This distinction provided the basis of the exclusivity principle laid down in *O'Reilly v Mackman*, but it has now

---

[29] Now known as a quashing order, a prohibiting order and a mandatory order respectively.
[30] [1983] 2 AC 237.
[31] See particularly *Wandsworth BC v Winder* [1985] AC 461; *Roy v Kensington and Chelsea and Westminster Family Practitioner Committee* [1992] AC 624; *Chief Adjudication Officer v Foster* [1993] AC 754; P Cane, *An Introduction to Administrative Law* (3rd edn, Oxford University Press, 1996), 99–104.

all but disappeared from view under the weight of exceptions to that principle enunciated in later cases.[32] A second strand in the cases defining the scope of judicial review rests on the contrast between governmental and non-governmental functions. This approach was first adopted in the *Takeover Panel* case[33] in which it was held that decisions of the Panel (a non-governmental, self-regulatory body) could be challenged under Order 53 because it was exercising a public function or a power with a public element. In later cases, this test has been elaborated in two ways.[34] One is to ask hypothetically whether the government would make provision for the exercise of the function if it was not being performed by the body in question.[35] The other is to ask whether the activities of the non-governmental body in question are an integral part of a governmental scheme of regulation.[36]

Yet a third strand in the case law on the meaning of 'public law claim' utilises an institutional distinction based on the source of a decision-maker's powers. In the *Takeover Panel* case the Panel's power was based neither on statute nor on contract but merely on the consent of those who submitted to its jurisdiction. Two of the judges indicated that if the Panel's power had been contractual (and in this sense 'private'), its decisions would not have been subject to judicial review. In other words, if the source of a body's power is contractual, the fact that it performs a public function will not render it amenable to judicial review.[37] This approach is of particular significance for cases involving the privatisation of government enterprises and contracting out of the provision of services by government. One typical result of privatisation is to transform the relationship between the provider and the consumer of a service from one based on statute to one based on contract; and a typical result of contracting out is to disrupt the statutory relationship connecting the consumer and the government entity by creating a contractual relationship between the consumer, or the government entity responsible for arranging for the provision of the service, or both, and the provider of the service. The issue then becomes whether the consumer can challenge (contractual) conduct of the service provider by way of judicial review.

A single judge of the High Court has held in this context that the *Takeover Panel* and *Aga Khan* cases[38] 'stand as authorities for the proposition that the courts cannot impose public law standards upon a body the source of whose power is con-

---

[32] An analogous distinction is used to determine the scope of application of the right to a fair trial under Article 6 of the ECHR. Article 6 applies to 'the determination of civil rights and obligations.' The case law on the meaning of 'civil' is complex, but on balance seems to draw the line between 'civil' and 'non-civil' in terms of entitlement-based 'rights' (the paradigm of which are 'private law rights' such as arise under property law and contract law) and discretion-based benefits (such as ex gratia payments and purely discretionary social welfare benefits). See Clayton and Tomlinson, above n 8, at 625–31. The appropriate domestic analogy is, of course, with rules governing the applicability of the requirements of (procedural) natural justice.

[33] *R v Panel on Takeovers and Mergers, ex parte Datafin* [1990] 1 QB 146.

[34] J Black, 'Constitutionalising Self Regulation' (1996) 59 *MLR* 24.

[35] Eg *R v Chief Rabbi of the United Hebrew Congregations, ex parte Wachmann* [1992] 1 WLR 1036.

[36] See eg *R v Disciplinary Committee of the Jockey Club, ex parte Aga Khan* [1993] 1 WLR 909 per Hoffmann LJ.

[37] Eg *Law v National Greyhound Racing Club* [1983] 1 WLR 1302.

[38] See above nn 33 and 36 respectively.

tractual and absent sufficient statutory penetration.'[39] The *Servite Houses* case involved a challenge to a decision of a housing association to close a residential nursing home in which a local authority, in discharge of statutory functions, had arranged for the applicants to live. The ground of challenge was that the applicants had been promised that they would be able to live there for the rest of their lives. The judge held that the decision was not amenable to judicial review on public law grounds because the respondent was entitled, under its contract with the local authority, to close the home.

Several points deserve notice. One is the reference by the judge to 'public law standards.' Although the public/private distinction was introduced in *O'Reilly v Mackman* on the back of a reform of court procedure, and although judicial review procedure has distinctive features, the procedural public/private distinction has brought a substantive public/private distinction in its wake. In other words, judicial review is to be understood not merely as a distinctive procedural regime, but also as the gateway to a distinctive set of substantive public law principles which provide grounds for challenging decisions that are amenable to judicial review, but not for challenging decisions that are not so amenable. This coupling of procedure and substance was not inevitable, and I will have more to say about it later. The second point to note is that the judge combined the institutional and the functional tests by holding that contractual power may be amenable to judicial review if it is an integral part of a statutory regime of service provision. In this respect, the fact that the relevant regime is statutory does not mean that this criterion is an institutional one based on the source of the power. Rather, the fact that a contractual function is embedded in a statutory regime indicates that the function is 'public' in the relevant sense.

Thirdly, it is instructive to compare the approach in *Servite Houses* with that in the later case of *Poplar Housing and Regeneration Community Association Ltd* v *Donoghue* in the Court of Appeal.[40] Poplar was a housing association created by Tower Hamlets LBC so that the council could transfer to it a substantial proportion of the council's (public) housing stock. Tower Hamlets had arranged for the applicant to be accommodated temporarily in one of Poplar's houses pending a decision as to whether it had a statutory duty to house her permanently. In due course the council decided that the applicant was not entitled to permanent housing; and as a result, Poplar sought a possession order against the applicant, who argued that in seeking the order Poplar was acting in breach of Article 8 of the ECHR. This argument raised the issue of whether Poplar was a public authority for the purposes of section 6 of the HRA. It was accepted by all parties that Poplar was not a pure public authority; and so the relevant questions were whether it was a hybrid public authority and whether the act of seeking a possession order was public or private. The Court of Appeal held that Poplar was bound by the HRA, effectively because it was an integral part of the arrangement by which the council fulfilled its statutory housing functions.

---

[39]   *R v Servite Houses, ex parte Goldsmith* [2001] LGR 55.
[40]   [2001] 3 WLR 183.

The fact patterns in these two cases are essentially similar. In particular, the challenged action in both cases was done in exercise of a contractual, or at least a contract-like, power. An explanation for the difference in outcome may lie in the fact that whereas the source of the power was directly relevant to the scope of judicial review in *Servite Houses*, it was only indirectly relevant to the scope of the HRA in *Poplar*. According to the rule that the judge in *Servite Houses* extracted from the *Takeover Panel* and *Aga Khan* cases, an exercise of contractual power will be subject to judicial review only if it is an integral part of a governmental activity. By contrast, a body can be a public authority under the HRA provided only that certain of its functions are public; and the fact that a decision was made under a contract is only one factor to be taken into account in determining whether it was a private or a public act.

In *R (Heather) v Leonard Cheshire Foundation*[41] (the facts of which were very like those of *Servite Houses*) the Court of Appeal, in holding that the Foundation was not a hybrid public authority for the purposes of the HRA, distinguished *Poplar* on the ground that the activities of the Foundation were not an integral part of the activities of the local authority in the way that the activities of Poplar were. Whereas Poplar was a statutory housing association formed to take over the council's housing stock, the Foundation is a long-established non-statutory charitable organisation specialising in the provision of residential care. However, the fact that the relationship between the Foundation and the council was essentially contractual did not figure (expressly at least) in the court's justification for its decision that the Foundation was not a public authority. This is not to say that the legal underpinning of an entity's activities may not be relevant to its status. In *R (A) v Partnerships in Care Ltd*[42] a non-governmental psychiatric hospital was held to be a public authority because statute imposed certain obligations in relation to the running of the hospital directly on its owners. The point would seem to be that contract does not weigh so heavily against a finding of publicness under the HRA as it does in the context of CPR Part 54.[43]

An institutional public/private divide is a much more prominent feature of EC law. Of most general significance, perhaps, is the law concerning the effect of directives in the domestic law of the Member States. Unlike EC regulations, directives are designed to be implemented by Member States rather than to affect the legal rights and obligations of citizens by their own force. However, in order to overcome problems caused by non-implementation or incorrect implementation, the European Court of Justice (ECJ) developed the doctrine of 'direct effect' of directives. According to this doctrine, once the date for implementation of a directive has passed, the directive is treated, as against *organs of the state* but not against citizens, as having

---

[41] [2002] EWCA Civ 366.

[42] [2002] EWHC 529; [2002] 1 WLR 2610.

[43] CPR Rule 54.1(2) defines 'a claim for judicial review' to mean 'a claim to review the lawfulness of (i) an enactment; or (ii) a decision, action or failure to act in relation to the exercise of a public function.' The first limb of this definition refers to claims under s 4 of the HRA. Because the rule is procedural, the reference in the second limb to 'public functions,' while no doubt meant to summarise the law relating to the scope of judicial review, does not supersede or modify it.

been correctly implemented.[44] This means that a citizen can challenge decisions and actions of the state and its organs that are inconsistent with the directive. The institutional aspect of the criterion that imposes obligations on states under unimplemented or incorrectly implemented directives is reinforced by the principle, clearly stated by Advocate-General Slynn in *Marshall v Southampton and South-West Hampshire Area Health Authority (Teaching)*,[45] that the state is directly bound by directives in relation to all of its activities, whether 'public' or 'private.'

The leading case on the meaning of 'organ of the state' is *Foster v British Gas plc* in which the ECJ offered the following definition of 'organ of the state':

> a body, whatever its legal form, which has been made responsible, pursuant to a measure adopted by the State, for providing a public service under the control of the State and has for that purpose special powers beyond those which result from the normal rules applicable to relations between individuals.[46]

This definition of 'organ of the state' assumes the existence of a 'core' state that is itself left undefined; and it is concerned with entities beyond that core. The definition is narrow in various respects. It applies only to entities to which 'special powers' have been expressly delegated by the state, and only to entities that provide a 'public service under the control of the state.' As a result, it identifies as public only entities that are both institutionally and functionally public. Institutionally, the entity must be a delegate of the state and under its control; and functionally, it must be providing a public service and have special powers for this purpose. At the relevant time, British Gas was a state-owned utility company. It was a vehicle for commercial activity rather than for what Advocate-General van Gerven called the 'exercise of authority in the strict sense,'[47] which he seems to have thought to be the characteristic of the state in its core sense. In his view, British Gas was a (non-core) state organ because it had legal powers that enabled and entitled it 'to decisively influence the conduct of persons.'

Another context within EC law in which the outer boundaries of the State need to be specified is that of public procurement. The Public Supply Contracts Regulations 1995, SI 1995/201 (which give effect to an EC Directive) govern contracting by 'contracting authorities.' The definition of this term contains both named entities and a general provision in the following terms:

> a corporation established, or a group of individuals appointed to act together, for the specific purposes of meeting needs in the general interest, not having an industrial or commercial character, and (i) financed wholly or partly by another contracting authority, or (ii) subject to management supervision by another contracting authority, or (iii) more than half of the board of directors or members of which or, in the case of a group of individuals, more than half of those individuals, being appointed by another contracting authority.

---

[44] For more detail see TC Hartley, *The Foundations of European Community Law* (5th edn, Oxford University Press, 2003), 206–19.

[45] [1986] 1 CMLR 688.

[46] [1990] 2 CMLR 833 at 857.

[47] *Ibid* at 851.

Like the definition adopted in *Foster*, this one identifies contracting authorities by combined institutional and functional criteria: they are entities that perform the function of meeting needs 'in the general interest' and in a non-commercial way; and they are in a relationship of 'close dependency' (understood in terms of sub-paragraphs (i), (ii) and (iii) in the definition) on another contracting authority.[48]

A third institutional approach to establishing the boundaries of the state is found in case law of the European Court of Human Rights. As noted earlier, only states are bound by the ECHR. In *Costello-Roberts v United Kingdom*[49] the question was whether the United Kingdom could be held responsible for acts of corporal punishment inflicted on a student by a teacher in an independent school. In holding the United Kingdom responsible the Court seems to have adopted a principle of vicarious liability—the State could not, by delegating internal discipline to school authorities, absolve itself of responsibility for acts of discipline that were inconsistent with rights of pupils under the Convention.

This brief survey of some of the areas in which current law embodies and utilises a public/private distinction presents a complex picture of various functional and institutional criteria combined in a number of different ways in various related areas of the law. At the same time as this patchwork of provisions has been developing, so also have critiques of the public/private distinction. It is to these that we now turn.

CRITIQUES OF THE PUBLIC/PRIVATE DISTINCTION

There was much criticism of the public/private distinction in the 1980s based on two main lines of attack. One was that the categories of public and private are so indeterminate and manipulable that they are little more than political slogans. This argument was one manifestation of a thorough-going realist/critical scepticism about legal concepts which, if taken seriously, would render impossible normative legal analysis of the sort I am engaged in here. So I will not address it in detail. The other main argument (identified particularly with feminist legal theory)[50] was that the public/private distinction is typically used as a shield to mask the extent of legal regulation of people's lives. The underlying idea here was that there are very few areas of life that are not subject to legal regulation; and that if something is regulated by law it is, in an important sense, public. For present purposes, the problem with this argument is that it does not help us to understand how the public/private distinction can operate within the law and not just as a marker of law's boundary. In other words, the public/private distinctions with which I am concerned in this chapter refer to different ways in which activities can be regulated

---

[48]   *R v HM Treasury, ex parte University of Cambridge* [2000] 1 WLR 2514.

[49]   (1993) 19 EHRR 112. See further Clayton and Tomlinson, above n 8, 189–90.

[50]   See, eg, N Lacey, *Unspeakable Subjects: Feminist Essays in Legal and Social Theory* (Oxford, Hart, 1998), ch 3.

by law. We might say, for instance, that although insurance markets are regulated by law, they provide a 'private' mechanism of loss distribution, by contrast with the 'public mechanism' of a social security system funded by taxes.

Even so, although the criticisms of the public/private distinction that will be examined here do not rest directly on either of these sorts of argument, they contain echoes of both lines of attack.

Dicey's Modern Influence

As noted above, Dicey was opposed to distinguishing between public and private both as a matter of substantive law and in designing adjudicatory institutions. His view was that governors and governed alike should be judged by 'ordinary courts' according to the same set of legal rules. His prime motivation was, it seems, a fear that the distinction would in practice operate to provide the governors with legal privileges and immunities not enjoyed by the governed. That he should have felt this way is not altogether surprising. In eighteenth century France the regional royal courts (*Parlements*) 'not only interfered to a considerable degree in executive government but also impeded such reforms as the monarchy sought to introduce.'[51] In 1790 the revolutionaries passed a law (which was confirmed in 1795 and is still in force) making it a criminal offence 'for the judges of the ordinary courts to … call administrators to account before them in the exercise of their official functions.' The Conseil d'Etat, an organ of the executive arm of government staffed by civil servants, was established in 1799 to deal with complaints by citizens against the government. But it was not until 1889 that citizens could complain to it directly rather than through a minister of the government. In 1879, 38 members of the Conseil resigned or were dismissed as the result of a purge of members thought not to be 'in total agreement with the government.'[52] The first edition of Dicey's *Introduction to the Study of the Law of the Constitution* was published in 1885.

Dicey's views influenced judicial thinking in England in the first half of the twentieth century. On the other hand, his ideas put no discernible brake in that period on the growth of government regulation, the development of the Welfare State, and increasing government participation in the economy. Nor did they restrain the development of statutory administrative tribunals, staffed in large part by non-lawyers, the sole function of which was to adjudicate disputes between citizens and government. The growth of tribunals in England was haphazard, and dissatisfaction with the resulting lack of system led to the establishment of a committee of inquiry. In its 1957 report the Franks Committee recommended that tribunals should be identified as part of the judicial arm, rather than the executive arm, of government.[53] In Diceyan spirit, the Committee rejected proposals for the

---

[51] Brown and Bell, above n 19, 45.

[52] *Ibid* at 5.

[53] Cmnd 218, 1957. In 1970 the US Supreme Court significantly judicialised social security administration procedures in *Goldberg v Kelly* 397 US 254, under the influence of Charles Reich's famous article 'The New Property' (1964) 73 *Yale LJ* 733.

establishment of a general administrative appeals tribunal and an administrative division of the High Court, the former on the basis that it would undermine the ultimate control of 'the superior courts' over adjudicative bodies and would introduce a dual system of law with 'all the evils attendant on this dichotomy.'[54] Not much more than a decade later in Australia, the Kerr Committee made recommendations that led to the establishment of the Administrative Appeals Tribunal (AAT).[55] For constitutional reasons, the AAT is technically part of the executive branch; but in many significant respects, in looks and behaves very much like a court.[56] It operates subject to ultimate control by superior federal courts.

At much the same time, there were some who, tapping into a deep vein of anti-Diceyan sentiment, lamented the absence in England of a separate system of public law and of a body like the Conseil d'Etat, that could, in resolving disputes between citizen and state, take proper account of the nature and modes of operation of government administration in a way that bodies staffed (entirely) by lawyers, and adopting court-like procedures and modes of thought, were unlikely to be able to do.[57] But this view has never attracted much support. The Kerr Committee in Australia rejected the French model, most fundamentally because (the Committee said) the 'political and administrative context' in which it operated was different from that in Australia.[58] In Britain, the Leggatt Review of Tribunals has recently recommended a rationalisation of appellate tribunals falling short of the establishment of an AAT-type body.[59] But it reaffirmed the Diceyan ideology of the Franks Committee: 'Tribunals are an alternative to court, not administrative, processes.'[60] More importantly, the role of Dicey's 'ordinary courts' in reviewing administrative activity has grown enormously both in volume of claims and symbolic importance in the past 25 years. While the tribunal system handles vastly more complaints against government than do the courts, it is the courts that tend to deal with those that have the broadest implications and the highest profile in political terms. Institutionally, the formal, external mechanisms for resolving complaints against government still basically conform to Diceyan principles of institutional design.

By the 1960s, however, anti-Diceyan thoughts had started to enter the judicial mind. Symptomatic of this trend were decisions of the House of Lords such as *Ridge v Baldwin*,[61] which established the principle that administrators must fashion themselves in the image of the courts by complying with the rules of natural justice; and *Conway v Rimmer*,[62] which established ultimate judicial hegemony

---

[54] Cmnd 218, 1957, paras 122,123.
[55] Commonwealth Administrative Review Committee Report, Parliamentary Paper No 144 of 1971.
[56] P Cane, 'Merits Review and Judicial Review: The AAT as Trojan Horse' (2000) 28 *Federal LR* 213.
[57] The most famous exposition of this view is that of JDB Mitchell, 'The Causes and Effects of the Absence of a System of Public Law in the United Kingdom' [1965] *PL* 95.
[58] See above n 55 at para 222.
[59] *Tribunals for Users: One System, One Service* (TSO, 2001), paras 6.9–11.
[60] At para 2.18.
[61] [1964] AC 40.
[62] [1968] AC 910.

over decisions about whether the 'public interest' required or justified non-disclosure of government-held information in court proceedings. Decisions such as these were taken as heralding the dawn of a new era of government legal accountability—a new 'public law.' In the 1970s Diceyan premises about the legal position of government were further undermined by the development of rules and principles of tort law concerned expressly with the liability of 'public authorities.' Many thought that the final nail had been inserted in the coffin of Dicey's intellectual and ideological legacy when, in *O'Reilly v Mackman*,[63] the House of Lords interpreted the 1977 amendments to judicial review procedure as having introduced a special regime for 'public law cases.' As we have seen above, this procedural public/private divide brought in its wake the idea that public law cases are subject not only to public law procedure, but also to substantive rules and principles of public law. The development of a substantive public/private divide in the English common law has no doubt been encouraged by the fact that such a divide plays an important part in EC and human rights law.

Perhaps the staunchest modern supporter of Dicey's opposition to a substantive public/private law divide is Carol Harlow.[64] Her basic argument is that subjecting the state to 'the ordinary law of the land' is likely to be a more effective way of resisting the creation of legal privileges and immunities than creating a separate regime of public law rules of state responsibility. In her view, a separate regime of public law rules and principles makes sense only if there are separate institutional arrangements for dealing with complaints against the state. She argues against such arrangements because they bring with them the need for criteria to delimit the jurisdiction of these separate complaint-handling bodies. In her view, neither institutional nor functional criteria of publicness reflect the 'interpenetration of public and private institutions and capital' that characterises contemporary society. Indeed, the effect of the public/private distinction is to conceal political issues behind a formalist façade. What is needed, she said, are procedures to enable courts to deal better with such political issues rather than to pretend that they arise only in 'public law cases' which, therefore, require the creation of separate procedural arrangements and separate substantive rules.

Experience in both France and England certainly provides good reason to avoid the sort of fruitless jurisdictional line-drawing that accompanies the existence of separate public law adjudicatory bodies and procedures. It is also hard to disagree that it is undesirable for the public/private distinction to be used to prevent the consideration of issues of public interest by classifying contexts in which they arise as 'private.' But none of this seems to be inconsistent with drawing some sort of public/private distinction, at least for some purposes. Unless we say (in effect) that 'everything is public' or, conversely, that 'everything is private'—which Harlow does not do—there is no reason to object to a public/private distinction as such, however much disagreement there may be about how it should be drawn in various circumstances.

---

[63] [1983] 2 AC 237.
[64] See especially '"Public" and "Private" Law: Definition without Distinction' (1980) 43 *MLR* 241.

The view that a distinction between public law and private law makes sense only in a particular political and constitutional context is elaborated by John Allison.[65] He argues that such a distinction is 'satisfactory' only in a system (like France in the eighteenth and nineteenth centuries) which displays four features: (1) a well-developed theory of 'the state' as a discrete administrative entity to which public law can be applied and which has characteristics (such as unique powers and the opportunity for their abuse) that justify and require subjecting it to special legal controls; (2) a 'categorical approach to law' according to which legal categories such as 'public' and 'private' are mutually exclusive; (3) a doctrine of separation of powers which ensures that those who decide disputes between citizen and state are independent of the administration but also expert in understanding its processes and needs; and (4) inquisitorial procedures for the resolution of disputes between the citizen and the state which enable the public ramifications of such disputes to be properly investigated.

Allison's analysis is complex and sophisticated, and full justice cannot be done to it here. A number of general comments are in order, however. First, there is a certain inevitability, if not circularity, about Allison's argument. He starts by asserting that the public/private distinction has been transplanted into English law (from French law). He then expounds the conceptual and institutional foundations on which he considers the French public/private distinction to have been built and notes the absence of each in the English legal system. Finally he concludes that the public/private distinction could operate satisfactorily in English law only if the conditions of its thriving in French law were reproduced in England. Thus reduced to its bare bones, the argument appears to depend for much of its force on the assertions that the French legal system provides the paradigm (if not the only instance) of a successful public/private distinction, and that it is this distinction that English law is and should be striving to reproduce. Neither of these assertions is (to say the least) beyond argument.

Secondly, it is clear that even if the concept of the state as a discrete administrative entity reflected the reality of eighteenth and nineteenth century French political life, it is in serious conflict with contemporary pluralistic understanding of the way society is organised and governed. There is a tendency in some writings critical of the public/private distinction to suggest (at least implicitly) that government participation in economic and social life and, conversely, the involvement of non-government entities in the tasks of governance, is—like our conscious awareness of these phenomena—a feature of the late twentieth century. One only has to think of the long history of professional self-regulation, for instance, or of state participation in the relief of poverty, to find grounds for doubting this suggestion. One of the most frequent criticisms of Dicey concerns his failure to recognise the many and various sites of governmental activity in nineteenth century England.[66] If it is indeed the case that a workable public/pri-

---

[65] See above n 18.

[66] Eg HW Arthurs, *Without the Law: Administrative Justice and Legal Pluralism in Nineteenth Century England* (Toronto, Toronto UP, 1985).

vate distinction can exist only where state and non-state occupy separate and non-overlapping spheres, it would surely be incapable of thriving in France as well as in England, either in the nineteenth or the twenty-first century. However, Allison's view appears to be that the public/private distinction operates successfully in France despite the realities—and our understanding of the realities—of governance in contemporary society.

There is, I think, a more fundamental point at stake here. Even if Allison is correct in identifying a theory of the state—as opposed, for instance, to a desire on the part of the executive and legislative arms of government not to be judged by lawyers—as the historical foundation of the French public/private distinction and of the institutional arrangements that give it practical effect, it is worth recalling (see p 253 above) that from 1873, the concept of 'public function' (*service publique*) has played a central role in the definition of the jurisdiction of the Conseil d'Etat and, hence, of the sphere of public law. This reflects the fact that the reason we want to impose special legal controls on the state is not because of what it is but because of what it does.[67] Unlike the concept of the state, that of a public function is radically evaluative. As Harlow puts it, no function is 'typically governmental in character.'[68] People can and do disagree about where the public ends and the private begins. But this does not prevent public/private operating 'satisfactorily' as a legal distinction any more than the radically evaluative nature of the concept of reasonableness (for instance) rules it out as a 'satisfactory' legal concept. What is essential, however, is that the evaluative nature of the functional public/private distinction should be recognised and that judgements about the nature of particular functions should be supported by normative arguments so that the political nature of the distinction is not hidden behind a formalistic screen.

Thirdly, a word needs to be said about Allison's contention that a satisfactory distinction between public and private law requires a 'categorical approach to law.' One example of the different approaches of French and English law is that the latter allows, while the former denies, the possibility of 'concurrent liability' in contract and tort. In French law there is either liability in contract or liability in tort, whereas in English law a person can be liable in both contract and tort in respect of one and the same incident. The possibility of concurrent liability certainly destabilises the distinction between contract and tort. However, it is important to note that contract and tort are not opposites in the way that public and private are. In this regard, public and private are more like reasonable and unreasonable than like contract and tort. In my view, the mere fact that English law is less 'categorical' than French law is of little or no relevance to whether the public/private distinction is likely to operate 'satisfactorily' in English law.

---

[67] N Bamforth, 'The Public Law-Private Law Distinction: A Comparative and Philosophical Approach' in P Leyland and T Woods (eds), *Administrative Law Facing the Future: Old Constraints and New Horizons* (London, Blackstone, 1997), ch 6. See also S Fredman and G Morris, 'Public or Private? State Employees and Judicial Review' (1991) 107 *LQR* 298, 309–12

[68] See above, n 64, at 257; see also RH Mnookin, 'The Public/Private Dichotomy: Political Disagreement and Academic Repudiation' (1982) 130 *U of Penn LR* 1428.

Finally, let us consider Allison's argument that the distinction between public law and private law can operate satisfactorily only if review of decisions is conducted by 'independent experts' following inquisitorial procedures. This argument can be helpfully rephrased in regulatory terms. A basic tenet of modern regulatory theory is that the more a regulator knows about the regulated activity, the more effective is its regulation likely to be in achieving regulatory goals. From this point of view, experts are likely to be more effective regulators than non-experts.[69] It is also widely believed that proactive investigation by the regulator is likely to generate more and better information about regulated activities than reactive, adversarial fact-finding. At the same time, it is important that the regulator remain independent of the regulated in order to avoid 'regulatory capture.' These are all good arguments. But what is their relationship to the public/private distinction? There is no obvious reason why expertise and independence would be more needed in the regulation of public activities than of private.

Regarding inquisitorial procedures, Allison argues that disputes which involve the state administration are likely to have 'far wider ramifications' than disputes which do not; and that inquisitorial procedures are better suited to the proper consideration of such 'polycentric' disputes. However, he also thinks that the first of these propositions is true only if one presupposes a theory of the state as a distinct entity; and that anyway, it is not only disputes involving the state that have wide ramifications.[70] Allison's hesitation at this point reflects the fact that polycentricity is a function more of the way we understand disputes than of their intrinsic nature. Indeed, the distinction between polycentric and bipolar disputes can itself be seen as a type of functional public/private distinction; and like the latter distinction, it is essentially evaluative. Bipolar disputes are those we are prepared to resolve in terms of the interests of the two parties, whereas polycentric disputes are those which we think ought only to be resolved by taking account of interests beyond those of the immediate parties.

In this light we can detect a serious tension in Allison's scheme. On the one hand he says that the public/private distinction will work satisfactorily only if inquisitorial procedures are available to resolve polycentric public disputes; while on the other hand he says that the public/private distinction will only work satisfactorily if publicness is understood institutionally in terms of a distinct state administration. However, these criteria fight against one another because Allison also accepts that not all—and not only—disputes involving the state will be polycentric. This suggests that far from being a condition of the satisfactory operation of the distinction between public and private law, the institutional concept of a distinct state administration fails to capture the very reason why we draw the distinction, which is to distinguish between activities and relationships in terms of the degree of society's *legitimate* interest in them. Ironically, perhaps, putting the matter in this way leads us to a different, and common, criticism of the public/private distinction: because

---

[69]   See eg contributions of Colin Scott and Martyn Hopper in J Black, P Muchlinski and P Walker (eds), *Commercial Regulation and Judicial Review* (Oxford, Hart, 1998); especially Scott at 59–61.

[70]   See above n 18, 191.

it operates in a binary way ('either public or private') it may fail to capture the complexity, subtlety and ambiguity of our value judgements about the proper relationship between the individual and society. This criticism is an application of a much more thorough-going objection to the binary fashion in which law organises and regulates social relationships. It is discussed further pp 269–75 below.

Integrationism

Carol Harlow thinks that no distinction should be drawn between public and private law, and that the law which governs relations between citizens should also govern relations between citizens and the state. Dawn Oliver, by contrast, argues that there is no distinction between public and private law because underlying all legal rules and principles (whether thought of as public law or private law) that regulate the exercise of decision-making power, whether by government or citizen, is a common set of legal values.[71] She recommends the adoption of an 'integrated approach to substance, remedies and procedure' that 'would enable the common law and equity to develop, with statutory provisions and European and human rights law, so as to promote the protection of individuals and public interests against abuses of all kinds of power.'[72] The values which, according to Oliver, underlie legal regulation of the exercise of power are autonomy (freedom of action), dignity, equal respect, status and security. In her view, these values support 'duties of considerate decision-making'[73] which apply as much to dealings between citizens as to dealings by government with citizens. Oliver's argument is not that there are no important differences between the state and citizens,[74] but only (it seems) that these differences should not be (and, indeed, are not)[75] reflected in a substantive distinction between public and private law. Nor does Oliver subscribe to the implausible view that all law is public, or that an activity is public merely by virtue of being regulated by law.[76]

There are, it seems to me, two main weaknesses in Oliver's position. The first arises from the role that the five 'values' play in the argument. These values are so abstract that it is not surprising that they can be said to underpin both public and private law. Nor does their ubiquity, by itself, suggest that there are no substantive differences between the two areas of law. For instance, two laws that struck the balance between autonomy and security differently might each nevertheless promote both values. Secondly, it is a recurring theme of Oliver's book that the state has no interests 'of its own' but is required in everything it does to act 'altruistically' in the 'public interest'; and that the law does and should reflect this important difference

[71] D Oliver, *Common Values and the Public-Private Divide* (London, Butterworths, 1999).
[72] *Ibid* at 248.
[73] *Ibid* at 27.
[74] *Ibid* at 12–13.
[75] Although Oliver generally denies that there is any distinction between public law and private law, her detailed exposition does not entirely support this denial: see eg *ibid* at 16, 110, 132,135.
[76] *Ibid* at 24–5.

between the state and citizens. It is hard to see how this view of the state can consistently co-exist with the proposition that there neither is nor ought to be any substantive public law/private law divide.[77] Oliver's position here is reminiscent of Clapham's suggestion, noted earlier, that unlike its citizens—who have a right to privacy—the state has no more than a claim to secrecy which can only be successfully asserted by demonstrating that the public interest demands secrecy.

Oliver certainly demonstrates that there are important parallels and similarities between the legal obligations resting on governmental decision-makers on the one hand, and non-governmental decision-makers on the other; and although Oliver does not make the point, her analysis does illustrate the impact of institutional arrangements on substantive law. The clearest example of this in English law is the distinction between common law and equity, which would not have developed in the way it did had there not been separate courts of common law and equity. Since the merging of the two sets of courts in the nineteenth century, a process has been underway of integrating the two bodies of law. It has nevertheless been found useful to see them as distinct components of a complex whole rather than as forming one undifferentiated mass of legal rules and principles. The history of the public/private distinction has been somewhat the reverse of this. In the absence of separate public law and private law courts, legal rules and principles governing the conduct of public decision-makers were not sharply differentiated from private law. On the contrary, the former were significantly influenced and fertilised by the latter. The development since 1977 of a distinct 'judicial review jurisdiction' has not created a rigid, substantive public law/private law divide (as Oliver seems to suggest), but it has brought certain important legal distinctions into sharper focus.

Instrumentalism

We have already noted the criticism that the public/private distinction operates in a binary fashion—either public or private. On the other hand, we have also seen that the HRA introduces the more flexible idea of 'hybrid' public authorities, which are defined as bodies some of whose functions are public. The concept of hybridisation is prominent in discussions of law and regulation that draw on ideas and insights from social theory. A hybrid is a product of mixing two or more elements. As Scott says:

> The term 'hybrid' has been used to describe arrangements which consist of a mixture of market and hierarchical ordering … Thus the concept precisely captures the notion of relationships … which are partly based on contractual notions of exchange and partly on … notions of hierarchical decision making.[78]

[77] For a useful discussion of this point in relation to property law see JW Harris, 'Private and Non-Private Property: What is the Difference?' (1995) 111 *LQR* 421 (the difference between private and non-private property is that the latter lacks the 'crucial feature of legitimate self-seeking exploitation').

[78] C Scott, 'The Juridification of Relations in the UK Utilities Sectors' in Black, Muchlinski and Walker (eds), above n 69, at 46 n 89.

Privatisation and contracting out have produced good illustrations of public/private hybridisation. In legal terms, the paradigmatic basis of private relationships is contract while the paradigmatic basis of public relationships is statute. One common result of privatisation and contracting out is that contractual relationships (for instance, between service-provider and customer, or between regulator and regulated) are embedded in, or operate as part or against the background of, a statutory regime that establishes duties of service provision or powers of regulation. It is not that contract and statute operate side-by-side in such a way that certain aspects of a relationship are governed by contract and others by statute. Rather the two elements are intertwined or blended with the result that the contract must be interpreted and applied in the light of relevant statutory provisions, and the statutory provisions must be interpreted and applied taking account of the contract.

Regulation scholars have been in the forefront of discussion of recent changes in 'the nature of the state' in terms of concepts such as hybridisation. A possible explanation for this it that unlike public lawyers, who tend to take an institutional (or 'constitutional') approach to understanding government, regulationists are concerned to describe and analyse certain social activities regardless of the institutional form they happen to take from time to time. They see regulation not as a function of *government* but rather as a form of *governance*—the latter being:

> characterised by interdependence between organisations (both state and non-state), a pattern of interactions within networks, observation of 'rules of the game' negotiated between the actors, and a degree of autonomy from the state.[79]

The careful observer now finds that regulation is not only something that the government imposes on citizens. Citizens may impose it on other citizens, and even on government itself.[80] Regulation can also be found 'inside government,' as government 'waste-watchers, quality police and sleaze-busters' keep a close eye on the activities of other parts of the government machine.[81]

The relevant question for present purposes concerns the implications of hybridisation for the distinction between public law and private law. In answering this question it is important, first, to observe that in the regulatory literature, hybridisation is typically understood in institutional terms. It describes the institutional structure within which certain tasks, understood in terms of the concept of 'governance,' are performed. It does not address what the tasks of governance are or should be, or where the boundaries of governance are or should be drawn. But it does assume, at least implicitly, that 'governance' describes a limited set of

---

[79] C Scott, 'The Governance of the European Union: The Potential for Multi-Level Control' (2002) 8 *European LJ* 59, 61. See also Freeman, above n 2.

[80] C Scott, 'Private Regulation of the Public Sector: A Neglected Facet of Contemporary Governance' (2002) 29 *J of Law and Society* 56. Scott conceptualises 'accountability' on three dimensions: upwards to a higher authority, horizontally to a 'broadly parallel institution' and downwards to 'lower level institutions and groups': 'Accountability in the Regulatory State' (2000) 27 *J of Law and Society* 38, 42.

[81] C Hood, C Scott, O James, G Jones and T Travers, *Regulation Inside Government: Waste-Watchers, Quality Police and Sleaze-Busters* (Oxford University Press, 1999).

social activities. So although the concept of hybridisation, thus understood, can be used to undermine an institutional public/private divide, it would not support any conclusion about the viability or desirability of a functional public/private divide. This perhaps explains why Julia Black, who accepts the hybridisation analysis, nevertheless argues that 'regulation' should be understood as a public function and subjected to a distinctive set of legal controls ('public law accountability') appropriate to its nature as such.[82] Of course, this view leaves open the very large question of how 'regulation' should be defined and understood.[83] But it does not entail wholesale abandonment of the public/private divide. To do that, it is necessary to go one step further by arguing that regulation (for instance) should be understood simply as a social function or activity, and that questions about how that activity or function ought to be controlled and held accountable should be answered in purely instrumental terms.

Such a radical instrumentalist argument is (at least) implicit in Colin Scott's contention that public lawyers who worry that practices such as privatisation and contracting out have generated an 'accountability deficit' fail to take account of new forms of and opportunities for accountability and control that such practices have generated and which may, in practice, be as effective as or even more effective than the modes of accountability that are no longer available.[84] Whereas for Black the nature of power is relevant to deciding how its exercise should be controlled, for Scott the only criterion for judging control mechanisms is whether they produce effective accountability.[84a] An obvious point to make about Scott's approach (described in this way) is that if it is to be of any use in practical reasoning, the notion of 'effective accountability' needs to be spelled out in terms of a normative theory about the nature and goals of accountability mechanisms against which the success (or failure) of particular accountability regimes can be assessed. Scott's principles of 'interdependence' and 'redundancy' could be understood as part of such a normative theory; although it is doubtful whether Scott intended them as such.

The public/private distinction can be understood as part of a normative theory of accountability under which the exercise of public functions should be subject to a particular accountability regime (different from that applicable to private activities) because they *are* public. In this account, the public/private distinction may cut either of two ways: it might be used to justify imposing more stringent controls on 'public' activities than on private activities, or less stringent controls. So, for instance, we might want to accord less contractual freedom to public contractors than to private contractors, but also relieve public contractors of certain contractual liabilities that rest on private contractors.

It is possible to understand the functional public/private distinction as utilised

[82]   J Black, 'Constitutionalising Self Regulation' (1996) 59 *MLR* 24.

[83]   On this see J Black, 'Decentring Regulation: Understanding the Role of Regulation and Self-Regulation in a "Post-Regulatory" World' (2001) 54 *CLP* 103; 'Critical Reflections on Regulation' (2002) 27 *Australian Journal of Legal Philosophy* 1.

[84]   Scott, 'Accountability in the Regulatory State', above n 80.

[84a]   *Ibid* 55.

by Black in precisely this way. On this basis, the difference between Scott's and Black's approach is that whereas Black thinks that the public/private distinction provides an attractive normative basis for a theory of accountability, Scott thinks that it does not.

For Scott, one reason why the public/private distinction is problematic is that as an empirical matter, the likely effectiveness of public law controls is questionable once it is recognised that accountability is achieved by a dense and complex network of relationships and techniques of control. This, he says, 'presents difficulties for public lawyers' because such networks are 'not directly 'programmable' with the public law norms (fairness, legality, rationality, and so on). Interventions to secure appropriate normative outcomes must necessarily be indirect and unpredictable in their effects.'[85] This empirical challenge is taken up by Anne Davies in her study of NHS contracting.[86] Her conclusion is that 'the success of contractualisation could be enhanced by creating a public law normative framework for internal contracts, based on the policy of using them as fair and effective mechanisms of accountability.'[87] Based on her empirical study, she identifies certain problems of regulation and enforcement of NHS contracts and argues that public law institutions and rules can contribute to their resolution in ways that the private law of contract probably could not. In his review of Davies' book, Peter Vincent-Jones draws attention to some empirical evidence that could be interpreted as pointing in a different direction.[88] Given the nature of empirical research in law,[89] it seems unlikely that the questions at stake here will ever be conclusively resolved. The meaning and goals of accountability, and judgements about the success of accountability mechanisms, are likely to remain contested and ultimately dependent on normative legal and political theories. Putting the point quite crudely, people who believe that a public/private distinction is normatively justified and an important accountability tool are unlikely to be shaken in this belief by the observable facts that the line between state and non-state is blurred, and that the social universe is characterised by complex and interacting networks of accountability. Nor will the assertion that it is difficult to impose public law values on complex accountability networks convince them to abandon the attempt to do so and instead to be satisfied with judging the 'success' of such networks according to other criteria.

Assume for the sake of argument, then, that some version of the public/private distinction can provide an acceptable normative approach to accountability and

---

[85] *Ibid* at 59–60.

[86] A Davies, *Accountability: A Public Law Analysis of Government by Contract* (Oxford, 2001). Davies' approach is based on the idea of contract as a tool of governance as opposed to exchange. See also J Freeman, 'The Contracting State' (2000) 28 *Florida State ULR* 155. Failure to draw this distinction is identified by Julia Black as the basis of the refusal of courts to subject the exercise of contractual power to judicial review: Black, above n 82.

[87] Davies, above n 86, 185.

[88] P Vincent-Jones, 'Regulating Government by Contract: Towards a Public Law Framework?' (2002) 65 *MLR* 611, 619–20.

[89] For a general discussion see J Baldwin and G Davies, 'Empirical Research in Law' in P Cane and M Tushnet (eds), *The Oxford Handbook of Legal Studies* (Oxford University Press, 2003) ch 39.

control of social decision-making. This poses the thorny question of whether and how this binary distinction can operate in the face of institutional hybridisation, which is more suggestive of a continuum. The problem can be illustrated by considering the HRA again. The provisions of section 6 recognise and are premised on institutional (but not functional) hybridisation, yet the issue to which the section is addressed—whether or not an entity is under an obligation to respect Convention rights—is binary. Or consider the *Takeover Panel* case:[90] the Takeover Panel was a hybrid entity in the sense that it performed regulatory functions, but its functions were not underpinned by statute nor was it institutionally part of the state. But the question the court had to decide was binary—whether or not the Panel was amenable to the (public law) judicial review jurisdiction.

A suggestive perspective on this issue is provided by Gunther Teubner's use of the idea of 'polycontexturality'.[91] His discussion is particularly pertinent for present purposes because while Teubner thinks that the public/private distinction can no longer be understood in terms of a state/non-state institutional dichotomy, he rejects the conclusion that the distinction should therefore be rejected. Rather social life should be understood in terms of distinctive activities—such as education, journalism and medicine—which Teubner calls by various names including 'spaces of social autonomy'. In his view, the task of law is to regulate social activities by striking a balance between conflicting public and private interests and values in relation to particular activities. The mechanisms by which Teubner sees this happening are (1) the 'fragmentation' of 'private law'—producing, for instance, education law, journalism law and medical law; and (2) its transformation into a form of 'constitutional law' of social activities which, in relation to each particular activity, reflects a distinctive mix of public and private concerns. A concrete example might help to explain Teubner's rather abstract discussion. A common objection to contracting-out of the provision of 'public services' is that the doctrine of privity of contract may make it difficult for citizens to complain about service failures. This objection might be overcome by modifying the doctrine of privity in this context to take account of the public interest in the delivery of such services. In other contexts, by contrast, where there was no such public interest in the performance of contracts, the doctrine of privity might be maintained. The result would be the creation of a set of laws of contract moulded to the distinctive characteristics of particular social activities.

Although Teubner does not put it in these terms, we might understand him (unlike Black) as rejecting *both* an institutional *and* a functional public/private divide, but accepting what might be called a 'values-based' public/private distinction. He sets up a dichotomy between 'political activities oriented toward the public interest' and 'profit-oriented economic activities' and suggests that instead of thinking about 'spaces of social autonomy' in terms of a bipolar distinction between 'politics and economics' we should think in triangular terms of the relationship between these two 'rationalities' and activities that are simply 'social'

---

[90] See above n 33.
[91] G Teubner, 'After Privatization? The Many Autonomies of Private Law' [1998] *CLP* 393.

rather than 'public' or 'private.'[92] An attraction of this approach is that it makes clear the normative nature and the distributional implications of the public/private distinction; and in so doing, it helps to explain the continuing attraction of the distinction in the face of institutional and functional hybridisation. The approach is, of course, diametrically opposed to Oliver's (see pp 268–69 above). Her solution to hybridisation is to argue that a single set of values, neither public nor private, applies or should apply to all social activities. It is also diametrically opposed to the approach of those who argue that 'the private is the political' and that all human life should be viewed in social terms;[93] or conversely that all human action, in the political sphere as much as in the non-political, is motivated by self-interest and is, in that sense, private.[94]

Returning, then, to the question of whether a binary public/private distinction can operate in the face of institutional and functional hybridisation, Teubner's analysis would support a positive answer to this question. By positing a polarity between the individual and society, and by associating each pole with a distinct set of values relevant to the regulation and control of human activity, a normative, values-based binary public/private distinction can be maintained even if the public/private dichotomy is rejected as a way of understanding and classifying social institutions and social activities. There is some evidence that this is the direction in which the law is moving. Consider again the *Takeover Panel* case for instance. There the jurisdictional question of the amenability of the Panel to judicial review was decided on the basis of a binary public/private distinction. By contrast, the court made it clear that whether a judicial review application against the Panel would succeed was a discretionary matter to be decided flexibly and partly on the basis of the (hybrid) nature of the Panel and of its activities.[95]

In the context of judicial review of interpretations of rules by regulators, Julia Black pushes this approach further by arguing that all such interpretations should be reviewed on the basis of their 'rationality.' She recommends adoption of this standard of review as part of 'a united set of public and private law principles.'[96] This ground of review would certainly have the benefit of flexibility, allowing the court to take account of the many forms of hybridisation that characterise contemporary governance regimes. However, the concept of rationality needs to be informed by a set of values. As Black says, we need to look 'at the type of function being exercised' and ask 'what duties and responsibilities should accompany the exercise of such functions and to whom they should be owed, what degree of autonomy should those exercising them have and what degree of judicial supervision should be exercised over them.'[97] Those questions can be answered only on the

[92] See especially *ibid* at 402.

[93] This line of argument is particularly associated with legal realism and critical legal studies (Horwitz, above n 18; Mnookin, above n 68, at 1436–39). In the public law literature, civic republicanism tends in this direction.

[94] DA Farber and PP Frickey, *Law and Public Choice: A Critical Introduction* (Chicago, Chicago UP, 1991); Mnookin, above n 68, at 1434–36.

[95] P Cane, 'Self Regulation and Judicial Review' [1987] *CJQ* 324; Scott, above n 69, at 38–41.

[96] See above n 56, at 157.

[97] *Ibid.*

basis of a set of values. A public/private distinction provides one way of thinking about such values. As we might say, adopting Teubner's terminology, the 'rationality' of individual autonomy (or of 'the economic') is different from the 'rationality' of social co-operation (or of 'the political').[98] In this view, legal regulation requires the striking of a balance between the demands of these two rationalities in the context of particular social activities.

CONCLUSION

We began with the observation that there is a paradox in legal thinking about the public/private distinction. On the one hand, it is deeply embedded in the law, but on the other it is widely rejected as a way of understanding social life. We have examined legal regimes in which both institutional and functional public/private dichotomies play an important part. We have surveyed various criticisms of the public/private distinction all of which, in their different ways, either explicitly or implicitly rest on a rejection of binary opposition between public and private institutions, and public and private functions, or both, in favour of some concept of hybridity.

Building on Teubner's work, I have suggested a resolution of the paradox initially highlighted by arguing that rejection of an institutional or functional public/private dichotomy in favour of a concept of hybridity is not inconsistent with retaining a values-based binary public/private distinction. Such a distinction embodies a particular theory about the way power ought to be distributed in society and about the forms that accountability for the exercise of power should take. Pointing to the phenomenon of institutional and functional hybridity does not by itself undermine a values-based public/private approach to the legal regulation and control of power. To do this, what is needed instead is a competing normative theory of accountability.[99] It is not enough to say that it does not matter whether accountability mechanisms are 'public' or 'private', so long as they are 'effective' or 'successful', because effectiveness and success can only be judged in the light of a normative theory about the way power ought to be distributed.

In brief, the resolution of the paradox lies in the observation that the supporters and the opponents of the public/private distinction are talking about different

---

[98] Teubner does not explicitly associate individual autonomy with market rationality and community interest with political rationality, but the association seems to be implicit in his analysis. It is, nevertheless, problematic. Human rights are, on the whole, concerned with non-economic aspects of individual autonomy.

[99] John Braithwaite offers such a competing theory in his 'republican' reinterpretation of the doctrine of separation of powers as a normative principle equally applicable to all power regardless of whether it is public or private: 'On Speaking Softly and Carrying Big Sticks: Neglected Dimensions of a Republican Separation of Powers' (1997) 47 *U of Toronto LJ* 305. Andrew Clapham's and Dawn Oliver's projects (see pp 254–56 and 268–69 above respectively) may be similarly understood. Underlying such approaches is the idea that *power* should be controlled, whatever its nature or source. See also M Hunt, 'Constitutionalism and Contractualisation of Government in the United Kingdom' in M Taggart (ed), *The Province of Administrative Law* (Oxford University Press, 1997), ch 2. For a contrary view see Black, above n 82, at 29–30.

things. In the view of the opponents, the distinction misrepresents the way power is distributed and exercised; while according to its supporters, it embodies an attractive normative theory of the way power ought to be distributed and its exercise controlled.

11

Courts in a Multi-Layered Constitution

NICHOLAS BAMFORTH*

MANY OF THE legal consequences of the UK membership of the European Union are highly visible, as are those associated with the bringing into national law—via the Human Rights Act 1998—of the European Convention on Human Rights. Courts must 'disapply' legislation if it contravenes EC law,[1] and short of that must interpret the legislation as far as possible in the light of parallel rules of EC law.[2] Legislation may not be set aside for incompatibility with Convention rights, but a court can make a declaration of that incompatibility under section 4 of the 1998 Act, opening the way for the legislation to be amended. Meanwhile, section 3 contains an obligation, analogous to that in play in cases involving EC law, to interpret legislation compatibly with Convention rights so far as this is possible.[3] By contrast, 'disapplication' and declarations of incompatibility are not permitted outside of the EC law and Convention contexts, and ordinary common law rules of statutory interpretation apply.[4] Proportionality review—albeit using differently formulated tests—is used in cases involving EC law[5] or Convention rights,[6] but not—at least, officially—in other cases. Furthermore, distinctive tests are used—depending upon whether a case involves EC law, Convention rights, or the ordinary common law—when assessing whether a litigant has standing and whether a body is public in nature.[7] These various contrasts provide clear illustrations of the impact of what has been categorised—in the

---

* I should like to thank Peter Leyland and Gordon Anthony for their helpful comments concerning drafts of this chapter.

[1] *R v Secretary of State for Transport, ex p. Factortame(2)* [1991] 1 AC 603; *R v Secretary of State for Employment, ex p. Equal Opportunities Commission* [1995] 1 AC 1.

[2] Case C-106/89, *Marleasing v La Comercial* [1990] ECR I-4153.

[3] On s 3, see *Poplar Housing Association v Donoghue* [2002] QB 48, paras [75] & [76] (Lord Woolf LCJ); *R v A.* [2002] 1 AC 45, paras [44] (Lord Steyn) & [162] (Lord Hutton); but cf para [108] (Lord Hope); *Wilson v First County Trust Ltd (No 2)* [2002] QB 74; *Mendoza v Ghaidan* [2002] EWCA Civ 1533; C Gearty, 'Reconciling Parliamentary Democracy and Human Rights' (2002) 118 *LQR* 248.

[4] According to the common law, this may still give effect to fundamental rights: see : *R v Secretary of State for the Home Department, ex p. Leech (No 2)* [1994] QB 198, 209; *R v Secretary of State for Social Security, ex p. Joint Council for the Welfare of Immigrants* [1996] 4 All ER 385; *R v Lord Chancellor, ex p. Witham* [1998] QB 575; *R v Secretary of State for the Home Department, ex p. Simms* [1999] 3 WLR 328.

[5] See, eg, *R v Chief Constable of Sussex, ex p. International Trader's Ferry* [1999] 2 AC 418.

[6] See Section 2 below.

[7] See the Miles and Cane chapters in this volume.

introductory essay in this volume—as a 'multi-layered' constitution: that is, one which contains multiple, but inter-connected and sometimes overlapping 'European' and 'national' layers. For the remedies which may be awarded by courts, and the tests and standards which may or must be employed, vary depending upon whether an EC law point, a Convention right, or the ordinary common law—affected by neither of the aforementioned things—is in play. At 'national' level, devolution provides a further illustration of the operation of the 'multi-layered' constitution, given the differing powers conferred on courts—under the Scotland Act 1998, Government of Wales Act 1998 and Northern Ireland Act 1998—to police each set of devolved institutions.

This chapter is concerned not so much with the details of these illustrations, as with the background to them. What is it, constitutionally-speaking, that causes courts to act 'differently' in cases involving EC law, Convention rights, and ordinary common law, and how far can or should they do so? Consideration of these questions highlights the true complexity of the 'multi-layered' constitutional structure. It is unsurprising that the answers should vary depending upon whether EC law or the Convention is involved. However, analysis also reveals that the answers are either hotly contested (in the case of both questions, in the EC law context) or unclear (in relation to the second question, in the Convention context) and that they may, depending upon one's perspective, rest as much on one's understanding of the constitutional norms which prevail within the 'national' constitutional layer as on one's understanding of the rules of the two 'European' layers.[8] It would be impossible in a single chapter to deal comprehensively with every issue posed for courts by the existence of a 'multi-layered' constitution: and, given that devolution is analysed elsewhere in this volume,[9] the focus will be on the impact of EC law and Convention rights. The first section of the chapter will analyse the competing arguments surrounding the role of courts in relation to EC law and the European Communities Act 1972, and the second section will consider the Convention and the Human Rights Act 1998. The third section will explore the notion of 'spill over': that is, the possibility that EC law or the Convention may influence judicial interpretation of statutes or the common law in 'non-European' contexts. Given the dualist nature of the domestic legal system, the possibility of judicial reliance on 'European' legal norms in cases which do not involve EC law or Convention rights begs important questions concerning the role of the courts and of those norms.[10] It will be argued in the final section of the chapter that the views of analysts and judges concerning the issues canvassed in this introduction are often driven by considerations which need explicitly to be

---

[8]   One's characterisation of the constitutional role of national courts can have important implications for one's view of their ability to develop the common law by reference to EC law and the Convention: see G Anthony, *UK Public Law and European Law: The Dynamics of Legal Integration* (Oxford, Hart, 2002).

[9]   See the Hadfield and Cornes chapters in this volume.

[10]   Particularly in the public law field, given the ambitious judicial development which has occurred following the creation of the application for judicial review procedure in 1977: see the essays collected in C Forsyth (ed), *Judicial Review and the Constitution* (Oxford, Hart, 2000).

built into theoretical accounts of the role of courts in public law cases. In a 'multi-layered' constitutional structure, such accounts will otherwise be incomplete.

THE RECEPTION OF EC LAW WITHIN THE UNITED KINGDOM

There is still considerable uncertainty—from the perspective of UK law—about why, exactly, courts should accord priority to rules of EC law where these are in conflict with provisions of domestic law, and about the circumstances—if any—in which national legislation which defies the requirements of EC law might nonetheless be given effect by the courts. It can therefore be said that while the *existence* of overriding EC law norms demonstrates that multiple layers are present within the contemporary constitution, it remains to be definitively confirmed *how* those layers inter-relate. Some accounts locate the answer within national law; some do so by reference to the requirements of EC law; and some employ a combination of norms of EC and national law. One's view of the nature and shape of the multi-layered constitution will depend—in the EC law context—upon which account one favours. Indeed, the contemporary constitution might appear to be *more* or *less* multi-layered depending upon the account adopted. For this reason, the divergent accounts will form the main focus of this section of the chapter.[11]

The first group of accounts focuses mainly or entirely upon national law. The three accounts falling within this group differ in terms of whether they regard the force of EC law at national level as being attributable mainly or entirely to the actions of Parliament or to the courts, and as to whether—if the answer lies with the courts—that answer can be categorised as political or legal in nature. The first account maintains that the overriding force given to norms of EC law by national courts is the result of Parliament's intentions as expressed in the European Communities Act 1972, which incorporated EC law at national level. Section 2(4) specifies that 'any enactment passed or to be passed ... shall be construed and have effect subject to the foregoing provisions of this section'. This refers back, crucially, to section 2(1), which allows relevant elements of EC law—including, by implication, EC law supremacy[12] and direct effect[13]—to be 'recognised and available in [national] law, and be enforced, allowed and followed accordingly'. Meanwhile, section 3 directs national courts to take judicial notice of the decisions of the European Court of Justice. In *R. v Secretary of State for Transport, ex p. Factortame(2)*,

---

[11] Only one of the accounts to be considered—that developed by Laws LJ in *Thoburn v Sunderland City Council* [2002] EWHC 195 Admin, [2002] 3 WLR 247—has explicit judicial support, in the form of his Lordship's own judgment in that case. Given the controversial nature of this account (see n 33 below), together with the constitutional magnitude of the debate, it is submitted that this cannot be conclusive of the matter. For a contrasting approach to questions considered in this chapter, see A O'Neill 'Fundamental Rights and the Constitutional Supremacy of Community Law in the United Kingdom after Devolution and the Human Rights Act' [2002] *PL* 724.

[12] Case 6/64, *Costa v ENEL* [1964] ECR 585.

[13] Case 26/62, *van Gend en Loos v Nederlandse Administratie der Belastigen* [1963] ECR 1; Case 41/74, *Van Duyn v Home Office* [1974] ECR 1337.

Lord Bridge used the 1972 Act in order to justify his conclusion that national statutes which were inconsistent with EC law must be 'disapplied' by the courts.[14] According to Lord Bridge:

> If the supremacy within the European Community of Community law over the national law of member states was not always inherent in the E.E.C. Treaty ... it was certainly well established in the jurisprudence of the European Court of Justice long before the United Kingdom joined the Community. Thus, whatever limitation of its sovereignty Parliament accepted when it enacted the European Communities Act 1972 was entirely voluntary. Under the terms of the Act of 1972 it has always been clear that it was the duty of a United Kingdom court, when delivering final judgment, to override any rule of national law found to be in conflict with any directly enforceable rule of Community law. Similarly, when decisions of the European Court of Justice have exposed areas of United Kingdom statute law which failed to implement Council directives, Parliament has always loyally accepted the obligation to make appropriate and prompt amendments. Thus there is nothing in any way novel in according supremacy to rules of Community law in those areas to which they apply and to insist that, in the protection of rights under Community law, national courts must not be inhibited by rules of national law from granting interim relief in appropriate cases is no more than a logical recognition of that supremacy.[15]

The suggestion that Lord Bridge explained the overriding force of EC law by reference to factors within the national constitutional layer—in particular Parliament's intentions—has been articulated by Sir Neil MacCormick (among others).[16] For the essence of the passage cited above is that Parliament has managed to bind *itself.* Lord Bridge did not go on to say whether this was a situation which was unique to the European Communities Act 1972, or but one example of a broader range of situations in which it might be possible for Parliament to do such a thing. As Paul Craig has suggested, Lord Bridge's judgment is open to a variety of interpretations, each of which has different implications for our analysis of the relationship between Parliament and the courts.[17] A narrower reading would suggest that the 1972 Act had unique effects, based upon the reception into domestic law—via section 2—of the unique EC law principles of supremacy and direct effect. In consequence, courts should read future statutes subject to the 1972 Act, possibly— although this is not settled—unless those statutes made it sufficiently clear that they were departing from the requirements of EC law. A broader reading would suggest that courts may now, as a general matter, depart from pre-existing constitutional norms whenever the intentions of Parliament are clear enough. Normatively, this reading rests on the assumption that the constitutional justifications for the existence of a legally sovereign national Parliament—as that term was traditionally

---

[14] N 1 above.

[15] N 1 above, 658–9.

[16] According to Sir Neil MacCormick, the House of Lords sought to explain its decision in *Factortame(2)* by reference to norms of domestic law *alone*: *Questioning Sovereignty: Law, State, and Nation in the European Commonwealth* (Oxford, OUP, 1999), pp 99–102; see also TRS Allan, 'Parliamentary Sovereignty: Law, Politics, and Revolution' (1997) 113 *LQR* 443, 445, 448.

[17] See further PP Craig, 'Sovereignty of the United Kingdom Parliament after *Factortame*' (1991) *YBEL* 221, 251–5.

understood—no longer exist.[18] However, other than the inference that Parliament's intentions must be clear enough, Lord Bridge's judgment *itself* offers us no real guidance as to when courts might use this broader reading to justify departing from pre-existing norms of constitutional law.

The second account—developed by Sir William Wade—categorises the recognition that EC law has overriding force as the political response of national courts to the reality of EU membership. Wade describes the decision in *Factortame(2)* as 'a revolutionary change',[19] which he explains—at least, at an analytical level—solely in terms of the behaviour of national courts.[20] He suggests that the rule whereby courts give effect to the most recently enacted statute of the Westminster Parliament regardless of the wording of any earlier statute concerning the same subject matter—part of the long-standing 'rule of recognition' in English law—has always been in the keeping of the courts. It is 'a rule of unique character, since only the judges can change it. It is for the judges, and not for Parliament, to say what is an effective Act of Parliament'.[21] If judges recognise that there should be a change, this is a technical 'revolution': something which happens 'when the judges, faced with a novel situation, elect to depart from the familiar rules for the sake of political necessity …. the rule of recognition is itself a political fact which the judges themselves are able to change when they are confronted with a new situation that so demands'.[22] This, according to Wade, is exactly what happened in *Factortame(2)*. Indeed, Wade suggests, Lord Bridge took it for granted that Parliament was able to bind its successors:[23] a possibility which, on his analysis, was presumably always inherent given the nature of the rule of recognition.[24]

The third account—articulated by Laws LJ in *Thoburn v Sunderland C.C.*—also explains the decision in *Factortame(2)* by reference to the role of national courts, but does so in legal rather than political terms. In his judgment in *Thoburn*, Laws LJ accepted a conclusion which was implicit in *Factortame(2)*: namely that the European Communities Act 1972 is not open to implied repeal.[25] *Factortame(2)* was, Laws LJ suggested, concerned with the primacy of substantive provisions of EC law. In *Thoburn*, by contrast, the court was concerned to identify 'the legal *foundation* within which those substantive provisions enjoy their primacy, and by which the relation between the law and institutions of the EU law and the British State ultimately rests'.[26] Laws LJ suggested that this foundation was domestic constitutional law, specifically the common law. For:

---

[18] Craig, n 17 above, pp 251–4.

[19] Wade & Forsyth, *Administrative Law* (8th edn, Oxford, OUP, 2000), p 28.

[20] Wade seems to rest his analysis on the consequences of Lord Bridge's reasoning in *Factortame(2)*—the possibility of 'disapplication' of a post-1972 statute—rather than on its content. For this reason, it is appropriate to analyse it separately from Lord Bridge's own explanation.

[21] Sir William Wade, 'Sovereignty—Revolution or Evolution?' (1996) 112 *LQR* 568, 574.

[22] N 21 above, 574.

[23] N 21 above, 573.

[24] See Wade's 'The Basis of Legal Sovereignty' [1955] *CLJ* 172, esp pp 187–192.

[25] N 11 above, paras [61], [68] and [69].

[26] N 11 above, para [66].

The common law has in recent years allowed, or rather created, exceptions to the doctrine of implied repeal .... There are now classes or types of legislative provision which cannot be repealed by mere implication. These instances are given, and can only be given, by our own courts, to which the scope and nature of Parliamentary sovereignty are ultimately confided. The courts may say—have said—that there are certain circumstances in which the legislature may only enact what it desires to enact if it does so by express, or at any rate specific, provision. The courts have in effect so held in the field of European law itself, in the *Factortame* case.[27]

Laws LJ argued that this turned on the common law's recognition of a hierarchy of statutes. 'Ordinary' statutes were open to implied as well as express repeal; 'constitutional' statutes, including the 1972 Act, were only open to express repeal. Laws LJ suggested that a 'constitutional' statute was one which '(a) conditions the legal relationship between citizen and State in some general, overarching manner, or (b) enlarges or diminishes the scope of what we would now regard as fundamental constitutional rights'.[28] Due to the legal development represented by this recognition, the 1972 Act was a 'constitutional' statute, immune from implied repeal,[29] and EC law could be recognised as having overriding force for this reason.

The significance—for our purposes—of these three accounts is that they explain the decision in *Factortame(2)* by reference primarily to the powers of institutions at *national* level. Those 'multi-layered' aspects of the contemporary constitution which can be associated with British membership of the EU are seen as resulting—constitutionally-speaking—from the actions of the Westminster Parliament and/or the national courts. For Wade, the decisive event appears to have been the response of the national judiciary to a significant political development, namely accession to the EU. Obviously, the fact of accession depended—historically speaking—on the actions of the executive and Parliament, but for Wade, the key constitutional moment came in the House of Lords' decision in *Factortame(2)*. This reflects Wade's long-standing view that Parliamentary Sovereignty can only be shed if the *courts* recognise, as a political matter, that this is the case. This might be triggered either by the overthrow of the governing institutions of a state, or by a more technical change such as the passage of a statute which triggers a unique judicial response.[30] The 'revolution' in the EC context is of the second variety, but—according to Wade—might encourage 'revolutionary' judicial behaviour in other contexts. It is, he suggests, now 'guesswork' to predict whether other limitations on sovereignty might be possible, and that sovereignty is—as a result of *Factortame(2)*—'now a freely adjustable commodity whenever

---

[27] N 11 above, para [60]. More broadly, Laws LJ talked, in the same paragraph, of it being the responsibility of the courts to develop (as a legal matter) the 'scope and nature' of Parliamentary Sovereignty—echoing his extra-judicial view in 'Law and Democracy', [1995] *PL* 72 at 85–8.

[28] N 11 above, para [62]. Laws LJ suggested *obiter* that examples of such statutes, apart from the 1972 Act, included the Magna Carta, the Bill of Rights 1689, the Acts of Union 1707, the Human Rights Act 1998, the Scotland Act 1998 and the Government of Wales Act 1998.

[29] N 11 above, para [63]. The contrast between 'legal' and 'political' developments and responses developed in this and preceding paragraphs is, of course, open to attack from a realist standpoint.

[30] N 24 above, esp at 187–92.

Parliament chooses to accept some limitation.'[31] According to Lord Bridge's own reasoning in *Factortame(2)*, by contrast, the House of Lords was merely *responding* in legal terms to a decisive event which had already occurred, namely Parliament's decision to pass the 1972 Act. Lord Bridge was thus keen to stress that the House of Lords was carrying out Parliament's will, unusual though the practical consequences may have been in relation to the traditional operation of Parliamentary Sovereignty. Craig shares Lord Bridge's view that the House of Lords was responding to Parliament's legislative initiative,[32] but appears to favour what was described above as a broader reading of Lord Bridge's judgment. In consequence, he seems to be in implicit agreement with Wade that courts may be able to recognise the existence of *other* constraints on Parliamentary Sovereignty, especially in the area of fundamental rights. For Craig, however, the reason for this lies *not* in the assertion that there has been a 'revolution', but rather—as noted above—in the fact that the underpinning constitutional justification for the continued existence of a legally sovereign Parliament may no longer exist. Craig's analysis thus focuses on the consistency of the contemporary constitutional architecture—at national level and viewed in the round—rather than on the specific assertion that *courts* may now be free to recognise further constraints on the Westminster Parliament.

Laws LJ's analysis in *Thoburn* has attracted critical comment,[33] and it can certainly be said—quite apart from the lack of authority cited in the judgment—that the reasoning may not be entirely consistent with Sir John's own previously stated extra-judicial views.[34] Nonetheless, it provides an important comparison with Wade's and Lord Bridge's accounts, given that it might well be felt to fall somewhere between the two. A key similarity with Lord Bridge's account is that both explain the overriding force of EC law as the result of a *legal* development at national level. Nonetheless, the two differ in that Laws LJ related his account to the role of the courts, whilst Lord Bridge placed decisive weight on the legal consequences of Parliament's actions in 1972. A second similarity is that under either approach, relevant provisions of the 1972 Act would still seem to be open to express repeal. Laws LJ stated in *Thoburn* that if a provision of EC law 'was seen to be repugnant to a fundamental or constitutional right guaranteed by the law of England, a question would arise whether the general words of the ECA [1972] were sufficient to incorporate the measure and give it overriding effect in domestic law'.[35] In other words, the status of EC law, resting—as it did for Laws LJ—on domestic common law, was not absolute, leading him to conclude that his

---

[31] N 21 above, 575 & 573. At 575, Wade suggests that it might be possible for courts to decide that Parliament can voluntarily limit its sovereignty at any time; or that accession to the EC was a unique legal event; or, as a middle course, that certain legal provisions—for example, those relating to fundamental rights—are capable of entrenchment, while others are not.

[32] N 17 above, pp 252–3.

[33] See, eg, G Marshall, 'Metric Martyrs and martyrdom by Henry VIII clause' (2002) 118 *LQR* 493.

[34] In 'Law and Democracy', n 27 above, 84–9, Sir John argues that the common law now recognises various examples of 'higher-order law'. *However*, he goes on to state that while section 2(4) of the European Communities Act 1972 is not open to implied repeal, this is because power has been devolved by Parliament to the EU, *not* because of 'higher-order law' analysis.

[35] N 11 above, para [69].

approach gave 'full weight' to the 'supremacy of *substantive* Community law' as well as to the supremacy of the United Kingdom Parliament, vouchsafed by the common law: reflecting the general responsibility of the courts to strike such a balance.[36]

Despite Lord Bridge's rather different reasoning in *Factortame(2)*, it seems plausible to suggest that he might reach a similar conclusion concerning a post-1972 statute which was explicitly incompatible with EC law, given that his judgment rested on the proposition that Parliament's specific intention in passing the 1972 Act must be deemed to take priority over Parliament's intentions as stipulated in other statutes—a proposition which might allow for a statute which was expressed with sufficient specificity to displace the 1972 Act.[37] In this respect, both Lord Bridge's and Laws LJ's accounts stand in stark contrast to Wade's. For given that, according to Wade, there has already been a 'revolution', with the House of Lords allying itself to the *political* reality of Britain's membership of the EU, it is uncertain what would be sufficient—empirically-speaking—to trigger a judicial 'counter-revolution'. Would an express repeal of the European Communities Act 1972 be enough, for example? Indeed, would anything be sufficient, given that— according to Wade—we now live in a constitutional world that is so unpredictable that we are effectively left to guess what new limitations on Parliamentary Sovereignty the courts may impose? The inability of Wade's account to provide any normative basis for assessing such points is perhaps its crucial weakness as a legal theory: the blunt assertion that courts are making essentially 'political' decisions when fundamental constitutional questions arise leaves us—as a matter of logic— with nothing to fall back on, at least in terms of orthodox legal analysis, when assessing what courts *ought* to do.

A further question concerns the potential for practical overlap between Lord Bridge's and Laws LJ's explanations. It is clear that, unlike Wade, both are content to tie their accounts to the law itself—not unsurprisingly, since both accounts form part of judgments delivered in actual cases. As some of the comments made by both judges might imply, however, it may sometimes be difficult *in practice* to delineate an exact distinction between the respective roles of the courts and Parliament—even though each account appears to presuppose that such a distinction can be drawn. This difficulty might, in fact, echo broader constitutional arguments concerning the relationship between Parliament and the courts. Perhaps the most prominent is Sir Stephen Sedley's extra-judicial assertion that the emergence of a powerful regime of judicial review in the late twentieth century might mean that:

> we have today ... a new and still emerging constitutional paradigm, no longer of Dicey's supreme parliament to which the rule of law must finally bend, but of a bi-polar sovereignty of the Crown in Parliament and the Crown in its courts, to each of which the Crown's ministers are answerable—politically to Parliament, legally to the courts.[38]

---

[36] N 11 above, para [70].

[37] It seems likely that this would require express repeal, but this is not absolutely certain.

[38] Human Rights: a Twenty-First Century Agenda' [1995] *PL* 386, 389. Sedley J (as he then was)

Perhaps less radically, it can be asserted that any legislation passed by Parliament in a common law system depends, by definition, upon the judiciary for its practical interpretation and application. In consequence, whilst it may be necessary for the sake of constitutional clarity to distinguish between the role of Parliament and that of the courts when explaining the overriding effect of EC law—not least, given the consequences which the theory adopted may have for the circumstances (if any) in which Parliament might be free to ignore the requirements of EC law—it may well be that the recognition of such effect operates, in practice, as a co-operative venture.

From the standpoint of the accounts considered so far—two of which, it should perhaps be reiterated, have been advanced by national judges as part of their judgments in cases—it seems clear that the priority to be accorded to EC law depends upon one's interpretation of domestic constitutional considerations. However, two further explanations of the overriding role of EC law have a rather different focus. The first is effectively the antithesis of the arguments so far considered, given that it seeks to tie the overriding effect of EC law overwhelmingly to the requirements of EC law *itself*.[39] This approach starts by stressing the unique nature of EC law. When explaining its recognition of direct effect in *van Gend en Loos*, the European Court of Justice stated that 'the Community constitutes a new legal order of international law for the benefit of which the states have limited their sovereign rights, albeit within limited fields …'.[40] The Court reiterated and expanded upon this argument in *Costa v ENEL* when proclaiming the principle of EC law supremacy: 'By contrast with ordinary international treaties', the Court asserted, 'the EEC Treaty has created its own legal system which, on the entry into force of the Treaty, became an integral part of the legal systems of the Member States and which their courts are bound to apply'.[41]

In consequence, while the European Communities Act 1972 acted as the mechanism by which EC law norms were brought into the UK, historically-speaking, the unique nature of those norms—as demonstrated in *van Gend* and *Costa*—was such that EC law was permanently entrenched in domestic law, rather than merely incorporated. It follows from this argument that severe constraints were thereby placed on the freedom of action of the Westminster Parliament. The 1972 Act could not be impliedly repealed—for the principles of EC law would disallow this—and, while the Act was in theory open to express repeal should Britain wish to leave the EC, practical obstacles might still be placed in the path of this course of action given that any withdrawal would need, logically, to be conducted in accordance with the rules of EC law. Since the EC Treaty contains no explicit provision allowing for unilateral withdrawal by a member state, an inter-governmental

suggested in *R v Parliamentary Commissioner for Standards, ex p. Fayed* [1997] COD 376 that Parliamentary privilege rested on 'a mutuality of respect between two constitutional sovereignties'—a point approved by Lord Woolf MR when the case reached the Court of Appeal: [1998] 1 WLR 669, 670.

[39] This argument would effectively be a more radical version of that put forward by the respondents—and rejected by Laws LJ—in *Thoburn v Sunderland City Council*, n 11 above, paras [53–7].

[40] N 13 above, 12.

[41] N 12 above, 593–4.

conference would probably need to be convened to renegotiate the Treaty to allow for any withdrawal—a possibility which could not be guaranteed, politically-speaking. From this standpoint, any Parliamentary attempt unilaterally to withdraw from the EC without renegotiation of the Treaty might therefore be subject to legal challenge based upon the dictates of the Treaty itself.

Straightforward though this approach is—not least because of its apparent consistency with the jurisprudence of the Court of Justice—it is open to criticism because it considers only half the picture, constitutionally-speaking. For, as Sir Neil MacCormick has argued, if the reception of EC law into the domestic legal systems of Member States is initially mediated via the rules of national constitutional law—in the UK, by the passage of the European Communities Act 1972—it is unclear why those rules should not *continue* to have a decisive effect until the Member State has clearly left the EU.[42] This criticism forms part of MacCormick's broader theory, which constitutes the second explanation referred to above. MacCormick suggests that the reception of EC law into domestic law involves an 'interlocking of legal systems, with mutual recognition of each other's validity, but with different grounds for that recognition'.[43] For the European Court of Justice, the overriding quality of EC law at national level derives—as the theory considered above suggests—from the nature of Community law itself, as the Court's decisions in *Van Gend en Loos* and *Costa* demonstrate. In MacCormick's words, EC law is—for the Court—'a distinct legal system of a new type ... that enjoys "primacy" or "supremacy" over the laws of the Member States'.[44] From this standpoint, the 'ultimate power of interpretation' of the powers 'transferred' to the EU by the Member States, and of the nature of the Member States' obligations, lies with the Court.[45] For national courts, *by contrast*, 'the ultimate validating ground' for the superior force of EC law 'is found in domestic constitutional law'.[46] MacCormick suggests that this standpoint is clearly evident in *Factortame(2)*, in Lord Bridge's assertion that the *Westminster Parliament* must have intended EC law to have overriding force at domestic level, given that it was *aware* of the nature of EC law when it passed the European Communities Act 1972.[47] MacCormick argues that

> [f]rom the Lords' point of view ... the reason for the binding character of Community law is the provision of domestic constitutional law that made valid the acceptance of Community membership and Community law through accession to the relevant treaties.[48]

---

[42] MacCormick, n 16 above, p 116 ff; see also Sir John Laws' analogous basis for refuting this argument in *Thoburn*: n 11 above, paras [58–9].

[43] MacCormick, n 16 above, p 102.

[44] MacCormick, n 16 above, p 94.

[45] *Ibid.*

[46] MacCormick, n 16 above, p 101. Conceptually, this is an aspect of the 'competence-competence' problem found in many Member States: see MacCormick's comparative analysis, n 16 above, pp 99–102.

[47] MacCormick, n 16 above, pp 94 and 100. Contrast this, however, with the 1971 Command Paper *The United Kingdom and the European Communities*, Cmnd 4715, paras 29 & 31.

[48] MacCormick, n 16 above, p 101.

A key difference between this argument and the other theories analysed so far is that MacCormick seeks to explain the relationship between EC law and national law in a way which is coherent in terms of the basic constitutional norms of *each*. MacCormick categorises his argument as 'pluralistic': he believes that EC law and national law are analytically distinct and partially independent legal orders, but that they overlap and interact in practice.[49] Analytically, the relationship between the two cannot be categorised as hierarchical. On the one hand, alterations in the constitutional powers of the EU institutions depend upon treaty-making *between* the Member States at international level. Furthermore, any amendment to the EC treaties will only take effect if it is passed into the national law of each Member State using the procedure *internal* to the Member State in question, in the same way that each Member State must amend its existing constitutional rules on joining the EU so as to allow EC law—including the principles of direct effect and EC law supremacy—to operate at national level.[50] On the other hand, considered in its *own* right, the EC's legal order is:

> neither conditional upon the validity of any particular state's constitution, nor upon the sum of the conditions that the states might impose, for that would be no Community at all. It would amount to no more than a bundle of overlapping laws to the extent that each state chose to acknowledge 'Community' laws and obligations.[51]

This characterisation of the relationship between the EC and national systems has a crucial practical consequence. For, as MacCormick points out, if each system ultimately has its own internal constitutional point of reference, the highest national court and the Court of Justice need not produce identical answers to the question whether an individual Member State might unilaterally secede from the EU. MacCormick believes that Lord Bridge's judgment in *Factortame(2)* can best be explained in these terms. The implication of Lord Bridge's reasoning is, MacCormick suggests, that 'the supremacy of Community law and with it the interpretative competence' of the Court of Justice will be upheld by domestic courts *so long as* the Westminster Parliament is content for Britain to remain within the EC.[52] If Westminster changed its mind and chose to withdraw Britain unilaterally from the EU, this would 'be valid in the perspective of UK law, whatever the Community organs might ... think, say, or do'.[53]

MacCormick's is the one theory—of those we have explored—that might be described as truly 'multi-layered' in nature. For MacCormick recognises that there may be overlapping, and possibly divergent, centres of constitutional gravity for courts in cases which involve EC law points.[54] It follows from this, although

---

[49]   MacCormick, n 16 above, p 119; for different versions of pluralism, see pp 117–21.

[50]   MacCormick, n 16 above, pp 117–9.

[51]   MacCormick, n 16 above, p 118.

[52]   MacCormick, n 16 above, p 100.

[53]   *Ibid*; see also the rather more vague formulation, below, p 94.

[54]   For a subtly different but analogous account of *Factortame(2)*, see TRS Allan, 'Parliamentary Sovereignty: Law, Politics, and Revolution' (1997) 113 *LQR* 443, 445–6. In relation to the EC level, see KJ Alter, *Establishing the Supremacy of European Law: The Making of an International Rule of Law in Europe* (Oxford, OUP, 2001), pp 52–63.

MacCormick does not develop the point at length, that a pluralist account would enable us to explain the effect of the European Communities Act 1972 and the *Factortame* litigation in a way which avoids talk of 'constitutional statutes' or 'revolutionary' switches in judicial allegiance. A key aspect of pluralist accounts is the recognition that the Court of Justice and national courts can operate with divergent points of constitutional reference. A pluralist could therefore maintain that while the outcome in *Factortame(2)* was, from the standpoint of the Court of Justice, a logical consequence of the application of the fundamental EC law principles of supremacy and direct effect (interpreted, by the Court, as deriving from the treaties), from the standpoint of the House of Lords it was—by contrast—a logical consequence of the drafting of the 1972 Act. Since domestic courts cannot recognise international treaties without an appropriate incorporating measure (on a standard dualist analysis)[55] sections 2 and 3 of the 1972 Act serve—for domestic courts—as the bridge across which the relevant EC law principles must cross in order to be enforceable and overriding at national level. The apparent immunity of the 1972 Act from implied repeal is therefore explained by the fact that sections 2 and 3 are drafted in such a way as to allow EC law to pass into national law with binding status in national courts, given that EC law—by its own lights—must take priority over national law. However, a unilateral British withdrawal from the EU would, as MacCormick claims, be upheld by domestic courts if it involved the express repeal of sections 2 and 3: for this would remove the means of access into domestic law of direct effect and supremacy, as well as of the judgments of the Court of Justice.[56] The Court could pronounce all it liked on the legitimacy of UK withdrawal *viewed from the standpoint of EC law*, but with sections 2 and 3 removed from the picture this need have no influence on domestic courts. It would be at this point, rather than at the stage at which Wade views it as necessary, that it would become appropriate to talk of the resolution of the dispute as turning on political factors.

MacCormick's argument is supported, at a general level, by Gordon Anthony's analysis of the reception of EC law and Convention rights into national law. Anthony argues that the 'dynamics of legal integration'—whether this involves the reception of EC law or Convention rights within domestic law—'are finally mediated by internal institutional considerations',[57] even though 'judicial recourse to those considerations is often prompted by the "external" dynamic of European law'.[58] A court's view concerning the proper ambit of its power as an institution of the *national* constitutional order will, in other words, have crucial implications for

---

[55] See, eg, *Maclaine Watson v Department of Trade and Industry* [1990] 2 AC 418, 476–7 (Lord Templeman).

[56] In principle, the question whether an act of express repeal would be required (implied repeal being insufficient) should turn on judicial interpretation. However, the matter appears to have been settled by the result in *Factortame(2)*. A post-1972 statute (the Merchant Shipping Act 1988) which appeared, without expressly saying so, to disregard the priority given to rules of EC law by sections 2 and 3 of the 1972 Act was effectively set aside by reference to those rules and the earlier Act.

[57] N 8 above, p 180. See also below, pp 12–15.

[58] N 8 above, p 47.

its evaluation of the legal legitimacy of governmental (or, if appropriate, legislative) action by reference to norms of EC law and Convention rights. Those norms have sometimes been taken by national courts to require an *adjustment* in national practices or in the relative freedom to act of different national institutions, but such adjustments tend ultimately to be made by reference to the pre-existing constitutional order at national level. This has allowed national courts, to date, to afford practical primacy to EC law—as in *Factortame(2)*—even though continued judicial reliance on constitutional orthodoxy has limited the extent to which EC law has become integrated at national level.[59] Anthony criticises this orthodoxy in normative terms, but his evaluation of existing judicial approaches would seem to allow for the possibility—in an extreme case such as unilateral British withdrawal from the EU—that national courts and the Court of Justice might arrive at different conclusions given their respective points of constitutional reference.

It has been argued in this section of the chapter that a variety of explanations can be advanced for the overriding influence of EC law before national courts. Some accounts tie the phenomenon to the national layer, although there is scope for disagreement as to the role of different institutions within this layer and the extent to which it might be possible for a member state unilaterally to disobey the requirements of EC law. Other accounts, by contrast, tie the phenomenon either to the nature of EC law itself, or to the interaction between the national and EC layers. Again, these accounts offer divergent views concerning the possibility that a member state might disobey the norms of EC law: for example, by unilateral withdrawal from the EU. It should be added that just as there might in practice be an overlap between the arguments advanced by Lord Bridge and Laws LJ concerning the roles of the courts and Parliament at national level, accounts which root the overriding power of EC law in the roles of institutions at national level need not be seen as inherently incompatible with MacCormick's 'pluralist' analysis. For the accounts which we have analysed tend to ignore pluralist analysis rather than to rebut it. The merits and demerits of the various accounts have been canvassed in this section of the chapter. The crucial point, in terms of our analysis of the 'multi-layered' constitution, is that each account offers a differing picture of the relationship between the national and EC layers (and, in many cases, of the role of institutions at national level), and that the variety of accounts which exist demonstrates the uncertainty which still surrounds our understanding of the multi-layered constitution in the context of EC law—whichever account one ultimately favours. One's understanding of the multi-layered constitution will therefore vary according to the account adopted. The reception of the Convention into national law, by contrast, involves a rather different set of considerations, which will be considered in the next section of the chapter.

---

[59] See also n 8 above, chs 3 & 4, esp pp 73–4.

THE HUMAN RIGHTS ACT 1998 AND THE COURTS

The decision of the House of Lords in *R. (Daly) v Secretary of State for the Home Department* provides a powerful illustration of the influence of the jurisprudence of the Court of Human Rights in domestic judicial review since the entry into force of the Human Rights Act.[60] For the House of Lords explicitly recognised that proportionality was now, in Lord Steyn's words, 'applicable in respect of review where [C]onvention rights are at stake'.[61] In reaching a similar conclusion, Lord Cooke relied heavily on the fact that the Strasbourg Court had condemned the *Wednesbury* standard of review in *Smith v United Kingdom* as offering inadequate protection to Convention rights, thereby violating the Article 13 right to an effective remedy.[62] A further illustration of the role of the Convention can be seen in *Porter v Magill*, where the House of Lords amended the standard of review for bias so as to give proper weight to Article 6.[63]

It would be wrong, however, to think that Convention rights—or decisions of the Strasbourg Court concerning those rights—have the same overriding significance at national level as do norms of EC law. This is due to the nature of the Convention and the drafting of the Human Rights Act. The Convention is binding on signatory states as a matter of international law, and the Strasbourg Court seeks to prescribe the minimum acceptable standards for the protection of Convention rights at national level.[64] Unlike norms of EC law, however, the Convention's reception within the domestic legal system of *any* signatory state turns to a considerable degree on the nature of the mechanism used in that state for bringing the Convention into national law.[65] The Convention contains no principles of supremacy or direct effect: unlike EC law, it has the authority at national level of a standard international treaty. In consequence, when giving effect to Convention rights via the 1998 Act, courts have been concerned not so much with the nature of the relationship between the European and national layers—the question which appears ultimately to be crucial when considering the limits of the courts' powers

[60] [2001] UKHL 26; [2001] 2 WLR 1622.

[61] N 60 above, para [27]. This begs two questions. The first is whether proportionality should be seen as a ground of review in its own right, in the manner of 'illegality' or 'procedural impropriety'. Doubt may be cast on this by the fact that, technically, the proportionality test is merely a *part of* a court's assessment of whether a public authority has violated its statutory duty under s 6(1) of the 1998 Act to act compatibly with Convention rights. Paul Craig categorises s 6 simply as creating a new head of illegality (*Administrative Law* (4th edn, London, Sweet & Maxwell, 1999), pp 556–7). The second is whether it is consistent with the Strasbourg case law for domestic courts to employ proportionality when determining whether an 'unqualified' Convention right has been violated: see further R Clayton and H Tomlinson, *The Law of Human Rights* (Oxford, OUP, 2000), paras 6.86–6.91, 6.123–6.147A.

[62] N 60 above, para [32], referring to *Smith v United Kingdom* (2000) 29 EHRR 493. As *Daly* demonstrates, the fact that Article 13 is not included in the list of Convention rights brought into English law by the 1998 Act (see s 1 and schedule 1) has not affected the ability of domestic courts, using s 2, to draw upon relevant Strasbourg case law.

[63] [2001] UKHL 67, [2002] 2 WLR 37.

[64] *Handyside v United Kingdom* (1976) 1 EHRR 737, paras 47–9.

[65] See C Gearty (ed), *European Civil Liberties and the European Convention on Human Rights: A Comparative Study* (The Hague, Martinus Nijhoff, 1997), chs 2 to 8.

in the EC law context—but with the degree of priority to be accorded to Convention rights *as they understand them and relative to* competing considerations inherent in the 1998 Act and in the domestic constitutional order more broadly.[66] One obvious consideration is that the drafting of the Act makes clear that there are limits to how far national courts may apply Convention rights.[67] According to sections 3 and 4, legislation must be interpreted so far as possible in the light of Convention rights, but must be applied as it stands if it is incompatible with them[68]—the court's only option in such a case being to consider whether to issue a declaration of incompatibility. This position is reinforced by the susceptibility of section 2(1)—which requires courts to 'take into account' relevant Strasbourg case law, but only in so far as they regard it is as 'relevant to the proceedings' in hand—to flexible interpretation.

The existence of competing considerations is evident in the Human Rights Act case law to date. In cases such as *Daly* and *Porter v Magill*, the House of Lords was content to amend the relevant standards of judicial review. As creations of the common law, such standards have always been open to judicial development, but the Human Rights Act provided the necessary impetus. Section 2(1) allowed the House of Lords to take full account of the Strasbourg case law, which appeared to require the developments concerned. Furthermore, those developments were not felt by the House of Lords to take judicial review impermissibly into territory traditionally reserved for elected bodies. In the *Alconbury* case, by contrast, Lord Hoffmann was concerned to avoid reaching a conclusion—based on a wide reading of Article 6—which would be 'undemocratic' in the sense that it would involve courts in reviewing the merits of specialist decisions, something which would go beyond their accepted constitutional role in judicial review.[69] Lord Hoffmann also suggested that since section 2(1) did not expressly bind national courts to follow Strasbourg decisions:

> if I thought ... that they compelled a conclusion fundamentally at odds with the distribution of powers under the British constitution, I would have considerable doubt as to whether they should be followed.[70]

More broadly, the idea of judicial restraint clearly underpins the notion of the 'discretionary area of judgment', initially articulated by Lord Hope in *Kebilene*.[71]

---

[66] See further MacCormick, n 16 above, pp 107–8.

[67] That Convention rights could be overridden by national legislation was made clear as the Human Rights Bill passed through Parliament: HL Deb, 5 February 1998, col 839 (Lord Irvine); HL Deb, 16 February 1998, col 771 (Lord Irvine). See also *R v Secretary of State for the Home Department, ex p. Simms* n 3 above, 341–2 (Lord Hoffmann).

[68] See also s 6(2)(a) concerning judicial review.

[69] *R (Alconbury) v Secretary of State for the Environment, Transport and the Regions* [2001] 2 WLR 1389, para [129]. See also Lord Slynn at para [50]; Lord Clyde at paras [159], [171].

[70] N 69 above, para [76]. See also Lord Hoffmann's approach in *Runa Begum v Tower Hamlets LBC* [2003] UKHL 5, [2003] 1 All ER 731, paras [35], [37], [42–6], [50] & [59].

[71] *R v Director of Public Prosecutions, ex p. Kebilene* [2000] 2 AC 326, 380–1. See also *Wilson v First County Trust (No 2)* [2002] QB 74, para [33]; *International Transport Roth v Secretary of State for the Home Department* [2002] EWCA Civ 158; *R v British Broadcasting Corporation, ex p. Prolife Alliance* [2003] UKHL 23. For critical analysis, see RA Edwards, ' Judicial Deference under the Human Rights Act' (2002) 65 *MLR* 859 and the Hunt chapter in this volume.

Lord Hope made clear that judicial deference to elected institutions should play an important role in Human Rights Act judicial review cases. Where difficult policy choices had to be made by the executive or the legislature between the rights of the individual and the needs of society, it would be appropriate for the judiciary to defer to the elected body. This notion of deference was a home-grown concept: it did not emanate from Strasbourg, even if it might in some situations implicate analogous factors to those involved in the Strasbourg Court's 'margin of appreciation' principle.[72] Given these various concerns, it is perhaps understandable that Laws LJ felt able to state in *R. (Mahmood) v Secretary of State for the Home Department* that the 1998 Act did not:

> authorise the judges to stand in the shoes of Parliament's delegates, who are decision-makers given their responsibilities by the democratic arm of the state. The arrogation of such a power to the judges would usurp those functions of government which are controlled and distributed by powers whose authority is derived from the ballot box.[73]

The weight which courts feel inclined to accord to the competing factors identified here will clearly vary according to the context: whether, for example, the recognition of a more intense form of review than officially existed hitherto will lead them into inappropriate territory. Equally, some judges might be keener than others to prioritise the demands of the Strasbourg case law over common law constitutional norms: for example, while Lord Hoffmann stressed in *Alconbury* that Convention rights could not override fundamental constitutional norms, the drafting of section 2(1) is such that other readings are possible.[74] The requirements and implications of the Strasbourg case law are also sometimes ambiguous: some commentators therefore criticised early Human Rights Act decisions for failing to distinguish clearly enough between issues going to the nature of proportionality review at Strasbourg level, and issues going to the proper measure of judicial deference.[75] For present purposes, such points clearly illustrate the fact that in the absence of EC law-style principles such as direct effect and supremacy in the Convention, judicial interpretation of the Human Rights Act is ultimately likely—particularly given the Act's drafting—to involve the striking of some sort of balance between giving effect to Convention rights as understood by *national* courts and remaining within the perceived dictates of *national* constitutional law.

---

[72] See *Kebilene*, n 71 above. See further the Hunt chapter in this volume.

[73] [2001] 1 WLR 840, para [33].

[74] For example, Lord Slynn's judgment in *R (Alconbury) v Secretary of State for the Environment, Transport and the Regions*, n 69 above, para [26] may allow for greater weight to be given to the Strasbourg jurisprudence; see also G Anthony, 'Interacting Legal Orders and Inter-Court Disputes: the ECHR Beds into UK Public Law', in G Amato, G Braisant and E Venizelos (eds), *The Constitutional Revision in Today's Europe* (London, Esperia, 2002), pp 577–606. The role of comparative—and particularly Commonwealth—case law might also be significant in judicial evaluations of the requirements of Convention rights. See *R v Home Secretary, ex p. Daly*, n 60 above, para [27]; D Feldman, 'Proportionality and the Human Rights Act 1998' in E Ellis (ed), *The Principle of Proportionality in the Laws of Europe* (Oxford, Hart, 1999), esp at pp 118–122, 142–4; R Clayton and H Tomlinson, n 61 above, paras 6.40, 6.74, 6.75–6.81.

[75] R Clayton, 'Regaining a Sense of Proportion: the Human Rights Act and the Proportionality Principle' [2001] EHRLR 504; C Gearty, n 3 above.

In other words, 'national' level concerns can assume a prominent role, without the need—as in EC law cases—to engage in difficult constitutional speculation concerning the reason for and extent of their prominence. As Laws LJ suggested in *Mahmood*,

> Much of the challenge presented by the enactment of the 1998 Act consists in the search for a principled measure of scrutiny which will be loyal to .. Convention rights, but loyal also to the legitimate claims of democratic power ....[76]

Attempts to strike such a balance are clearly at the centre of the courts' task in interpreting the Human Rights Act—making clear that a very different 'multi-layered' exercise is in play from that involved in national cases which turn on points of EC law. Both the Human Rights Act and the European Communities Act 1972 require national courts to have regard to the case law emanating from the European layer, but in the Strasbourg context this does not have overriding effect at national level, the power of the Strasbourg jurisprudence clearly being mediated—in so far as UK courts are concerned—by national constitutional considerations.

THE 'SPILL OVER' EFFECT

The dualist nature of the domestic legal system might perhaps suggest that the impact of EC law standards and Convention rights ought to be confined to cases falling within the scope of the European Communities Act 1972 and the Human Rights Act 1998 respectively. However, prior to the coming into force of the 1998 Act, courts sometimes—but not always—used standards which would be enforced in cases involving EC law as a justification for developing domestic law consistently even when EC law was *not* involved, and employed Convention-style reasoning despite the fact that the Convention had not then been brought into domestic law.[77] As Gordon Anthony asserts:

> On some occasions, the courts ... seemingly viewed the processes of change attributable to European law and domestic law as separate and distinct. However, on other occasions, the courts ... permitted a fusion of domestic and European legal standards to occur'.[78]

This latter possibility—sometimes referred to as 'spill over'[79]—raises the possibility that, now that the 1998 Act is in force, national law might be developed by reference to Convention norms even where the Act does not officially have a role to play. The possibility of 'spill over' is therefore of considerable interest when evaluating the role of courts in a 'multi-layered' constitution: for it suggests that, despite the boundaries which the 1972 and 1998 Acts formally place around the

---

[76] N 73 above, para [33].

[77] G Anthony, n 8 above, pp 6–9, 17–22, chs 5 & 6. Perhaps the most obvious example is *M v Home Office* [1994] 1 AC 377, where the availability of interim relief against ministers acting in official capacity in cases involving EC law was used to justify its extension to cases with no EC element.

[78] N 8 above, p 3.

[79] Anthony, n 8 above, p 54; see also his 'Community Law and the Development of UK Administrative Law: Delimiting the 'Spill-over' Effect' (1998) 4 *EPL* 253.

situations in which European norms may be employed, courts might allow such norms in practice to influence the development of domestic law on a broader basis. These issues can be illustrated by considering in greater detail the role of proportionality in judicial review.

Before the Human Rights Act came into force, proportionality was not officially recognised as a ground of review save in cases involving EC law.[80] This was reaffirmed by the House of Lords in *R. v Secretary of State for the Home Department, ex p. Brind*, where Lord Bridge suggested that it would be a 'judicial usurpation of the legislative function' for a court to require that a statutory discretion be exercised in accordance with Convention rights (and thus reviewed using proportionality), given that this would amount to the judiciary bringing the Convention into national law.[81] Richard Clayton and Hugh Tomlinson thus categorise *Brind* as being based upon a 'strict "dualist" view': a treaty that had not then been brought into national law by Parliament 'could only be relevant if [a] statute was ambiguous'.[82] Nonetheless, it is very often suggested that proportionality was employed *in practice* by the courts at this time.[83] This argument is based on a series of cases (including *Brind* itself) involving fundamental rights, in which an approach labelled 'anxious scrutiny' was used regardless of the ground of review that was formally in play. The phrase 'anxious scrutiny' comes from Lord Bridge's assertions in *R. v Secretary of State for the Home Department, ex p. Bugdaycay* that a court 'must ... be entitled to subject an administrative decision to the more rigorous examination, to ensure that it is in no way flawed, according to the gravity of the issue' and that 'when an administrative decision ... is said to be one which may put the applicant's life at risk, the basis of the decision must surely call for the most anxious scrutiny.'[84] Perhaps the most broadly cited formulation of this approach—at least, in the context of *Wednesbury* unreasonableness—was found in *R. v Ministry of Defence, ex p. Smith*, where Sir Thomas Bingham MR suggested that:

> The court may not interfere with the exercise of an administrative discretion on substantive grounds save where the court is satisfied that the decision is unreasonable in the

---

[80] Eg, *Stoke-on-Trent C.C. v B&Q* [1991] Ch 48 (Hoffmann J); [1993] AC 900 (HL); *R v Ministry of Agriculture, Fisheries and Food, ex p. First City Trading* [1997] 1 CMLR 250.

[81] [1991] 1 AC 696, 748 (Lord Bridge). See also 750F (Lord Roskill); 760–6 (Lord Ackner); 766–7 (Lord Lowry); see also *R v Secretary of State for the Environment, ex p. NALGO* (1993) 5 Admin LR 785, 798, 800; P Craig, 'Unreasonableness and Proportionality in UK Law', in E Ellis (ed), n 74 above, pp 90–91; G de Búrca, 'Proportionality and *Wednesbury* Unreasonableness: the Influence of European Legal Concepts on UK Law', in M Andenas (ed), *English Public Law and the Common Law of Europe* (London, Key Haven, 1998), pp 59–66.

[82] N 61 above, para 2.33. There is clearly a typographical error in the text: Clayton & Tomlinson refer to 'an incorporated treaty'.

[83] J Jowell, 'Is Proportionality and Alien Concept?' (1996) 2 *EPL* 401; G de Búrca, n 81 above, pp 66–71; P Craig, n 81 above, pp 91–3, 96–9.

[84] [1987] 1 AC 514, 531; see also Lord Templeman at 537. For general analysis, see M Hunt, *Using Human Rights Law in English Courts* (Oxford, Hart, 1997), chs 5 & 6; R Clayton and H Tomlinson, n 61 above, paras 2.30–2.40; P Craig, n 81 above, at pp 96–9; M Fordham, 'What is 'Anxious Scrutiny'?' [1996] *JR* 81; M Beloff and H Mountfield, 'Unconventional Behaviour? Judicial Uses of the European Convention in England and Wales' [1996] *EHRLR* 467.

sense that it is beyond the range of responses open to a reasonable decision-maker. But in judging whether the decision-maker has exceeded this margin of appreciation the human rights context is important. The more substantial the interference with human rights, the more the court will require by way of justification before it can be satisfied that the decision is reasonable ....[85]

Where a decision interfered heavily with a fundamental right, the decision-maker was thus required to produce a strong justification to convince the court that the decision fell within the range of reasonable responses. As Sir Thomas went on to make clear, however:

[t]he greater the policy content of a decision, and the more remote the subject matter ... from ordinary judicial experience, the more hesitant the court must necessarily be in holding a decision to be irrational ....[86]

Supporters of the notion that 'anxious scrutiny' resembles or entails proportionality analysis can invoke many examples from the pre-Human Rights Act case law. In *Brind* itself, Lord Templeman—when considering whether it was *Wednesbury* unreasonable to prohibit the broadcast of the voices of leading members of prescribed terrorist groups on radio and television—asserted that it was better to ask whether a reasonable minister could reasonably conclude that this interference with freedom of expression was justifiable, rather than whether the Home Secretary had acted irrationally or perversely (the traditional *Wednesbury* test). This meant that:

[i]n terms of the Convention, as construed by the European Court, the interference with freedom of expression must be *necessary and proportionate* to the damage which the restriction is designed to prevent.[87]

Paul Craig therefore suggests that Lord Templeman 'reasoned in a manner directly analogous to proportionality' in *Brind*, and that Lord Bridge—while refusing explicitly to recognise proportionality—employed it covertly by making clear that only an *important* competing public interest would be enough to justify the restriction of freedom of expression, given freedom of expression's importance as a human right.[88] Sir Thomas Bingham MR's formulation in *Smith* might also be understood in terms of proportionality. For the standard which a respondent was required to meet in order for their decision to survive scrutiny was related to the seriousness of the interference with human rights, enabling Craig to

[85] [1996] QB 517, 554. This test was originally propounded extra-judicially by Sir John Laws in 'Is the High Court the Guardian of Fundamental Rights?' [1993] PL 59, 69. See also the analogous approach employed in 'illegality' cases: *R v Secretary of State for the Home Department, ex p. Leech (No. 2)*, n 3 above, 209, 216–7; *R v Secretary of State for Social Security, ex p. Joint Council for the Welfare of Immigrants*, n 3 above; *R v Lord Chancellor, ex p. Witham*, n 3 above; *R v Secretary of State for the Home Department, ex p. Pierson* [1998] AC 539, 575 (Lord Browne-Wilkinson); *R v Secretary of State for the Home Department, ex p. Simms*, n 3 above, 340 (Lord Steyn), 341–2 (Lord Hoffmann). See also M Fordham and T de la Mare, 'Anxious Scrutiny, the Principle of Legality and the Human Rights Act' [2000] JR 40.

[86] N 85 above, 556.

[87] N 85 above, 751E–F (emphasis added).

[88] P Craig, n 81 above, p 92.

argue that the real question was whether the interference with a given right was the least restrictive possible in the circumstances—a proportionality-related inquiry.[89] Perhaps the most obvious overlap between 'anxious scrutiny' and proportionality was found in *R. v Secretary of State for the Home Department, ex p. Simms*.[90] This was technically an illegality case, but Lord Steyn considered whether the respondent's policy restricting prisoners' communications with journalists was necessary in a democratic society in the sense that a pressing social need could be shown for it, and asked whether the restrictions were no more than proportionate to the legitimate aim pursued—a proportionality test frequently employed by the Strasbourg Court.[91] Lord Steyn went on to equate this test with Sir Thomas Bingham MR's formulation from *Smith*.[92] Lord Hobhouse condemned the respondent's policy as *both* unreasonable *and* disproportionate, and like Lord Steyn went on to cite with approval Sir Thomas Bingham's test from *Smith*.[93] At least in the context of *Simms* itself, both judgments therefore treated Sir Thomas Bingham's formulation as analogous to—if not synonymous with—a proportionality test.

From the standpoint of the 'multi-layered' constitution, the question whether a form of proportionality review was in use in these cases is significant because an affirmative answer would suggest that the dualist position articulated in *Brind*— that Convention-style proportionality review could not be deployed without Parliament bringing the Convention into national law—was in practice disregarded by the courts in the cases in issue. Instead, a 'European' norm—proportionality—influenced judicial decision-making outside the areas where this was formally permitted at the time, suggesting that judicial practice reflected 'multi-layered' influences rather more than orthodox theory allowed for. For an affirmative answer to be given, however, we would need to be clear that a sufficiently close relationship did indeed exist between 'anxious scrutiny' and Convention-style proportionality. This requires us to consider the intensity and clarity of review under each heading, and the implications of this for the role of the courts: interrelated issues about which there is no definite consensus of opinion.

The intensity of review refers to the closeness with which a court will scrutinise the impugned decision. That *Wednesbury* review can vary in intensity is clear from the fact that some *Wednesbury* cases involve 'anxious scrutiny' and others do not. However, the intensity of review would appear, from Sir Thomas Bingham MR's judgment in *Smith*, to vary even within 'anxious scrutiny': for the *more* substantial the interference with fundamental rights, the *more* the court will require by way of justification in order to be satisfied that the decision under review was reasonable.

---

[89] N 81 above, pp 92–3, 97. See also G de Búrca, n 81 above, pp 70–1. Proportionality has also been associated with *Wednesbury* outside of the 'anxious scrutiny' pocket: see Taylor LJ's description of proportionality as merely 'a facet of irrationality' in *R v Secretary of State for Health, ex p. US Tobacco* [1992] 1 QB 353, 366.

[90] N 3 above. The case was decided after the Human Rights Act was passed but before it came into force.

[91] N 3 above, 336–40.

[92] N 3 above, 340.

[93] N 3 above, 352–3.

However, proportionality can also vary in intensity. When using proportionality, the Strasbourg Court habitually asks whether an interference with a 'qualified' Convention right

> corresponded to a 'pressing social need', whether it was 'proportionate to the legitimate aim pursued', [and] whether the reasons given by the national authorities to justify it are 'relevant and sufficient'…[94]

The intensity with which this standard is applied varies depending upon the nature and drafting of the Convention right in issue. The Court has made clear, in the context of Article 8, that where an interference affects:

> a *most intimate* aspect of private life … there must exist *particularly serious* reasons before interferences on the part of public authorities can be legitimate.[95]

The Court has also suggested that its evaluation of the 'necessity' of an interference will be connected with the nature of a 'democratic society', the hallmarks of which include 'pluralism, tolerance and broadmindedness' towards unpopular groups and practices.[96] In relation to Article 10, the Court has made clear that in deciding whether a restriction on freedom of expression was 'necessary' in a 'democratic society', it could not overlook the 'duties and responsibilities' which that Article specifically states are owed by those exercising the right.[97] Finally, the Court employs a looser proportionality test—based on the concept of a 'fair balance'—when dealing with Article 1 of the First Protocol than it does in relation to Articles 8 to 11.[98] Given that both proportionality and 'anxious scrutiny' can vary in intensity, it might therefore be felt that the crucial issue, at least in cases involving Convention rights, is not so much the identity of the ground of review which is *formally* in play as the *intensity* of the review itself, whatever name review is conducted under.[99]

Nonetheless, the House of Lords asserted in *Daly*—its post-Human Rights Act response to the decision of the Court of Human Rights in *Smith v United Kingdom* (the appeal from *Smith* before the Court of Appeal)—that proportionality is more intensive than 'anxious scrutiny' and should be used in Human Rights Act cases. In *Smith v United Kingdom*, the Strasbourg Court had found that Sir Thomas Bingham MR's 'anxious scrutiny' standard was too restrictive, and that the claimants had been denied an effective remedy contrary to Article 13.[100] This led Lord Cooke

---

[94] *Sunday Times v United Kingdom* (1979) 2 EHRR 245 at para 62, citing *Handyside v United Kingdom*, paras 48–50.

[95] *Dudgeon v United Kingdom*, (1981) 4 EHRR 149, para 52 (emphasis added).

[96] *Handyside v United Kingdom*, n 94 above, para 49; *Dudgeon v United Kingdom*, n 95 above, para 53; *Smith v United Kingdom*, n 62 above, para 87.

[97] *Handyside v United Kingdom*, n 94 above, para 49.

[98] R Clayton and H Tomlinson, n 61 above, paras 6.45, 18.26, 18.76–18.81.

[99] It is clear from *Daly* that the intensity of proportionality review will vary: see Lord Steyn, n 60 above, para [28]. Furthermore, while the domestic standard of review was found to be inadequate from the standpoint of Article 13 in *Smith v United Kingdom*, n 62 above, this has not always been the case: compare *Vilvarajah v United Kingdom* (1991) 14 EHRR 248; *Chahal v United Kingdom* (1996) 23 EHRR 413; *Hatton v United Kingdom* (2002) 34 EHRR 1.

[100] N 62 above, paras 136–8.

to suggest in *Daly* that while *Wednesbury*-related 'anxious scrutiny' and proportionality would often produce the same results, the Strasbourg Court's decision in
Smith marked the 'quietus' of the view that the two were 'substantially the same'.[101]
Lord Steyn observed that, although there was an overlap between the two standards,[102] the intensity of review was 'somewhat greater' using proportionality.[103]
Indeed, Lord Steyn categorised the fact that proportionality sometimes went
beyond Sir Thomas Bingham MR's formulation as one of the concrete differences
which existed between the two standards. For under proportionality, the intensity
of review was to be:

> guaranteed by the twin requirements that the limitation of the [claimant's] right was
> necessary in a democratic society, in the sense of meeting a pressing social need, and the
> question whether the interference was really proportionate to the legitimate aim being
> pursued.[104]

To reach any general conclusion about the similarity or difference between the
two standards based only upon the intensity of review would, however, be insufficient. For it is important also to consider the clarity with which review is
conducted—something which in turn has implications for the institutional role of
the courts. It might well be said that opinion is divided not so much as to the existence of differing degrees of judicial clarity concerning the nature of review
conducted under the 'anxious scrutiny' and proportionality headings, but as to the
significance of this phenomenon. It seems clear that full-scale proportionality
review—whatever the intensity with which it is conducted—requires courts in
principle to engage in a much clearer *comparative* assessment of the weights to be
ascribed to rights and to the competing policy justifications for restricting them
than is the case with 'anxious scrutiny', under which the weight accorded to particular rights is frequently difficult to gauge.[105] This can clearly be seen in *Smith*. As a
general matter, Sir Thomas Bingham MR's 'anxious scrutiny' formulation offers
no guidance as to how much weight the court should accord human rights *relative
to* matters of policy. We are told that the closeness with which a court will review a
decision should vary depending upon the level to which that decision interferes
with a right and the degree to which it involves matters of policy. However, we are
told nothing about the *comparative* degree of priority to accord to rights and
policy in a case where both are involved. This is reflected in the Court of Appeal's

---

[101] N 60 above, para [32].
[102] N 60 above, para [26].
[103] N 60 above, para [27]; see also Lord Bingham at para [23].
[104] N 60 above, para [27].
[105] See, generally, PP Craig, n 61 above, pp 546–52, n 81 above, pp 94–99; D Feldman, 'Proportionality and the Human Rights Act 1998', in E Ellis (ed), n 74 above, pp 127–9. For examples, see *R v Secretary of State for the Home Department, ex p. Bugdaycay*, n 84 above, 531–4 (Lord Bridge), 537–8 (Lord
Templeman); *R v Secretary of State for the Home Department, ex p. Brind*, n 81 above, 748–9 (Lord
Bridge); 750–1 (Lord Templeman); 757–9 (Lord Ackner); 763–6 (Lord Lowry). This criticism does not
apply so strongly to judicial usage of 'anxious scrutiny' in the 'illegality' cases considered at n 85 above,
in which rights considerations appear to have been given a positive weight. This is unsurprising, given
that courts are generally less sensitive in 'illegality' cases to the charge that they are interfering inappropriately in executive decision-making.

handling of the case. The appellants were arguing that the Ministry of Defence's policy—whereby lesbian, gay or bisexual members of the armed forces would automatically be discharged from military service—was *Wednesbury* unreasonable. Sir Thomas Bingham acknowledged that the case concerned 'innate qualities of a very personal kind', that '[t]he applicants' rights as human beings are very much in issue',[106] and that their arguments were of 'very considerable cogency'.[107] He noted, however, that the discharge policy had been supported by Parliament and by the professional advice available to the Ministry of Defence, that the Ministry had not had the chance to consider any alternatives, that Parliament was itself reviewing the policy,[108] and that the applicants' claim involved the possibility of a major policy change.[109] In consequence, the policy could not be categorised as *Wednesbury* unreasonable. It may be observed, however, that while Sir Thomas Bingham's judgment contains a perfectly coherent statement of the competing rights and policy arguments in *Smith*, these arguments were never weighed *against* one other so as to explain why the Ministry's policy was not unreasonable.

This appears to stand in sharp contrast to proportionality, which—as Gráinne de Búrca has argued—in theory requires 'the *express* articulation and *explicit* weighing of the specific aims of a measure in relation to its impact on a right or interest invoked by the applicant'.[110] Rights and policy must be balanced *against* one another, with a specific weight assigned to each. From this viewpoint, the intellectual focus of proportionality is sharper than that involved in the typical 'anxious scrutiny' case, whatever the intensity of review in play. It might be argued that this difference of focus is reflected in Lord Steyn's suggestions in *Daly* that proportionality—unlike 'anxious scrutiny '—'may require the reviewing court to assess the balance which the decision maker has struck, not merely whether it is within the range of rational or reasonable decisions',[111] and that proportionality 'may require attention to be directed to the relative weight accorded to interests and considerations.'[112] These differences at the level of clarity might, in turn, be felt to reflect differing perceptions of the appropriate institutional roles of courts under each heading of review.

Nonetheless, some theorists have down-played the significance of differences at the level of clarity. For example, Mark Elliott has argued—using a comparison between the judgments at Court of Appeal and Court of Human Rights levels in *Smith*—that the distinction between the two approaches 'is one of degree rather than of type'.[113] Elliott suggests that 'anxious scrutiny' offers the executive a 'substantial margin of freedom, thereby permitting judicial intervention only if

---

[106] N 85 above, 556D See also Simon Brown LJ in the Divisional Court, below at 540–1.

[107] N 85 above, 557.

[108] N 85 above, 558.

[109] *Ibid.*

[110] N 81 above, pp 54–5 (emphasis added); see also P Craig, n 81 above, pp 99–100.

[111] N 60 above, para [27].

[112] *Ibid.*

[113] 'The Human Rights Act 1998 and the Standard of Substantive Review' (2001) 60 *CLJ* 301, 308 & 313.

the lack of balance' between the right and the competing policy objective in play:

> is so great that as to be manifestly unreasonable. In contrast, the proportionality doctrine requires much closer scrutiny of the balance; in turn, a much lower level of imbalance is needed in order to trigger intervention by the reviewing court.[114]

That this may not be *radically* significant can, however, be seen—Elliott argues—by considering the practical operation of the two standards. For proportionality—like 'anxious scrutiny'—can still in practice involve a relatively unstructured weighing of competing interests in practice, suggesting that 'far from representing wholly distinct modes of judicial review, they constitute different points on—or, more accurately perhaps, sections of' a spectrum.[115] This being so, the availability of proportionality in Human Rights Act cases should not be seen as heralding the demise of 'anxious scrutiny' (or presumably even traditional *Wednesbury*) review in non-Human Rights Act cases: rather, the official recognition of proportionality merely allows for more intense judicial scrutiny where Convention rights are involved.[116]

An evaluation of the merits of the competing positions would lie beyond the scope of the present chapter.[117] Their importance, for present purposes, lies in the constitutional significance which each would ascribe to the possible 'spill over' of proportionality now that the Human Rights Act is in force. It is important here to separate analytical, institutional and normative viewpoints (in so far as such a separation is possible). Elliott's argument operates from an analytical viewpoint: his major concern is that, as a matter of legal logic, proportionality and 'anxious scrutiny' are insufficiently distinctive—considered as approaches to judicial review—to justify the conclusion that the former might 'replace' the latter outside of the Human Rights Act. Other theorists might of course argue differently,[118] but the key point for Elliott would appear to be that 'spill over' is not a radically significant issue analytically-speaking. As Elliott acknowledges, however, things might be seen differently from an institutional viewpoint—that is, a viewpoint which is concerned with the appropriate role of the courts in the national constitutional structure. The institutional viewpoint which Elliott articulates is clearly dualist in nature: he suggests that courts might have felt inhibited—in the absence of express Parliamentary approval—about openly recognising the existence of proportionality review prior to the coming into force of the Human Rights Act 1998.[119] The Act provided a sufficiently solid constitutional foundation for the recognition of proportionality review, explaining why such recognition only

---

[114] N 113 above at 313.

[115] N 113 above at 315.

[116] N 113 above, at 314–5, 322ff.

[117] See further the Taggart chapter in this volume. For a critique of Elliott's approach, see G Anthony, n 74 above.

[118] Elliott's argument is intended as a riposte to Paul Craig's suggestion that *Wednesbury* review 'might be caught in the "pincers" of the tests used in EC law and the HRA' (n 61 above, p 586; see also P Craig, n 81 above, pp 96–9).

[119] Save in EC law cases, in which Parliamentary approval might be inferred from the European Communities Act 1972.

occurred in *Daly*.[120] As Elliott suggests, however, this argument might prove to be something of a two-edged sword in terms of the legitimacy of 'spill over': for, just as it might be said that that the Act permits the judicial recognition of proportionality, it might equally be said to limit the extent of that recognition to cases falling *within* the scope of the Act itself.[121] From this viewpoint, one's view concerning the preferable reading of the Act will determine one's position concerning the permissible extent of 'spill over'. However, normatively-speaking, further arguments are possible. For example, Gordon Anthony takes Elliott to task for focusing excessively on the dictates of domestic law, instead of acknowledging the positive weight which 'European' legal norms can have on the re-shaping of national law.[122] From this standpoint, 'national level' constitutional constraints should presumably be capable of being ignored or over-ridden by national courts if such an approach is necessary in order to encourage a normatively desirable outcome, namely consistency between all levels of the 'multi-layered' constitutional structure.

This dispute concerning the significance of 'spill over' has been paralleled, in the case law since the Human Rights Act came into force, by judicial disagreement as to whether such a phenomenon is occurring in practice.[123] If it is, then the dualist view that an Act of Parliament must exist in order to permit the use of 'European' norms in individual cases might be felt to have been surpassed in practice: begging the much broader question whether a court's *own* view concerning its place in the 'multi-layered' constitutional structure is not now the key issue when determining the influence of European norms via the process of 'spill over'. If this is the case, then the significance of national measures such as the 1972 and 1998 Acts might in fact be less significant than we would at first assume—a conclusion with radical consequences for our preceding discussions. As we have seen, however, it may equally be felt—in a more 'neutral' sense—that the differences between 'anxious scrutiny' and proportionality are insufficiently great that they should generate significant constitutional questions. In consequence, the role of courts within a multi-layered constitution leaves many questions unanswered. Such questions may only be resolved by reference to normative criteria, and it is to these that we turn in the next section of the chapter.

THE MULTI-LAYERED CONSTITUTION AND PUBLIC LAW THEORY

It has been argued that the courts are now required to take account—in different ways, depending upon the issue in play—of the multi-layered nature of the

---

[120] N 113 above, pp 310–1.

[121] Such an abrupt distinction between permission for and prohibition of judicial activity might, in practice, be seen as somewhat artificial, however: see further P Craig and N Bamforth, 'Constitutional Analysis, Constitutional Principle and Judicial Review' [1991] *PL* 763.

[122] N 74 above, pp 16–28.

[123] Compare *R (Medway Council and Kent County Council) v Secretary of State for Transport* [2002] EWHC 2516 Admin; *R (Association of British Civilian Internees) v Secretary of State for Defence* [2003] EWCA Civ 473.

contemporary constitution. Where appropriate, national courts give priority to norms of EC law or Convention rights. The degree of priority—and its practical consequences—depends upon a court's understanding of the role of EC law or the Convention within national law: in other words, upon that court's interpretation of the requirements imposed, at national level, by the existence of a multi-layered constitution. Of course, this phenomenon influences judicial decision-making *throughout* domestic law. It is, however, particularly important in the public law context given the consequences it has for the way in which we determine the *proper* role of the courts, normatively-speaking: that is, for how we evaluate the role of the courts from the standpoint of public law theory. It will be argued in this section of the chapter that the various questions highlighted in previous sections must be resolved, ultimately, by reference to such issues.

In two well-respected analyses of public law theory—namely Carol Harlow and Richard Rawlings' *Law and Administration*[124] and Martin Loughlin's *Public Law and Political Theory*[125]—the competing approaches to the proper roles of the courts, Parliament and the executive have been divided into three groups. Harlow and Rawlings talk of red-light, green-light and amber-light theories; Loughlin talks of conservative normativist, functionalist and liberal normativist theories.[126] Both accounts devote a large amount of attention to the Westminster Parliament, the executive, and the national courts. The appropriateness—or inappropriateness—of judicial decisions and decision-making tends to be assessed in terms of how far the courts appear to be willing to trespass into areas more appropriately reserved for (or, according to perspective, inappropriately dominated by) Parliament and/or the executive. Neither account, however, pays sustained attention to the impact of EC law or the Convention at national level, even though both phenomena have important constitutional consequences for the present-day role of national courts. This absence is perhaps unsurprising: both books approach public law theory via an analysis of its historical development, and EC law can rightly be seen as a late entrant, historically-speaking, into the field. Furthermore, both books were published before the Labour government came to power in 1997, explaining the lack of discussion of Convention rights other than in the context of existing amber-light/liberal normativist theories. It will be argued in this section of the chapter that, given the multi-layered nature of the contemporary constitution, it is now rather more difficult to assess the role of the courts—and to offer guidance concerning that role—using just the three approaches mentioned above. In Human Rights Act cases and in cases involving EC law, national courts are subjected to a series of pressures to comply with the jurisprudence of the Strasbourg and Luxembourg courts. The attitudes with which these pressures are dealt

---

[124] (2nd edn, London, Butterworths, 1997), esp chs 1–4.

[125] (Oxford, Clarendon Press, 1992.)

[126] Harlow and Rawlings seem to treat Loughlin's categorisation as working in parallel to their own: see *Law and Administration*, n 124 above, pp 37–8 (n 10), 67. For a critique of Loughlin's categorisation, see Paul Craig, book review, (1993) 13 *Leg St* 275. For the sake of simplicity, the two characterisations will be treated as analogous in this section of the chapter.

with are often related to the three approaches, but such an overlap is not inevitable and is sometimes non-existent. This being so, the three approaches cannot provide a complete theoretical explanation of the role of national courts in the contemporary, multi-layered constitution.

To understand this argument, it is necessary first to sketch out the three competing theoretical approaches. Useful summaries of each have been provided by Adam Tomkins. Tomkins characterises red-light theorists/conservative normativists as believing:

> (1) that law is autonomous to and superior over politics; (2) that the administrative state is something which needs to be kept in check by the law; (3) that the preferred way of doing this is through rule-based adjudication in courts; and (4) that the goal of this project should be to enhance individual liberty ... an idea of liberty which is best realized by having small government.[127]

As Tomkins's fourth point reveals, red-light theory/conservative normativism rests on a particular ideological perspective. As Carol Harlow and Richard Rawlings therefore suggest, for such theorists, 'the primary function of administrative law should be to control any excess of state power and subject it to legal, and more specifically judicial, control'—behind which lies 'a preference for a minimalist state'.[128] Traditionally, such theorists have favoured the notion of a balanced constitution, with the executive being controlled politically by Parliament and legally by the courts. However, the apparent decline of Parliamentary power legitimated the onset, during the later stages of the twentieth century, of greater judicial intervention.[129] Nowadays, when it comes to the control of state power, 'the emphasis' under this approach to public law is 'on courts rather than government'.[130]

According to Harlow and Rawlings, green-light theorists—functionalists, in Loughlin's terminology—are 'inclined to pin their hopes on the political process' rather than on judicial control of executive power and the idea of a balanced constitution.[131] For Tomkins, such theorists believe:

> (1) that law is nothing more than a sophisticated (or elitist) discourse of politics ..; (2) that public administration is ... a positive attribute to be welcomed; (3) that the objective of administrative law and regulation is not merely to stop bad administrative practices, but to encourage and facilitate good administrative practices ... and ... that the

---

[127] A Tomkins, 'In Defence of the Political Constitution' (2002) 22 *OJLS* 157 at 158; see also M Loughlin, *Public Law and Political Theory*, n 125 above, pp 60–61 (note that Loughlin is only talking only about *conservative* normativism at this point).

[128] N 124 above, p 37.

[129] N 124 above, pp 45–7; see also M Loughlin, n 125 above, p 180.

[130] N 124 above, p 67; M Loughlin, n 125 above, p 189. Note Harlow and Rawlings' observation (infra, p 158) that courts nonetheless insist in judicial review cases that they are not engaging in independent value judgments, but are instead asserting Parliament's sovereign will. This is perhaps no coincidence.

[131] N 124 above, p 67. As Loughlin demonstrates (n 125 above, pp 190–206), caution is however necessary at this point: for different functionalist writers have subtly divergent views concerning the role of courts and the law.

best institutions to achieve these aims will not necessarily be courts ...; and (4) that the goal of this project should be to enhance individual and collective liberty where liberty is conceived of as something which is, if not constituted by the state, then ... at least facilitated by it, and ... certainly not necessarily threatened by it.[132]

An important aspect of the green-light/functionalist position is hostility to the courts, which are seen as opposed to the values of administration, and as unrepresentative and therefore undemocratic mechanisms for regulating executive action.[133] Supporters of this position are therefore keen, according to Harlow and Rawlings, to promote 'alternative, democratic forms of accountability'.[134] While red-light theorists favour external, retrospective, *judicial* controls over decision-making, green-light theorists favour prospective, internal, *political* controls, causing Harlow and Rawlings to emphasise the 'characteristic reliance of green light theorists on political and administrative institutions'.[135] The logical consequence of this reliance is, of course, a demand for judicial restraint: courts should not seek to substitute themselves for the rightful decision-maker chosen by Parliament.[136] This view of the appropriate roles of the various institutions is explained by the green-light theorists'/functionalists' enthusiasm for interventionist government—the fourth aspect identified by Tomkins in his summary. Harlow and Rawlings characterise early theories within this school as:

> *administration centred*—the role of administrative law was not to act as a counterweight to the interventionist state but to facilitate legitimate government action—and *collectivist* in character, advancing the claim to promote the public interest or common good.[137]

Loughlin seemingly goes further, arguing that functionalism 'has a certain affinity with a political theory of socialism'.[138] Having characterised courts as unrepresentative and predominantly conservative bodies which were inclined to stand in the way of the democratic will, green-light theorists/functionalists were naturally hostile to extensive judicial review of executive action.

According to both Harlow and Rawlings and Loughlin, amber-light theory or liberal normativism has emerged in recent years as a consensus position, with theorists who might previously have fallen into other camps coming to favour at least some components of this approach.[139] Tomkins characterises such theorists as believing:

> (1) with red-light theorists that law is both discrete from and superior to politics; (2) that the state can successfully be limited by law, although that law ought properly to allow for

---

[132] N 127 above, pp 158–9; see also M Loughlin, n 125 above, pp 60–1.

[133] C Harlow and R Rawlings, n 124 above, pp 72–3.

[134] N 124 above, p 74; see also M Loughlin, n 125 above, pp 189, 204–5.

[135] N 124 above, p 76. See also M Loughlin, *Sword and Scales: An Examination of the Relationship Between Law and Politics* (Oxford, Hart, 2000), pp 208–13, ch 15.

[136] N 124 above, p 79.

[137] N 124 above, p 71; see also M Loughlin, n 125 above, pp 167–8.

[138] N 125 above, p 105; see also below, pp 133–7.

[139] C Harlow and R Rawlings, n 124 above, p 90; M Loughlin, n 125 above, ch 9.

the administration to enjoy a degree—albeit a controlled degree—of discretionary authority; (3) that the best way of controlling the state is through the judicial articulation and enforcement of broad principles of legality; and (4) that the goal of this project is to safeguard a particular vision of human rights.[140]

Amber-light/liberal normativist theorists thus stress the use of principles, the structuring of administrative discretion, the notion that rights may sometimes trump policy considerations, and reliance on a combination of fire-watching (internal) and fire-fighting (external) controls over public power. Such theorists focus on judicial remedies, like their red-light counterparts, but prioritise the constitutional role of the judiciary to a far greater extent. Given that amber-light theory/liberal normativism is a middle position, it is perhaps unsurprising that there has been speculation concerning the degree to which it is distinctive from its rivals. Tomkins suggests, for example, that on the one hand, amber-light theory/liberal normativism is part of the broader idea of liberal-legalism, which is not confined to administrative law and instead concerns the role of courts in all areas of the constitution;[141] on the other hand, due to its stress on the role of courts, amber remains a 'shade of red'.[142]

There is, it must be said, a degree of ambiguity about the coherence of the three approaches described above,[143] and about the extent to which players in contemporary public law—whether judges or theorists—can easily be characterised using such terms of reference.[144] It remains the case, however, that the three approaches have been widely seen as providing a useful and illuminating guide—even if only a rough guide, in which certain boundaries are contestable—to the ways in which we think about public law. This being so, it is important to consider the extent to which they can properly explain the multi-layered constitution which now exists. Cause for doubt on this front is provided by the fact that the analyses of and arguments about many of the cases discussed so far in this chapter seem to be guided, not just by competing perspectives concerning the proper role of national courts as opposed to the Westminster Parliament and the national government, but also by competing views concerning the appropriate role of national courts *in the light*

---

[140] N 127 above, p 159.

[141] However, it should be noted that Loughlin does not himself deploy the term 'liberal-legalism' in his book, *Sword and Scales* (n 135 above).

[142] N 127 above, p 158. Note also Loughlin's suggestion that both amber- and red-light theories have their origins in normativism, n 125 above, pp 62 ff, 102–4.

[143] See P Craig, n 126 above.

[144] Two examples will demonstrate this. First, Harlow and Rawlings and Loughlin both suggest that Sir William Wade has shifted from the red- to the amber-light camp in recent years (*Law and Administration*, n 124 above, ch 4; *Public Law and Political Theory*, n 125 above, pp 213–4, 221, 223). However, Wade's own view—both of theory in general and of the theoretical stance attributed to his work—may not entirely match up with this: see Wade & Forsyth, n 19 above, pp 6–7, 8–9. Secondly, Michael Taggart characterises Sir John Laws as a contemporary Diceyan ('Reinvented Government, Traffic Lights and the Convergence of Public and Private Law. Review of Harlow and Rawlings: *Law and Administration*' [1999] *PL* 124 at 132)—suggesting, using the above analyses, that he should perhaps be seen as a red-light theorist/conservative normativist. However, Sir John Laws' extra-judicial writings—for example his discussion of fundamental common law rights in 'Law and Democracy', n 27 above—are not necessarily consistent with this view.

of the requirements of EC law and/or the Convention, mediated via the domestic constitution.[145] In other words, one's opinion about the exact nature of the multi-layered constitution—about whether, for example, EC law takes priority over domestic law due to factors of a national or purely European character, or about how far domestic courts can rely upon the jurisprudence of the Strasbourg Court where that jurisprudence appears to challenge arrangements of a long-established constitutional nature at national level—can be just as, if not more, influential in cases involving either EC law or Convention points than the bare answer to the question whether one is a red-, green- or amber-light theorist.

The words 'can' and 'bare' are used in the preceding paragraph since there is frequently, in practice, an overlap between a particular theorist's position in terms of the red-light/green-light/amber-light scale and their view concerning 'multi-layered' issues. Given their emphasis on the importance of individual rights, amber-light theorists would, for example, tend to be more intuitively sympathetic to Convention norms—and to their importance in domestic law—than might theorists falling within other camps.[146] Murray Hunt's analysis of the actual and potential use of Convention rights by national courts in the period prior to the enactment of the Human Rights Act is a justifiably influential example of such an approach.[147] Nonetheless, a proper understanding of the role of the courts requires us to recognise that there is, as a matter of *logic*, a conceptual distinction between 'multi-layered' issues and red-light/green-light/amber-light issues, even if the two frequently overlap in practice. Three practical examples will illustrate this. First, regardless of the divisions between the red-light, green-light and amber-light schools concerning the appropriate allocation of powers between institutions at the national level, views still vary in practice—even within each school—concerning the nature, extent and desirability of European influences. For example, some theorists within the green-light/functionalist camp have, historically-speaking, accorded greater significance to the reception of EC law norms within domestic law than have others.[148] More recently, other green-light theorists have come to support a role for courts in cases involving Convention rights, if only for pragmatic reasons.[149] Equally, it is not inevitable—even within the amber-light/liberal normativist camp—that every theorist will attach the same significance to the Convention. This can be shown by considering the work of Trevor Allan. Allan is rightly regarded as a leading figure in contemporary amber-light/liberal normativist thought. However, when discussing fundamental constitutional rights, he is keen to emphasise the role played by domestic common law, rather than the

---

[145] See further M Taggart, n 144 above, pp 128–9, concerning the restructuring of modern government.

[146] See, for example, J Jowell and A Lester's analysis of proportionality in 'Beyond *Wednesbury*: Substantive Principles of Judicial Review' [1987] PL 368.

[147] M Hunt, n 84 above.

[148] See M Loughlin, n 125 above, pp 195–7, concerning JDB Mitchell and his growing sympathy for European institutions (and parallel disillusionment with domestic political institutions), by contrast with other functionalists (infra, pp 197–206) who did not share this concern.

[149] M Taggart, n 144 above, p 136.

Convention, as a guarantor of individual rights—an approach which appears to differ considerably from that employed by Murray Hunt.[150] In consequence, the degree of overlap between one's position in terms of the red- to green-light spectrum and in terms of 'multi-layered' issues would seem to be contingent rather than necessary.

Secondly, the red- and green-light approaches sometimes fail to provide a basis for determining how questions of a 'multi-layered' nature should be answered. This is well illustrated by the debate concerning the constitutional basis on which national courts must accord priority to EC law, considered in section 1 above. As Martin Loughlin perceptively remarks, conservative normativism/red-light theory:

> lived on as the dominant tradition in public law thought throughout the twentieth century, even though the political environment [was] transformed. [It] ... fastened on to such ideas as sovereignty, the universal rule of ordinary law, and a conception of the rule of law which places the judiciary beyond reproach and ... tried to re-order the world through this ideological grid. On occasion, this can be seen starkly, as when, in debates over European Community relations, words like 'federalism' come to be treated with the same sort of disdain which ... Dicey reserved for *droit administratif.*[151]

These comments neatly capture the impression of unreality, when considering the role of EC law, which is ultimately conveyed (albeit without any display of disdain) in Wade's analysis of *Factortame(2)*—an analysis which concludes with what amounts to an intellectual shrugging of the shoulders in Wade's assertion that academics should 'turn a blind eye to constitutional theory' and follow the judges in bowing to the winds of political change.[152] The fact that Wade—as someone who is characterised as a leading defender of red-light theory—regards it as appropriate to conclude his analysis at this point must surely raise questions about the ability of the red-light approach, *in and of itself,* to provide a satisfactory account of the role of national courts in EC law cases. A related but not identical point can be made about green-light theory/functionalism. Michael Taggart has implied that, in so far as Harlow and Rawlings refer to the roles of EC law and the Convention when articulating their preferred green-light approach, little attention seems to have been paid to the possibility that these European influences might challenge their hostility to the public law-private law distinction at national level.[153] If correct, Taggart's point would suggest that—at least for some influential theorists—there is no necessary connection between their approach to the influx of European norms at national level and their approach to other, 'national' level questions.[154]

---

[150] See, eg, TRS Allan, *Law, Liberty and Justice: The Legal Foundations of British Constitutionalism* (Oxford, Clarendon Press, 1993).

[151] M Loughlin, n 125 above, p 233.

[152] HWR Wade, n 21 above, p 575.

[153] N 144 above, pp 129–30. EC law and the Convention are generally mentioned only in passing by Harlow and Rawlings: n 124 above, pp 23–5, 123–4, 170–5.

[154] One might perhaps also that while there *are* direct links between the red-light/amber-light/green-light approaches and underpinning (and competing) political philosophies, 'multi-layered' issues have at least a veneer of political neutrality, in that they are concerned with 'technical' questions

Finally, there are examples in the case law of situations where there is either no correlation—or no connection at all—between a court's affiliation measured in terms of the red-light/green-light/amber-light scale and its approach to questions of a 'multi-layered' nature. Domestic courts were careful—prior to the entry into force of the Human Rights Act 1998—to stress that the explicit emphasis which was placed on the role of common law fundamental rights in the case law of the 1990s was a factor which was distinct from, although frequently parallel to, the requirements of the Convention.[155] One such case—namely *Brind*—is an excellent illustration of a lack of correlation. For the House of Lords was keen to stress the importance of common law fundamental rights—arguably demonstrating an amber-light leaning—while simultaneously rejecting the idea that the Convention could be relied upon directly at national level.[156] An example of a complete lack of connection arises in the EC law context. In *Factortame(1)*, the House of Lords ruled that national law did not allow for the granting of interim relief against a Minister of the Crown acting *qua* Minister.[157] However, after the European Court of Justice ruled that interim relief must be granted if it was the sole obstacle to the effective enforcement of a directly effective EC law right, the House of Lords altered both its reasoning and its conclusion when the case returned to it as *Factortame(2)*.[158] The sole motivating factor behind their Lordships' shift of position was the perceived need to respond to the judgment of the Court of Justice. The only decisive issue for the House of Lords was, in other words, a 'multi-layered' one, which was capable of determining the case in and of itself.

To enable us to engage in a theoretical assessment of the role of courts which is suitable in a 'multi-layered' constitution, it is tentatively submitted that we need to consider what might be termed notions of 'minimalism' and 'maximalism' alongside the now traditional red-light, green-light and amber-light perspectives. Both 'minimalism' and 'maximalism' relate to the reception of EC law and the Convention. A 'minimalist' perspective would suggest that the European Communities Act and the Human Rights Act merely provide basic, outline frameworks for national courts, within and around which they are free to give such priority as they deem appropriate to rules of EC law or Convention rights.[159] Furthermore, in determining the appropriate level of priority, a national court might well seek to invoke European norms on the basis that, in the absence of any specific legislative prohibition at national level, this is a useful or normatively desirable thing to

to do with the *structure* of the national constitution. One's answer to a question of the second type may be influenced by one's political perspective, but as the examples discussed in the text suggest, this connection is neither necessary nor inevitable.

[155] See, eg, *R v Secretary of State for the Home Department, ex p. Brind*, n 81 above; *Derbyshire County Council v Times Newspapers* [1993] AC 534.

[156] The formulation adopted by the House of Lords was that the Convention could only be employed as an aid to interpretation when resolving ambiguities in statutes.

[157] *R v Secretary of State for Transport, ex p. Factortame (1)* [1990] 2 AC 85.

[158] N 1 above, following Case C-213/89, *R v Secretary of State for Transport, ex p. Factortame* [1990] ECR I-2433.

[159] See also G Anthony, n 8 above, pp 77–9, 157–8 , although note that Anthony employs the reverse interpretation of the term 'minimalist' to that used here.

do.[160] Supporters of this perspective may, in consequence, feel comfortable with the idea of national courts openly employing proportionality review in cases which involve no EC law or Convention point. A 'maximalist' perspective would, by contrast, suggest that the 1972 and 1998 Acts should be recognised as setting clear boundaries around the areas in which courts may develop national law to reflect EC law or the Convention. Analytically, supporters of this viewpoint would be committed to a strongly dualist approach: courts should only employ 'European' standards of review such as proportionality in those areas in which the relevant domestic statutes permit them to do so.[161] A key issue for maximalists concerns the range of powers which the 1972 and 1998 Acts should properly be read as construing upon national courts. Given that the 1972 Act does not expressly state that national courts should accord priority to EC law over subsequent national statutes—although it would, on one reading, have been possible prior to *Factortame (2)* to infer that the Act had such consequences—a maximalist would presumably have regarded it as entirely correct for the House of Lords to have avoided reaching a 'radical' conclusion on this point in *Factortame(1)* until the European Court of Justice had made it clear that such a conclusion was unavoidable.

The minimalist and maximalist standpoints outlined here fall at opposite ends of a spectrum, on which most judges and theorists would seem likely in reality to occupy some sort of middle position. Whilst it lies beyond the scope of this chapter to delineate all such positions, it is to be hoped that—by analysing the positions falling at each end of the spectrum—a start will have been made. For present purposes, the key point to reiterate is that while a theorist's position concerning 'multi-layered' issues will frequently overlap with their position on the red-light/green-light/amber-light scale, this need not—for the analytical reasons highlighted above—necessarily be the case. In consequence, it is necessary for us to consider whether a theorist or a judge is a minimalist or a maximalist—quite apart from their position in terms of the red-light/green-light/amber-light scale—in order properly to analyse their stance viewed against the backdrop of the contemporary, multi-layered constitution.

CONCLUSION

A number of questions have been considered in this chapter. It has been argued that the force of 'European' norms depends, in the contemporary constitution, on

---

[160] The conclusion that something is 'useful' need not be for explicitly political reasons and could indeed be for reasons which appear to be entirely legal—for example, to ensure consistency between different areas of domestic law.

[161] Lord Hoffmann's views concerning proportionality, the impact of EC law at national level, and the nature of the changes made to domestic law by the Human Rights Act 1998 might be categorised as broadly maximalist in approach: see his judgments in *Stoke-on-Trent CC v B&Q*, n 80 above (as Hoffmann J); *R v Secretary of State for the Home Department, ex p. Simms*, n 3 above, 341–2; *R (Alconbury) v Secretary of State for the Environment, Transport and the Regions*, n 69 above, para [76]. For further examples of a 'maximalist' approach, see G Anthony, n 8 above, pp 105–10.

whether an EC law or Convention issue is in play—but that, in both contexts, the exact force of the relevant norm will depend upon the explanation one adopts as to *why* it should be accorded some degree of priority. While the possible explanations vary, many—at least, many of the more plausible explanations—would appear to tie the force of the relevant norms to factors which operate within the 'national' layer of the constitution. Whatever one's explanation of the force of either EC law or Convention rights at national level, it therefore seems likely that—in explaining that force—one will refer back to the 'multi-layered' nature of the contemporary constitution. It is inevitable, within any constitution, that uncertainty—if not disagreement—will exist concerning the respective powers of different institutions, and this is certainly the case in a 'multi-layered' constitution. As in many areas falling within their field, public lawyers must therefore make use of normative criteria in order to determine which explanation is preferable. An absence of theory—or a recourse to the notion that fundamental constitutional questions are 'all politics'—cannot, as the discussion of EC law in this chapter has indicated, provide us with an adequate answer. This being so, it is ventured that a combination of red-light/green-light/amber-light theory and minimalist and maximalist arguments must be employed in order to offer a coherent normative justification for the role of courts in a multi-layered constitution.

12

Reinventing Administrative Law

MICHAEL TAGGART*

I have not the slightest doubt that the adoption of a written constitution, providing generous opportunities for judicial review of legislation, would revolutionise the study and transform the status of constitutional law in this country. Great issues of state would be determined in a judicial forum, and the attention of newspaper readers would be diverted from the criminal courts to the drama of the latest constitutional law case. Fortunes would await the specialist practitioners of constitutional law. The university courses would devote a second year to the subject. Animation would intrude into the discussion class; the case method of teaching would make its appearance; books, Ph.D. theses and law review articles would pour forth in spate; the political and social philosophies of our judges would be dissected (with the greatest of respect, of course); and we might ultimately come to rival Italy, where more than half the judges of the Constitutional Court are university professors.[1]

S O SPOKE ONE of the leading public law scholars of the post-Second World War period about the likely impact of an entrenched UK Bill of Rights. More than 40 years on, notwithstanding the fact that the United Kingdom has neither a written Constitution nor a curial power to invalidate statutes,[2] Professor de Smith anticipated the air of excitement and controversy surrounding the constitutional reforms of the Blair Government, one of which has been the 'incorporation' of the European Convention on Human Rights. What Lord Steyn described recently as 'renaissance constitutionalism'[3] is as much in the air in the United Kingdom as in other parts of the common law world.

This chapter is about administrative law, and its place in the multi-layered constitution. The argument is that the central tenets of the 'classic model' of administrative law are being undermined by constitutionalism from within the United Kingdom and internationalisation without, and by the constitutional

* I would like to thank, with the usual disclaimer, Matt Lewans and Paul Rishworth for comments. I benefited from the research assistance of Joshua Pringle, and thank him and the New Zealand law firm of Chapman Tripp for that assistance. This chapter owes a good deal to conversations and teaching with David Dyzenhaus and Murray Hunt, and the example set by Brian Simpson.
[1] SA de Smith, *The Lawyers and the Constitution* (London, G Bell & Sons Ltd, 1960), 10–11.
[2] E Barendt, 'Is there a United Kingdom Constitution?' (1997) 17 *OJLS* 137.
[3] Lord Steyn, 'The New Legal Landscape' (2000) 6 *EHRLR* 549 at 552.

methodology that is an integral part of these phenomena. It is argued that British administrative law is in the process of being reinvented.

The first part of this chapter sets out briefly the central tenets of the 'classic model' of administrative law. The legendary *Wednesbury* case,[4] which is taken to exemplify that model, is considered in the second part. In the third part, the *Wednesbury* case is reconsidered in the light of the Human Rights Act 1998. The analysis of how that case would be decided today illustrates the extent to which administrative law is being reinvented. The final part considers briefly the vital element of justification in this process.

THE CLASSIC MODEL OF ADMINISTRATIVE LAW

Carol Harlow has described the key elements of the 'classic model' of judicial review that prevailed in the United Kingdom up to the 1960s as:[5]

- restricted grounds of review coupled with a strict application of the doctrine of precedent;
- highly individualistic orientation and conspicuously marked by judicial restraint;
- interest-oriented, a fact reflected in the law of locus standi;
- the absence of any substantive distinction between public/private law;
- remedy-oriented.

This restrictive attitude to judicial review was manifested in terms of proof and onus of proof.[6] The common law's aversion to requiring decision-makers to give factually supported and legally reasoned decisions, which flowed from the freedom judges enjoyed in that regard,[7] meant that reasoned decisions were rarely given by inferior decision-makers (unless, of course, required by statute[8]). Discovery was very limited.[9] Disclosure of error was restricted to what would appear on the face of the record or could be deposed to by way of affidavit. Judicial review proceeded on the papers. Permission to issue interrogatories or to cross-examine deponents was rarely granted.[10] There was and still is no duty on respondents to

---

[4]   *Associated Provincial Picture Houses Ltd v Wednesbury Corporation* [1948] 1 KB 223 (CA) (hereafter referred to as *Wednesbury*).

[5]   C Harlow, 'A Special Relationship? American Influences on Judicial Review in England' in I Loveland (ed), *A Special Relationship? American Influences on Public Law in the UK* (Oxford, Clarendon Press, 1995), 79, 83.

[6]   See M Fordham and T de la Mare, 'Identifying Principles of Proportionality' in J Jowell and J Cooper (eds), *Understanding Human Rights Principles* (Oxford, Hart Publishing Ltd, 2001), 27, 32.

[7]   See generally M Taggart, 'Should Administrative Tribunals be Required to State Findings of Fact?' (1980–81) 9 *NZULR* 162; 'Should Canadian Judges be Legally Required to Give Reasoned Decisions in Civil Cases' (1983) 33 *UTLJ* 1.

[8]   This was first done on a widespread basis in the Tribunal and Inquiries Act 1958. See generally AP Le Sueur, 'Legal Duties to Give Reasons' (1999) 52 *Current Legal Problems* 150.

[9]   See *O'Reilly v Mackman* [1983] 2 AC 237 at 280, per Lord Diplock (HL).

[10]   *George v Secretary of State for the Environment* (1979) 38 P & CR 609 at 615, per Lord Denning MR (CA); *Minister of Energy v Petrocorp Exploration Ltd* [1989] 1 NZLR 348 (CA). Admittedly in *O'Reilly v Mackman*, above n 9 at 282 Lord Diplock referred to *George's* case, saying it 'may well be for the reasons given by Lord Denning … it will only be in rare occasions that the interests of justice will require

file an affidavit to explain why a decision was made.[11] Indeed, there is an obscure but strongly supported common law doctrine against permitting litigants to 'to probe the mental processes of the administrator.'[12] The danger of not filing affidavits informing the court of the basis of the decision is that the respondent may not discharge the evidential onus put upon them by the applicant's case. But where the threshold that the applicant must meet is very high—as the stated *Wednesbury* unreasonableness test is—the respondent will often get away with uninformative or otherwise self-serving affidavits.[13]

In these ways the classic model purported to keep the judges' noses out of the tent of politics—restricting who could seek judicial review, avoiding 'policy' issues, ensuring the dispute was justiciable, restricting the proof and requiring the satisfaction of high thresholds for intervention, deferring to legitimate authority, and ensuring that the remedy matched the wrong. All of this is exemplified by the *Wednesbury* case,[14] which has become the emblem of the classic model of administrative law.

WEDNESBURY: THE CASE

Behind the emblem that is *Wednesbury* lies the case that gave it the name. There is a school of thought that study of the case is irrelevant to understanding the emblematic significance of *Wednesbury*. This is not a view I share. The common law develops by the adjudication of cases. A contextual understanding of the *Wednesbury* case and speculation how it might be decided today, throws important light on what has changed and what has remained constant in the last half century.

Some Context[15]

The cinema emerged at the very end of the nineteenth century, and quickly became an extremely popular form of mass entertainment.[16] Initially, the two

---

that leave be given for cross-examination of deponents' in judicial review applications, but he went on to point out that since a rule change in 1977, cross-examination should be allowed whenever the justice of the case requires. There is little evidence of any subsequent liberalisation in the United Kingdom.

[11] *New Zealand Fishing Industry Association Inc v Minister of Agriculture and Fisheries* [1988] 1 NZLR 544 at 554, per Cooke P (CA).

[12] *United States v Morgan*, 313 US 409, 422 (1941), per Frankfurter J. See the cases referred to in Taggart, above n 7, at 37 n 148 and *Comalco New Zealand Ltd v Broadcasting Standards Authority* [1995] 3 NZLR 469 (HC), upheld on appeal: (1995) 9 PRNZ 153 (CA). See generally N Nathanson, 'Probing the Mind of the Administrator: Hearing Variations and Standards of Judicial Review under the Administrative Procedure Act and other Federal Statutes' (1975) 75 *Col LR* 721.

[13] See, eg, JAG Griffith, 'Judicial Decision-Making in Public Law' [1985] *PL* 564.

[14] *Wednesbury*, above at n 4.

[15] With the notable exceptions of *Roberts v Hopwood* [1925] AC 578 (HL) and *Liversidge v Anderson* [1942] AC 206, leading administrative law cases have not received the same amount of contextual attention that private law cases have. See AWB Simpson, *Leading Cases in the Common Law* (Oxford, Clarendon Press, 1995).

[16] R Vorspan, '"Rational Recreation" and the Law: The Transformation of Popular Urban Leisure in Victorian England' (2000) 45 *McGill LJ* 891, 956.

matters of concern in the *Wednesbury* case, the Sabbath and entry of children to cinema, were dealt with by the general prohibition on Sunday entertainment (in place since 1780)[17] and the common law privilege of cinema owners to decide who to admit and who to exclude from their cinemas.[18]

Apparently, the initial impetus for statutory regulation of the cinema industry was public safety. The Cinematograph Act 1909[19] was prompted by a series of deadly cinema fires in the preceding two years.[20] This Act covered the exhibition of 'inflammable films,' and was intended, in the words of its long title, 'to make better provision for securing safety at cinematographic and other exhibitions.' A major side-effect of this Act was to increase markedly the number of cinemas and the amount of capital invested in the industry.[21]

The licensing was in the hands of local authorities, and licences were granted to such persons or companies as the licensing authority thought fit, and subject to such conditions as it might determine.[22] The power to impose conditions generated a number of reported cases. However, with one exception, legal attempts to restrict the powers of licensing authorities to matters of public safety failed.

The leading early case, which set the pattern, is *London County Council v Bermondsey Bioscope Co Ltd*.[23] There the imposition of a condition that the licensed cinema should be closed on Sunday, Good Friday and Christmas Day, survived legal challenge. The Divisional Court rejected the argument that to be valid the conditions had to relate to public safety. The scope of the discretion was wider than that, the court said, as long as the condition reasonable (or not unreasonable), and hence within the licensing authority's power. As regards the prohibition on Sunday opening, which was the basis of the impugned prosecution for breach of licence, this condition did no more than restate the general law against Sunday entertainments and so was within power.

The interests of children were also a reoccurring theme in the cinema licensing case law. It was found to be reasonable to require licensees to undertake not to give sweets to children as an enticement into the cinema.[24] Also upheld were licence conditions designed to ensure that only appropriate films were shown to unaccompanied children under the age of 16 years.[25]

---

[17]   Sunday Observance Act 1780 (Geo III, c 49). See generally J Wigley, *The Rise and Fall of the Victorian Sunday* (Manchester, Manchester University Press, 1980), especially Appendix III (listing the major statutes relating to Sunday observance in Britain). For the modern legal position in the United Kingdom, see A Bradney, *Religions, Rights and Laws* (Leicester, Leicester University Press, 1993), ch 6.

[18]   *Said v Butt* [1920] 3 KB 497 at 502, per McCardie J (KB) (theatre not movie house). See generally MW Turner and FR Kennedy, 'Exclusion, Ejection, and Segregation of Theater Patrons'(1947) 32 *Iowa LR* 625 and SC Isaacs, *The Law Relating to Theatres, Music Halls, and other Public Entertainments, and to the Performers Therein, Including the Law of Musical and Dramatic Copyright* (London, Stevens & Sons Ltd, 1927), 85–94.

[19]   9 Edw 7, c 30.

[20]   A Field, *Picture Palace: A Social History of the Cinema* (London, Gentry, 1974), 18–22.

[21]   See M Chanan, 'The Emergence of an Industry' in J Curran and V Porter (eds), *British Cinema History* (London, Weidenfeld and Nicolson, 1983), 39, 49.

[22]   Cinematography Act 1909, s 2(1).

[23]   *London County Council v Bermondsey Bioscope Co Ltd* [1911] 1 KB 445 (KB). See also *Ellis v North Metropolitan Theatre* [1915] 2 KB 61 (KB).

[24]   *R v Burnley Justices* [1916–17] All ER Rep 346 (KB).

[25]   *Mills v London County Council* [1925] 1 KB 213 (KB). Cf *Ellis v Dubowsky* [1921] 3 KB 621 (KB).

Not all conditions of this ilk were upheld, however. A condition barring entry into a cinema after 9 pm of any child under 10 years old, as well as any children between 10 and 14 years old who were not accompanied by a parent or guardian, was held to be ultra vires. A majority of the Divisional Court in *Theatre de Luxe (Halifax) Ltd v Gledhill*[26] held these conditions did not reasonably relate to the use of the premises. The future Lord Atkin dissented, but in terms that supported reasonableness review by the court.[27] The majority judgment was out of step with the case law, and was uniformly distinguished or doubted. In *Wednesbury*, Lord Greene MR took the view that the majority in *Gledhill's* case put 'much too narrow a construction upon the licensing power given by that Act [of 1909], which, of course, is not the same Act as we have to consider here.'[28]

By the end of the Second World War, the cinema was a booming business. The crest of the wave of popularity was 1946, when attendance at British cinemas reached the giddy height of 1,635 million patrons, grossing £118.3 million, in what was the last year before facing competition from television.[29]

The Case

The facts of *Associated Provincial Picture Houses Ltd v Wednesbury Corporation*[30] are so well known that it might be thought gratuitous to recite them. But familiarity has bred contempt, and a closer look throws new light on the case.

Wednesbury is one of the smaller industrial towns in the Midlands, in the centre of the district that was known in the time of the industrial revolution as 'the Black Country'.[31] Famous for its coal mining and iron ore, when the coal ran out in the nineteenth century, iron and steel production took over as dominant industries in Wednesbury, until those industries too fell on hard times during the first quarter of the twentieth century. In 1951 the population of Wednesbury stood at just over 34,000, having increased little over the previous 50 years.

---

[26] [1915] 3 KB 49 (KB).

[27] Sir Robin Cooke, 'The Struggle for Simplicity in Administrative Law' in M Taggart (ed), *Judicial Review of Administrative Law in the 1980s: Problems and Prospects* (Auckland, Oxford University Press, 1986), 1, 15 (suggesting that Lord Greene reinterpreted what Atkin LJ had said and meant in the earlier case).

[28] *Wednesbury*, above n 4, at 232.

[29] See P Corrigan, 'Film Entertainment as Ideology and Pleasure: A Preliminary Approach to a History of Audiences' in Curran and Porter, above at n 21, at 30; HE Browning and AA Sorrell, 'Cinemas and Cinema-going in Great Britain' (1954) 117 *Journal of the Royal Statistical Society, Series A (General) Part II* 134. Thereafter, there is a clear correlation between the rapid expansion of TV licences and declining cinema patronage: see *ibid* (Table 2).

[30] *Wednesbury*, above at n 4.

[31] The information in this and the following paragraph is drawn from JF Ede, *History of Wednesbury* (Wednesbury, Wednesbury Corporation, 1962). Wednesbury is in the county of Staffordshire in the West Midlands, about eight miles northwest of Birmingham. While I am not aware of any study of the cinema and cinema-going in Wednesbury, there is for Birmingham. See J Richards, 'The Cinema and Cinema-going in Birmingham in the 1930s' in JK Walton and J Walvin (eds), *Leisure in Britain 1780–1939* (Manchester, Manchester University Press, 1984), 31 and D Maynall, 'Palaces for Entertainment and Instruction: A Study of the Early Cinema in Birmingham, 1909–18' (1985) 10 *Midland History* 94.

Church and religion pervade the history of the town. The first known church at Wednesbury dates from the beginning of the thirteenth century, and a census in 1894 showed that 30 per cent of the then population of 25,000 attended church regularly. Almost certainly that percentage would have dwindled by the 1940s.

There had been a Picture House on Walsall Street, Wednesbury since 1915.[32] It was built and owned by Associated Provincial Picture Houses Ltd (APPH), and had seating for 900 patrons. APPH was a subsidiary of Provincial Cinematograph Theatres (PCT), which by the late 1920s was a leading cinema chain with nearly 100 cinemas throughout England. In 1929 PCT/APPH was bought by Gaumont–British Picture Corporation, although thereafter PCT/APPH continued to trade in their names.[33] The original Wednesbury Picture House was demolished in 1938 to make way for a new Gaumont cinema, with a wide auditorium seating 1,594, at a cost of £45,000.[34] This is the cinema which was the subject of the litigation.

By virtue of the Sunday Entertainments Act 1932, in certain circumstances a local authority was empowered to allow cinemas to open on Sundays, 'subject to such conditions as the authority thinks fit to impose.'[35] In 1946 Wednesbury Corporation granted the Gaumont cinema permission to operate on Sundays under the 1932 Act, subject to the condition that no children under fifteen years of age would be admitted on Sundays, regardless of whether or not they were accompanied by an adult.

The Picture House sought a declaration that the defendant's decision was ultra vires and/or unreasonable. As is so often the case in administrative law cases, there was a happy coincidence of the applicant's financial interest and the public interest in ensuring that a public authority acts lawfully. Obviously the primary motivation for the challenge was financial, as such a condition not only directly limited the pool of potential Sunday patrons, by excluding children under 15 years of age,[36] but also would have dissuaded many parents from patronizing the theatre on Sunday due to the need to make alternative arrangements for the care of their children.[37] Of course, that was exactly what the Corporation intended.

[32] The information in this paragraph is taken from A Eyles, *Gaumont British Cinemas* (London, Cinema Theatre Association, British Film Institute, 1996), ch 3, 97, 220.

[33] The Gaumont 'empire' of cinemas was vast. In 1929 it owned or controlled 270 cinemas. Competition was stiff in the 1930s, and by the end of that decade Associated British Picture Corporation and the Odeon theatre group were snapping at Gaumont's heels. In 1941 Odeon took over Gaumont, but the two cinema chains were not allowed by the Board of Trade to merge until the late 1950s. See D Crow, 'The British Film Industry: The Advent of Leviathan (1927–36)' (1954) 23 *Sight & Sound: The Film Quarterly* (April-June 1954, No 4) 191.

[34] It was renamed 'Odeon' in March 1964, and taken over by an independent operator in 1972, when it was renamed 'Silver.' The cinema doors closed for the last time on 19 April 1974, and it became a Bingo Hall.

[35] Sunday Entertainments Act 1932, s 1(1).

[36] It appears from various studies that children aged between 5–9 went to the cinema on average three times a month, and those aged between 10–15 went about 4½ times a month. See Browning and Sorrell, above n 29, at 134.

[37] British statistics from slightly earlier (which may not, of course, reflect the composition of audiences in Wednesbury) show that 57 per cent of regular cinema-goers were 18–40, although that group made up 42 per cent of the population. Moreover, more women attended regularly than men. It is this 18–40 year old group that would be most heavily hit by the condition prohibiting children attending Sunday cinema. For figures, see Corrigan, above n 29, at 33. See also S Harper and V Porter, 'Cinema Audience Tastes in 1950s Britain' (1999) 2 *Journal of Popular British Cinema* 66, 67–68.

There was much concern around this time about the impact of the cinema on children. Indeed, at the end of 1947 the Home Office and the Department of Education set up a Departmental Committee to consider the effects of cinema attendance on children under the age of 16 years, with a view to seeing whether changes were necessary to conditions of admission.[38] But local authorities were not imposing conditions as to entry by children on other days,[39] so one is drawn back to the significance of Sunday.

It is highly likely that the councillors of Wednesbury were reacting to fears, expressed long and loud by churches throughout Britain, that the cinema was rivalling the church, and Sunday cinema would draw townspeople away from the church and from traditional forms of recreation (as distinct from amusement), especially those based around the church.[40] Apparently some local authorities only allowed Sunday cinema after church services or in the evening.[41] The blanket prohibition on cinema admission of children all day on the Sabbath can only mean that Wednesbury Corporation thought that children (no doubt, with their parents) should do other things on the Sabbath, whether this be church-going, reading, walking or just spending 'quality time' together.[42]

It appears from several places in the judgment that the 'the well-being and the physical and moral health of children' was a relevant factor for the Corporation.[43] This was a 'relevant' or 'germane' factor that the local authority 'can properly have in mind,' 'a matter of public interest,' and therefore not something the courts can interfere with. It is not clear from the judgment how the court was informed that the physical and moral well-being of the children was taken into account by the local authority, or how the decision was intended to further that objective. There is no reference to affidavit evidence from councillors or officials in the reported judgment. Perhaps it was a matter of surmise. It certainly could not be brought under the rubric of judicial notice.

That surmise was coupled with an implicit interpretation of the open-ended discretion that the physical and moral well-being of the children was germane to the imposition of conditions on Sunday cinema openings. The Corporation took

[38] See *Report of the Departmental Committee on Children and the Cinema* (Cmd 7945, May 1950) and for a useful summary see G Keir, 'Children and the Cinema' (1950–51) 1 *British Journal of Delinquency* 225. This report led directly to the provision in the Cinematograph Act 1952 giving the Secretary of State power to make regulations concerning, inter alia, 'the health and welfare of children in relation to attendance at cinematograph exhibitions': s 2(1)(b). See ERH Ivamy, 'The Legal Background of the Motion Picture Industry' (1953) 20 *The Solicitor* 35, 37.
[39] Exceptionally, one local authority did impose a condition that cinemas close (to all patrons of whatever age) on Thursdays. Professional opinion viewed this as ultra vires: (1933) 97 *JP* 629.
[40] See generally J Richards, *The Age of the Dream Palace: Cinema and Society in Britain 1930–1939* (London, Routledge & Kegan Paul, 1984) 1–2, 50–53. For evidence of this in particular localities, see P Wild, 'Recreation in Rochdale, 1900–40' in J Clarke, C Critcher and R Johnson (eds), *Working-Class Culture: Studies in History and Theory* (London, Huchinson of London, 1979), 140 and Richards, above n 31 (Birmingham).
[41] See (1948) 112 *JP* 378.
[42] For the recreational options on Sunday, see Richards, above n 40, at ch 3.
[43] *Wednesbury*, above n 4, 230 (see also 233). The court quoted from *Harman v Butt* [1944] KB 491, 499, per Atkinson J (KB)('the defendants were entitled to consider matters relating to the welfare, including the spiritual well-being, of the community and of any section of it').

into account a relevant 'implicit' consideration.[44] That foredoomed the judicial review application. The rest of the judgment, as famous as it has become, was really surplus to requirements.

Sunday Entertainments Act 1932

It is necessary to look a little more closely at the Sunday Entertainments Act 1932. As noted above, public entertainment of any kind, including cinema showings, was illegal on the Sabbath. The Act in force went back to 1780, but its antecedents went back much further. As regards cinemas, several local authorities imposed a condition on licences granted under the 1909 Act that cinemas not open on Christmas Day, Good Friday or Sundays. As regards Sundays, this prohibition was otiose but harmless as long as everyone was aware of the general statutory prohibition.[45] However, in due course, some local authorities (particularly in London) forgot about the general prohibition and on occasions relaxed the licence prohibition on Sunday cinema exhibitions.[46] Moreover, there were many unauthorised breaches of the 1780 Act, particularly by cinemas in seaside towns at holiday times.[47] This all came to a legal head when the London County Council's practice of approving licensee applications to open on Sundays was correctly held by the Court of Appeal to be contrary to the Sunday Observance Act 1780 and hence unlawful.[48] This created difficulties, not the least of which was the spectre of common informers seeking substantial fees for identifying Sunday-opening cinemas.[49] Something had to be done quickly, and the upshot was the Sunday Entertainments Act 1932.[50]

The long title of the Sunday Entertainments Act 1932 states in relevant part it is 'to permit and regulate the opening and use of places on Sundays for certain entertainments.' It legalised such Sunday openings as had been purportedly permitted earlier and prescribed a procedure by which any licensing authority could apply for an order allowing Sunday opening in that licensing area. For those municipalities

---

[44] Lord Greene MR says as much in this passage: '[i]f, in the statute conferring the discretion, there is to be found expressly or by implication matters which the authority exercising the discretion ought to have regard to, then in exercising it must have regard to those matters' (*ibid* at 228). This pre-dates the modern splitting of relevant considerations into mandatory considerations and permissive ones (see below text following n 91). In *Wednesbury*, although Lord Greene suggests the physical and moral well-being of children is a mandatory relevant consideration ('must have regard to'), nothing turned on the future distinction because the court assumed or inferred that the local authority did take it into account.

[45] See *London County Council v Bermondsey Bioscope Co Ltd*, above n 23.

[46] This occurred elsewhere, and certainly did in Birmingham and neighbouring Smetwick: Richards, above n 40, at 52.

[47] 'Sunday Entertainments' (1949) 207 *LT* 212.

[48] *R v London County Council, ex parte Entertainments Protection Association Ltd* [1931] 2 KB 215 (CA).

[49] Above n 47, at 213.

[50] There is a tangled history. 'In all, two Parliaments, three Governments and four Bills were necessary to deal finally with the matter' of Sunday cinema opening: SG Jones, *Workers at Play: A Social and Economic History of Leisure 1918–1939* (London, Routledge & Kegan Paul, 1986), 175. See also 'Sunday Entertainments' (1932) 96 *JP* 640.

desiring Sunday cinema openings, an elaborate scheme was installed by regulations providing for a vote at an advertised public meeting and, if required, a polling of local electors.[51] By April 1946, 115 Orders had been made by Parliament at the request of local communities. In nearly 70 per cent of these cases, a public meeting had voted against the initiative, only to be overruled by the poll of electors.[52]

Without archival work, it cannot be said with any certainty what prompted the Wednesbury electors to vote for Sunday cinema opening or what motivated the councillors to impose the condition. What we do know is that Birmingham, Wednesbury's more populous neighbour, had agreed to open its cinemas on Sunday as early as 1932, over the spirited opposition of churches and moralists.[53] Elsewhere in Britain, the factors at play included the profound effect of the Second World War on social attitudes and mores, the decline of organised religion and the extraordinary popularity of the medium, especially among the working classes.[54] What is clear is that after the Second World War the local electors in Wednesbury succeeded in gaining an Order authorising Sunday cinema opening in the town.

Leading counsel for the cinema made the most of this, and put his best argument in two parts: 'It is material that in the present case there had been a poll of the electorate in favour of Sunday opening,' and 'No reasonable authority could have imposed the condition preventing the persons who have voted for Sunday performances taking their children under fifteen with them.'[55] In other words, the councillors of the town should not be able to frustrate the wishes of the majority of local electors who favoured Sunday opening, by imposing a condition that meant their children (and likely some parents as well) would be denied the fruits of that victory. By the mid-1940s, secularisation of English life was well advanced but not yet complete or universal. And there is reason for thinking that the town had 'strong ecclesiastical traditions.'[56] In the telling phrase of Harry Hopkins, which on its own probably explains the result in *Wednesbury*: 'the shed skin of Sabbatarianism was not yet wholly cleared away.'[57]

Lord Greene MR—Vinerian Scholar, Fellow of All Souls and long-time standing counsel to the University of Oxford[58]—swiped that submission aside, saying '[t]he

[51] See Sunday Cinematograph Entertainment (Polls) Order 1932, SR & O 1932/828. See generally 'Sunday Cinema Polls' (1947) 211 *JP* 204, 219 and 236 (3 Pts).

[52] *Ibid* at 204.

[53] Richards, above n 31.

[54] See P Addison, *Now the War is Over: A Social History of Britain 1945–51* (London, British Broadcasting Corporation and Jonathan Cape Ltd, 1985), ch 5; J Chapman, 'British Cinema and "The People's War"' in N Hayes and J Hill (eds), *'Millions Like Us'? British Culture in the Second World War* (Liverpool, Liverpool University Press, 1999), 33: J Richards, 'Cinema-going in Worktown: Regional Film Audiences in 1930s Britain' (1994) 14 *Historical Journal of Film, Radio & Television* 147.

[55] *Wednesbury*, above n 4, at 225–6, argument of Gallop KC. Constantine Gallop, a graduate of University College London and Balliol, was a brilliant student, placed first in the First Class Honours lists in the Bar finals and at UCL. He took silk in 1946. See *Who Was Who: 1961–1970* (London, A & C Black, 1972), 410.

[56] See Cooke, above n 27, at 13 and Ede, above n 31, at chs 3, 6 and 10.

[57] H Hopkins, *The New Look: A Social History of the Forties and Fifties in Britain* (London, Secker & Warburg, 1963), 210.

[58] AB Schofeld, *Dictionary of Legal Biography 1845–1945* (Chichester, Barry Rose Law Publishers Ltd, 1998), 182.

vote was merely for opening the cinema on Sunday "subject to such regulations as the authority thinks fit to impose".'[59] The authority had been given a 'discretion…without limitation.' It was a discretion to be exercised executively not judicially, and furthermore there was no appeal provided to the courts. The discretion was 'entrusted' to a 'responsible body,' the local authority, which 'was entrusted by Parliament with the decision on a matter which the knowledge and experience of that authority can best be trusted to deal with.'[60]

From the very beginning of cinema licensing in 1909, there was concern over the scope of local authorities' power to impose conditions on licences. For many years, The *Justice of the Peace and Local Government Review* ran an advisory service, regularly fielding questions from subscribers about the ability to impose conditions under the Acts of 1909 and 1932. Indeed, in 1940 one subscriber anticipated the question to arise in the *Wednesbury* case—can children be excluded altogether from a licensed Sunday cinema exhibition—and the opinion ventured was in the negative, such a condition would be ultra vires.[61] The refrain over this long period was that these discretions, although wide, were not unlimited.[62] The well-worn phrase from *Sharp v Wakefield* was routinely invoked: '[d]iscretion means that something is to be done within the rules of reason and justice, not according to private opinion; according to law and not humour. It is not to be arbitrary, vague or fanciful, but legal and regular.'[63]

Lord Greene agreed, of course. The ideal of the Rule of Law, not of men or women, demanded (and still demands) agreement.[64] But the Master of the Rolls went on to ask: 'what does [reasonably] mean?,'[65] and answered famously by ascribing a special, administrative law meaning to the term 'unreasonable,' to which the geographical epithet 'Wednesbury' has attached thereafter.[66] *Wednesbury* unreasonableness meant to the Master of the Rolls 'something so absurd that no sensible person could ever dream that it lay within the powers of the authority' or 'so unreasonable that no reasonable authority could ever have come to it.'[67] Of course, he really had no need to add, '[t]o prove a case of that kind would require something overwhelming.'[68]

---

[59]   *Wednesbury*, above n 4, at 225 (in arguendo).

[60]   *Ibid* at 229–30.

[61]   See (1940) 104 *JP* 196.

[62]   For a selection see (1931) 95 *JP* 587; (1932) 96 *JP* 284; (1933) 97 *JP* 629; (1935) 99 *JP* 494; (1936) 100 *JP* 739, 769; (1938) 102 *JP* 866; (1943) 107 *JP* 418.

[63]   [1891] AC 173 (HL).

[64]   I think this is what Sir John Laws must have meant when he referred to the 'rule of reason' as one of two underpinnings of the *Wednesbury* case: J Laws, 'Wednesbury' in C Forsyth and I Hare (eds), *The Golden Metwand and the Crooked Cord: Essays on Public Law in Honour of Sir William Wade QC* (Oxford, Clarendon Press, 1998), 185, 186. For criticism of Laws' characterisation, see below at nn 86–87 and accompanying text.

[65]   *Wednesbury*, above n 4, at 229.

[66]   See *Hawkins v Minister of Justice* [1991] 2 NZLR 530 at 534, per Cooke P (CA) ('the geographical epithet adds nothing').

[67]   *Wednesbury*, above n 4, at 229–30.

[68]   *Ibid* at 230.

It is part of the *Wednesbury* legend that the decision was delivered *ex tempore* late on a Friday afternoon;[69] the inference being that the judgment was 'tossed off' and considered run-of-the-mill. This might have explained the infuriating repetition in the judgment—*seemingly* the same thing said four times and in four different ways! But it appears the judgment was held off over the weekend and delivered on the following Monday.[70] Probably, Lord Greene was as surprised as anyone that the case gained admission to the Pantheon of leading public law cases.[71] It may be an illustration of the modern tendency, disparaged by Lord Radcliffe, to discover leading cases 'before they have proved that they have in them the quality to lead.'[72]

Back to the Future

In the *Wednesbury* litigation it is unlikely that the Wednesbury Gaumont cinema was acting simply only out of its own parochial financial interest. As one of over 300 cinemas in the Gaumont chain,[73] it is likely that Head Office wanted a precedent in its favour to prevent the spread of this aberrant licensing practice. Counsel for APPH is reported to have said that '[s]o far as his clients knew, no other local authority in the kingdom had taken the same line as Wednesbury.'[74] What the Gaumont chain may have been resisting was the spectre of 'tin-pot dictatorships' of councils dotted all over Britain, each a law unto themselves, imposing increasingly bizarre conditions.[75] This concern harkens back to one of the hallowed administrative law cases of the late nineteenth century, *Kruse v Johnson*.[76]

---

[69] M Beloff, 'Wednesbury, Padfield, and All That Jazz: A Public Lawyer's View of Statute Law Reform' (1994) 15 *Statute LR* 147, 157.

[70] *Ibid.*

[71] In addressing law students in Birmingham in 1938, Sir Wilfrid Greene spoke against lifting principles out of the context of cases in which they were applied. He said: 'The desire for simplification is a perennial weakness of the human mind, even the mind of judges; and the temptation to take a statement of principle out of its context of fact is one always to be resisted, particularly if the recital of facts fills many dreary pages in the report and the principle is concisely stated in the head-note. But it is a temptation that must be resisted by those who fully understand the proper use of precedent in the judicial method': 'The Judicial Office' (Presidential address to the Holdsworth Club, Faculty of Law, University of Birmingham, 13 May 1938), 12. This lecture was published at the time, but it was not included in the volume of selected Presidential addresses published to celebrate the 50th anniversary of the Holdsworth Club. See BW Harvey (ed), *The Lawyer and Justice: A Collection of Addresses by Judges and Jurists to the Holdsworth Club of the University of Birmingham* (London, Sweet & Maxwell, 1978).

[72] Lord Radcliffe, *Not in Feather Beds: Some Collected Papers* (London, Hamish Hamilton, 1968), 211, 216–17.

[73] By 1948 the commonly owned but separately run Odeon and Gaumont chains operated 317 and 304 cinemas respectively. The rival Associated British Cinemas chain had 442 cinemas. See A Eyles, 'Exhibition and the Cinema-going Experience' in R Murphy (ed), *The British Cinema Book* (London, British Film Institute, 1997), 217, 219–21.

The Gaumont chain started in Birmingham, and was headquartered there until 1939. In this and several other ways, Birmingham was 'in the forefront of cinema development in Britain in the 1930s.' See Richards, above n 40, at 36.

[74] 'Sunday Entertainment for Children' (1949) 113 *JP* 599, 600.

[75] The flavour of this is evident from *ibid* ('We find it very difficult to accept the view that it is for each elected local authority to determine, within its own (often accidental) boundaries').

[76] [1898] 2 QB 91 (DC, seven-judge bench). This case was relied upon in *London County Council v Bermondsey Bioscope Co Ltd*, above n 23.

In its own time *Kruse's* case was as famous and influential as *Wednesbury*, which replaced it in the administrative law catechism. It involved a challenge to a newly-created by-law prohibiting the playing of music in public within 50 yards of a dwelling house. The two persons convicted of this offence were associated with the Salvation Army, and it seems clear that the police employed the by-law to stop Salvationists from singing hymns in public.[77] The primary challenge to the validity of the by-law was on the ground of unreasonableness. Despite considerable unease within the legal profession as to the potential tyranny by tin-pot local bodies, each promulgating different local rules, a specially constituted Divisional Court upheld the by-law (by a majority of six to one).

The case is famous for its expression of judicial restraint, emphasising the need for 'benevolent interpretation' of the by-laws of elected local authorities. This golden thread runs through *Wednesbury*, and stitches the emblem on the classic model of administrative law. The classic model was long on rhetoric, as is shown by Lord Chief Justice Russell's listing of the grounds upon which the courts would intervene:[78]

> But unreasonable in what sense? If, for instance, they are found to be partial and unequal in their operation as between different classes; if they were manifestly unjust; if they disclosed bad faith; if they involved such oppressive or gratuitous interference with the rights of those subject to them as could find no justification in the minds of reasonable men, the Court might well say, 'Parliament never intended to give authority to make such rules, they are unreasonable and ultra vires.'

In saying that the courts will protect formal equality—each treated alike as are similarly situated—the court held out the hope that inconsistency of treatment could be combated. I suspect the *Wednesbury* case was not argued under the breach of equality head of unreasonableness (discussed in *Kruse*) because the Sunday Entertainments Act appeared to recognise that individual local authorities could impose different conditions from one another. That was the compromise adopted by the legislature in 1932: regularisation of Sunday cinema openings in areas where this had been illegally allowed, and elsewhere allowing a 'local option' by poll. There was already in the 1909 Act a broadly conferred and much exercised power to impose licence conditions on the other six days of the week. An expressly conferred additional power to impose conditions in relation to *Sunday* openings must have been intended to allow local attitudes and feelings to come into play.

Was *Wednesbury* Rightly Decided?

The *Wednesbury* case is almost universally portrayed as the product of post-war deference by the judiciary; an exemplar of the self-induced lethargy that blotted

---

[77] See DGT Williams, 'Subordinate Legislation and Judicial Control' (1997) 8 *Public Law Review* 77, 79–81 and generally R Vorspan, '"Freedom of Assembly" and the Right of Passage in Modern English Legal History' (1997) 34 *San Diego LR* 921.

[78] Above n 76, at 99–100.

the judicial escutcheon in the middle decades of the twentieth century. I think one has to be careful to separate the case from its emblematic character. Situated in its time and place, it seems to me the result was almost inevitable on the facts and the law.[79] More importantly for our purpose, however, the logic of the classic model of administrative law also compelled the result. The high threshold for judicial intervention, coupled with the lack of transparency and difficulties of proof, almost guaranteed non-intervention.

WEDNESBURY TODAY

It is oft-remarked that the *Wednesbury* case would not be decided the same way today. That is true, but trite. The motivating forces—the hangover of Sabbatarianism and Parliament's reluctance to legislate on that moral issue at one fell swoop, across the entire United Kingdom—are not present today. Since the Second World War the decline of organised religion and the secularisation of society has continued apace. Today it would be as unthinkable to banish children from the cinema on Sunday on the basis of age and Sabbatarianism as it was for Lord Greene to contemplate the dismissal of a school teacher on the ground of natural red hair colour.[80] But the important point in revisiting *Wednesbury* today, is to identify what has changed from a legal perspective, rather than to note changes in social attitudes or mores. In this section, I will examine how a case, identical to *Wednesbury*, would be dealt with by an English court today.[81]

'Righting 'Administrative Law

This is no place for a primer on developments in administrative law since the mid-twentieth century, but something must be said about the tremendous growth of the subject.[82] So rapid have been the developments since the mid-1960s that Lord

[79] Cf Sir Stephen Sedley, 'Sounds of Silence: Constitutional Law Without A Constitution' (1994) 110 *LQR* 270, 279; *R v Secretary of State for the Home Department, ex parte Daly* [2001] 2 AC 532, at 549, per Lord Cooke of Thorodon (HL).

[80] The 'red haired school teacher' illustration of *Wednesbury* unreasonableness (above n 4, at 229) has passed into legal folklore.

[81] I am using *Wednesbury* here to bring out the different methodology of constitutionalism and internationalisation, in contrast to the classic model of administrative law. This is, however, quite artificial because so much has changed in the world and in the law since then. If nothing had changed legally then, as Mark Aronson pointed out to me, the result would be the same today as in 1947. But if everything else in law stayed constant (ie prohibition on Sunday cinema exhibitions, subject to override by poll, broad discretionary power) except for the modern injection of human rights law, this would in my view make a difference in terms of limiting the breadth of the discretion so as to be compatible with the HRA. It is hoped that the disadvantage of this artificiality is offset by the utility of the analysis.

[82] For chapter and verse see the trinity: P Craig, *Administrative Law* (4th edn, London, Sweet & Maxwell, 1999); SA de Smith, H Woolf and J Jowell, *Judicial Review of Administrative Action* (5th edn, London, Sweet & Maxwell, 1995); HWR Wade and C Forsyth, *Administrative Law* (8th edn, Oxford, Oxford University Press, 2000).

Diplock felt able to say in the early 1980s that 'any judicial statements on public law if made before 1950 are likely to be a misleading guide to what the law is today.'[83] According to the orthodox account, in the mid-1960s the judges awoke from their 'long sleep' and set about renovating the house of judicial review.[84] To list only a few developments; prerogative powers are no longer immune from judicial review; the concept of jurisdiction was first expanded and then collapsed into a flexible error of law standard; the administrative/judicial dichotomy has withered under the fairness sunlamp; the concept of legitimate expectation has emerged first as a procedural doctrine and latterly as a substantive one; evidential and factual review has sprung up.

Amid all this expansion, paradoxically the *Wednesbury* formula not only survived but became a mantra, repeated literally thousands of times all over the common law world. Nor has the tide of citation been stemmed by stern criticism.[85] In part, this is because the dicta have a protean quality; it is 'a legal formula, indiscriminately used to express different and sometimes contradictory ideas.'[86] As such, it is ideally suited to flexible application and, indeed, susceptible to reinvention.

This is no better exemplified than by Sir John Laws' description of the *Wednesbury* case as reflecting 'the rule of reason,' whereby intrusions upon individual freedom by public authorities 'must be objectively justified.'[87] Of course, this stands the case on its head. As shown above, the inscrutable Corporation never explained or justified its decision and the court was complicit in this non-transparency by assuming the answer to the very question to be decided and inferring what the Corporation must have thought and done. *Wednesbury* is the antithesis of the rule of reason.

What are missing from *Wednesbury* to complete the desired reinvention are a rights-centred approach and the creation of the justificatory mechanisms to instantiate the Rule of Law. In fairness to Laws LJ, it must be said that he has been willing to do the necessary spadework on both fronts, both judicially and extra-judicially.[88]

---

[83] *R v IRC, ex parte Federation of Self-Employed and Small Businesses Ltd* [1982] AC 617, at 649.

[84] The quoted phrase is Sedley's (above n 79) but the sentiment is shared by all leading administrative textbook writers (see above n 81). An American political scientist has deployed statistical analysis to show that, despite this claim of judicial passivity, large numbers of claimants on both appeal and review succeeded against the government in this period. See S Sterett, *Creating Constitutionalism? The Politics of Legal Expertise and Administrative Law in England and Wales* (Ann Arbor, University of Michigan Press, 1997), ch 2.

[85] See the comprehensive critique by Thomas J in *Waitakere City Council v Lovelock* [1997] 2 NZLR 385 (CA).

[86] The quotation is from Justice Felix Frankfurter in *Tiller v Atlantic Coast Railroad Co*, 318 US 54, 68 (1943). Sir Roger Ormrod gave *Wednesbury* as an example of this process in 'Words and Phrases and their Influence on the Law in Practice' in P Wallington and RM Merkin (eds), *Essays in Memory of Professor FH Lawson* (London, Butterworths, 1986), 145, 149. See also DGT Williams, 'Law and Administrative Discretion' (1994) 2 *Indiana Journal of Global Legal Issues* 191, 210.

[87] Above n 64, at 186, 191.

[88] See, eg, the material referred to in M Hunt, *Using Human Rights Law in English Courts* (Oxford, Hart Publishing, 1997), 164–74; *R v Ministry of Agriculture, Fisheries and Food, ex parte First City Trading* [1997] 1 CMLR 250 (QB); *Chesterfield Properties Plc v Secretary of State for the Environment* [1998] JPL 568, 579–80 (QB). See also the discussion of an unpublished paper by Sir John Laws in R Thomas, 'Reason-giving in English and European Community Administrative Law' (1997) 3 *European Public Law* 213, 220.

The 'Righting' of administrative law is a large and complicated topic, which cannot be done justice here.[89] It predated the Human Rights Act 1998, but that legislation now confirms and requires the application of a methodology that profoundly challenges the tenets of the classic model of administrative law. Two colleagues and I argued a few years ago that such a domestic human rights instrument fundamentally changes the traditional administrative law grounds for review of discretionary decision-making.[90] A public authority must comply with the Human Rights Act unless required to do otherwise by statute. Within that vague limit, however, the authority must exercise its discretion compatibly with rights in the Human Rights Act. Some of the rights are not absolute but rather are qualified by limitations, and this entails a 'balancing exercise,' whereby the private right and public interests are weighed by the judge.[91]

The focus of this right-centred inquiry differs from that under the classic model of administrative law. The starting point is the right allegedly infringed by the exercise of discretionary power by the public authority. Next is the inquiry into whether the right has been reasonably or justifiably limited in terms of the express qualifications on the right. If it has not *and* exercise of the discretionary power in conformity with the right is not precluded by the statute, then the public authority *must* decide in accordance with the Human Rights Act. When this stage is reached the right is a constitutional trump, preventing the decision-maker from exercising the discretionary power in a way that infringes the right. We called this a decisive consideration in order to distinguish it from traditional administrative law analysis.

It is elementary that in the legal control of discretionary power there is a hierarchy of considerations.[92] At the top is the mandatory relevant consideration: this may be expressly provided in the statute or may be implied. Such considerations must be taken into account by the decision-maker and given genuine consideration. In the middle is the permissive relevant consideration, which is one that the decision-maker may lawfully take into account but is not obliged to do so. Last of all, at the bottom, is the irrelevant consideration, and it is unlawful for the decision-maker to take this into account at all. As regards the two types of relevant considerations, the weight given each consideration is for the decision-maker, not the court, unless it can be said that the decision-maker has acted unreasonably.

---

[89] See generally Hunt, above n 88 and M Loughlin, 'Rights Discourse and Public Law Thought in the United Kingdom' in GW Anderson (ed), *Rights and Democracy: Essays in UK-Canadian Constitutionalism* (London, Blackstone Press, 1999), 193.

[90] J McLean, P Rishworth and M Taggart, 'The Impact of the New Zealand Bill of Rights on Administrative Law' in *The New Zealand Bill of Rights Act 1990* (Auckland, Legal Research Foundation Inc, 1992), 62–97. What follows is a summary of that argument drawn from M Taggart, 'Tugging on Superman's Cape: Lessons from Experience with the New Zealand Bill of Rights Act 1990' [1998] *PL* 266, 274–79.

[91] See *Bahamas District of the Methodist Church in the Caribbean and the Americas v Symonette* [2000] 5 LRC 196 (PC, Bahamas) at 217: 'Human rights conventions and equivalent constitutional provisions recognise that the protection afforded to rights ... is not absolute ... Broadly stated, a balancing test is then called for'.

[92] See generally J McLean, 'Constitutional and Administrative Law: The Contribution of Lord Cooke' in P Rishworth (ed), *The Struggle for Simplicity in the Law: Essays for Lord Cooke of Thorodon* (Wellington, Butterworths, 1997), 221, 227–30.

The Human Rights Act methodology sketched above supersedes this analysis. If the discretionary power can be exercised in conformity with the (reasonably limited) right, it must be so exercised. In contradistinction to traditional administrative law theory, this is not just something a decision-maker may or must have regard to, it is a legal impediment to exercising the power in a way that infringes the Human Rights Act.

Often in the past in administrative law cases, 'rights' issues were not visible at the abstract level of principle or were lost sight of amid the flexible application of doctrine in particular contexts or the clamour of controversy. For example, who spoke for the 'rights' of the children or their parents or the majority of electors who voted for Sunday cinema opening in *Wednesbury*? What weight was given to the 'right' of the cinema owner to invite whomever it liked onto its property?[93] The 'rights centred-ness' of the Human Rights Act entails that arguments about context, policy, justiciability and deference generally must relate to the definition of the right or its prescribed limitations. This is a more focused, consistent and transparent methodology than that prevalent in traditional administrative law adjudication, where 'rights' issues can be swept over in conclusory findings that the exercise of the power was or was not *Wednesbury* unreasonable.

As Jeffrey Jowell and Anthony Lester demonstrated 15 years ago, the mantra of *Wednesbury* unreasonableness in administrative law has obscured the underlying role of administrative law in protecting rights.[94] The claim here is not that administrative law methodology could not recognise rights or appropriately balance them against other interests. It is rather that the judges had considerable leeway in how they approached and resolved such issues in traditional administrative law terms. There was no accepted methodology that required rights issues to be identified and approached in the same manner and sequence (definition of right, limitations on right, relation to statute, etc). The Human Rights Act changes all that.

By section 6 of the Human Rights Act 1998 it is unlawful for a public authority to act in a way which is incompatible with the European Convention on Human Rights (ECHR), unless compelled to do so by statute (in which case a declaration of incompatibility may be made). The number of instances in which a statute will require a discretionary power to interfere with a reasonably limited right is likely to be relatively small. So the argument made here will likely be available in the

[93] Susan Sterett has shown that judges were most active on review and appeal in areas where the individual's property rights were threatened by the state: above n 84. She does not, however, consider the *Wednesbury* case in terms of property rights; nor did the Court of Appeal in *Wednesbury*. The trial judge, Henn Collins J, took the view that the 1932 Act did not abridge rights but extended them by waiving the Sunday observance prohibition: *Associated Provincial Picture Houses, Ltd v Wednesbury Corporation* [1947] 1 All ER 498, at 499 (KB).

It all depends on starting point, of course. Some American legal scholars would view the local authority's action there as expropriating without compensation the right of the cinema owner to admit and exclude whomever it likes on whatever day it likes. See above n 18. That the British have never viewed the situation this way, but rather as clearly within the 'police power' of local government to regulate licensed activity, is suggestive of further comparative common law research on licensing and property rights. See *Sky City Auckland Ltd v Wu* [2002] 3 NZLR 621 (CA).

[94] J Jowell and A Lester, 'Beyond *Wednesbury*: Substantive Principles of Administrative Law' [1987] *PL* 368.

preponderance of cases where public authorities exercise discretionary powers in such ways as to infringe Convention rights. Certainly, should a *Wednesbury* case reappear today, there would appear to be scope to exercise the condition-imposing power in ways that would not unreasonably infringe rights so that it could not be said that rendering the discretion compatible with the Convention would empty it of content and trigger section 6(2) of the Human Rights Act 1998.

Wednesbury under the ECHR and the Human Rights Act 1998

Although somewhat artificial, there is value in looking at how a case on all fours with *Wednesbury* would be decided today under the Human Rights Act 1998.[95]

Wednesbury Corporation is a public authority, and as such cannot lawfully 'act in a way which is incompatible with a Convention right.'[96] The actions of the Corporation in *Wednesbury* essentially constitute a specific restriction upon the liberty of a certain class of persons (children under 15) to attend the cinema on a certain day of the week, together with a restriction on the freedom of cinema operators to admit such persons on that day. Is this compatible with Convention rights?

To invoke the Human Rights Act a person must be a 'victim' of an unlawful act, as defined in the ECHR.[97] The jurisprudence of the European Court of Human Rights establishes that persons or companies claiming to be victims of a violation of one or more of the Convention rights must be able to show that they were 'directly affected' by the measure complained of.[98] The excluded children and the cinema owner are victims under this test, but neither the children's parents nor various representative bodies would likely qualify.

Several rights might be invoked on the facts of *Wednesbury*,[99] but I will focus on the rights to freedom of expression and respect for family life.

The right to hold and express opinions includes the freedom to receive information and ideas without interference by public authorities. Prima facie, exclusion of children from the cinema interferes with the right of those children to receive information and ideas.[100] Although Article 10 provides that '[t]his Article shall not prevent States from requiring the licensing of … cinema enterprises,' a licence condition excluding children from cinema admission exceeds the obvious

---

[95] A more realistic situation today would be local authority imposed curfews for children. See Criminal Justice and Police Act 2001, ss 48–9.

[96] Human Rights Act 1998, s 6. It is not necessary to explore here the issue whether the interpretive principle in s 3 provides broader catchment than s 6.

[97] *Ibid* s 7, cross referencing to ECHR Article 34.

[98] See eg, *Open Door Counselling Ltd and others v Ireland*, judgment of 29 July 1992, Series A, No 242; (1993) 15 EHRR 244.

[99] The other Convention rights of possible relevance to this situation are: Article 5 (right to liberty and security); Article 11 (freedom of assembly and association); Article 14 (prohibition of discrimination); Article 1 of the First Protocol (peaceful enjoyment of property).

[100] ECHR Article 10 has been held to protect someone who is prevented from receiving information: *Autronic AG v Switzerland*, judgment of 22 May 1990, Series A, No 178; (1990) 12 EHRR 34; *R (Farrakhan) v Secretary of State for the Home Department* [2002] EWCA Civ 606; [2002] 3 WLR 481.

limitation of freedom of expression necessarily consequent upon introduction of a licensing scheme.[101] For the limitation to pass muster, it must comport with Article 10(2), being a restriction 'prescribed by law and necessary in a democratic society, in the interests of … the protection of health or morals.'

The first issue is whether the imposition of a condition pursuant to a broad open-ended discretion is 'prescribed by law.' Initially, the European Court of Human Rights spoke tough—affirming the Rule of Law ideal that law be accessible, knowable, sufficiently precise to guide action, with foreseeable consequences—but tempered this with realism: 'many laws are inevitably couched in terms which, to a greater or lesser extent, are vague and whose interpretation and application are questions of practice.'[102] There is nothing in subsequent jurisprudence from the European Court to suggest that the broad discretion to impose conditions on cinema licences would not satisfy the 'prescribed by law' test.[103] The second issue is, assuming the condition at issue in *Wednesbury* was imposed today, whether it would be upheld as necessary to protect the health or morals of children? The answer to this is surely no. The European Court, in cases concerning whether or not Article 10 has been justifiably restricted, have taken what amounts to a balanced, proportional approach; essentially asking whether the scope of the impugned restriction is too broad or intrusive, extending further into the realms of merits-based review in more egregious cases. The condition would not be considered a proportionate response, and likely no permissible margin of appreciation would be able to save the condition.

The same result would be reached under Article 8, which protects 'family life.'[104] The argument here is that the decision of parents and children to accompany each other to the cinema is a 'family' matter within the protected sphere of 'family life.' There is no single definition of 'family life' in the European jurisprudence. Whereas the separation of parent(s) and child is very short term—a matter of hours—compared to the immigration cases that routinely raise Article 8 challenges, it is not implausible to invoke this Article. But even if an infringement was made out, Article 8 contains similar qualifications to Article 10 and the Corporation would fare no better today in attempting to justify its condition.

But the important lesson is that the burden of justification and persuasion—

---

[101] See FG Jacobs and RCA White, *The European Convention on Human Rights* (Oxford, Clarendon Press, 1996), 230–32.

[102] *Sunday Times v United Kingdom*, judgment of 26 April 1979, 270 Series A, No 30; (1979–80) 2 EHRR 245, at 270.

[103] In the European sequel to the House of Lords' decision in *R v Home Secretary, ex parte Brind* [1991] 1 AC 696, the Commission on Human Rights held a statutory discretionary power satisfied the 'prescribed by law' requirement if its scope and manner of application could be understood with sufficient clarity: *Brind v United Kingdom* (Application 18714/91), 9 May 1994, (1994) 77 ADR 42. The same fudging has occurred in Canada with the identical phrasing in s 1 of the Charter of Rights and Freedoms. See *Slaight Communications Inc v Davidson* (1989) 59 DLR 416 (SCC).

[104] The cinema, not being human and not capable of having a family, cannot be considered to be a 'victim' for the purposes of s 7 of the Human Rights Act 1998, and thus could not raise this Article on its own behalf. This problem could be solved easily by joining a party to the proceeding who could lay claim to the status of 'victim', eg, a family affected by the Corporation's prohibition being the obvious example.

that the right has been reasonably limited—falls squarely on the public authority. Wednesbury Corporation could not today maintain its inscrutability. It would have to justify the restriction on the children's right to freedom of expression or lose the litigation. The methodology of rights adjudication forces the local authority to give reasons and to back those up with as much evidence as possible, including sociological evidence.

As noted above, in 1947 the Wednesbury Corporation could have put forward a formidable case. A so-called 'Brandeis brief', containing sociological and economic evidence,[105] could have included studies on the impact of the cinema on children, and information about the church-going habits of the population, the variable 'take-up' of the opportunity to permit Sunday openings elsewhere in the country and the varying conditions imposed by other licensing authorities where Sunday cinema opening was allowed. The Corporation never had to do this. Indeed, it never had to give any reasons or provide any evidence at all as to why it did what it did. Not only did the classic model not require justification, it actively discouraged it. It was for the challenging cinema to discover and show legal error, and to get over a very high threshold. The collectivity could sit tight-lipped. What rights-centred adjudication has done—and this is revolutionary—is to fundamentally and irrevocably change the methodology, and hence the rules, of the public law game.

This leads on to another important difference between rights adjudication in administrative law guise today and the position in 1947. Back then it was APPH, simultaneously pursuing its private financial interest and the public interest in ensuring lawful administration, which appeared and was heard. In so far as the interests of the children, their parents, or the majority of electors who had voted for Sunday cinema opening were heard at all, it fell to counsel for the cinema to advocate for them. The reported argument suggests it was done, at best, obliquely. There were no other plaintiffs, neither in court nor 'maintaining' the action.[106] No intervenors appeared, and no amicus curia was appointed.[107]

Imagine the scene today if such a condition was imposed. Children and parents' rights groups would gather under the banners of human rights for children and family 'choice'. The Human Rights Act and the ECHR would be bandied about, buttressed by reference to the International Covenant on Civil and Political Rights (ICCPR)[108] and the ratified but unincorporated Convention on the Rights of Children (CRC).[109]

[105] On the 'Brandeis brief' see DM Walker, *Oxford Companion to Law* (Oxford, Clarendon Press, 1980), 148.

[106] The reference here is to the tort and crime of maintenance, whereby someone without a legally recognisable interest in the subject matter of a civil action provides financial assistance to a party to that action.

[107] I am not saying that the Rules of Court allowed all of this in the 1940s. The point is that the absence of such is consistent with the classic model of administrative law.

[108] 999 UNTS 171. See D Fottrell, 'Reinforcing the Human Rights Act: the Role of the International Covenant on Civil and Political Rights' [2002] *PL* 485.

[109] United Nations Convention on the Rights of the Child 1989, 1577 UNTS 3. The ECHR makes few explicit references to children and has been said to 'lack even the most basic recognition of the rights of children': U Kilkelly, *The Child and the European Convention on Human Rights* (Aldershot, Dartmouth, 1999), 3. This makes reference to the CRC all the more important.

ICCPR Article 19 and CRC Article 13 regarding freedom of expression are in very similar terms to ECHR Article 10. Moreover, CRC Article 3 provides that '[i]n all actions concerning children … undertaken by … administrative authorities … the best interests of the child shall be a primary consideration.' Case law in New Zealand and Canada treat this ratified but unincorporated international legal obligation as a relevant consideration that administrative decision-makers must take into account; in other words, a mandatory relevant consideration.[110] Interestingly, this is little more than the Court of Appeal did in *Wednesbury*: reading the broad discretion as 'implicitly' recognising the relevance of the best interests of the children. Again, the difference today is that we have fundamentally different perceptions of what is good for children and who should determine that issue (as between the parents/care-givers, the children and the state), than was the case in England immediately after the Second World War.

Today, 'victims' (in terms of the requirements of the Human Rights Act and ECHR) would be found by children's and parents' rights groups to take representative actions, and the groups themselves would seek standing. Amicus curiae might be appointed by the court. If the English legal establishment was unpersuaded, a trip to Strasbourg might be embarked upon. But court action would be only one strand of a co-ordinated strategy of lobbying and public campaigning. At the international level, these same non-governmental organisations (NGOs) would complain to the Human Rights Committee and the Committee on the Rights of the Child at the periodic reviews of the United Kingdom's performance under the ICCPR and CRC, and likely provoke adverse comment. This would be used to flay the government, and on it goes …

This bears the hallmark of what Abram Chayes called 'public law litigation.'[111] The object of such litigation is the vindication of constitutional rights or statutory policies.[112] Suffice it to say here, this model of litigation rejects almost all of the constraints of judicial method and procedure contained in the classic model of administrative law. For complex reasons, pressure groups are increasingly bringing political/policy disputes to court, for resolution there rather than in the legislature or elsewhere in government and society.[113] 'Bringing rights home' has given these groups in British society, and the individuals represented by them, legal pegs in the form of rights upon which to hang administrative law challenges. A further dimension is added by the increasing imbrication of human rights instruments—domestic, regional and international—each influenced by, and building upon, the instruments that have gone before. It is part of the complex

---

[110]   *Tavita v Minister of Immigration* [1994] 2 NZLR 257 (CA); *Baker v Canada (Minister of Citizenship and Immigration* [1999] 2 SCR 817; (1999) 174 DLR (4th) 193 (SCC); *Minister for Immigration and Ethnic Affairs v Teoh* (1995) 183 CLR 273, at 304, per Gaudron J (HCA).

[111]   See A Chayes, 'The Role of the Judge in Public Law Litigation' (1976) 89 *Harv LR* 1281. See also C Harlow, 'Public Interest Litigation in England: The State of the Art' in J Cooper and R Dhavan (eds), *Public Interest Law* (London, Blackwell, 1986), 90. Cf RL Marcus, 'Public Law Litigation and Legal Scholarship' (1988) 21 *Michigan Journal of Law Reform* 647.

[112]   Chayes, above n 111, at 1284.

[113]   The pioneering book in the United Kingdom is C Harlow and R Rawlings, *Pressure Through Law* (London, Routledge, 1992).

process of globalisation, which is being played out in various ways as regards human rights law.[114]

To some, the international human rights lobby is a bogey, pushing the envelope of politics onto (for the most part) an unsuspecting and naïve British judiciary.[115] Perhaps even more worrying, from this point of view, is the minority of judges who are already aboard 'the rights band-wagon.'[116] Importing 'rights talk' and the paraphernalia of constitutional adjudication from the USA and Europe (with the foreshadowed legalisation of politics and politicisation of the judiciary) is said to undermine the tenets of the *English* Constitution.[117] Critics of these developments sometimes become unlikely supporters of the reasoning and result in *Wednesbury*. For example, it has been said of JAG Griffith, a principal supporter of the 'Political Constitution,'[118] that his criticisms of Lord Greene's judgment 'strangely echoes Griffith's own views.'[119]

The indigenousness of *Wednesbury* is an attraction also to those on the political Right. Here there is support for 'fundamental rights,' but of the home grown variety, rooted in English soil and history, mixed with a good deal of scepticism of what is to be gained from reliance on European sources.[120] This cashes out in a preference for *Wednesbury* terminology over the Euro-speak of proportionality. For this to be a viable option the monolithic skin of the *Wednesbury* standard has to be shed to reveal that it has always been a chameleon, taking its hue from the nature of the issues involved. On this basis, five years ago Sir John Laws was prepared to pronounce *Wednesbury* 'alive and well.' [121]

Indeed, *Wednesbury* is far too healthy for the liking of some commentators. Those who do not share all the qualms of the Left about the judiciary adjudicating rights or the Right's suspicion of regional and international human rights standards, worry that the *Wednesbury* standard will continue to license human rights

---

[114] See C McCrudden, 'A Common Law of Human Rights?: Transnational Judicial Conversations on Constitutional Rights' (2000) 20 *OJLS* 499; reprinted in K O'Donovan and GR Rubin (eds), *Human Rights and Legal History: Essays in Honour of Brian Simpson* (Oxford, Oxford University Press, 2001).

[115] See, eg, C Harlow 'Public Law and Popular Justice' (2002) 65 *MLR* 1, especially 9,12–13, 16–18.

[116] C Harlow, ' Export, Import: The Ebb and Flow of English Public Law' [2000] *PL* 240, 251.

[117] See further M Taggart, ' "The Peculiarities of the English": Resisting the Public/Private Law Distinction' in P Craig and R Rawlings (eds) *Law and Administration in Europe—Essays in Honour of Carol Harlow* (Oxford, Oxford University Press, 2003), 107.

[118] JAG Griffith, 'The Political Constitution' (1979) 42 *MLR* 1.

[119] C Harlow and R Rawlings, *Law and Administration* (2nd edn, London, Butterworths, 1997), 82. For JAG Griffith's recent views on Lord Greene, see 'Judges and the Constitution' in R Rawlings (ed), *Law, Society, and Economy: Centenary Essays for the London School of Economics and Political Science 1895–1995* (Oxford, Oxford University Press, 1997), 289, 290–91.

[120] See, eg *R v Lord Chancellor, ex parte Witham* [1998] QB 575 (QB). See also the scepticism of Lord Hoffmann: 'A Sense of Proportion' in M Andenas and F Jacobs (eds), *European Community Law in English Courts* (Oxford, Clarendon Press, 1998), 149.

[121] Laws, above n 64, at 201. But in a recent case Laws LJ appears to turn his back on *Wednesbury* in favour of the flexibility of proportionality: *R (on the application of ProLife Alliance) v British Broadcasting Corporation* [2002] EWCA Civ 297; [2002] 2 All ER 756, at 767, per Laws LJ (CA). In a similar vein, see *R (Farrakhan) v Secretary of State for the Home Department*, above n 100, at 500–1, per Lord Phillips of Worth Matravers MR (CA); *R v Secretary of State for the Home Secretary, ex parte Daly*, above n 79, at 547 (Lord Steyn) and 549 (Lord Cooke of Thorodon).

infringements.[122] While acknowledging many of the advances made in recent times towards flexible, rights-respecting applications of *Wednesbury*, their worry is the atavistic tendencies of some judges to revert back to *Wednesbury* non-transparency when the going is perceived to get tough.[123]

Will this mean that the name *Wednesbury* will disappear from the lips of lawyers and from the law reports? If it does, in my view, it will simply be replaced by another term, likely contenders being proportionality or 'margin of appreciation,' expressing much the same ideas. The central idea behind *Wednesbury* is that judges are not, and should not pretend to be, ready, willing and able to adjudicate upon every dispute between citizen and the state. Some of these disputes are not justiciable in the strict sense, nor do many of the others fall within the training or expertise of the judges. The trick, as Goldilocks learnt the hard way, is to get the temperature of constitutional porridge 'just right.'[124]

Inevitably, as seems now to be recognised on all sides, this involves a sliding scale, with non-justiciability at one end and close scrutiny at the other, and the development of criteria to pin a dispute accurately on the scale.[125] What this requires is the articulation of a theory of deference—with fine calibrations of democratic legitimacy, expertise and comparative competence—for the first time in UK public law.[126] This would allow, for instance, in a case like *Wednesbury*, the democratic credentials of an elected council to be balanced with the democratically evidenced wishes of the majority of local electors wanting Sunday cinema.

TOWARDS A CULTURE OF JUSTIFICATION

As hinted at earlier, the classic model of administrative law never lived up to the Rule of Law rhetoric. The law presupposes that there are reasons for the decisions reached and that the administrative process is rational and not arbitrary, but did not insist on the statement of findings of fact and reasons for decisions.[127] It is only in the last decade or two that any progress has been made in changing the common law in this regard. The English courts (and for that matter those in Australia and New Zealand) have not yet gone as far as the Supreme Court of Canada in recognis-

---

[122] Hunt, above n 88, at 241.

[123] *Ibid* at 25.

[124] The allusion to Goldilocks was suggested by a heading in Martin Shapiro's 'The "Globalization" of Judicial Review' in LM Friedman and HN Scheiber (eds), *Legal Culture and the Legal Profession* (Colorado, Westview Press, 1996), 119, 132.

[125] The case law and literature is increasing rapidly. See generally P Craig, 'The Courts, the Human Rights Act and Judicial Review' (2001) 117 *LQR* 589; I Leigh, 'Taking Rights Proportionately: Judicial Review, the Human Rights Act and Strasbourg' [2002] *PL* 265; M Elliott, 'The Human Rights Act 1998 and the Standard of Substantive Review' [2001] *CLJ* 301.

[126] Hunt, above n 88, at 215; Craig, above n 125; J Jowell, 'Beyond the Rule of Law: Towards Constitutional Judicial Review' [2000] *PL* 671. For a discussion of some of these issues outside the United Kingdom, see M Taggart, 'The Contribution of Lord Cooke to Scope of Review Doctrine in Administrative Law: A Comparative Common Law Perspective' in Rishworth, above n 92, at 189.

[127] See above n 7 and accompanying text.

ing a generally applicable common law duty to give reasons on administrative deci-sion-makers,[128] but it seems only a matter of time before the exceptions swallow the hoary general rule that reasons need not be given.[129] The constitutionalisation of administrative law requires this step.[130]

That will not please everyone.[131] Some view requiring reasons for discretionary decision-making (or the imposition of lawyers' reasoning processes) as threaten-ing the very nature of discretion.[132] On one positivistic view, there is a tension between administrative decision-making and the giving of reasons. Frederick Schauer has argued that giving reasons involves a commitment to the generality of the reason and its application in similar circumstances.[133] He points out that on this conception 'giving a reason is like setting forth a rule'[134] and that makes it problematic to require reasons in circumstances where the power of particularism is strong—where 'case-by-case decision making and flexibility are thought impor-tant.'[135] That describes exactly the orthodox conception of discretionary power in administrative law that underpins the 'no fettering' rule, and views notions of review for inconsistency and an estoppel doctrine as anathema.

Moreover, many lawyers view the sphere of discretion as a lawless void, and they are quite happy about that.[136] Discretion is the hole in the middle of the dough-nut, to use Dworkin's metaphor,[137] where 'culture, tradition and myth' rather than rationality determine outcomes.[138] If law intruded, then judges would be on a slippery slope to determining, for example, the merits of such trivia (or 'high policy,' depending on your point of view)[139] as conditions on opening cinemas on Sunday: about which they know nothing and care less, and would be needlessly redoing what has been done by those that do know and care. There is a strong res-onance here with what was said and done in the *Wednesbury* case.

---

[128] *Baker v Canada (Minister of Citizenship and Immigration,* above n 110 .

[129] See P Craig, 'The Common Law, Reasons and Administrative Justice' [1994] *CLJ* 282. For an overview of the then current state of the law in the United Kingdom, Canada, Australia and New Zealand as to the common law requirement on administrators and judges to give reasoned decisions, see M Taggart, 'Administrative Law' [2000] *New Zealand Law Review* 439, 439–42.

[130] See Jowell, above n 126, at 680–81.

[131] This section draws upon D Dyzenhaus, M Hunt and M Taggart, 'The Principle of Legality in Administrative Law: Internationalisation as Constitutionalisation' (2001) 1 *Oxford University Com-monwealth Law Journal* 5, 27–29.

[132] Cf R MacDonald and D Lametti, 'Reasons for Decision in Administrative Law' (1990) 3 *Cana-dian Journal of Administrative Law & Practice* 123.

[133] F Schauer, 'Giving Reasons' (1995) 47 *Stan LR* 633, 642–44.

[134] *Ibid* at 651.

[135] *Ibid* at 659.

[136] David Dyzenhaus got me to see this clearly.

[137] R Dworkin, *Taking Rights Seriously* (Cambridge, Harvard University Press, 1977), 31: 'Discre-tion, like the hole in a doughnut, does not exist except as an area left open by a surrounding belt of restriction.'

[138] JL Mashaw, 'Small Things Like Reasons are Put in a Jar: Reason and Legitimacy in the Adminis-trative State' (2001) 70 *Fordham LR* 17, 26: 'The [administrative state] … is the institutional embodi-ment of the enlightenment project to substitute reason for the dark forces of culture, tradition, and myth.'

[139] In *Wednesbury,* above n 4, at 230 Lord Greene MR referred to the dispute as 'a matter of high public policy.'

A variation on this objection is that the imposition of a duty to give reasons will or may lead to excessive or unpredictable judicial intervention. In the American administrative law context, Martin Shapiro demonstrated that the evolved reasons requirement there confers upon reviewing judges considerable discretion to choose any point on a continuum from mild procedural review (you can reach any decision you please, as long as you give reasons) through intermediate review (you must give adequate reasons for the decision reached) to full substantive review (you must reach the best reasoned decision). According to Shapiro, the 'procedural veneer' of reason-giving requirements is 'an ideal cover' for judges intent on substantive review.[140]

Of course, exactly the same tension between correcting administrative errors and preserving administrative expertise exists in other common law jurisdictions. The non-transparent and instrumental selection by judges from a flexible range of review standards that Shapiro complains about is illustrated on the other side of the Atlantic by the flexible (for which read variable) application of *Wednesbury* unreasonableness.[141] In other words, reason-giving will not necessarily solve one of the enduring paradoxes of administrative law—*quis custodiet ipsos custodes* (who guards the guardians?). But coupled with a formal and explicit calibration of review standards, accompanied by criteria to guide selection, judicial discretion can be acceptably constrained.[142]

CONCLUSION

Constitutionalism requires justification of alleged rights-infringing behaviour and the adoption of a constitutional methodology of proportionality, balancing of rights and interests, and reasoned elaboration. Internationalisation accentuates that development by reinforcing, and in some instances adding to, the rights that claim recognition from the courts.[143] At least as regard 'rights' recognised by domestic human rights instruments or by the common law itself, the new constitutional methodology is firmly in place.[144] In a legal system without a 'capital C'

---

[140] M Shapiro, 'The Giving Reasons Requirement' [1992] *University of Chicago Legal Forum* 179, 181–89 reprinted in M Shapiro and A Stone Sweet, *On Law, Politics and Judicialization* (Oxford, Oxford University Press, 2002) 228. See generally S Shapiro and R Levy, 'Heightened Scrutiny of the Fourth Branch:Separation of Powers and the Requirement of Adequate Reasons for Agency Decisions' [1987] *Duke LJ* 387.

[141] See Jowell and Lester, above n 94; Laws, above n 64.

[142] See *International Transport Roth Gmbh v Secretary of State for the Home Office* [2002] EWCA Civ 158; [2002] 3 WLR 344, at 372–78, per Laws LJ (dissenting)(CA).

[143] See Dyzenhaus, Hunt and Taggart, above n 131.

[144] Due to space constraints, the argument in this chapter is limited to administrative law cases involving alleged infringements of rights recognised in domestic, regional or international human rights instruments or by the common law. There is an important debate, yet to occur in the United Kingdom, about whether or not British public law will bifurcate into human rights law and general administrative law (ie, the area left when you subtract rights-centred litigation). Some will argue that the unreformed or classic model of administrative law should survive in the latter area. I can see no advantage in maintaining an administrative law rump, cut off from developments in human rights law. But that is a matter for another day.

constitution, such as the United Kingdom, rights-based adjudication takes place, by default, through administrative law proceedings. Consequently, administrative law is in the throes of adjusting to that enhanced role. I have described that process as the reinvention of administrative law, because of the magnitude of the departure from the classic model of administrative law. The emblem of the classic model, *Wednesbury* unreasonableness, is also in the process of being reinvented. It appears likely that *Wednesbury* unreasonableness will be either replaced altogether by proportionality or blended with it somehow.[145] The hard work of fashioning doctrines, procedures and techniques adequate to the task required by constitutionalism has only just begun.

[145] See eg, *Association of British Civilian Internees—Far Eastern Region* v *Secretary of State for Defence* [2002] EWCA Civ 473 (CA).

13

Sovereignty's Blight: Why Contemporary Public Law Needs the Concept of 'Due Deference'

MURRAY HUNT

INTRODUCTION

SINCE THE COMING into force of the Human Rights Act 1998 (HRA), one of the central concerns of courts and commentators concerned with public law has been the extent to which the advent of explicit human rights adjudication has affected the traditional grounds of judicial review. The focus of debate has largely been the extent to which the traditional *Wednesbury* approach to judicial review must now be replaced by the proportionality test which is required under the European Convention on Human Rights (ECHR), and the extent to which this has changed the nature of adjudication in public law.[1] Indeed, so much analysis has there been of this in the courts and in the journals that there is now a palpable weariness setting in amongst the discussants, and a growing consensus that the matter has now been settled beyond doubt and need no longer detain us.[2]

It is certainly true that at a purely doctrinal level the topic long since ceased to be very interesting. A number of masterly analyses have been produced explaining the way in which the proper application of a proportionality test requires a highly structured and sophisticated analysis quite different from anything that was ever required under the more traditional grounds of judicial review.[3] That the courts

---

[1] See eg Paul Craig, 'The Courts, the Human Rights Act and Judicial Review' (2001) 117 *LQR* 589; Mark Elliott, 'The Human Rights Act 1998 and the Standard of Substantive Review' (2001) 60 *CLJ* 301; Ian Leigh, 'Taking Rights Proportionately: Judicial Review, the Human Rights Act and Strasbourg' [2002] *PL* 265; Richard Clayton, 'Regaining a Sense of Proportion: The Human Rights Act and the Proportionality Principle' [2001] *EHRLR* 504.

[2] See eg Tim Owen, 'Assessment of Fact, Due Deference and the Wider Impact of the Human Rights Act in Administrative Law' in J Jowell and J Cooper (eds), *JUSTICE/UCL Seminars* (Oxford, Hart Publishing, 2003).

[3] See eg Michael Fordham and Tom de la Mare, 'Identifying the Principles of Proportionality' in J Jowell and J Cooper (eds), *Understanding Human Rights Principles* (Hart Publishing, 2001), 77–89; David Feldman, 'Proportionality and the Human Rights Act 1998' in Evelyn Ellis (ed), *The Principle of Proportionality in the Laws of Europe* (Hart Publishing, 2000); Garreth Wong, 'Towards the Nutcracker Principle: Reconsidering the Objections to Proportionality' [2000] *PL* 92.

are now required to follow this approach whenever Convention rights are in play, rather than the less rigorous approach followed before the HRA, has also now been authoritatively established at the highest level in a number of cases.[4] What is there left to say?

There is one important aspect of this debate, however, which has yet to be satisfactorily addressed by courts and commentators and which is not going to go away: the question of 'deference'. When is it appropriate and when is it not appropriate for courts to interfere with decisions made by other wielders of constitutional power, be they legislative, executive or administrative? More importantly, what *approach* should courts take to identifying the circumstances in which judicial interference is appropriate or inappropriate? This, after all, is the inescapable central question of public law in any legal system with a pretence to constitutionalism of any kind: what are the proper boundaries to the respective powers of the different branches of government, and who decides on where those boundaries are drawn? Despite the pride which leading protagonists often take in the anti-theoretical nature of English legal practice,[5] this subject is one of those doctrinal outcrops where the submerged assumptions of legal theory repeatedly defy practitioners' and judges' habituated techniques for keeping them conveniently concealed beneath the waterline.

This chapter attempts to sketch out the beginnings of a framework for approaching this inescapable and central question of public law. It takes as its point of departure the landmark decision of the House of Lords in *Daly*, which takes an important step towards a culture of justification in English public law, yet simultaneously appears to contain the means of its own undoing in Lord Steyn's teasing observation at the end of his seminal judgment that 'in law, context is everything'.[6] It asks how this elliptical but important statement should be translated into a judicial approach which remains true to the underlying vision of constitutionalism which animates the judgment, at the same time as recognising the limits to the legitimate judicial role in a modern constitutional democracy.

It is argued that in trying to work out how to achieve this delicate task, a false doctrinal step was taken in English law with the introduction of spatial metaphors into the language of judicial review, presupposing that there is a 'discretionary area of judgment' or a 'margin of discretion,' within which primary decision-makers are simply beyond the reach of judicial interference. Such an approach, it is argued, is entirely at odds with the notion of review for justification: it treats cer-

---

[4] Most notably *Daly v Secretary of State for the Home Department* [2001] 2 WLR 1622; *R v Shayler* [2002] 2 WLR 754.

[5] See, eg, Lord Hoffmann's pride in the pragmatism of English practice in his 2001 COMBAR Lecture, 'The Separation of Powers' [2002] JR 137, 138, para 5: 'Anyone who thinks it is a denial of justice for the Lord Chancellor to sit as one of five members of an appellate committee in a case in which he has not the slightest personal interest would be more comfortable in a state founded on theoretical or religious principles than in an old democracy whose institutions have been shaped by the way things work in practice'. The paradox of such a robust defence of legal pragmatism in a lecture invoking a highly formalistic theory of the separation of powers to justify limits to the judicial role is symptomatic of the continued vitality of the Diceyan account.

[6] *Daly*, above n 4, at para 28.

tain areas of decision-making, or of a particular decision-maker's responsibilities, as being beyond the reach of legality, and within the realm of pure discretion in which remedies for wrongs are political only. It also tends to prevent the proper articulation of what may be perfectly legitimate reasons for deferring, obscuring them behind a vocabulary of spaces and boundaries which are asserted as if the underlying assumptions about the constitutional division of powers were not contentious.

The chapter attempts to show that this false doctrinal step can be traced back to the central problem which continues to blight contemporary public law and to prevent its evolution into a mature system regulating the legality of the exercise of power in a modern polity. The blight is cast, it is argued, by English lawyers' weakness for the alluring idea of 'sovereignty' as a foundational concept. The conceptual neatness of sovereignty-derived thinking too readily seduces them into a conceptualisation of public law in terms of competing supremacies, which in fact bears little relation to the way in which public power is now dispersed and shared between several layers of constitutional actors, all of which profess an identical commitment to a set of values which can loosely be termed democratic constitutionalism.

The idea of sovereignty casts a double blight. On the one hand, the idea of the sovereignty of *Parliament* lives on, as vital as ever in contemporary accounts of our constitutional arrangements, notwithstanding the demonstrable fact that Parliament's power is now subject to a number of constitutional constraints which should long ago have made this claim embarrassingly at odds with both legal and political reality. On the other hand, the idea of the sovereignty of *the individual*, and of a correspondingly sovereign role for *the courts* in protecting the supposedly inviolable areas of the individual's life against democratic incursion, now increasingly features in contemporary accounts of public law, notwithstanding the explicit recognition in this country's institutional arrangements that Parliament has an important role in both the definition and protection of fundamental rights and values. The very language of our constitutional discourse therefore permits the co-existence of what should be the radically opposed narratives of democratic positivism (rooted in the sovereignty of Parliament) and liberal constitutionalism (rooted in the sovereignty of the individual and the courts' task in protecting that sphere).

Most damaging of all, however, is the strange persistence of the Diceyan attempt to accommodate both types of sovereignty within a single constitutional account. This leads to a public law of competing supremacies, in which the debate is always about how to define the boundaries of the respective areas of supremacy of the courts on the one hand and the political branches on the other, but the only justificatory arguments available within the model are irreconcilable premises which are selectively invoked depending on whether it is interference or non-interference which requires to be justified. This problem pervades our administrative law and has doomed many of its concepts to be built on constantly shifting sands. In terms of the current debate, it will be argued that this underlying conceptualisation translates inevitably into a spatial language of areas or margins of discretion, exclusive zones within which the branch concerned is the master of all it surveys and is free from any interference by any other branch.

The chapter goes on to argue for an alternative approach which does not seek to delineate respective zones of competence, or to decide who has the power to define those boundaries, but which begins from the premise that in today's conditions both the courts and the political branches share a commitment *both* to representative democracy *and* to certain rights, freedoms and basic values, including those which are enshrined in the ECHR. In place of Diceyan constitutionalism with its irreconcilable premises, this approach attempts to root itself in a more coherent vision of constitutionalism which combines a non-positivist role for courts in articulating and furthering the fundamental values to which society is committed, at the same time as giving a meaningful role to the democratic branches and the administration in the definition and furtherance of those values.

It argues that the time has come to move beyond a public law conceptualised in terms of parallel or competing sovereignties, indeed to abandon the language of sovereignty altogether in favour of the language of *justification*, which attempts to reconceive our conceptions of law and legality away from formalistic concepts such as the historic will of Parliament, the separation of powers and ultra vires towards more substantive concepts of value and reason.[7] The crucial mediating concept for doing this, it is argued, is that of 'due deference'—the idea that in certain circumstances there may be good reasons why it is appropriate for courts not to interfere with decisions of the legislature, executive or administration, or of a lower court or tribunal, but that such deference from the courts must be *earned* by the primary decision-maker by openly demonstrating the justifications for the decisions they have reached and by demonstrating the reasons why their decision is worthy of curial respect.

After explaining how the 'due deference' approach would work in practice, the chapter goes on to demonstrate both the shortcomings and the dangers of the spatial approach, and the relative advantages of the due deference approach, by reference to some recent decisions in three specific contexts in which, on a crude approach, courts might be expected to recognise the existence of a wide 'discretionary area of judgment': immigration control, town and country planning, and social and economic policy. Each of these is, in a broad sense, a 'context' in which the European Court of Human Rights has indicated that it will afford a wide 'margin of appreciation' to the national authorities due to the nature of the subject matter, and there are already many instances of domestic courts translating this directly into a wide discretionary area of judgment, or margin of discretion, for primary decision-makers in these areas of decision-making. In each of them, however, there are some indications of the emergence of a less crude approach, though as yet no consistent formulation of the theoretical basis on which such an approach could be sustained.

---

[7]   The thinking behind this chapter is indebted to the work of David Dyzenhaus, and in particular his efforts to build on Etienne Mureinik's conception of legality as 'a culture of justification': see eg D Dyzenhaus, 'Law as Justification: Etienne Mureinik's Conception of Legal Culture' (1998) 14 *SAJHR* 11.

THE PROBLEM: WHAT DOES *DALY* REQUIRE?

In one sense, the unanimous decision of the House of Lords in *Daly*[8] is a totem of the most dramatic change which the HRA requires of our traditional public law: the abandonment of the deferential *Wednesbury* standard in all cases involving Convention rights, and in its place the unequivocal embrace of proportionality. Lord Steyn's short speech on this subject[9] contrasted the approach which had been taken in the Court of Appeal in *Mahmood*[10] with the approach which was now required under the Human Rights Act. Lord Phillips MR's formulation of the approach to be adopted to assessing the proportionality of an interference with Convention rights in *Mahmood* was that 'the court will ask the question, applying an objective test, whether the decision-maker could reasonably have concluded that the interference was necessary to achieve one or more of the legitimate aims recognized by the Convention.'[11]

The House of Lords in *Daly* considered that to be couched in language reminiscent of the traditional *Wednesbury* ground of review, whereas under the proportionality approach which was now required 'the intensity of review is somewhat greater.'[12] Examples of the concrete differences this might make in practice were that the proportionality approach may require the reviewing court to assess the balance which the decision-maker has struck, not merely whether it is within the range of rational or reasonable decisions; and it may require attention to be directed to the relative weight accorded to interests and considerations. The greater intensity of review under the proportionality approach was said to be guaranteed by the twin requirements that the limitation of the right was necessary in a democratic society, in the sense of meeting a pressing social need, and the interference being really proportionate to the legitimate aim being pursued. However, there was an important qualification: this shift to a greater intensity of review did not mean that there had been a shift to 'merits review'. Lord Steyn endorsed the observation of Jeffrey Jowell[13] that even under the HRA judges and administrators will remain fundamentally distinct.[14] To that extent, 'the general tenor' of the observations in *Mahmood* were said to be correct. Then came Lord Steyn's teasing conclusion that 'in law, context is everything'.[15]

Lord Steyn's great insight in his speech in *Daly* is not so much the fact that HRA adjudication requires a different approach from the traditional *Wednesbury* approach: this much had been obvious since the decision of the European Court of Human Rights in *Smith and Grady v United Kingdom*,[16] holding that the

---

[8] [2001] 2 WLR 1622.
[9] *Ibid* at 1634B-1636C
[10] *Mahmood v Secretary of State for the Home Department* [2001] 1 WLR 840.
[11] *Ibid* at 857, para 40.
[12] [2001] 2 WLR 1622 at 1635D, para 27.
[13] J Jowell, 'Beyond the Rule of Law: Towards Constitutional Judicial Review' [2000] *PL* 672.
[14] *Daly*, above n 12, at 1636B, para 28.
[15] *Ibid.*
[16] (2000) 29 EHRR 493.

inadequacy of judicial review for the purposes of determining the applicants' Article 8 claim in *Smith v Ministry of Defence*[17] was in breach of ECHR Article 13. The real insights in *Daly*, it is suggested, are twofold and are crucially interrelated.

First, Lord Steyn explicitly recognises that, although applying the proportionality approach may only make a difference to the outcome in a handful of cases, it will not be possible to identify those cases unless the approach itself is properly applied. It is therefore crucial to the effective protection of Convention rights that the highly structured proportionality approach is properly understood and applied by both decision-makers and reviewing courts wherever Convention rights are in play.[18] This should finally lay to rest the oft-repeated but banal observation that there is no real difference between *Wednesbury* and proportionality, because a decision which is disproportionate is also bound to be one to which no reasonable decision-maker could come. The real point is, as Lord Steyn makes clear, that proportionality is not so much a 'test' or a 'standard' as a new type of *approach* to adjudication which subjects the justification for decisions to rigorous scrutiny in order to determine their legality. Understood in this way, *Daly* is a major landmark on the road to the development of a true 'culture of justification,' a destination to which English public law has been feeling its way for several years, but now at an accelerated pace thanks to the HRA.[19]

The second insight in *Daly* is in the crucial observation that there is a difference between a proportionality approach and a full 'merits review.' This is of the utmost significance, because, as will be argued below, it preserves the very basis on which the meaningful existence of administrative law depends: the recognition by judges that in judicial review they do not have *primary* responsibility, but a secondary responsibility to ensure that the primary decision-maker has acted in accordance with the requirements of legality.[20] *Daly* delivers this crucial insight, but leaves entirely open the question of how it should be worked out in practice. Public law's big task for the next few years will be how to give practical effect to this second insight in *Daly*, in a way which does not forfeit the first. In other words, what approach should courts adopt to determining precisely how the 'context' of a particular decision affects the appropriate intensity of review?

Daly itself does not give us any answers to this question. Predictably, in the wake of the decision in *Daly* a number of courts have interpreted the 'context' qualification to Lord Steyn's statement of principle in order to justify continuing to apply the traditional *Wednesbury* standard. Lawyers representing defendant authorities

---

[17] [1996] QB 517.

[18] *Daly*, above n 12, at 1636, para 28: 'It is therefore important that cases involving Convention rights must be analysed in the correct way.'

[19] This first insight is an important step on the way to making more explicit the embrace by English courts of an attitude of 'constitutionalism': see Lord Steyn's 2002 Robin Cooke Lecture, 'Democracy Through Law' for the emerging contours of this judicial commitment. See also Lord Bingham, 'The Evolving Constitution' [2002] EHRLR 1.

[20] See D Dyzenhaus, (1998) 14 *SAJHR* 11 at 24–25 for a salutary reminder, from a South African perspective, that an instrumentalist approach to the justification for judicial review (contingent on whether the legislature or executive are good or bad at a particular point in time) will lead to inconsistency on this point.

in public law proceedings merely preface their familiar *Wednesbury* submissions with the words 'in context ....' If the more important insight in *Daly* is not to be lost, it is a matter of some urgency that a much more sophisticated approach be developed, one which attempts to articulate the sorts of contextual factors that will be relevant to the appropriate intensity of review, and is explicit about precisely how those factors relate to the degree of deference which is appropriate in the particular context.

In a recent contribution to this debate, Jeffrey Jowell has argued that two views are emerging about the extent to which courts should defer to Parliament and other bodies exercising public functions.[21] The first contends that courts should in principle bow to the decisions of the legislature and those exercising power on its behalf on matters of public interest (sometimes referred to as matters of public 'policy' or 'expediency'). The second contends that judges should assess those decisions by the standards of legality under domestic administrative law, allowing little or no 'discretionary area of judgment' to the primary decision-maker.[22]

It is certainly true that a review of both the literature and of HRA judgments reveals a mixture of utterances from a democratic positivist's perspective on the one hand, with its formalistic notion of the separation of powers and romantic attachment to the idea of parliamentary sovereignty, and a liberal constitutional-ist's perspective on the other, with its equally romantic judicial supremacism about the priority of individual rights and the sovereignty of the courts as their ultimate guardian. From the democratic positivist's perspective, Parliament remains the supreme law-giver in our constitutional arrangements and is there-fore the final arbiter of the meaning of Convention rights, and can exercise its sov-ereignty by defining what those rights mean in particular contexts.[23] For the democratic positivist, it is only an expression of the same foundational premise that in this legal universe Parliament can also delegate to executive and adminis-trative decision-makers a zone of decision-making which is beyond the reach of judicial review because it is within some irreducible core of discretionary judg-ment. From the liberal constitutionalist's perspective, on the other hand, the courts are the final arbiter of whether a Convention right has been or is being vio-lated, as they are the guardians of the area of inviolability into which public authorities cannot step, and there is therefore no room for judicial deference to democratic decision-makers, including Parliament.[24]

More interesting by far, however, than the existence of this spectrum of views is the fact that, despite their radically different theoretical underpinnings, the two views are often espoused by the same judge or commentator, depending on the issue they are addressing or whether they are seeking to justify judicial interference

---

[21] J Jowell, 'Due Deference under the Human Rights Act' in Jowell and Cooper (eds), above n 2.
[22] Jowell's preferred intermediate position, which rests on a distinction between constitutional competence and institutional competence, is considered further below.
[23] See eg K Ewing, 'The Human Rights Act and Parliamentary Democracy' [1999] *MLR* 79; JAG Griffith, 'The Common Law and the Political Constitution' [2001] *LQR* 43.
[24] See eg Clayton and Leigh, above n 1.

or abstention in a particular case.[25] This is the contemporary manifestation of our Diceyan inheritance: a constitutional discourse which selectively invokes democratic positivism and liberal constitutionalism in order to justify or explain a particular decision, but which lacks an overarching coherent vision of democratic constitutionalism in which the apparent contradiction of these foundational commitments is explicitly confronted and an attempt made to reconcile them without resort to the language of sovereignty.

The doctrinal vehicle which has so far emerged in English public law to address the central question of deference identified by Lord Steyn in *Daly* is, it will be argued, a product of this Diceyan prison, and unless an alternative approach is developed which is capable of transcending the language of sovereignty, we are in danger of perpetuating the Diceyan account into the era of the HRA.

THE FALSE STEP: EMERGENCE OF THE SPATIAL METAPHOR

Concerns about the Margin of Appreciation

In the period following the enactment of the HRA and its coming into force, there was a great deal of speculation as to whether the Strasbourg concept of the margin of appreciation would have any role to play in national courts under the Act. For public lawyers who hoped that the HRA might herald a more principled approach to judicial review, the particular concern was that English courts would simply substitute the language of the margin of appreciation for the language of *Wednesbury* review, leaving matters much the same as they had been before the HRA was passed. This concern led to the publication of articles arguing that the doctrine of the margin of appreciation was a doctrine of a supranational court and therefore had no direct application by national courts when they came to adjudicate on Convention issues under the HRA.[26] These arguments explicitly acknowledged,

---

[25] Many examples could be cited, but for present purposes it suffices to contrast Lord Hoffmann's invocation of liberal constitutionalism in his robust defence of the sovereign role of the courts in defending the individual's personal sovereignty against invasion by the majority (see eg *R v Secretary of State for the Home Department, ex parte Simms and O'Brien* [2000] 2 AC 115; 'The Separation of Powers', above n 5, at paras 12, 13 and 17), and his invocation of, amongst other things, democratic positivism as a justification for treating as non-justiciable by the courts certain decisions 'entrusted by Parliament' to executive or administrative decision-makers (see eg *Secretary of State for the Home Department v Rehman* [2001] UKHL 47, [2001] 3 WLR 877; *Alconbury Developments Ltd v Secretary of State for the Environment, Transport and the Regions* [2001] 2 WLR 1389; 'The Separation of Powers', above n 5, at paras 9–11). Although Jowell does not agree with Lord Hoffmann's view that courts should defer on democratic grounds to the legislature on matters of public policy, the reliance on both democratic positivism and liberal constitutionalism is also evident in his account, in which the courts' constitutional role is said to be derived not from the very nature of democracy itself but from an exercise of Parliament's sovereign will in enacting the HRA.

[26] See eg R Singh, M Hunt and M Demetriou, 'Is there a Role for the "Margin of Appreciation" in National Law after the Human Rights Act?' [1999] *EHRLR* 15; D Pannick, 'The Discretionary Area of Judgment' [1998] *PL* 545; A Lester and D Pannick (eds), *Human Rights Law and Practice* (Butterworths, 1999), para 3.2.1.

however, that some of the underlying ideas that inform the margin of appreciation, being considerations of when it may not be appropriate for a judicial decision-maker to interfere with the decision of a primary decision-maker, would inevitably have some role to play in judicial review under the HRA.

The Wrong Turn

The argument that the margin of appreciation itself is of no direct application under the HRA was won before the Act came into force. In *Kebilene*, the issue was directly addressed by Lord Hope who said that the 'technique' of the margin of appreciation, being an integral part of an international supervisory jurisdiction, is not available to national courts when they are considering Convention issues arising in their own countries.[27] However, Lord Hope went on, quite rightly, to observe that a similar question arose for national courts in the application of the principles contained in the ECHR. He observed that the questions which the courts will have to decide in the application of those principles will involve questions of balance between competing interests, and issues of proportionality. Recognising that this could potentially involve the courts in revisiting difficult choices made by the executive or the legislature between the rights of the individual and the needs of society, Lord Hope sought to spell out how courts should approach the difficult question of the limits of their legitimate role. He said:

> In some circumstances it will be appropriate for the courts to recognize that there is an area of judgment within which the judiciary will defer, on democratic grounds, to the considered opinion of the elected body or person whose act or decision is said to be incompatible with the Convention.

He also adopted Lester and Pannick's label of the 'discretionary area of judgment' as a convenient and appropriate description of 'the area in which these choices may arise.'

So Lord Hope chose an explicitly spatial solution to the problem: the concept of an *area* of judgment, within which the judiciary *will* defer. This clearly contemplates there being a zone or area of decision-making in which a decision-maker is immune from any interference by the court (and it follows that the decision-maker must therefore be immune from any review by the court within that area, as there is no point in any review if there can be no interference at the end of it). It is, in other words, a 'justiciability' doctrine, premised on the idea that certain issues are simply not amenable to judicial determination. The task then becomes identifying the circumstances in which such a discretionary area of judgment will be recognised by the courts. Lord Hope offered some assistance in this respect, by giving some examples: it would be easier to recognise such an area of judgment where

---

[27] [2000] 2 AC 326 at 380G. For similar acknowledgements of the inappropriateness of the margin of appreciation doctrine due to its supranational nature, se Lord Steyn in *Brown v Stott* [2001] 2 WLR 817 at 842 and Simon Brown LJ in *Porter v South Bucks District Council* [2002] 1 All ER 425 at 438–39, paras 25–27.

the rights at stake are qualified rights, where the Convention itself requires a balance to be struck; or where the issues involve questions of social or economic policy. It would be less easy where the rights at stake are stated in unqualified terms, or are of high constitutional importance, or of a kind where the courts are especially well placed to assess the need for protection.

This idea of there being a discretionary area of judgment, or a margin of discretion, within which courts will defer to primary decision-makers, has now gained widespread acceptance. It is frequently relied upon by advocates representing defendants to judicial review proceedings, and is now very frequently referred to by judges. Although, as will be seen below, some judges have conspicuously avoided referring to it,[28] and others use it in a slightly different sense from the non-justiciability sense in which Lord Hope appeared to use it in *Kebilene*,[29] it is by now sufficiently well established to have become a significant part of the public law landscape, and one which therefore demands particularly rigorous examination to ascertain whether it can really do the job for which it has been chosen.

What is Wrong with the Spatial Approach?

So long as it is distinguished from Strasbourg's margin of appreciation, and the 'width' of the margin or area of judgment is acknowledged to be variable depending on the context, what is wrong with this approach to what is acknowledged to be probably the most difficult question in contemporary public law? There are a number of problems with the spatial approach.

First, it fails to make clear whether the area which is identified as being a 'discretionary area of judgment' is, quite literally, a non-justiciable area, beyond the reach of law and in the realm of pure politics, or rather is an area within which decisions are still subject to scrutiny by the courts by the application of legal standards, albeit that in the course of conducting that scrutiny the reviewing court might decide that the decision, or aspects of it, are worthy of the court's respect. In other words, this approach fails to draw a clear distinction between deference as submission and deference as respect.[30] Deference as submission occurs when the court treats a decision or an aspect of it as non-justiciable, and refuses to enter on a

---

[28] Lord Steyn, for example, has consistently preferred to speak in terms of courts according a degree of deference to the legislature or executive where the context justifies it (see eg *Brown v Stott*, above n 27); and Lord Woolf has also consistently referred to paying degrees of deference to Parliament depending on the context (see eg *R v Lambert* [2001] 2 WLR 211 at 219, para 16; *Poplar Housing Association Ltd. v Donoghue* [2002] QB 48 at 70–71, para 69).

[29] Lord Bingham, for example, in both *Brown v Stott*, above n 27 and *Shayler*, above n 4, uses the language of a discretionary area of judgment but, crucially, does not suggest that the courts will automatically defer to any decision within that area, but rather suggests that they will *give weight* to decisions within that area—that is, they will accord such decisions the appropriate degree of deference. This significantly opens up the need to articulate the factors which will determine the degree of deference which is appropriate in the circumstances.

[30] The distinction is drawn by David Dyzenhaus in 'The Politics of Deference: Judicial Review and Democracy' in Michael Taggart (ed), *The Province of Administrative Law* (Hart Publishing, 1997), ch 13.

review of it because it considers it beyond its competence. Deference as respect occurs when the court gives some weight to a decision of a primary decision-maker for an articulated reason, as part of its overall review of the justifications for the decision.

Secondly, an approach based on spatial metaphors of 'areas' or 'margins' tends to pre-empt the articulation of the real reasons for deferring to an assessment of a primary decision-maker. As will be argued below, there are good reasons and bad reasons for deferring to a primary decision-maker, and what is important is that an approach be adopted which requires the explicit articulation and evaluation of those reasons. The spatial approach encourages courts to focus on a single factor which defines the nature of the context in which the decision-maker is operating and allows its approach to be determined by that factor. For example, a decision-maker who is taking decisions in the national security context is likely to be accorded a wide margin or area of discretionary judgment on that account alone, rather than have the court carefully examine the various possible reasons for why a degree of deference may be appropriate to certain aspects of the decision. The 'area' in which the decision-maker operates maps nicely onto a wide 'area' of discretion, to the exclusion of other factors which ought to be considered. In short, there is nothing in the spatial approach which encourages the articulation of the various factors which are relevant to the deference inquiry, and requires them to be rigorously related to the specific aspects of the decision to which they are relevant.

Thirdly, an awareness of the history of the development of modern public law should alert us to the dangers inherent in this spatial approach. Much of the progress of modern public law has been in rolling back what were formerly considered to be zones of immunity from judicial review, reformulating the considerations which were thought to justify total immunity and reintegrating them into substantive public law as considerations which affect the particular, contextualised application of what have increasingly become accepted as universally applicable general principles. That progress has been hard fought for, but it is constantly threatened by the failure to ground deference theory in anything other than crudely formalistic notions of the separation of powers and the supposed continued sovereignty of Parliament.

Fourthly and finally, there is no avoiding the multi-textured nature of the issues which fall to be adjudicated. Because rights and values are transcendent of context, cases cannot be neatly classified into categories according to the kind of subject matter they raise, and then a particular standard of review applied to them. This means that the relevant features which pull in different directions as far as the intensity of review is concerned are often present in the same case. Questions of fair trial, non-discrimination or the liberty of the individual (all matters on which courts consider themselves to have a special role) may arise in 'areas' of decision-making, such as national security or social and economic policy, in which the courts have traditionally been reluctant to interfere with primary decision-makers. It is too simple to suppose that cases can be classified according to their subject matter and the intensity or standard of review decided upon according to that categorisation: the nature of the subject matter of the decision is just one of a number of variables in play which may affect the degree of deference which is appropriate. Any approach to the limits of judicial review must be sufficiently sophisticated to reflect this basic truth.

Parallel Criticism of Strasbourg's Spatial Approach

Much of the above criticism of the spatial approach in domestic public law is reflected in critical contemporary commentary about the margin of appreciation doctrine in the jurisprudence of the European Court of Human Rights.[31] In its early days the margin of appreciation doctrine was often used by the European Court in a crude and blanket way, which attracted criticism of the Court for resorting to a standardless doctrine as a substitute for coherent legal analysis of the issues at stake.[32] Ronald St John Macdonald, for example, a former judge of the European Court, has said that the doctrine of the margin of appreciation had on occasion permitted the Court's evasion of its responsibility to articulate the reasons why its intervention in particular cases may or may not be appropriate.[33] The dangers of too readily conceding a wide margin of appreciation to national decision-makers has also been acknowledged by the European Court's Deputy Registrar Paul Mahoney:

> Cession, in inappropriate contexts, of over-broad discretion to national authorities to restrict the guaranteed human rights would run counter to the universality of human rights and would defeat the purpose of the Convention—which is to remove protection of human rights from the 'reserved domain' of the State and to make it instead an international responsibility. ... Some ten years ago Judge Ganshof van der Meersch urged that a margin of appreciation should not be conceded in a general fashion. As a matter of principle the Court should be extremely circumspect before deferring to the national authorities when they have interfered with the enjoyment of one of the guaranteed rights. Judicial self restraint should itself be exercised with restraint if the universal standards are not to be diluted or sacrificed in favour of national diversity.

Conceding a margin of appreciation 'in a general fashion' is precisely what the European Court is doing when it presumes a wide margin of appreciation in a particular context (eg 'the planning sphere'). To focus on one relevant factor (the nature of the subject matter) and found a presumption upon it about the

---

[31] See eg P Mahoney, 'Marvellous Richness of Diversity or Invidious Cultural Relativism?' (1998) 19 *Human Rights Law Journal* 1; C Ovey, 'The Margin of Appreciation and Article 8 of the Convention' *ibid* at 10; J Schokkenbroek, 'The Basis, Nature and Application of the Margin of Appreciation Doctrine in the Case-Law of the European Court of Human Rights' *ibid* at 30; Y Arai, 'The Margin of Appreciation Doctrine in the Jurisprudence of Article 8 of the European Convention on Human Rights' (1998) 16 *Netherlands Quarterly of Human Rights* 41.

[32] Lord Lester, 'The European Convention on Human Rights in the New Architecture of Europe: General Report,' *Proceedings of the 8th International Colloquy on the European Convention on Human Rights* (Council of Europe, 1995), 227, 236–37.

[33] R St J Macdonald, 'The Margin of Appreciation' in R St J Macdonald, F Matscher and H Petzold (eds), *The European System for the Protection of Human Rights* (Martinus Nijhoff, 1994), 83–124.

appropriate degree of restraint in cases arising in that area is bound to lead to overdeference to national decision-makers. It may well be the case that, often, the conflicting rights in issue in that area of decision-making will be of the sort where it is not appropriate for the Court to become embroiled in the balancing of local interests. But fundamental rights can cut across all manner of subject matter areas, and the margin of appreciation needs to be sensitive enough to accommodate that.

Rather than automatically assume a wide margin of appreciation in particular subject matter areas, subject only to possible narrowing by having regard to other factors, contemporary commentators on the Strasbourg case law favour the adoption of a more sophisticated criteria-based approach. This would involve the European Court in avoiding any presumption about the width of the margin of appreciation, and instead identifying what Paul Mahoney has called 'some practical criteria for situating the bounds of the margin of appreciation in concrete cases.' This criteria-based approach is more sensitive to the many different features of the context, and does not start by ascribing great weight to a particular factor, by presuming a wide margin of appreciation on the basis of the subject matter area alone. As Schokkenbroek has said:

> a sufficient degree of flexibility can be maintained as long as the Court bases the exercise of its supervisory function on a series of relative factors which may properly determine the scope of the review it will carry out, not on a straightjacket of absolute rules.

'DUE DEFERENCE' AS AN ALTERNATIVE APPROACH

If, as seems to be the case, the doctrine of the discretionary area of judgment, or the margin of discretion, has now effectively become the direct domestic equivalent of the Strasbourg doctrine of the margin of appreciation, the question arises whether there is any alternative approach which would avoid the pitfalls identified above. One alternative is that advocated by Jeffrey Jowell, who has sought to chart something of a middle course between, on the one hand, those arguing for recognition of a discretionary area of judgment whenever the courts are called upon to decide a matter of 'public interest' or 'policy' and, on the other hand, those who see Convention questions as a matter of hard-edged legality which is always a question for the court and therefore see little or no room for a discretionary area of judgement.[34] Jowell argues that both of these extreme views are erroneous, because they rest on a mistaken notion of the relative competence of courts and other institutions in the new constitutional order which he considers to have been introduced by the HRA. He argues for an intermediate position, in which there is some limited room for deference by the courts, but which is a function not of the courts' relative *constitutional* competence (which on Jowell's account has been transformed at a stroke by the enactment of the HRA), but of their relative *institutional* competence to decide certain types of question. The argument is that, now

---

[34] J Jowell, 'Due Deference under the Human Rights Act' in Jowell and Cooper (eds), above n 2.

that the courts enjoy a new constitutional competence which they have never previously had, it is never justifiable for them to defer on democratic grounds alone, but *only* on institutional grounds.

Jowell's rejection of the two extremes, one of which requires courts to defer submissively and the other of which leaves no room for deference at all, is entirely correct. His suggested alternative, however, concentrates on one important and undoubtedly relevant factor (relative institutional competence) to the exclusion of all others. In particular, it excludes from the deference inquiry important normative considerations about what the court's proper role is, by assuming that those normative questions have been settled by the HRA itself. So, for example, by saying that it is never justifiable for a court to defer to a primary decision-maker on democratic grounds (the democratic legitimacy of judicial interference for the protection of human rights having been settled by the HRA), Jowell appears to factor out democratic considerations from deference theory altogether. But a rich conception of legality and of the rule of law should not only be able to legitimate a role for courts in enforcing legal standards on public decision-makers; it ought, at the same time, to have space for a proper role for democratic considerations, including a role for the democratic branches in the definition and furtherance of fundamental values. This brings us back to one of Lord Steyn's important insights in *Daly*: an acceptable approach to articulating the limits of judicial review in a constitutional democracy is crucial to defending the legitimacy of its very basis.

By the same token, Jowell's approach rules out normative considerations which pull in the opposite direction, away from deference. Institutional constraints on judicial decision-making ought not necessarily to constrain a court to defer if it considers it to be its constitutional role to decide a particular question. Questions of institutional competence are inseparable from deeper normative questions of institutional design. Courts as institutions are designed in a particular way because of an underlying notion of their function. If, as Jowell suggests, courts now have the constitutional competence to decide all questions concerning compatibility of public action with fundamental rights, they ought not to be constrained by institutional limitations: rather, institutional considerations ought to follow from the answer to the underlying normative question about the court's function. Institutional competence constraints can often be resolved, in that procedures can be changed (as they sometimes are) in order to accommodate what is required procedurally in order for the court to fulfil its constitutional function.[35]

Jeffrey Jowell's focus on institutional competence, therefore, whilst certainly identifying one important and relevant factor in the deference inquiry, ultimately

---

[35] See eg the indications in the House of Lords decision in *R v Shayler* [2002] UKHL 11, [2002] 2 WLR 754 that, in a judicial review of a refusal to authorise disclosure by a former member of the security services, the High Court should use its inherent power to devise a procedure for enabling it to see material too sensitive to be disclosed to the individual's legal advisers, for example by the appointment of a special advocate to represent the individual, even where there was no statutory provision for such a procedure: see Lord Bingham at 776, para 34 and Lord Hutton at 800, para 113; and see to the same effect Lord Woolf MR in the Court of Appeal in *Secretary of State for the Home Department v Rehman* [2000] 3 WLR 1240 at 1250–51, para 31.

cannot on its own be determinative of when courts should and when they should not pay a degree of deference to a decision. It cannot be a matter solely of institutional competence, divorced from deeper normative questions of what courts ought or ought not to be doing in a modern constitutional democracy. Deference theory needs grounding in something more explicitly normative, in which courts are encouraged not only to articulate their reasons for deferring or not deferring, but to theorise them in terms of what justifies or limits judicial intervention. This requires nothing less than reconfiguring public law in terms of a culture of justification, as argued for by Mureinik and Dyzenhaus.[36] In a culture of justification, as Lord Steyn recognised in *Daly*, all exercises of power require justification, but the very nature of 'justification' dictates the court's role in reviewing legality. Justification requires reasons, that is, rational explanations for why a particular decision has been taken. The task of a court reviewing for legality in a culture of justification is to subject those reasons to careful scrutiny and to decide whether or not the decision is *justifiable*. In deciding how much weight it should accord to the primary decision-maker's justificatory arguments it should have regard to a variety of different factors which might be in play and which are relevant to the question of whether any and if so how much deference might be due from a judicial decision-maker. On this approach, one of the explicitly normative considerations to be taken into account in assessing the appropriate degree of deference is the degree of democratic accountability of the primary decision-maker, and the extent to which the affected interests have already had the opportunity of genuinely participating in a democratic process directed at balancing the competing interests.

Democratic arguments, however, must not be treated as determinative of the justification question, as reasons which pre-empt judicial involvement altogether, because the court would then be abdicating its task of deciding whether justification has been made out. The whole notion of 'precluded areas,' to which the spatial approach gives life, is quite at odds with the very concept of 'review' for legality: invocation of the discretionary area of judgment amounts to a claim of non-justiciability, an argument that the decision is not suitable for judicial resolution at all, rather than an argument that the decision is *justifiable* in a democratic society. An argument that an issue is within the decision-maker's discretion is the very opposite of justificatory. It amounts to telling courts that a matter is none of their business, which is difficult to reconcile with modern conceptions of legality and the political branches' own professed commitment to the rule of law and to respect for fundamental rights and values. Dyzenhaus seeks to incorporate this important point into his theory of deference by arguing for recognition of a concept of due deference which distinguishes between 'deference as submission' and 'deference as respect.'[37] Submissive deference is what happens in the Diceyan model of constitutionalism: judges submit to the intention of the legislature, on a positivist

---

[36] See D Dyzenhaus, 'Law as Justification: Etienne Mureinik's Conception of Legal Culture' (1998) 14 *SAJHR* 11.

[37] D Dyzenhaus, 'The Politics of Deference: Judicial Review and Democracy' in M Taggart (ed), *The Province of Administrative Law* (Hart Publishing, 1997), ch 13, 286.

understanding of that intention. Deference as respect, on the other hand, requires judges to pay 'a respectful attention' to the reasons which are offered by a primary decision-maker as justifications for a particular decision.

But at the same time as distinguishing respect from submission, and therefore abstention, following review for legality, from non-justiciability, the concept of due deference also, and crucially, distinguishes review for legality from review for correctness. It does so by preserving an important distinction between a decision which is justifiable and one which is justified. As Dyzenhaus says:

> in the administrative law context, there is an important distinction between a judicial test which asks whether a non-judicial decision-maker's decision can be shown to be justifiable and one which asks whether it is justified. When a judge asks whether the decision-maker's decision is justified, he is usually asking whether the decision coincides with the decision the judge would himself have given. Here the reasons of the decision-maker hardly matter since the issue is coincidence of content rather than the relationship between reasons and content. But when the judge asks whether the decision is justifiable, he is asking whether the decision-maker has shown it to be defensible, taking all the important considerations into account. And that of course makes the reasons for decision very important.[38]

Any theory of deference must not only avoid the submissive approach which flows if one starts from the premise of parliamentary sovereignty, but must also preserve this important distinction between judicial and primary decision-makers on which the very existence of a coherent public law depends. Many of the attempts to grapple with this difficult problem have started by asking the wrong question. The debate about whether proportionality is a question of law or fact, or mixed law and fact, for example, is not helpful, and merely substitutes one set of labels for another without getting to the difficult underlying normative question of why it is that courts ought sometimes to feel constrained in substituting their own decision for that of another decision-maker. Similarly, characterisation of the question of whether an interference is proportionate as being an 'objective' question does not get to the real question. Whether the question of the proportionality of an interference is a question for the court or for the decision-maker is simply the wrong question to ask. It is a question for both of them. The amount of deference which ought to be given to the decision-maker on the various constituent elements of the decision taken should be built into the correct approach to assessing proportionality. Even the language of intensity of review or differential standards of review is not enough in itself, because it too expresses a conclusion about the appropriate degree of intrusion. What is needed instead is a vocabulary which flushes out the underlying, inescapably normative considerations which explain the court's inclination or disinclination to interfere with any particular decision.

How, then, without resorting to the spatial approach, should courts approach the deference question in a way which steers between the two extremes of judicial submission and judicial supremacism? Because of the transcendent quality of

---

[38] (1998) 14 *SAJHR* 11, 27–28.

rights and values, capable in principle of cutting across all substantive areas of public decision-making, and the large number of variables which are in play which interact with each other in different ways, courts should approach the deference question in a focused, issue-specific way, asking first what is the specific issue on which the primary decision-maker has made a decision to which a claim for deference is being made. Having carefully identified the issue in respect of which the claim for deference is made, the court should ask, in relation to each specific issue which it has identified, how much, if any, deference it ought to give the primary decision-maker who has made a decision on that particular question. At the stage of determining the degree of deference which is due to the decision-maker on the relevant aspects of its decision, the court should articulate the sorts of factors which might warrant a degree of deference from a judicial decision-maker, and identify the specific factors which are in play when deciding how much deference is due in the particular circumstances of the case.

A number of different factors are likely to be relevant to this inquiry into the appropriate degree of deference, though no single factor is likely to be determinative: the outcome of the inquiry is likely to depend on the interaction of a number of different factors. The nature of the right in question and the nature of the particular context are certainly relevant factors: naturally courts feel a greater legitimacy in pronouncing on fair trial rights and other procedural guarantees which are considered to be at the core of the judicial function, and feel a very real diffidence in relation to issues which involve striking balances between a variety of different interests or between different groups, which they consider to be more in the nature of a 'political' judgment. To focus exclusively on these two considerations, however, would be too narrow and would prevent articulation of the underlying considerations which inform received ideas about the respective functions of the judicial and the political branches.

The relevant factors would certainly include the relative expertise of the decision-maker in the subject matter in question: does the primary decision-maker possess some expertise in the particular subject matter, for example in scientific, technical or academic matters, which is central to the issue to be decided and which a reviewing court cannot pretend to possess? They would include also the relative institutional competence of the primary decision-maker to determine the type of issue in question: is the court's adjudicative decision-making process simply not equipped to conduct the type of decision-making which preceded the primary decision-maker's decision? Again, this question must be closely tied to the issue which has to be decided: for example, if one of the issues is a highly factual question such as the degree of impact on visual amenity, which the primary decision-maker decided after actually visiting the site in question itself, that is an issue on which appropriate deference ought to be paid to the finding of the primary decision-maker. This should not be a particularly controversial proposition: it is well established, even in the context of the exercise of a full appellate jurisdiction in which an appeal court has jurisdiction over fact and law, that allowance should be made by the appellate court for the advantage which the first instance decision-maker had in actually seeing the witnesses in question give their live evidence. To this extent, due deference on grounds of relative institutional competence is a well established feature of even appellate adjudication.

The relevant factors in the deference inquiry should also include the degree of democratic accountability of the original decision-maker, and the extent to which other mechanisms of accountability may be available in the increasingly layered context in which power is exercised in contemporary conditions. The mere fact that a decision has been taken by a democratically accountable decision-maker should never in itself be determinative, but in a democratic society a reviewing court should give careful consideration to whether other avenues of accountability are available and more appropriate, and to how well democratic mechanisms are working in practice when deciding the degree of deference which is due to a decision-maker.[39] A similar and to some extent overlapping consideration which is also relevant to the deference inquiry is the extent to which the primary decision-maker has conscientiously conducted a thorough compatibility inquiry: without reducing scrutiny of justification to a merely procedural protection by making this factor determinative, the degree of respect which is due to a measure should be influenced by the seriousness of the engagement with the proportionality question by the primary decision-maker, and the opportunities which have been afforded to the various interests in the process leading to the decision.

There is a limit, however, to how far it is possible to go in describing an approach or methodology in the abstract. The real test of the above critique of the spatial approach to deference and the advocacy of a 'due deference' alternative is whether it would make any difference in practice. The remainder of this chapter therefore turns to consider recent decisions in 'contexts' where courts have been traditionally submissive to primary decision-makers, in particular immigration control, town and country planning, and social and economic policy, to illustrate the operation of the two approaches in practice.

PRACTICAL EXAMPLES OF WHY 'DUE DEFERENCE' MATTERS

Immigration Control

One context in which it is instructive to compare the two approaches is that of immigration control, an area of government action in which the courts have traditionally been mainly deferential to the executive. Indeed, it was this context that yielded the formulation of the approach to be adopted to assessing the proportionality of an interference with Convention rights which was the subject of the

---

[39] The degree of deference which is due may well therefore be contingent on the strength of democratic institutions at a particular point in time, and the extent to which Parliament is performing the role envisaged for it in the HRA, of giving proper scrutiny to executive claims that legislation is compatible with Convention rights; a point made by Nick Blake, 'Importing Proportionality: Clarification or Confusion' [2002] *EHRLR* 19, 26.

House of Lords' unanimous clarification in *Daly*. *Mahmood* was a challenge by way of judicial review to the Home Secretary's decision to remove an illegal entrant who was married to a British citizen.[40] One of the grounds of challenge was that the decision to remove was in breach of the illegal entrant's right to respect for his family life under ECHR Article 8. It was in the context of explaining how the court should now approach the issue of whether the Secretary of State's decision contravened Article 8, compared to before the HRA was in force, that Lord Phillips MR formulated the approach that the House of Lords in *Daly* felt required clarification.

Lord Phillips MR held that even after the HRA, where the court reviews an executive decision which is required to comply with the ECHR as a matter of law, it remains the case, as before, that the role of the reviewing court is supervisory: the court would only intervene where the decision fell outside the range of responses open to a reasonable decision-maker.[41] In performing the exercise of deciding whether the decision of the executive was permitted by the HRA, he held, invoking Lord Hope in *Kebilene*, that the court had to bear in mind that, just as individual states enjoy a margin of appreciation under the ECHR, 'so there will often be an area of discretion permitted to the executive of a country before a response can be demonstrated to infringe the Convention.' It was therefore on this explicitly spatial approach, drawing a direct analogy with the Strasbourg margin of appreciation, that Lord Phillips MR adopted the formulation in terms of the reasonableness of the decision-maker's conclusion that the interference was necessary,[42] and went on to conclude that 'there were reasonable grounds' for the Secretary of State's conclusion that deportation was necessary in the interests of an orderly and fair control of immigration and that there had been no violation of the right to respect for family life.[43]

The approach in *Mahmood* can be contrasted, however, to the approach taken by a differently constituted Court of Appeal in the same context in *B v Secretary of State for the Home Department*, which is much closer to the 'due deference' approach advocated above.[44] *B* was a statutory appeal on a point of law from a decision of the Immigration Appeal Tribunal (IAT), dismissing an appeal against the Home Secretary's decision to deport the appellant on grounds that it was conducive to the public good, following B's conviction for offences of indecency. The appellant had been in the United Kingdom since the age of seven, had grown up here, and lived the whole of his adult life here. One of the grounds on which he challenged the decision to deport him was that it was in breach of ECHR Article 8 because it was a disproportionate response to his offending.

The Court of Appeal unanimously held that the question of the proportionality of an interference with an Article 8 right was a question of law, and as such it was a

---

[40] *R (Mahmood) v Secretary of State for the Home Department* [2001] 1 WLR 840.
[41] *Ibid* at paras 37–38.
[42] *Ibid* at para 40.
[43] *Ibid* at para 67.
[44] [2000] Imm AR 478.

question for the court to decide afresh, even if answering it involved taking a much closer look at the merits than was usual on such an appeal.[45] Significantly, however, the Court of Appeal in *B*, like the House of Lords in *Daly*, was also careful to distinguish this greater intensity of review from a full 'merits review,' by accepting that within the court's own assessment of proportionality, a degree of deference might be due to the IAT's appraisal of certain aspects of the merits of the decision.[46] Characterising proportionality as a question of law for the court to decide was not inconsistent with paying 'proper regard' to the IAT's view. The question, however, was what such a 'proper regard' involves. The Court of Appeal in *B* began to answer this important question by distinguishing between different aspects of the IAT's decision according to whether it (the court) was 'as well placed as that tribunal' to evaluate them.[47] It held that findings of primary fact derived chiefly from oral testimony were to be treated with the respect always accorded to such findings by appellate courts,[48] but in relation to all the other aspects of the IAT's decision (inferences of fact, propositions of law, and reasoning leading to its conclusion), it held that the court was as well placed as the tribunal to decide what to make of them.

The approach adopted by the Court of Appeal in *B* is a good example of the 'due deference' approach being applied in a context, deportation for the public good, in which traditionally courts have generally preferred to adopt a submissive stance rather than subject decisions to proper scrutiny for justification.[49] Although proceeding on the premise that the proportionality of an interference with a Convention right is a question of law for the court, it nevertheless preserves the notion of 'due deference' to a primary decision-maker where it is warranted, and seeks to articulate the reasons why some degree of deference may be due to a decision-maker on certain aspects of its decision.[50] This, not the spatial approach, is the approach which follows from the House of Lords decision in *Daly*.[51]

[45] *Ibid* at paras 6, 18, 31, 36 and 47.

[46] *Ibid* at para 18.

[47] *Ibid* at paras 25–27.

[48] See Sedley LJ at para 26; Simon Brown LJ at para 47: in forming its own view on whether the proportionality test is satisfied, the court 'will give such deference to the IAT's decision as appropriately recognises their advantage in having heard the evidence.'

[49] In *R v Secretary of State for the Home Department, ex parte Isiko* [2001] UKHRR 385 at paras 30–31, the approach in *Mahmood* was expressly preferred by the Court of Appeal over the approach in *B*; but this does not survive *Daly*, as *Isiko* is one of the examples cited by Lord Steyn, [2001] 2 WLR 1622 at 1634F, para 25, of the passage from *Mahmood* being followed by other courts.

[50] See in particular Sedley LJ's formulation at [2000] Inn AR 478, para 18, in terms of 'how much deference is due to the IAT's appraisal of [the merits].'

[51] However, notwithstanding the very clear correction of the *Mahmood* and *Isiko* approach by the House of Lords in *Daly*, the Court of Appeal in *R (on the application of Samaroo) v Secretary of State for the Home Department* [2001] EWCA Civ 1139, [2001] UKHRR 1139 has reverted in this context to the approach of recognising a 'discretionary area of judgment' or a 'margin of discretion' in the statutory decision-maker (see paras 29–30 and 35), the effect of which goes a long way towards rehabilitating the *Mahmood* approach. Whether the Court of Appeal's approach in *Samaroo* is compatible with *Daly*, particularly in light of its approving citation of the very passages from the High Court's decision in *Samaroo* that were cited by Lord Steyn in *Daly* [2001] 2 WLR 1622 , at 1634F para 25, as examples of the erroneous *Mahmood* passage being followed by other courts, has yet to be considered by the House of Lords.

The immigration control context also affords one of the most considered attempts so far by an English court to grapple with the question of due deference under the HRA. *International Transport Roth v Secretary of State for the Home Department* [52] concerned a challenge by road hauliers to the penalty regime contained in Part II of the Immigration and Asylum Act 1999 imposing fixed financial penalties on those responsible for clandestine entrants to the United Kingdom (those who arrive concealed in a vehicle). The measures were a response to the large increase in the number of clandestine entrants to the United Kingdom, which had increased from less than 500 in 1992 to more than 16,500 in 1999. [53] The challenge was to the legality of the legislative scheme itself, on the ground that it was in breach of ECHR Article 6(1) and Article 1 of Protocol 1, and it rested on features of the scheme which it was argued were disproportionately burdensome on carriers: first, the burden of establishing blamelessness lies on them; secondly, the penalty was fixed, there being no flexibility whatever either for degrees of blameworthiness or mitigating circumstances; and thirdly, there was no provision for compensation even where a carrier was eventually determined not to be liable but his vehicle had been detained in the meantime. [54]

The Court of Appeal, by a two to one majority, upheld the declaration of incompatibility awarded by Sullivan J below. Not surprisingly, in a case involving a direct assault on the compatibility of primary legislation in an area of great political sensitivity, and in which the evidence of the effect of the legislation showed that it had been effective in achieving its goal of reducing the number of clandestine entrants, the case produced a careful consideration of the question left open in *Daly*: when should courts defer to democratic decision-makers and when is it appropriate for them to interfere with their decisions? On this question, although Laws LJ's dissent contains the most detailed treatment, it will be argued that his analysis, while containing certain truths, ultimately fails to escape the conundrums in which the modern day Diceyan remains trapped, whereas the analysis of Simon Brown LJ contains important insights which begin to lay the foundations for the future development of a 'due deference' approach.

The prominence given to the question of deference in Laws LJ's dissent reflects his entirely correct perception that the development of principle to assist in determining the degree of deference which ought to be paid to democratic decision-makers [55] is one of the most important challenges which the common law must meet. [56] For him, the issue at the heart of the case was what was the quality of any deference owed by the courts to the legislature in deciding whether the legislation

---

[52] [2002] EWCA Civ 158, [2002] 3 WLR 344.

[53] *Ibid* at para 1.

[54] *Ibid* at para 24.

[55] Laws LJ's analysis focuses exclusively on *democratic* decision-makers. The problem of when to accord due deference in administrative law generally is much wider than this, including as it does administrative tribunals and other primary decision-makers (eg planning inspectors, special educational needs tribunals) who may not be democratic or otherwise politically accountable but have an expertise in their area.

[56] [2002] 3 WLR 344 at para 75.

violated the carriers' Convention rights, and this was therefore an opportunity to try to identify the principles according to which the proper degree of deference to the legislature falls to be measured. After reviewing some of the formulations in the main cases to have considered the question,[57] Laws LJ sought to draw together 'the principles now being developed by the courts for the ascertainment of the degree of deference which the judges will pay, or the scope of the discretionary area of judgment which they will cede, to the democratic powers of government.'[58]

He identified four such principles:[59] first, greater deference will be paid to Acts of Parliament than decisions of the executive or subordinate measures; secondly, there is more scope for deference where the right at stake is qualified and therefore the ECHR itself requires a balance to be struck; thirdly, greater deference will be due where the subject matter is peculiarly within the constitutional responsibility of the democratic powers; and fourthly, greater or lesser deference will be due according to whether the subject matter lies more readily within the actual or potential expertise of the democratic powers or the courts. Applying these principles to the case at hand, he held that the assessment of the evidence as to the pressing need for effective control on clandestine entrants to the United Kingdom is 'obviously far more within the competence of government than the courts.'[60]

There is much in Laws LJ's analysis in *Roth* which would be present in a proper 'due deference' approach. He correctly identifies the centrality of the deference question for contemporary public law. He begins to identify some of the sorts of factors that are undoubtedly of great relevance to the deference inquiry: what is the degree of democratic accountability of the decision-maker being reviewed; what is the nature and importance of the right which is at stake; and what is the relative expertise of courts and decision-makers in the particular context? He also explicitly talks in terms of 'degrees of deference,' making clear that the amount of deference which ought to be paid to any particular decision is likely to vary according to a number of different factors.

Yet Laws LJ's approach leads him to a conclusion which is striking in its submissiveness to Parliament and the executive: in concluding that the assessment of these matters ('the social consequences which flow from the entry into the UK of clandestine illegal immigrants in significant numbers') is obviously far more within the competence of government than the courts,[61] and that the principles of deference in this case require the balance struck by the democratic powers to be accepted,[62] Laws LJ effectively abandoned his scrutiny of the justification for the measure before it had begun in any meaningful sense. Whatever the proper outcome to the case ought to have been, it was clearly the sort of case which required the application of a judicial methodology for carefully testing its justification in

---

[57] *Kebilene* (above n 27), *Brown v Stott* (above n27), *Lambert* (above n 28) and *Poplar v Donoghue* [2002] QB 48 (none of them, it will be noted, administrative law cases in the classic sense).

[58] [2002] 3 WLR 344 at para 81.

[59] *Ibid* at paras 83–87.

[60] *Ibid* at paras 87, 109.

[61] *Ibid* at para 87.

[62] *Ibid* at para 107.

order to determine its legality. If 'the principles of deference' operate to pre-empt effective scrutiny of justifications for decisions interfering with Convention rights, we shall indeed have lost Lord Steyn's important first insight in *Daly* that the key to the effective protection of Convention rights in our contemporary constitution is to subject the exercise of all public power to a rigorous process of public justification of the reasons for that decision.

This raises the question whether there is something about Laws LJ's approach to deference which leads inevitably to an unduly submissive approach by courts. The answer, it is suggested, lies in the premises from which he proceeds, which are set out in the preamble to his judgment and reveal a strong attachment to an ultra-Diceyan universe of co-existing supremacies, separation of powers and territorial divisions between constitutional actors.[63] Laws LJ's entire analysis in *Roth* is posited on a supposed antithesis between a system based on parliamentary supremacy on the one hand and a system based on constitutional supremacy on the other. In the former, which it is said the British system was, pure and simple, until not very long ago, Parliament is sovereign and constitutional rights cannot exist. In the latter, the Constitution, of which the courts are guardians, is sovereign, and parliamentary supremacy cannot exist. The British system in its present state of evolution is said to be at an 'intermediate stage' between these two: Parliament remains the sovereign legislature, but the common law has come to recognise and endorse the notion of constitutional or fundamental rights, now given a democratic underpinning by the HRA. This is said to give rise to an inevitable tension between the maintenance of legislative sovereignty and the vindication of fundamental constitutional rights. Deference is one of the means by which courts seek to mediate between these respective claims in our 'intermediate Constitution.'

As an eloquent exposition of the modern-day Diceyan position this could not be bettered: it rests upon a conception of the rule of law which seeks to accommodate within the same account both the sovereignty of Parliament and the sovereignty of judges in upholding constitutional rights. But these premises are a fundamentally unstable basis on which to attempt to construct a coherent theory of judicial review, and, it is suggested, they inevitably commit the modern-day Diceyan to an approach to deference which is likely to pre-empt effective scrutiny, for at least two reasons, both of which are apparent from Laws LJ's reasoning in *Roth*.

First, the prior assumption of an antithesis between constitutional rights and parliamentary sovereignty leads to a mischaracterisation of the nature of the adjudicative task when a court has to decide whether power has been exercised incompatibly with a constitutional right. Laws LJ describes this adjudicative task as a matter of balancing the claims of the democratic legislature on the one hand and the claims of the constitutional right on the other. But in rights adjudication, properly understood as Lord Steyn envisaged it in *Daly*, there is no such antithesis: assessment of the claims of the democratic powers is integral to the court's assess-

---

[63] *Ibid* at paras 69–79.

ment of whether the right has been violated. The court does not decide, first, the claim of the individual constitutional right (independently of democratic considerations) and then, having done so, weigh them against the claims of the democratic legislature. To proceed from this assumption is to overlook one of the single most important features of current constitutional arrangements, which is that Parliament, in the HRA, has committed itself and also the executive and the administration to act compatibly with Convention rights in everything they do. In short, the deference question arises as an integral part of the court's assessment of legality.

Secondly, Laws LJ's premises commit him to an explicitly territorial approach to the constitutional division of powers between the courts and democratic decision-makers: certain subjects, such as the defence of the realm and the security of the state's borders (including immigration control), are said to fall within the special constitutional responsibility of the executive, and certain other matters, such as criminal justice, within the special responsibility of the courts.[64] The amount of deference which is appropriate will be influenced by whether the content of the measure in question is within one or other of these areas of special responsibility. The problem with this approach is that the areas of special responsibility are defined by reference to subjects which cut across each other: so, for example, the question of what is required for a fair hearing (which is peculiarly within the province of the courts) may arise in the area of immigration policy which is peculiarly within the province of the executive.[65] Indeed, the questionable utility of this attempt to differentiate areas of responsibility is shown by the fact that one of the special constitutional responsibilities that Laws LJ attributes to the courts is 'the maintenance of the rule of law'.[66] A more transcendent responsibility it is hard to imagine.

By contrast, Simon Brown LJ's approach to the question of deference in *Roth* is much less threatening to the *Daly* commitment to law as justification, because it does not pre-empt effective scrutiny. Crucially, Simon Brown LJ regards the question of how much deference ought to be accorded to a decision-maker as an integral part of determining legality. His starting point in *Roth* was that he recognised a high degree of deference due by the court to Parliament in determining the legality of the scheme, but against the background assumption that under the HRA courts cannot abdicate their function as the guardian of human rights and accordingly must interfere if satisfied that the legislature has overstepped the limit of what is justifiable.[67] But crucially, and in keeping with Lord Steyn's landmark judgment in *Daly*, the court can only know if Parliament has overstepped that limit if it conducts a proper scrutiny of the justifications for the decisions (some-

---

[64] The underlying territorial notion manifests itself in the language used: at one point, for example, (*ibid* at para 86) Laws LJ states that 'there are no tanks on the wrong lawns.'

[65] As pointed out by Jonathan Parker LJ, *ibid* at para 139. In *Carson v Secretary of State for Work and Pensions* [2003] EWCA Civ 797 (17 June 2003) at para 73, Laws LJ appears to have accepted this: 'the powers of the courts and the powers of the other branches of government, if they do not overlap, at least may operate in the same field, they are not marked off by walls without windows.'

[66] *Ibid* at para 85.

[67] *Ibid* at paras 26–29.

thing which Laws LJ's approach prevented him from doing). Having carried out that scrutiny, and 'affording all such deference as I believe I properly can to those responsible for immigration control and for devising and enacting the legislation necessary to achieve it,' Simon Brown LJ felt that he had no alternative but to find the legislative scheme unfair to carriers in the sense that it imposed an excessive burden on them for the pursuit of the social goal, and he therefore agreed that a declaration of incompatibility should be granted.

In stating that he had accorded all such deference to Parliament and the executive as he believed he properly could, Simon Brown LJ was clearly presupposing that deference is not a matter of submission to democratic decision-makers in areas of policy which are peculiarly within their responsibility, but rather is something which has to be earned by the primary decision-maker, and the degree to which it is earned depends on a variety of factors which the court has to weigh carefully in reaching its overall decision as to how much respect is deserved. Although by no means articulated exhaustively, the factors which Simon Brown LJ clearly took into account in reaching his conclusion on deference included the importance of the social goal being pursued and the fact that Parliament and the executive are democratically accountable.[68] Ultimately, however, although these factors appeared to lean in favour of upholding the balance struck by Parliament, they were not sufficiently weighty to earn the court's respect given the extent of the interference with the rights of the carriers.

Gypsies and the Law of Town and Country Planning

Another context in which the question of how courts should approach the deference question arises in an acute form is that of the law of town and country planning as applied to Gypsies. On the one hand, town and country planning is a context (in the broad sense) in which the courts have traditionally been reluctant to interfere with decisions of planning inspectors, for a combination of reasons including the extent of public participation in the modern plan-making process, the further opportunities to challenge decisions in a well-developed appellate structure, the expertise of planning inspectors, and the democratic accountability of both local planning authorities and the Secretary of State responsible for the planning system. On the other hand, important and fundamental rights of Gypsies are at stake in planning decisions concerning where they may station their caravans. Because their traditional way of life involves an itinerant lifestyle, which has

---

[68] In deciding on the degree of deference which was due, Simon Brown LJ does not appear to have explicitly taken into account as a factor the degree to which ministers in Parliament had sufficiently considered the possibility of achieving the same objective by other means. This was a factor which was, rightly, taken into account by Sullivan J at first instance at paras 170–73. Laws LJ, on the other hand, at [2002] 3 WLR 344, para 114, expressly ruled it out as a relevant factor on the basis that for a court to evaluate the quality of ministerial evaluation of the policy options would contravene Article 9 of the Bill of Rights 1688, a position now approved by the House of Lords in *Wilson and Others* v *Secretary of State for Trade and Industry* [2003] UKHL 40.

now been recognised as being an integral part of their ethnic identity,[69] administrative decisions about whether or not to grant them permission to station their caravans in a particular place, or whether or not to enforce against them if they are camped on land without authorisation, are decisions which unavoidably impinge on the important cultural rights of a minority as well as on the fundamental right of the individuals themselves to respect for their home and family life. Given these competing pulls towards and away from deference, how should courts approach their task of deciding such cases?[70] Two recent decisions in this context demonstrate well the contrast between the possible approaches to the deference question.

Buckland and Boswell v Secretary of State for Environment, Planning and the Regions was an appeal by two Gypsy families under section 288 Town and Country Planning Act 1990 against a refusal to grant temporary planning permission for the use of a Green Belt site for the stationing of caravans.[71] An inquiry was held, and the planning inspector visited both the site itself and other Gypsy sites. The inspector defined the main issue in the appeal as being:

> whether general or personal need for Gypsy accommodation and the personal circumstances and rights of the Appellants as Gypsies amount to very special circumstances sufficient to outweigh the degree of harm due to inappropriateness in the Green Belt and any other harm in relation to the rural location of the site [which was in a Special Landscape Area], the safety of the road access and noise from the M42.[72]

At the beginning of the inquiry, the inspector apparently circulated what the judge described in his judgment as 'a list of the considerations which he believed needed to be covered.' These included (under the sub-heading 'Case Law'), 'Rights as defined in ECHR, especially Arts 2 on education and 8 on respect for family life and home.'

The inspector adopted the conventional framework for making decisions about proposed development in the Green Belt, incorporating the Convention rights of the Gypsies as, in effect, material considerations to be weighed in the overall balance along with other planning factors. Since it was common ground that the proposed development was inappropriate to its location in the Green Belt, the Inspector proceeded on the basis that the proposed development could only be justified by very special circumstances sufficient to override harm by inappropriateness and any other adverse planning effects. He concluded that there were:

> no very special circumstances, by way of need for Gypsy accommodation or the personal needs or circumstances of the Appellants, sufficient to outweigh the harm that would

---

[69] *Chapman v United Kingdom* (2001) 33 EHRR 399 at para 73.

[70] The issue may come before a court in a number of different ways: for example, on an appeal against an enforcement notice (under the Town and Country Planning Act (TCPA) 1990, s 288) or a refusal of planning permission (under TCPA, s 289) where an inspector has refused the first level appeal; on an application for an injunction to restrain a breach of planning control (under TCPA 1990, s 187B); on an application for a possession order under CPR Pt. 55; on an application to commit for contempt for breach of an injunction or other order. Although there are many procedural routes, the issue will very often be the same.

[71] [2001] EWHC Admin 524, [2001] 4 PLR 34.

[72] *Ibid* at para 4.

occur for the duration of the permission sought due to inappropriateness in the Green Belt, the detrimental impact on the Special Landscape Area, and the threat to road safety.[73]

One of the grounds of appeal to the High Court was that the inspector had misdirected himself on the issue of proportionality. It was argued that the inspector had to consider whether the interference with the claimant's Article 8 rights was proportionate, and that it was a consequence of the House of Lords decision in *Daly* that on a section 288 or 289 appeal the High Court should satisfy itself that the right balance had been struck by the inspector. Sullivan J unequivocally rejected that submission.[74] Relying on the elliptical paragraph 28 of Lord Steyn's speech in *Daly*, he held that town and country planning was a different 'context' from that of prisoners' rights, and one in which it was not appropriate for the appellate court to decide for itself whether the right balance had been struck:

> 'Striking that balance was a matter for the inspector, using his own planning expertise in the light of all the evidence, including, most importantly in so many planning cases, the site visit'.[75]

Invoking the House of Lords decision in *Alconbury*, upholding the limited scope of rights of appeal to the courts in planning cases, and the approach of the European Court in *Chapman*, he held that it was entirely compatible with Article 8 for the inspector to adopt the conventional Green Belt approach to the case, because the balancing exercise required by that Article was incorporated into the balancing exercise which was carried out in the application of the conventional approach. What mattered was not whether the word 'proportionality' was mentioned in the decision letter, but whether the inspector had in fact carried out the requisite balancing exercise.

The decision in *Buckland and Boswell* is a practical example of the approach to deference grounded in a formalistic notion of the separation of powers. The reason for Sullivan J's unhesitating rejection of the argument that the court should satisfy itself that the right balance had been struck was that he considered that it would be 'to embark on a merits review'.[76] He could see nothing between forbidden merits review and the traditional approach. As a result, he treated the question of compatibility (whether there had been a violation of Convention rights) as a matter exclusively for the inspector.[77] The reasons he gave for this were a combination of reasons of institutional competence and constitutional legitimacy. The considerations articulated by the European Court in *Chapman*, which underpinned its recognition of a presumptively wide margin of appreciation, were said by Sullivan J to apply equally to the ability of the High Court to review inspectors' decisions.[78] Like the European Court, the High Court does not do site visits, does

---

[73] *Ibid* at para 15.
[74] *Ibid* at paras 46–59.
[75] *Ibid* at para 59.
[76] *Ibid* at para 56.
[77] *Ibid* at para 59.
[78] *Ibid* at para 57.

not hear evidence and is not familiar with many of the policy considerations that may be relevant. Also, on the normative side, Sullivan J clearly thought that this was entirely as it should be, because the regulatory framework was designed in such a way that some of the questions which go to make up the Article 8 question are decided at an earlier stage. The planning enquiry process ensures that arguments as to whether there really is a pressing social need and whether a refusal would be proportionate can all be addressed in detail in an appropriate forum. The elaborate plan-making process meant that full account was taken of conflicting social needs when policies were being framed; and then on an individual appeal the inspector, applying the conventional approach to development in the Green Belt, conducted a balancing exercise in determining the appeal. This, Sullivan J thought, was enough. As he said in relation to one of the joined appeals[79]:

> the statutory process must enable Article 8 rights to be addressed, but it does not follow that they must be addressed in full at each and every stage of the process so that finality is never achieved.[80]

The approach to deference adopted in *Buckland and Boswell*, focusing primarily on questions of institutional competence, will inevitably lead to an unduly submissive stance by courts in the planning context. It is to be contrasted, however, with the approach adopted by the Court of Appeal in *Porter v South Bucks District Council*,[81] which is much closer to the due deference approach advocated in this chapter. The Court of Appeal in *Porter* had to grapple directly with the question of how its former approach to the availaibility of a particular remedy in the planning context now had to change as a result of the HRA where Article 8 rights were engaged. Local authorities wishing to evict Gypsies from unauthorised encampments have increasingly been resorting to the power in the planning legislation to apply for an injunction to restrain a breach of planning control.[82] Before the HRA, the well established approach of the courts when dealing with such applications

---

[79]   *Ibid* at para 135.

[80]   *Wychavon District Council v Smith* (one of four conjoined appeals with *Buckland and Boswell*), [2001] EWHC Admin 524 at paras 135–36. The *Wychavon* case was a local authority's appeal by way of case stated against a decision by magistrates that certain occupiers of Gypsy caravans were not guilty of failing to comply with a breach of condition notice under TCPA 1990, s 187A . The issue was whether the magistrates were entitled to conclude that the Gypsies had made out the statutory defence that they had taken all reasonable measures to secure compliance with the Notice on the ground that they did not have a suitable site to remove their caravans to. Applying the same approach of looking at the regulatory framework overall to see if there were adequate procedural safeguards to protect the applicants' Article 8 rights, Sullivan J held that the magistrates were not entitled so to hold: 'an interpretation of the subsection [giving the statutory defence] which does not enable the magistrates to consider questions of need and availability of suitable alternative sites is not in breach of the Convention, because the magistrates' court is not the stage in the regulatory framework where such questions should be addressed.'

[81]   [2001] EWCA Civ 1549; [2002] 1 All ER 425.

[82]   TCPA 1990, s 187B which provides: '(1) Where a local planning authority consider it necessary or expedient for any actual or apprehended breach of planning control to be restrained by injunction, they may apply to the court for an injunction, whether or not they have exercised or are proposing to exercise any of their other powers under this Part. (2) On an application under subsection (1) the court may grant such an injunction as the court thinks appropriate for the purpose of restraining the breach.'

for injunctive relief was to treat the court's discretion as being narrowly circum-scribed by the fact that the planning authorities had already decided what consti-tutes a breach of planning control.[83] The courts in such cases regarded the planning authorities as having already struck the balance between the general public interest and the interests of the individuals who were to be evicted, and saw any role for the courts in considering questions such as the availability of alterna-tive sites, or the hardship which would be caused by an injunction, as a usurpation of that policy-making function, and contrary to the will of Parliament which had entrusted those powers to the planning authorities. In other words, like Sullivan J in *Buckland and Boswell*, they adopted an entirely submissive approach to the deci-sions of the planning authorities, subject only to a residual power to correct mani-fest errors or perverse decisions.

The justification for this submissive approach was again rooted largely in a for-malistic notion of the separation of powers, premised on there being respective areas of responsibility of the courts and the political branches within which each has exclusive competence. It is exemplified by the decision of Hoffmann J at first instance in *Mole Valley*:

> There can be no doubt that requiring [the Gypsies] to leave the site would cause consid-erable hardship. This court, however, is not entrusted with a general jurisdiction to solve social problems. The striking of a balance between the requirements of planning policy and the needs of these defendants is a matter which, in my view, has been entrusted to other authorities.[84]

The invocation of Parliament's 'entrusting' the functions to the planning authori-ties demonstrates again the attraction of the rhetoric of parliamentary sovereignty to justify judicial restraint.

The central issue in *Porter* was whether this approach survived the coming into force of the HRA, or whether the fact that Article 8 was engaged in such cases meant that the court now had to make an independent judgment in deciding whether or not to grant an injunction. In each case, the judge below had granted the injunc-tions sought, and the question for the Court of Appeal was therefore whether those judges had directed themselves correctly about the approach they should take to the exercise of their discretion. The arguments made to the Court of Appeal covered

---

[83] The leading authorities were two Court of Appeal decisions, *Mole Valley District Council v Smith* [1992] 3 PLR 22 (decided under the predecessor power to grant injunctions) and *Hambleton District Council v Bird* [1995] 3 PLR 8.

[84] Cited with approval in the Court of Appeal in the same case [1992] 3 PLR 22 at 31. See to similar effect Lord Donaldson MR at 32 ('it is not for the courts to usurp the policy decision-making functions of the Secretary of State ... by a side-wind') and Balcombe LJ at 33 ('the court is being asked to reverse the decisions of the authorities to whom Parliament has entrusted the relevant decision, not on grounds of illegality, but on grounds of policy'). The reasoning of Pill LJ in *Hambleton* [1995] 3 PLR 8 at 15 was to precisely the same effect: the fact that the granting of an injunction is dependent on the court's discretion 'does not however entitle a judge ... to act as a court of appeal against a planning decision or to base a refusal to grant an injunction upon his view of the overall public interest.' The judge below in that case was criticised for having taken upon himself the role of assessing the benefits and disbenefits to the public as a whole, thereby 'taking upon himself the policy function of the plan-ning authorities and housing authorities and their powers and duties.'

the entire spectrum of possible positions identified above.[85] At one extreme, it was argued on behalf of some of the authorities that the court ought not to interfere with the balance struck by the planning authority between the interests of the Gypsy and the interests of the wider community, unless that balance had been struck in a *Wednesbury* unreasonable way: in other words, the court should submit to the planning authority's striking of the balance, subject only to the court's conventional public law jurisdiction to interfere with manifestly perverse decisions. At the other extreme, it was argued on behalf of some of the appellants that the court was bound to consider afresh all facts and matters, including all issues of policy as to whether planning permission should be granted and all questions of hardship for the Gypsies concerned were they to be removed. Between these two extremes, the other appellants argued for the 'due deference' approach: accepting that *some* deference had to be paid by the courts to the planning judgments arrived at by the planning authority, but very much less than had hitherto been thought appropriate. On this approach, the question for the court faced with an application for such an injunction was how to decide what degree of deference was due in the circumstances to the determinations of the planning authorities.

The Court of Appeal in *Porter* had no hesitation in rejecting the two extreme positions, that the court itself was now the primary decision-maker, or that the court was required to submit to the balance struck by the planning authorities subject only to review for *Wednesbury* unreasonableness.[86] It held that the court considering whether or not to grant an injunction which would have the effect of evicting Gypsies from land is not entitled to reach its own independent view of the planning merits of the case: it is required to take these as having been decided within the planning process. However, in deciding whether or not to grant the injunction, the Court of Appeal held that the court must consider for itself a variety of factors which must be weighed in the balance. These factors include, for example, questions of hardship for the defendant and his family, including the impact on the family's health and education; the availability of alternative sites; the planning history of the site; the need to enforce planning control in the general interest; the degree and flagrancy of the breach of planning control; whether other enforcement measures had been tried in the past; whether there was any urgency in the situation; health and safety considerations; previous planning decisions; the local planning authority's decision to seek injunctive relief; and the degree of environmental damage resulting from the breach of planning control.

The Court of Appeal also recognised that the weight to be given to these considerations in the balancing exercise may vary depending on a number of other factors. For example, the relevance of previous planning decisions will depend on matters such as how recent they are, the extent to which considerations of hardship and availability of alternative sites were taken into account, and the strength

---

[85]   They are summarised at [2002] 1 All ER 425 at para 4 of the Court's judgment.

[86]   The approach which is to be taken by a court considering an application for an injunction under TCPA 1990, s 187B is set out at [2002] 1 All ER 425, paras 38–42.

of the conclusions reached on land use and environmental issues.[87] Similarly, the relevance and weight of the local planning authority's decision will depend on the extent to which they can be shown to have had regard to all the material considerations and to have properly posed and approached the Article 8(2) questions as to necessity and proportionality.[88]

Having identified these various factors as being relevant to the striking of the necessary balance between the competing interests, the Court of Appeal held that the approach to section 187B contained in the Court of Appeal's decision in *Hambleton,* which precluded consideration by the judge of questions of hardship, was not consistent with the court's duty to act compatibly with Convention rights contained in section 6(1) of the HRA.[89] It held that proportionality requires that the injunction not only be appropriate and necessary for the attainment of the public interest objective sought (the safeguarding of the environment), but also that it does not impose an excessive burden on the individual whose private interests (the Gypsy's private life and home and retention of his ethnic identity) are at stake. The court's task in answering that question was acknowledged not to be an easy one, involving as it inevitably does the striking of a balance between competing interests of a very different character, but the task was unavoidable under the HRA, and 'provided it is undertaken in a structured and articulated way, the appropriate conclusion should emerge.'[90]

The Court of Appeal in *Porter* therefore adopted an intermediate position on the question of deference, explicitly rejecting both the 'primary judgment' approach of those who would have the courts substitute their own decision on the merits, and at the same time the crudely submissive approach of those who would regard the questions to be decided as having been 'entrusted' to the local planning authority and the planning inspector. Although the language of 'due deference' is not explicitly used by the court in *Porter*, it avoids altogether the use of the spatial metaphor in any of its forms, and is therefore liberated to articulate the range of factors which need to be taken into consideration when deciding the appropriate degree of deference to be paid, as well as the considerations which affect the weight which is to be given to the various reasons for deferring. The Court of Appeal's decision in *Porter* therefore contains the seeds of an approach to deference which offers a promising route towards realising the full potential of the House of Lords decision in *Daly*.[91]

---

[87] *Ibid* at para 38.
[88] *Ibid* at para 39.
[89] *Ibid* at para 41.
[90] *Ibid* at 42. Applying the new approach to the facts of the particular cases, the Court of Appeal held that in three of the four cases the judges below had determined the applications for an injunction by reference to the old approach which involved them in deferring excessively to the planning authorities' own views as to how the balance between the competing interests fell to be struck.
[91] The Court of Appeal's approach has now been unanimously approved by the House of Lords, [2003] UKHL 26, [2003] 3 All ER 1.

Social and Economic Policy

In the context of what might be broadly described as 'social and economic policy,' courts have recently begun to scrutinise more carefully claims for deference based solely on the fact that the decision being challenged is one taken within such a context. In *Poplar Housing Association v Donoghue*, the Court of Appeal came close to treating this fact as determinative of the question whether the statutory procedure obliging a court to make an order for possession of an assured shorthold tenancy if the appropriate notice had been given was in breach of the right to respect for private life, family life and home in ECHR Article 8.[92] Although Lord Woolf CJ expressed his conclusion in terms of degrees of deference to Parliament, his reasoning was based primarily on the need for courts to recognise that the legislation represented the striking of a balance by Parliament between those in the position of the person resisting possession and the needs of those dependent on social housing as a whole. The economic and other implications of any policy in this area were said to be extremely complex and far-reaching, and the question of whether the restrictions on the court's powers were legitimate and proportionate were said to be 'the area of policy where the court should defer to the decision of Parliament,' on the basis that the correctness of that decision was more appropriate for Parliament than the courts.

In *Wilson v First County Trust*, however, which concerned the compatibility with ECHR Article 6 of a provision of the Consumer Credit Act 1974 imposing a statutory bar on a lender enforcing an agreement in certain circumstances, the Court of Appeal rejected a similar claim for deference on the basis that the legislation was concerned with social issues, and the issues fell within an area in which courts should be ready to defer, on democratic grounds, to the considered opinion of the elected body or person. The Court of Appeal's response was a robust and significant statement of the distinction between deference as submission and deference as respect, and of the centrality of reasons in a culture of justification:

> We recognize the force of those arguments. But, unless deference is to be equated with unquestioning acceptance, the argument that an issue of social policy falls within a discretionary area of judgment which the courts must respect recognizes, as it seems to us, the need for the court to identify the particular issue of social policy which the legislature or the executive thought it necessary to address, and the thinking which led to that issue being dealt with in the way that it was. It is one thing to accept the need to defer to an opinion which can be seen to be the product of reasoned consideration based on policy; it is quite another thing to be required to accept, without question, an opinion for which no reason of policy is advanced.[93]

Similarly, in *Mendoza v Ghaidan*, in which the Court of Appeal were required to re-visit, in light of the coming into force of the HRA, the House of Lords' interpre-

---

92   [2001] EWCA Civ 595, [2002] QB 48 at paras 69–72.
93   [2001] EWCA Civ 633, [2002] QB 74 at 93–94, para 33. See, however, the unanimous criticism by the House of Lords of the use made of Hansard in support of this approach: [2003] UKHL 40 at paras 51–67, 110–18, 139–45.

tation of the term 'spouse' in the Rent Act 1977 as excluding same-sex partners,[94] an argument based on *Poplar* that the court ought to defer to Parliament's striking of the balance between a number of competing interests was given short shrift by the Court of Appeal.[95] The argument was made in the context of whether there was an objective and reasonable justification for treating same-sex partnerships differently from other-sex partnerships in relation to Rent Act protection: it was argued that it fell within the legitimate ambit of the state's discretion or judgement to arrange its housing schemes and the disposition of its housing stock by doing so.

A unanimous Court of Appeal held, however, that any principle of deference to the will of Parliament could not assist in this case, for three reasons. First, because once discrimination had been established, it was not enough to discharge the burden of objective and reasonable justification to claim that what had been done fell within the permissible ambit of Parliament's discretion: a much more positive argument was required to discharge the burden that arose. Secondly, while courts should only enter with trepidation on questions of social or economic policy such as the general organisation of housing policy, the court had no hesitation in saying that issues of discrimination have high constitutional importance and are issues that the courts should not shrink from: in such cases deference has only a minor role to play. Thirdly, once it was accepted that the court is not simply bound by whatever Parliament has decided, the court had to scrutinise the justifications offered, including to see whether the means chosen to achieve the end are logically related to forwarding that end. It found that they were not, and held that the statutory term was to be interpreted in such a way as to include same-sex partners in order to avoid a breach of ECHR Article 14 in conjunction with Article 8.[96]

CONCLUSION

The above practical examples taken from the three specific contexts of immigration, planning, and social and economic policy, demonstrate how the two different

---

[94] In *Fitzpatrick v Sterling Housing Association* [2001] 1 AC 27.

[95] [2002] EWCA Civ 1533, [2003] 2 WLR 478 at paras 16–21. The decision is under appeal to the House of Lords.

[96] See also *Gurung, Pun and Thapa v Ministry of Defence* [2002] EWHC Admin 2463 (27 November 2002), concerning the exclusion of Gurkhas from the scheme of ex gratia payments made to former Japanese Prisoners of war, in which the Ministry argued (at para 40) that it would not be constitutionally legitimate for the courts to alter the criteria on the basis of which the payments were made, because the court was not properly equipped to undertake the task of balancing conflicting claims to scarce resources, and this would be a usurpation of the functions of Parliament in the control and approval of public expenditure. That argument was rejected by McCombe J who held that the exclusion of the Gurkha claimants from the compensation arrangements on the basis of a distinction based on race was irrational and inconsistent with the common law principle of equality that is 'the cornerstone of our law' (para. 55). Cf the decision of Stanley Burnton J in *Carson v Department of Work and Pensions* [2002] EWHC. Admin 978, concerning the non-payment of annual pension uprate to UK pensioners resident abroad, at paras 68–70, that questions concerning the allocation of scarce resources and foreign relations are non-justiciable. The Court of Appeal in the same case, however, [2003] EWCA Civ 797, considered that the case had nothing to do with foreign relations (para 66) and treated the allocation of scarce resources as going to the degree of deference rather than justiciability (paras 72–73).

approaches to the question of deference can make a very real difference to the out-come of cases. It is not a question of one approach leading to deference and the other to interference; it is a question of how to ensure that Lord Steyn's first insight in *Daly*, that unlawful decisions can only be identified if the process of review for justification is properly carried out, is not lost by adopting an approach to defer-ence which pre-empts such review.

Despite the persistence of the language of discretionary area of judgment and margin of discretion, there are some encouraging signs in some recent cases that courts are beginning to feel their way towards a concept of due deference and to leave behind some of the surrogates for this issue which dominated the early days of HRA adjudication, including the spatial metaphor. The lesson of this review, it is suggested, is that, in place of the language of discretionary area of judgment, or margin of discretion, or latitude, English courts should now adopt, as an integral part of their assessment of legality, an explicit due deference approach, premised on the assumption that power in our Constitution is shared amongst the various actors rather than to be parcelled out according to some inflexible and outdated idea of the separation of powers and co-existing supremacies.[97] This will require the explicit articulation of a number of matters which at present are too often buried beneath inappropriate doctrinal tools: the sorts of factors that might war-rant a degree of deference from a judicial decision-maker; the specific factors which are in play in a particular case; why the court considers that they require a degree of deference to a particular decision, or an aspect of it; and just how much deference the court considers to be due in the circumstances.

The argument which has been made in this chapter is part of a much wider need for a thoroughgoing reconceptualisation of public law, in response to the modern landscape of power, and the manifest inadequacy of the existing conceptual framework in contemporary conditions. Until this is done, the development of a coherent and mature system of public law fit for a modern constitutional democ-racy will continue to be blighted by our collective failure to understand the nature of our inheritance and move beyond its paralysing confines. The explicit adoption of a 'due deference' approach to determining the limits of the judicial role should help to facilitate the reconfiguration of our public law around the concept of justi-fication, at the same time as building meaningful democratic considerations into a theory of deference which does not depend on crude notions of sovereignty and authority for its underlying conception of legality. If such an approach is adopted, it may yet be possible to avoid the perpetual lurching between democratic posi-tivism and liberal constitutionalism to which Dicey committed us and from which we have yet, despite the significant institutional reforms of recent years, to make a very convincing escape.

---

[97] See Lord Hoffmann in *R v BBC ex p Prolife Alliance* [2003] UKHL 23 at paras 74–77 for an exam-ple of how an approach rooted in a formalistic notion of the separation of powers turns complex ques-tions of deference into bright-line jurisdictional questions for the courts to decide as a question of law. This explains the apparent paradox that an approach which leads inexorably to the submissiveness of Lord Hoffmann's judgment in *Rehman* above can at the same time be critical of the deference approach for 'its overtones of servility or gracious concession' (Prolife, para 75).

14

Civil Liberties and Human Rights

CONOR GEARTY

INTRODUCTION

T HE IDEA OF civil liberties is old fashioned and perhaps also unfashionable, especially in contrast to the energy generated by its younger, newly arrived sibling, human rights law. The purpose of this chapter is to show that it would be wrong to write off the concept as a relic of a past, pre-human rights age. The argument here is that the subject of civil liberties stands on the brink of a remarkable renaissance, precisely (albeit perhaps also paradoxically) because of the enormous breadth, depth and range of the Human Rights Act 1998 (HRA). Civil liberties law is capable of being presented as a coherent set of ideas rooted in an underlying political philosophy which in turn reflects a particular way of looking at the world. While the European Convention on Human Rights (ECHR) is clearly far more broadly based than is civil liberties law, it is the latter that gives that Convention its main theoretical integrity.

An awareness of civil libertarian principles greatly assists in identifying the appropriate way in which the courts should go about interpreting the HRA. It also allows a signalling to the judges, in a far more coherent fashion than has yet properly emerged, about when they can afford, indeed when they are obliged, to take an activist approach and when in contrast a certain restraint is called for. With the topic of civil liberties in this way retrieved from the margins, the chapter will conclude with some thoughts on the subject's perceived vulnerabilities. It was these alleged weaknesses which gave rise to the perception of the need for the new discourse rooted in human rights in the first place, and so—having attempted freshly to rediscover the old subject within the new—the time is right in this chapter to revisit these supposed difficulties. It will be argued that these problems are in fact more apparent than real, and that they are in any event rather less severe than the difficulties that also circumscribe the concept of human rights.

CIVIL LIBERTIES, 'HUMAN RIGHTS' AND THE ECHR

We start with the setting of parameters. Civil liberties is a discipline primarily engaged with the law and practice concerned with those freedoms which are essential to the maintenance and fostering of our representative system of government.[1] At the very centre of such freedoms, the entitlement upon which the utility of the remaining liberties depend, and which gives them added zest and meaning, is the right to vote. Here we have an example of a civil liberty, indeed we would say the key civil liberty, which is realisable only through positive state action: our right to vote cannot exist in the abstract; it requires a large state machinery to make it work. Furthermore, a properly functioning representative democracy will insist that each vote carries a broadly equal weight, and will not permit certain affluent electors to buy the power to be heard at the expense of other interests; the electoral playing field should be an equal one. In contrast, other civil liberties are particularly valuable in that they make meaningful the exercise of this core right to vote, but they are reliant more on state inaction than action.

The freedom to think for oneself, to believe what one wishes and to say what one wants are essential if a democratic assembly is going to be truly and properly representative. Their importance is, however, broader than this. Such civil liberties affect the general political atmosphere, the democratic health of the community, in a way which matters whether or not a vote is imminent or a voter likely to be influenced one way or the other. The right to associate with others and to assemble together are essential for the same reasons. Access to relevant information can also be seen to be an important civil liberty, both because the uninformed vote is a less effective one and because the discourse upon which a properly functioning democracy depends should be a well-informed one. Finally, it surely goes without saying that a state which arbitrarily kills, imprisons or tortures its citizens so chills the political atmosphere that it cannot be described as democratic, regardless of how free speech formally is or how regularly secret votes are polled: freedom cannot be constructed on such authoritarian foundations. Adherence to these core civil liberties produces an assembly that is both representative and accountable (through the ballot box and through the political energy that the prospect of the vote inspires) for the power that it exercises. It also guarantees a vibrant political community even at those times (the great majority) during which a vote is not imminent. Civil liberties also requires as a matter of basic principle that the relationship between the individual and the state be regulated

---

[1] See on this point the work of K D Ewing whose recent writings have elaborated on the nature of the British constitution and on the place of civil liberties (and social rights) within it: see especially his 'Human Rights, Social Democracy and Constitutional Reform' in CA Gearty and A Tomkins (eds), *Understanding Human Rights* (London, Mansell, 1996), ch 3; 'The Politics of the British Constitution' [2000] *PL* 405; 'Constitutional Reform and Human Rights: Unfinished Business' (2001) 5 *Edinburgh Law Review* 1; and 'The Unbalanced Constitution' in T Campbell, K D Ewing and Adam Tomkins (eds), *Sceptical Essays in Human Rights* (Oxford, Oxford University Press, 2001), ch 3. Also valuable is the work of J Griffith: see in particular his 'The Common Law and the Constitution' (2001) 117 *LQR* 42.

by law, so some principle of legality is as essential to the subject as is a commitment to representative government.

The degree of synchronisation between the content of civil liberties law that has just been delineated and the ECHR will be immediately apparent to those with even the broadest sense of what the latter document contains. Under Article 3 of the First Protocol, the 'High Contracting Parties undertake to hold free elections at reasonable intervals by secret ballot, under conditions which will ensure the free expression of the opinion of the people in the choice of the legislature.' The basic essentials for a properly functioning democratic society are established in the body of the ECHR itself, with Article 2 declaring that 'Everyone's right to life shall be protected by law,' Article 3 prohibiting in absolute terms 'torture' and 'inhuman or degrading treatment or punishment,' and Article 4 forbidding 'slavery,' 'servitude,' and the performance of 'forced or compulsory labour'. The 'right to liberty and security' in Article 5 is necessarily more complex and qualified than the prohibitions that appear in Articles 2 to 4, but a clear consequence flowing from it is that persons cannot consistently with the ECHR be held without trial, or with no expectation of a trial, on the basis of their political beliefs. Any trial that does occur must satisfy the procedural requirements of Article 6, which among other safeguards, guarantees defendants a 'fair and public hearing … by an independent and impartial tribunal established by law.' Having ensured that there should be no drastic punishment lurking in the shadows of a seemingly free society, the ECHR then goes on to consolidate its vision of an 'effective political democracy' with a series of guarantees dealing with the civil liberties of thought, conscience and religion (Article 9), expression (Article 10) and assembly and association (Article 11). The provisions are widely drawn and intended to complete the spectrum of rights which underpins the democratic state from the moment an idea is first hatched, through its articulation, translation into a political platform and thence, via the right to vote, into a legislative assembly where, if it can command sufficient support, it will be translated into law.

A consequence of thinking about liberty, expression, assembly and so on, and also the entitlement to vote, as civil *liberties* rather than human *rights* is to focus attention away from the possibility of these being absolute entitlements vested in human beings as such and to divert the analytical spotlight instead on to their utility as part of the essential fabric that goes into the making of our democratic tapestry. This is where civil liberties can make its most important contribution to political and legal reasoning, for the absence of any assertion of absolutism is the most powerful (non) claim that the subject makes on our attention. As we have seen, civil liberties are defined by reference to an underlying political philosophy rooted in representative democracy, which definition at the same time permits, also by reference to that same underlying ideological premise, exceptions to be made to them. With this singular intellectual swoop, civil liberties law rises above the endless debates provoked by rights-talk, about when this kind of reckless speech should be allowed and when not, about why this assembly should be restricted and this other not: human rights law has no coherent way of answering these questions without drawing on some deeper set of principles. Civil liberties law, in contrast, has the benchmark of democratic necessity readily to hand. If it has an intuition, then it is not the quasi-religious concept of respect for human dignity but rather the robustly tangible notion that we should belong to a self-governing community of equals.

The exceptions to and derogations from rights that feature so prominently in many of the ECHR Articles can now be seen in their proper context. The ECHR is far from being a simplistic statement of rights in an unqualified form. An 'effective political democracy' (as the recitals to the ECHR call it) is not required to prove its worth by committing suicide, so '[i]n time of war or other public emergency threatening the life of the nation any High Contracting Party may take measures derogating from its obligations under this Convention to the extent strictly required by the exigencies of the situation, provided that such measures are not inconsistent with its other obligations under international law'[2] and provided also that torture, slavery, servitude or retrospective punishments are not deployed.[3] The taking of life is also not permitted in any circumstances other than, significantly and again rightly from the point of view of principle, 'in respect of deaths resulting from lawful acts of war.'[4] In the same vein is Article 17, prohibiting 'any State, group or person any right to engage in any activity or perform any act aimed at the destruction of any of the rights and freedoms set forth herein or at their limitation to a greater extent than is provided for in the Convention.'

While not all Convention rights are explicitly qualified, each of the freedoms of thought, conscience, religion, expression, assembly and association set out in Articles 9 to 11 is subject to a variety of widely drawn exceptions all of which must, however, be 'in accordance with' or 'prescribed by' law and also be 'necessary in a democratic society' for the realisation of the aim in question. The principle of legality is as we earlier mentioned a key part of civil liberties. The idea that a right, which is itself necessary in a democratic society (if it were not it would not be in the ECHR in the first place) being restricted on the basis of an overriding and somehow deeper democratic necessity is contradictory only if the question is addressed solely as one of human rights. If we see these fundamental freedoms as civil liberties, we are guided to look at them not as individual rights standing alone but rather as the building blocks of a democratic society; on this basis we can recognise them as political freedoms rather than personal entitlements. Once understood like this, it becomes clear that they may on occasion have to yield to the greater good of the political community as a whole.[5] Of course this focuses attention on the tricky questions of when such qualifications should be made and who should make them, but these are practical difficulties rather than principled objections. The problem of the partisan exercise of discretion—a key area in any analysis of civil liberties practice—is, however, explicitly addressed in Article 14,

---

[2] ECHR Article 15(1).
[3] ECHR Article 15(2).
[4] *Ibid.*
[5] See Murray Hunt, ch 13 above.

under which the 'enjoyment of the rights and freedoms set forth in this Convention' is guaranteed against 'discrimination on any ground such as sex, race, colour, language, religion, political or other opinion, national or social origin, association with a national minority, property, birth or other status.'

When we turn to the case law of the European Court of Human Rights we find a bench of judges that has generally been alive to the deep civil libertarian roots in the charter that it is their responsibility to interpret.[6] In its first judgment on the guarantee of free elections, the European Court described the Article as one which 'enshrines a characteristic principle of democracy' and therefore as 'of prime importance in the Convention system.'[7] Dismissing an argument that because the Article began with a reference to the obligations of the High Contracting Parties it could not therefore empower ordinary people in the way that other Convention rights did, the Court described the construction of the Article as derived from 'the desire to give greater solemnity to the commitment undertaken' and to 'the fact that the primary obligation in the field concerned is not one of abstention or non-interference, as with the majority of the civil and political rights, but one of adoption by the State of positive measures to "hold" democratic elections.'[8] The European Court noted that Article 3 'applies only to the election of the "legislature," or at least of one of its chambers if it has two or more' but remarked that the 'word "legislature" does not necessarily mean only the national parliament, however; it has to be interpreted in the light of the constitutional structure of the State in question.'[9] These words were to prove particularly prescient in light of the Court's later holding, by 15 votes to two, that the inability of a British citizen resident in Gibraltar to vote in elections to the European Parliament involved a violation of Article 3 of the First Protocol by the UK Government.[10]

The European Court has been just as principled and robust in its defence of freedom of expression in the political sphere, an area in which it has had many more cases through which to develop its views. The leading case remains the 1986 decision in *Lingens v Austria*.[11] The applicant was the publisher of a magazine in Vienna which printed a couple of pieces critical of the then Austrian Chancellor and accusing him of protecting former members of the Nazi SS for political reasons and of aiding their participation in Austrian politics. At the private suit of the Chancellor, the publisher was convicted of criminal defamation, fined, and issues of his magazine were confiscated. The relevant law under the Austrian Criminal Code was extremely broad, covering:

[a]nyone who in such a way that it may be perceived by a third person accuses another of possessing a contemptible character or attitude or of behaviour contrary to honour or

---

[6] See generally A Mowbray, 'The Role of the European Court of Human Rights in the Protection of Democracy' [1999] *PL* 703; C A Gearty, 'The European Court of Human Rights and the Protection of Civil Liberties: an Overview' (1993) 52 *Cambridge Law Journal* 89.

[7] *Mathieu-Mohin and Clerfayt v Belgium* (1987) 10 EHRR 1, at para 47.

[8] *Ibid* at para 50.

[9] *Ibid* at para 53.

[10] *Matthews v United Kingdom* (1999) 28 EHRR 361.

[11] (1986) 8 EHRR 407.

morality and of such a nature as to make him contemptible or otherwise lower him in public esteem.[12]

There were more severe punishments if the defamation was printed or broadcast and, though there was a defence where truth could be proved, the nature of the crime made this very difficult in most circumstances. In unanimously condemning as a breach of ECHR Article 10 the intimidatory action launched by the Chancellor, the Court laid down some important general principles which have acted as its key benchmarks in subsequent cases:

> [t]he Court has to recall that freedom of expression, as secured in paragraph 1 of Article 10, constitutes one of the essential foundations of a democratic society and one of the basic conditions for its progress and for each individual's self-fulfilment. Subject to paragraph 2, it is applicable not only to 'information' or 'ideas' that are favourably received or regarded as inoffensive or as a matter of indifference, but also to those that offend, shock or disturb. Such are the demands of that pluralism, tolerance and broadmindedness without which there is no 'democratic society.'
>
> These principles are of particular importance as far as the press is concerned. Whilst the press must not overstep the bounds set, *inter alia*, for the 'protection of the reputation of others', it is nevertheless incumbent on it to impart information and ideas on political issues just as on those in other areas of public interest. Not only does the press have the task of imparting such information and ideas: the public also has a right to receive them.…
>
> Freedom of the press furthermore affords the public one of the best means of discovering and forming an opinion of the ideas and attitudes of political leaders. More generally, freedom of political debate is at the very core of the concept of a democratic society which prevails throughout the Convention.
>
> The limits of acceptable criticism are accordingly wider as regards a politician as such than as regards a private individual. Unlike the latter, the former inevitably and knowingly lays himself open to close scrutiny of his every word and deed by both journalists and the public at large, and he must consequently display a greater degree of tolerance.[13]

This is the European Court at its most principled, and therefore most fearless. The case law which has followed in the years since *Lingens* bears testimony to the robustness of the Court's conception of political liberty.[14] One decision, *Jersild v Denmark*,[15] is particularly of interest from a theoretical perspective. The applicant was a journalist working for the Danish Broadcasting Corporation. He made a programme which featured a group of self-avowedly racist youths, who were living in the Copenhagen area. During the interview with them that was broadcast, the youths made several derogatory and racist remarks about black people in general and immigrant workers in particular. Under the Danish Penal Code, racially insulting remarks were prohibited by law, and the public prosecutor subsequently instituted proceedings against both the three youths and the applicant, together with the latter's head of department, for having aided and abetted the making of

---

[12] See Austrian Criminal Code, art 111.
[13] *Lingens*, above n 11, paras 41–42.
[14] See especially *Castells v Spain* (1992) 14 EHRR 445.
[15] (1994) 19 EHRR 1.

the remarks. All five were convicted before the local courts. The applicant and his boss appealed to the Danish Supreme Court where, however, their convictions were upheld. The journalist then took his case to Strasbourg.

The European Court held by 12 votes to seven that the applicant had been a victim of the violation of his Article 10 rights. While recognising 'the vital importance of combating racial discrimination in all its forms and manifestations'[16] the majority nevertheless saw the case as one primarily concerned with press freedom. 'Although formulated primarily with regard to the print media,' the principles the Court had developed in earlier cases 'doubtless appl[ied] also to the audio-visual media.'[17] Having regard therefore to the particular nature of the medium before it, and taken as a whole, 'the feature could not objectively have appeared to have as its purpose the propagation of racist views and ideas.'[18] The item 'was broadcast as a part of a serious Danish news programme and was intended for a well-informed audience' and did not require a counter-balancing point of view to that of the youths within the programme itself, particularly when 'the natural limitations on spelling out such elements in a short item within a longer programme' were taken into account.[19] The *Jersild* decision is rightly celebrated for the depth and maturity of its commitment to media freedom. Its civil libertarian roots are evident not only in its ringing endorsement of the role of the broadcasting media in our political culture, but also in its recognition that speech of this nature has limits. The European Court had 'no doubt that the remarks in respect of which the [youths] were convicted were more than insulting to members of the targeted groups and did not enjoy the protection of Article 10.'[20] The freedom of expression protected by Article 10 was qualified by its underlying role in a liberal democratic state, and the unfocused apolitical stirring up of hatred could not hide under its tolerant umbrella.

The civil liberties guaranteed in ECHR Article 11 have tended to be overshadowed by the breadth the European Court has accorded to Article 10. Thus in *Steel and others v United Kingdom*,[21] a case involving a number of persons who were involved in political 'direct action' of various sorts, was analysed as raising a series of Article 10 freedom of expression issues rather than the right to assembly under Article 11. Of the three kinds of action before the European Court, however, the conduct that came closest to the peaceful communication of political views was the type that secured the Court's sympathy and ultimately a favourable ruling. These were the three applicants who had been arrested for handing out leaflets outside a conference devoted to the sale of fighter helicopters. The protest had been 'entirely peaceful' with there having been no significant obstruction or attempt to obstruct those attending the conference or to take any other kind of

---

[16] *Ibid* at para 30.
[17] *Ibid* at para 31.
[18] *Ibid* at para 33.
[19] *Ibid* at para 34.
[20] *Ibid* at para 35, citing earlier Commission decisions in *Glimmerveen and Hagenbeek v The Netherlands* (1979) 18 D & R 187 and *Künen v Germany* (reported as *X v Federal Republic of Germany*) (1982) 29 D & R 194.
[21] (1998) 28 EHRR 603.

action that might have provoked those attending to violence.[22] The Court was unanimous that their arrest had infringed their Article 10 rights.[23] The remaining two applicants were not so lucky; their noisy and intrusive protests (obstructing a grouse shoot and breaking into motorway construction sites) had not been without any risk of disorder and had interfered markedly with the rights of others, and the Court accordingly found against them. The Strasbourg judges seem to have got the civil libertarian balance right; the more the communication of political ideas is achieved through conduct rather than words, then the greater the interest of the state in controlling that expression is bound to be. Where the action is not peaceful, the chances are that it is not protected by Article 10 (or 11). The European Court is not saying that there is no (moral) right to engage in disruptive direct action, merely that there is no civil liberty to do so if the price a democracy must pay for such tolerance is legal anarchy.

Where Article 11 undoubtedly comes into its own as a discrete civil libertarian protection is in relation to its guarantee of freedom of association. This is a civil liberty that is analytically more clearly distinct from freedom of expression than is freedom of assembly. Its importance lies in its protection of one of the key attributes of a healthy democratic culture, the political party. The point has become important recently in relation to Turkey, where the attempt to ban domestic political organisations opposed to the government has brought the country before the European Court. The first and most important of these cases was *United Communist Party of Turkey and others v Turkey.*[24] The Turkish Constitutional Court had by order dissolved the Communist Party and transferred its assets to the Treasury, with the founders and managers of the Party being banned from holding like offices in any other political body. In Strasbourg, the Government argued that it was faced with 'a challenge to the fundamental interests of the national community, such as national security and territorial integrity'[25] and that this justified the action it had taken, which it admitted was draconian. The European Court was unanimous in its disagreement. The safeguards set out in Article 10 and 11 applied 'all the more in relation to political parties in view of their essential role in ensuring pluralism and the proper functioning of democracy.'[26] Furthermore, '[t]he fact that their activities form part of a collective exercise of freedom of expression in itself entitles political parties to seek the protection of Articles 10 and 11 of the Convention.'[27] The free expression of opinion implicit in the guarantee of the right to vote in Article 3 of the First Protocol would be 'inconceivable without the participation of a plurality of political parties representing the different shades of opinion to be found within a country's population.'[28] It followed that 'only

[22] *Ibid* at para 64.
[23] *Ibid* at para 110. Article 5 was also infringed: see para 64.
[24] (1998) 26 EHRR 121. See also *Socialist Party and others v Turkey* (1998) 27 EHRR 51. Cf *Refah Partisi (The Welfare Party) v Turkey* (2003) 37 EHRR 1.
[25] *United Communist Party v Turkey,* above n 24, at para 49.
[26] *Ibid* at para 43.
[27] *Ibid.*
[28] *Ibid* at para 44.

convincing and compelling reasons'[29] could justify restrictions on a party's freedom of association, none of which could be found in this case. This did not mean that 'the authorities of a State in which an association, through its activities, jeopardises that State's institutions' were not entitled to fight back: 'some compromise between the requirements of defending democratic society and individual rights is inherent in the system of the Convention.'[30] But in this case the ban on the Party had been so immediate that no pattern of subversive action could be pointed to.[31]

To say that the ECHR is rooted in a commitment to civil liberties that is both rational and principled is not to say that mistakes are never made. There have been suggestions that its evaluation of whether emergency measures derogating from basic freedom have been justified has sometimes erred too much on the side of the state authorities.[32] Certainly the European Court has not always got the application of its principles right in its political speech and association cases. During the Cold War period, for example, the European Commission had not found objectionable under the ECHR a ban on the German Communist Party.[33] A couple of cases in the 1980s upheld Germany's controversial prohibition on the employment of extremists in the civil service.[34] Britain's and Ireland's media restrictions on members of a lawful political party, Sinn Féin, were likewise found to pass muster at around the same time.[35] In vain did the Turkish lawyers in the Article 11 cases we have discussed seek to catch the European Court's eye with some of these embarrassing skeletons from the ECHR's past. A different kind of error from the perspective of principle can be seen in *Bowman v United Kingdom*,[36] where restrictions on the funding of political campaigns designed to prevent the well resourced securing an undue advantage at election time were analysed in very narrow terms by the Court, in a way which seemed not to appreciate the importance of the principle of political equality.[37] Viewed overall, however, the record of the European Court in the sphere of political freedom is not a bad one. The European Court is generally appreciative that civil liberties are at the core of the ECHR and it has usually sought to assert them in a manner that has been principled and coherent.

---

[29] *Ibid* at para 46.
[30] *Ibid* at para 32.
[31] *Ibid* at para 58.
[32] See *Brannigan and McBride v United Kingdom* (1993) 17 EHRR 539.
[33] *German Communist Party v Federal Republic of Germany*, App 250/57 (1957) 1 *Yearbook of the European Convention on Human Rights* 222.
[34] *Glasenapp v Germany* (1986) 9 EHRR 25; *Kosiek v Germany* (1986) 9 EHRR 328. See now *Vogt v Germany* (1995) 21 EHRR 205.
[35] *Brind v United Kingdom* (1994) 18 EHRR CD 76; *Purcell v Ireland* (1991) 70 D & R 262.
[36] (1998) 26 EHRR 1.
[37] See C A Gearty, 'Democracy and Human Rights in the European Court of Human Rights: A Critical Reappraisal' (2000) 51 *NILQ* 381.

CIVIL LIBERTIES IN BRITAIN

As we have already observed, a commitment to civil liberties disguised as human rights of the type introduced by the Human Rights Act 1998 is a relatively new idea for legal practitioners in the United Kingdom. On the traditional British model, the individual has generally been free to assert his or her civil liberties unless constrained by law from doing so: human rights (of any sort) have simply not come into the equation. In some ways the HRA introduces an awkward note into this well-established constitutional law, with its references to human rights and Convention rights as though these were separate from traditional civil liberties. We have already argued that, however it is described, the ECHR is itself deeply rooted in civil libertarian principle. The substance of the HRA is also in large part designed further to promote civil liberties. The biggest claim that the HRA can make for the attention of civil libertarians lies in its determined protection of the principle of parliamentary supremacy.[38] This is a counter-intuitive point for human rights lawyers, and it may signal a parting of the ways between civil liberties and human rights as the latter term is generally understood. But it is immediately appreciated by the theorist of civil liberties that there would be little point in the protection of the right to vote, and of such freedoms as those of assembly, association and expression, if the political community in which these entitlements were exercised was one in which the ultimate decisions were taken not by the representatives of the people but by an elite guardianship of unelected officers: there is more to the exercise of civil liberties than the right to make irrelevant political noise.[39] As is well known, the key interpretive power in the HRA is set out in section 3(1), under which it is declared that:

> [s]o far as it is possible to do so, primary legislation and subordinate legislation must be read and given effect in a way which is compatible with the Convention rights.

But where this possibility does not arise, the courts must leave the legislation alone and enforce it, albeit the senior courts may in appropriate circumstances issue a (non-binding) declaration of incompatibility, the effect of which is to put pressure on the executive and legislative branches to consider changes to the offending law.[40] The civil libertarian's theoretically well-grounded commitment to parliamentary sovereignty leads him or her to be more inclined than the human rights lawyer to set limits to what is 'possible' under section 3(1) and causes him or her also and for the same reason to be more relaxed about the issuance of declarations of incompatibility.[41] Rather than abuse the concept of legislative supremacy,

---

[38] See A Tomkins, ch 3, above.

[39] See KD Ewing, 'The Bill of Rights Debate: Democracy or Juristocracy in Britain?' in KD Ewing, CA Gearty and B A Hepple (eds), *Human Rights and Labour Law: Essays for Paul O'Higgins* (London, Mansell, 1994), ch 7.

[40] HRA, ss 4, 10 and Sch 2.

[41] See CA Gearty, 'Reconciling Parliamentary Democracy and Human Rights' (2002) 118 *LQR* 248.

therefore, civil libertarians are inclined to celebrate it as the realisation of the essence of their subject in its highest form.

To state the civil libertarian position in these stark terms is certainly to distinguish it from the notion of human rights, particularly when this idea is considered as a set of abstract guarantees of human dignity rather than in the qualified, civil-liberties-oriented form that we have been examining in the ECHR. But it is also to expose civil liberties to counter-attack as involving a commitment to parliamentary sovereignty that is unduly naïve, even gullible, in the optimistic assumption that it would seem to make about the nature of representative government. Rule by the majority has not turned out to be the Nirvana of sensitive, fair and just decision-making that this approach, and the early democratic idealists identified with it, assumed it would be. The 'mistakes' of the European Court of Human Rights, discussed earlier, are few in comparison with the transgressions on civil liberties for which the British legislative branch in the full exercise of its sovereignty must take responsibility. The right to vote has been suspended in war-time. The right of prisoners sentenced to more than a year in jail to sit in the Commons was hurriedly removed in 1981 when just such a person—the Irish Nationalist Bobby Sands—was returned by the constituents of two Northern Ireland counties while he was on hunger strike in the Maze prison (a protest from which he was subsequently to die).[42] The system of local taxation introduced by Parliament in 1988—and immediately labelled a poll tax by its opponents—was perceived by some to be an indirect attack on the right to vote by appearing to identify those exposed to local taxation primarily by reference to the electoral register.[43]

These explicit and implicit attacks on the right to vote have been serious, but it has been in the context of the protection of the civil liberties of expression, assembly and association that Parliament has been at its most cavalier. The political freedoms of particular persons and groups have been effectively suspended, particularly during war-time and also during periods of great internal conflict, such as occurred during the general strike in 1926 and in the depression years of the early 1930s.[44] The Cold War of the post-war decades produced its own litany of illiberal parliamentary actions, as did the counter-terrorism crisis which overlapped with the end of the Cold War and which is still ongoing.[45] Laws like the Emergency Powers Act 1920 and the anti-terrorism legislation passed with disconcerting frequency since 1974 further undermine the optimistic, civil libertarian assumption that democracy and justice are inextricably linked, particularly when the secondary legislation promulgated under such measures and the exercise of official discretion under them is also taken into account.[45a] It is clear from our

[42] Representation of the People Act 1981.

[43] Local Government Finance Act 1988. The tax did not long survive: see Local Government Finance Act 1992.

[44] See generally KD Ewing and CA Gearty, *The Struggle for Civil Liberties: Political Freedom and the Rule of Law in Britain, 1914–45* (Oxford, Oxford University Press, 2000).

[45] See generally KD Ewing and CA Gearty, *Freedom under Thatcher: Civil Liberties in Modern Britain* (Oxford, Clarendon Press, 1990).

[45a] See now Cabinet Office, Draft Civil Contingencies Bill (2003).

perspective a century on that an early and influential democratic socialist theorist like Eduard Bernstein was being ridiculously idealistic when he wrote that 'the idea of the oppression of the individual by the majority' was 'absolutely repugnant to the modern mind' and that the 'more democracy prevails and determines public opinion, the more it will come to mean the greatest possible degree of freedom for all.'[46]

With Bernstein's assumption no longer available to us, we are brought squarely to the key theoretical challenge facing the civil libertarian: there is no guarantee that the representatives of the people acting collectively and in the exercise of their untrammelled power will preserve for all the civil liberties upon which a properly functioning representative democracy depends; nor is there any guarantee that such an assembly will respect the equal dignity of all the people. It was in an attempt to resolve this conundrum that certain democratically-minded utilitarians developed the idea of human rights in its modern, broadest form, as a kind of fence of basic principle surrounding and circumscribing the political playing field, limiting the freedom of manoeuvre of the democratic body so as to prevent unethical excess, both in the field of civil liberties and in relation to any irretrievable damage that might otherwise be done by such a body to human dignity.[47] To this extent it is true to say that the idea of human rights in this strong form is for many more an answer to anxieties about parliamentarian majoritarianism than it is an independent idea in its own right. It is clear that this 'human rights' solution begs a whole series of questions about who is to say what is excessive in the actions of the parliamentary branch, about why the officials around the political game should be more trusted to know right from wrong than the popularly elected players, and other queries of this sort. Attractive though abrasive responses along these lines are, they do not in themselves directly address the concerns that have led the human rights advocates to the position they find themselves in. If there is to be no ring-fence at all, is the untrammelled power of the legislative branch a matter of no concern to the civil libertarian? Are the excesses which the civil libertarian knows the legislature to be capable of and to have done to be discounted as neither here nor there? Is every reduction in civil liberties promulgated by Parliament to be greeted with a fatalistic shrug of the shoulders, and the remark that our democratic leaders always know best? It is to these questions that we turn in the final part of this chapter.

CIVIL LIBERTIES, THE JUDICIARY AND THE POLITICAL PROCESS

The civil libertarian is of course concerned with attacks on political freedom whatever their source, but a full explanation of his or her position requires a prior questioning of three assumptions that are all too easily made in this area, particularly (it has to be said) by the advocates (in the reactive but nevertheless strong sense

---

[46] E Bernstein, *The Preconditions of Socialism* (H Tudor ed and trans), (Cambridge, Cambridge University Press, 1993), 141.

[47] R Dworkin, *Taking Rights Seriously* (London, Duckworth, 1977), ch 7.

described above) of human rights. First, it is surely wrong to assume that applying a theoretical construct to a real situation (whether based on 'human rights' or 'civil liberties') can ever be other than messy, incomplete and therefore from the per-spective of principle unsatisfactory. Secondly, it is equally incorrect to assume that the judges are likely to be more effective guardians of human rights than the leg-islative branch, merely because they are outside and not within the maelstrom of politics. Thirdly, and mirroring our second false assumption, it is wrong to deny that the legislator has any effective engagement with civil liberties and human rights merely because legislation antagonistic to either or both ideas often gets passed. When these ideas have been more fully explored, it will be possible to develop a more mature understanding of the strengths as well as the limitations of the continued deployment of the concept of civil liberties in a sphere which, it is admitted, is now more often than ever before attracting the language of human rights, albeit a language which, as we have seen is the case with the ECHR, is redo-lent with civil libertarian principle.

Turning now to the first assumption we have identified, it is surely right to assert that however pure their abstract articulation, all concepts inevitably lose some-thing in their translation into practice. Not only is this bound to happen, but it is also right that it should: a set of ideas imposed from above invariably either fails entirely or succeeds only through distorting reality to fit its ideology and therefore comes at too high a human cost. As we have earlier demonstrated in our discus-sion of the abstract idea of civil liberties, the subject comes embedded in the socie-ty to which it is applied, with exceptions and protections built in for the security and the well-being of the state. It is inevitable that departures from civil libertarian principle will occur from time to time, with inappropriate controls on freedom being imposed, and other anti-civil libertarian tactics being deployed in the pur-suit of popular (and sometimes not so popular) goals. The civil libertarian does not welcome this, but knows that it can happen. The price for constructing the foundations of the subject in the real world of politics is that the hurly burly of that chaotic environment can sometimes seem to erode the structure and threaten the entire model. If the answer to this—that what the civil libertarian must do is not just shrug the shoulders but fight back, protect principle and gradually rese-cure what has been lost by engaging in the political arena (marching, campaign-ing, writing, debating, appearing on the television and so on)—is thought unsatisfactory, then this is because life itself is unsatisfactory. There may be many weaknesses in rooting civil liberties in the contingent world of politics but there is certainly one enduring strength—the subject is always connected to the commu-nity whose political freedom it seeks to protect and with the members of that com-munity whose civil liberties are at the core of its concern.

Declarations of 'human rights' from on high can in contrast seem rather grand, staid affairs, interventions from the minaret, the pulpit or the ivory tower bellowed at the mob below, but rather lost in all the noise. In his or her purest and most uncompromising form, the human rights ideologue rather resembles the spoilt child: 'I know what is right, now do as I tell you.' Politics, like adulthood, is not like this. If this were what the human rights referee were doing in real life, making decisions without regard to how the political match was unfolding, then he or she would soon find him- or herself being wholly ignored, their rulings initially rejected as fatuously unrealistic and then quite quickly ignored completely. In practice, of course, in order to get noticed and not disappear completely off the political radar, the human rights referee does seek to engage with the world in which he or she finds him- or herself, does try in translating human rights ideas into practice to take account of the mood and spirit of the times and the political atmosphere into which these adjudications on what is right and wrong are delivered. No human rights lawyer or advocate proposes anything other than some type of contextualised approach these days. The problem that emerges however is that, without a strong and mature set of theoretical foundations, such attempts at *realpolitik* can easily collapse into a kind of fatalistic quietism, with all executive and legislative interventions being upheld as necessary and right, simply because they have happened.

These remarks thus lead us directly to recall what we have described as the second questionable assumption that is commonly made by human-rights-based critics of the civil libertarian's commitment to parliamentary sovereignty, namely that the judges around the parliamentary playing field are able efficiently and in a principled manner to do this job of adjudication. That this is not the case can be shown not only (or even necessarily) by demonstrating the theoretical impossibility of the demands made of such officers, but also, and more gloomily, by glancing at the evidence. Turning first to the judicial record on civil liberties prior to implementation of the HRA, it is certainly the case that the rhetoric of this part of state power has been supportive of civil liberties. Indeed the Victorian father of contemporary English constitutional law erected an entire theory of government around the principled excellence of the judiciary in this regard.[48] The empirical narrative tells a rather different story, however. The judiciary's hostility to parliament in the seventeenth century, and its enthusiastic avowal of royal power, was one of the key factors underlying Parliament's assertion of its omnipotence in the aftermath of the 'Glorious Revolution.' When the courts finally reconciled themselves to the reality of parliamentary sovereignty, during the first half of the nineteenth century,[49] they found that they were wholly unprepared for the next phase in Parliament's development, namely democratisation. Their hostility to a constitution rooted in the exercise of power by other than the propertied was still capable of being spotted in the law reports as late as 1910,[50] and their antipathy to the entitlement of women to vote was manifest in their rejection of a series of sometimes quite cleverly constructed legal challenges that were launched in the late Victorian and Edwardian periods: it was apparently 'a principle of the unwritten

[48] See AV Dicey, *Lectures Introductory to the Study of the Law of the Constitution* (2nd edn, London, Macmillan, 1885).

[49] See eg *Edinburgh & Dalkeith Railway v Wauchope* (1842) 8 Cl and F 710; 8 ER 279. J Goldsworthy, *The Sovereignty of Parliament: History and Philosophy* (Oxford, Oxford University Press, 1999) is an excellent account.

[50] *Amalgamated Society of Railway Servants v Osborne* [1910] AC 87, especially the speech of Lord Shaw of Dunfermline.

constitutional law of the country that men only were entitled to take part in the election of representatives to Parliament.'[51]

Nor have the courts excelled at the protection of the liberties of expression, assembly and association in the face of the kind of legislative hostility to which we have already referred. The story is a depressing one, altogether too long to recount here, with there being only a few dissents and not much more to show by way of a response to the endless cases legitimising the exercise of state power in ways that were inimical (at times grievously so) to individual liberty.[52] Indeed the courts went even further, on many occasions plundering the common law for novel forms of state repression that not even the more reactionary of Cabinet members had dared put before Parliament.[53] The process continued with depressing consistency throughout the democratic era, beginning with the First World War and working its way through the various crises of the twentieth century. Eventually the end of the Cold War in 1989 and the great alleviation in the level of subversive violence that occurred with the IRA ceasefire in 1994 provided some space for a realignment of judicial practice in line with the still frequently deployed language of civil liberties. For the first time, decisions such as in *DPP v Jones*[54] and *Redmond-Bate v DPP*[55] showed a judicial branch sensitive to the underlying importance of the exercise of civil liberties, in the context of association and assembly in the first case and assembly and expression in the second.

The 1990s may come in retrospect to be seen as an Edwardian-style golden age, when freedom thrived in the gap between the end of the Cold War and the start of the new counter-terrorist world order that was inaugurated with the attack on the World Trade Centre and the Pentagon that occurred on 11 September 2001. It was in this liberal atmosphere, and perhaps marking its highest point, that the Human Rights Act 1998 took full effect, on 2 October 2000. There is certainly some evidence that the Act has led to a stronger commitment to political speech in certain cases than might otherwise have been apparent.[56] But can it seriously be said that the pre-HRA cases would have been decided differently if the judges involved in them had had access to a human rights charter? Following the events of 11 September 2001, we have seen a hardening of attitudes on the bench, the beginnings of a

---

[51] *Nairn v University Court of the University of St Andrew* (1907) 15 SLT 471, at 473 per Lord McLaren. See subsequently *Nairn v University Court of the University of St Andrews* [1909] AC 147. Earlier cases include *Chorlton v Lings* (1868) LR 4 CP 374 and *Chorlton v Kessler* (1868) LR 4 CP 397.

[52] See generally *The Struggle for Civil Liberties*, above n 44.

[53] The classic examples are *Elias v Pasmore* [1934] 2 KB 164; *Thomas v Sawkins* [1935] 2 KB 249; and *Duncan v Jones* [1936] 1 KB 218.

[54] [1999] 2 AC 240. But see H Fenwick and G Phillipson, 'Public Protest, the Human Rights Act and Judicial Responses to Political Expression' [2000] *PL* 627. See further the same authors' 'Direct Action, Convention Values and the Human Rights Act' (2001) 21 *Legal Studies* 535.

[55] *The Times*, 28 July 1999.

[56] *R v BBC, ex parte ProLife Alliance* [2002] EWCA Civ 297, [2002] 2 All ER 756 is an outstanding example but the decision has since been overturned in the House of Lords in a manner which shows little understanding of the importance of the principles of political freedom [2003] UKHL 23; [2003] 2 All ER 977. Compare *R v Shayler* [2002] UKHL 11, [2002] 2 All ER 477. But see the disappointing decision on the right to vote of prisoners in *R v Secretary of State for the Home Department, ex parte Pearson and Martinez* [2001] EWHC Admin 239.

return to the routine deference of the past. Given the context of the current 'war on terrorism', the majority of the important cases so far have involved state action against foreigners suspected of various wrongdoings. Thus, the HRA has proved of no help to the asylum seekers held in Oakington whose victory, secured before Collins J on Article 5(1) grounds just four days before 11 September 2001, was shortly afterwards unanimously overturned by a Court of Appeal presided over by the Master of the Rolls Lord Phillips.[57] The same fleeting victory was also accorded the American leader of the Nation of Islam Louis Farrakhan by the Administrative Court, which deployed ECHR Article 10 against the Home Secretary's refusal to allow him to visit the United Kingdom only to have the ruling overturned by a Court of Appeal that was once again headed by the Master of the Rolls.[58]

Secretary of State for the Home Department v Rehman[59] is particularly instructive demonstration of the general point. The case was concerned with the legal basis upon which the Home Secretary could lawfully deport a person on the ground that it was for the public good in the interests of national security. The Special Immigration Appeals Commission had held that conduct could only constitute a threat to national security if it were targeted at the United Kingdom, its citizens or its system of government, and had concluded that the Secretary of State had failed to prove to a high civil balance of probabilities the acts which were said to have endangered national security in this particular case. The Court of Appeal allowed the Home Secretary's appeal against this decision[60] and the matter was further appealed to the House of Lords where oral argument was heard on 2 and 3 May 2001. The speeches in the case dismissing Rehman's appeal were however not handed down until 11 October, exactly one calender month after the attacks on the World Trade Centre and the Pentagon in the United States. In accepting a very broad definition of the risk or danger to the security or well-being of the nation, the five law lords in the case took an extremely deferential approach to the powers of the Home Secretary in this area, both in relation to his judgment of what constituted a risk to national security and as regards his assessment of the risk posed by individuals being considered for expulsion. The tone of the decision recalls cases of a similarly restrictive nature from the same court legitimising the exercise of state power in a way inimical to civil liberties during both World Wars,[61] the Cold War,[62] and arising out of the conflict in Northern Ireland.[63] Of many quotes that could be taken from the case, it is perhaps Lord Hoffmann's 'postscript' that best captures the atmosphere on the bench:

[57] *R v Secretary of State for the Home Department, ex parte Saadi and others* [2001] EWHC Admin 670, [2001] EWCA Civ 1512, [2002] 1 WLR 356, [2001] 4 All ER 961 for the unsuccessful appeal to the House of Lords, see [2002] UKHL 41; [2002] 4 All ER 785.
[58] *R v Secretary of State for the Home Department, ex parte Farrakhan* (2002) 152 NLJ 708.
[59] [2001] UKHL 47, [2001] 3 WLR 877, [2002] 1 All ER 122.
[60] [2000] 3 WLR 1240.
[61] *R v Halliday, ex parte Zadig* [1917] AC 260; *Liversidge v Anderson* [1942] AC 204.
[62] *Chandler v DPP* [1964] AC 763.
[63] *McEldowney v Forde* [1971] AC 632; *R v Secretary of State for the Home Department, ex parte Brind* [1991] 1 AC 696.

I wrote this speech some three months before the recent events in New York and Washington. They are a reminder that in matters of national security, the cost of failure can be high. This seems to me to underline the need for the judicial arm of government to respect the decisions of ministers of the Crown on the question of whether support for terrorist activities in a foreign country constitutes a threat to national security. It is not only that the executive has access to special information and expertise in these matters. It is also that such decisions, with serious potential results for the community, require a legitimacy which can be conferred only by entrusting them to persons responsible to the community through the democratic process. If the people are to accept the consequences of such decisions, they must be made by persons whom the people have elected and whom they can remove.[64]

The decision, and Lord Hoffmann's remarks, are not wholly unexpected. Only those who expect the courts to impose human rights and/or civil liberties protection from on high are entitled to feel let down, but such disappointment reflects a degree of political immaturity, a desire for a benevolent parent to step in and solve a squabble between siblings. Politics is not like this, and civil liberties—like all of life—are part of politics. It is fortunate that the legislative branch has been less pusillanimous than the judiciary in meeting the challenge to civil liberties that has been precipitated by the executive response to the events of 11 September 2001. For the third assumption that the civil libertarian would want to challenge, that the legislature is and always has been uninterested in the protection of civil liberties and human rights, is the most deeply entrenched of all. To some extent the critics of parliamentary sovereignty do of course have a point. As we have already detailed at depressing length, the record here is not honourable from a civil libertarian perspective. But nor is it as dishonourable as is so frequently asserted. Whatever it might mean to say that there has never been a 'culture of rights' in this country, it is certainly the case that the legislature has frequently displayed at least a degree of sensitivity to rights when faced with executive initiatives restrictive of rights and liberty. This is not to say that such sensitivity inevitably or even invariably wins the day. Much depends on the atmosphere of the times and the general political climate: the Official Secrets Act 1911 and the first Prevention of Terrorism Act in 1974 were notably unscathed by their passage through Parliament. However, when the circumstances are right, the legislature can and does win important concessions which both affect the content of proposed laws and constrain executive action in the future. The defence of the realm and emergency powers legislation passed at the onset of, respectively, the First and Second World Wars were strongly influenced in both these ways by the parliamentary debates that accompanied and followed their enactment.[65] The Incitement to Disaffection Act 1934 was seriously undermined by parliamentary hostility.[66] In more recent times, both the Police and Criminal Evidence Act 1984 and the Police Act 1997[67] were strongly affected and modified by the parliamentary debate that surrounded their enactment.

---

[64]   Above n 59 above, para 62.
[65]   For the details see *The Struggle for Civil Liberties*, above, n 44, at chs 2 and 8.
[66]   *Ibid* at 243–52.
[67]   KD Ewing and CA Gearty, *A Law Too Far: Part III of the Police Bill 1997* (Civil Liberties Research Unit, King's College London, 1997).

The Government's legislative proposals in the aftermath of 11 September were markedly improved from the civil libertarian perspective by the changes that were conceded as a result of a strong parliamentary engagement with the relevant issues of principles. Much of the Act in its final form may still be thought deplorable, particularly those provisions which permit the detention of non-residents without charge,[68] which greatly expand state power in relation to terrorism[69] and access to communications data,[70] and which allow for the implementation of the third pillar of the European Union without effective democratic scrutiny. It is also right to decry the fact that the legislation, which is long and complex, was pushed through Parliament at alarming speed. Yet despite all this, important amendments on matters of substance were achieved. Proposals to introduce retrospective criminal legislation on bomb hoaxes were dropped even before the Bill was published after the idea had provoked a strong and very critical response. An expansion of the law to include incitement to religious hatred was omitted after a strongly negative report on the proposal from the Home Affairs Committee of the House of Commons.[71] That body's critical appraisal of the Government's plans also led to other beneficial changes such as the 'sunset' provision limiting the life of the internment power to five years,[72] with its renewal on an annual basis also being required to be based on an annual review by an independent person.[73]

Following other critical reports from another parliamentary body, the Joint Committee on Human Rights, the Government found itself having strongly to defend its assertion that there was 'a public emergency threatening the life of the nation' sufficiently grave to warrant the derogation from ECHR Article 5 that the Home Secretary had judged was necessary in order to be able lawfully to introduce its new detention powers.[74] As a result of legislative pressure, the Act in its final form provides for a committee of privy counsellors to conduct a review of the whole measure[75] and this body was established in April 2002.[76] Of course none of this is perfect, and a parliamentary body operating at the level of civil libertarian perfection would have done much more.[77] But in the context of the time, one of unparalleled anxiety and concern about the future, it was not a bad performance on the whole, and certainly not one which justifies any claim that Parliament is too

---

[68] Anti-terrorism, Crime and Security Act 2001, Pt 4. See generally A Tomkins [2002] *PL* 205.

[69] See in particular Anti-terrorism, Crime and Security Act 2001, ss 117–120.

[70] *Ibid*, Pt 11.

[71] Home Affairs Committee, First Report, *The Anti-Terrorism, Crime and Security Bill 2001* (HC 351, 2001–02).

[72] See Anti-terrorism, Crime and Security Act 2001, s 29.

[73] *Ibid* s 28. The task has been assigned to Lord Carlile of Berriew who is also responsible for review of certain of the powers in the Terrorism Act 2000.

[74] Human Rights Act 1998 (Designated Derogation) Order 2001, SI 2001/3644. The two Joint Committee on Human Rights reports are at HL Paper 37, HC 372 and HL Paper 51, HC 420 respectively.

[75] Anti-Terrorism, Crime and Security Act 2001, s 122.

[76] Its members are Lord Newton of Braintree (chair), Chris Smith MP, Joyce Quinn MP, Sir Brian Mawhinney MP, Alan Beith MP, Terry Davis MP, Baroness Hayman, Lord Holme of Cheltenham and the retired law lord Lord Browne-Wilkinson.

[77] But see further D Feldman, 'Parliamentary Scrutiny of Legislation and Human Rights' [2002] *PL* 323.

simply and always the lapdog of the executive branch. The contrast with the narrow ruling of the Special Immigration Appeals Commission in the first case arising under the new detention powers in the 2001 Act is stark, with the appellants succeeding on the basis that the Government had not also allowed for the detention without trial of British residents or derogated from Article 14 as well as Article 5.[78] On all other substantive matters the executive was successful. It is depressing to think that this human rights victory was only achieved because the Government has not been as repressive as it might have been.[79]

CONCLUSION

The argument in this chapter has been that, far from being rendered redundant by the Human Rights Act 1998, the need to think seriously about civil liberties has never been more important than it is at present. With the seeming collapse of socialist alternatives to liberalism, and the start of a war against terrorism that promises never to end, the state's commitment to civil liberties, indeed to representative democracy itself, cannot afford to be taken for granted. The HRA begs difficult questions of fit and compatibility of all branches of law, but it does so particularly in the field of public law. The attraction of the civil libertarian perspective is that it identifies for the judges, legal practitioners, parliamentarians and political activists a clear pathway through the HRA, and one moreover that is both firmly rooted in a theory of representative government and solidly grounded in the ECHR itself and the Strasbourg case law. The HRA does not in itself provide such guidance; it needs to be extracted from it by the kind of reasoning in which we have engaged here and for which (we would claim) the concept of civil liberties has provided such valuable theoretical support.

The benevolent power of the ECHR system lies in the clarity with which the protection for civil liberties has been accorded so distinct a priority, both within the document itself and in the case law under it. Without a clear grasp of principle, discussion about what it is right for the judges to do under the HRA quickly collapses into a fatuous question-begging set of queries about the proper remit for the 'discretionary area of judgment' to be accorded the legislature, and this then quickly produces passivity where there should be activism (and quite possibly activism where there should be passivity, though this is a different point). On the analysis provided here, it is the job of all three branches of government to uphold those principles of civil liberties without which our society would not be the self-governing community of equals that its claim to be a representative democracy

---

[78] *A and others v Secretary of State for the Home Department,* Special Immigration Appeals Commission, 30 July 2002.

[79] According to counsel for nine of the detainees quoted in the *Guardian*'s report of the appeal proceedings in the case, the Government 'botched' the new legislation by permitting British citizens to remain free of the threat of detention: *Guardian,* 9 October 2002. The Commission decision on this point was afterwards overruled by the Court of Appeal [2002] EWCA Civ 1502; [2003] 1 All ER 816.

suggests that it is. Properly read, the HRA requires such a commitment from all three branches. If this is what is meant by a 'culture of rights' then we should all be unqualifiedly in favour of it.

15

Standing in a Multi-Layered Constitution

JOANNA MILES*

It is surely absurd and unworkable to have different tests of standing according to whether the judicial review application is based upon: (i) ordinary common law principles; or (ii) common law principles matching or embodying [European Convention] rights; or (iii) directly effective European Community law; or (iv) convention rights; or (v) a combination of any of those four grounds.[1]

T HE CURRENT LAW of standing is multi-faceted, the applicable rule being determined by the jurisdictional source of the legal argument being made. This multi-faceted system is a product of piecemeal accretions to the jurisdiction of domestic courts over the last 30 years, most recently those made by devolution and human rights legislation. It may be said that we now have a 'multi-layered', rather than unitary, constitution. The courts are required to interpret and apply laws deriving from several sources, each commanding a different level of constitutional authority. They are called on to interpret and apply measures emanating from the institutions of the European Community, in some cases disapplying domestic legislation which cannot be read and applied compatibly with those measures. They enforce the duty of public authorities to act compatibly with the European Convention of Human Rights(ECHR), ensuring 'so far as it is possible to do so' that the domestic legislation under which those authorities act is read and given effect compatibly with Convention rights, and having a discretion to make a declaration of incompatibility if the interpretive route cannot provide the compatibility sought. They are responsible for policing the limits to the competence of the new devolved institutions, declaring as ultra vires (in some instances, prior to enactment) any measure which exceeds the competence of the body in question. And they continue to exercise their traditional public law jurisdiction, reviewing the validity of the actions and decisions of statutory and non-statutory inferior

* I am grateful to Albertina Albors-Llorens, John Allison, Ivan Hare, Tom Hickman and Edwin Simpson for their assistance in the preparation of this chapter; all errors are mine. Manuscript submitted August 2002.

[1] Lord Lester of Herne Hill, Hansard, HL Deb, 24 Nov 1997 vol 583, col 828, on the introduction into UK law of the 'victim test', by the Human Rights Act 1998, s 7.

bodies by reference to the familiar, but recently invigorated, standards of administrative law. In each part of their jurisdiction, the courts have different substantive laws to apply, and, often, persons wishing to invoke those laws will face different rules regarding standing and intervention. Should those same claimants wish to take their cases to either of the two European courts, they face further standing and intervention rules. Even in a case that falls squarely within the remit of what we might call 'traditional' or 'ordinary' domestic administrative law, the malleable 'sufficient interest' test can be stretched or restricted according to the nature of the complaint and the character of the claimant and, underlying it all perhaps, the theory of standing adhered to by the judge.

It is instructive to reflect on the current state of the law of standing with various questions in mind. What purposes are served by standing rules? What is the proper relationship between standing law and the rules permitting third party intervention? Can the deployment of the different tests be justified by reference to the subject matter of the disputes to which they relate, or are those tests based on inconsistent views about the type of interest sufficient to move the court, such that their co-existence can fairly be condemned as 'absurd'? Most basically, do we have a clear idea of the role that we want the courts to play, and that it is constitutionally appropriate for them to play, in judicial review? If so, what implications ought such an idea to have for the standing and intervention rules? Can the multiple standing and intervention rules encountered by UK litigants be satisfactorily sustained within our legal system (or systems)?

Before turning to those questions, the current standing and intervention rules are illustrated with a hypothetical case involving Greenpeace in order to demonstrate the variety of rules that will be encountered by such a body wishing to be heard in court in this multi-layered system. The survey is not comprehensive in regard to the details of all the rules, but provides a flavour of the current situation. An interest group is used for this exercise, since such claimants test (if not exceed) the outer limits of most standing and intervention rules. We shall see that an organisation such as Greenpeace receives very different treatment depending on the issue raised and the court in which it seeks to raise it.

A CASE STUDY: GREENPEACE AT HOME AND ABROAD

The Secretary of State, acting pursuant to an Act of the Westminster Parliament passed to implement a European Community directive, authorises an activity which Greenpeace believes will cause damage to the environment and to the health of residents in specific localities in the United Kingdom. Will Greenpeace have standing to challenge any aspect of this situation on any grounds, or be permitted to intervene in a challenge brought by another?

A. STANDING RULES

1 'Ordinary' Judicial Review in England, Wales and Northern Ireland: the 'Sufficient Interest' Test

Standing to argue traditional, domestic ultra vires grounds in judicial review of the Secretary of State's action before these courts is governed by the 'sufficient interest' test.[2] That rather flexible language sustains various approaches to standing. In some cases, the courts adopt a strict analysis, tying the question of standing to the topography of the statutory power whose exercise is being complained of, the ground of complaint, and the relationship of the claimant to the issue.[3] Even having opened the court door, a claimant cannot necessarily put forward every argument that might objectively be made, but may be permitted to challenge the decision on only some grounds.[4] Elsewhere, the courts take a much broader view, apparently willing to find that a claimant has standing simply by virtue of the seriousness of the illegality alleged,[5] or the public interest in having the matter judicially reviewed,[6] most fundamentally to uphold the rule of law.[7] Standing in such cases may be regarded as having been diluted to the most attenuated of concepts, though judges deny the existence of a universal citizen's action.[8] Many of these latter cases in the England and Wales courts[9] have involved applications from interest groups of various sorts. The case law suggests that Greenpeace will often be accorded standing in relation to issues falling within its expertise. That expertise, the likelihood that some Greenpeace members live within range of the activity causing concern (whom it may therefore be said to be representing) and the importance of the issue at stake, seem likely to afford the organisation a 'sufficient interest' in the matter.[10]

---

[2] Supreme Court Act 1981, s 31(3); Judicature (Northern Ireland) Act 1978, s 18(4).

[3] *R v Secretary of State for the Environment, ex parte Rose Theatre Trust Co* [1990] QB 504.

[4] *Re McBride's Application for Judicial Review* [1999] NI 299.

[5] See *Inland Revenue Commissioners v National Federation of Self-Employed and Small Businesses Ltd* [1982] AC 617 at 633, 647 and 662–63.

[6] *R v Felixstowe Justices, ex parte Leigh* [1987] QB 582; *R (on the application of Rusbridger and Toynbee) v Attorney-General* [2002] EWCA Civ 397, 2002 Westlaw 346980 (March 21, 2002), rev'd on other grounds [2003] UKHL 38; *R v Her Majesty's Treasury, ex parte Smedley* [1985] QB 657.

[7] Lord Diplock in the *IRC* case, above n 5 at 644; *R v Secretary of State for Foreign Affairs, ex parte World Development Movement* [1995] 1 WLR 386, at 395.

[8] *R v Secretary of State for the Environment, ex parte Rose Theatre Trust Co* [1990] QB 504, at 520; *R v Somerset County Council, ex parte Dixon* [1998] EnvLR 111, at 117.

[9] Interest group cases in Northern Ireland are rare: P Maguire, 'The Procedure for Judicial Review in Northern Ireland' in B Hadfield (ed), *Judicial Review: a Thematic Approach* (Dublin, Gill and Macmillan, 1995).

[10] *R v Her Majesty's Inspector of Pollution, ex parte Greenpeace (No2)* [1994] 4 All ER 329; though they do not necessarily have standing to pursue any environmental matter: *ibid* at 351f–g.

2. 'Ordinary' Judicial Review in Scotland: 'Title and Interest to Sue'

It is doubtful whether Greenpeace would have standing to make a similar challenge in Scotland. The two-part Scottish rule 'title and interest to sue' is similar to
the narrower interpretations of the 'sufficient interest' test. *Title* to sue rests on 'the
individual or body seeking to challenge the minister's act or decision [showing]
that, having regard to the scope or purpose of the legislation or measure under
which the act is performed or the decision is made, he or they have [a right of chal-
lenge] conferred on them by law, expressly or impliedly.'[11] Empowering legislation
may be held to confer title on any member of the public to challenge the legality of
executive action, but a pursuer with *title* may still lack *interest* to sue, for example if
its interest in the matter is purely ideological.[12] Whilst the Scots courts may be
receptive to associational standing, which may offer Greenpeace some hope, the
sort of public interest standing recognised by the English courts may not be
accepted in Scotland.[13] The perceived divergence of attitude between English and
Scottish courts is apparently encouraging attempts at forum shopping within the
UK to avoid the restrictive Scottish rule, in one case by Greenpeace itself.[14]

3. Standing in EC Law Cases at Home and in Luxembourg

Domestic Challenges and EC Treaty Article 234[15] References

Those same 'sufficient interest' or 'title and interest' rules determine Greenpeace's
entitlement to challenge the implementing domestic measures– the Act of Parliament included[16]—on EC law grounds in the domestic courts.[17] Those domestic
proceedings also give Greenpeace access to the European Court of Justice if the
national court makes a reference under EC Treaty Article 234 regarding the proper
interpretation or validity in EC law of the underlying Community measure,[18] thus
enabling Greenpeace to seek review of the EC measure via the domestic courts.

Direct Challenge to the EC measure in Luxembourg EC Treaty under Article 230(4)

However, it would not ordinarily be possible for Greenpeace, or (in the vast majority of cases) any of its members, to obtain direct review of the validity of the Euro-

---

[11]   *Rape Crisis Centre v Secretary of State for the Home Department* 2001 SLT 389, per Lord Clark.
[12]   *Scottish Old People's Welfare Council* 1987 SLT 179.
[13]   Lord Hope of Craighead, 'Mike Tyson comes to Glasgow' [2001] *PL* 294; cf Lord Clyde and DJ
Edwards, *Judicial Review* (Edinburgh, W Green, 2000), ch 10.
[14]   *R v Secretary of State for Scotland, ex parte Greenpeace*, 24 May 1995, unreported; see C Munro,
'Standing in Judicial Review' 1995 SLT 279.
[15]   Consolidated Version of the Treaty Establishing the European Community.
[16]   *R v Secretary of State for Transport, ex parte Factortame (No 2)* [1991] AC 603.
[17]   Eg *R v Secretary of State for the Environment, ex parte Greenpeace* [1998] Env LR 415.
[18]   Case 158/80 *Rewe-Handelsgesellschaft Nord mbH and another v Hauptzollamt Kiel* [1981] ECR
1805.

pean measure in the European courts. The standing of non-privileged natural and legal persons to bring such actions is restricted by the extremely narrow construction of the 'individual concern' element of the 'direct and individual concern' test, governing such applicants' access to the European courts.[19] *In general*, the applicant has to prove membership of a closed class of persons affected by the impugned measure.[20] Measures affecting wide and uncertain classes of persons (often true of measures in the environmental field) are thus almost immune from direct challenge by private persons. There is no scope for the sort of public interest/interest group standing permitted in England.[21] Greenpeace might try to bring itself within one of the special categories of individual concern, perhaps by virtue of its having participated by right in a formal consultation exercise with the EC institutions regarding the adoption of the impugned measure.[22] But communications between Greenpeace and the EC institutions not forming part of such a process will not afford the group standing.[23] In the absence of this possibility, Greenpeace will be forced to challenge the underlying EC measure domestically via EC Treaty Article 234, and so to wait until the measure has been implemented by some challengeable domestic measure or decision (if any) over which the domestic courts have jurisdiction.[24]

4. Judicial Review on Human Rights Grounds

Since the passage of the Human Rights Act 1998 (HRA), standing in cases relying on human rights arguments, especially those relying directly on Convention rights, merits separate consideration. There are various arguments that Greenpeace might wish to make against the domestic measures on human rights grounds, but whether they have standing to make the arguments is problematic.

Judicial review under HRA, section 6

The new public law illegality argument created by section 6 of the HRA—acting incompatibly with Convention rights—can be invoked in judicial review and other

---

[19] For 'privileged' applicants—Member States, Community institutions—see EC Treaty Article 230(2) and (3).

[20] *Plaumann v Commission* [1963] ECR 95, reaffirmed in Case C-50/00P *Unión de Pequeños Agricultores v Council*, [2003] QB 893, rejecting AG Jacobs' opinion; the Court of First Instance decision in Case T-177/01 *Jégo-Quéré et Cie. SA v Commission*,[2003] QB 854, seems destined to be overturned. There are a few further categories of 'individual concern': see for examples Joined Cases 67/85, 68/85, 70/85 *Van der Kooy v Commission* [1988] ECR 219, para 14; Case C-358/89 *Extramet Industrie v Council* [1991] ECR I-2501, para 13; Case C-309/89 *Codorniu SA v Council* [1994] ECR I-1853, para 19. See A Albors-Llorens, 'The Standing of Private Parties to Challenge Community Measures' (2003) 62 *CLJ* 72.

[21] Case T-585/93 *Stichting Greenpeace Council v Commission* [1995] ECR II-2205, on appeal Case C-321/95 P [1998] ECR I-1651.

[22] See tests set out in Case T-122/96 *Federolio v Commission* [1997] ECR II-1559, para 61.

[23] See above n 21.

[24] There may sometimes be no such domestic measure, effectively rendering the EC measure immune from private challenge: AG Jacobs, *UPA v Council*, above n 20, at para 43.

proceedings only by a 'victim' of the alleged illegality, matching the standing rule of the European Court of Human Rights.[25] A 'victim' is one whose own Convention rights have been, or are at risk of being, violated by the impugned act or measure, either directly or indirectly. The European Court's interpretation of the test has not been consistent, but whilst broader than the EC law 'individual concern' test, its scope is clearly more limited than the standard sufficient interest test is capable of being. In particular, despite occasionally generous interpretation of 'victim,'[26] it affords no scope for public interest challenges.[27] As for other forms of representative standing, organisations such as Greenpeace may act in Strasbourg on behalf of any of their members who are victims, but only if they can positively identify those member-victims and demonstrate that they have their authority to act on their behalf.[28] However, *domestic* civil procedure rules only permit representative applications to be made by parties which have standing to make the claim in their own right. So it seems that, where the group itself cannot claim victim status, interest groups will be unable (as organisations) to bring section 6 proceedings in the domestic courts, even on behalf of their own members.[29] One option is to reverse the formal roles by finding an individual victim prepared to lend his or her name to an action which Greenpeace could informally support and direct.[30]

Standing to Make Human Rights Arguments Outside the Victim Test

However, Greenpeace may remain able itself to make human rights arguments on other grounds under the standard sufficient interest test (if not in Scotland). The literature is full of speculation regarding the ways in which non-victims, who are nevertheless regarded as having a 'sufficient interest,'[31] might complain about the violation of the rights of others, some of which are set out here.[32]

[25] Human Rights Act 1998, s 7(1), (3), (7); this applies equally in devolution cases where Convention rights are relied on: eg Scotland Act 1998, s 100.

[26] *Open Door and Dublin Well Woman v Ireland* (1992) 15 EHRR 244; see also *R (on the application of H) v Ashworth Hospital Authority* [2001] EWHC Admin 872; [2002] 1 FCR 206; cf failure to establish victim status in *R (on the application of Rusbridger and Toynbee) v Attorney General* [2002] EWCA Civ 397; at first instance: 2001 Westlaw 753344 (22 June 2001); contrast remarks of Lords Steyn and Rodgers [2003] UKHL 38 at paras 21 and 55.

[27] *Klass v Germany* (1978) 2 EHRR 214, para 33.

[28] *Confédération des Syndicats Médicaux Français v France* (1986) 47 DR 225; Rules of Procedure of the European Court of Human Rights, Rules 36 and 45; cf the 'democratic link' which Peter Cane demands of associational claimants: below n 56.

[29] Civil Procedure Rules, Part 19.6. See *In re Medicaments and Related Classes of Goods (No 4)* [2001] EWCA Civ 1217, [2002] 1 WLR 269: Clayton and Tomlinson regard this decision as '[difficult to justify] in the context of Convention case law': *The Law of Human Rights: First Annual Supplement* (Oxford, OUP, 2001), para 22–23; however, the fault seems to lie in the domestic rules' failure to permit representation in the manner allowed in Strasbourg.

[30] For the risks entailed with front man claimants see Loux, below n 46.

[31] *R v Secretary of State for Social Security, ex parte Joint Council for the Welfare of Immigrants* [1997] 1 WLR 275; contrast *McBride*, above n 4; the claimants' differing levels of expertise might justify the difference of approach: see Hare, below n 51.

[32] M Elliott, 'Human Rights and the Standard of Substantive Review' [2001] 60 *CLJ* 301; M Fordham, 'Human Rights Act Escapology' [2000] *JR* 262; R Clayton and H Tomlinson, *The Law of Human Rights* (Oxford, OUP, 2000), paras 22.44–22.49; S Grosz, J Beatson and P Duffy, *Human Rights: the 1998*

R (on woappy Rusbridge + Toynbee)
s 3 LHRA v AG (2003)

(i) HRA and related arguments

Non-victims can arguably seek declarations regarding the interpretation of primary legislation thought to be potentially incompatible with Convention rights, inviting the court to engage in the interpretive exercise required by section 3 of the HRA, and if that fails, to issue a declaration of incompatibility.[33] Section 7 only restricts standing to claim that a public authority has acted in a way made unlawful by section 6 and the associated remedies in section 8. Where a declaration of incompatibility is sought, that cannot be the claimant's argument since to be unlawful under section 6 the incompatible action must not have been required by primary legislation; in declaration cases the legislation *does* require such action, so no section 6 question arises. In similar vein, it has been argued that non-victim claimants can assert Convention rights via section 3 as part of a traditional illegality argument in relation to powers whose source is statutory.[33a] The legislation empowering the defendant authority, interpreted in accordance with section 3 to confer a power to infringe Convention rights only to the extent that the Convention allows, restricts the authority's power—and so gives grounds for a traditional illegality argument—without any need to refer to section 6, and so again avoiding the victim test. The victim test is thus left little if any exclusive area of substantive operation. Greenpeace may thus be able to make arguments against the Secretary of State's action resting on, for examples, ECHR Articles 2 and 8, via an ultra vires argument supported by HRA, section 3.

(ii) Common Law and EC Rights Jurisprudence

The HRA aside, the common law has its own jurisprudence of human rights, with an emergent doctrine of proportionality, which places its own limits on the legality of public action.[34] It seems clear that the courts remain determined to maintain and develop common law-based human rights review, despite the availability of direct Convention-based review under the HRA.[35] This jurisdiction opens up increasingly wide possibilities for non-victim claimants, though the common law has yet to recognise 'environmental rights' as such, so may offer no assistance here.

Act and the European Convention (London, Sweet and Maxwell, 2000) para 4.42–4.44; M Supperstone and J Coppel, 'Judicial Review after the Human Rights Act' [1999] *EHRLR* 301; D Feldman, 'Remedies for Violations of Convention Rights under the Human Rights Act' [1998] *EHRLR* 691.

[33] This was apparently conceded in *R (on the application of Rusbridger and Toynbee) v Attorney General* [2003] UKHL 38, per Lord steyn, para 21. Cf recent suggestions that s 4 declarations will not 'ordinarily' be available to non-victims: *Re S (Minors) (Care Order: Implementation of Care Plan)* [2002] UKHL 10, [2002] AC 291, para 88.

[33a] Compare the responses to the arguments made in *R (Howard League for Penal Reform) v Secretary of State for the Home Department* [2002] EWHC 2497 (Admin); [2003] 1 FLR 484 and *R (Medway Council) v Secretary of State for Transport* [2002] EWHC 2516 (Admin); 2002 Westlaw 31523297, para 20.

[34] *R v Secretary of State for the Home Department, ex parte Pierson* [1998] AC 539; *R (on the application of Daly) v Secretary of State for the Home Department* [2001] UKHL 26, [2001] 2 AC 532.

[35] See *Daly*, above, n 34.

In some cases, EC law will also afford a basis for human rights arguments.[36] Sufficiently interested non-victims will be able to invoke these arguments in the domestic courts.

5. Judicial Review of Legislation and the Devolution Settlement

We have seen already that Greenpeace may have standing to challenge the validity of Acts of the Westminster Parliament in the English courts on EC law grounds, and probably to seek a declaration of incompatibility with Convention rights. If the case, for example, involved an Act of the Scottish Parliament, the limitations on the legislative competence of the Parliament would render that legislation vulnerable to further challenge, for example on Convention grounds.[37] Standing to seek concrete review of devolved legislation post-enactment is governed by the ordinary rules of each jurisdiction discussed above, amended only where the victim test holds sway.[38] Owing to the restrictive nature of the Scottish standing rules, Greenpeace may therefore be unable to challenge legislation of the Scottish Parliament in the Scottish courts, and it is doubtful whether an English court (before which Greenpeace might have standing) would have jurisdiction over the matter. One other novel feature of the devolution scheme is the possibility of abstract review by the Judicial Committee of the Privy Council of the validity of devolved legislation, both before it comes into force and post-enactment in a freestanding application absent any concrete dispute.[39] However, it is only possible for law officers of the United Kingdom and of the devolved government to make the referral,[40] so this new mode of challenge, unlike concrete, dispute-based post-enactment challenge, is unavailable to non-governmental claimants.

B. INTERVENTION RULES

Instead of bringing its own claim, Greenpeace might intervene in proceedings begun by another. This option of course depends upon such proceedings having been commenced, and on Greenpeace being aware of those proceedings early enough to organise an effective intervention.[41]

---

[36] See Grosz, Beatson and Duffy, above, n 32, at paras 4.35–4.36.
[37] Scotland Act 1998, s 29.
[38] *Ibid,* s 100.
[39] Eg Scotland Act 1998, s 33, Sch 6 paras 4 and 34.
[40] Contrast countries where pre-enactment review can be initiated by elected representatives: A Page, 'Constitutionalism, Judicial Review and "The Evident Utility of the Subjects Within Scotland" ', in L Farmer and S Veitch (eds), *The State of Scots Law: Law and Government After the Devolution Settlement* (Edinburgh, Butterworths, 2001), 17–18.
[41] See the Public Law Project's findings regarding obstacles to intervention: below n 54.

1. Intervention in 'Ordinary' English Judicial Review Proceedings, HRA and Domestic EC Cases

The Civil Procedure Rules' intervention provision[42] covers ordinary judicial review proceedings, HRA and domestic EC review. 'Any person' may apply for permission to file evidence or to make representations at the hearing.[43] Whether permission to intervene will be granted and if so under what conditions is left to the discretion of the judge in his management of the case.[44] It is also possible for interested parties to intervene (more cheaply and quickly, and without the court's permission) via a witness statement filed as part of one of the parties' case.[45]

2. Intervention in Scotland

The HRA has prompted the belated adoption of rules permitting intervention by persons 'directly affected' and by public interest interveners in judicial review proceedings before the Court of Session.[46] Unlike the English rules, these Rules provide in detail for the form and procedure for applications to intervene and for the purpose of the proposed intervention. So although Greenpeace may lack standing to bring a claim in Scotland, it will be able to seek permission to intervene.

3. Intervention in Abstract Review of Devolved Bodies' Measures

Although standing to initiate this form of review is highly restricted, the Privy Council has unfettered discretion to allow interventions in those proceedings.[47]

4. Intervention before the European Courts

Should an EC-based domestic case be referred to the European Court of Justice under EC Treaty Article 234, all those who intervened in the national proceedings, but only those, are entitled to make submissions to the European Court of Justice; it is not possible for other interested parties, save the Commission and Member States, to intervene in those proceedings by the time they reach the Court, even if

[42] Northern Ireland courts remain governed by the Rules of the Supreme Court (Northern Ireland) 1980, SR 1980/346, as amended.

[43] Rule 54.17.

[44] Practice Direction: Judicial Review, para 13.2 gives no further guidance to putative interveners. Cf the Scottish provisions: below n 46.

[45] This mode of intervention was employed by the Public Law Project in *R v Lord Chancellor, ex parte Witham* [1998] QB 575.

[46] SSI 2000, No 317, Act of Sederunt (Rules of Court of Session) (Amendment No 5) (Public Interest Intervention in Judicial Review) 2000; see A Loux, 'Writing Wrongs: Third-party Intervention Post-incorporation' in A Boyle, C Himsworth, H McQueen and A Loux (eds), *Human Rights and Scots Law: Comparative Perspectives on the Incorporation of the ECHR* (Oxford, Hart, 2002).

[47] Judicial Committee (Devolution Issues) Rules 1999, SI 1999/665, rule 5.54.

the Article 234 reference is the first they hear of the case.[48] Those wishing to inter-vene in a direct action under EC Treaty Article 230 must be able to show an inter-est in the result, and the intervention must support the form of order sought by one of the parties.[49] Whilst organisations such as trade associations and trade unions, which can show that the decision will have an impact on their members' rights, are regularly permitted to intervene, public interest intervention by non-governmental organisations of the sort familiar to the Strasbourg and domestic courts is almost unheard of, 'almost precluded by the stringency of the rules.'[50] Greenpeace may therefore again be excluded from participation in the direct chal-lenge, but appear at Luxembourg as an intervener in an Article 234 case.

THE FOUNDATIONS OF STANDING AND INTERVENTION RULES

Having outlined the rules currently operating in the multi-layered UK/European system, we turn our attention to the questions posed at the start of the chapter, to examine the rationale, if any, for those rules and to identify criteria against which the appropriateness of the prevailing situation, and of given rules to a given juris-diction, can be evaluated.

Some Initial Observations

It may be helpful to start by sketching out some basic ideas about the roles of, and relationship between, standing and intervention rules, and to note that, to the extent that both sets of rules raise similar questions, they should be developed consistently with each other.

The Roles of Standing and Intervention Rules: Initial Observations

In discerning the purposes to be served by standing rules, it is essential to avoid misleading arguments which relate not to standing but to some other canon of judicial restraint. It is easy to conflate standing with matters which are more prop-erly described in terms of the ripeness, mootness or justiciability of the dispute, or with the appropriateness or otherwise of the remedy sought, perhaps given a delay in making the application, or with a simple lack of merits. It is important to tease out these distinct arguments, in particular because calls for wider standing are often opposed on these sorts of confused bases, and it can be too readily assumed that the problems that these separate doctrines are designed to tackle are an

---

[48] Articles 37 and 39 of the Statute of the Court of Justice are inapplicable to Article 234 proceed-ings; see D Denman, 'Third Parties and Art 234 References' [2001] *JR* 211.

[49] Statute of the Court of Justice, Article 37.

[50] C Harlow, 'Access to Justice as a Human Right' in P Alston (ed), *The European Union and Human Rights* (Oxford, Oxford University Press, 1999), 197.

unavoidable 'secondary infection' that will be contracted from allowing wider standing.[51]

Standing is also often considered with a view to efficiency and economy with judicial resources, and a concomitant concern for access to justice, ensuring that cases deemed most important reach the court promptly. By limiting the types of persons with standing, it is hoped that time will be devoted to the most pressing cases. This exercise clearly rests on a fundamental evaluation of the types of cases with which the courts should be chiefly concerned, whether because of an assessment of those cases' intrinsic importance or because of the courts' qualification (or otherwise) to deal with them. However, putting that issue to one side for now, narrow standing rules (for example excluding interest group claimants), often justified on this resource-saving basis, may fail to promote the resource-saving objective. A directly affected claimant is not necessarily best equipped to put the argument, and where one measure affects a large constituency, the courts may face numerous ill-argued cases brought by individual victims. It may be preferable to allow interest group actions, so that the courts are presented with prompt, focused and well-informed cases, whose resolution will benefit all members of the affected class.[52] In any event, a standing rule must be clear and straightforward to apply if it is not itself simply to attract protracted litigation; experience teaches that that goal is rather elusive, particularly where the test requires a detailed contextual analysis of the claimant and his case.[53]

Turning to intervention, it is proper to ask first for what purpose the putative intervener is applying to be heard. This may affect our view of the propriety of the intervener being heard at all, and, if it is to be heard, may affect both the mode of the permitted intervention, and the scope of the argument or evidence which is allowed to be adduced, and the status of the intervener in the proceedings.[54] The intervener may be seeking to provide the court with information or expertise, empirical or legal, to inform its decision; or (or additionally) it may wish to protect its own interests, or interests belonging to a particular constituency, or to assert some view of the public interest. Where the interests represented (or information provided) by the intervener coincide with those of one of the parties to the claim, and the evidence or argument that the intervener wishes to introduce supports that of the original party, it may be possible (without seeking the court's permission) to intervene by way of written evidence submitted by that party. But

[51] See I Hare, 'The Law of Standing in Public Interest Adjudication' in M Andenas and D Fairgrieve (eds), *Judicial Review in International Perspective* (The Hague, Kluwer, 2000); cf C Himsworth, 'No Standing Still on Standing' in P Leyland and T Woods (eds), *Administrative Law Facing the Future* (London, Blackstone, 1997), 201–2.

[52] For further discussion of this point and reference to the parliamentary debates, see J Miles, 'Standing under the Human Rights Act: Theories of Rights Enforcement and the Nature of Public Law Adjudication' (2000) 59 *CLJ* 133, 144–47; Hare argues that standing rules should be developed in pursuit of this pragmatic objective: above n 51.

[53] Hare, above n 51.

[54] See generally *A Matter of Public Interest: Reforming the Law and Practice on Interventions in Public Interest Cases* (London, Justice/Public Law Project, 1996), 17–22; *Third Party Interventions in Judicial Review: an Action Research Study* (London, Public Law Project, 2001), 4–6; P Bryden, below n 105.

where the intervener wishes to introduce a different perspective on the matters before the court, it will be necessary to apply for separate intervener status; if the purpose of the intervention is one of information rather than interest representation, representation by way of written submissions may be adequate.[55]

To the extent that the intervener's purpose is one of interest representation, questions about the true representativeness of the intervener may arise. There is no problem when a materially affected person seeks to intervene; such a person can claim a relationship with the issues at stake akin to that held by those with victim status and as such is clearly a proper person to be heard by the court. Potential difficulty arises where the application to intervene comes from an intervener who purports to represent the interest-holder in question, but who is itself prevented by the standing test from bringing any claim directly. Peter Cane's analysis of representative standing provides guidance here:[56] if it is felt proper that there be a 'democratic link' between a *claimant* and a constituency which it purports to represent, there is arguably no less a need for such a link to exist if the interests of that constituency are to be put before the court by means of an *intervention* in an application made by some other person. By contrast, if the intervention is more in the manner of a conventional *amicus curiae*, providing the court with empirical or legal expertise without representing any particular perspective, such link between intervener and a constituency (if any) may be considered unnecessary.

Having clarified the pertinent issues, we get a better view of the purposes standing and intervention rules can and should serve. Such rules should be essentially concerned with *who* can be heard in court in relation to what sorts of issue. A rule may be highly restrictive of the class of persons entitled to move (or intervene before) the court, or it may confer a right on all citizens to complain (or intervene) in relation to every public decision and action. But whether narrow or entirely open, the rules should be based on a view about (1) the appropriateness and legitimacy of different types of claimant or intervener asserting their concern for the particular issue in the judicial (rather than political) sphere, and (2) the character of the courts' jurisdiction and the place of the courts within the constitutional balance. Identifying the basis of the current rules in these terms is not easy. The vague language used to formulate standing tests, such as 'sufficient interest' or 'individual concern,' means that the tests do not attract an obvious interpretation; intervention rules are even more broadly framed, conferring a large measure of discretion on the judge to determine the source and scope of interventions to be permitted. Needless to say, the normative basis of the standing and intervention rules is rarely, if ever, articulated by the legislature creating the jurisdictions either of the court or of the authorities under challenge. It is left to the court to discern the proper scope of its own function, and to determine whether the given claimant or intervener has a right to engage in the judicial as opposed to the political process in the particular case.

---

[55] *Ibid.*

[56] 'Standing up for the Public' [1995] *PL* 276; 'Standing, Representation and the Environment', in I Loveland (ed), *A Special Relationship? American Influences on Public Law in the UK* (Oxford, Clarendon Press, 1995).

The Relationship Between Standing and Intervention Rules: Initial Observations

Some parts of the courts' jurisdiction—HRA cases being an obvious example—allow for wider intervention than standing.[57] If the putative intervener's interest in the matter would be insufficient to afford him standing in relation to the type of decision under challenge, it might be asked whether such a person or group ought to be allowed to intervene where a claim is brought by someone with standing. For example, if only a victim can move the court, it might be felt inconsistent for that court, once moved, to admit evidence and arguments from non-victims.[58]

The HRA requires us to augment Harlow and Rawlings' useful set of metaphors for different models of judicial review proceedings. The original trio are: the 'drainpipe'—the traditional bipolar adversarial dispute, where standing and intervention rules are narrow, as are the grounds for review, the opportunity for discovery and the available remedies; the 'freeway'—where all aspects of the process, including standing and intervention, are much broader, the grounds for review more intensive, the range of available remedies allowing for greater judicial creativity and control; and the hybrid, compromise model represented by the 'funnel'—where standing is broad, but the opportunities for discovery and intervention are narrow, and the grounds for review and remedies traditional.[59] English law has perhaps recently developed from the hybrid to the extent that it is increasingly receptive to third party intervention; we might say that the cup of the funnel is larger.

Enter the Human Rights Act 1998. The Government, through Parliament, adopted the Strasbourg model,[60] reassuring interest groups that they would get their HRA day in court by intervention.[61] So the funnel remains wide, receptive to interventions from all quarters, but now has a 'lid' for cases under the HRA. That lid can only be lifted by a victim, but once opened, potentially allows a large number of persons and interests to be represented before the court. The original 'funnel' model was regarded as problematic; it was felt that reception of broader standing would inevitably put pressure on the system, leading to demands for more intensive standards of review and improved information mechanisms for the court, via more generous intervention and disclosure.[62] The added feature—increased opportunity for intervention but only after the 'lid' has been lifted—may appear to create an inconsistency. One possible justification for the availability of wide intervention alongside narrow standing in the human rights context is suggested in the next section.[63] The necessity for and propriety of permitting wide interest representation before the court at all is addressed in more detail later.

[57] Intervention in abstract devolution review is similarly situated alongside a very narrow standing test.
[58] See Lord McCollum CJ in *In re Northern Ireland Human Rights Commission* [2001] NI 271 at 280e, implicitly overturned by the House of Lords' decision, below n 138.
[59] C Harlow and R Rawlings, *Pressure Through Law* (London, Routledge, 1992), 310–17.
[60] ECHR Article 36(2); Lord Lester, '*Amici Curiae*: Third Party Intervention before the ECHR', in F Matscher and H Petzold (eds), *Protecting Human Rights: the European Dimension*, (2nd edn, Cologne, Heymann, 1990).
[61] See the Lord Chancellor, Hansard, HL Deb, 24 November 1997, vol 583, col 833–4.
[62] R Rawlings, 'Courts and Interests' in I Loveland (ed), above n 56, at 109.
[63] Below text to n 75.

The Relationship Between Standing and Intervention Rules and the Subject Matter of the Litigation

It is apparent from the Greenpeace examples that the standing and intervention rules in different areas of the courts' jurisdiction vary. The question to be asked here is whether those variations can be justified by reference to the subject matter falling within those discrete areas of the courts' jurisdiction. It may well be appropriate for a single legal system to operate different standing rules in relation to different substantive areas; the admission of wide standing rules in some areas is therefore not necessarily inconsistent with there being narrower rules elsewhere.[64] However, an immediate difficulty with the current situation arises from the fact that the formally separate areas of jurisdiction are in substance far from discrete. Moreover, as we have just seen, the intervention and standing rules within the *same* jurisdiction may allow for a different range of persons to be heard in court. Two areas are examined here: human rights law and EC law.[65]

Human Rights Cases

The HRA endeavours to reserve section 6 complaints to victims, but arguably fails to achieve this in substance owing to the probability that non-victims who are otherwise regarded as having a 'sufficient interest' (or, rather less likely, 'title and interest to sue') can make traditional ultra vires arguments with the assistance of section 3 of the HRA, and the likelihood that those courts will continue to allow non-victims to make arguments which turn on rights recognised at common law. If this analysis is right, then domestic law, at least outside Scotland, contains a direct conflict which Lord Lester would likely condemn as 'absurd.'

In developing a standing test to govern access to human rights arguments, it is important to bear in mind the different attitudes that may be held in relation to the nature of rights and the relationship of the rights-holder and others in relation to those rights. A comparison of individualist and communitarian approaches to rights and public law may be helpful here.[66] A narrow victim test supports the individualist view that rights are the property of their holders, and that only those persons should be entitled to move the court in relation to an alleged violation. Other than in the case where that victim is legally incompetent, as for example in the case of minor children, a 'benevolent' third party should not be permitted to bring the matter to court, unless (perhaps) it can demonstrate that it has the clear, ongoing authorisation of the victim to bring the case on his behalf. This view, (perhaps at its broadest permitting what Peter Cane calls 'associational' standing[67]), is reflected in some interpretations of 'sufficient interest' outside the

[64]   P Craig, *Administrative Law* (4th edn, London, Sweet & Maxwell, 1999), 715.
[65]   The different standing rules for abstract and concrete devolution review invite similar analysis.
[66]   For fuller analysis, see Miles, above n 52, at 148–52. See also D Feldman, 'Public Interest Litigation and Constitutional Theory in Comparative Perspective' (1992) 55 *MLR* 44.
[67]   Above n 56.

HRA.[68] By contrast, a communitarian analysis supports the broader view of 'sufficient interest' taken in non-HRA cases, and so justifies non-victims' continuing ability to make human rights arguments. On this view, the focus is not on the particular victim, but a wider concern about governmental illegality—public wrongs rather than private rights—in which anyone may assert an interest sufficient to move the court.[69] Such a wider standing rule (which may be felt to amount to no standing rule at all) would recognise a collective public right to have government held legally accountable for its actions, including in individual rights cases (and in other areas), and so permitting 'surrogate' and 'public interest' standing.[70] Cases such as *Joint Council for the Welfare of Immigrants* support this analysis in a rights context under the standard 'sufficient interest' test.[71]

The parliamentary debates do not suggest that the victim test was selected with either or indeed any such view in mind,[72] so the justification (if any) for having the different standing tests for human rights arguments is one for the courts to explore in the light of their perception of the prevailing political theory relating to rights enforcement, part of what Feldman calls the 'constitutional ethic.'[73] As the law stands, assuming that non-victims can make at least some of the human rights arguments suggested in the Greenpeace case study, there is tension between the victim test and the scope of non-victim review, betraying inconsistent views about the entitlement of non-victims to concern themselves with rights-violations. The courts cannot deal with the tension by reinterpreting the 'victim' test; whilst susceptible of quite broad interpretation, its language offers less scope than the standard test to bring *its* interpretation into line with *them*. So perhaps the common law should prefer its narrower interpretations of 'sufficient interest' over its more expansive cases in rights-based situations, effectively matching the victim test. Many would regard that as a retrograde step and one that the courts are unlikely to make, but short of legislative removal of the victim test, it may be the only acceptable means of alleviating the tension. The alternative, effectively side-lining the victim test by fully exploiting non-victim review, whilst arguably preferable on policy grounds, may give insufficient weight to the victim test's place in the HRA scheme.[74]

---

[68] See the discussion of standing to make a discrimination argument: *McBride*, above n 4; and *R v Legal Aid Board, ex parte Bateman* [1992] 1 WLR 711.

[69] Sedley J, as he then was, in *R v Somerset County Council and ARC Southern Ltd, ex parte Dixon* [1998] Env LR 111, at 121, though he does not advocate a completely open door—'in the majority of cases' the claimant will need an interest greater than that of the rest of the public, at 117.

[70] Cane, above n 56.

[71] Above n 31; see also *R v Secretary of State for Social Services, ex parte Child Poverty Action Group* [1990] 2 QB 540; these cases may alternatively be justified as ensuring justice for individuals who encounter difficulty moving the court to protect themselves, and so supplements the individualist approach; the communitarian approach would not require the claimant to demonstrate victim support.

[72] For analysis, see Miles, above n 52, at 142–47. See also the *Response to the Northern Ireland Human Rights Commission's Review of Powers Recommendations* (Northern Ireland Office, May 2002), in which the Commission's recommendation that it be exempted from the exclusionary effect of the victim test is rejected at para 70–72.

[73] Feldman, above n 66.

[74] Though victims alone could claim discretionary damages awards: HRA, s 8. A scheme offering wide access to judicial review plus victim-only damages (a sort of public/private split) is not

The clash between victim standing and wide intervention, by contrast, may be more apparent than real. There is a distinction between the question of who can bring the court's attention to an alleged illegality, and what the court does, and from whom the court hears, once that allegation is before it. So, in this context, a victim's autonomy is protected to the extent that a non-victim is prohibited from bringing his complaint to court, but if a victim chooses to move the court, he initiates a process in which others may properly become involved. David Feldman has argued that the victim test fails to recognise the 'collectivist' philosophy which informs the content of many of the Convention rights, which may accordingly be perceived as satisfying public as opposed to purely individual purposes and requiring a balance to be struck between individual and wider public and social interests.[75] However, even if we are stuck with victim standing, third party interventions may help ensure that courts are better equipped to address those wider, collective issues which are central to determining the success of victims' complaints; and, as we shall see, such interventions may also better equip the courts to develop and expound the law more generally.

European Community Law Cases

The European Community context generates a similar tension, here deriving from the mismatch between national and supranational levels. As the case study showed, a challenge to the validity of a measure of the EC institutions may reach the European courts via several routes, one of which allows (in England, if not Scotland) very broad standing, the other extremely narrow standing. Damages actions brought in the European courts against Community institutions under EC Treaty Articles 235 and 288 may also involve impugning the validity of an EC measure, and yet there a straightforward victim standing test applies. The inconsistencies are exacerbated by the fact that access to the Article EC Treaty 234 route is determined by different rules in each Member State.

Since identical legal issues can find their way to the European courts by all of these routes it is impossible to find any rationale for the variety of standing tests in the subject matter of the litigation.[76] The rationale for the narrow EC Treaty Article 230 rule might be to preserve the European courts' resources by giving national courts primary responsibility for resolving EC law disputes. But where the national court is minded to rule the challenged EC measure invalid, it is obliged to make a reference.[77] The European Court of Justice thus has no control over the number

inconsistent, but it seems clear that that was not the scheme intended; the pervasive force of s 3, denying victims much of their exclusivity, was perhaps overlooked. Thanks to Tom Hickman for this point. See cases above n 33a.

[75] D Feldman, 'The Human Rights Act and Constitutional Principles' (1999) 19 *LS* 165, 173–78, 193–94.

[76] Craig has identified a rationale for the varying approaches taken by the European Court of Justice to its own Article 230(4) standing rule: 'Legality, Standing and Substantive Review in European Community Law' (1994) 14 *OJLS* 507; but that does not account for the divergence of standing rules at issue here.

[77] Case 314/85 *Foto-Frost* [1987] ECR 4199.

of Article 234 references that it receives and so its resources may be drawn upon in any event.

One way of resolving the tension between national jurisdictions, and between national and supranational levels, would be to harmonise the national rules governing standing and procedure for the bringing of EC law claims, and, where the case involves a challenge to the validity of an EC measure, to tie in such rules with those governing direct access to the European Court of Justice under Article 230. The Court is unlikely to encroach on domestic autonomy in this area, and the Commission's suggestions for harmonisation specifically in standing to argue environmental matters were not well received.[78] But it is the Court's own Article 230 standing rule which is out of line with the generally more open rules found in many national jurisdictions and even in its own Article 235 jurisdiction,[79] so if any change is to be made, it should perhaps be in the Court's own practices; but given the outcome of the recent flurry of judicial activity in this area, that seems unlikely to occur by way of judicial re-interpretation of the test. We are therefore likely to be left with a mismatch between jurisdictions that cannot be explained by reference to the issues being litigated.

STANDING AND INTERVENTION RULES AND THE CONSTITUTIONAL ROLE OF THE COURTS

A second perspective from which the appropriateness of standing and intervention rules may be judged relates to the constitutional role of the courts, the associated issue of the public's right to participate in legal proceedings, and the limits of the courts' practical competence.[80] Two closely related questions help frame this debate: (1) are the courts rights defenders only, or law enforcers generally? (2) are the courts essentially dispute-resolvers or more generally expounders of the law?

Rights Defenders or General Law Enforcers?

The traditional model casts courts as resolvers of bipolar disputes between directly affected parties. The victim test reinforces this orthodoxy, though as we have seen is accompanied by the possibility of wide intervention and sits rather uncomfortably alongside the opportunities for human rights review potentially open to non-victim claimants. However, one effect of a *generally* narrow standing rule (as opposed to one that operates exclusively in the *human rights* field) premised on

---

[78] Himsworth, above n 51, at 214–17; C Harlow, 'Access to Justice as a Human Right', in P Alston, M Bustelo and J Heenan (eds), *The European Union and Human Rights* (Oxford, Oxford University Press, 1999), 200.

[79] See AG Jacobs' Opinion in Case C-50/00P *UPA v Council*, above n 20, at para 85.

[80] Many of the issues explored here have also been canvassed recently by Carol Harlow, below n 111, who takes a more sceptical view of the ability of the legal system to accommodate wide standing and intervention.

the model of a bipolar dispute initiated by a materially affected claimant[81] is that several key areas of modern governmental activity may thereby be excluded from the scope of judicial review, at least that instigated by private persons.[82] Complaints relating to environmental, cultural, economic or international matters[83] may involve no individuated claimant, or class of claimant, who satisfies such a standing rule. The flexible sufficient interest test can accommodate these cases; a more restrictive rule, based on individual rights or material interests, as opposed to the vindication of some broader public or ideological interest, may not.

So narrow standing rules effectively put some issues beyond the courts' reach, and so, it might be said, beyond legal as opposed to political accountability. Commentators such as Trevor Allan would not regard that as a bad thing.[84] For Allan, judicial review should be concerned primarily with individual right and interest, as protected by the rule of law principles of due process and equality; beyond that, he would allow for judicial review only to resolve 'general questions of constitutional authority,' such as jurisdictional disputes between different levels of government.[85] It is from that primary focus on individual rights that the institution of judicial review derives its legitimacy, and as a result of which the judiciary can claim a constitutional function distinct from and balancing those of the political arms of government. That focus does not steer the judiciary clear of political controversy, and the courts must not shirk their constitutional responsibility to adjudicate on the individual's claim just because the case is controversial.[86] Indeed, the fact that an individual right is at stake is all that is required to render the matter justiciable; there is no need or justification in Allan's view for any separate 'political question' or justiciability doctrine.[87] Moreover, save for allowing representative standing to enable some claimants to assert the rights of others, this understanding of judicial review would largely dispense with the need for rules of standing.[88]

This view deprives the courts of any basis on which legitimately to adjudicate on cases raising no question of individual right, such as the *Fire Brigades Union*[89] and 'Pergau Dam' cases.[90] The propriety of judicial review in cases such as these, and the standing of the claimants to bring them, has attracted a range of academic comment. Allan maintains that judicial review is out of place here, even where there may be concern about the adequacy of the mechanisms supposed to ensure

---

[81]   Contrasted with a purely 'ideologically' motivated claimant: see Stewart, below n 122.

[82]   On the relevance of Attorney General relator actions, see below n 98.

[83]   *R v Secretary of State for Foreign and Commonwealth Affairs, ex parte Rees-Mogg* [1994] QB 552; *R v Her Majesty's Treasury, ex parte Smedley* [1985] QB 657; *R v Secretary of State for Foreign Affairs, ex parte World Development Movement* [1995] 1 WLR 386; *R v Secretary of State for the Environment, ex parte Rose Theatre Trust Co* [1990] QB 504. For discussion of utilities regulation, a sphere where these sorts of claims may arise, particularly on environmental grounds, see Peter Leyland, ch 8 above.

[84]   TRS Allan, *Constitutional Justice* (Oxford, Oxford University Press, 2001).

[85]   *Ibid* at 172.

[86]   TRS Allan, *Law, Liberty and Justice* (Oxford, Oxford University Press, 1993), 225.

[87]   Above n 84, at 163.

[88]   Above n 86, at 234; see *ibid* n 98 regarding representative standing, which he would at least allow for bodies such as the Equal Opportunities Commission.

[89]   *R v Secretary of State for the Home Department, ex parte Fire Brigades Union* [1995] 2 AC 513.

[90]   *World Development Movement*, above n 83.

political accountability for the challenged decision.[91] If the courts adjudicate in cases where no question of individual right is at stake, they allow themselves to become a surrogate political forum for those who lost their battle in the political process and so stray into a non-justiciable mire. Absent a claim of individual right, the court has no readily defensible, specifically 'legal' as opposed to simply 'political' basis for deciding the case, and so for asserting that its interpretation of the relevant statute should be regarded as any more authoritative that than of the executive or legislature.[92] So although government must at all times act in accordance with the law, for Allan and others *judicial* review will not always be an appropriate control mechanism.[93]

However, other commentators argue that, even assuming that the orthodox mechanisms of political accountability worked (and so excluding any argument for judicial review based on a perceived need to compensate for a democratic deficit), there remains a distinct function properly to be played by the courts in policing the limits of governmental powers even where no individual is directly or singularly affected. And with that function necessarily comes a wider standing rule to ensure that the matter can be brought before the court. In Lord Diplock's words, it cannot be said:

> that judicial review of the actions of officers and departments of central government is unnecessary because they are accountable to Parliament for the way they carry out their functions. They are accountable to Parliament for what they do so far as regards efficiency and policy, and of that Parliament is the only judge; they are responsible to a court of justice for the lawfulness of what they do, and of that the court is the only judge.[94]

The disagreement turns on the fundamental issue of what counts as a 'legal' and in that sense justiciable dispute. Allan describes the 'Pergau Dam' case as one where 'it is not clear that legal and political objections could be sufficiently distinguished' to justify judicial review,[95] such that the court arguably found itself improperly encroaching on executive discretion. By contrast, Ivan Hare, an advocate of broad standing rules, says of the case that 'it would be difficult to think of a challenge more closely formulated in rigorous legal terms,' the only point involving 'one of strict statutory construction.'[96]

Approaching the issue from a slightly different tack, perhaps intended to be more sympathetic to Allan's theory of individual rights, Peter Cane has advocated a theory of *public* rights, on the basis of which a 'legitimate area of activism' might be carved out for the courts, and corresponding limits on the competence of the political arms of government might be created.[97] The vindication of such public

---

[91] Above n 84, at 172–73, in relation to the *Fire Brigades Union* case; cf Feldman above n 66, at 50 regarding the use of judicial review to support representative democracy.

[92] Above n 84, at 195–96.

[93] Above n 86, at 223. See also Harlow, below n 111, at 5.

[94] In the *IRC* case, above n 5, at 644.

[95] Above n 84, at 195. See also the view of Carol Harlow that this case constitutes 'a new high watermark in the substitution of legal for political accountability,' below n 111, at 5.

[96] Above n 51, at 309.

[97] Cane in Loveland (ed), above n 56, at 142–45.

rights should be open to private citizens under broad standing rules.[98] However, this approach is problematic. Identifying what 'rights' might fall within the scope of such a theory is contentious, Cane's criterion being that the importance of the rights and interests in question is such that they should be judicially protected against undue governmental encroachment except by express legislative provision.[99] Suggested examples include freedom of information, basic constitutional principles such as 'no taxation or expenditure without Parliamentary approval,' and possibly environmental rights. As Cane acknowledges, the identification (and content) of rights which can and should be afforded judicial protection would have to rest on some underlying, inevitably contested, political theory regarding the appropriate division of judicial and executive/legislative competence.

Whatever is the proper answer to this question regarding the scope of the courts' jurisdiction, it should be addressed head on, as commentators discussed here have done, via a theory of justiciability or carefully reasoned theory about the purpose of judicial review, and not evaded by unreflectively adopting a standing rule whose *effect* is to exclude these controversial areas from judicial review. However, it is important to note that wide standing rules per se are not a cause of justiciability problems. One could (subject to one's view of the issues addressed in the previous section) have a wide standing rule to allow non-victim claimants to make perfectly justiciable human rights arguments, but accompany that with a justiciability rule which excluded from court cases not involving individual rights. Conversely, claims brought by individual victims may take the courts into highly contentious political territory that, absent the human rights dimension, might have been regarded by some as non-justiciable.[100] But it is the subject matter of the application, and the argument which it is proposed to be made, that determines justiciability, not the identity of the person making it.

Dispute Resolvers or Expounders of the Law?

As the foregoing discussion implies, whether the courts are confined to the vindication of individual rights or enforce the law more generally, the breadth of standing and intervention rules may also depend upon the characterisation of the courts' role and their relationship with the other branches of government. This perspective on standing and intervention has received considerable attention in the American literature. Giradeau Spann used the term 'expository justice' to describe a model of the US federal courts' function which could be contrasted with the traditional 'dispute resolution' model.[101] Under the traditional model, the

---

[98] The availability of actions by the Attorney General may be more apparent than real, particularly where the putative defendant is a part of central government: *ibid.*

[99] *Ibid* at 150. Cf the restricted scope of public right actions such as the Scottish *actio popularis*: Clyde and Edwards, above n 13, at para 10.23.

[100] eg *Hatton v United Kingdom* (2002) 34 EHRR 1.

[101] G Spann, 'Expository Justice' (1983) 131 *UPa LR* 585; see also O Fiss, 'The Forms of Justice' (1979) 93 *Harv LR* 1.

courts' role is perceived as being primarily that of resolving bipolar disputes, only incidentally expounding the law and then only to the extent necessary to deal with the individual cases before them. By contrast, the expository justice model views the courts' primary function as being to give 'operational meaning to principles that would otherwise remain abstract, rhetorical and elusive,'[102] in particular where those principles are the very broad statements found in constitutional documents such as a Bills of Rights, or in this jurisdiction the ECHR.[103] It is necessary for the courts to ensure that those principles are understood in a way that is relevant to current social conditions, at least keeping pace with social evolution.[104] The courts' exposition of the law is therefore crucial, governing not just the immediate dispute before the court, but having wide-ranging implications for a number of groups within society beyond those represented by the immediate parties to the claim. It may accordingly be desirable for the courts to be equipped with information and argument from sources other than the immediate parties.

It has been said that whenever the public perceive that governmental power is being exercised over them—here by what may be felt by them to amount to judicial law-making—they will seek involvement in the relevant decision-making process. The nature of the issues before the court often reflects the pluralist nature of modern society. Judicial decisions about the meaning and proper application of a given legal principle—which will often involve weighing the claims of two or more sets of rights or interests—may therefore be felt to enjoy greater legitimacy if participation by a wide range of parties and interests in the courts' proceedings is permitted.[105]

In the EU context, the population governed by the European Court of Justice's decisions is especially large and diverse, so opportunity to intervene in proceedings before the Court may be regarded as particularly important. Seen in this light, the rules regarding intervention in cases brought by way of a reference under EC Treaty Article 234 (in particular) are too restrictive. It will be recalled that only those private persons who appeared in the national proceedings are permitted to make representations to the European Court of Justice. This exclusion of newcomers is ostensibly based on the view that Article 234 proceedings are non-contentious, designed simply to ensure a uniform interpretation of Community law.[106] But this characterisation of the proceedings surely understates the significance of Article 234 decisions. Given the declaratory, and sometimes prospective[107] nature of the judgments, it might be thought that a wider circle of non-governmental interests should be represented in court than those which

---

[102] *Ibid* at 592.
[103] In cases described by Spann as 'statutory' rather than 'constitutional' (a dichotomy that does not as easily translate into the UK context), the courts' function is seen as key to the operation of the separation of powers.
[104] *Ibid* at 600. Cf the 'living instrument' approach to the interpretation of the ECHR: *Tyrer v United Kingdom* (1979–80) 2 EHRR 1.
[105] P Bryden, 'Public Interest Intervention in the Courts' (1987) 66 *Can Bar Rev* 490.
[106] Case C-181/95 *Biogen v Smithkline Beecham* [1996] ECR I-717, paras 4–6, quoted by Denman, above n 48.
[107] Case 149/77 *Defrenne v SABENA* [1978] ECR 1365; Spann identifies prospectivity as characteristic of an expository system.

fortuitously appeared at the national level, not least since different national systems will have standing and intervention rules of varying degrees of generosity.

In this jurisdiction, cases in which the courts have been receptive to broader standing have often turned on 'legislative' rather than 'adjudicative' facts,[108] where the case concerns the validity of some general measure or policy in its application to a wide class of persons, rather than on the particular treatment of one individual. Contrast abstract devolution cases, where a peculiarly narrow standing rule applies.[109] Legislative facts will be central in any references made by the law officers to the Privy Council. The court's role here may be regarded as particularly expository, such cases often requiring interpretation of broadly framed provisions, for example where it is argued that the legislation is incompatible with Convention rights. The standing rule may accordingly be felt to require counter-balancing by non-governmental intervention to provide wider interest representation before the court and so, it might be felt, better exposition of the law.

So the expository nature of many judicial decisions and the consequent claim of civil society to be involved in judicial decisions affecting it has clear implications both for the scope of standing rules—unlike the dispute resolution model, the expository justice model does not suggest any particular relationship between claimant and issue[110]—and, perhaps more so, for the nature of the evidence which courts are willing to admit and for the nature and scope of interventions which they allow. But allowing wider participation and evidence is far from uncontroversial. As Carol Harlow has recently demonstrated, the difficulty lies in managing an opening-up of the courts' procedures in a way which will enhance, rather than undermine, the legitimacy and quality of their decisions, and improve rather than stultify their processes.[111]

The Democratic Implications of Wider Participation in Judicial Proceedings

An initial judgment has to be made about the constitutional appropriateness of the courts embracing their (inevitable) expository function by developing their procedures in this way; and this gives us a slightly different perspective on the issues raised by Trevor Allan, viewed not from the bench, but from the place in the democratic system, and in the judicial system, of individual members of civil society.

David Feldman has argued that the law relating to standing and intervention must be developed compatibly with the wider constitutional context, in particular the scope afforded to members of civil society to participate in formal political debate.[112] Where a dispute concerns the scope and enforcement of individual

---

[108] For this distinction see KC Davis, 'An Approach to Problems of Evidence in the Administrative Process' (1942) 55 *Harv LR* 364, 402–3. For an example, see *R v Secretary of State for Employment, ex parte the Equal Opportunities Commission* [1995] 1 AC 1.

[109] See Page, above n 40, at 16–18.

[110] Even in a traditional system, the concept of 'dispute' may be contentious, turning on a determination about the types of 'injury' cognisable for these purposes: Spann, above n 101, at 624–27.

[111] C Harlow, 'Public Law and Popular Justice' (2002) 65 *MLR* 1. See also S Hannett, 'Third Party Intervention: In the Public Interest?' [2003] *PL* 128.

[112] Above n 66.

rights and material interests, there is no constitutional difficulty in allowing affect-ed individuals, or their representatives, to assert those rights in court, whether by initiating proceedings or by intervening in proceedings already begun.[113] Matters become more complicated where the claimant is purporting to act in the name of the 'public interest' or to assert an ideological interest.[114] If the political system is firmly rooted in representative democracy and responsible government, claims by private individuals or groups either to be heard directly in the political forum (rather than through an elected representative) and to litigate matters of public or purely ideological interest in court may be viewed with suspicion. Such claims become 'an alternative or supplement to orthodox political processes, taking the courts beyond their core function of adjudicating on individuals' rights and duties'[115] and, we might add, using access to the courts to give the claimants a powerful, direct voice which the representative political system has deliberately denied them.

However, he goes on to observe that a given political system, the product of years of evolution, is unlikely to adhere uncompromisingly to a single theory. So, for example, where a formally representative/responsible political system is never-theless receptive to public involvement in policy-making, the prevailing political theory may be more accommodating of participation than the formal under-standing of the constitution implies, and so participation by the wider public (usually in the form of interest groups) in court—whether to challenge the man-ner of the group's consultation by a policy- or decision-maker, or to challenge the substance or implementation of policy—may be regarded as being more conso-nant with the prevailing 'constitutional ethic,' properly understood.[116] Moreover, if the system permits public interest claims to be made by private claimants not materially affected by the matters under dispute, it must perforce afford similarly interested groups and individuals the opportunity to seek permission to intervene in those proceedings since the claimant can claim no greater right (than prompt-ness) to put his arguments before the court than any other person.[117]

This approach may be compared with that of commentators and judges[118] who have argued that the courts should widen opportunities for participation in their proceedings precisely in order to compensate for 'democratic deficit' and so for lack of popular participation elsewhere in the system. This argument has been

[113] The propriety of *surrogate* claimants turns in part on whether an individualistic (what Feldman calls a 'liberal individualistic') or communitarian view of rights enforcement is taken.

[114] Assuming for the sake of argument that Allan's objections to this sort of litigation can be over-come. The concept of 'public interest' is problematic. It may be more accurate to talk not of a single 'public interest', but of a compromise amongst a plurality of affected interests: Stewart, below n 122, at n 371. Some 'public interest' claims may therefore amount to 'maxi-private-interest litigation', though for some claims, for example those relating to impact of government action on future generations, 'whose interests may not be represented under a strictly liberal individualist regime,' the concept of 'public interest' may remain apt: Feldman, above n 66, at 55.

[115] Feldman, above n 66, at 48.

[116] *Ibid.*

[117] Bryden, above n 105, at 527.

[118] Lord Mustill, in *R v Secretary of State for the Home Department, ex parte Fire Brigades Union* [1995] 2 AC 513, at 567F-H.

particularly prevalent in the European context.[119] However, Feldman allows room
for this sort of argument, such evolutive challenges to current practices being necessary to allow for constitutional development.[120] Changes in one part of the system—whether in the judicial or another branch of government, may trigger
change elsewhere.

For example, moves by the European Commission to enhance participation by
civil society, in particular non-governmental organisations, in European policy-
making[121] may place irresistible pressure on the European Court of Justice, or failing that,[121a] the Inter-Governmental Conference, to expand standing under EC
Treaty Article 230(4). The link between wider participation at the policy formation or decision-making stage and increased standing and intervention rights has
been argued many times before.[122] At the very least, it might be argued that the
existing category of individual concern covering those involved by right in a consultation process should be expanded to cover consultees more generally, to
achieve compatibility with the wider participation at the policy-making stage.

In the domestic context, Harlow notes consultation by government in relation
to the development of policy, seen as a key aspect of the 'modernising government'
programme, which is being deployed in an increasing range of areas, supplement-
ing representative democracy.[123] Furthermore, it can be argued that the Government's express endorsement of intervention in judicial proceedings as an
appropriate tactic for interest groups deprived of the right to move the court
under the HRA[124] justifies extending participation in this sphere and endorses the
courts' receptiveness to such applications. Even outside the human rights context,
Harlow diagnoses the courts' acceptance of broad standing and intervention in
cases not involving individual rights as indicative of a developing form of 'public
interest litigation' of the type described by Abram Chayes, in which it is implicitly
regarded as constitutionally appropriate for civil society to litigate rather than
lobby.[125]

So, to summarise the position thus far. In proceedings relating to individual
rights and interests, matters falling squarely within the jurisdiction of the courts as

---

[119] C Harlow, 'Towards a Theory of Access for the European Court of Justice' (1992) 12 *YEL* 213,
and 'Public Law and Popular Justice,' above n 111, at 13; contrast her view of the propriety of NGO
involvement in domestic litigation: since the domestic democratic deficit is less acute, it is asked
whether interest groups, whose own democratic nature might be questionable (see Cane, above n 56)
ought to be granted standing. This concern seems to be downplayed in the international sphere on the
basis that some input from civil society in the otherwise state-dominated arena is better than none.

[120] Above n 66, at 51.

[121] *European Governance: a White Paper* (COM (2001) 428 final); *Consultation Document: Towards a
Reinforced Culture of Consultation and Dialogue* (COM (2002) 277 final). The absence of discussion in
these papers of NGOs' participation in judicial proceedings to determine the validity of EC measures is
striking, given the emphasis otherwise placed on the rule of law, NGOs' central role in the functioning
of civil society and representative democracy, and the concern to bring the people closer to Europe.

[121a] Albors Llorens suggests that prospects of judicial reform are now non-existent, above n 20.

[122] Classically, by R Stewart 'The Reformation of Administrative Law' (1975) 88 *Harv LR* 1667; see
Craig, above n 64, at 715–16.

[123] Above n 111, at 11.

[124] Eg Lord Chancellor, Hansard, HL Deb, 24 November 1997, vol 583, col 832.

[125] Above n 111.

it is traditionally understood, there is no constitutional difficulty in allowing those individually affected to participate in court. The expository nature of the court's function may make it desirable that the variously affected individuals (ie perhaps including those affected by the legal point, if not the particular facts, in dispute) be involved as interveners. Whether persons other than those individuals (and their duly authorised representatives) can intervene or bring a claim as ideologically-motivated surrogates will turn on the debate between individualism and communitarianism (or collectivism) and on the arguments surrounding participation considered here. Once we enter the sphere of pure 'public interest' litigation, those latter arguments, together with the debate between Allan and others, come to the fore.

The Institutional Problems of Wider Participation in Judicial Proceedings

However, even if a sound case can be made for widening participation in the courts' proceedings in the various terms discussed above, there may remain problems relating to the courts' institutional competence which justify further caution. Lon Fuller's classic discussion of the problems created by polycentric disputes is important here.[126] Many public law cases involve polycentric issues, which raise problems for courts called upon to expound the relevant law, because their traditional (dispute resolution model) procedures are better suited to handling bipolar disputes. It is said that in order to appreciate the full implications of the decision it is called on to make, a court would have to transform itself into something more like a Royal Commission or public inquiry, or indeed a Parliament, than a court of law; at its worst, the 'freeway' would become a political 'free-for-all.'[127] Such a transformation would, it is said, render any procedural distinction between the judicial and the political forums of government rather thin. Moreover, it would also be likely to fail in its goal of ensuring adequate participation by *all* interested parties. The net result would be similar to that produced by the traditional system—an ill-informed decision reached on the basis of incomplete participation and which has unforeseen repercussions for some of the many affected individuals—but at the further cost of undermining the distinctiveness and legitimacy of the courts' function. So, Fuller would argue, the court must exercise restraint by deciding cases on bases which do not demand an appreciation—which the court cannot have—of likely external repercussions.

However, John Allison claims[128] that the suggested restraint may not be a virtue, since however restrained the court may be, its decision will necessarily have ramifications that it cannot foresee. Cases brought by individual victims and which therefore appear on their face to be bipolar may on closer examination involve genuinely polycentric problems. The problem of polycentricity is insidious; a court may fail to appreciate the polycentric nature of the case before it and so be

---

[126] L Fuller, 'The Forms and Limits of Adjudication' (1978) 92 *Harv LR* 353.
[127] Harlow, above n 111, at 17.
[128] J Allison, 'The Procedural Reason for Judicial Restraint' [1994] *PL* 452.

unaware of the need to exercise the recommended restraint. Indeed, Allison argues that Fuller's concept of adjudication—an adversarial contest based on the proofs and arguments of the two parties, the old 'dispute resolution' model—itself actually *aggravates* the problem, by depriving the courts of the wherewithal to detect these aspects of a case. The central complaint—ill-informed judicial decision-making—must be addressed either way. One way of ameliorating the situation would be to introduce 'correctives' to the system of a type advocated by the promoters of the expository justice and public law litigation model (notably third party intervention and Brandeis briefs) which allow information to be brought before the court from sources beyond the immediate parties.[129] Where that information includes non-legal, for example socio-economic data, it will additionally be necessary to ensure that it is properly interpreted by judges, whose background as lawyers (rather than as administrators) may not previously have exposed them to these sorts of materials.

It is important to bear in mind in this debate what the substantive law invoked by the claimant in each type of case requires of the court, and to note in doing so that the suggested interventions will not take the courts into non-justiciable subject matter. Rather, they will provide information essential to proper resolution of the issues squarely before the court. The standard of review has in recent years become increasingly intensive, both under the HRA, under EC law and at common law: the former two involve proportionality review; common law review also shows signs of accepting a true proportionality test within the scheme of, or alongside, *Wednesbury*. Certainly, the admission into domestic law of a proportionality doctrine has been accompanied, under the HRA in particular, by the concept of a discretionary area of judgment for executive decision-makers and legislators.[130] However, even allowing for that self-denying ordinance, the courts cannot abdicate their responsibility to police the limits of that area, and to do so sufficiently closely to satisfy the demands of the ECHR.[131] If they are to engage sensibly in proportionality review, however intensively applied,[132] the courts may need relevant specialist information which the immediate parties to the claim may not be equipped to put before the courts themselves. For example, a court may be unable properly to determine the justifiability of a prima facie infringement of a victim claimant's Convention-protected interest, and so the scope of his Convention right, if it does not have before it information pertinent to weighing that interest against the legitimate aim, such as the rights of others, sought to be pursued via the infringement.[133]

---

[129] A Chayes, 'The Role of the Judge in Public Law Litigation' (1976) 89 *Harv LR* 1281; 'Public Law Litigation and the Burger Court' (1982) 96 *Harv LR* 4. For English proposals, see Allison, above n 128, at 468–72.

[130] eg *R v DPP, ex parte Kebilene* [2000] 2 AC 326, 381A-E, per Lord Hope.

[131] *Smith v United Kingdom* (2000) 29 EHRR 493; Article 13 was not incorporated by the HRA, but the courts are likely to have regard to it in fashioning the standard of review, since they may otherwise incur criticism from Strasbourg.

[132] See Allison, above n 128.

[133] See Loux, above n 46, 335–38; see also Feldman's arguments re the collective nature of Convention rights, above n 75.

The substantive grounds of review themselves may therefore make the courts more receptive to third party intervention, especially by way of written submission, and may also demand a more favourable attitude towards evidence generally in judicial review cases.[134] The courts' experience of proportionality in EC law has encouraged a more generous approach to disclosure in that field.[135] Some judges clearly consider that recent developments in the nature of judicial review, not least their freeing from the '*Wednesbury* straitjacket,' mean that a different approach to evidence will be required. Munby J adverted to such developments to support the existence of a power to order cross-examination and receive oral evidence in judicial review proceedings.[136] It seems likely that the domestic courts will continue to encourage interventions and allow wide standing where the rules permit them to do so. Even before the HRA came into force, the English courts had indicated a willingness to broaden their information base by accepting interventions.[137] The House of Lords recently endorsed the value of third party interventions in a case concerning the Northern Ireland Human Rights Commission's capacity to intervene in legal proceedings involving Convention rights.[138] Lord Woolf remarked that 'the successful introduction of human rights into ... domestic law ... is substantially dependent upon the courts giving proper effect to those rights,' a task in which the Commission and other interveners would be able to give 'substantial assistance to enable the courts to fully appreciate what is involved in properly applying human rights in the litigation which comes before them.'[139] Whilst the power to admit interveners may be exercised sparingly,[140] and when allowed generally confined to paper, interventions have been permitted in a number of recent high profile cases.[141]

---

[134] For the standard position on disclosure see: *R v Secretary of State for Home Affairs, ex parte Harrison* and *R v Secretary of State or the Environment, ex parte London Borough of Islington and the London Lesbian and Gay Centre* reported at [1997] *JR* 113 and 121; *R v Secretary of State for Foreign and Commonwealth Affairs, ex parte World Development Movement* [1995] 1 WLR 386, at 396–97.

[135] N Green, 'Proportionality and the Supremacy of Parliament in the UK' in E Ellis (ed), *The Principle of Proportionality in the Laws of Europe* (Oxford, Hart Publishing, 1999), 157–63.

[136] *R (on the application of G) v Ealing London Borough Council (No.2)* [2002] EWHC Admin 250, *Times*, 18 March 2002, especially paras 14–15, though he felt that rarely would oral evidence be required.

[137] See eg comments of Henry LJ in *R v Ministry of Defence, ex parte Smith* [1996] QB 517, at 564E-F. Cf reservations regarding use of Brandeis briefs: A Henderson, 'Brandeis Briefs and the Proof of Legislative Facts in Proceedings under the Human Rights Act 1998' [1998] *PL* 563.

[138] *In re Northern Ireland Human Rights Commission* [2002] UKHL 25; [2002] HRLR 35. This power is important given the express legislative prohibition on the Commission making Convention-based arguments as a claimant (save where it can itself claim victim status): Northern Ireland Act 1998, s 71(1), which preserves for the Commission the power to bring proceedings relating to the law and practice of human rights which do *not* involve the type of argument falling within the preserve of the victim test.

[139] *Ibid* at para 34.

[140] *Ibid* per Lord Slynn at para 25.

[141] Eg *R (Pretty) v Director of Public Prosecutions (Secretary of State for the Home Department intervening)* [2002] UKHL 61, [2002] 1 AC 800, see para 51 for list of non-governmental interveners. For analysis of this development see Hannett, above n 111.

The recent, pre-HRA, *Source Informatics* case provides an interesting illustration of some of the potential benefits of allowing intervention.[142] Various parties sought to intervene in a judicial review of the lawfulness of Department of Health guidance regarding the legality of doctors and pharmacists selling anonymised prescription data to pharmaceutical companies. The claimants had failed at first instance, and several interested parties applied to intervene in the substantive appeal in order to introduce public interest and human rights arguments that the claimants were not proposing to put. The Court of Appeal allowed the interventions on the ground that it ought not to decide the case on as narrow a basis as had the court of first instance; it was in no one's interests for the Court of Appeal to give a decision leaving as many unanswered questions and uncertainties as had the first instance decision. It was recognised that, despite careful case management, the Court may simply not have the time to produce a definitive ruling on all the issues. However, the interventions would at least provide the Court with information which would better qualify it to identify what those issues *were*, and so which would enable the court to state clearly the limits of the decision that it *was* able to make and to indicate what were the remaining areas of uncertainty. The interventions put the Court of Appeal in the position that Allison would wish it to be, better able to appreciate and respond to the nature and extent of the polycentric problem before it.

In developing their procedures in this way, the courts of course need to be aware of their inherent institutional limitations. Deciding where and on what basis the line between legitimate and excessive intervention in court proceedings should be drawn is very difficult, something that it is not readily susceptible to a priori rules, but rather a matter for the court to regulate in its discretion. It is unfortunate then that the courts do not more regularly make their decisions about applications to intervene explicit; we are often left with what Sarah Hannett describes as a 'justificatory vacuum'.[142a] Carol Harlow cautions that intervention cannot legitimate judicial law-making[143] and that it is 'fallacious' to suppose that the populace can participate in all decision-making.[144] But the line between legitimate, ie (in this context) informed, exposition and development of existing legal principles, and undemocratic judicial legislation is a difficult and delicate one to identify: one person's policy leap will be another's development of existing principle.[145] Moreover, the courts remain distinct from the legislature by virtue of various, characteristically *judicial* constraints on their activities: they are politically independent, obliged to reach substantively rational, expressly justified decisions in response to applications initiated without their control; they cannot choose issues that they address or reach decisions simply on the basis of personal preference; they cannot

---

[142] *R v Department of Health, ex parte Source Informatics Ltd* [2000] COD 114 for a report of the intervention applications; substantive appeal reported at [2001] QB 424.

[142a] Above n 111.

[143] Above n 111, at 11. For a contrary view in the human rights context, see Loux above n 46, 340–41.

[144] Above n 111, at 14.

[145] Contrast Lord Woolf's view of the Court of Appeal's activities in *Heil v Rankin* [2001] QB 272 with that of Carol Harlow [2001] QB 272, paras 41–48; (2002) 65 *MLR* 1, at 11.

take huge leaps into the dark, being constrained by the incremental common law method and the doctrine of *stare decisis*.[146] The doctrines of ripeness and mootness generally steer them clear of making advisory declarations, though there will be some occasions in public law cases where there is deemed to be good reason in the public interest for making such declarations, cases turning on legislative rather than adjudicative facts being particularly likely to fall into this category.[147] As for the scope of the participation afforded, even with improved mechanisms for alerting putative interveners to impending litigation in which they might wish to intervene,[148] allegations of selectivity in the interests represented before the court may be unavoidable.[149] However, given the inevitably expository nature of the courts' judgments, wider interest representation in court, albeit necessarily incomplete, is arguably better than none. As Abram Chayes pithily remarked, the court is probably in no worse position than the legislature itself in this regard, and to suggest otherwise 'is to impose democratic theory by brute force on observed institutional behaviour'.[150]

CONCLUSION

If standing and intervention rules, and associated procedural rules regarding disclosure of evidence and cross-examination, are to be developed and applied on other than purely pragmatic grounds, some clear understanding of the purpose of these rules must be reached. They must be developed coherently with an understanding of the nature of the substantive law to which they relate, and so of the proper relationship of putative claimants and interveners to the subject matter of the claim, and with an understanding of the nature of the courts' constitutional function generally, and particularly in the public law context.[151] Of course, many of the issues discussed in the course of this chapter are not unique to public law. As Peter Cane notes,[151a] cases in the private law courts will often raise polycentric issues too, not least in the human rights sphere. The scope for representative claims to be made in private law, and under the victim test, is currently far more restricted[152] than is effectively allowed for by the non-victim sufficient interest test in public law cases, though *intervention* in private law cases is possible at the courts' discretion. Nor are human rights claims, in particular, unique to the jurisdiction of the various divisions of the High Court—the HRA can be invoked at

---

[146] Fiss, above n 101, at 12–17; Spann, above n 101, at 647 *et seq*.

[147] *R v Secretary of State for the Home Department, ex parte Salem* [1999] 1 AC 450. Cf varying attitudes towards the declarations sought in the *Rusbridger* context, above n 26 (HL).

[148] As proposed by the Public Law Project, see above n 54.

[149] The court does not ultimately control the appointment of *amici* to redress imbalance in the interest representation before the court: Loux, above n 46 at 337 and Justice/PLP, above n 54, at 35.

[150] Chayes (1976), above n 129, at 1311.

[151] See Miles, above n 52, for an attempt to examine current judicial review and HRA review in the context of some of the models discussed here.

[151a] See ch 10 above.

[152] Civil Procedure Rules, Part 19.6.

any time in any court. Harlow concludes that it is illogical in these circumstances to develop the procedures of the Administrative Court alone, and in the absence of a constitutional court, whose procedures could perhaps have been satisfactorily tailored to accommodate wide opportunities for intervention, allowing intervention in all courts may be too unwieldy unless they are carefully controlled and confined largely to paper.[153] Such interventions ought at any rate to be permitted in those courts whose judgments have precedential value, in particular in the appellate courts, since it is there that exposition of the law is paramount and it is those decisions which will guide those of the lower courts and tribunals.

In the public law context, the current patchwork of rules faced by those who wish to appear before public law courts in UK jurisdictions, particularly in the human rights context, is somewhat difficult to reconcile by reference to the criteria suggested here. Lord Lester's admonition of the resulting absurdity was not adequately addressed during the parliamentary debates on the Human Rights Bill. His concerns may find support from the judiciary who, if experience of the reception into English administrative law of the demands of EC remedial law is any indication, might be expected to do their best to eradicate the inconsistencies.[154] We will see over the next years whether and to what extent the courts' interpretation and application of those rules alleviate the tensions.

[153] Above n 111.
[154] See *M v Home Office* [1994] 1 AC 277.

Index

Please note that references to Figures and other non-textual materials are in *italics*